HEIGHTS OF JUSTICE

HEIGHTS OF JUSTICE

Discourse from
Boston College Law School

Edited by

Lawrence A. Cunningham

ASSOCIATE DEAN FOR ACADEMIC AFFAIRS
PROFESSOR OF LAW AND BUSINESS
BOSTON COLLEGE LAW SCHOOL

CAROLINA ACADEMIC PRESS
Durham, North Carolina

ISBN 1-59460-233-6
LCCN 2006922243

CAROLINA ACADEMIC PRESS
700 Kent Street
Durham, NC 27701
Telephone (919) 489-7486
Fax (919) 493-5668
www.cap-press.com

Printed in the United States of America

*Dedicated to
Darald and Juliet Libby,
with eternal gratitude
for your generous support.*

CONTENTS

Acknowledgments   xi
Style Note   xiii
Introduction   xv

PART I EDUCATION AND PRACTICE

A.   Dialogue
     1. A Culture of Conversation   3
     2. Theory and Practice   15
     3. A Theory-Practice Spiral   27
     4. Comparative Law   41

B.   Roles
     5. Self-Awareness and Critical Reflection   53
     6. Ethics in Externships   63
     7. Analytical Feedback on Student Writing   73
     8. Fundamental Structure in Legal Writing   81

C.   Lawyering
     9. Professionalism   89
     10. Civil Disobedience   97
     11. Rebellious Lawyering   109
     12. Multicultural Lawyering   123

PART II INSTITUTIONS AND LEGITIMACY

A.   Separation of Powers
     13. Statutory Violations and Equitable Discretion   135
     14. Judges v. Legislators as Sources of Law   149

B. Federalism
    15. Federal Prosecution of State and Local Officials   163
    16. Corporate Federalism   175

C. Contemporary Lawmaking
    17. Private Standards in Public Law   189
    18. Uncertain Risk   203
    19. Third World Environmental Issues   213

Part III Law and Society

A. Democratic Order
    20. Democracy, Taxes and Wealth   227
    21. The Overlooked Middle   239
    22. Federal Fraud Protection in the Labor Market   253
    23. The Public's Right to Know   267

B. Equality and Difference
    24. Deportation, Social Control, and Punishment   283
    25. Girls in the Juvenile Justice System   297
    26. Patients' Bill of Rights   307
    27. Transracial Adoption   317

Part IV Convention and Critique

A. Aspirations
    28. Situated Decisionmaking   333
    29. Trade and Inequality   347
    30. The Apogee of the Commodity   359

B. Affiliations
    31. Fiduciary Relationships   375
    32. Marriage as Partnership   389
    33. Consensual Amorous Relationships   399

C. Lawmakers
    34. The Article 2 Merchant Rules   407
    35. Lessons from the Article 8 Revision   421
    36. Copyright Opinions   431
    37. Copyright and Time   445

Part V Courts and Beyond

A. Supervision
    38. Origin of the Appeal   463
    39. Judicial Integrity   479
    40. A More Independent Grand Jury   493

B. Examination
    41. Maximum Sentence Enhancements   509
    42. Catholic Judges in Capital Cases   521
    43. Behavioral Science Evidence   533

C. Circumvention
    44. Doctrine in Dispute Resolution   551
    45. Advance Pricing Agreements   565

Index of Contributions   577
Index   583

Acknowledgments

Thanks to all my colleagues at Boston College Law School for their overwhelming support of this project. I appreciate their trusting me to reproduce, selectively, portions of their considerable contributions to legal scholarship. Whether or not I succeeded in vindicating that trust by faithfully rendering their work in my selections, I encourage readers inspired by the scholarship appearing in this anthology to consult the original contributions.

An asterisk footnote accompanying each selection provides citations to the original printed version and to a subsequent Internet version of each article. Complete versions of many papers by professors of Boston College Law School are available from the Boston College Legal Research Series on the Legal Scholarship Network: http://www.ssrn.com/link/boston-college-public-law.html.

Thanks to Deena Frazier, Bibliographic Access & Resources Librarian, for developing our Internet-based scholarly repository, to which she has posted complete versions of all pieces excerpted in this book. In turn, thanks to Gloria Tower, Law Library Assistant, and John Gordon, Publication Support Specialist. Thanks to my secretary, Jeannie Kelly, for helping to prepare many of the pieces contained in this book. For production assistance at various stages, thanks to Meg Daniel, Linda Lacy, Elizabeth Rosselot, Katy Morrissey and Keith Sipe. Thanks finally to John Garvey, Dean of Boston College Law School, for his unwavering financial and intellectual support of this project.

Acknowledgment is also made to those organizations holding copyright to the works contained in this volume.

L.A.C.

STYLE NOTE

Three types of academic contributions appear in this anthology. Some pieces are short essays adapted substantially as originally published; others are longer papers from which discrete sections were so adapted; and other longer pieces suggested more of a cascading selection, including portions from throughout the piece.

In all cases, stylistic conformity within this book required applying minor technical editorial conventions. Key examples were occasionally adding or modifying section headings and in rarer cases modifying paragraph length toward a uniform standard.

Footnotes are removed; selected references appear in concluding pages to each piece, along with suggestions for further reading of works by each author. In the references, books appear by author and title (with date) and articles appear by author, title, journal and date (the journal name preceded by volume number and succeeded by page number).

INTRODUCTION

Heights of Justice explores political, social, economic and procedural attributes of justice, as applied law. Themes combine theory and practice to articulate moral and ethical values that facilitate a rational application of law. This application seeks to foster legal arrangements imbued by values associated with the Jesuit tradition, including the dignity of persons, advancing the common good and compassion for the underprivileged. Actions in the name of justice exhibit commitment to serving others; legal scholarship in this vein is dedicated to providing intellectual and professional sustenance necessary to achieve these objectives.

For lawyers, pursuit of these objectives begins in law school. Legal education ideally entails dialogue and intellectual discovery. Dialogue includes making connections between seemingly different classifications, such as theory and practice, or clinical training and feminist jurisprudence. Such iteration, along with parallel exchanges using interdisciplinary and comparative inquiry, often produces surprisingly powerful insights. One example is how seeming dichotomies sometimes turn out not only to be false, but to reflect a mutually-complementing spiral. Engaging discussion of this kind among teachers and students broadens pedagogical range, rendering law not merely a system of rules but a pathway to justice. When such conversations continue into reflective legal practice, inventive conceptions of justice emerge that deepen the meaning and value of lawyering.

In justice's political dimension, institutional legitimacy is a cornerstone. An example is the relationship between governmental branches, especially between the judiciary and legislatures. Finding harmony in this relationship, whether through inquiry into the nature of equity or when addressing such charged topics as bioethics, lends a sense of justice to these institutional dynamics. Similar inquiries illuminate the relationship between central and local authorities in a federal republic. One virtue of federalism is that it enables central authority to promote democratic legitimacy by policing or pressuring local authorities. Contemporary lawmaking is complex, incorporating executive branch agencies (such as the Food and Drug Administration and the Securities and Exchange Commission), private actors (such as the American Dental

Association and the Financial Accounting Standards Board) and international organizations (such as the World Bank). Suitable institutional arrangements to ensure political justice are essential to incorporate such participants.

Institutional legitimacy depends, further still, on the content of resulting social and economic policies. This need creates an intersection of law and society requiring attention to principles of both democratic order and equality. At the center of this intersection are matters of wealth distribution, influenced by tax policy, and socio-political factors such as family structures and trade unions. In an information age, how information is shared is central to organizational legitimacy, of both government and large enterprises such as public companies. Equality plays a complex role in this democratic process, influencing such important issues as immigration and deportation policy and health care delivery. Questions of equality must deal with the role of difference, apparent in such settings as treatment of girls versus boys in juvenile justice systems and in transracial adoptions (white parents adopting black babies).

Convention helps to promote institutional legitimacy and the values of democracy and equality. Convention's virtue, however, depends upon its endless critique. For example, accepted models of decision-making or international trade law must be tested, sometimes refashioned, and only then do they remain legitimate. Slavery, a convention, withered only under critique. Associated methods of discourse promote justice. This occurs independent of the intellectual tradition used for study, such as pragmatism, liberalism, utilitarianism, or Aristotelean virtue ethics, to name a few major approaches. When applied to lawmakers, discourse pitting convention against critique advances justice too, whether assessing the drafting of commercial codes or writing judicial opinions resolving copyright disputes.

In adjudication, justice entails supervision, starting with the appeal and involving judicial review of official conduct, such as prosecutors in grand jury proceedings. Judges also must police themselves and their courtrooms; they frequently must reconcile legal mandates with moral values when these collide, or oversee expert witnesses when assessing probity of proffered evidence. Courts' infirmities in adjudication invite pursuing alternative paths to justice, such as mediation. Blazing such passages may require doctrinal adjustment, the pursuit of which promotes justice. Bolder paths to justice include pre-dispute contracting, a recent innovation in international tax law. This shows capacity of contemporary institutions to respond justly to needs of an endlessly changing world.

While justice may be a vague concept, it is powerful and pervasive. Its infinite complexity inclines scholars to recognized categories of justice. Roughly, leading examples are political justice, distributive justice, corrective justice, and procedural justice (fairness in administration). These rough categories are contested, overlapping, and often essentially tools of convenience. While these conceptions have some utility, practical justice would suffer from attempting to classify its manifestations into such pigeon holes. Instead, *Heights of Justice* is organized to reflect the preceding illustrations.

This arrangement generates considerable coherence in the topics featured. This collection of scholarship is unusual because it is all generated by members of a single law faculty, Boston College Law School. Each contributor pursues an individual scholarly arc. Each develops an individualized body of knowledge that gels, when viewed in total. This volume captures a different coherence, one across colleagues of a school. This unusual feature means both (1) the collection presents an organic whole, readable in the sequence presented and (2) it will enrich readers who prefer to skip around, and these readers likely will wish to study further works of particular scholars. In preparing this introduction and in selecting excerpts for inclusion, I serve as a reader, interpreter and narrator of the works. Commentary and content thus filter through a different lens than the original materials, making me, not each author, responsible for any omissions of nuance or subtlety.

I. Legal Education and Practice

Contributions collected in the book's opening section reflect upon the meaning of legal education, teaching, writing and thinking about justice. The first series of works addresses dialogue in legal education, the second builds on these foundations to explore roles in the legal academy, and the third extends these insights into the practice of law.

A. *Dialogue.* Conventional wisdom denominates law school's principal task as teaching students to "think like lawyers." Gregory Kalscheur demonstrates how restricting such a conception is and pushes, instead, for law schools to celebrate the fundamental human drive to ask questions and to follow our curiosity wherever it takes us. Professor Kalscheur elucidates the thought of Bernard Lonergan and James Boyd White to enhance understanding of meaning and value in conceiving law as a social and cultural activity. Envisioning law school as a process called "re-horizoning," he emphasizes how traditions of the Society of Jesus enable law schools within a Jesuit university, such as Boston College, to provide unique ways to establish cultures of authentic conversation.

In a classic work that Professor Kalscheur draws upon, Mark Spiegel first provides working definitions of theory and practice and then explains how division into these categories does not reflect a natural order but a choice. By discussing development of the case method and the legal realist challenge to it, he shows how traditional approaches to legal education can be seen either as theoretical or as practical. Professor Spiegel explains that these labels are thus contingent products of our age, explores why we persist in this labeling and what difference this makes for legal education and its capacity for enrichment.

Provisionally adopting Professor Spiegel's working definitions of theory and practice so dissected, Phyllis Goldfarb deepens the theme using two movements in law's academy: clinical education (seen as practical) and feminist jurisprudence (seen as theoretical). She identifies underlying methodological kinship to illustrate how problematic the theory-practice label remains. By studying the ethical impulse that sparks both clinical education and feminism, Professor Goldfarb discerns a theory-practice spiral, growing through mutual affinities. This discovery opens a new ethical vision to reinvent the nature of moral theory as anchored in the concrete reality of specific people in our lives, not one orbiting around the abstract "generalized others" of traditional philosophy.

Dialogue in legal education is the animating theme of Hugh Ault's ensuing essay, which explores comparative law as a directive force in reshaping legal education. A world-renowned comparative tax scholar, Professor Ault recounts his pioneering development of a comparative law course at Boston College Law School decades ago. The essay is contextualized in the broad framework of change in legal education during the last decades of the twentieth century. That is when law professors became increasingly inventive, law became increasingly interdisciplinary, and critical theory from legal history, philosophy, economics and other fields enriched the tapestry of legal rules and their operation to generate deeper insights into legal systems.

B. *Roles.* The second series of pieces in this section builds upon these transformative enterprises to explore varying conceptions of roles in legal education. Noting the sociological foundations of the concept of role, Filippa Anzalone reflects on learning theory, showing how teachers are more effective when self-aware. The piece is a phenomenology of discovery about learning theory, a report of applied knowledge aimed at excellence in pedagogy and a study of how contemporary reflective practice and criticism continue to transform legal education and the professor's role in it.

The contribution featuring Alexis Anderson explores challenges facing various participants in law school externship programs, centering on ethical issues of confidentiality. The piece uses cases to illuminate the roles of students and supervisors in the field and on the faculty. It provides protocols to teach students skills and professional habits necessary to provide competent client representation.

Jane Kent Gionfriddo, a former President of the Legal Writing Institute, presents a theory of written analytical feedback on student writing for law practice. She envisions legal writing teachers playing the dual role of legal educator plus reader in law practice. Professor Gionfriddo illustrates how her theory works, using a specific legal problem showing student communication and teacher feedback, along with commentary on why the feedback succeeds pedagogically.

Judith Tracy extends Professor Gionfriddo's framework to demonstrate how using samples in the classroom enhances analytical development. Balancing the roles of legal educators engaging students to pursue justice while training them as professionals, she explores teaching methods producing imminent engagement. These emphasize the specific roles of audience and writer, not monolithic off-the-rack exercises.

C. *Lawyering.* Legal education does not stop at law school, but demands continued nurturing. In the practice of law, a theme of roles continues. But as Daniel Coquillette explains, it is impossible for lawyers in practice to separate professional ethics from personal morality. Yet these sometimes conflict. Emphasizing how professional identity as lawyers is the center of the lawyer's personal morality, Dean Coquillette's meditation focuses on our ultimate motivation for obeying rules in all roles. He critically examines three theories of professional behavior—goal-based, rights-based, and duty-based—to guide lawyers into justice's humanistic roots, away from instrumentalism.

Recognizing the impossibility of drawing sharp lines between the lawyer and one's self, Judith McMorrow considers latitude lawyers have in committing acts of civil disobedience. Such conduct may be proper under certain circumstances for non-lawyers, yet remain improper for lawyers. Professor McMorrow develops a theory and prescribes a norm of special caution for lawyers. Its premise is the correlation between the rule of law and positive law, meaning that lawyers bear special obligations to act in accordance with law to promote democratic legitimacy. This limits lawyerly civil disobedience, guided by the standard of special caution.

The question of roles likewise contributes to defining the nature of lawyering. Paul Tremblay works through competing conceptions of poverty lawyering, dubbed "rebellious" lawyering and "regnant" lawyering. Regnant lawyering is the conventional approach, emphasizing client autonomy and calling for the lawyer to advance the client's interests here and now. Rebellious lawyering takes a broader and longer view, conceiving of the lawyer's role as driving a "justice-based allocation of resources away from clients' short-term needs in favor of a community's long-term needs." Professor Tremblay develops a theory of justice aimed at refashioning legal ethics into this model of lawyering.

Building on themes of critical self-reflection, Carwina Weng examines scholarship on multicultural lawyering to discover a focus on learning about culturally-different clients. The literature wrongly overlooks the human inclination towards unconscious cultural blindness and discrimination against those who are different. To address this oversight, she calls for a new conception of multicultural lawyering, one demanding self-analysis of one's culture and its influences. Professor Weng contributes a framework for learning cultural self-awareness, using cognitive and social psychology to lend completeness to cross-cultural lawyering.

II. Institutions and Legitimacy

The delivery and administration of justice depends upon existence of legal institutions. In a democracy, these require components that provide balance and fairness to systemic efficacy and legitimacy. Traditional notions of separation of powers and federalism support these structures in the United States. Increasingly administrative agencies and private actors, both within the United States and globally, play critical though inchoate roles. Scholars explore advanced attributes of these legal power structures in this section.

A. *Separation of Powers.* The relationship between the judicial and legislative branches of government in generating law and justice is a central theme of United States jurisprudence. The first pair of contributions in this section considers aspects of this relationship. Both reflect how it is the role of legislatures to express political will and of courts to mediate it.

Zygmunt Plater examines the role of equitable discretion in the modern statutory context. He starts with an unsettling proposition: courts, even courts in equity, lack discretion to permit violations of statutes to continue despite broad mandates to "balance the equities." Resolving this separation of powers puzzle involves dissecting equitable powers into three distinct balancing exercises: a threshold balance, a balance on the question of contending conducts, and a balance in tailoring equitable remedies. Equity defers to legislation in the second but retains discretion as to the first and third. So the thrice-balanced method facilitates equity in the age of statutes, mediating the roles of courts and legislatures.

Charles Baron explores, more directly, the relative desirability of law being made by courts or legislatures, using the law regarding the "right to die" to illustrate. Common law responded, in the absence of legislation, to technological advances in prolonging human life. Legislators sidestepped difficult questions while case law incrementally evolved responsive legal principles. The interaction exhibits law's magisterial dialectic process. Neither branch is institutionally subservient to the other. The interaction between them promotes public confidence that results yield more just law.

B. *Federalism.* Public confidence is a component of democratic legitimacy; it is a critical function of federalism. Likewise a central theme of United States jurisprudence, the second pair of contributions in this section considers aspects of the federal-state relationship. Both reflect federalism's flexibility enabling it to promote public confidence and democratic legitimacy.

George Brown explores federal prosecutions of state and local officials for political corruption. These actions pose difficult issues of how federalism relates to state autonomy and local sovereignty. He examines *Sabri v. United States,* which endorses such actions without appreciating the significant constitutional issues they pose, and links it to the widely-publicized campaign finance reform case (*McConnell*). Questioning conventional rationales such as justifiable protection of federal funds, Professor Brown explains that endorsing these federal actions promotes anti-corruption imperatives grounded in principles making Congress "the guardian of the democratic process."

Reneé Jones explains federalism on similar grounds of public confidence in lawmaking. She focuses on federalism in corporate law, implicated by the Sarbanes-Oxley Act of 2002 that suggests a "creeping federalization of corporate law." She explains that a realistic federal threat to state jurisdiction is critical to development of legitimate corporate law among states. Professor Jones uses Sarbanes-Oxley to ground one prong of her theory of dynamic federalism. This is a relationship between state and federal regulation that enables each to reinforce the other's efficacy. In this context, enabled by the federal preemptive threat, federal legislation induces state courts to jurisprudential shifts congruent with democratic principles garnering popular support.

C. *Contemporary Lawmaking.* The federal preemptive threat inherent in federalism, and the separation of powers concept, play defining roles in the broader stage of law production found in the administrative state. Each piece in this part grapples with this complex, radial, production of law in contemporary society, including the role of private actors.

Mary Ann Chirba-Martin examines public safety when private associations establish standards—endorsed by federal agencies—that may not be in the public interest. The illustration is dental amalgam fillings, which the American Dental Association (ADA) champions as safe while the Food and Drug Administration (FDA) essentially defers. Judicial capacity to provide a forum to resolve contending interests is limited. So only state legislatures can produce law necessary to assure appropriate safety and dissemination of information—and they are constrained by the threat of federal preemption in doing so.

Federal administrative agencies increasingly leverage their regulatory function by adopting private standards as public law. This phenomenon, well illustrated by how the Securities and Exchange Commission adopts private accounting standards for public companies, poses issues of both public access to materials and legitimacy of the process. In my contribution to this volume, I offer an analytical framework to promote the legitimacy of this process and, for the federal government, nominate the Director of the Federal Register to implement its objectives.

In emerging areas of international practice in which law as yet plays little formal role, innovative and creative approaches are essential to establish legitimacy and promote justice. David Wirth explores the example of how private organizations from the United States and abroad, together with donor country governments, have reoriented both the procedures for developing and the content of third world development agendas financed by the World Bank. He fashions a partnership advocacy model to guide those efforts, with particular attention to assuring democratic accountability to the poor in developing countries who are the ostensible, but rarely the actual, beneficiaries of donor lending operations. Professor Wirth then defines a principled role for American lawyers in such partnerships.

III. Law and Society

Law must respond to the needs of societies it governs to achieve justice. Two series of papers in this section illustrate how. The first, presented as democracy, seeks systemic solutions in contexts of taxation, mediating institutions, the workforce and public access to governmental information. The second series, denominated as equality, addresses specific instances that focus on immigrants, girls, patients and infants.

A. *Democracy.* Democracy and wealth are inextricably bound, each facilitating and simultaneously threatening the other. James Repetti demonstrates how wealth concentration impairs economic growth, due to reduced opportunities, and frustrates democratic processes. Particularly when wealth concentration arises from inheritance, tax policy should be used to offset these adverse effects, with proceeds from such transfers allocated to fund education that nurtures human capital.

A sub-theme of tax policy aimed at nurturing human capital is the idea of the middle class, a classification embracing a more general middle. Thomas Kohler laments a systemic tendency to overlook this vast "middle," comprised of families, religious congregations, service and fraternal groups, grassroots political clubs, and unions—all of which mediate relations between individuals and institutions. Mediating bodies—"little platoons" of society as Edmund Burke called them—inculcate habits central to self-rule at individual and social levels. This is why Tocqueville stressed associations as mediating groups with potential to act as "schools for democracy."

Extending this concern about the overlooked middle, Kent Greenfield considers federal law concerning candor. It protects against fraud in capital markets by theorizing that accurate information facilitates optimal capital allocation. A similar rationale, perhaps even stronger, justifies equivalent protection against fraud in labor markets, but neither federal nor state law provides it. Professor Greenfield explains why common law and state regulation are inadequate, requiring a federal statutory approach.

Information is central to capital and labor markets and increasingly to all citizens in a democracy. The venerable doctrine called the public's right to know underscores this theme when addressing information held by government. Mary-Rose Papandrea demonstrates judicial reluctance to promote this right when the executive branch asserts secrecy on grounds of national security. Yet the public's right to know, grounded both in the First Amendment and the Freedom of Information Act, is essential to political justice, particularly amid national crisis when government activities are directed at non-citizens.

B. *Equality*. Non-citizens are part of numerous groups often put in law's shadows, denied access to justice even though equality demands it. In the case of non-citizens, a critical moment of justice arises in deportation proceedings. Daniel Kanstroom explains how deportation is often an automatic consequence of criminal conviction, yet constitutional protections provided in criminal proceedings do not apply in deportation proceedings. To maintain constitutional legitimacy, Professor Kanstroom says, the Constitution's criminal law protections should be incorporated into the deportation system. One model for doing so appears in the juvenile justice system.

The juvenile justice system's goal is individualized rehabilitative justice, yet juveniles sometimes likewise are denied justice through blindness to notions of equality of treatment. Effects can be particularly pernicious for girls. Francine Sherman documents the disparities girls face in the juvenile justice system and explains legal remedies to provide redress. While differences between male and female offenders have undermined equal rights challenges in the adult arena, differences among individuals are acknowledged in juvenile courts, and dispositions can be driven by those individual needs.

If equality means addressing gender-specific needs of girls in the juvenile justice system, broader conceptions of equality play an overlooked role in politically-driven proposals for a "patients' bill of rights." While assigning due process rights to patients of privately-funded health plans, Dean Hashimoto explains that the proposals never appreciated how Medicaid-managed care systems often do not provide equal treatment for the poor or other minorities. Any patients' bill of rights should safeguard such patients by extending protections to such managed care programs based on a principle of equality, Professor Hashimoto says.

Principles of equality are complex. From whose viewpoint should equality be assessed? Ruth-Arlene Howe confronts such questions in one of her classic articles on the trans-racial adoption debate — chiefly the adoption by white couples of black children. Her thesis is that the increase in such adoptions reflects less an interest in the equality of all persons participating in the process than it does an elevation of the interests of white adults above the needs of black children. Professor Howe urges a shift from seduction by the rhetoric about trans-racial adoption to crystallizing culturally-sensitive approaches to meeting needs of black children in foster care.

IV. Convention and Critique

Conventional wisdom is often long on convention and short on wisdom. Papers in this section critique and expose such limitations. In legal discourse, this facilitates evolving legal conventions towards more just formulations, whether the topic is decision-making, international trade, slavery, relationships or lawmaking.

A. *Aspirations*. Pragmatism, a hearty philosophy for centuries, occasionally comes under rebuke for lacking rational principles to resolve difficult questions. Catharine Wells defends pragmatic analysis of legal decision-making. She presents two models of normative decision-making that purport to distinguish between types of decision-making but shows how these describe interdependent parts of any decision-making process. Professor Wells concludes that pragmatic decision-making should be appreciated as elucidating contextual elements of all forms of deliberation, not as rejecting rationally structured decision-making procedures.

Confronting the concept and meaning of justice head-on is an ambitious project. Taking the leap, Frank Garcia explores various theories of justice in the tradition of liberalism, including communitarian, libertarian, and fairness-based accounts. From this analysis, Professor Garcia articulates a Rawlsian framework of justice that he expands to evaluate contemporary international trade law. His compelling conclusion, contrary to convention, is that traditional liberal justifications of the international order justify asking wealthier states to adopt redistributive policies in international trade law.

Effects of injustice persist long after corrections are made. This is among the major lessons in our legacy of slavery. Deep wounds heal slowly, and wounds of the soul may never heal. Anthony Farley critically reviews the realities of slavery to conclude that "the black is the apogee of the commodity," a trait sustaining inherited injustices marked by the trauma of "white-over-black." Despite energetic search for empowerment and reparations by community leaders, such as the Black Panthers, this morally bankrupt legacy makes a mockery of accepted aspirational notions, such as the rule of law, designed to win struggles against injustice. Achieving justice is even more perplexing than many conventional theorists may think.

B. *Affiliations.* Legal classifications are often pivotal in conceptions of justice and applications of law. How should relationships be treated, according to arms'-length norms of the market place or the relational strictures of fiduciary obligation? A trio of pieces provides perspective on the law and nature of affiliations.

Scott FitzGibbon consciously sets out to develop a theory of affiliations, specifying its architecture and articulating associated ethical obligations. This exercise entails engaging with the distinction between contract and fiduciary law. Applying virtue ethics, this account refutes utilitarian theories that deny any difference between contract and fiduciary duty. Accounting for the ethics, psychology and anthropology of affiliations, Professor FitzGibbon provides a basis for sustaining attributes that distinguish the worlds of contract and trust.

Law has struggled for centuries to classify the nature of marriage, as rooted in status or in contract. By reviewing evolving legal doctrines and social dimensions of three features of modern matrimonial arrangements—ante-nuptials, cohabitations, and property settlements—Sanford Katz concludes that marriage is a special model of contract, partaking of components of consensual free exchange along with social constraints directed through state agents. The result is a law of marriage in flux, blending private and public law, individual and communal values, local and national concerns.

The complexion of marriage as straddling the zones of private individual autonomy and public policy becomes more acute in amorous consensual relationships between teachers and students. Elisabeth Keller explores the jurisprudential terrain anchored in freedoms of association and privacy but constrained by societal norms.

C. *Lawmakers.* Justice is a performance as well as a structural process, meaning lawmakers are central figures. They write laws, both in legislation and judicial opinions. Studying these actors in action are two pairs of pieces, one on statutory commercial law and the other on judge-made copyright law. Bismark reportedly quipped that those who like laws (or sausages) should not witness how they are made; those who like justice insist upon seeing.

The Uniform Commercial Code is among the most ambitious and successful modern legislative initiatives, covering a broad range of commercial transactions in its dozen different articles. Among the most famous of these statutes is Article 2, on sales, brainchild of Karl Llewellyn, a prolific and provocative law professor in his day. A peculiar feature of Llewellyn's work in Article 2 is a distinction between merchants and non-merchants. Ingrid Hillinger demonstrates, contrary to common belief, that the merchant rules did not codify trade customs but codified Llewellyn's conceptions of rational commercial rules. Reconceived as statements of policy not reality, they invite asking how law shapes practice and why the merchant rules should not apply to non-merchants.

Ontological issues appear in legislative drafting exercises of all kinds, including statutory updates of the UCC in light of technological change. James Rogers cites changes in securities trading during the latter twentieth century, when electronic means of recording proliferated. Commercial law reformers rewrote the law in putatively media-neutral terms, updating the law suitable for paper transactions to expressly cover paperless transactions. Professor Rogers explores the limits of this strategy, speculating that changes in the medium ineluctably change the content, meaning a shift from print to digits bears ontological effects obscured by such legislative updating.

Two copyright law scholars examine judicial approaches to the subject. The judge's job is to assess and, despite objective principles, this is an art. The reality of the judicial art is most pronounced when most reliant upon judgment, which is the field of copyright law that entails making aesthetic judgments. Alfred Yen develops this exquisite insight by exploring major movements from aesthetic theory and showing how they correspond to the analytic premises of judicial opinions in copyright disputes. Accordingly, the aesthetic nature of legal reasoning requires explicit consciousness of aesthetics in judging.

Judges in copyright disputes often face arguments that the venerable fair use doctrine permits a copycat to use a work without payment or constraint. The multi-factor judicial inquiry leaves out, surprisingly, the length of time since a work's first publication. Joseph Liu examines this omission, showing how time is as important a factor in fair use analysis as traditional factors. Incorporating time facilitates dynamic judicial accounting for policy stakes, such as authorial incentives and public access, while also injecting public-regarding values into copyright jurisprudence.

V. Courts and Beyond

Adjudication is the high-water mark of justice. Assuring its integrity is central. Mechanisms include the appeal and other structural arrangements designed to promote integrity; judicial inspection reinforces these structures. Enduring limitations of adjudication yield to searches for superior pathways to justice.

A. *Supervision.* Inherent in the American system of justice is the possibility of appeal, a quintessentially supervisory conception enabling superior courts to review lower court judgments. Mary Sarah Bilder uses cultural history to explain that appeals are a foundational feature of American jurisprudence. They are not merely legal procedures, rooted in common law, as convention has it, but a transatlantic characteristic of Western European legal culture. Professor Bilder defines an American "culture of appeal" as a central attribute of justice rooted in legal, religious, political, and literary ideas dating to the 1630s.

If the appeal is an emblem of equitable justice, then appellate review of official actors is critical to justice. As Robert Bloom explains, the concept of judicial integrity is a hallmark of our Constitutional order, and sanctions judicial exercise of supervisory powers that, in turn, promote the integrity of persons acting under official license. He laments, however, that a series of Supreme Court pronouncements mistakenly retreats from the doctrine of judicial integrity, diminished in part by reduced exercise of such supervisory powers.

Specific judicial supervision is essential to police practices of prosecutors exercising executive branch powers. A common example occurs when prosecutors seeking a grand jury indictment possess but do not disclose exculpatory evidence during the proceeding. Michael Cassidy demonstrates how historical appreciation of the grand jury's role, combined with the supervisory powers of federal courts, mandates judicial review. Short of this, state legislative and judicial action can supervise prosecutorial discretion in grand jury proceedings by mandating disclosure of exculpatory evidence in specified cases.

B. *Examination.* Structures contribute partial promotion of justice in adjudication; courts also must exercise examination, of legislators, themselves, and participants in litigation.

Courts exercise considerable discretion when imposing sentences on criminal defendants, although various legislative schemes often exert limitations on this discretion. Difficult issues arise as to what due process safeguards are relevant to sentencing, as distinguished from substantive elements of a crime. Frank Herrmann explores the landscape, encouraging applying full due process safeguards to all types of sentencing schemes. Critical in such exercises is how judicial supervision of sentencing laws can be achieved without provoking legislative efforts to negate this power through artful drafting of criminal statutes.

A slight but lethal swing in the penal pendulum occurring towards the end of the twentieth century brought death as a penalty back to the forefront of social thought. This penalty poses profound moral issues for Catholic judges sitting in capital cases. John Garvey provides a framework to reconcile legal requirements with religious conviction by inquiring into theories of cooperation in morally impermissible behavior. His model establishes that Catholic judges cannot enforce the death penalty, either by sentence or upon jury recommendation, but face more difficult balancing when reviewing lower court orders or petitions for *habeas corpus*.

Adjudication requires establishing evidentiary grounds for conclusions, whether by judges or juries. Among difficult contexts is evidence provided by expert witnesses, designed to educate fact finders in arcane areas. Social scientific evidence poses greatest complexities. Mark Brodin measures this form of proof against specific reliability standards and general requirements for admitting expert testimony. He finds that much of this testimony should be excluded. It does not assist juries, can distort the accuracy of the fact-finding process and imperil a proceeding's fairness.

C. *Circumvention.* Judicial dispute resolution may be recognizable as a common means of adjudication, but alternatives proliferate. Obstructing these pathways are doctrinal entanglements or administrative obstacles, which two scholars in concluding pieces show can be removed.

Ray Madoff reflects upon mediation's appeal, observing its varying success in fields ranging from divorce (where it has worked well) to wills (where it has not). She theorizes mediation's relative success in divorce law is due to doctrinal revolutions such as the no-fault principle and its relative failure in wills settings as owing to the unseen hand of doctrine, a wills law that encourages opting for judicial disputation. To increase successful mediation for wills dispute resolution, doctrinal changes are necessary.

Innovations for dispute resolution increasingly take one step back in the process to prevent disputes from arising. This occurs in international tax law when parties agree with governments in advance on the tax treatment of complex cross-border transactions. Diane Ring puts this fascinating "advance pricing agreement" procedure under the lens of administrative theory, to test the theory, including examining its lessons for academic accounts of the administrative state. She finds in this inquiry a certain justice in this innovation enabled by the administrative state, an exercise in cooperation that epitomizes emerging models of collaborative governance.

Coda

Justice is law's deep bed, whether the topography is called distributive, corrective, political or procedural justice, or located on the more textured terrain of social, economic, or racial justice. Normative moral theories and behavioral practices interact with law in complex ways. Ethical lawyers grapple with value and meaning in all aspects of their spiritual, intellectual, moral, and professional lives, whether in formal legal education or practicing law. Contributions to this anthology animate how these theories and practices ascend to the heights of justice.

Lawrence A. Cunningham
Associate Dean for Academic Affairs
Boston College Law School
March 15, 2006

PART I

EDUCATION AND PRACTICE

A. DIALOGUE

CHAPTER ONE

A CULTURE OF CONVERSATION[*]

Conventional wisdom holds that the principal task of a law school is to teach law students to "think like lawyers." What does this task entail? Articulated relatively neutrally, [by Derek Bok] this component of a law school's work emphasizes "training students to define the issues carefully and to marshal all the arguments and counterarguments on either side." Attaining this sharpness of mind, however, often is experienced as coming with a significant cost; [Carrie Menkel-Meadow has said] (not entirely cynically) ... that "law makes [one's] mind sharper by narrowing it." ...

... I contend that this short-sighted narrowing of mind is symptomatic of a crisis of meaning and value in the law and legal education. This narrowness of perspective in the study and practice of the law stems from a tendency to see the law simply as a set of instrumental rules to be manipulated, and the lawyer simply as a technician skilled in the manipulation of those rules. A crisis in meaning and value results when law students arrive at law school and experience themselves being formed to play the restricted role of skilled technician, a role disconnected from larger questions of human aspiration. Instead of being introduced to the law as a deeply human activity that itself involves a search for meaning and value, law students can experience law school as an alienating trade school. In short, law school can be experienced as a form of narrow training that diminishes something central to the human person: the fundamental human drive to question and to follow those questions wherever they lead....

The Crisis of Meaning and Value in Legal Education.... Our failures to engage in honest and open discussions which analyze world issues, community concerns, and classroom queries create in us myopic thought patterns that restrict our reasoning ability, and as a consequence, our ability for legal analy-

---

* **Gregory A. Kalscheur, S.J.**, *Law School as a Culture of Conversation: Re-imagining Legal Education as a Process of Conversion to the Demands of Authentic Conversation*, 28 LOYOLA UNIVERSITY OF CHICAGO LAW JOURNAL 333 (1996), http://papers.ssrn.com/abstract_id= 749345.

sis. In our failure to open our minds and face important issues with sincerity, we handicap ourselves in our very purpose for being here....

Law school then becomes an institution whose primary focus is the development of a high level of analytical rigor and technical competence with respect to these rules. Technical competence and analytical rigor are, of course, of great importance and are not problematic in themselves. The separation of technique from concern for human values, however, is a problem. The inculcation of a technical legal rationality that occupies the great bulk of the student's time and life in law school can cause the ability and desire to ask questions falling outside that model of legal rationality to atrophy....

[U]nderstanding of the law as a set of rules to be manipulated and law school as the process of attaining mastery in the application of a set of technical skills stems in large part from the presuppositions underlying the development of the "case method" of legal study by Harvard Law School Dean Christopher Columbus Langdell in the latter part of the nineteenth century. Langdell's dream was to make the law a respectable discipline within the university setting by demonstrating that law was best understood as a "science" — a system of rules that was self-sufficient, that operated with deductive certainty, and that was not subject to change....

Langdell's highly formalistic understanding of "legal science" has not survived the twentieth-century critique launched by the Legal Realists of the 1930s and '40s and carried on by today's Critical Legal Studies movement. With their emphasis on exposing the degree to which the law allows for a wide range of significant judicial choice in legal decision making, the Realists and their CLS successors effectively demolished the Langdellian idea that the law possesses an internal, almost geometric logic, that compels particular decisions in particular cases.

Still, Langdell's conception of the identity of the lawyer as one who has mastered the technical skills of deploying, manipulating, and applying legal rules (now understood non-formalistically) in particular situations of human conduct has, to a great extent, survived. Moreover, this conception of the identity of the lawyer continues to permeate the law school experience....

The emphasis on technical mastery and analytic rigor that characterizes the contemporary law school, of course, should not be discarded. Still, the separation of technical skill from human aspirations and values—its disjunction from the fundamentally human search for purpose and meaning in life—narrows the vision of the law student in a way experienced as humanly diminished. Moreover, education that generates this myopia promotes an impoverished understanding of the law, the legal process, and what it is to be a lawyer. Such an impoverished understanding of the law makes it more difficult for us to see the law as something we create, as an activity that constitutes us and our communities, and as a process of questioning through which we can criticize the law and seek to move the communities it constitutes in new directions.

In order to avert this crisis, [according to Elizabeth Dvorkin] "what is needed is a way of bringing together mastery with aspiration, intellect with experience, rigor with value, pragmatism with idealism, competence and skill with caring and a sense of meaning." The work of Bernard Lonergan and [James Boyd] White allows us to bridge these dichotomies in a way that can ground a re-humanized vision of the law and of legal education....

Law as a Meaning-Making Activity Constitutive of Character and Community. The potential for a fruitful exploration of the law in a Lonerganian framework is evident in the relationship between Lonergan's discussion of the constitutive function of acts of meaning and White's understanding of the law as a form of "constitutive rhetoric." Lonergan contends that human reality—the real world in which we live—is "in large measure constituted through acts of meaning." The world of immediacy, that which is experienced simply through sense and consciousness, is tiny. Thus, the real world is one we encounter only through the mediation of meaning; indeed, it is a world that is constructed by means of acts of meaning. "Beyond the world we know about, there is the further world we make," and "what we make, we first intend."

Thus, cultural achievements like language, religion, and art, as well as social institutions like the state, the law, and the economy are all constituted—made real—by intentional human acts of meaning. Moreover, not only do our intentional acts of meaning transform our natural, social, and cultural environments, but through our intentional acts of meaning we also constitute and transform ourselves. Our intentional acts of meaning shape the characters we come to possess. Accordingly, in this vast field where meaning is constitutive, human responsibility is greatest and human freedom reaches its highest point....

Because the constitutive function of meaning forces us to confront, in our lives as individuals and communities, this "moment of existential crisis" when we recognize that we make ourselves through the choices and decisions inherent in our intentional acts of meaning, "reflection on meaning and the consequent control of meaning" is crucial. There is, Lonergan stresses, nothing fixed or immutable about the reality we construct through our acts of meaning. We change social and cultural entities like the law—indeed, we change ourselves—through changes in meaning....

In a similar fashion, White elaborates a conception of the law as an activity "by which meaning and community are established." He contends that the law usefully can be viewed as a meaning-making activity concerned with the art of constituting character, community, and culture in language. The life of the law is therefore "a life of art, the art of making meaning in language with others." This conception of the law is driven by White's hope that it can serve as a ground upon which criticism of particular laws and the legal culture can rest, and additionally can help us understand what lawyers and judges at their best might do....

For White, the law is not simply a body of rules to be managed and applied; rather, it is an activity involving a set of resources for thought and argument. It is a language that our culture makes available for speech and argument on those occasions that the culture deems as legal. Thus, it is all of the technical and non-technical resources—rules, constitutions, statutes, judicial opinions, maxims, general understandings, conventional wisdom—"that a lawyer might use in defining his or her position and urging another to accept it." And while the law is an activity that works through this inherited language, as given by an established culture in an existing community, White's central claim is that in using these materials, the activity that is the law transforms them.

Law as a Form of Common Sense Knowing Subject To General Bias. White's conception of the law can also be brought into fruitful dialogue with Lonergan's analysis of practical common sense. In this realm of common sense, intelligent inquiry generates spontaneous questions about what to do, and about how things relate to us, rather than to one another. These questions give rise to an accumulation of insights about practical, everyday issues, and then to spontaneous collaboration among people in testing and improving those insights. Common sense both "aims at mastering the concrete and the particular," and achieves that aim "in a concrete and particular manner." It does this by bringing to bear in any particular context "an habitual but incomplete set of insights that [is] completed with appropriate variations in each concrete set of circumstances that calls for speech or action." Thus, common sense "consists in a set of insights that remains incomplete, until there is added at least one further insight into the situation in hand."

The activity of the law can be understood as a particular form of this sort of practical common sense. The resources of the legal culture, such as the Constitution, statutes, and judicial opinions, are, in a sense, an accumulation of past insights. This set of accumulated insights remains incomplete until it is brought to bear in an individual case. Within the context of that case, those accumulated insights are tested, evaluated, and improved in the creative search for the new insight which will guide action and govern decision in that case. Thus, for example, White describes the law as an activity in which people interact with a body of authoritative legal material (in Lonerganian terms, the accumulation of past insights) and the circumstances and events of the actual world in a given instance. Moreover, as with Lonergan's description of common sense, the law is a process of intellectual development that is always incomplete, "that is ever to be completed differently in each concrete situation": "One's knowledge of the law, [like one's knowledge of a language,] is never complete.... The speaker of ordinary competence constantly invents new ways to use the language." ...

Biases impede the proper operation of practical common sense by preventing or distorting the further question that is inherent in intelligence itself. The reflective moment in the human cognitional process can only move to judgment and affirm an insight as true or false, good or bad, to be done or not to be done, when the knower can affirm that there are no further pertinent questions to be asked. Bias, however, cuts off this process of questioning too soon.

Lonergan identifies several types of question-distorting biases. Individual bias, for example, is a refusal to ask all the relevant questions as a result of a distorted egoism. It involves a refusal to move to "the self-abnegation involved in allowing complete free play to intelligent inquiry." Thus, a person operating out of individual bias will give free rein to the "Eros of the mind, the desire and drive to understand," where his own interests are concerned, but he will fail to give serious consideration to the further relevant questions prompted by that desire to understand when those questions diverge from his own interests. Group bias operates in a similar fashion with respect to a group or a class.

General bias, in contrast, is a bias of practical common sense itself; it is refusal on the part of common sense to recognize and appreciate the important further pertinent questions that are raised by other fields, by other realms of inquiry. As Lonergan explains, common sense

> is incapable of analyzing itself, incapable of making the discovery that it too is a specialized development of human knowledge, incapable of coming to grasp that its peculiar danger is to extend its legitimate concern for the concrete and the immediately practical into disregard for larger issues and indifference to long-term results.

This short-sightedness of common sense, this impatience with any kind of theoretical knowing, can lead to a long-term cycle of decline.... Thus, Lonergan concludes that practical common sense needs to be guided, but is incompetent to choose its own guide.

The law, too, can suffer from this general bias of short-sightedness. For example, some judges and legal practitioners increasingly seem to conclude that—at least at the nation's elite law schools—legal education has taken a turn toward esoteric theory which offers little by way of practical insight to those laboring in the trenches of the law. This narrow focus on practical issues sets up a misleading oppositional relationship between "theoretical" and "practical" scholarship that exemplifies general bias and that fails to see the critical interaction that must exist between theory and common sense practice, between the general and the particular....

Both of these overreactions—a focus on theory alone or on particulars alone—are manifestations of a general bias that precludes the exploration of all further relevant questions, thereby preventing us from realizing illuminating insights.

A general bias of short sightedness is also inherent in a conception of the law as simply a system of institutionally established and managed rules. "Law is in this sense objectified and made a structure." Such a static view of the law fails to capture the way in which the law itself is transformed by its creative application in ever-new concrete situations. Similarly the law can be seen as a machine-like bureaucratic component of the structures of government....

To the extent that a bureaucratic ends-means rationality takes over the law and excludes any consideration of how a given decision will affect the course of the law over the longer term, general bias is apparent....

The Cultural Context of Cosmopolis as a Check on Bias. For Lonergan, the exaltation of common-sense practicality that slides into the longer cycle of decline must be countered by culture.... Culture ... acts as a counterbalance to the general bias of common sense....

Lonergan sometimes refers to this cultural counterbalance as cosmopolis. Cosmopolis is the particular conception of culture that provides the necessary context for critical reflection on common sense knowing. It "is founded on the native detachment and disinterestedness of every intelligence," and "its business is to prevent practicality from being short-sightedly practical and so destroying itself." Cosmopolis performs this function by recognizing that we need others and their questions and insights in order to overcome bias. Cosmopolis, therefore, can be described as the intersubjective cultural community that offers to common sense "the corrections and the assurance that result from learning accurately the tested insights of others and from submitting one's own insights to the criticism based on others' experience and development."

While Lonergan sees the cultural context of cosmopolis as a check on common sense that somehow remains outside common sense, White's view of the law as a culture of argument brings the function of cosmopolis within the activity of the law itself. Thus, for example, the lawyer's recognition of the law as a form of constitutive rhetoric within a culture of argument "should define the lawyer's own work as far less manipulative, selfish, or goal-oriented ... and as far more creative, communal, and intellectually challenging." ...

The Law School as a Culture of Conversation Promoting Conversion. If the conception of the law articulated by White truly is to include a cultural check on the problems of bias inherent in the process of practical common sense, the sort of attitude and character displayed by the ideal judge must be inculcated within the legal culture more generally. Thus, White's way of looking at the law must also affect the teaching and objectives of American law schools—the prospective lawyer's point of entry into the legal culture of argument. Indeed, White contends that seeing law as a form of constitutive rhetoric demands a different method of teaching in the law school....

Law school, then, is not about learning the rules and how to manipulate them. Rather, it is about acquiring certain habits of mind, a certain ability to question and converse with the resources available in the legal culture, with one's clients, and with one's colleagues. Moreover, through this process of questioning and conversation, the law school itself can be seen as an important component of the cosmopolis that works to reverse general bias....

Further, the law students' interaction with professors and legal scholarship during their time in law school helps to give the students the sort of broader, "cosmopolitan" perspective that can assist them in warding off the deleterious effects of general bias. As writers and scholars, rather than full-time practitioners, law professors have "the chance to stand back from the world of detail and of practice and to try to see something in it, to find something to say about it, of a more general nature than would likely emerge from the press of life in practice."

Lonergan's notions of horizon and conversion are helpful tools for understanding how this "cosmopolitan" habit of mind that is open to pursuing all of the further pertinent questions is acquired. Law students may well arrive at law school with horizons—pre-existing structures of knowledge and experience—that block unfettered operation of the unrestricted desire to know. Because of one's history, education, experience, and personal development, certain questions may be blocked from one's field of vision.

Law school, ideally, provides opportunities for students to experience "re-horizoning." Such a conversion to a new horizon can take place through the case analysis that is such a major component of the law school experience. Instead of studying cases simply as structures in which doctrinal rules are embodied, learning to read a judicial opinion (in many ways, the primary work of law school) should largely be a process of learning to engage in a new form of questioning. It can be a special kind of reading that is really a form of conversation with a text....

Learning to enter into a judicial opinion in this way is a process of giving oneself over to the questions prompted by the unrestricted desire to know. Such study requires the student to learn how to keep putting questions to the text, to the facts, to the parties involved, and to the judge, and to follow those questions wherever they may lead.

Moreover, through the process of critically analyzing a series of opinions in this way, through the enterprise of responding to questions raised by the teacher, and through the experience of engaging in conversation and argument with fellow students in and out of class with respect to legal issues, the law student begins to engage in a process that Lonergan calls dialectic; a process that can have a powerfully "re-horizoning" effect. This process of dialectic is a technique that brings conflicts to light and promotes conversion by making subjective differences objective....

The conversion that Lonergan envisions, and that law school can foster, is a process of finding out for oneself and in oneself what it is to be intelligent, to be reasonable, and to be responsible; in short, conversion entails ever more whole-hearted fidelity to the unrestricted desire to know. The process of dialectic involved in legal education understood as part of a culture of argument and conversation contributes to this sort of conversion....

Conversion and the Demands of Authentic Conversation. Lonergan contends that the formula for achieving detachment from bias and moving to a horizon open to greater fidelity to the unrestricted desire to know is "a continuous and ever more exacting application of the transcendental precepts. Be attentive. Be intelligent. Be reasonable. Be responsible." ...

Conversation conducted in accord with these rules promotes "re-horizoning" by keeping the conversation partners faithful to the demands of the unrestricted desire to know and by inviting them to explore the new possibilities for thinking and living that are encountered in an authentic conversation.

Conversation in its primary form is an exploration of possibilities in the search for truth. In following the track of any question, we must allow for difference and otherness. At the same time, as the question takes over, we notice that to attend to the other as other, the different as different, is also to understand the different as possible.

To learn to converse in this way is to learn to explore possibilities, difference, and otherness; through the encounters revealed by that exploration, conversion to a new horizon becomes conceivable as an option....

The Role of the Jesuit Law School. This vision of legal education does not require a radical overhaul of the law school curriculum. Indeed, as we have seen, the case method that typically dominates law school instruction can be an ideal vehicle for opening students to the practice of authentic conversation.

Therefore, implementation of this vision essentially demands that teachers and students approach the study of the law with a new attitude, with a conscious intentionality of striving to see their endeavor as a conversational search for meaning and value and with a commitment to establishing a classroom atmosphere in which such conversation takes place.

Such an understanding of the nature and purpose of legal education obviously places rigorous demands on both students and teachers. It is rooted in a desire to integrate the study of the law with the fundamental human drive to question and in an understanding of the law that sees law not as a set of rules to be manipulated, but as an activity through which we constitute ourselves and our communities. While this vision is certainly not uniquely Catholic or Jesuit, I believe that the commitments and traditions of the Society of Jesus may give law schools that operate within the context of Jesuit universities unique motivations and opportunities to implement this vision.

Striving to make the law school a culture of authentic conversation through which we can imagine new possibilities for constituting good lives and good communities by encountering the imaginative visions of others is consistent with the Society's recent articulation of a commitment to establishing a culture of dialogue as part of its characteristic way of proceeding. Moreover, encouraging imaginative encounters with new possibilities for living is also consistent with the Society's traditions of imaginative pedagogy rooted in the Spiritual Exercises....

While the typical authentic conversation in the law school context will rarely be a dialogue that can be characterized as "spiritual conversation," true fidelity to all of the questions that present themselves in our law school conversations, and genuine openness to the convictions of the others whom we encounter, will inevitably bring questions of God into play. The religiously and ideologically pluralistic context of the contemporary law school is not, of course, a forum for classroom catechesis. Still, we should guard against an understanding of legal conversations that would preclude us from giving ourselves wholly to the questions which might arise, and from following those questions wherever they lead.

Second, a Jesuit law school that nurtures the practice of authentic conversation is participating in a pedagogy of the imagination that is rooted in the Spiritual Exercises. I have attempted to describe the sort of authentic conversation that can be part of the law school culture as a process of questioning and an exchange of convictions through which we encounter, explore, and imagine possibilities, difference, and otherness. By introducing us to such a process of conversation, law school can teach us to engage in a new form of questioning that allows us to approach legal problems with a reconstructive and critical imagination.

This sort of school of the imagination is also central to the Spiritual Exercises. Ignatius repeatedly directs the retreatant to put himself or herself into the proper disposition for prayer through the use of imagination.... Ignatius consistently invites the retreatant to enter imaginatively into the concrete details of the scene that is the subject of a given contemplation.... Such techniques of imaginative prayer are so central to the Spiritual Exercises that they have been described as a form of decision-oriented mysticism rooted in the act of imagining....

Through an application of the case method that is open to the demands of authentic conversation, the law school experience can foster the development of this sort of moral imagination. Accordingly, as part of the Society's commitment to develop a culture of dialogue, and given their roots in the educational traditions of the Society, law schools operating within the context of Jesuit universities are ideally situated to begin the process of re-imagining the law school as a culture of dialogue fostering conversion to the demands of authentic conversation.

Conclusion. Bernard Lonergan's analysis of the constitutive function of meaning, the operation of practical common sense, and conversion as movement toward a new horizon as a result of detachment from bias, along with White's conception of the law as an activity of constitutive rhetoric within a culture of argument and conversation, suggest that law school can be understood as a process of "re-horizoning" for greater fidelity to the unrestricted desire to know. To the extent that a law school constitutes itself as a community in which authentic conversation about the law is encouraged and in which the skills necessary for such conversation are modeled and taught, the law school can serve as a community which fosters the development of a culture of argument.

Through the dialectical process and conversational questioning that are part of this culture, the law school can be an effective component of a cosmopolis of legal culture with the potential to combat the problems of general bias inherent in the law as a species of practical common sense. Finally, by striving for greater fidelity to unfettered operation of the fundamental human desire to know, the understanding of legal education I have tried to articulate might make it increasingly possible for law schools to train students to "think like lawyers" without sacrificing the students' fundamentally human desires to think and act like persons searching for meaning and value in fully integrated lives.

Principal References

Quotations from original source materials by James Boyd White are from Heracles' Bow: Essays on the Rhetoric and Poetics of the Law (1985) and those by Bernard J. F.

Lonergan are from: Insight: A Study of Human Understanding (rev. stud. ed. 1958); Dimensions of Meaning, in Collection (F.E. Crowe, S.J. ed., 1967); and Method in Theology (1994).

Additional Selected References

William A. Barry, S.J., Allowing the Creator to Deal with the Creature: An Approach to the Spiritual Exercises of Ignatius of Loyola (1994).

Derek Bok, A Flawed System, Harvard Magazine (May–June 1983), at 45.

Frank P. Braio, Towards the Re-Horizoning of Subjects: Re-Structuring Classical-Modern Educational Perspectives, in 13 Method: J. of Lonergan Stud. 99–109 (1995) (reviewing Bernard Lonergan, Topics in Education, in 10 Collected Works of Bernard Lonergan (Robert Doran & Frederick E. Crowe eds., 1993)).

Elizabeth Dvorkin et al., Becoming a Lawyer: A Humanistic Perspective on Legal Education and Professionalism (1981).

Harry T. Edwards, The Growing Disjunction Between Legal Education and the Legal Profession, 91 Michgian Law Review 34 (1992).

David Granfield, The Inner Experience of Law: A Jurisprudence of Subjectivity (1988).

M.H. Hoeflich, Law, Culture and the University: An Inaugural Discourse, 40 Syracuse Law Review 789 (1989)

Anthony T. Kronman, Jurisprudential Responses to Legal Realism, 73 Cornell Law Review 335 (1988).

Anthony T. Kronman, The Lost Lawyer: Failing Ideals of the Legal Profession (1993).

Carrie Menkel-Meadow, Narrowing the Gap by Narrowing the Field: What's Missing from the MacCrate Report—Of Skills, Legal Science and Being a Human Being, 69 Washington Law Review 593 (1994).

Antonio T. de Nicolas, Powers of Imagining, Ignatius de Loyola: A Philosophical Hermeneutic of Imagining through the Collected Works of Ignatius de Loyola (1986).

Mark Spiegel, Theory and Practice in Legal Education: An Essay on Clinical Education, 34 UCLA Law Review 577 (1987).

James P. Walsh, S.J., Imagining: A Way of Life, in Jesuit Education and the Cultivation of Virtue 27–28 (William J. O'Brien ed., 1990).

James Boyd White, When Words Lose Their Meaning: Constitutions and Reconstitutions of language, Character, and Community (1984).

James Boyd White, Law Teachers' Writing, 91 Michigan Law Review 1970 (1993).

James Boyd White, Justice as Translation: An Essay in Cultural and Legal Criticism (1990).

Further Reading
(selected work by Gregory A. Kalscheur, S.J.)

John Paul II, John Courtney Murray, and the Relationship Between Civil Law and Moral Law: A Constructive Proposal for Contemporary American Pluralism, 1 Journal of Catholic Social Thought 231 (2004).

CHAPTER TWO

THEORY AND PRACTICE*

... Most discussions of legal education do not see the question of what is theoretical and what is practical as a problem. Commentators assume we know which labels are appropriate for which things and what these labels mean. The issue, for them, is how to strike the balance between the theoretical and the practical. Those who favor more practice argue that the balance has been struck too far in favor of theory; those who favor more theory argue that legal education is too professional or practical at the expense of theory.... [But stating] the question that way obscures the choices already made. Most types of legal education have elements of both theory and practice, however those terms are defined. In addition, how we choose to define the terms "theory" and "practice" strongly influences how we perceive various aspects of legal education....

The development of legal education in the United States is a [frequently-told] story.... The tension between theory and practice, academic and practitioner, is a constant theme in those accounts. [R]ather than redescribing this conflict, [this essay] challenges the way the conflict is characterized. I argue that each of three major educational traditions within legal education—the case method, legal realism, and clinical education—can be viewed as either theoretical or practical depending upon what aspects are emphasized and upon the perspective of the observer.

Before beginning my argument, I wish to preliminarily define the terms "theory" and "practice." By "theory" we commonly mean a set of general propositions used as an explanation. Theory has to be sufficiently abstract to be relevant to more than just particularized situations. By "practice" we commonly mean the doing of something. Practice also is associated with the idea of repetition; therefore, practice sometimes is equated with the gaining of skills because one gains skills by repetition.

---

* **Mark Spiegel**, *Theory and Practice in Legal Education: An Essay on Clinical Education,* 34 UCLA LAW REVIEW 577 (1987), http://papers.ssrn.com/abstract_id=780444.

[T]hese preliminary definitions of theory and practice are used as background for my discussion of the case method, legal realism, and clinical education. It is important to emphasize, however, that I am not attempting to give the one correct definition of theory or practice. Indeed, ... I argue [below] that there are different traditions which make any attempt at definition contingent upon the choices made by the individual choosing the definition.

The Case Method. American legal education did not begin with Harvard Law School and Christopher Columbus Langdell. [I]n addition to the apprenticeship system there were proprietary private law schools and college-based legal education predating Langdell. Langdell, however, established the University-based professional school and the dominance of the case method.

The "theoretical" part of the development of the case method began with Langdell's famous equating of law with "science." According to Langdell, "[l]aw considered as a science ... consists of certain principles or doctrines." Conceived this way, the study of law is theoretical because it involves learning underlying general principles.

But why the case method? Assuming that law has certain underlying principles and that the appropriate way to learn how to become a lawyer is to study these principles, why not study them via lectures or by reading treatises or other learned books? Here a second connection with science becomes critical. Science involved not only the notion that there were basic principles underlying a discipline but also a methodology. The case method, according to Langdell, was a methodology that emulated the scientific method.

The methodological link had two aspects. First, Langdell argued that cases were the law's raw empirical data.... Second, Langdell maintained that learning principles from cases involved the same kind of inductive reasoning as scientific reasoning. The substantive equation of law and legal education with natural science has not survived, but the methodological link has lasted. It is no longer, however, a methodology that seeks to discover the true principles of the law by looking at "experimental" case data. Instead, the case method teaches students to think like lawyers.

The transition from characterizing the case method as a way of learning the scientific principles of the law to viewing it as a teaching of analysis did not take long. By the 1890's, some twenty years after Langdell began at Harvard, his disciples were justifying the case method because it taught analysis. For example, [William A.] Keener, who introduced the case method to Columbia Law School, wrote: "By this method the student's reasoning powers are constantly developed...." Ames, Langdell's successor at Harvard, stated that the object of the "Harvard method" was not teaching the knowledge of law but the "power of legal reasoning." By 1913, when Josef Redlich did a study of the case method for the Carnegie Foundation, one of the main findings was that "the real purpose of scientific instruction in law is not to impart the content of the law, not to teach the law, but rather to arouse, to strengthen, to carry to the highest possible pitch of perfection, a specifically legal manner of thinking."

Although the shift in justification of the case method from discovering principles to learning analysis could have been perceived as a shift from theory to practice, the case method still was viewed as scientific and theoretical. Redlich, who was critical of the case method for its narrowness, still believed that "[i]t emphasizes the scientific character of legal thought … and demands that law, just because it is a science, must also be taught scientifically." Moreover, according to Redlich, Langdell's great advance over the Inns of Court and the apprenticeship system was that he substituted for this earlier training "a genuine theoretical instruction in the common law."

A further study of legal education was conducted for the Carnegie Foundation in 1921 by A.Z. Reed. Reed, like Redlich, was critical of the case method for its narrowness. He likewise was concerned about the Harvard model being indiscriminately applied by all schools, based on a myth that the bar was homogenous. However, he also saw the case method as "theoretical," even while recognizing that it no longer was designed to teach legal principles but rather to "master judge made laws in the future."

Is the situation different today? Criticism about the narrowness of the case method continues and it is doubtful whether anyone today considers its methodology "scientific." However, for a large segment of legal educators there is still the tendency to consider the case method theoretical. Articles about legal education continue to refer to the case method as theoretical. While none of the authors expressly define theory and its relation to the case method, their use of the term illustrates that the conception of the case method as theoretical is a background assumption that needs no explication.

An example is provided by a comprehensive study of legal education by Professors Gee and Jackson. In a long historical article, Gee and Jackson discuss how the case method was a response to dissatisfaction with the apprenticeship system. They then go on to state that the case method served the need of providing a consistent education in legal theory and a means of analysis. According to them, what Langdell accomplished was to ensure the dominance of the theoretical over the practical….

… Keener, who was an exponent of the case method, justified the case method by emphasizing its practical side:

> The student is required to analyze each case, discriminating between the relevant and the irrelevant, between the actual and possible

grounds of decision. And having thus discussed the case, he is prepared and required to deal with it in its relation to other cases. In
other words, the student is practically doing as a student what he will
be constantly doing as a lawyer.

... In our time, William Twining summed up the view of the case method as
practical by stating succinctly: "The introduction of the case method ... involved a crucial switch from emphasis on knowledge to emphasis on skill."

[Anthony] Chase argues that the development of the case method was the
development of a clinical methodology of law. Whether one agrees with Chase's
equation of the case method with clinical instruction, his argument is sound
that one's view of the case method as theoretical or practical may turn on with
what one compares it. As compared to the apprenticeship system, the case
method is systematic, more abstract, and arguably theoretical. As compared
to the lectures of Thomas Jefferson's day, the case method is narrow, more concerned with methodology rather than principles, and arguably practical.

Legal Realism. Characterizing the case method as teaching doctrine plus
some skills is not a new story. For critics of the case method, the theoretical
aspects of legal education, if any, stem from the realists, not from Langdell.
While all theory in legal education is not "realist" theory, legal realism opened
up the possibility of combining the study of law with other disciplines by arguing that law is not self-contained. From that perspective the law and economics movement is as much a product of legal realism as is critical legal studies. The realists exposed the myth of underlying doctrinal principles and
attempted to bring social science theory to the law schools.

Legal realism cannot be labeled either theory or practice in the same way
as the case method. Legal realism was not a unified movement or an educational model. Nevertheless, an important concern of the realists was legal education. And different "realist" ideas for legal education can be viewed as theory or practice depending upon which representatives are selected and what
aspects are emphasized.

In discussing the "practical" side of realism's relation to legal education, the
obvious starting points are Frank and Llewellyn. Frank wrote a series of articles in which he advocated more "practical" training in law schools. His proposals were derived from his insight that rules do not determine case outcomes;
the "fact" level is crucial. Therefore, immersion in facts is critical to understanding the world of the lawyer and to becoming a lawyer. Practical work
would illustrate how the world of action was different from the world in books.
For Frank, however, this view did not lead to law student as empirical social
scientist. Instead, he proposed that law students become participant-observers.

Karl Llewellyn's "practical" side was more interesting and complex. He divided legal theory into three branches: the study of the ends and values involved in law (legal philosophy); the use of empirical description (legal science); and the study of the craft aspects of law, such as the machinery of justice and methods of lawyers and judges (jurisprudence). Like Frank, Llewellyn believed that the study of craft was not limited to empirical social science study—that was the job of the legal science branch of legal theory. Llewellyn also was interested in the transmission of skills. His idea of learning skills had both an aesthetic and a theoretical dimension. Learning a craft was learning an art and, as such, had important humanistic value. Moreover, as Llewellyn's tripartite division of legal theory illustrates, skills were an integral part of theory.

The "practical" side of Llewellyn and Frank was not merely a fringe element of their thinking, but derived directly from their critique of formalism and the case method. For these scholars, the narrowness of the case method limited our definitions both of law and of lawyering.

Besides Frank and Llewellyn, is there any support for the claim that realism had a practical side? As an academic intellectual enterprise, realism's most prominent "positive feature" was its attempt to integrate other disciplines, particularly the social sciences, into the study of law. But, as Professor Schlegel has shown, even the social scientists had their practical agenda. The scholarly tradition of natural science and objective rigorous research was accompanied by a pragmatic reformer tradition. Empirical facts were necessary not merely to understand the underlying principles but to confirm the need for reform. In this sense, the addition of social science was practical.

Even within the scientific tradition there is an ambiguity. To be scientific is to be rigorous. While the addition of social sciences to the study of law was broadening as compared to the case method, science also has a technical side that, combined with the pragmatic concerns of the scientific realists, can change legal education from a humanistic enterprise to the learning of technique. As Calvin Woodard has stated, this focus on making the law useful transformed legal scholarship and education "from an inductive science based on the case method into an applied science based on practical considerations."

None of the above discussion is meant to prove that either the case method or legal realism is either theoretical or practical. What it intends to illustrate is the contingent nature of such labels. From one perspective Langdell brought law schools into the intellectual world of the University; from another perspective Langdell professionalized legal education and centered its methods in the world of practice. From one perspective legal realism brought social science theory to legal education; from another it created the "social engineer—

a craftsperson who embodies both scientific rationality and the skills of practical implementation."

Clinical Education. Where does clinical education fit within this labeling process? Both by definition and history it starts on the practical side of the spectrum. By definition it is practice because it involves doing. Moreover, it appears to concern itself more with particulars than with the general. Its focus is the world of practical ends rather than abstract knowledge.

Clinical education, at least in the early stages of development during the 1960's, was more akin to the second coming of the apprenticeship system than to an educational movement. Its initial development was largely a response to two forces: student complaints about the lack of relevance of the second and third year of law school, and CLEPR grants. Little thought was given to basic questions concerning what clinical education had to offer law students and law schools other than the opportunity for the earlier acquisition of real life experience. If there was an explicit educational rationale, it was related to some connection between providing service and learning.

In the 1970's, pressure developed for additional skills training in law school. Chief Justice Burger began giving speeches about the inadequacy of trial advocacy. The Clare and Devitt Commission proposals and the development of the National Institute of Trial Advocacy lawyer training programs were responses to Chief Justice Burger's concerns. There also developed a broader focus on lawyer competency which included skills in addition to trial advocacy. For example, the ABA Task Force on Competency recommended that law schools provide instruction in interviewing, counseling, and negotiation.

Clinical education was a natural partner of this increased emphasis on skills and competency. One of the original rationales for clinical education was skills training. For many, skills, by definition, can only be learned by performance. Clinical education provided opportunities for performance, and hence clinical education was the place to center skills training. This equating of clinical education with skills training further reinforced the idea that clinical education is inherently practical.

But neither the definitional approach nor this history captures the whole picture. Just as the case method and legal realism embody elements of both theory and practice, so does clinical education. Gary Bellow, in an influential article published in 1973, described clinical education as a methodology. For Bellow, clinical education's underlying method was student performance of a role within the legal system and the use of this experience as the focal point for intellectual inquiry. By focusing attention on methodology, Bellow tried to bring to the forefront the learning issues that were submerged beneath issues such as funding and credit allocations. In so doing he was able to get beyond the notion that since doing is practice, clinical education's inherent nature is practical.

If clinical education is a methodology, it conceivably can be used to teach any of the substantive subjects in the curriculum. If these substantive courses are "theoretical" the use of a different methodology should not change the theoretical status of the courses. Under Bellow's definition of clinical education there is nothing inherently limiting about clinical education other than using the student's performance as a starting point for inquiry. Some may see the student's practice experience in legal services as limiting, but clinical education does not require placement in only legal services offices. This placement is not inherent in the nature of the methodology. Moreover, Bellow's conceptualization of clinical education as methodology directly linked it to the tradition of case method teaching as methodology. If the case method could be theoretical, why not this newer method?

Another important rationale for clinical education that emerged at this time was the teaching of professional responsibility. The primary funding source for clinical education, the Council on Legal Education for Professional Responsibility, had the term "professional responsibility" in its title during the 1960's, but it was not until the mid-1970's that a significant shift occurred toward using clinical education to teach professional responsibility. This link with professional responsibility could be characterized simply as a widening of the practical domain of clinical instruction. The teaching of ethics or professional responsibility has comparable intellectual status within legal education as has clinical education. Moreover, ethical issues frequently are considered the domain of the practitioner. On the other hand, professional responsibility can be approached as an exploration of philosophy which would be as theoretical as any other part of law school. Starting the inquiry into these issues from performance does not change this and, indeed, arguably strengthens the possibility of meaningful theoretical discussion....

... [D]espite its history, clinical education is not one thing and does not have one essential nature. Clinical education can be a methodology similar to the case method, or it can be an exploration of theory borrowed from other disciplines similar to legal realism. Clinical education can be considered either theory or practice in the same way that the case method and legal realism can be either. That is, the characterization can be determined more by what features are emphasized and by the perspective of the person answering the question than by the object of the question.

This is not really surprising. Much of the question of categorization as theory or practice reflects a false dichotomy that demands that things be seen in either/or terms. Either you are contemplative or you are not; either you are dealing with general propositions or you are not. Reality is, obviously, much more complex. Any activity or educational method involves a mixture of contemplation and action, truth seeking and practical ends, general statements and specifics. Clinical education is no exception; therefore, there is a choice involved in how we view clinical education....

Practice. Given the many words written about the "basic dichotomy" in legal education between theory and practice, it is surprising that little attention has been devoted to attempting to specify what an author means when he or she uses these terms. If these terms had one unique meaning, this failure to "define" would be of little significance. However, these terms do not have singular definitions. Indeed, there are at least two different ways of looking at these terms, each of which signifies very different world views. For lack of better labels I will call one "scientific" and the other "normative."

At the beginning of this essay, theory was defined as a set of general propositions used as explanation. This definition embodies two ideas: generality and explanation. Theory has to be sufficiently general to be relevant to more than just particularized situations. A theory that applied to only one instance would not be a theory at all, but would be simply a description of that one instance. It is not sufficient, however, for theory to be simply general; it must also explain. This understanding of theory as explanation connects theory with truth. Under the classical version the relationship of theory to truth is an exclusion of activities having a practical end from the domain of theory. Theoretic truth was truth recognized as having value in itself, free from the distortion allegedly caused by the need to achieve practical ends. Related to the classical view of theory as truth is the notion that theory involves contemplation. By retreating into the world of the mind we are able to perceive in a more detached manner.

Under the scientific view, theory has come to have a highly structured definition derived from assumptions about what counts as truth. Contemplation, by itself, is no longer considered sufficient to produce theory. Instead, propositions must be set forth in a logical order which explains how they are deduced from the theory.

One may define properties and categories, and one still has no theory. One may state that there are relations between properties, and still one has no theory. One may state that a change in one property will produce a definite change in another property, and one still has no theory. Not until one has properties and propositions stating relations between them, and the propositions form a deductive system—not until one has all three does one have a theory.

Furthermore, the propositions must be stated with sufficient precision so that they are testable and capable of verification by empirical experiment.

Since only factual statements can be proved or disproved, normative statements are excluded from scientific theory. Normative statements may be interesting, even illuminating, but they do not count as theory because they cannot lead to discovery of truth. They are merely an expression of a subjective position.

This scientific definition of theory has been challenged in a number of ways. The assumptions that there can be separation between objective and subjective, fact and value, particular and general, that allows for the discovery of "irrefutable truth" [in Hannah Arendt's phrase] have been questioned not only in the social sciences but also within the natural sciences and mathematics. In addition, under the classical tradition, theory not only distinguished [as Richard Bernstein put it] "appearance from reality, the false from the true," but also provided an "orientation for practical activity." We have lost this vision of theory and it is argued that we need to reclaim it.

This particularized definition of theory also affects practice. Under the scientific view practice is a specific kind of doing. It is the technical application of theoretical knowledge. Many of the same writers who challenge the scientific understanding of theory also challenge this conception of practice. They argue that we have lost a critical distinction between the technical and the practical. Practice at one time was not simply the application of technique, but it was the domain in which judgment was exercised. Moreover, practice was different from technical expertise because it expressly asked [to quote Gadamer,] "the question of the good too … about the best way of life or about the best constitution of the state."

The separation between the scientific and the normative views of theory and practice is part of our tradition of legal education. Langdell's system not only attempted to emulate scientific methodology, but also mimicked science's aspirations to be seen as value-free. The realists, in turning to social science, also were interested in making law a value-free social science. The legal process school was still another attempt to insulate law and the legal education from choices about substantive values. And today the law and economics school sees itself as working within a scientific paradigm which allows it to avoid normative statements....

Some of the proposals to reform legal education further illustrate the influence of the scientific view. The suggestion that we should divide our students into two streams after the first or second year of law school—those who are seeking truth and those who are seeking the financial rewards of private practice—is based upon the idea that the pragmatic orientation of the students going into practice is inconsistent with the pursuit of truth. This assumes both a conception of truth that is in accord with the scientific vision and a view of practice that is technocratic.

The scientific vision of theory and practice also influences our perception of clinical education [which] usually is equated with skills training. However, if one accepted the possibility that practice was something other than acquisition of technical skills—that it included the study of judgment and a critical assessment of values and institutions—clinical education might be viewed differently.

First, clinical education can be used to explore and to think about lawyer decisionmaking. Theory as applied to the real world is partial. The dilemma of practice is how to decide when there is no universal rule that provides the answer. Studying decisionmaking is one way to explore this gap.

Second, clinical education can be used to apply a critical perspective to a student's own lawyering experiences and to connect those experiences to the political, social, and psychological dimensions of lawyering. Studying decisionmaking requires an understanding of the assumptions about ourselves and the world of lawyering which govern our decisions. It is the exploration of these assumptions and the connection between them and our behavior that can lead to the critical insight that comes from trying to figure out what is this activity and what does it mean to me. It also can lead to the exploration of the major ethical dilemmas of the lawyer's role. Finally, it can lead to the exploration of the meaning of these activities for society—is this an appropriate and just way to organize our institutions....

... I am not arguing the superiority of either the normative or the scientific view. What is critical to my argument is recognizing that the choice involved has much to say about how we perceive clinical education. Acknowledging the scientific model as only one point of view rather than the only correct view opens up the possibility that what we mean when we say clinical education is "practical" is contingent. If the scientific view is selected, clinical education is likely to be equated with the learning of technocratic skills; if the normative view of theory is selected then clinical education can be viewed as something other than technical skills application....

[T]he way we label aspects of legal education as "theory" or "practice" and what we mean by those labels involves choices on our part and ... those choices have affected how we view and use clinical education.... [A]s long as the dialogue in legal education is characterized as how much theory (traditional courses) vs. how much practice (skills training), the framing of the issue determines the answer. Traditional courses are at the core with some practice at the periphery. We might argue about the relative size of the core and the periphery, but that would be the extent of the dialogue. By definition we know what is central. On the other hand, perhaps, if the issue were perceived so that we agreed that little of what we do within legal education has a unitary nature of theory or practice and that our conceptions of theory and practice can be broadened, then we might just ask how the total package of legal education should be structured without allowing a priori labeling to determine the answers we reach.

Selected References

James Barr Ames, in Proceedings of the 7th Annual Meeting of the Association of American Law Schools, 31 Rerpot of the 31st Annual Meeting of the American Bar Association 1012 (1907).

Hannah Arendt, The Life of the Mind (one vol. ed. 1981).

Gary Bellow, On Teaching the Teachers: Some Preliminary Reflections on Clinical Education As Methodology, in Clinical Education for the Law Student (1973).

Richard Bernstein, The Restructuring of Social and Political Theory (1976); Praxis and Action (1971); & Beyond Objectivism and Relativism (1983).

Anthony Chase, The Origin of Modern Professional Education: The Harvard Case Method Conceived as Clinical Instruction in Law, 5 Nova Law Journal 323 (1981).

Roger Cramton, The Current State of the Law School Curriculum, 32 Journal of Legal Education 321 (1982).

Jerome Frank, A Plea for Lawyer-Schools, 56 Yale Law Journal 1303 (1947) & Why Not a Clinical-Lawyer School, 81 Pennsylvania Law Review 907 (1933).

Hans-Georg Gadamer, Hermeneutics as Practical Philosophy, in Reason in the Age of Science (G. Lawrence trans. 1981).

E. Gordon Gee & Donald W. Jackson, Bridging the Gap: Legal Education and Lawyer Competency, 1977 BYU Law Review 695.

Thomas C. Grey, Langdell's Orthodoxy, 45 Pittsburgh Law Review 1 (1983).

William A. Keener, The Inductive Method in Legal Education, 17 Report of the 17th Annual Meeting of the American Bar Association 482 (1894).

Anthony T. Kronman, Foreword: Legal Scholarship and Moral Education, 90 Yale Law Journal 955 (1981).

Christopher Columbus Langdell, A Selection of Cases on the Law of Contracts (1871).

Karl Llewellyn, The Study of Law as a Liberal Art, in Jurisprudence: Realism in Theory and Practice (1962).

Josef Redlich, The Case Method in American University Law Schools (1914).

A. Z. Reed, Training for the Public Profession of the Law (1921).

Henry Schlegel, American Legal Realism and Empirical Social Science: From the Yale Experience, 28 Buffalo Law Review 459 (1979).

William Twining, Pericles and the Plumber, 83 Law Quarterly Review 396 (1967).

Calvin Woodard, The Limits of Legal Realism: An Historical Perspective, 54 Virginia Law Review 689 (1968).

Further Reading (selected work by Mark Spiegel)

The Rule 11 Studies and Civil Rights Cases: An Inquiry Into the Neutrality of Procedural Rules, 32 Connecticut Law Review 155 (1999).

Lawyers and Professional Autonomy: Reflections on Corporate Lawyering and the
  Doctrine of Informed Consent, 9 Western New England Law Review 139 (1987).
Lawyering and Client Decision-making: Informed Consent and the Legal Profession,
  128 Pennsylvania Law Review 41 (1979).

CHAPTER THREE

A THEORY-PRACTICE SPIRAL[*]

Should law school classes cultivate professional skills or should they advance a broad intellectual agenda? This question has remarkable staying power in ongoing debates about the crux of a legal education. The form of the inquiry presumes a distinction between legal theory and legal practice.

This Article concerns the relationship between theory and practice in legal academia. In particular, it examines the relationship between theory and practice from the standpoint of two movements within law's academy: clinical education and feminist jurisprudence. Although the former is often thought of as a practical movement, and the latter a theoretical movement, I hope to demonstrate the fundamental methodological similarity of the two movements, and hence, the problematic nature of the theory-practice label. Ironically, the methodological similarity of the two movements is found in their responses to the problematic nature of the theory-practice relationship.

This Article also examines the ethical impulse that sparks clinical education and feminism. I suggest that each movement's perceptions of the theory-practice relationship are embedded in ethical concerns and have far-reaching ethical implications....

Because feminists and clinical educators recognize the interlacing of theory and practice, they view this Article's opening question—whether law school classes should cultivate professional skills or advance a broad intellectual agenda—as an unintelligible inquiry. An explicit recognition of the theory-practice relationship by all legal educators would shift their focus to the inquiry that preoccupies clinical and feminist legal educators: how can legal education more effectively illuminate the ethical dimensions of daily life and work, and how can it better inculcate in students a sense of moral responsibility for professional and personal choices? The pervasiveness of injustice in our world, and the power of lawyers to aggravate or alleviate it, makes this an

* **Phyllis Goldfarb,** *A Theory-Practice Spiral:The Ethics of Feminism and Clinical Education,* 75 MINNESOTA LAW REVIEW 1599 (1991), http://papers.ssrn.com/abstract_id= 749365.

urgent inquiry. I hope this Article represents a step toward encouraging all legal educators to acknowledge and address this crucial question....

Reading Antigone. Sophocle's *Antigone* opens in the midst of crisis. Antigone and her older sister Ismene have suffered the loss of their brothers, Polynices and Eteocles, who have killed one another while fighting for the throne of Thebes. Having assumed the throne, their uncle Creon has issued an edict declaring that Eteocles, the ruler whom the Theban people had favored, would be given an honorable state funeral, while Polynices, who had returned from expulsion to forcibly seize the throne, would be denied all last rites. The edict forbade anyone to bury Polynices on pain of death.

As the curtain lifts, Antigone is informing Ismene that she has decided to defy Creon's edict. In a previous conversation in which Antigone had tried in vain to dissuade Polynices from doing battle, Polynices had asked his sisters to bury him when he met his death. Antigone now declares that her obligation lies with her dead brother and with the holiest laws of the gods which impose an obligation to bury one's deceased kin, not with the law of the king. Frightened by Antigone's defiance, Ismene insists that because they are only women, they are too weak to resist men and the state. When Ismene refuses to assist Antigone in defying the decree, informing her that she is "bound to fail," Antigone speaks harshly to her. Ismene responds by assuring Antigone that she loves her.

This conversation shapes Antigone's central conflict, and the drama unfolds towards its somber conclusion. Among its many themes, the play seeks to unravel the complex relationship between law and morality. This philosophical inquiry is captured in the struggles of its characters. Antigone elevates her religious responsibility to her deceased brother over her responsibility to obey the law. Polynices' rejection of Antigone's pleas that he not go to war has not affected the primacy of her responsibility to their relationship. This choice is consistent with her previous behavior in insisting on the primacy over her own life of her responsibility to her relationship with her exiled Oedipus, whom she had cared for until his death. In contrast stands Creon's insistence until near the play's end that his duty to consistently apply law and policy outweighed his familial relationships with Polynices or Antigone.

A Feminist's Reading. A feminist reader of *Antigone* might note that, although only Ismene explicitly evokes gender to support her stance, tying her refusal to resist the state to her womanhood, the genders of the other characters are more than incidental features. [T]he play challenges the possibility of transforming moral discourse by including both voices when the power to declare truth is so unevenly distributed. Because Creon commanded the force of law, his truth could officially annihilate Antigone's truth, casting it as deviant and dangerous. If not for the depths of tragedy that befell his family, Creon was unlikely to have recognized the partiality of his view. Antigone, then, underscores the reasons that feminists value double vision: they acknowledge the need for genuine dialogue across differences while remaining sharply cognizant of the societal structures that impeded its accomplishment....

Antigone, or any number of other lived or vicariously lived situations, readily provide the impetus for such a theoretical project. Feminist theorizing begins with the concrete experiences of particular women, such as Antigone, whose situations crystallize the relationship of their needs and interests as they view them to state authority as they encounter it. These experiences are then questioned, probed, examined, explored, and analyzed, a process that produces tentative theoretical conceptions. Once formulated, these theories are continually held up to the light of new experiences for evaluation, refinement, modification, and development. In short, feminist thinkers view concrete situations as containing strong theoretical potentialities. Theory then circles back to guide future behavioral choices which, in turn, test and reshape theory. This method of analysis is an essential feature of feminism....

A Clinician's Reading. Examining whether a clinical educator would bring any special perspective to a reading of *Antigone* is an effort less obvious than the above. Legal clinicians, having drawn in the past on a variety of theoretical foundations for their work, are likely to have a more diffused focus than feminist readers focused on gender. Nevertheless, clinicians might find in Antigone a justification of clinical methods. They might compare the possibilities for insight immanent in study and deliberation alone with the possibilities for insight immanent in Antigone's situation.

Some teachers are drawn to clinical settings due to a deeply-held belief that experiencing a conflict between one's personal morality and a prescription of law or law practice provides a bone-deep entryway into exploring the relationship between law and morality, or constructing a theory of state power and how it operates. Confronting such a situation, clinicians believe, brings the values at stake and the potential consequences of various courses of action into sharp relief. Thus, a person facing an actual conflict is more likely to notice and contemplate the breadth and depth of the concrete consequences that may flow from the situation....

The stories underlying the cases that find their way into law school clinics may resemble Greek tragedies: their characters confronting trying circumstances and behaving wisely or foolishly, nobly or ignobly. The complexity, richness, and texture of these cases do not easily lend themselves to simply stated understandings or moral summaries. Clinic students, as well as clients, may find themselves standing in Antigone's position, experiencing distaste, perhaps even a powerful visceral resistance, toward the prescribed form or custom of law practice. They may also find themselves standing in Creon's position, uncritically accepting the practices of law without attention to consequences. Alternatively, they may feel, like Ismene, a deep ambivalence about their personal and civic responsibilities. The value of clinical methods depends on using Antigone's, Creon's, Ismene's, and others' standpoints as starting points for inquiry....

Why The Readings Converge. Despite differences in content, both the feminist and clinical readings adopt a similar approach to the theoretical enterprise. Both feminist theorists and clinical educators see experiences like Antigone's and Creon's as containing, among other things, powerful theoretical possibilities. Both movements also see theory as containing powerful practical possibilities for informing future behavior and experience. This ongoing feedback relationship suggests that what has appeared dichotomous is actually dialectic. The theory-practice split is really a theory-practice spiral.

Clearly, clinical education and feminist theory demonstrate not the inherent separation between theory and practice, but the eternal interplay of good theory and good practice. In fact, clinicians and feminists share concerns about the soundness of theory uninformed by, and untested in, the bright light of the real-world, as well as the soundness of practice unshaped by, and unattached to, the firm roots of consciously-developed theory.

[T]he methodologies of feminism and clinical education both emphasize, as the reading of Antigone illustrates, direct personal experience as theory's starting point, as well as its returning point for testing and rebuilding. To reiterate the methodological premise of both movements, each conceives of the relationship between explanation and experience, theory and practice, in the shape of a spiral.

Use of Experience. Clinical education has a predominantly pedagogical identity, generating considerable attention to the learning process. In the interest of effective learning, clinical students engineer and participate in events which they carefully analyze, soon thereafter, and others who observed or participated in the same events may join in the examination. Feminists, on the other hand, though concerned with the learning process, generally do not identify with pedagogy in the same way as clinical educators. Without the demand of short-term learning objectives, feminists rely on the delayed retelling of experience to those who may or may not have shared analogous events, but who rarely shared the actual events.

Feminists rely on the consciousness-raising process of storytelling about a broad range of life experiences as one source of experiential data. Clinic educators and students rely on a narrower band of experience, their own engagement in professional work, as their primary source of data. Clinic students, for purposes of learning, deliberately choose this band of experience, which they could otherwise avoid or postpone. Feminists, on the other hand, generally examine their own and others' unavoidable, everyday experiences for purposes of learning.

Feminists generally place more importance than clinicians on acquiring second-order experience, that is on enlarging personal experience by seeking out stories of others' experiences and discussing these stories in group settings. Although a clinical classroom may sometimes resemble this feminist process, dressing for a time in consciousness-raising garb, clinics attend primarily to first-order experience, the students' direct involvement in events. Feminist methods of interpreting experience also tend to include more group involvement and feedback than do clinical methods of interpretation. Inquiry into a clinic student's experiences often occurs in a community of two, in a discussion between supervisor and student.

Despite these distinctions, each movement uses its experiential data similarly, generating insight by asking questions that examine the meanings and implications of the data. The movements are alike in the essential authority that they accord to the data of experience in their respective intellectual endeavors.

Role of Affect. Because experience contains both cognitive and affective content, exploring an experience fully requires exploring not only its cognitive, but also its affective dimensions. Feelings often provide windows to thought, and analyzing the causes and consequences of particular affective reactions often is a valuable step toward comprehending experience. When feminism and clinical education claim that experience precedes explanation, and that explanation must remain open to experience, they are tacitly recognizing the role of affect in experience and, therefore, in human understanding. Feminists and clinicians, in their respective settings, devote time to bringing this role to the surface, rather than submerging it, in order to facilitate understanding.

Interpersonal Dynamics. One reason that experience inevitably includes cognitive and affective dimensions is that experience generally occurs in an interpersonal setting, and other persons arouse in us both cognitive and affective responses. Because feminists recognize the political content of personal interaction, they counsel attention to the social identity and experience-based points of view of the persons who are interacting, as one contribution to a full understanding of the events that the interaction engenders. Although the standard clinical vocabulary does not include explicitly political language to describe the interpersonal dynamics of law practice, clinicians frequently study the nature of these dynamics in at least implicitly political terms, and view such study as essential to conscious participation in, and careful evaluation of, the events that transpire.

Hierarchy and Collaboration. Recognition by clinicians and feminists of the socially charged quality of interpersonal dynamics has consequences for the implementation of their respective methods. Clinical educators not only attend to relationships created by a legal event such as the attorney-client relationship, but they consider the student-teacher relationship as well. Because clinical teachers and clinical students are involved in a collaborative enterprise, and because they jointly consider and decide issues that the teacher did not preconceive, the power in their relationship is less imbalanced than it can be in many teacher-student relationships. Although the teacher's evaluation of students and her insistence on the completion of certain lawyering tasks essential to effective representation inevitably retain hierarchical overtones, other more egalitarian features of the clinical process diminish their impact.

Likewise, feminist teaching retains as few aspects of authoritarian control as possible. Feminist teachers endeavor to create a cooperative classroom climate that welcomes students and other persons to share their life experiences as the basis for further inquiry and speculation. In so doing, the feminist classroom recreates, in part, the collaborative, questioning spirit of the consciousness-raising method. For feminists, the teaching medium has ethical weight and is part and parcel of the learning message.

Because first-order engagement in lawyering is the central feature of clinical curricula, clinicians need not work as hard as feminists to shape a climate that invites personal experience into the learning inquiry. As a result, clinicians are more likely than feminists to view the collaborative exploration of the meaning of experiences as indigenous to their teaching enterprise, rather than as a conscious outgrowth of an ethical choice. Nevertheless, many clinicians view the less hierarchical, more cooperative nature of clinical programs as an important contribution to law school education.

Interdisciplinary Inquiry. Feminists and clinicians resist the compartmentalization of ideas that impedes awareness of their interconnection, and view wide-ranging thought as essential to truth-seeking. Consequently, both have adopted interdisciplinary methods. Each movement engages the services of many disciplines to further understanding of their own and others' concrete observations and experiences.

Feminist legal thinkers can locate interdisciplinary assistance with relative ease because scholars who identify their work as feminist and share similar values and approaches are at work in virtually every field. To the contrary, clinical educators do not constitute a readily identifiable, cross-disciplinary move-ment. Because the work of clinical legal educators has no tidy analogue in other disciplines, legal clinicians comb other disciplines for whatever assistance they can find. For clinicians, exploring the relationship of law to society requires such assistance, just as for feminists, comprehensively grasping the pervasive impact of socializing forces such as gender requires interdisciplinary treatment. Real life, the focus and source of each movement's analysis, suffers too much distortion when viewed though a single disciplinary prism. Rather, under-standing and improving real lives compels careful synthesis of all trustworthy knowledge, no matter its name or disciplinary address.

Contextual Reasoning. The Aristotelian practical reasoning process em-ployed by each movement, moving as it does from specific to general, links the particulars generated and examined by clinical and feminist methods to the conceptual insights of many disciplines. Moreover, Aristotelian-style rea-soning links these particulars to each movement's normative concerns. Clin-icians and feminists worry, as did Aristotle, about the outcomes produced by applying principles to a limited factual context rather than developing a full contextual understanding before rendering judgment.

Attention to context means that feminists and clinical participants must ex-plicitly acknowledge as relevant pieces of the context the norms they bring to the details of events. As feminists and clinicians have indicated, only by ex-amining their normative structures can people truly comprehend and evalu-ate their behavioral choices. Acknowledging one's normative inclinations as a facet of the exercise of judgment conforms with the feminist's concern for can-dor in decisionmaking and for persistent appraisal of the soundness of one's judgment. This self-conscious examination also conforms with the clinician's concern for vigilant attention to the ethics of lawyering practices.

Critical Inquiry. Critique is inherent in the feminist enterprise. Feminists closely scrutinize the norms and ideologies embodied in institutional arrange-ments and compare these norms to their own ethical values. Although fewer clinical scholars have risen to this challenge, such scrutiny is inherent in the clinical project as well. No one concerned with the power allocations in legal process can avoid such critical institutional assessment. Taking this obligation seriously frees thinkers to envision and implement better institutional choices.

For feminists and clinicians, the need to consult the subtleties of varied ex-periences and a broad array of knowledge sources emerges from the urgency of knowing. Both clinicians and feminists find more at stake in this quest than intellectual integrity alone. The quality of living itself is the weight in the bal-ance. Clinicians are deeply concerned with the conditions that trigger the legal process, with the consequences of legal process for their clients, and with the effect of legal process on all who encounter it. Feminist legal thinkers are concerned with these issues as well, because they are issues that implicate trenchant questions of fairness, justice, and equality. The concern with consequences, and with concepts that may generate better consequences, is an animating force of each movement.

Moral Judgment. From an Aristotelian perspective, feminist methodology and clinical methodology each represent a species of activist moral philosophy. Both movements view engagement in an ethically-conscious practice as a prerequisite to the knowledge and development of ethical judgment. Although the practices of each movement are not equivalent, each conceives of an ethical practice as involving engagement in activity in which one learns reflectively from and with others. Although perhaps eliciting and attending to somewhat divergent details, each views reasoning from the details of real events to principled resolution as the appropriate manner of engaging and developing moral judgment.

Insistence on contextual development does not undermine the capacity of feminists and clinicians to make moral judgments. Rather, this is the feature of feminist and clinical methods that makes moral judgment possible. It is in this sense that feminists and clinicians, while ethically scrupulous, are the opposite of ethical relativists. They have made a moral judgment that moral judgments must be as carefully and flexibly tailored as possible to actual lived situations. In other words, feminists and clinicians require elaborate knowledge of the many-faceted realities and novelties of a situation before passing judgment and taking action. Feminists and clinicians do not use their sensitivity to the harm that faulty judgments can unleash to evade making judgments, but to highlight the importance of taking extraordinary care in developing the requisite knowledge from which to undertake the task of judgment....

Enriching the Traditional Law School Classroom. Those who malign lawyers' character and competence turn to law schools to help solve both problems. By exposing students to law as it operates through people, processes, and institutions, and by promoting practices of critical reflection, law schools can do something about lawyer's competence and perhaps even more about lawyer's character. By supporting and taking seriously both clinical and feminist methods, as this Article describes them, law schools would cultivate habits of attention to matters of ethical consequence and improve the moral training of lawyers.

Taking clinical and feminist methods seriously might cause the proliferation of a few, or a few more, courses in clinical education and feminist jurisprudence in the law school curriculum. To my mind, this would be an eminently desirable result. Another way for legal education to take these movements seriously is to import the lessons of both methodologies into the traditional classroom.

If teaching doctrine is the aim of traditional education, then teaching "doctrine in a vacuum" frustrates that aim. Legal rules and principles grow out of historical, social, cultural, and ethical contexts. For students to understand fundamentally and work creatively with rules and principles, they must appreciate the contexts from which these rules and principles emerged. Adopting the clinical and feminist emphasis on the development of context as a prelude to understanding would enrich the traditional classroom environment.

One way to develop more context for legal rules and principles is to diversify the learning materials of the law school classroom. Feminists and clinicians would urge classroom elaboration of the stories of the persons who become the textbooks' cases, whether through visits to the class of persons involved in litigation, examination of story-illuminating materials such as case histories, transcripts, and pleadings, or imaginative role-playing by students based on historical materials. Students could then probe these materials to ascertain whether they included the positions of all interested persons and communities and, if not, seek to remedy the exclusions.

Use of interdisciplinary tools, as advocated by feminists and clinical educators, would inform students' thinking beyond the concrete history of the case itself. With interdisciplinary assistance, a student could consider a number of important questions: What were the structural forces—historical, social, and cultural—alive in the era and region in which the case was born? What were the patterns of social conflict and conditions of social distress that may have affected its birth? How did the conduct and outcome of the case affect these conditions? How can professionals and institutions respond to the individual and social problems that they encounter?

With this broad and deep contextual background, feminists and clinicians would require students to reason from the concrete reality of the cases to principled conclusions. Feminists, in particular, would have students consider the reasoning advanced and the conclusions desired by the full array of interested persons before making any decisions, encouraging students to rethink doctrine from a variety of vantage points. Students then would compare their decisions and decisionmaking processes to the actual reasoning and judgment in the case. In doing so, they would have to reflect on questions of fairness and justice. Was the decision and the process of decision in this case just? From whose perspectives? Can I defend my decision and my process of decision? Can I critique them? What is my defense or critique of the court's reasoning and holding?

Cross-disciplinary attention to the tools of the humanities, particularly literature and philosophy, would help students think critically about these questions of justice, fairness, and truth. Wrestling with their internal conflicts concerning ethical processes and outcomes, an active experience on which students must reflect intensively, can help students develop the cognitive and affective capacities of moral judgment needed to resolve their conflicts. In this way, students, guided by whatever tools are available, confront and articulate the inchoate philosophies by which they live and make choices. By doing so, they come to understand themselves and others and can begin to develop a conscious process of moral reasoning....

The feminist and clinical movements view the nature of justice and community as the stakes of education, a sensibility that the classroom can actively tap. To stimulate this sensibility, feminists and clinicians would reduce the traditional hierarchy of the classroom. A teacher wedded to this aim would not be the omniscient fount of knowledge, but would facilitate the students' active responsibility for making sense of their experience of the legal and interdisciplinary materials. Authoritarianism conflicts with the values of this project and impedes its possibilities of success. An atmosphere of open exploration, where students and teachers exchange their views and insights on matters of deep and abiding interest, encourages students to assume responsibility for developing the understanding of self and others that this classroom approach requires.

If legal education followed this methodological course, it would come to resemble feminist and clinical methodologies in yet another manner. The classroom would employ particular intellectual practices, and insight would flow from participation in these practices. These practices involve relating to diverse texts and materials in a way that brings one's own and others' perspectives into view, and critically reflecting on these perspectives in light of such materials. The experience of the classroom method would constitute the source of insight, and the experience of further classes and materials would test and develop these insights. This classroom methodology links theory and practice in the spiral that inspires feminism and clinical education. Plainly, the lessons of these movements can enlighten legal education generally.

Reexamining Ethics. The methodologies of the feminist and clinical education movements suggest that the story of Antigone, a case in a law school clinic, or other richly specified narratives represent promising springboards for inquiry into broad questions about law and morality. The considerable and sundry details of such narratives express the subtleties and complexities of the morally charged situations in which humans find themselves. Unlike many children's tales, a single lesson does not surface readily from these narratives. Rarely do these real-life or life-like contexts provide easily grasped answers to obvious questions. Rather, they suggest multiple interpretations and analyses. The narratives contain painstaking renderings of competing viewpoints that check our natural tendencies to oversimplify and overlook details and perspectives that unsettle the neat conclusions that we desire. We must actively engage the full breadth and depth of these narratives to honestly and effectively further our analysis. What we will come to know as a result of this inquiry will be altered by the contextualized process through which we have come to know it.

I have sought to demonstrate that such a theory-building practice is a distinctly ethical project. Clinical and feminist methods represent possibilities for rescuing the morally significant details that are systematically excluded from the culture's storehouse of standard stories. Acute empirical sensitivity—foregrounding the stories of those whom cultural structures have generally relegated to the background, and supporting the voices often rendered barely audible—can help to accomplish this goal. Working through the cognitive dissonance created by the infusion of these previously neglected perspectives expands our understanding and promotes both a critique of the societal structures that obscured such knowledge and an interest in dismantling these knowledge-distorting structures. This is why Abraham Heschel would have prophets take philosophers to the slums. From the feminist-clinician-prophet-philosopher's vantage point, the distinction between epistemology and ethics collapses.

From feminists' and clinicians' relentless demand for elaborate concrete detail and for special attention to the data provided by those whom society frequently disempowers comes a reconceived notion of what qualifies as ethical inquiry. This notion of ethical inquiry is a process grounded in our experiences of social and institutional interactions and concerned with the way people actually respond to the moral choices presented by everyday life and work. The focus of ethical theory is no longer the justification of actions affecting the "generalized others" of traditional philosophy, but the justification of actions affecting the "concrete others" with whom we are enmeshed. Ethical systems emerge from this network of relationships when we seek to resolve and explain our resolutions of the quotidian dilemmas that we encounter in the complex, nuanced, temporal context in which they arise. This ethical theory, then, responds to the experiences central to daily personal situations and requires reflection on such situations to develop moral consciousness.

In the hands of feminists and clinicians, ethics becomes a sustained practice of empirical attention and reflection on the actions of people in actual situations. Ordinary life expresses and creates ethical theory, which is understood as having an inescapably social character. The better our context-sensitive empiricism, the better our moral deliberations, and the more precise the articulation of our ethical principles will be.

Conclusion. As exemplified by the reading of Antigone, feminism and clinical education are independent movements that, in response to different conditions, have formulated reciprocally reinforcing methodologies. In this Article, I have explored the dramatic likeness between feminist methods and clinical methods, a likeness rooted in their independent efforts to foster collaborative critical inquiry into the ethical dimensions of interpersonal and institutional experiences. I have sought to enhance that likeness by considering the implications of a direct application of feminist methods to clinical education and, conversely, of clinical methods to feminist jurisprudence. Although motivated by different aims, each set of methods illuminates the relationship between theory and practice, a relationship conveyed by the image of a spiral.

Selected References

Anthony G. Amsterdam, Clinical Legal Education—A 21st-Century Perspective, 34 Journal of Legal Education 612 (1984).

David R. Barnhizer, The University Ideal and the American Law School, 42 Rutgers Law Review 109 (1989).

Katharine T. Bartlett, Feminist Legal Methods, 103 Harvard Law Review 829 (1990).

Drucilla Cornell, The Poststructuralist Challenge to the Ideal of Community, 8 Cardozo Law Review 989 (1987).

Richard Delgado, Storytelling for Oppositionists and Others: A Plea for Narrative, 87 Michigan Law Review 2411 (1989).

Gerald E. Frug, The City as a Legal Concept, 93 Harvard Law Review 1057 (1980).

Carol Gilligan, In a Different Voice: Psychological Development and Moral Theory (1982).

Abraham Heschel, Who is Man? (1965).

David Luban, Epistemology and Moral Education, 33 Journal of Legal Education 636 (1983).

Catharine MacKinnon, Feminist Discourse, Moral Values and the Law—A Conversation, 34 Buffalo Law Review 11 (1985).

Carrie Menkel-Meadow, Two Contradictory Criticisms of Clinical Education: Dilemmas and Directions in Lawyering Education, 4 Antioch Law Journal 287 (1986).

Martha Minow & Elizabeth Spelman, In Context, 63 USC Law Review 1597 (1990).

C. Segal, Tragedy and Civilization: An Interpretation of Sophocles (1981).

William Simon, Visions of Practice in Legal Thought, 36 Stanford Law Review 469 (1984).

Mark Spiegel, Theory and Practice in Legal Education: An Essay on Clinical Education, 34 UCLA Law Review 577 (1987).

Mark Tushnet, Scenes from the Metropolitan Underground: A Critical Perspective on the Status of Clinical Education, 52 George Washington Law Review 272 (1984).

Robin West, Jurisprudence and Gender, 55 Chicago Law Review 1 (1988).
James Boyd White, The Study of Law as an Intellectual Activity, 32 Journal of Legal Education 1 (1982).

Further Reading (selected work by Phyllis Goldfarb)

Picking Up the Law, 57 Miami Law Review 973 (2003).
Describing without Circumscribing: Questioning the Construction of Gender in the Discourse of Intimate Violence, 64 George Washington Law Review 582 (1996).
A Clinic Runs Through It, 1 Clinical Law Review 65 (1994).
Beyond Cut Flowers: Developing a Clinical Perspective on Critical Legal Theory, 43 Hastings Law Journal 717 (1992).

CHAPTER FOUR

COMPARATIVE LAW*

Legal education in the United States is in the midst of a period of change and growth. In keeping with common law tradition, there has been no abrupt, violent break with the past. But ... a gradual process has been at work producing profound changes in a system which had been relatively stable for some time. Many of these changes had long been advocated as necessary or desirable and had been implemented to varying degrees at leading law schools....

As one aspect of the change, more and more attention is being paid to the contribution which other disciplines, primarily economics and behavioral sciences, can make to a fuller understanding of the legal system. As a related development, it had been recognized in theory for many years that the law in books might be different from the law in action, but only a few law schools actually made efforts to explore the law in action and relate it to the law in books. It is only in the past few years that law schools generally have embarked on serious efforts to investigate the social and economic background of legal rules as well as the social and economic consequences of legal rules in operation....

Changes have taken place in the methods of law teaching as well as in the curriculum. The traditional casebook and case method is now routinely supplemented by lectures, written work, work on specially constructed problems, and field work. Teachers are increasingly inventive in finding the technique best adapted to the subject matter.

Perhaps the most pervasive change has been the breaking down of traditional artificial and arbitrary classifications of subject matter. Thus, while torts, contracts, property, crimes and so on, have not been abolished, there is increasing emphasis on how they are related to each other. And stepping back one step, there is emphasis on how civil procedure is related to all of them. Stepping back still further, it is recognized that the techniques and re-

---

* **Hugh J. Ault**, *The Importance of Comparative Law in Legal Education: United States Goals and Methods of Legal Comparison*, 27 JOURNAL OF LEGAL EDUCAITON 599 (1975) (co-authored with Mary Ann Glendon), http://papers.ssrn.com/abstract_id=771505.

sources of the social sciences are indispensable to the understanding of legal rules in operation.

Thus, the doors of the law schools have been opened to the behavioral scientists and economists. Recognizing the need to make arbitrary divisions of subject matter for convenience in teaching, and, at the same time, the need to relate all these subject matter areas to each other, to procedure and to the social sciences, the law schools have increasingly turned to courses which attempt to give the advanced student at least a tentative method for organizing his or her knowledge about the legal system....

Finally, a number of courses in the law school curriculum have come to try to fulfill a function of stimulating students to think creatively about legal problems by providing new insights into the legal system. Legal history and legal philosophy are increasingly being taught as courses which add a new dimension to the traditional analysis of legal problems. This final step back puts such distance between the student and substantive law that it has often been said that such courses have no place in a law school curriculum. But the hope cherished by those who advocate such courses is that distance will lend perspective and that the so-called perspective courses will enable students to become better lawyers.

Sometimes the lines between traditional subject matter areas are erased, and a professor in one course, say in criminal law, attempts to provide the procedural, sociological, historical, philosophical, or economic dimensions. Professors so inclined are increasingly aided by modern casebooks which make available material beyond the traditional cases and notes. But there are difficulties. In many cases a law teacher's recognition of the need for additional information precedes the availability of results of social scientists. And even when results of such investigations are accessible, problems remain of "translating" them into a form which can be understood by law students. Another difficulty is that the great mass of material to be covered and the pressure of time in most substantive courses tends to limit what any ambitious professor can do with historical, economic, or philosophical materials.

When seen as a perspective course, comparative law presents a kind of perspective not found in legal history or in jurisprudence. These latter perspectives are most useful in provoking the student to engage in examining the premises of legal rules and, indeed, of legal institutions. But ... when the law is under constant pressure to adapt to rapid social and economic change, and when the basic assumptions of the system are constantly being challenged and tested, there is also a need for new and alternative models of solutions to social problems. Because comparative law is a source of such models, it can be said that if comparative law did not exist it would have to have been invented.

Comparative law in the curriculum of the American law school has … a variety of functions. Courses offered under titles including the words "comparative law" may place differing emphasis on any of a number of aims. Some courses may actually attempt to prepare a student for professional work with a foreign legal system. Others specialize in area studies. Since the occupational hazard of the field is facile comparison, much of the effort of comparative law teachers and writers has been directed toward developing methods of teaching and research which avoid this common pitfall.

Whatever the principal emphasis of their courses, most American teachers of comparative law would probably say that at the very least their goal is to make the American law student a better lawyer within his or her own legal system. That is, comparative study should enable them to think more precisely and creatively about legal problems which they will encounter in law school and in practice.

Interestingly enough, this seems [true] of legal philosophy and legal history courses too. These courses are seen [not] as independent disciplines forming discrete subject matter areas in the law school curriculum, [but] as courses which deepen the students' understanding of the legal system and the legal process. Indeed, one might say this trend in legal history, legal philosophy, and comparative law, is simply [a way] to recognize frankly the traditional classification of subject matter in the law school curriculum for what it is—an arbitrary division for convenience in teaching and studying, but which must be reassembled and integrated by the student (with or without help) so that the relationships between the parts are understood.

If comparative law—or legal history, or legal philosophy—is seen as a perspective course, it is easy to see that the perspective it lends to any given aspect of the legal system can be introduced in either or both of two ways. It can be taught as a separate course with the hope that the insights and methods of analysis it affords will be carried over by the student into other areas. It can also be integrated into a course in a particular subject matter area to enrich the study of that area by adding yet another dimension to the particular problem being studied. It is the purpose of this report to describe the techniques and results of experiments with both kinds of courses.

The Comparative Legal Analysis course which has been taught by the authors for five years at Boston College Law School is of the first type. The title of the course was chosen to emphasize that the concern of the course is with a method of analysis rather than with substantive law. The principal emphasis of the course is on the study of the process of growth and change in legal systems and the complex interaction between doctrine and policy in this process.

Comparative law as a perspective course differs from the traditional basic course in comparative law as a matter of emphasis. Comparative law taught as a basic course has as its principal goal to give law students an introduction to comparative method and to the workings of one or more foreign legal systems, and as a by-product to give him or her more understanding of the American legal system. In comparative law as a perspective course these priorities are reversed. The emphasis is on the insight which the study of the foreign "model" can give into the student's own legal system.

This approach has implications for the course materials used. The traditional basic course uses materials and problems selected to facilitate entry into the workings and habits of thought of foreign legal systems. In the perspective course, the organizing principle is quite different and will be described in detail below. The problems are selected to illustrate the process of growth and change. They all involve settled legal doctrine under pressure to adapt to changed social and/or economic conditions.

A subsidiary concern of the course has to do with the accurate identification of social and economic context and with the complexities of the relationship between law and social change. None of the concerns of the course are unique to a course in comparative law, but comparative models do afford some unique opportunities to gain new insight into the fundamental tension which exists in every legal system between the need for certainty and predictability on the one hand and the need for a mechanism for growth on the other.

Thus, in a sense the goal of the course is extremely modest. It does not aim to give a student a working knowledge of any other legal system. On the other hand, the goal is almost overwhelmingly ambitious, since it is nothing less than to make the student think about all legal problems in an entirely new way, to add an additional layer of perception to his or her analysis of legal problems. In this sense its ambitions are no less than those of a modern legal philosophy or legal history course. The idea is to give new depth to legal analysis by using all the illumination that other disciplines can furnish.

In general the attempt is made to give the students some perspective on the operation of their own legal system by exposing them to a range of legal techniques which differ from those familiar to them from their common law training. When the aim of the course is thus stated, some approaches which have traditionally been used in the teaching of comparative law are clearly eliminated. The course is not intended to be a historical overview of the development of another legal system, or an introduction to problems of dealing with foreign legal systems as a practicing attorney.

In order to use the comparative technique to provide students with a perspective on their own legal system, some important initial decisions must be made as to what to compare and the methodology of comparison. As mentioned above, the problems were chosen to illustrate the tension between legal doctrine and broader policy considerations which typifies a legal system during a period of change and transition. [In general, we] have drawn our materials from the French and German systems—for the two usual reasons and a third. The availability of the materials and the familiarity of the teachers with the languages and techniques would have been determinative. But French and German materials are particularly useful in a course with the aim of illuminating American legal problems, because they present common social problems which appear in countries at broadly comparable stages of social and economic development.

Initially, we spent a substantial amount of time during the first few hours of the course on a general introduction to French and German legal institutions, covering such matters as the reception and influence of Roman law, the development of the codes, court structure, the judicial process, stare decisis, etc. While it would probably be undesirable to thrust the student into the consideration of problems within a foreign legal system without some such preparation, we found that the material could be handled in large part by outside reading and that it was not necessary to spend as much class time on general background as we had originally thought.

In class we found it helpful to use a "case of first impression" to dramatize differences in the judicial process and in the relations between courts and legislatures. For this purpose we traced the development of the right of privacy in French, German, and American law.

After this (abbreviated) general discussion of the French and German systems, we undertook an examination of a series of selected problems. Since our comparative technique was fundamentally the same in all of the examples, it is perhaps useful to spend some time discussing this approach in general terms before returning to the specific problems. Basically, we would begin our discussion of a given legal problem by attempting to articulate the common social problem which the legal systems under consideration were dealing with or reacting to.

Obviously such an inquiry has many facets and can be illuminated by learning and techniques from other disciplines. However, in the beginning, we attempted to select problem areas in which the common social problem was relatively easy to define and then moved on to an examination of the various legal techniques that the systems used to accommodate the competing social interests which had generated the problem. It is a truism that in comparable societies the legal results in a given situation will be substantially similar in a large percentage of cases; however, in cases where the result is similar the interest is in the differing techniques which the systems under consideration have used in order to achieve the desired result.

Here the discussion centered on the doctrinal starting points ... available in the systems under consideration, and on the legal institutions (courts, administrative agencies, legislatures) which dealt with the existing legal doctrines and principles. The analysis centered on the problem of the extent to which the system's doctrinal starting point generated the conclusion in a particular situation, and the extent to which non-doctrinal policy considerations could be accommodated in the solution. The problems selected provided examples ranging from cases where the force of doctrine was such that it alone appeared to determine results, to cases where doctrine was merely something which had to be dealt with, while the result appeared to be determined by the pressure of other forces.

One clear danger of such an approach is an inadequate understanding of the functioning of a particular legal doctrine in practice in a foreign system. To what extent, for example, do various procedural devices make the particular legal rule difficult to apply? To what extent do general business or social norms make it practically difficult for a clearly expressed legal sanction to be applied? We recognize the difficulties of this type of analysis but nonetheless believe that some useful general comparative observations can be made. A discussion of four specific topics which we have covered under this general analytical format, will illustrate how the method worked.

Contract Formation. We begin with a series of relatively straightforward problems from the law of contracts in order to accustom the students with the method of analysis and to put them at ease in dealing with unfamiliar materials. The warm-up consists of a few pitches right over the plate—enforceability of promises, offer and acceptance, limits on enforceability of promises. First, we consider a problem familiar to all first year law students—the question of when a promise will be enforced by the legal order. An analysis of the various policies operating in the area leads relatively quickly to a conclusion that all the social orders under consideration are faced with the same fundamental problem—how to structure a legal mechanism for determining what promises will and what promises will not be enforced by the system.

A discussion of the agreement theory in the civilian system and the doctrine of consideration in the common law system brings out two points of fundamental importance: 1. In some situations, the doctrinal starting point (for example, consideration) leads to the result that certain promises which have high social utility are not enforced, *e.g.*, the firm offer problem. 2. Some promises which, under strictly doctrinal analysis would be enforceable, are nonetheless not enforced because of overriding policy considerations.

As soon as the students have begun to feel at home in the area of contracts, we introduce a common social problem involving the contractual relationship to which no system has evolved an entirely satisfactory solution—the problem of economic duress. After discussing the difficulties of defining the problem, the many possible doctrinal analyses of the problem, the competing policy considerations, and the tentative efforts the systems have made to deal with it, the student gets or should get a feeling of how comparative analysis can illuminate discussion of the open-ended problems which will form the subject matter of the latter part of the course.

Agency Problems. The specific topic covered involves the complex of legal doctrines generally denominated "agency" in common law. Here, as in the problem of contract formation, the initial discussion centers on the common problem faced by all systems which recognize some notion of agency relationship How to weigh the relative interests of the principal and the third party dealing with the agent in situations where the agent has no authority or exceeds his authority.

Here the French and American doctrines of apparent authority which developed to protect the third party are contrasted with the German approach of abstracting the external power to represent from the internal limitations placed on that power by the principal. This topic illustrates nicely the general point that the doctrinal starting point from which a particular problem is approached will in turn determine the points of stress in the actual operation of the legal system.

For example, under the abstract approach of German law, the third party's knowledge of internal limitations creates a difficult conceptual problem; if the internal limitations are truly of no effect as a limitation on an agent's authority, then the third party's knowledge of those limitations should be irrelevant. On the other hand, there is clearly no social utility in protecting a third party who is acting in bad faith, and a complex problem of the interaction of doctrine and policy is created.

For the French and American systems, starting the analysis from the agent's apparent authority, the existence of limitations known to the third party clearly obviates any appearance of authority and the problem is easily solved within the doctrinal framework of those two systems, without external policy considerations.

From the agency materials, the course moves to a study of the trust and the devices which have been developed in French and German law to fulfill functions performed by the trust in common law. Particular attention in this area is paid to differing policies toward restraints on alienability; the danger of doctrines assuming a life of their own; and the interesting history of the reception of the trust idea in Louisiana.

Matrimonial Property. After the trust materials, the course moves on to common social problems with which all of the systems under consideration are currently struggling. Picking up the theme sounded in the economic duress materials, the analysis becomes increasingly difficult and the difficulties are frankly acknowledged. Indeed, part of the perspective function of the course is to develop skill in perceiving these difficulties. The social problem itself is hard to identify—indeed too hastily "naming" the problem may produce the illusion that the problem has been solved. As the analysis becomes more refined, it may be seen that the social and economic contexts of a particular problem are not really comparable, raising questions about the utility of models from one system for another. Also, the policy aims of the systems under consideration may be entirely different. So, in this section, in addition to the difficulties experienced previously at the level of doctrine, the more complex problem of determining the proper subjects for comparison must be faced.

All of these difficulties are present in studying the way in which the law affects the property relationships of spouses in the French, German, English, and American systems. Yet, in this section of the course, the main emphasis is not on the technical difficulties of comparison but rather on two other themes which have been present from the beginning—the relationship between law and social change, and the relationship between law and behavior. In the first section of the matrimonial property materials, the subject for consideration is traditional systems of matrimonial law and the changes which occurred in them after the Industrial Revolution. After having spent a fair amount of time discussing this process of change which has run its course in the systems under consideration, we examine the way in which all four systems have reacted to changes in the ideology of marriage and the role of the married woman in their particular society. One of many interesting aspects of this subject for the American law student is the role which comparative law studies have in fact played in this area on the continent.

The matrimonial property materials lead naturally into the final problem of the course. Like economic duress and matrimonial property, the last problem involves policy conflicts and social tensions which can never be completely reconciled, but at best are kept in uneasy equilibrium. This is the problem of identification and recognition of the appropriate corporate constituency. Here, the ultimate complicating factor is that the most interesting model comes from Yugoslavia, a society which is not really at a comparable level of economic development with France, Germany, and the United States, and in which the economy is planned.

Problems of Corporate Constituency. The contract and agency units were typical of situations in which there is a general consensus in the legal systems being considered as to the outlines of the common problem. Thus they were concerned primarily with analysis of the differing doctrinal responses which give content to the units. The problems in the definition of corporate constituency are much more complex. Here we find no consensus in the systems under consideration as to the appropriate constituency.

Should it be limited to shareholders and should the aim of the corporation be simply profit maximization, with other interests being represented by external regulation (either legislative or through litigation, *e.g.*, class actions)? Or should the corporate constituency be internalized and if so, in what form and through what legal institutions? And which of the various competing constituencies should be represented and in what proportion? The analysis of the competing social considerations and the variety of legal techniques available should broaden the student's perception of a threshold area of legal analysis. The hope is, of course, that by this time the student will have been provoked to bring some of the methods of comparative legal analysis to bear on other threshold areas of the law....

It seems to us that the format we have used is adaptable to the capabilities and interests of many different teachers. Problems involving the dynamics of change can be found in all legal systems and in all subject matter areas. We have found it easy to add and subtract problems as the course has developed and we have been able to successfully integrate the contributions of a number of guest lecturers with our basic themes.... [Our first-hand experience in developing comparative law in the U.S. law school curriculum should] illuminate the fundamental problem which all law courses, regardless of their denomination, are at bottom dealing with: the complex interaction of doctrine and policy in an evolving legal system....

Selected References

Adolf A. Berle, The Modern Corporation and Private Property (1968).

Abram Chayes, The Modern Corporation and the Rule of Law, in The Corporation in Modern Society 26–46 (E. Mason ed. 1966).

John P. Dawson, The Oracles of the Law (1968).

Henry M. Hart, Jr. & Albert M. Sacks, The Legal Process: Basic Problems in the Making and Application of Law (Tent. ed. 1958).

John N. Hazard, Area Studies and Comparison of Law: The Experience with Eastern Europe, 19 American Journal of Comparative Law 646 (1971).

Otto Kahn-Freund, Comparative Law as an Academic Subject, 82 Law Quarterly Review 40 (1966).

Albert Kiralfy, ed., Comparative Law of Matrimonial Property (1972).

K. W. Ryan, An Introduction to the Civil Law (1962).

Rudolf B. Schlesinger, Comparative Law: Cases, Texts, Materials (3d ed. 1970).

Arthur Taylor von Mehren, The Civil Law System: Cases and Materials for the Comparative Study of Law (1957).

Detlev F. Vagts, Reforming the "Modern" Corporation: Perspectives from the German, 80 Harvard Law Review 23 (1966).

John Minor Wisdom, A Trust Code in the Civil Law Based on the Law Restatement and Uniform Acts: The Louisiana Trust Estates Act, 13 Tulane Law Review 70 (1938).

Further Reading (selected work by Hugh J. Ault)

Introduction to United States International Taxation (Aspen 2005) (with Paul R. McDaniel & James R. Repetti).

Comparative Income Taxation: A Structural Analysis (Kluwer 2d ed. 2004) (with Brian J. Arnold).

U.S. Exemption/Territorial System vs. Credit-Based System, 32 Tax Notes International 725 (2003).

U.S. Corporate Taxation Reform from an International Perspective, 30 Japan Tax Law Review 185 (2002).

Corporate Integration, Tax Treaties, and the Division of the International Tax Base: Principles and Practices, 47 Tax Law Review 565 (1992).

B. ROLES

CHAPTER FIVE

SELF-AWARENESS AND CRITICAL REFLECTION[*]

… In recent years, the legal academy's discussions of pedagogy have focused on learning theory. There is a fresh interest in the learning styles of law students and a sense that understanding them only improves the quality of law teaching. Although knowledge of student learning and thinking styles is helpful to both teacher and student, I argue it is only one part of the equation in improving legal pedagogy. We need to think as well about the learning style differences of law professors, and the resultant differences in teaching styles. In this essay, I argue that self-awareness of one's own learning preferences, thinking style and intelligences, together with rigorous critical reflection about pedagogy, is the best first step toward improving law school teaching. At the risk of oversimplification, I am arguing that learning about one's own unique styles in relationship to others will make one a better teacher.

Law School Pedagogy and Its Goals. In 1870, Christopher Columbus Langdell had a revolutionary idea. He traded the one-sided, teacher-centered lecture of the law school classroom for the more dynamic pedagogy of the case method and Socratic dialogue. Instead of passively listening to an instructor, a veritable sage on the stage, the law students Langdell envisioned would be active partners in their education, attempting to uncover the universal principles and legal rules underlying appellate decisions through the progressive techniques of question and answer. In Langdell's view, the case method would create true lawyers, who would master legal principles and then apply them to the "ever-tangled skein of human affairs." In his zeal to transform the study of law into a respectable university degree program, Langdell launched a trend that was to last for over a century. The case book method and Socratic dialogue were enthusiastically embraced by legal pedagogues at the start of the

---

 * **Filippa Marullo Anzalone**, *It All Begins with You: Improving Law School Learning Through Professional Self-Awareness and Critical Reflection*, 24 HAMLINE LAW REVIEW 324 (2001), http://papers.ssrn.com/abstract_id=718101.

twentieth century; they have been the dominant teaching techniques in American law schools since then.

In the 21st century, the legal pedagogy of 1870 has lost much of its luster and appeal. The world at large, and the teachers and learners who populate law schools, have changed markedly since Langdell's day. A century ago, higher education was a man's world. Socratic dialogue was a logical pedagogical choice for a small class of men from similar social and economic backgrounds. Teachers and students looked alike, talked alike, and communicated easily with one another. But today, women make up over fifty percent of the nation's law students. Educational research has noted that women participate less in so-called Socratic classes where the instructor uses rapid questioning and answer techniques, but they participate more in classes with a discussion format.

In addition to gender diversity, racial, ethnic, and cultural diversity characterizes today's legal academy and law school classroom. But while the composition of the classroom has evolved, what goes on in it, to a significant degree, has not. Law is no longer viewed as an empirical science and the intellectual hegemony of legal education is increasingly questioned. Thoughtful legal educators have looked at law school pedagogy and found that traditional approaches emphasize doctrinal analysis at the cost of the development of interpersonal and problem solving skills. Some scholars have called for envisioning new paradigms of learning in the legal academy.

Along with changes in their learner populations, law schools have experienced changes in the learning environment. Although critics argue that law schools continue to prepare nineteenth century gentlemen for membership in the bar, a number of pedagogical innovations have been suggested, and there are "frequent calls for legal educational reform." Writing from a clinical perspective more than fifteen years ago, Anthony Amsterdam stated that legal education:

> was too narrow because it failed to develop in students ways of thinking within and about the role of lawyers—methods of critical analysis, planning, and decision-making which are not themselves practical skills but rather the conceptual foundations for practical skills and for much else, just as case reading and doctrinal analysis.

In response to criticisms and changes in the learner population, law schools have made strides in changing classroom techniques. The American Bar Association Commission on Women in the Professions stated that "the first year curriculum could be improved by the use of a greater variety of teaching methods in light of the diversity of learning styles in [the] student body." In fact, substantial work is underway in this area. In addition, there have been efforts to tailor a number of upper level and clinical courses to diverse learning styles. Another intriguing development is the institution of academic support programs to address the diversity of learning styles and to overcome some of the barriers the modern law school poses for a diverse student body.

Other articles have identified the particular skills required to be an effective practitioner and then examined ways to help students develop those skills. In fact, a variety of teaching methods are used in the law school classroom of today. One of the methods, borrowed from medical education, is problem solving. Problem-based learning enables a student to apply what he or she has learned and to take responsibility for his or her own learning. Legal educators are experimenting with a number of teaching techniques and are manifesting heightened concern about striking the right balance between the traditional academic approach and learning by doing. Some articles have suggested the use of games, both in and out of the classroom ... A handful of articles examines the use of technology in teaching and another group looks at teaching methodology and accommodations for learner disabilities. Other scholarship has considered the role and place of legal work and other out of classroom experiences (known as internships and externships) in the enterprise of legal pedagogy.

In addition to experiments that alter the traditional law school classroom, some commentators urge law faculty to teach students to use critical self-assessment and to practice self-consciously. To accomplish this, some legal educators have adopted instructional formats that encourage reflective, critical practice. Although the choice of teaching methodologies and techniques is of utmost importance, the pedagogical goal of encouraging law students to become reflective practitioners has greater significance. One of the more exciting and recent developments in legal pedagogy has been the introduction of students to the concept of reflective practice.

Legal education's goal is to turn uninitiated novices into competent attorneys. However, by concentrating solely on the law school curriculum, the legal academy may be defining its challenge too narrowly. Learning is not restricted to problem solving, and the identification and management of external problems should not be its sole focus. Chris Argyris argues that most people really do not know how to learn, and this is especially true of well-educated professionals. Legal educators should consider modeling critical reflection themselves. Argyris suggests that professionals become more self-conscious about their own behavior by examining how it may contribute to problems in their own organizations. By analogy, we law professors, as professionals, should reflect on our own demeanor in the classroom to begin to identify the ways in which we may inadvertently contribute to dissonance in the classroom. Of course, the principal goal of faculty self-reflection is to give legal educators the information they need to change how they act. Through interactions with teachers who model self-reflection, students will discover the importance of their inner selves by identifying with those teachers. If legal educators are charged with teaching critical self-reflection through self-knowledge to nascent professionals, we need to model it as well.

… Whatever the techniques, however, self-reflection empowers students, teachers, and practicing lawyers to become more aware of what they do and, thus, more able to improve what they are doing. Modeling self-reflection and assigning self-reflective projects to students demands a certain level of comfort with self-disclosure. Such self-disclosure does not come naturally to all teachers and students. Designing projects that stimulate self-reflection and evaluating students' self-reflection is not without its hazards. Some students (and faculty members) are more comfortable with disclosure than their peers or colleagues. They write or tell stories with more flourish. They may be more adept at self-examination or have more insight into their own psyches or behavior than others. There is a real danger when using reflective exercises and assignments that faculty will unwittingly reward the students who write the most sensational narratives or reveal fantastic details of an experience with dramatic fanfare. Knowing the right mix of coaching and guidance to offer students is essential. How much we ourselves reveal or how much we show the way to our students plays a profound role in encouraging learner self-reflection and communicating the tools of life-long learning to our students.

Most legal educators have neither the time nor the desire to become applied learning theorists. How, then, does a law professor improve his or her teaching? What piece of the puzzle have we been ignoring by focusing solely on students' diverse learning styles? What should a faculty member know about him or herself to improve his or her teaching? Does critical reflection play a role in this exploration? If so, what are some of the drawbacks of critical reflection, and is it for everyone? …

Why Self-Assessment? Without being aware of it, most of us are probably teaching in the style that we are most comfortable learning. Many of us do not even know how we learn best or how we prefer to learn. The rationale for self-assessment is this: in learning about himself or herself, a law professor learns how he or she learns, and he or she becomes familiar with styles and preferences other than her own. By reviewing the literature on applied learning theory, and by expanding her methodological repertoire, an instructor would be engaging in healthy and transformative critical reflection about his or her pedagogy in particular and, hopefully, about accepted law school teaching methodology in general.

Learning and teaching are not solely cognitive activities. Being mindful of the emotional, as well as the cognitive, realm would enhance classroom rapport and help to establish a successful learning environment. Self-assessment is an important attribute of emotional intelligence, a kind of master aptitude that can either facilitate or hinder learning. Self-knowledge on the part of the instructor contributes to emotional "synchrony" between teacher and learners. Classrooms with a high level of synchrony are classrooms where students seem generally happier, more interested, and enthused; there is a feeling of mutuality between teacher and learners that sets the stage for learning. Self-awareness allows an individual to experience or change his or her feelings. It can help an individual to develop a sense of self-efficacy, a readiness to learn, that will have a profound effect on his or her ability to learn.

Self-assessment, and the self-knowledge about one's own learning and thinking preferences that it would produce, would be a form of reflection and action, a praxis, and a conscious move away from the didactic norm of education.

Exploring Critical Pedagogy. Critical pedagogy helps teachers look at teaching contextually.... The philosophical roots of critical pedagogy are found in the works of Hegel, Marx, and the Frankfurt School of critical theory. Since critical pedagogy views the educational process as an effort by dominant social groups to impose a particular value system on students, a teacher may either impose those dominant values in the classroom, or act as an agent of change, liberation, and transformation. Through this prism, teaching is a political act and a key concern of critical pedagogy is that educators recognize the innate imbalance of power in our institutions and classrooms. Critical pedagogy has synthesized the thinking of critical theorists, postmodernists, and feminist critical pedagogues to form a general theory of adult learning, informed by perspectives of race, class, gender, and social inequities.

A major theme of critical pedagogical theory, germane to the goal of improving law school teaching, is that [as Habermas put it] while "all institutions are educative, not all are true learning communities." A basic understanding of critical pedagogy informs the legal educator's critically reflective practice by giving legal educators a baseline for action. One of the first steps in effecting change and transforming our teaching is an understanding that law schools must be committed to learning. Critical pedagogy views liberation practice as an antidote to the oppression and control that are hallmarks of traditional education.

The tradition of critical pedagogy, with its distinct political perspective on both individual and institution, offers a unique prism for a law professor's initial foray into critical reflection about his or her teaching and the larger community's influence on it. However, critical pedagogy must be approached with a reflective frame of mind and with discriminating caution. How can law faculty avoid the paralysis that questioning comfortable assumptions can engender as they begin an inquiry into themselves to improve their teaching? Critical pedagogy gives law professors a means of questioning institutional and individual assumptions and belief systems in the legal academy by providing a political framework within which to envision their unique roles. The perspective of critical pedagogy alone is inadequate. Another element of critical reflection is that of reflective practice.

The Importance of Reflective Practice for Professionals. Reflective practice is significant for law teachers on a number of levels. Law professors can use it to examine their own practices as teachers, thereby modeling reflective practice for their students and colleagues as a positive lifelong educational approach to professional life. Law professors can also use reflective practice as a teaching technique, encouraging their students to apply it in their careers as practicing attorneys.

Reflective practice is a method that law faculty can use in their quest to transform classroom dynamics. By first defining and understanding our own unique qualities, strengths, weaknesses, and learning preferences, we will improve our professional practice of teaching. The process of self-discovery may be difficult and even humbling. Modeling critical reflection means that we earnestly deliberate about others' views, even those diametrically opposed to our own. To do otherwise is to destroy the crucial element of trust that is essential to critical reflection.

The Adult Learning and Education Model as a Tool for Critical Reflection. The word "pedagogy" is derived from the Greek, meaning "to teach a child." When we employ the pedagogic model, we are using a form of teaching and learning with a venerable history. Pedagogy can be traced to one of the earliest known formal institutions of learning, the monastery schools of the seventh century. The model's origins lie in a didactic teaching construct that is concerned primarily with the transmittal of knowledge. Because of the frustrations he encountered in trying to adapt the pedagogic model for use with adults, Malcolm Knowles popularized the word "andragogy", also derived from the Greek, meaning to teach adults.

Andragogy moves away from the bottom line, banking concept of education that [in Paolo Freire's words] "transforms students into receiving objects." Andragogy views learners as unfinished beings who, when confronted with a disorienting experience, can choose to either ignore or grapple with the experience. If the choice is made to deal with the incongruence, learning occurs.

Some experts distinguish instrumental from communicative learning. Instrumental learning uses the scientific method of problem solving; it is a form of learning in which the student grasps concepts and tests hypotheses. It is task oriented learning. Communicative learning is intuitive. It is concerned with contextual meaning and validation of values, morals, and ideals. Communicative learning uses metaphor and thematic patterns to convey information.

In adulthood, a learner spends considerable time and energy reassessing prior learning. Through this self-assessment, the adult learner takes the learning of his or her formative years and, ideally, transforms it with an adult understanding. The learner uses the scientific method of deductive logic (instrumental learning) and the validation and justification of belief systems (communicative learning) to further refine and differentiate the meaning schemes of earlier understanding. This type of transformative learning is reflective learning. It involves looking at earlier assumptions and reworking them; it is what Jack Mezirow calls the "assessment and reassessment of assumptions" and earlier formed meaning perspectives. A learner's culture can either animate or impede transformative thought and critical reflection. In a traditional law school culture, law teachers encounter a number of barriers to learning. Some of these are the assumptions held by our colleagues, our students, and perhaps ourselves about how learning is best accomplished. Students', peers', and our own assumptions about roles can often stymie creativity in the classroom, and can lead to dissatisfaction with our teaching and doubts about the effectiveness of our work.

The Appropriate Role For Law Professors. "Role" is a sociological concept. Both popular literature and the entertainment industry have been fertile grounds for fostering conceptions about roles in law school. At the same time, institutional and cultural forces have shaped rather rigid roles and suggested the professorial demeanor that many law professors have adopted at various times in their careers. Legal educators can transform their teaching by critically reflecting on their teaching and improve student learning by rearticulating the assumptions underlying the law school as a learning environment.

Dewey wrote that all people "require moral sanction in their conduct: the consent of their kind." This "consent" is usually derived from the customs, habits, and traditions of a particular society or social group. Many law professors have unwittingly and unselfconsciously accepted the images proffered by their peers and colleagues because they are a customary ethos in a particular institution, or because the roles match what the students seem to expect.

Douglas McFarland has unearthed startling dichotomies between the ways professors see themselves and how students and practitioners view the ideal law professor. From the results of his empirical research on the self-images of law professors and the persona of the "ideal law professor" as identified by students and practicing lawyers, McFarland draws some fascinating conclusions about the reasons for the discordant views of the bench and the academy on the subject of legal education.

Finding one's authentic voice through rigorous self-assessment and critical reflection is one way for law teachers to resist the impulse to adopt a preconceived role. The purpose of this rigorous self-analysis is, of course, to be able to engage more authentically and more meaningfully with students to improve their learning. It is important that a teacher establish a relationship of trust with students and focus on what will help them learn. Through rigorous and honest self assessment, coupled with a critical scrutiny of the larger organization, an instructor will become more reflective and thoughtful about the organization's mission, and the pedagogical process set up to achieve institutional goals, and, thereby, become a better teacher.

Self-reflection is a necessary ingredient in the transformational process of adult personality development. However, one has to get into the water to learn how to swim. Thus, in our efforts to improve our teaching to enhance student learning, we must first carefully consider our own natural proclivities and inclinations to understand and improve our teaching. Examination of our own aptitudes, thinking, personality and learning styles and emotional intelligence may help us to discover a genuine self. Our quest to find our legitimate voice, the deliberations we go through on our way to finding a true and comfortable demeanor, become part of the heuristics of personal professional development that we model for our students. In order to learn, an adult must be able to identify and be consciously aware of the desired change. By defining our objectives and modeling self-reflective behavior to effectuate personal development and change, we are, in effect, saying to our students, "This is my problem and this is how I am thinking it through." We are presenting transparent "scripts" for our students that they can internalize and use as their own in their individual quests for professional development and life-long learning. The communication of authenticity from this struggle may be as important to our students' autonomous learning as the substantive content of our courses....

Selected References

American Bar Association, Commission on Women in the Profession (1998).

Anthony G. Amsterdam, Clinical Legal Education—A 21st Century Perspective, 34 Journal of Legal Education 612 (1984).

John Barell, Teaching for Thoughtfulness: Classroom Strategies to Enhance Intellectual Development (1991).

Stephen D. Brookfield, Becoming A Critically Reflective Teacher (1995).

Roger Cramton, The Current State of the Law Curriculum, 32 Journal of Legal Education 321 (1982).

John Dewey, Experience and Education (1938).

Jerome Frank, A Plea for Lawyer Schools, 56 Yale Law Journal 1302 (1947).

Paolo Freire, Pedagogy of the Oppressed (rev. ed. 1993).

Steven I. Friedland, How We Teach: A Survey Of Teaching Techniques In American Law Schools, 20 Seattle Law Review 1 (1996).

Malcom Knowles, The Modern Practice of Adult Education: From Pedagogy to Andragogy (rev. ed. 1980).

Douglas McFarland, Students and Practicing Lawyers Identify The Ideal Law Professor, 36 Journal of Legal Education 93 (1986).

Jack Mezirow, Transformative Dimensions of Adult Learning (1991).

Myron Moskovitz, Beyond the Case Method: It's Time to Teach With Problems, 42 Journal of Legal Education 241 (1992).

Deborah L. Rhode, Missing Questions: Feminist Perspectives on Legal Education, 45 Stanford Law Review 1547 (1993).

Paul J. Spiegelman, Integrating Doctrine, Theory and Practice in the Law School Curriculum: The Logic of Jake's Ladder in the Context of Amy's Web, 38 Journal of Legal Education 243 (1988).

Robert Stevens, Law School: Legal Education in America from the 1850s to the 1980s (1983).

Paul F. Teich, Research On American Law Teaching: Is There A Case Against The Case System?, 35 Journal of Legal Education 167 (1986).

James Boyd White, Doctrine In A Vacuum: Reflections On What A Law School Ought (And Ought Not) To Be, 36 Journal of Legal Education 155 (1986).

CHAPTER SIX

ETHICS IN EXTERNSHIPS[*]

[A]lthough far more joins in-house and externship clinical programs than separates them, an externship is, in at least some respects, a distinct clinical format, one with unique characteristics that shape the nature and resolution of the ethical issues faced by each of the externship players. For that reason, the literature on professional responsibility issues as they present in in-house clinics is of only limited help. An independent investigation of how ethical dilemmas arise and how they should be resolved in externship settings is in order.

... Two factors drive our analysis of externship ethical dilemmas: the first is structural, the second, pedagogical. As to structure, the fact that our externs are undertaking legal work certainly does not warrant special treatment for externships; lawyering is the bread and butter of in-house clinics, too. Rather, it is the tripartite nature of externship practice that proves the distinctive trait. Externships, by definition, involve a collaboration of three parties: the extern, the field supervisor, and the faculty supervisor. Ethical dilemmas encountered by any one of these parties affect all three partners to the union. Each of the participants in this triangular relationship plays a special role critical to the analysis of professionalism questions....

Th[is] tripartite structure is not the only unique feature of externships. Externships also present special pedagogical opportunities to explore ethics in practice in ways that are distinct from opportunities afforded by their in-house clinical cousins.

Professionalism issues, of course, are either an explicit or implicit part of pedagogy in every externship program. Many externship programs include a seminar component, which in some cases satisfies students' professional responsibility graduation requirements.... But ethics is a pervasive part of all clinical education. If our contention that externship ethics pedagogy is unique is to have any force, it must mean that externship participation exposes stu-

---

    * **Alexis Anderson**, *Ethics in Externships: Confidentiality, Conflicts, and Competence Issues In the Field and in the Classroom*, 10 CLINICAL LAW REVIEW 473 (2004) (co-authored with Arlene Kanter and Cindy Slane), http://papers.ssrn.com/abstract_id=599084.

dents to ethical questions in some qualitatively different fashion than does participation in in-house clinics. And that is precisely our experience....

[An] explicit and primary pedagogical focus on ethics shapes how the externship players perform their professional roles. Externship directors want their students to embrace as fully as possible their professional responsibilities. It is important to the externs' development that they consider themselves more than mere non-lawyer assistants. If they perceive themselves as having responsibilities akin to those of front-line lawyers, they will both better comprehend their field supervisors' plight and be better prepared for the day when they become full-fledged lawyers themselves. The externship programs' focus on ethics also provides a natural forum for field supervisors desirous of consultants to assist them in dealing with thorny ethical dilemmas.

Like ethics issues generally, these themes are best tested in the context of specific ethical problems. [Among others,] we investigate how externship programs can best manage lawyers' professional duty to preserve client confidences....

Confidentiality. Confidentiality—the quintessential element of the lawyer-client relationship. Lawyers promise it, clients rely on it, state disciplinary boards demand it. As extern students embark on their field placements, they become part of the legal team obligated to protect information related to the representation of clients. Their placement supervisors, whether they operate in the private or the public sector, routinely communicate and reinforce the demands of this professional duty to their new charges.

Why, then, is there any problem? After all, law students practicing in live client clinics grapple effectively with these responsibilities daily. It is not the student status of externs that complicates the application of these professional duties in externship programs. Rather, it is the connection of externs to their greater law school communities that causes the rub. Commonly, the extern submits journals to the externship faculty member (who typically is not part of the client's official legal team), participates in seminar discussions with fellow externs placed in other settings, and seeks guidance on ethical dilemmas and supervision matters both from fellow students and the faculty supervisor. Each of these facets of the externship experience forces students to make very complicated and challenging decisions about their confidentiality responsibilities.

At first blush there appears to be an easy answer to the extern's dilemma. Surely the student's professional duties must trump the needs of outsiders who might desire to be brought into the "loop." Classmates' and faculty's interests in receiving a full accounting of the client's business should take a backseat to the rights of clients to have their secrets protected. Therefore, the extern's lips must remain sealed.

While that straightforward ethics analysis has a visceral appeal, it misses the point when applied in the externship setting. [E]xternship faculty members ask students to reflect upon their experiences in their journals, in connected seminar classes, and in individual discussions with the faculty supervisor. Indeed, the legitimate pedagogical goals of most externship programs depend upon students developing a nuanced understanding of the lawyering role and its attendant ethical dilemmas. To accomplish those objectives, programs invite (and sometimes require) externs to seek guidance on their ethical questions in journal entries and in seminar, to share their angst over the difficult professional issues they encounter, and to discuss with their fellow students and externship faculty possible resolutions to the puzzles they face. Externs engage in those tasks at the same time that they must remain ever-mindful of their ethical duties.

From the faculty supervisor's perspective, navigating the confidentiality morass can be equally challenging. Remember our starting premise: faculty supervisors are not part of the lawyer-client relationships at the field placements. While externs are part of the lawyering team, the externship faculty members are merely curious outsiders. But that very definition flags the faculty member's problem. On the one hand, ensuring that students comprehend and execute appropriately all ethical constraints, including their duty of confidentiality, is a clear imperative. On the other, faculty also take their consultative role seriously and want to assist their students who are struggling with ethical dilemmas; they are constrained, though, in their ability to provide sage counsel by the need to respect the confidentiality of the externs' workplaces.

Field supervisors are caught in this tension as well. They bear the immediate burden of maintaining their clients' secrets. While that responsibility exists regardless of the externship overlay, field supervisors frequently experience heightened concern about their ability to protect client confidences because of their involvement in externship programs. They are aware that their externs are submitting journals and discussing their work with externship faculty and seminar colleagues. Efforts to assist these supervisors in their search for protocols designed to help ensure professional compliance by externs are long overdue....

[*Case Scenario: Breach of the Duty.*] At the beginning of each meeting of a Corporate Counsel externship seminar, the professor asks students for an update on placement activities. Georgia, who works in the in-house legal department of a large, publicly traded company, responds to the professor's inquiry in a despairing tone: "Things have been pretty awful for the last two weeks." "What's the problem?" the professor asks. "It seems as though no one has any time for me," Georgia responds. "They're all too busy working on the merger." "Is the merger public knowledge?" the professor asks with trepidation. Georgia hesitates as she begins to grasp the significance of the question; "No, it isn't," she replies.

This scenario proves an apt departure for our discussion of the professional responsibilities related to confidentiality because it raises the issues in their most pristine form. The analysis must begin with a determination of the roles of the respective parties. Let us start with Georgia. [S]he is functioning as a member of a lawyering team—in this case externing in the office of the general counsel of the corporation. The team of which she is a part has a client—the corporation. And that client has a secret—the impending merger, news of which it has not yet publicized.

What then are Georgia's ethical duties? This extern has become privy to client confidences as a direct result of her externship duties in the corporation counsel's office. Certainly were she an assistant general counsel employed by the corporation, there would be no doubt that she must not divulge confidential information to outsiders. Why, then, is there any question but that Georgia's obligations should be the same?

First, we can eliminate what are not distinguishing factors.... Georgia's externship status does not absolve her of professional responsibilities. Nor is her conduct excused because her disclosure was undoubtedly innocently made, without intent to prejudice her client. The professional duty to maintain client confidences exists whether lawyers intend to cause their clients harm or are guilty only of innocent slips.

Next, the inquiry should proceed to an analysis of the role of Georgia's audience. In our scenario, Georgia has shared her client's secret with her peers and professor of the Corporation Counsel seminar. She might have shared the information just as easily (and, for purposes of our discussion, just as improperly) in a journal entry submitted to the faculty supervisor overseeing her externship. In either case, Georgia has divulged confidential information to persons outside the corporation's legal team.

Hasn't Georgia done just what most externship directors would suggest when their students experience nagging problems at their placements that seem to elude their own remedial efforts? Her field supervisor is so enmeshed in the merger project that he does not recognize her malaise. So, Georgia has turned to the one community that might both empathize with her plight, and, perhaps, assist her in resolving the work issue. To ignore her plea for understanding seems particularly cruel, at worst, and pedagogically questionable, at best.

How then might we balance the conflicting needs of the partners to this scenario? Certainly, the corporation has a legitimate interest in protecting its secrets. In addition, as a practical matter, it would become very difficult for externship programs to place their students were externs to become known for leaking confidential information, for field supervisors would almost certainly be loathe to participate in externship programs if they concluded that law schools were not supporting their efforts to practice consistent with all professional duties. In short, both good practice and pragmatic considerations demand that externs comply with all professional duties to maintain confidentiality.

With that principle established, let us turn to an examination of the role of the faculty supervisor and Georgia's seminar colleagues in this dilemma. The seminar members, student and faculty alike, have a legitimate interest in fostering for externs an atmosphere of free exchange of ideas and of mutual support. But there are practical considerations at issue here, too. Many programs' seminar discussions focus on questions about supervision, lawyering roles, and professional responsibility. Thus, faculty supervisors routinely encourage their students to share their work-related concerns in their journals and during seminar.

The crux of the problem, then, becomes what is shared with outsiders to the legal work setting. Concerned and well-intentioned though they may be, fellow classmates and the faculty supervisor cannot receive confidential information. However, that constraint does not mean that the needy extern cannot communicate her work issues with her class and in her journal. Prophylactic measures could have allowed all the actors in this externship vignette to accomplish their goals and helped to avoid the problem that has befallen Georgia.

But what to do when the proverbial cat is already out of the bag? We should assume that the externship program in our scenario tried to sensitize its students to the demands of practice, including the ethical constraints surrounding confidentiality. Now that Georgia has breached that duty, we need to explore what the response to that lapse should be, both by the extern and by the externship faculty. We can only imagine the faculty supervisor's shock when the disclosure occurred. With one misstep, Georgia has shared highly sensitive corporate insider knowledge with the entire seminar class. What remediation would be appropriate?

A *mea culpa* undoubtedly would be forthcoming. Like other externs, Georgia was so focused on her personal plight of inadequate supervision and felt so relieved that she at last had the ear of colleagues who could assist her that she neglected her professional duties. Would her apology, coupled perhaps with a request to her audience that the information not be shared and that no trading be done, suffice? No; even if we include a stern warning from the externship professor, Georgia's lapse has inflicted client harm—a leak of highly sensitive client information has occurred.

Although charting an appropriate course of action under the circumstances may be challenging, all involved will benefit from the endeavor. As ugly as the occurrence may seem, it provides the seminar group with a rich teaching moment. One can envision a much more sophisticated discussion of the demands of confidentiality stemming from this regrettable scenario. Not only would Georgia's peers have a new appreciation for the reach of their professional duties, but they might well assist Georgia and the faculty supervisor in determining appropriate next steps. Both must decide whether to inform the field supervisor (and, therefore, indirectly "the client" in the context of this in-house counsel placement) of the disclosure and, if so, how.

To whom and in what way should the players in an externship program disclose breaches of the duty of confidentiality? Field supervisors, who bear ultimate responsibility for students' work for placement-site clients, have become embroiled in ethical problems by such lapses. As Comment 16 to Model Rule 1.6 provides: "A lawyer must act competently to safeguard information relating to the representation of a client against inadvertent or unauthorized disclosure by the lawyer or other persons who are participating in the representation of the client or who are subject to the lawyer's supervision." Thus, Georgia's disclosure has exposed her supervising attorney to inquiry as to his own competence and adequacy of his supervision. Her direct site supervisor has a duty to "make reasonable efforts" to ensure that Georgia's conduct is compatible with his own professional obligations, and "shall be responsible" for any such lapses, if he "knows of the conduct at a time when its consequences can be avoided or mitigated but fails to take reasonable remedial action."

Georgia and her faculty supervisor essentially have two options: leave the field supervisor in the dark or come clean. The first option may have some initial appeal; after all, it avoids what would surely be a difficult conversation with the field supervisor, and, under a strict reading of Model Rule 5.1, if the supervisor were never to learn of the lapse, his lack of timely knowledge of the incident would absolve him of personal professional liability. However, such an interpretation seems ill-advised on both pragmatic and ethical grounds. Just as Georgia inadvertently let slip the secret, others in the seminar also might lapse, despite earnest admonitions to keep quiet about the merger. If so, the damage might well snowball beyond control. In addition, were the field supervisor to learn subsequently of the breach, any constructive relationship that the law school and externship program had fostered with the placement would be unalterably severed.

Prompt candor seems the only choice. This approach empowers the supervising attorney to take whatever remedial steps he feels are advised, thus repairing—as much as possible—the damage caused by the breach, and thereby saving himself from disciplinary action. It also allows him to implement additional assessment mechanisms to assist him in determining if public disclosure is required.

Girding oneself to have that conversation would not be easy. While time would be of the essence, particularly given the sensitivity of the confidential information at issue, Georgia and her faculty supervisor surely would want to discuss first how to reveal her lapse and decide which of them should inform the field supervisor of the situation. Furthermore, they would want to consider strategies for eliciting from the field supervisor his suggestions for addressing the issue, including his recommendations for remedial measures to be undertaken with the seminar group. Resolution of those questions would undoubtedly depend on the nature of the relationships among all the externship cast members, but the conversation should occur....

Best Practices. We would be foolish to assume that any one method, or even combination of techniques, will ensure that the players in externship programs will never run afoul of their duties to maintain workplace confidences. Ethical dilemmas over preserving client information undoubtedly will still occur, despite everyone's best intentions and superior training, as we saw in the second case study. However, the ability of the players to respond promptly and appropriately to those dilemmas will be enhanced if the program develops protocols designed to protect confidentiality. These protocols should support all the partners in the externship relationship in their efforts to comply with their professional duties. We offer suggestions for each of the players here, including: 1) materials for sensitizing externs to their new responsibilities; 2) mechanisms for alerting field supervisors to their duties to train their students in the particular nuances of confidentiality within their practice settings; and 3) means for supporting the externship faculty in their ongoing mission to ensure program compliance.

Extern Protocols. A starting premise has to be that externs should receive as much information as possible about the professional duties of confidentiality, and as soon as practicable. By definition, externs are still students learning their professional craft. Not all programs require a professional responsibility course as a co-requisite or pre-requisite to enrollment, and even in those that do, it is likely that instruction in the doctrinal ethics course will focus on the Model Rules and the Model Code, not on the local variations on the confidentiality rules in particular jurisdictions. Compiling materials that will help externs to accelerate their confidentiality learning curve is the necessary first step. Such a packet would likely include the professional rules governing lawyers for the jurisdiction in which the extern will work, any special confidentiality provisions unique to the externs' placement, and disciplinary rulings and ethics opinions from the relevant jurisdiction that clarify the interpretation of the rules. Many programs also reiterate the externs' professional duties at the program's commencement, in a list of course requirements, in program manuals for students, and in instructions about journal writing. Field supervisors, in their supervisory meetings with their externs, and faculty directors, in seminars and in journal feedback, can reiterate these duties.

But providing written materials for student review, without more, will not guarantee that externs will be sufficiently sensitized to their professional duties. Rather, externship faculty should develop teaching modules designed to test externs' grasp of confidentiality requirements. The Appendix includes sample seminar materials addressing hypothetical disclosures of placement-site information, which could be assigned reading for a program's initial, mandatory class on confidentiality and how to "talk shop." The seminar discussion would then focus first on whether, in revealing the information at issue in a journal entry or in a seminar presentation, the student in each hypothetical breached workplace confidentiality. If so, the conversation would turn to how to remedy each ethical misstep. Similarly, an early, focused, journal assignment ... could require externs to identify who their clients are, or where no clients exist, any others to whom they owe a duty of confidentiality, and to solicit their field supervisors' comments on their own experiences in dealing with confidentiality issues. These assignments and classroom activities can help students both to understand the abstract ethical principles involved and to implement their mandate in practice.

Helping students navigate a safe course through these confidentiality constraints is anything but easy. The recurring tension implicit in externship programs, between ensuring compliance with ethical practice standards, on the one hand, and maximizing experiential learning and reflection, on the other, makes providing crisp guidance to externs difficult. It is a given that faculty will ask their externship students to reflect on their placement activities; identifying an acceptable format for that information sharing, one that is respectful of confidences, is the critical next step. At every turn, of course, faculty need to model ethically appropriate ways for their students to "talk shop." For years, the accepted approach has been to redact client identifiers, to use initials or pseudonyms, and to massage the facts. However, that approach has come under recent scrutiny as some commentators have questioned whether such quick fixes are effective in ensuring that workplace confidences are not divulged, particularly in small legal communities....

Field Supervisor Protocols. On-site supervisors know what measures are best designed to protect their workplace confidences. Furthermore, in externships, they are the front-line lawyers who must deal with ethical issues as they develop. Familiarity with the externship program's expectations for its students will help field supervisors as they discharge their responsibilities in this regard. Many externship clinics have developed field supervisor manuals, which detail both the program's educational goals and the law school's efforts to ensure extern compliance with professional norms. Field supervisors would also benefit from reviewing copies of the materials faculty supervisors provide to students detailing their externship responsibilities. An invitation to field supervisors to participate in an early seminar dedicated to exploration of confidentiality constraints would undoubtedly be a win-win, as well, sending an unmistakable message that all parties have consistent ethical expectations.

Faculty Supervisor Protocols. Externship faculty members are involved whenever any ethical lapse comes to light. While the measures previously discussed are designed to minimize confidentiality breaches, externship faculty will still face dilemmas over confidential client or workplace information.... Identifying in advance resources available to faculty supervisors when they confront particularly thorny questions is critical. The externship faculty's law school community is a natural first place to establish connections, as both clinical and non-clinical faculty can be an invaluable resource when ethical questions arise. For instance, externship faculty could invite those colleagues teaching doctrinal ethics courses to serve as consultants to the externship program.... Collegial support is [also] available from other members of the national network of externship clinicians, and beleaguered externship faculty may also obtain much needed direction by requesting advisory opinions from state bar association ethics committees....

Conclusion. This year marks the twenty-fifth anniversary of a path-breaking text in legal education, Gary Bellow's and Bea Moulton's *The Lawyering Process.* One of the first of its kind, the book quickly became a standard resource for many clinicians, particularly in-house clinical faculty. Bellow and Moulton offered their clinical colleagues more than insights into skills training; indeed, they reframed the core clinical curriculum to include an explicit focus on the ethical dimension of lawyering. Their approach remains relevant today; even a glance at the testimonials in the Fall 2003 issue of the *Clinical Law Review,* which was devoted to the book's anniversary, demonstrates the currency of the ethics questions with which Bellow and Moulton urged clinicians and their students to engage.

While *The Lawyering Process* did not expressly deal with externships, it did help all clinicians to develop an appropriate sensitivity to the ethical dilemmas inherent in clinical practice. We owe a debt to Bellow and Moulton and to the generation of clinicians who have followed in their footsteps since 1978, expanding upon Bellow and Moulton's discussion of ethics in the in-house clinical setting and extending the ethical focus to the externship context. Our contributions here build directly on the scholarship of these able predecessors. We are grateful, too, for the community of clinicians who provide a source of support as we struggle with the ethical challenges inherent in our externship programs, and for opportunities to grapple with such questions in conferences and in our writing. We hope that our discussion here will encourage externship faculty, field supervisors, and externs to engage in rich dialogue about their respective roles and the important ethical responsibilities that flow from those roles. That dialogue should begin early in each externship cycle, during the application process, with the implementation of careful conflicts-checking procedures designed first to identify, and then to avoid or cure, conflicts of interests occasioned by students' prior or contemporaneous legal work, personal interests or convictions, or responsibilities to third parties. It should continue as the externship progresses....

Selected References

David R. Barnhizer, The Clinical Method of Legal Instruction: Its Theory and Implementation, 30 Journal of Legal Education 67 (1979).

Gary Bellow & Bea Moulton, The Lawyering Process (1978).

Kate Bloch, Subjunctive Lawyering and Other Clinical Extern Paradigms, 3 Clinical Law Review 259 (1997).

Kathleen Butler, Shared Responsibility: The Duty to Legal Externs, 106 West Virginia Law Review 51 (2003).

David Chavkin, Am I My Client's Lawyer? Role Definition and the Clinical Supervisor, 51 SMU Law Review 1507 (1998).

Lawrence K. Hellman, The Effects of Law Office Work on the Formation of Law Students' Professional Values, 4 Georgetown Journal of Legal Ethics 537 (1991).

Lisa G. Lerman, Professional and Ethical Issues in Legal Externships: Fostering Commitment to Public Service, 67 Fordham Law Review 2295 (1999).

James E. Moliterno, Legal Education, Experiential Education and Professional Responsibility, 38 William & Mary Law Review 71 (1996).

J. P. Ogilvy, Guidelines with Commentary for the Evaluation of Legal Externship Programs, 38 Gonzaga Law Review 155 (2002/3).

Robert F. Seibel & Linda H. Morton, Field Placement Programs: Practices, Problems and Possibilities, 2 Clinical Law Review 413 (1996).

Paul R. Tremblay, Client Counseling and Moral Responsibility: Client-Centered Counseling and Moral Activism, 30 Pepperdine Law Review 615 (2003).

CHAPTER SEVEN

ANALYTICAL FEEDBACK ON STUDENT WRITING[*]

... Legal writing classes train students in legal analysis because accurate and precise analysis is the foundation for good writing in law practice. Legal writing classes do not teach students to write to a general audience; rather, they teach students to write to an audience in law practice. To provide students with an intimate sense of this audience's needs, therefore, legal writing classes require students to work on simulated problems as if they are practicing attorneys. Placed in this situation, students experience, and therefore internalize, why producing analysis that is accurate and precise is so critical to the success of their document.

[S]tudents placed in this "real life" environment are forced to confront and explore the critical premise that lawyers solve problems within the specific analytical constraints of our legal system, and that these constraints do not allow them to work with ideas in any way that they choose. Specifically, lawyers' ideas in large part come from analyzing legal authority, and therefore it is this authority that tends to dictate the outcome for the client. Lawyers are not free to pick which pieces of this authority form the basis of their analysis; instead, which pieces are controlling, or even relevant, depends upon the operative jurisdiction and our legal system's rules on the hierarchy among kinds of authority. When lawyers interpret this authority, then, they must stay within reasonable limits, using standard methods of legal analysis, even as they make creative or novel arguments. Their analysis is further constrained by the specific facts of the client's case because a lawyer may not "make up" facts that would be more helpful than the ones that actually took place. And finally, the procedural aspects of a client's case may affect the range of analysis that is appropriate.

---

[*] **Jane Kent Gionfriddo,** *The "Reasonable Zone of Right Answers:" Analytical Feedback on Student Work* 40 GONZAGA LAW REVIEW 427 (2005), http://papers.ssrn.com/abstract_id= 680761.

Working within these constraints as a "practicing attorney," students come to realize that their analysis must fall within a "reasonable zone of right answers (or explanations)" if it is to be useful to the document's audience. The audience in law practice depends upon writing based on ideas that are accurate because they fall within a range of analysis, even if creative or novel, that "reasonably" interprets relevant, controlling legal authority, and "reasonably" predicts or makes an argument as to how that interpretation affects the problem of the client. Ideas outside this "reasonable zone" are incorrect, and the student will be forced to confront the stark reality that the consequences of such a mistake can be serious. In the fast-paced environment of law practice, for instance, a supervisor may quickly act on a document's analytical errors, with dangerous results to the client or embarrassing ones for the supervisor.

Students also learn that an analysis that is technically "accurate" in the sense that it is within the "reasonable zone" is just the first step. They discover that their analysis must also be sufficiently precise … to convey a correct impression to the reader of their document. Vague analysis may not be "wrong" per se but will be ultimately incorrect if it fails to capture and communicate critical nuances and this failure results in the reader's misunderstanding the ideas on the page. A supervisor who acts upon such a misunderstanding may end up in the same embarrassing or even dangerous situation as one who bases action on analysis that is actually wrong. Analogously, a judge who misunderstands the underlying substance of a written argument may be less likely to come to the conclusion desired by the attorney-author of the document….

The focus on teaching legal analysis within the constraints of law practice affects the theory behind legal writing teachers' written feedback on student draft documents. A legal writing teacher's feedback on a draft document must assist students in learning this process of legal analysis—"thinking like a lawyer"—and in acculturating students into the new community of law practice where analysis expressed on the page of the document has such a profound effect, either positive or negative, on the reader. The legal writing teacher, therefore, encounters challenges that are somewhat different from those of a teacher who is giving commentary on written ideas in other rhetorical contexts. To illustrate these challenges, and their effect on the teacher's feedback, let's begin by comparing two teachers. First, let's imagine a teacher of a first-year legal writing course making written comments on a draft of an objective memorandum to a hypothetical work supervisor. Second, let's imagine a teacher of a freshman English composition course writing a critique of a draft essay on "telling the truth versus lying."

It is true that teachers in both situations must recognize the intimate connection between thinking about ideas and expressing those ideas. Obviously, without ideas there is no piece of writing. In both situations, sophisticated teachers recognize that they need to focus their feedback on the ideas themselves, at least until the student has sufficiently generated and developed thoughts on the subject at hand.

Beyond this similarity, however, there are significant differences in the two settings as to the relative freedom of student-authors to generate and develop those ideas, and these differences do affect teacher feedback on student written work in some critical ways. In the assignment in the freshman English Composition class, an essay on "telling the truth versus lying," the student-author must think through how she feels about the subject of "lying," including what her opinions are on what "telling the truth" and "lying" mean. She must then develop a thesis and provide support for her ideas, including confronting counterarguments. The teacher can support the student throughout this process by using written feedback. This feedback can help the student focus and expand her thoughts; develop a sharper thesis; elaborate on supporting points; clarify points that are not clear enough to an unknowledgeable reader (or perhaps even to the student-author); rethink aspects of the argument that are not logically thought out or presented; organize ideas logically; and ultimately, down the line, express ideas grammatically and even elegantly.

But in this circumstance there is no absolute range of "right and wrong" answers, whatever the teacher's own moral beliefs about "telling the truth versus lying," and there is little risk that the reader of the document will be harmed in some way or act in a harmful way to others as a result of what the student says or does not say or how precisely she says it. This gives the teacher greater freedom in choosing the role or roles that he assumes as the person giving the feedback to the student-author. It allows the teacher, if the teacher believes it desirable, to focus more on the student's own process in coming up with her own ideas, ideas that are constrained only in the sense of logic and sufficient development.

In contrast, the legal writing teacher—and the law student-author—function within a set of more severe constraints imposed by the nature of legal analysis and its use in the practice of law. Here, the teacher's paramount responsibility must be both to the student's analytical process and to the resulting analysis as expressed in writing, because this is what it means to work with ideas within this context. Even though each student has her own personal method of thinking and composing, she must still follow certain prescribed methodologies when working with legal analysis and this process must result in a written analysis that is sufficiently precise to be useful in law practice.

In commenting on student written work in this context, therefore, the teacher needs to provide feedback in the role of an expert legal thinker (and writer). He must be an expert as the legal educator, who assists the student in understanding the process of legal analysis and how to use it well to solve legal problems. At the same time, he must be an expert as the lawyer in law practice who is interested in the results of that process as they appear "on the page" of the document, given the kind of document being written and for what purpose in law practice. Given the complexities of this dual role, it is thus the teacher, and not other students for the most part, who has the expertise to provide students with useful feedback on their written work.

In the role of legal educator, the legal writing teacher must make comments specifically designed to help the student identify the analytical skills she understood—which resulted in the successes of the draft—and what skills she was still struggling with—which resulted in the document's problems. For these comments to help the student sufficiently, the teacher must read the draft document from the point of view of someone who has a complete knowledge and understanding of what the legal authority says, of the range of reasonable analysis that legal authority supports, and of how that analysis might reasonably affect the client's problem. The teacher must then confront directly whether the student appears to have understood the process to arrive at an analysis in the "reasonable zone of right answers" (even if, as in advocacy, it might creatively push the limits of legal authority) and has expressed a correct analysis precisely enough to allow the reader to grasp it accurately and easily from what is on the page.

Such comments, therefore, initially help the student learn the fundamental skills of legal analysis, both in the sense of a theoretical understanding and also in the practical sense of being able to use these skills to reach a good result. They also help the student confront that murkiness "on the page" more often than not reflects murkiness in thinking. As the course progresses, these comments assist the student to begin to self-identify analytical successes and problems in her own work and then attempt to fix problems increasingly independently.

In deciding on how to comment from the point of view of educator, the teacher must first gauge how much direction the specific student needs. To make this assessment, the teacher should consider the following: the student-author's analytical successes and problems throughout the whole draft; any knowledge that the teacher has about the particular student-author's process or resulting analysis; where the draft falls within the course's whole curricular sequence; the analytical requirements of the legal problem being worked on; and the teacher's experience with the kinds of problems students at certain stages of law school have with certain analytical skills.

To hit the right level of comment, the teacher needs to refrain from the following extremes. On the one hand, a teacher should in general not just "give" the student the analysis because this will result in the student just "filling in the blanks" as she revises, without her ever confronting what was wrong in the first place and how to correct it. Students who revise in this manner tend not to raise the level of their analysis; moreover, they may lose a sense of control over their own document because they end up feeling that they are just regurgitating an unthinking "answer" that is required by the teacher. On the other hand, if the teacher simply provides very general comments or asks very general questions that do not provide sufficient guidance to identify the problem and how to fix it, especially when students encounter difficult analytical skills for the first time, the student may end up feeling frustrated and defeated, which in turn will significantly undermine the student's ability to revise the document successfully.

In addition to providing comments as an educator, the legal writing teacher should provide comments from the point of view of a lawyer or judge in law practice, a reader who does not have the same familiarity with the analysis as the author. In this role, the teacher should read and give feedback as if he does not have knowledge of the analysis and will be taking action based exclusively on the ideas as communicated on the page of the document. Sometimes this kind of comment will simply describe the problems that the reader in law practice would encounter as he or she reads the ideas as expressed on the page of the document; sometimes this kind of comment will be written in the first person to convey more intimately and vividly the personal reaction of the reader. In either form, this type of comment compels the student to confront how the ideas as written will affect, desirably or adversely, the reader's ability to grasp the document's ideas and then to proceed to future action. In this matter, the student comes to realize why thinking about and expressing ideas precisely in law practice makes so much difference, thereby giving her a strong motivation to revise her work.

The precise balance between these dual roles of educator and lawyer in practice depends in the first instance on the number of drafts the student submits. A curriculum that calls for several drafts of an assignment before the final document will allow the teacher more freedom in giving written comments. During very early drafts, for instance, the teacher will be able to focus more on the student's individual process of idea generation and analysis and less on how those ideas might affect the ultimate audience. Knowing that he will have other chances to help the student on subsequent drafts, the teacher can comment in a fashion that focuses on the student's analysis in a more open-ended manner that allows the student room to make some mistakes without risking that she will have no further chance to correct these misapprehensions. Even at this point, however, the teacher must still be sure to alert the student to the kinds of analytical mistakes that might completely undermine the usefulness of the document, such as a serious misunderstanding of the analytical process or the adverse results of using that process incorrectly. To help the student focus on the analytical process that will generate an appropriate analysis, the teacher might choose to refrain from making comments from the point of view of a reader in law practice at this early stage, and leave that to a subsequent draft.

Much more common in first-year legal writing courses, however, are curricula that allow one draft and a final product for some or all major assignments, since the majority of courses do not have the resources to allow teachers to give feedback on several drafts of assignments. In this situation, the student hands in a piece of writing that, even though not a "final" product, is the kind of draft document that is the best work that the student can achieve at that particular point in the curriculum, given the student's skill level. In giving feedback on a document in this situation, the legal writing teacher should assume both roles of educator and lawyer in practice. When the teacher makes comments from both these points of view, he ensures that the student-author has sufficient support to see where she has succeeded in producing the analysis as well as in communicating it to the audience in law practice so that the document achieves its purpose.

Giving feedback in this dual role, of course, still requires that the legal writing teacher help the student-author with her own process of thinking and writing, so that she has the opportunity to develop a unique, individual voice that may not be the voice of the teacher. It still requires that the teacher recognize when the student has presented a novel analysis that the teacher did not initially anticipate, but that is within the "reasonable zone of right answers." A teacher needs to exercise a high degree of sensitivity in this situation, again, to ensure that the student retains a sense of control over the document, which in the final analysis is the student-author's and not the teacher's piece of work. But in giving feedback on just one draft before a final memo, the teacher must balance sensitively these important concerns with the overarching goal to ensure that the student's analytical process achieves a result within the "reasonable zone" of accuracy and precision.

Thus, the rhetorical context within which the legal writing teacher operates places him in a very tricky situation, one that requires a high degree of sophistication. In making comments on a draft document, the teacher must never lose sight of the ultimate goal of ensuring a correct analytical process that yields high quality results useful in law practice, even as the teacher supports the student in retaining a sense of her own voice and control as the author of the document....

Legal writing teachers should play a dual role in providing written feedback on their students' draft law practice documents. They should give comments from the point of view of an expert legal educator to ensure that the their students learn the fundamental skills of legal analysis, both in the sense of a theoretical understanding and also in the practical sense of being able to use these skills to reach a good result. Legal writing teachers should also take the point of view of an expert lawyer, to convey to students a sense of how ideas on the page will affect, desirably or adversely, their reader in law practice. Students who receive feedback from both these points of view internalize, in a sophisticated manner, both the analytical process and its place in law practice; as a consequence, they are much more likely to succeed as legal thinkers and writers in the legal profession.

Selected References

Linda L. Berger, Applying New Rhetoric to Legal Discourse: The Ebb and Flow of Reader and Writer, Text and Context, 49 Journal of Legal Education 155 (1999).

Debra R. Cohen, Competent Legal Writing—A Lawyer's Professional Responsibility, 67 Cincinnati Law Review 491 (1999).

Richard K. Greenstein, Teaching Case Synthesis, 2 Georgia State University Law Review 1 (1985–86).

Richard Hyland, A Defense of Legal Writing, 134 Pennsylvania Law Review 599 (1986).

Mary Kate Kearney & Mary Beth Beazley, Teaching Students How to "Think Like Lawyers": Integrating Socratic Method With the Writing Process, 64 Temple Law Review 885 (1991).

Philip C. Kissam, Thinking (By Writing) About Legal Writing, 40 Vanderbilt Law Review 135 (1987).

Richard K. Neumann, Jr., A Preliminary Inquiry into the Art of Critique, 40 Hastings Law Journal 725 (1989).

Carol M. Parker, Writing Throughout the Curriculum: Why Law Schools Need It and How to Achieve It, 76 Nebraska Law Review 561 (1997).

Teresa Godwin Phelps, The New Legal Rhetoric, 40 Southwestern Law Journal 1089 (1986–87).

David S. Romantz, The Truth About Cats and Dogs: Legal Writing Courses and the Law School Curriculum, 52 Kansas Law Review 105 (2003).

Suzanne E. Rowe, Legal Research, Legal Writing, and Legal Analysis: Putting Law School into Practice, 29 Stetson Law Review 1193 (2000).

CHAPTER EIGHT

FUNDAMENTAL STRUCTURE IN LEGAL WRITING*

Legal educators are charged with the responsibility of engaging students intellectually in thoughtful inquiries about the role of law and lawyers and the pursuit of justice. They also are responsible for preparing each student for life as a professional lawyer who serves others. Balancing these two features of legal education is challenging; it requires creative curriculum development and teaching techniques, which incorporate intellectual discourse and the practical training of practitioners. The reputation of a law school and the measure of its success depends on many characteristics, including the degree of competence and confidence with which its graduates are equipped as they begin and pursue their legal careers.

Consequently, an essential component of legal education is the development of a law student's ability to research legal problems, analyze legal authority, and write legal documents. As such, instruction in these skills generally begins in the first year of law school. Those who teach legal reasoning and writing (LR&W) explicitly introduce students to the fundamentals of these tasks. Ideally, further development of the skills of legal analysis and written expression of that analysis occurs in other 1L courses, as well as throughout the curriculum, and then continues as a part of the practitioner's life.

LR&W educators have approached their task by conscientiously reflecting on and re-examining what they do and how they do it, in order to design the most effective curricula and utilize the most meaningful teaching methodologies. They seek to engage students by recognizing that these skills must be learned incrementally and by structuring the course so that students can internalize the fundamentals which will enable them to successfully approach legal problem solving and expression.

---

* **Judith Tracy**, *Teaching Fundamental Structure in Legal Writing Through the Use of Samples*, 21 TOURO LAW REVIEW 297 (2005), http://papers.ssrn.com/abstract_id=786609.

An essential component of an LR&W curriculum is teaching students how to prepare legal documents which reflect the conventions of the practicing professional. Teachers want students to be able to apply what they learned from the LR&W course assignments to what they will be called upon to do as upper-level law students, legal interns, summer associates and, ultimately, as practitioners. This article describes how the use of sample documents can be incorporated into the introductory LR&W curriculum to maximize opportunities for students to identify and apply a structure to their legal writing and adapt it for future assignments in and beyond law school....

Teachers of legal reasoning and writing want to equip their students with the skills which will enable them to engage in valid legal analysis and to express that analysis effectively in writing. This is a cooperative effort between teacher and student. It requires thoughtful curriculum design, using appealing assignments which keep pace with the students' development, accompanied by meaningful feedback. It also requires the students' trust in the course and commitment to the learning process, which teachers must earn and conscientiously work to maintain. Teachers can begin this process by reassuring students that what they are learning as legal thinkers and writers are additional skills. Although teachers should communicate to students that legal analysis and writing require a particular rhetorical and professional approach, they should emphasize that the acquisition of these new skills will not invalidate or compromise other analytical and writing techniques used in other contexts. This is accurate because it appropriately acknowledges both the substantial abilities and experiences students currently bring to law school, which will enhance their capacity to be effective legal writers, and the fact that legal analysis and writing is characterized by particular conventions and expectations.

To effectively teach the skills necessary to become successful legal thinkers and writers, the curriculum should advance students' self-confidence.... First, teachers can provide a curriculum that reflects how lawyers approach analysis and writing in practice. Second, teachers can give their students opportunities to self-identify valid techniques for presenting legal authority to a reader. Incorporating samples into the first-year legal reasoning and writing curriculum can advance these goals.

In terms of simulating how lawyers approach legal problems, teachers should explain that lawyers first objectively analyze a client's legal situation before advising that client about an appropriate adversarial position and course of action. Lawyers consider the client's facts in conjunction with a thorough and objective analysis of the relevant law, such as statutes, regulations, cases, and administrative rulings. Only then can the lawyer assess the client's possible and practical options and provide advice. The best choice, ranging from a vigorous adversarial pursuit of the matter to a recognition that immediate resolution would be best, will be determined by the objective analysis as applied to the facts, and this will dictate what advocacy documents the lawyer prepares. Given the realities of practice, even though students may arrive in law school eager to assume an advocacy role immediately, they first should be taught to undertake objective analysis and writing, so that they develop the skills which are critical to responsible lawyering.

This understanding of how a lawyer approaches a client's problem is reflected in the method used to teach legal reasoning and writing. Teachers of legal reasoning and writing typically design their curricula so that students begin with objective analysis and writing, and the course progresses in later stages to introduce advocacy techniques. Often the first assignment in the course requires students to analyze and synthesize a limited body of authority relevant to a hypothetical problem, such as a common law problem in which the focus is on reading and understanding case law.

Within the context of this assignment, students are taught how to identify the legal issues, read and analyze relevant authority and derive an overall understanding of the issues based on a thorough synthesis of that authority. Through this process, students begin to develop fundamental analytical skills. Students learn how to read a case and understand the holding and the explicit reasoning, as well as what was implicit in the case, which taken together fully explains the outcome. Students learn how courts interpret and apply prior cases, how to synthesize a group of cases to articulate what they teach collectively about the legal issue, and how to apply that analysis to the facts of the hypothetical problem. Then, students learn how to transform that analysis into a written document, such as an office memorandum in which they set forth the analysis and apply it to hypothetical facts to suggest a course of action for the client.

This written presentation should also reflect the realities of practice and the expectations of the practicing lawyer. Thus, to arrive at the analysis of the legal issues in the problem, students read the relevant cases one after the other; worked through each one to understand the facts, outcome, and reasoning; and, finally, understood what the cases taught them as a group about the issues. But, to be useful, the written presentation should not document this process. The reader does not want to hunt for the analysis in a series of case descriptions. Rather, the lawyer expects a coherent expression of the analysis derived from the synthesis of those cases. The writer's task is to convert the analytical process into a structure that presents the information in a way which most effectively and efficiently educates the reader, provides a clear explanation of the legal analysis and instills confidence in the reader that the application of the analysis to the client's situation is reliable.

One way to equip students with the ability to prepare clear, logical and re-liable presentations of legal analysis, consistent with what will be expected of them in practice, is to provide them with sample memoranda. Samples can be used to demonstrate, generally, the structure and organizational approach expected in an objective legal document. The use of samples allows students to identify for themselves and then internalize useful and efficient techniques for presenting legal analysis, rather than being told abstractly how to prepare the material. Further, a well-structured sample memorandum can provide the essential basis for the preparation of an advocacy memorandum. Finally, it is legitimate and reasonable for students to want to see examples of the kinds of documents they are being asked to prepare, especially because the document is probably unlike anything that most first-year law students have previously seen or written.

Perhaps because of the alien nature of legal writing for the beginning law student, and the teacher's difficulty in explaining how to organize the legal document, many teachers of legal reasoning and writing teach students to apply a formula to express their analysis. This is often referred to with an acronym. The most commonly used acronym is IRAC (Issue, Rule, Applica-tion, Conclusion), or some variation of that. However, the imposition of a formula may create a misimpression among students that all analyses can be expressed and fully explained within it and that there is only one way in which lawyers present information. Admittedly, a formula may be useful because it provides students with a stated way to express their analysis and it offers teach-ers a way in which to evaluate the students' presentation; *i.e.*, by determining whether the formula was followed. Although the limitations of the IRAC for-mula or its variations have been acknowledged—for example, as a tool which represents only one approach and as one which must be adaptable to differ-ent analyses or more sophisticated presentations—its broad application sug-gests widespread acceptance.

Rather than teaching students to apply a formula, the use of sample mem-oranda which present different analyses enables teachers to equip students with the ability to identify and then apply a more general, and yet logical, ap-proach to structure. This approach reinforces two realities: that there is no one structure which fits all presentations; and that lawyers need to approach analysis and its written presentation considering not only their audience and purpose, but also the content, because the nature of the analysis will deter-mine the structure of its written presentation. Some teachers who use for-mulas have acknowledged these limitations, for example, when they recom-mend that the acronyms be modified for particular assignments. Rather than present and then qualify the utility of the formulas, teachers can provide students with instruction about structure which provides them with confidence about how to select an appropriate structure on their own and recognizes the need for flexibility. This approach helps the students effectively provide their readers with worthwhile documents.

While students want to prepare a document which responds to the needs of its audience, they, nevertheless and predictably, may react to being taught the necessity of structure in legal writing—and, indeed, to spending time writing objective legal analysis at all—with skepticism or even resistance. Teachers may tell a class that an organized presentation is essential to effective communication among lawyers, but students may still express concerns that their use of a structure will be confining, will make them mechanical rather than creative writers, and will deprive them of individuality. This reaction tends to be exacerbated when teachers explain the presentation of legal analysis by relying on an imposed formula that, by its nature, appears rigid. The credibility of the formula is further undermined when the teacher attempts to modify or manipulate it.

The use of different samples can respond to these concerns by demonstrating what the structure should be, while showing that different approaches and analyses can generate very different documents that are far from mechanical. The samples should be presented as examples, as opposed to the way in which a formula is taught, to minimize the risk that students will try to artificially and mindlessly force their analysis into the form they see in the sample, similar to an attempt to force analysis into a formula. This attempted replication inevitably would lead to an awkward and unsuccessful presentation, because that particular organization would not fit the relevant analysis and would not reflect the student's individual approach to the matter. However, careful use of samples as a teaching device will enable students to employ a meaningful structure for an assignment. This will both reinforce the need for a discernable organization and demonstrate that the analysis dictates how the material will be presented....

Samples can be used at various times within the first-year LR&W curriculum to further different pedagogical goals, as described in the examples which follow. When students are provided with a sample memorandum on a subject with which they are unfamiliar, they will react to it as the reader. They will react as the audience whom the author set out to educate. They will know immediately whether the document successfully educated them and, if it did, they will be able to dissect how the author achieved that and apply those techniques as they become the writer. On the other hand, when a student studies a sample memorandum which presents analysis with which he or she is familiar because, for example, it addresses part of the assignment with which the class has been working, then the sample provides a different learning experience. Here, the student will be able to see how the process by which the analysis was developed—through reading and class discussion of the authority—as transformed into a structure which successfully explains that analysis. Further, if students are given a sample memorandum on a matter on which they have already written, the sample will serve to confirm their work and will become part of the critiquing and feedback process.

Regardless of the pedagogical goal to which a sample is directed, teachers must actively engage students with each sample, discussing and dissecting the structure identified in the document. This will facilitate the students' ability and willingness to internalize the purpose of structure so that an appropriate format for the particular assignment can be created. Teachers will have advanced the likelihood that students will continue to meaningfully organize future law school and practice assignments. Further, interaction with the samples will be worthwhile because the students have been directly engaged with the product....

Selected References

Judith D. Fischer, Bareheaded and Barefaced Counsel: Courts React to Unprofessionalism in Lawyers' Papers, 31 Suffolk Univeristy Law Review 1 (1997).

Debra Harris & Susan D. Susman, Toward a More Perfect Union: Using Lawyering Pedagogy to Enhance Legal Writing Courses, 49 J 185 (1999).

Joseph Kimble, On Legal-Writing Programs, 2 Persp. Teaching Legal Res. & Writing 43 (1994).

Robert MacCrate, Report of the Task Force on Law Schools and the Profession: Narrowing the Gap, Legal Education and Professional Development—an Educational Continuum, 1992 A.B.A. Sec. Legal Educ. & Admiss.

Carol McCrehan Parker, Writing Throughout the Curriculum: Why Law Schools Need It and How to Achieve It, 76 Neb. L. Rev. 561 (1997).

J. Christopher Rideout & Jill J. Ramsfield, Legal Writing: A Revised View, 69 Washington Law Review 35 (1994).

Suzanne E. Rowe, Legal Research, Legal Writing, and Legal Analysis: Putting Law School into Practice, 29 Stetson Law Review 1193 (2000).

C. Lawyering

CHAPTER NINE

PROFESSIONALISM*

Recently I went to a little shop in Georgetown to buy my wife a teapot. The owner was a charming old lady with a sweet smile. We started talking, and she asked me what I did.

"Oh," I said, "I'm a law professor."

She smiled again and asked, "Does that mean you train lawyers?"

"Why yes," I replied.

"Well," she said, "perhaps you can help me answer this question: if a litigator, a divorce lawyer, and a corporate counsel all jump at the same time from a ten story window, who hits the ground first?"

"Gosh," I said, "I don't know!"

With the same sweet smile she looked up and said, "Who cares?"

The profession of being a lawyer has been the focus of my academic work as a legal historian and as a specialist in legal ethics. More important, it has been the business of my life, as it has been the business of your lives. I have taught for twelve years in four law schools and have practiced law for ten years. I believe that my profession, and your profession, is in deep trouble today. The question is, "Who cares?"

Notice my choice of words. It is not our "occupation," our "career," or our "vocation" that is in trouble. It is our "profession." There is a big difference among these terms. "Occupation," from the Latin *occupatio*, refers to "means of passing one's time"—simply a way to pass the time each day. I hope we all are doing more than this! "Career" is somewhat more elevated. It comes from the Latin carraria, or "vehicle," and refers to a forward motion through life. It shares the same root word as "careen"—the way vehicles are driven in Boston. Some of us are certainly "careening" through life, and yet, there should be more. Finally, there is "vocation," from the Latin *vocare*, meaning "to call." Historically, it refers to a divine call in the sense of being fit for something, talented in something.

---

* **Daniel R. Coquillette,** *Professionalism: The Deep Theory* 72 NORTH CAROLINA LAW REVIEW 1271 (1994), http://papers.ssrn.com/abstract_id=753492.

Simply passing your time in an occupation, or careening through life in a career, or even being called by your talent to a particular job does not require anything from you. But being a "professional" most certainly does. Here the root is the Latin *professio*, or "declaration," referring to a vow, a declaration of belief—an avowal made by you. All of you have taken "professional" oaths. These oaths require you to uphold the rule of law and to obey the regulations of the bar. They are not equivocal. You took these oaths in open court. If your word means anything, you are committed to this formal "profession" of obedience and to other "professional" duties.

This obligation is a deeply personal one. It is a delusion of young, inexperienced lawyers to think that they can separate their personal from their professional lives and their personal from their professional morality. The current jargon refers to this dichotomy as "role-defined" ethics. It is true intellectual rubbish. As Aristotle observed:

> The man, then, must be a perfect fool who is unaware that people's characters take their bias from the steady direction of their activities. If a man, well aware of what he is doing, behaves in such a way that he is bound to become unjust, we can only say that he is voluntarily unjust.

You cannot be a bad person and a good lawyer, nor can you be a good person and a lawyer with sharp practices. A lawyer who behaves like a jerk in court is not an "aggressive advocate" with an "assertive strategy," but a jerk.

I was told that W.C. Fields once paused by a tombstone that read, "Here lies a lawyer and an honest man" and remarked, "How did they get two bodies under there?" We can't split ourselves down the middle. Indeed, the word "integrity" itself comes from the Latin root *integritas*, as in "integral" and "integration." It means "wholeness" or "oneness." There is just one of each of us.

This means our professional identity as lawyers is at the center of our personal morality. And where do we get this identity? From our legal education, both at law school and, equally importantly, from the bar itself. Some of the most important lessons I have learned about professional ethics came not from my law professors but from my law partners and, indeed, from my professional adversaries in the heat of trial.

I believe our profession is in crisis today not because the American Bar Association has a bad media strategy, but because we have lost sight of the "deep theory" of professionalism in the classroom, in the office, and in the courtroom. What is a "deep theory?" Let me explain.

"Deep theory" focuses on our ultimate motivation for obeying rules. There are three common categories: "goal-based," "rights-based," and "duty-based."

Goal-based deep theories focus solely on political or economic outcomes. Examples include Marxism, fascism, and utilitarianism. If obedience to a rule promotes your goal, then obey it. If it doesn't, then don't, unless you might get caught. Suppose you obey the ABA Model Rules because if you don't, you might get disbarred, and you won't be able to afford that new car. That's a goal-based deep theory. From Marx to Machiavelli, goal-based theories have been easy to understand and implement. Best of all, they require no intrinsic test of the means that you employ to achieve your goal.

Recent developments in legal education, particularly legal realism and critical legal theory, have emphasized the function of law as an "instrument" to achieve particular political, social, or economic ends. This is legal education with a goal-based deep theory. The older ideals of a "neutral" rule of law have been debunked as, at best, a pious myth, and, at worst, a deliberate effort by the powerful to exploit the weak under an illusion of "fairness" of principle. Many students become convinced that professionalism means being willing to pursue the ends of others, irrespective of the means. It ultimately puts the client, for good or bad, in the driver's seat, and the ideal of justice becomes secondary.

This goal-based deep theory of education is very old. Indeed, it goes back to Greek philosophical schools known as the "Pre-Socratics." One of these schools taught that all morality is relative: What's good for you is good for you, and my notion of goodness is entirely personal as well. There is no objective standard of a good person or of good conduct. This school was called the Cynics, from which we derive the pejorative word "cynical." The Pre-Socratics, however, did not treat such notions of moral relativism as inherently bad, and neither do many modern American law teachers.

If you subscribe to the School of Cynics, or moral relativism, your goal in teaching is to equip each student to pursue as ably and effectively as possible her individual view of what is good. The Greek Pre-Socratics called this doctrine the Sophist School. The Sophists taught rhetoric, logic, and advocacy. If you used these skills to promote a military dictatorship, such as Sparta, well fine. If you used them to support a democracy, such as Athens, fine again. If your view of the good led you to become a swindler, well, that was your business, too. Cynicism and Sophism, in the classical Greek sense, are alive and well in American law schools today. Moral relativism and its corollary—a theory of "professional" teaching that equips each future lawyer to pursue whatever ends she or her client may choose—may be found everywhere. Thus, moral relativism and goal-based deep theories go hand in hand.

In the final analysis, however, democracies are poor settings for goal-based deep theories. As you may have noticed, democracies have trouble getting anything done efficiently. At least in the short run, totalitarian regimes—even very evil regimes—can pursue some ends better than democracies. Our faith in a democratic rule of law cannot be solely instrumental. Consequently, most democratic systems, including our own, have historically been founded on rights-based deep theories rather than goal-based theories.

The focus in a rights-based deep theory is on human freedom. Perhaps the most famous modern rights-based deep theory is that of John Rawls. He asks us to imagine ourselves in an "original position," a kind of meeting before we are born—ignorant of our sex, race, size, health, intelligence, social, or economic class. What ground rules would we all agree to? Rawls postulates at least two. Put roughly by Ronald Dworkin they are "that every person must have the largest political liberty compatible with a like liberty for all" and "that inequalities in power, wealth, income, and other resources must not exist except insofar as they work to the absolute benefit of the worst-off members of society." These so-called "principles of justice" in turn become touchstones to test the validity of all positive laws.

The trouble with rights-based deep theories is that they are excellent for defining the parameters of personal freedoms, but are less helpful in making critical choices within our own area of freedom. We can live an almost totally depraved life in complete accord with the Constitution and laws of the United States. Indeed, one could argue that we have a legal "right" to lead a depraved life. Put bluntly, rights-based deep theories are powerful tools for defending the freedoms of clients and of other people in general. As professionals, however, they do not really help us personally, because they fail to answer the affirmative questions such as what exactly we must do to be a good person and a good lawyer.

This leaves us with duty-based deep theories. Many of them have fancy names, like "Neo-Platonism," "Neo-Kantianism," and "Neo-Thomism." In fact, duty-based deep systems are familiar because they are founded on the great classical and religious traditions that we so widely share.

A key tenet of a duty-based system is that good acts do not necessarily lead to good results, at least not in this life. All great religions put us on notice that a good, even holy, life will not necessarily be free from cruel blows and bitter disappointments. If we measure our success by achievement, such as political or economic power, or by glory, we cannot ensure these results by being virtuous. Indeed, goal-based philosophers such as Machiavelli argue that we actually can be rewarded for doing evil, particularly if we pretend to do good in public and do evil in secret.

Here is a true historical irony. If we go back to the origins of our professional traditions in the Inns of Court, or to the foundations of the American legal profession and the first American law schools, we will discover a duty-based deep theory for the formalization of legal education in the Anglo-American tradition. Law was initially taught as a humanistic study in both American and English universities. The Inns of Court—the ultimate source of the "barrister ideal" in English law—strengthened the identification of individual lawyers with the system of justice. Maintaining this identity was seen as a professional duty. The diaries and legal papers of early American lawyers, including John Adams, Thomas Jefferson, and Alexander Hamilton, show that they shared these ideals.

I do not have time here to trace the details of how American legal education left its roots for the more modern emphasis on goal instrumentalism. But I do believe this shift lies at the heart of our identity crisis as a profession. This is not a superficial problem. It cannot be solved by required ethics courses or media consultants. It requires a major reexamination of what we, as lawyers, are doing with our lives every day.

Now here is the good news. While the task of refocusing legal education on its humanistic roots and on the duties of professionalism is a vast one, we, as individual lawyers, can act now. These are, after all, our lives and our profession.

[Consider] a true story. The ABA Ethics Committee usually spends its time wrestling with complex cases of conflict of interest or confidentiality. Last spring, however, we had a case that was simplicity itself. A lawyer's secretary was out sick, and the "temp" erroneously put a top secret client report into an envelope addressed to the opposing attorney. (The demand letter that was supposed to go to the opposing attorney went into the client's envelope.) The lawyer discovered the mistake after the mail had been dispatched but before it had been delivered. He called the lawyer on the other side and asked him to please return the envelope unopened, as it contained privileged, confidential client material. The other attorney refused to return the letter without his client's consent and the client said, "Open it."

The ABA Ethics Committee argued about this case for two days. Twenty years ago, I experienced a similar incident. The senior partner of my firm mistakenly received a top secret report from the opposing side. He took two minutes to return the letter unopened, observing that the integrity of the legal process rested in mutual trust between lawyers and that "we could lose any client, but not our self-respect."

Self-respect demands that we get away from the intellectual tyranny of instrumentalism. We are not just means to someone else's ends. We have a far prouder heritage, which, unfortunately, has been obscured in the classroom. This heritage is founded on our ancient duties: to protect the rule of law as an ideal, to serve the system of justice on which our democracy is based, and to study and promote humanism—the mutual bonds of our humanity on which peace itself ultimately depends.

[Finally,] there is a more important point. This profession does not belong to the law professors. It belongs to you and me as lawyers. Each day, and each hour, in our own professional lives, we possess the power to return to our profession's fundamental duties and roots. In countless small acts, such as returning envelopes, we can return the dignity. We can return the sense of self-respect. The ultimate answer to the question "Who cares?" has to be, "We do."

Selected References

ABA Committee on Ethics and Professional Responsibility, Formal Opinion 92-368 (1992).

Aristotle, The Ethics of Aristotle 91 (J.A.K. Thompson trans., Penguin Books 1955) (1953).

J.H. Baker, An Introduction to English Legal History (3d ed. 1990).

Harold J. Berman, Law and Revolution: The Formation of the Western Legal Tradition (1983).

F.H. Bradley, Ethical Studies (1990).

Roger C. Cramton, The Ordinary Religion of the Law School Classroom, 29 Journal of Legal Education 247 (1978).

Ronald Dworkin, Taking Rights Seriously (1977).

A.C. Ewing, Ethics (1965).

Lawrence M. Friedman, A History of American Law (1973).

Alan Harding, A Social History of English Law (1965).

E.W. Ives, The Common Lawyers, in Profession, Vocation and Culture in Later Medieval England 181 (Cecil H. Clough ed., 1982).

Immanuel Kant, Theory and Practice Concerning the Common Saying: This May Be True in Theory But Does Not Apply in Practice, in The Philosophy of Kant (Carl J. Friedrich ed., 1949).

Niccolo Machiavelli, The Prince (W.K. Marriott trans., 1958).

Alasdair MacIntyre, A Short History of Ethics (1966).

Sir Robert Megarry, Inns Ancient and Modern (1972).

1 Sir Frederick Pollock & Frederic W. Maitland, The History of English Law Before the Time of Edward I (2d ed. 1898).

John Rawls, A Theory of Justice (1971).

Bertrand Russell, A History of Western Philosophy (1945).

Further Reading (selected work by Daniel R. Coquillette)

Portrait of a Patriot: The Political and Legal Papers of Josiah Quincy, Jr. (2005).

Real Ethics for Real Lawyers (Carolina 2005).

The Anglo-American Legal Heritage: Introductory Materials (Carolina 2nd ed. 2004).
Lawyers and Fundamental Moral Responsibility (Anderson 1995).
Francis Bacon (Stanford 1992).

CHAPTER TEN

CIVIL DISOBEDIENCE*

Lawyers work with, under, for, and around the law as their professional livelihood. Lawyers are called "officers of the court," "officers of the law," and "ministers," and swear allegiance to support and defend the Constitution of the United States. Even the title "lawyer" reinforces the relationship between the person and the law. The very nature of law binds the lawyer to the content of law because, as every lawyer knows, the law is not a series of set rules plucked from universal concepts of right and good. Rather, law is an ongoing process that reflects shifting societal views. This ever changing nature of the law forces lawyers to be active participants in the shaping of Law. Because the lawyer plays a significant role in the shaping of law and benefits materially from and has special knowledge of the law, scholars and aspirational codes assert strongly and persuasively that the lawyer has special obligations both to uphold the law and to strive to make the law just.

If indeed lawyers have two special obligations—to uphold the law and to work to assure the law is just—then we understandably are confused about whether a lawyer should engage in civil disobedience or should counsel clients to engage in civil disobedience. Civil disobedience is the public and nonviolent violation of law for which the actor accepts punishment willingly. Civil disobedience is a commonly accepted method of attempting to make the law more just. If the lawyer's primary obligation is to take all necessary steps to make the law just, then the lawyer would be free to engage in civil disobedience or counsel clients to do so. If the lawyer's primary obligation is to uphold the law, then the lawyer's ability to engage in civil disobedience or counsel clients to do so might be reduced.

The purpose of this essay is to propose and justify a theory of the proper role of the lawyer faced with issues involving civil disobedience. I begin with an initial assumption that in certain circumstances an individual, including a

* **Judith A. McMorrow**, *Civil Disobedience and the Lawyer's Obligation to the Law*, 48 WASHINGTON & LEE LAW REVIEW 139 (1991), http://papers.ssrn.com/abstract_id=751924.

lawyer as an individual, may feel morally compelled to engage in acts of civil disobedience....

Given the assumption that civil disobedience sometimes is morally proper, the more difficult question concerns whether civil disobedience might be proper in certain circumstances for general (nonlawyer) citizens, yet still improper for the lawyer, either as individual or as counselor.... [B]y becoming a member of the legal profession the lawyer takes on special responsibilities, which require the lawyer to make certain personal and professional sacrifices.... [The] American legal system, with its Constitution, Bill of Rights, and emphasis on democracy, causes many people to see a close correlation between the rule of law (the notion that there are certain principles of justice with which both governments and individuals must comply) and positive law '(the pronouncements of legislatures, courts, and administrative entities).... [I]n light of this close identification between positive law and the rule of law, lawyers have a special obligation to act in accordance with the law. Because lawyers are essential agents of the positive law and voluntarily enter into that agency relationship, lawyers must recognize that legal professionals are more identified with the positive law than general citizens. Consequently, to protect the rule of law, lawyers have a special obligation to exercise caution before engaging in civil disobedience....

The Lawyer and Special Duties. If we decide that lawyers should never be held to different standards than those standards imposed on the general public, then determining the lawyer's role in civil disobedience is easy. Lawyers would be just like everyone else: if a certain situation did not warrant an act of civil disobedience by a general citizen, a lawyer would be wrong to commit an act of civil disobedience; if a particular circumstance justified an act of civil disobedience committed by a citizen, a lawyer also would be justified in engaging in civil disobedience.

Attorneys, however, have been held to special standards. For example, the attorney-client privilege can protect a lawyer from criminal sanctions for failing to reveal known information even though a nonlawyer possessing the same information might be criminally liable. More commonly, the lawyer may have affirmative obligations not applicable to general citizens. For example, a lawyer may have a special duty to disclose lawyer wrongdoing, to rectify the consequences of having offered material evidence that the lawyer later learns was false, and to disclose known adverse legal authority.

Lawyers even give up some essential attributes of our free society when representing a client. For example, under the provisions of professional regulation a lawyer's right to comment on pending cases is limited. A state may constitutionally impose a character and fitness requirement on persons seeking admission to the bar and may compel a bar applicant to take an oath of office stating that the applicant believes in the form of government in the United States and is loyal to the government, even if a similar oath could not be demanded of general citizens. State bars may also constitutionally exclude applicants who believe in the violent overthrow of the government and have a specific intent to bring revolution about.

The dominant ethic of our adversary system, as well as a dominant theme taught in law school, is that the lawyer should "represent a client zealously within the bounds of the law." This representational ethic requires the lawyer to engage in ... role-differentiated behavior. The extent to which lawyers should engage in role-differentiated behavior is debatable, but I know of no legal theorists who argue that a lawyer has no special obligations whatsoever. By accepting the role of lawyer, the lawyer takes on additional responsibilities which, in turn, may require that the lawyer give up certain freedom of action.

Consequently, there is nothing conceptually startling about the idea that a lawyer may have special obligations or limited rights as a lawyer, distinct from or in addition to one's obligations or rights as a general citizen. The difficulty lies in transforming the general notions about special obligations into mandates for concrete responsibilities in practice. Given that a person may feel compelled to engage in civil disobedience and given that in theory lawyers may have special obligations, we can now address the harder question of what special obligations ought to be imposed on the lawyer.

Ideal of "Rule of Law." Even assuming that civil disobedience is a morally appropriate method for citizens to challenge unjust laws, a necessary predicate to effective civil disobedience is a functioning legal and social system. We have in our jurisprudence two closely related concepts that support our legal system. First, most members of our society believe in the rule of law. The phrase "rule of law" carries mythic connotations for most of us, including lawyers. Functionally, the rule of law requires that both individuals and government are subject to the same general rules of fair play. The rule of law encompasses ideas of fair administration, procedural due process, and (for some) substantive fairness. The rule of law, however, must be implemented. In our legal system we implement the rule of law through a defined process of democratic decisionmaking. We established a Constitution, including a Bill of Rights, that establishes a democratic republic. This political system was designed to be relatively close to the ideal of the rule of law in light of our pluralistic society and flaws of human nature.

The result of this law making process is positive law—the legislation produced by our legislative process and decisions by courts and administrative [agencies]. The ideal of the rule of law—of fair administration, procedural due process and certain just results—pervades our political myth and legal system. As a result, rightly or wrongly many people tend to closely correlate the ideal of the rule of law with the enactments and pronouncements of our political system.

Because lawyers are involved intimately with the law and indeed swear to uphold and defend the Constitution of the United States, the reasonable assumption is that lawyers do accept the legitimacy of our legal system. Our legal system, however, occasionally (and sometimes systemically) causes or allows an injustice. Sometimes—often in painful circumstances—our positive law deviates more than a *de minimus* amount from the ideal of the rule of law. What is the proper response of the lawyer when the legal system perpetuates an injustice?

... [W]hen a person engages in the public, nonviolent breaking of law and submits to punishment willingly, that person is demonstrating respect for the general concept of the rule of law. In other words, by submitting oneself to punishment, the individual is acknowledging that all persons should be subject to law. Consequently, if the lawyer engages in civil disobedience and accepts any punishment that may accrue, the lawyer is not denying the underlying validity of the rule of law. Yet given that the lawyer in this instance simultaneously acts both as an agent of the law and violator of the law, it seems too simplistic to stop at this point. It is one thing to say that a general citizen can both show respect for an institution and defy some of its dictates. It is more troublesome, however, to assert that lawyers can legitimately uphold and defy the law simultaneously.

Lawyers and the Rule of Law. Civil disobedience by definition requires persons to rebel against something. That "something" is an acknowledged legitimate political system that the actor believes has erred. Despite the error, there nonetheless remains an underlying structure—a foundation—of legitimate law-making. Those who uphold that foundation of the political system are necessary and arguably play a morally correct role. At the risk of being labeled naive, lawyers are those who uphold the foundation of the legal system.

Our legal system, like a corporation, cannot act except through individual agents. Lawyers are, along with judges and police officers, the most common agents of the law. Much of the force of law comes not from judicial opinions and legislatures, but from the lawyers' interpretation and advice to clients about what the law means. Consequently, by serving as the conduit and translator of the law, the lawyer is a major actor in implementing both the law and the rule of law.

If the rule of law means, in ordinary language, that rules have some moderate constraining force on the individual predilections of decisionmakers ("rule of law not men"), then the individual actors who are charged with implementing the law must take seriously the goal of having something beyond purely individual choice govern the implementation of law. If these essential actors implement the law, we cannot help but look to them for affirmation—or disaffirmation—of the legitimacy of our system. The legitimacy of a legal system, in turn, is closely correlated to why people obey the law. When these essential actors—lawyers and judges—disregard law unequivocally, individual citizens cannot help but question the legitimacy of our political system and the ideal of the rule of law. Adherence to the rule of law then becomes a central definition of being a [lawyer].

The lawyer's special role in the law derives not just from the fact of the lawyer's involvement with the law, but also from the nature of the lawyer's involvement. Lawyers voluntarily enter into this agency relationship with the law. Lawyers *choose* to study law, *choose* to take a bar exam and become admitted to a bar, and *choose* to take an oath of office. Lawyers then accept the benefits that flow from being a lawyer and take advantage of the opportunities that accompany professional status. Like a bond of sisterhood, lawyers take on the special responsibility to protect and care for the rule of law. Because of the close identification our society makes between the positive law and the rule of law, lawyers cannot defy the positive law without raising at least the *possibility* of harming the rule of law.

Any legal system must maintain a core level of acceptance and legitimacy to function effectively. Even so, in times of social turmoil our United States legal system has been able to tolerate a certain amount of civil disobedience. As proponents of civil disobedience aptly observe, our society has benefited as a result of that civil disobedience. No solid evidence exists that a *de minimis* amount of civil disobedience, including disobedience by lawyers, will cause permanent harm to the rule of law. Unfortunately, however, no empirical studies indicate how much civil disobedience is tolerable before causing harm to the concept of law. Logic and intuition tell us that dangers exist if society, in effect, institutionalizes civil disobedience, particularly when conducted by the law's own agents—the lawyers.

We must recognize, however, that the lawyer's relationship to the law may enhance the effectiveness of civil disobedience. Lawyers are systemically part of the power structure, and the lawyer's intimate connection with the law may make the lawyer an even more effective symbol of civil disobedience. Consequently, perhaps more of the general public will notice the underlying message of civil disobedience when "even lawyers" will rock the boat and disobey the law. Yet the general public may have another reaction: if even lawyers feel they are not bound by the law, why should we be bound? St. Thomas Aquinas, the most noted spokesman on natural law, recognized that even when a law is unjust by being contrary to human good it may bind in conscience "in order to avoid scandal or disturbance." What more compelling disturbance exists than the disturbance of an eroding legal system? This obligation to obey an unjust law "is not based on the good of *being* law-abiding, but only on the desirability of not rendering ineffective the just parts of the legal system."

We do not know whether onlookers will see the civilly disobedient lawyer as upholding the rule of law or whether they will confuse the rule of law with the positive law. The question becomes how to deal with this uncertainty. Caution is the usual way in which we deal with uncertainty. To minimize harm to the rule of law, philosophers argue that certain preconditions, guidelines of caution, should be met before *anyone* engages in civil disobedience. For example, John Rawls places three conditions on engaging in civil disobedience. First, Rawls argues that civil disobedience should be limited to "instances of substantial and clear injustice, and preferably to those which obstruct the path to removing other injustices." Second, before engaging in civil disobedience an individual should ascertain that "normal appeals to the political majority have already been made in good faith and … they have failed." … Finally, "[i]n certain circumstances the natural duty of justice may require a certain restraint" to avoid too many groups with equally sound cases from simultaneously engaging in civil disobedience and thereby diminishing the effectiveness of their disobedience In addition to these conditions, every person electing to engage in civil disobedience must consider whether it is "wise or prudent" in certain circumstances.

Here again we turn to the concept of lawyer as agent of the law. Whatever liberties a general citizen might undertake in applying these conditions, certainly lawyers as agents charged with protecting and implementing the law have a special duty to err on the side of caution in evaluating each of these steps. Consequently, those who argue for civil disobedience—and the lawyer's ability to counsel and engage in civil disobedience—should have the burden of proving that such conduct is an exception to the norm of obedience.

Before engaging in civil disobedience a lawyer should take special care to examine whether the law or policy being opposed produces a clear and substantial injustice. Is the injustice far removed from the ideal of the rule of law? Because of the lawyer's special knowledge of both the law in general and the particular law at issue, a lawyer may have a broader basis than the general citizen to make this assessment.

Similarly, lawyers also have a special obligation to pursue "legitimate" means of redress. Any person who has pursued a controversial issue in judicial or legislative forums knows the disparity between the myth and the reality of American political and legal action. To pursue legal change requires enormous amounts of time, money, and expertise. Because of their special relationship to the law, lawyers have a greater expertise to pursue legal and legislative change. Given that as individuals lawyers have only a limited amount of time, energy, and expertise to give, there is a powerful utilitarian basis for saying that lawyers' efforts should be directed at making legal change for which others may lack the necessary expertise. Consider the fair or proper allocation of activity when a natural disaster strikes. A strong argument can be made that a doctor facing a natural disaster should devote his or her energies to giving medical care rather than to working in an office assisting in arranging the transport of supplies. Similarly, when injustice occurs, the lawyer has a special duty to use his or her expertise to correct that injustice.

That a lawyer has a special duty to obey the law does not force the lawyer into a position of blind adherence to law. Lawyers cannot ignore unjust laws by pointing to the general legitimacy of the system. The very reasons that bind a lawyer so strongly to the rule of law also impose on the lawyer a duty to make the law just. Because of their special relationship with the law, lawyers arguably have a special duty to respond not just to active injustice—but also to passive injustice—those instances in which public officials and private citizens (including themselves) fail to prevent wrong-doing or harm. Our legal system possesses, however, an ability to tolerate a significant amount of "legal" dissent and significant—though imperfect—avenues of reform. Expansive interpretations of the First Amendment allow for vigorous public debate. Consequently, a person—including a lawyer—can take part in a public or mass protest without engaging in civil disobedience. When individuals or groups— including lawyers—exercise constitutionally protected rights, such as the right to assemble peacefully and protest,they are using lawful means to attempt to persuade the larger community to embrace the protesters' goals.

Similarly, the United States legal system makes room for the "test case," in which individuals perform an act to create a controversy in order to give the legal system an opportunity to change the offending law. The test case method allows an individual to mount a direct challenge to a law by violating the law and bringing the dispute to court. Test case litigation is possible in instances of "direct" civil disobedience, in which the individual is challenging the very law being broken. Additionally, test case litigation requires that the individual have some good faith basis for believing that his or her position is justified by the extension, modification, or reversal of existing law.

The ABA Model Rules of Professional Conduct implicitly endorses the rationale behind the test case technique of challenging the existing law when it states that a lawyer "may counsel or assist a client to make a good faith effort to determine the validity, scope, meaning or application of the law." Similarly, both the Model Rules and ABA Model Code of Professional Responsibility provide that lawyers may make a good faith argument for the extension, modification, or reversal of existing law, again creating a legal outlet for challenging law and reflecting the fluidity of our legal system. Because so many volatile issues have a constitutional basis for challenge, [as Professor Levinson put it] "the range of moral issues that cannot be tied in good faith to a constitutional provision is relatively narrow."

Identifying a "special obligation" to obey the law, however, does not indicate that it is never right for a lawyer to break the law. Perhaps a lawyer who feels compelled to commit an act of civil disobedience, but who is uncertain what effect disobedience as a lawyer would have on the legal system, may feel compelled to resign from the bar. Perhaps a lawyer as individual would conclude that, even using the "extra caution" above, civil disobedience was appropriate. Thus, in correspondence with the idea of civil disobedience, the lawyer would willingly subject him or herself to the punishment of the law. The next question to consider is whether the lawyer should be subject to any additional professional sanction for engaging in civil disobedience?

Professional Regulation and Civil Disobedience. How should the obligation to obey the law affect how lawyers regulate themselves? Because only licensed attorneys may practice law, state bars control who may be admitted to practice and what justifies expulsion from the practice. All jurisdictions have adopted a code or standard of ethics. The two dominant models, the ABA Model Code of Professional Responsibility (Model Code) and the ABA Model Rules of Professional Conduct (Model Rules), provide two ways to address the question of the lawyer's relationship to the law. Both models contain broad ambiguities. Those ambiguities, however, are both tolerable and appropriate.

The Model Code prohibits a lawyer from engaging in "illegal conduct involving moral turpitude" or engaging in "conduct prejudicial to the administration of justice." The ABA formal pronouncements under the Model Code reject any distinction between professional and personal conduct, stating that a lawyer must comply with applicable rules at all times whether or not the lawyer is acting in a professional capacity. In contrast, the Model Rules state that it is professional misconduct for a lawyer to "commit a criminal act that reflects adversely on the lawyer's honesty, trustworthiness or fitness as a lawyer in other respects" or to "engage in conduct that is prejudicial to the administration of justice." This language reflects a conscious policy in the Model Rules to cover only offenses that "indicate lack of those characteristics relevant to law practice." Although both statements are sufficiently vague to allow for a variety of interpretations, the Model Rules seem to narrow the range of possible illegal conduct that would affect a lawyer's professional status.

Which vision, the full or part-time lawyer, is correct? Is an individual a lawyer, and therefore charged with upholding the integrity of the rule of law, only when doing lawyer-like things? Or, like a priest or a parent, do lawyers hold their role all the time?

As a practical matter one cannot draw sharp lines between the lawyer and personal self. Lawyers struggle constantly with the question of how to reconcile personal beliefs with their role in the legal system. One cannot humanly shed all personal perspectives when acting as a lawyer, even when one might have a responsibility to minimize them. Certainly some acts performed in the privacy of one's home and late in the evening might spill over to one's role as a lawyer. For example, most would question the fitness of a lawyer to practice law if that lawyer had sought to embezzle funds, even if the embezzlement concerned strictly personal business dealings. That act shows a defiance of the basic rules of how to allocate rights and responsibilities in our society....

... [A] lawyer does not avoid the problem of special responsibility simply by asserting publicly that the act of civil disobedience is being done as a citizen, not a lawyer. Nonetheless, this does not mean that the formal bar mechanism should sanction all attorneys who engage in civil disobedience. The bar as a regulator of conduct suffers from serious limitations. The lawyer's system of self-regulation struggles under mixed motives—or at least a strong perception of mixed motives. One reason lawyers work to develop codes is altruistic: they seek to develop standards to educate both lawyers and the public, to reinforce notions of right and wrong, and to provide a method of deterring misconduct. Those with a more jaundiced view see the system of self regulation as motivated by economic and class self-interest.

Even assuming that the altruistic goals dominate, the codes evidence the struggle to identify which altruistic goal should dominate. Should the codes serve primarily to educate lawyers, reinforce their notions of right and wrong, or deter the most harmful conduct? The codes have evolved from the 1908 "Canons of Professional Ethics," which were largely aspirational, to the 1969 "Model Code of Professional Responsibility," which contained a blend of aspirational and directive statements, to the 1983 "Model Rules of Professional Conduct," which contain only a limited number of aspirational statements. This evolution from "ethics" to "responsibility" to "rules of conduct" indicates that the bars have functionally—and perhaps properly—recognized the inherent limits of trying to use aspirational goals rather than concrete standards. These self developed standards, which require group approval and, consequently, a certain measure of consensus, inevitably focus on the lowest common denominator. Even assuming that lawyers would all agree that they should exercise special caution before engaging in civil disobedience, lawyers inevitably will disagree about what constitutes special caution. The resolution of that issue is grounded in how much one believes our legal system deviates from the norm of perfect justice, how much one weighs the harm caused by the injustice, and other variables not subject to even quasi-objective proof. As a system based on consensus, lawyer regulation is particularly ill-suited to be a directive basis for setting standards of caution.

Lawyer self-regulation can pick up the most egregious cases of repeated defiant acts, and the current standards are sufficient to capture those instances. For example, [a Virginia] state bar committee suggested that a single act of civil disobedience did not call into question an attorney's fitness to practice law, but concluded "that frequent and/or continual misdemeanor convictions of this nature may result in more serious professional consequences."

The standard of special caution, then, is one that each lawyer should assume individually. The law is not well suited to command all aspects of moral behavior. Given that law and morality do not always dictate the same behavior and given the possible existence of unjust laws within a valid legal system, individual lawyers must define some standards for themselves....

Conclusion. As essential agents of our legal system, lawyers have a special obligation to exercise special caution before engaging in civil disobedience. Because of the limitation of the concept of self-regulation, this standard appropriately is not incorporated into narrow "rules" of conduct, but should be part of the individual lawyer's consideration when evaluating an unjust law. When counseling a client the primary focus is no longer on the lawyer and his or her special relationship with the law. Rather, the primary focus is on assisting the client to make a fully informed decision. The lawyer cannot "tell" a client to engage in civil disobedience because that is a uniquely personal decision and because to do so would violate the lawyer's duty to respect the decision-making authority of the client. To evaluate the legal consequences of engaging in civil disobedience, however, the lawyer will likely have to engage in a wide-ranging discussion about the necessity defense and jury nullification—both of which are "legal" ways of curing "illegality." Because of the reality of the complex conversation, placing any practical limitations on the lawyer as counselor is inherently problematic. We can only urge the lawyer to respect the idea of the rule of law, to respect the inherently personal nature of the decision for the client, and to respect the client's autonomy.

Selected References

Francis A. Allen, Civil Disobedience and the Legal Order, 36 Cincinatti Law Review 1 (1967).

Lindsey Cowen, The Lawyer's Role in Civil Disobedience, 47 North Carolina Law Review 587 (1969).

John Finnis, Natural Law and Natural Rights (1980).

Eugene R. Gaetke, Lawyers as Officers of the Court, 42 Vanderbilt Law Review 39 (1989).

H.L.A. Hart, Positivism and the Separation of Law and Morals, 71 Harvardd Law Review 593 (1958).

Steven H. Hobbs, From The Shoulders of Houston: A Vision for Social and Economic Justice, 32 Howard Law Journal 505 (1989).

Harold Levinson, To a Young Lawyer. Thoughts on Disobedience, 50 Missouri Law Review 483 (1985).

Lewis F. Powell, Jr., A Lawyer Looks at Civil Disobedience, 23 Washington & Lee Law Review 205 (1966).

John Rawls, A Theory of Justice (1971).

Judith Shklar, The Faces of Injustice 5 (1990).

Harlan F. Stone, The Public Influence of the Bar, 48 Harvard Law Review 1 (1934).

St. Thomas Aquinas, Treatise on Law (Summar Theologica, Questions 90–97).

Charles Warren, A History of the American Bar (1911).

Richard Wasserstrom, Lawyers as Professionals: Some Moral Issues, 5 Human Rights 1 (1975).

Charles Wolfram, Modern Legal Ethics (1986).

R. George Wright, Legal Obligation and the Natural Law, 23 Georgia Law Review 997 (1989).

Ethics Opinions

ABA Comm. on Ethics and Professional Responsibility, Formal Op. 336 (1974).

Virginia Legal Ethics Opinion No. 1185, Virginia Lawyer Register, October 1989, at 14, col. 1.

Further Reading (selected work by Judith A. McMorrow)

The (F)Utility of Rules: Regulating Attorney Conduct in Federal Court Practice, 58 SMU Law Review 3 (2005).

The Advocate as Witness: Understanding Context, Culture and Client, 70 Fordham Law Review 945 (2001).

Rule 11 and Federalizing Lawyer Ethics, 1991 Brigham Young University Law Review 959.

Who Owns Rights? Waiving and Settling Private Rights of Action, 34 Villanova Law Review 429 (1989).

Chapter Eleven

Rebellious Lawyering[*]

The professional responsibilities of progressive lawyers are becoming less clear as we explore them more deeply. The debate about the proper ethical stance for lawyers representing the poor and disadvantaged is important and necessary, but it has yet to yield a coherent picture of how such lawyers ought to treat clients and their disputes. Because of the inherently political character of representing the disadvantaged, the peculiar vulnerability of those clients, and the absence of ordinary economic constraints on the attorney-client relationship, most would agree that the duties of progressive lawyers representing subordinated clients are different from those of lawyers representing more powerful clients. The precise nature of that difference, however, continues to perplex us.

Different "models" have been offered in an effort both to outline the implementation of progressive practice and to craft theoretical bases for such practice. One significant school of thought urges a "rebellious" approach to lawyering for the subordinated. The rebellious view builds upon an obligation to empower clients that largely translates into concepts of mobilization, organization, and deprofessionalization. A connected but slightly different view urges more zealous attention to the *legal* needs of clients, and criticizes what it perceives as superficial or mass produced legal work coming from busy poverty law offices.... I have proposed an ethic for legal services lawyers that seeks to reconcile the legal needs of the client community with those of individual clients, and that explains, while perhaps not justifying, the phenomenon of mass produced justice for poor people. Each of these efforts has struggled with the inevitable tensions between individual service and community goals, and between the politics of legal instrumentality and the politics of community organizing. Most arrive at a fairly critical assessment of present progressive practice.

---

[*] **Paul R. Tremblay**, *Rebellious Lawyering, Regnant Lawyering, and Street-Level Bureaucracy*, 43 Hastings Law Journal 947 (1992), http://papers.ssrn.com/abstract_id=770867.

These discussions of progressive lawyers' professional obligations commonly tend to include relatively unflattering comments about the lawyers themselves. Poverty lawyers have been described as oppressors, as domineering, as unreflective, as poor lawyers, or as unfeeling bureaucrats. This element of the literature implies that the problem with poverty law is at least in part a problem with poverty lawyers themselves, and that improvement depends upon those lawyers changing their attitudes and practices.

This Essay takes a somewhat more apologetic view of poverty lawyers. I suggest that experience teaches us that poverty lawyers are generally good, energetic lawyers committed to social justice and to lessening the pain of poverty. No doubt there are poverty lawyers who are oppressive, paternalistic, mediocre, or unfeeling bureaucrats. This, however, is not the problem with poverty lawyering. Rather, the defects in poverty lawyering are structural, institutional, political, economic, and ethical. Teaching poverty lawyers to change their attitudes may be critically important, but those attitudes and the resulting behavior are largely products of the conditions under which poverty lawyers work. Our mission as teachers and practitioners should be to develop practice patterns and proposals that account for the street-level experiences of those legal services lawyers who work on the front lines.

This Essay examines the notions of rebellious lawyering and "regnant" lawyering as they are affected by the daily triage obligations of legal services offices. I argue that rebellious lawyering constitutes a justifiable, justice-based allocation of resources away from clients' short-term needs and in favor of a community's long-term needs. Experience from comparable resource allocation debates in the medical field and in bioethics, however, reminds us of the difficulties we face in making such distributive choices at an individual level.

A generally overriding "ethic of care" operates to hinder the efforts of individual, street-level providers to postpone offering immediate relief in order to enhance a later, and perhaps more effective, benefit. By contrast, what we describe, and criticize, as regnant lawyering is better seen as the tendency of care providers to favor the present and identifiable over the future and unnamed. This may not justify regnant lawyering—in fact, an ethical analysis would likely conclude that short-term efforts unjustifiably work to the detriment of the client community in the long run—but it helps to explain regnant lawyering's persistence. We must therefore confront this apparent preference for the "rescue mission" if we are to arrive at an accepted rebellious role for poverty lawyers.

Because the rebellious view aims to defer rewards, it must rely less upon client demand for its justification and impetus. For this reason, I believe a significant element of the rebellious approach—the participatory, client-centered emphasis on client voice—may conflict with its collectivist strain. Unless we advocate a more paternalistic or interventionist approach in the representation and translation of our clients' "voices"—quite plainly a *non sequitur*—we may have to conclude that increased client-centeredness will lead to more, rather than less, conventional lawyering.

The Rebellious and Regnant Views Described. Rebellious lawyering is lawyering that seeks to empower subordinated clients. Its proponents recognize that being represented by a lawyer is seldom an experience that leaves a client feeling or being empowered. Most lawyers dominate lawyer-client interactions with their expertise in technical matters, their use of mysterious legal language, their depersonalization of disputes, and their greater perceived importance. Dominance by lawyers is pervasive in our profession, but it is especially pronounced with poor or more dependent people, and least prominent with powerful or corporate clients. Rebellious lawyering is therefore attentive to the elements of the attorney-client relationship and its interpersonal qualities that might further disenfranchise those who are oppressed.

A second element of rebellious lawyering addresses substance rather than process. Not only is the attorney-client *relationship* disempowering to clients, but the *services rendered* by lawyers also disempower clients. Lawyers are socialized to view disputes in the context of law, to perceive disputes as cases, and to cast persons in roles such as plaintiffs, defendants, or "deep pockets." Lawyers see clients as persons to be *helped*, as powerless persons who need to have problems solved through the intervention of the lawyer and her skills. Even if the result of such intervention were good for the client's material existence, that gain might come at the expense of the client's sense of control over her life, her self-esteem, her *power*. The rebellious perspective, though, also questions whether the lawyer's intervention is in fact good for the client's material existence. Formal legal intervention may bring short-term benefits such as a successful lawsuit, administrative appeal, or beneficial settlement. Little long-term benefit, however, may result from legal intervention, because the oppressive, unfair, or even unlawful conditions which led to the dispute do not change. Long-term rewards are not only ignored, they are *sacrificed*, as energies are applied elsewhere, and thus lost.

The rebellious idea of lawyering for the subordinated seeks to address the three defects in conventional lawyering just described: the interpersonal domination of clients by lawyers; the disempowerment that accompanies reliance on litigation-based dispute resolution or its equivalent; and the inefficacy of intrasystemic remedies to achieve meaningful change in the lives of poor clients. It first proposes a restructuring of the attorney-client relationship. By increasing participation and collaboration between client and lawyer the rebellious idea of lawyering attempts to overcome the oppressive character of most law office interactions. I shall refer to this as the "client voice" theme of rebellious lawyering. It then de-emphasizes conventional lawyering remedies to minimize the second and third problems. It urges a *collective* response to the issues faced by poor clients. A rebellious lawyer will encourage clients to organize, to connect, and to work for power and change extra-systemically as well as intra-systemically. I will refer to this as the "collectivist" theme of the rebellious view. As I discuss below, there is some tension between the "client voice" and the "collectivist" themes.

Regnant lawyering is not necessarily all lawyering that is not rebellious. As employed by Gerald Lopez, the term describes that strain of legal activity characteristic of liberal and progressive lawyers who care about social justice, but who are too enmeshed in their law oriented environment to perceive its limitations and harms. Regnant lawyering is client-centered, but in an instrumental way; it seeks to improve the lot of the disadvantaged by increasing their access to rights and to institutionally defined remedies. It can include empathic and client-centered lawyering on behalf of individual poor clients, or thoughtful impact litigation on behalf of a class of poor persons.

Indeed, regnant lawyering may be perversely dangerous precisely because it is benign and well-intentioned. Its impact upon dependent clients is harder to resist because the subordination happens in a supportive and caring context, and the perpetrator of the subordination is one who the client views as a helper or a champion. Not only may clients be misled about the efficacy of the work performed on their behalf, but regnant lawyers themselves are apt to misunderstand the effects of their work. Well-intended public interest lawyers litigating important lawsuits may well have no reason to suspect that their efforts are anything but "good" for their clients. A significant contribution of the rebellious literature is its insight for practicing lawyers into the subtly counterproductive impact of their traditional activity.

The "Deferral Thesis": Rebellious Lawyering as a Future-Oriented Undertaking.... The rebellious literature is clear and emphatic in its belief that poverty lawyers are not sufficiently rebellious in their practices; the literature is one of exhortation and advocacy for this point of view. That exhortation, however, must confront two separate matters. The first is whether its predictions are accurate and reliable: will rebellious lawyering produce the empowering changes its adherents claim? The second is a more complex ethical inquiry: who benefits from this new lawyering? Is it present clients presently, present clients in the future, future clients, or unempowered persons generally? The attractiveness, and thus the implementation, of the rebellious view will differ based on how one views these two matters....

If a more political practice is effective, then the question becomes for *whom* is it effective? I argue that a rebellious practice generally defers present benefits in return for promises of long-term reward. I will refer to this argument as the "deferral thesis." This premise is critical to my discussion below; if I am wrong about this, most of what I have to say will be of little interest to the ethical assessment of the rebellious stance. But I think the premise is correct. I cannot claim that the literature is abundantly clear on this point, nor can I claim that the deferral thesis is *always* true. In fact, there are many instances in which we see immediate rewards from the more political practice. A rent strike, for example, might prove to be a far more effective device than a traditional lawsuit for the establishment of tenants' rights against an oppressive landlord....

At one level the argument that rebellious lawyering is future oriented is rather self-evident. To a large extent the justification offered for adopting a more political and collectivist practice stance is that the deferral of temporary (and perhaps illusory) benefits ultimately will result in gaining more substantial, meaningful benefits. This argument echoes the normative vision invoked to justify legal services offices focusing on impact litigation at the expense of individual service cases. Though the justification for impact work stresses *efficiency*, that value usually favors the long view over the short view, particularly when more clients will be benefited overall by sacrificing service needs for impact goals. Similarly, the writing about empowerment readily accepts a gradual increase in power for dependent or subordinated persons as a worthwhile replacement for the kind of benefits ordinary lawyering might bring.

If the deferral premise were this straightforward, I could now turn to the complications caused by the sacrifices that the rebellious stance asks clients to make. But I read the empowerment literature as leaving the question of whom rebellious lawyering will benefit unanswered. I therefore present a brief argument to persuade the reader that the rebellious view privileges the long perspective, which may, perhaps, be contrary to the claims of some of the writings about it. Part of the difficulty I encounter is in separating the two strands of empowerment theoretics—the "collectivist" theme and the "client voice" theme.

The collectivist argument values mobilization. Some writers appear to contend that mobilization is preferable to litigation, even for the immediate client. Steve Bachmann's ACORN story of a client seeking to obtain a stop sign on her street is such an example. Gary Bellow's Tulare County deposition story is a less simple but powerful example of political rebellious lawyering that benefits clients in the same way that effective litigation would, while also empowering them and altering their political consciousness. Other rebelliousness advocates imply that mobilization is an effective method for clients to redress their grievances.

I think that mobilization cannot be expected consistently to play the same kind of immediate, short-term role that more traditional litigation and administrative hearing remedies currently play. I believe that, if pressed, rebelliousness advocates would agree that the most important function of mobilization is the creation of political influence that impacts upon the ability of community members to control bureaucracy—even in the absence of professional assistance. If mobilization has already occurred, the organized group may well be in a position to effect change, or to exert influence, in as direct a way as more traditional (for example, legal) avenues may provide. If mobilization has not yet occurred, the rebellious view urges lawyers to spur collective activity. But this process will take energy, resources, expertise, and time. Unless the poverty lawyer is expected to do both at the same time, the mobilization effort will occur at the expense of other benefits the clients might wish to obtain through conventional means. Doing both at the same time is, of course, out of the question, because reliance upon the conventional remedy usurps the power of mobilization and because poverty lawyers do not have the *time* to do both....

[T]he "client voice" theme challenges paternalistic, lawyer-driven handling of client cases and urges increased client collaboration in and control of the activity surrounding the client's dispute. Greater deference to client expertise, and less to lawyer expertise, is likely to empower the client. The concern that arises in this context is once again one of deferred or sacrificed rewards. I have argued that rebellious writers have overlooked the risk clients incur in rejecting technical lawyer expertise. That risk may be worth taking, but the literature has not explicitly framed the matter as one of informed consent. To the extent that the rebellious view privileges the empowerment of clients over their chances of success in the immediate controversy, that stance must also be viewed as one which favors long-term power development over short-term instrumental gain.

Justice Theory and the Rescue Mission. If we accept the deferral thesis as generally descriptive of the future oriented character of rebellious lawyering, we then confront an ethics debate that the medical field has engaged in for many years—the debate about whether and how a profession (or a society) can accommodate present needs and interests as well as the claims of future or long-term needs and interests. [T]heorizing ... in bioethics about this topic leads us to realize three things. First, it is important that future interests be accounted for in present decision-making. Second, it is difficult to devise a scheme that protects future interests and yet is client-centered. We can fairly expect that existing clients, and particularly clients in crisis, will not find it easy to forego immediate benefits, especially if they are not the obvious or reasonably assured beneficiaries of the future returns. Therefore, client-driven decisions must be replaced with decisions coming from another source, perhaps from lawyers acting as trustees for future clients or the client community. This conclusion has sobering consequences for the "client voice" theme. Finally, it is equally troublesome to expect immediate care providers to develop and implement allocational schemes that sacrifice present interests in favor of future interests.

Each of these three conclusions deserves further explanation and elaboration. All of these concerns can be framed in terms of considerations of distributive justice. Distributive justice questions regularly receive substantial attention within medicine. By contrast, distributive justice questions in law are far less prominent. [The] resource allocation questions with which medicine struggles are much more unavoidable in the context of poverty law than in the area of private lawyering. The relatively and visibly finite resources available to address the vast array of legal problems facing individuals who cannot pay for legal services requires that allocation decisions be made all the time, even if the decision-makers do not realize that they are doing so.

Matters of distributive justice often are viewed from three perspectives. *Macroallocation* questions concern broad societal or governmental decisions about how much ought to be allocated to competing arenas, such as legal matters versus health care, welfare versus defense, and so forth. Determining the size of the Legal Services Corporation (LSC) budget, for instance, would be a macroallocation matter. *Mesoallocation* questions concern how to distribute the allocated resources—for instance, how the LSC budget is distributed among various programs, applicants, and uses. *Microallocation* decisions reach the street level or the bedside: how an individual provider distributes the available resources among her various present and potential clients or patients.

The vision of rebellious lawyering described above represents a bundle of mesoallocation and microallocation recommendations that have as their purpose the introduction of future oriented values into the lawyering scheme. The future benefit versus present benefit tension that the rebellious view presents is prominent in medicine as well, and has received much attention from bioethicists. The most evident parallel example in medicine is the choice whether to allocate resources to preventive medicine or to crisis, or "rescue," medicine. The debate about that choice is instructive for those of us seeking a fair and ethical justification for rebellious lawyering.

How can medicine justify spending funds for preventive measures when many have ongoing acute needs that cannot be met? Several justice related concepts may be offered in support of that choice. A prominent justification is efficiency. If available evidence shows that more individuals may be made healthy by preventive means than by rescue measures, a mesoallocation policy favoring prevention garners support. There are weaknesses to this efficiency argument, however, notably the questionable nature of its utilitarian basis. Another justification is a Rawlsian "social contract" theory of justice, which factors the needs of future generations into present decision-making. Ronald Green points out that Rawls begins by assuming "rational voters in a hypothetical contract situation," each of whom is ignorant of who she is and how she is affected by the proposed policy, and thus engages us in a moral conversation that must include others who may not yet be born. Practices which maximize present gain at the expense of future individuals become morally troublesome when viewed from this perspective.

It is not surprising to find justice-based justifications for a future-oriented public policy. At the level of theory, the argument that it is morally correct to consider the harm caused to others by giving attention to certain individuals has a logical, as well as a prudential, attractiveness. This attractiveness supports in large measure the force of the rebellious view. These arguments echo those made by David Luban in his justification of focused case pressure in legal services and of lawyer activism in class action contexts. But rescue medicine has its moral defenders, and an assessment of rebellious lawyering must confront the ethical imperatives that favor clients in the here-and-now.

A large part of rescue medicine's defense appears to be visceral in nature. The bioethicist Edmund Pellegrino writes, "[T]here is an inescapable immediacy about the call for help of a sick person that overshadows all other more remote social needs, no matter how important." James Childress reports that "[o]ur society often favors rescue or crisis intervention over prevention because of our putative preference for known, identified lives over statistical lives." But Childress and others also have attempted a more principled justification of the immediacy concern, one that builds upon this visceral and compelling concern for the here-and-now. Childress distinguishes Max Weber's two measures of behavior, *zweckrational* ("goal-rational") and *wertrational* ("value-rational"), in his defense of the rescue mission. "There is … an important distinction between *realizing* a goal and *expressing* a value," and both, according to Childress, are important ends and substantial justifications. While sacrificing the immediate in favor of the future may be a perfectly appropriate *goal*, " 'we have (rationally defensible) worries about the sort of moral character represented by people who propose to stand pat and let present victims die for the sake of future possibilities.'" The symbolism and the values expressed by the sacrifice may be unacceptable. In this connection, Childress quotes Charles Fried: "[S]urely it is odd to symbolize our concern for human life by actually doing less than we might to save it."

Childress and Fried do not need to persuade us that their position on the question of rescue versus preventive medicine is correct to be relevant to the discussion of rebellious lawyering. It does seem that the urgency about which Fried and Childress worry is less dramatic in lawyering. We are not, for the most part, talking about life and death sacrifices when immediate conventional lawyering is deferred in favor of mobilization. Moreover, the sacrifices I see in the rebellious stance are less clearly present generation versus future generation, although this matter is not fully clear. What I have described as the future oriented approach of the rebellious stance can be seen as benefitting *existing* clients later, or benefitting *other*, as yet unnamed, future clients. How that outcome is predicted will substantially affect the symbolism of sacrifice that the above writers find so troubling.

Whatever one thinks about Childress' defense of the rescue medicine preference, two important consequences follow for our purposes. The first concerns the role of the client and of client choice in the resource allocation scheme. If one rejects the "value-rational" defense, either because it applies less visibly to legal resource decisions or because one finds it unpersuasive relative to the justice based theories favoring the long view, one must acknowledge that allocation decisions favoring future gain can feasibly be made only by persons not subject to present deprivation. If present recipients or applicants for scarce resources were to "vote" on the question of present versus future application of those resources, we could not reasonably expect the vote to be in favor of deference to the future.

I think this point is fairly self-evident, but one example from bioethics might be helpful in understanding the difficulty inherent in devising a scheme that requires sacrifice by those subject to it. A slightly different tension from the rescue/prevention dilemma in medicine is the tricky issue of clinical trials. In medical research, a "randomized clinical trial" (RCT) is thought to be an important element in ascertaining the efficacy of a given therapeutic procedure or medication. The "randomized" character of the research means that studies are performed "blind," with certain subjects receiving the intended treatment while others are offered a placebo or an alternative treatment. Though RCTs are intended generally to be employed among multiple treatments whose effectiveness is in question, there is much evidence that clinicians believe (and expect to prove by the experimentation) that one treatment is superior. The trials in many cases therefore call for some sacrifice from patients in the interests of "science," which is another way of saying in the interests of future patients. Ian Robinson captures the ethical tension in the following questions:

> [I]s it possible to have a randomised controlled trial in which the obligations of the clinical scientist to the collectivity do not ethically undermine the obligations of the clinical healer to individual patients participating in the trial? In brief, is it possible to reconcile the scientist's duty to all present and future patients with the healer's duty to present patients?

RCTs remain morally troublesome because of this tension. Some bioethicists have argued that patients need not be asked to consent to the trials, claiming that those patients will benefit ultimately from the experimentation. They also assert that patients are apt not to consent to participation if nonrandomized treatment is available, and that absent their consent the medical research will be impossible. This view is not the accepted one among medical ethicists, most of whom agree that RCTs are justified only when conducted with the knowing consent of the affected subjects. Implicit in the literature, however, is the understanding that patients, while informed about the risks of RCTs, are not necessarily offered the choice of full treatment or RCT participation; instead, the choice is between participating or not participating in the RCT. It is apparent that, except with an RCT that compares two equally risky treatments, patients will opt, when allowed the choice, for treatment rather than a placebo, or for conventional "healing" medicine rather than scientific research medicine.

In similar fashion, we cannot expect clients, if offered a free and informed choice, willingly to sacrifice their present benefits for future benefits unless the promised benefits are substantially assured and will accrue to those clients themselves. This does not deny the possibility of altruism and self-sacrifice, at least on occasion; it does, however, suggest that rebelliousness may need to be imposed from above....

Recalling the "value-rational" concern for the symbolism of not aiding the dying, we must confront the visceral strength of the emotional response doctors have when asked to make social justice choices at the bedside. While those responses may not require us to reject the long view, they do cause us to pause before seeking to establish the long view policy through street-level lawyers. There is much to be said for a "moral division of labor," in which the individuals who impose the long view are not those who have to treat the individual client or patient. This would not mean a rejection of collective activity, mobilization, or other aspects of the rebellious stance. It does mean, however, that the choices about how to proceed with a community of clients would need to be imposed upon street-level lawyers via some administrative or similar authoritative structure to overcome the natural preference for the here-and-now.

Some Reflections on the Fate of Rebellious Lawyering in the Context of Street-Level Reality. One reasonable conclusion to be drawn from bioethical experience with the prevention/rescue dilemma is that rebelliousness may need to be imposed upon, rather than chosen by, individual lawyers and clients. The "moral division of labor" approach may be the best way to avoid the preference for the here-and-now. The imposition of rebelliousness in legal circles, however, may be much more difficult than the imposition of a prevention ideology in medicine. Reimbursement schemes in medicine have a powerful impact on the behavior of individual physicians, and reimbursement mechanisms are almost uniformly imposed from without. For example, in 1987 Oregon legislators amended the state Medicaid program to cease covering organ transplants. The state concluded that the funds saved by this change would provide regular prenatal care to fifteen hundred pregnant women. This simple example demonstrates how macroallocation decisions can be made from above, thereby relieving the individual physician of having to justify to her patient the decision not to perform a transplant.

This kind of macroallocation mechanism is far less likely to occur within poverty law contexts. For subordinated clients who must pay for private counsel, insurance coverage for legal expenses is unlikely to be available. The resource allocation decisions that must be made within that context therefore will be negotiated directly between the attorney and her client, without the third-party influences offered by an insurer. For subsidized practice, macroallocation might occur at the level of the funding source, such as the LSC. Putting aside, for the moment, the ferociously unsympathetic attitude of the current and recent administrations to anything closely resembling collective lawyering efforts for the poor, even the most progressive federal administration is likely, at best, to send regnant, not rebellious, messages to its field offices.

We cannot realistically hope that rebellious lawyering will be imposed by the government agencies that fund poverty law. This presents serious consequences for the success of the endeavor. Advocates of the rebellious view must develop incentives for lawyers to adhere to the long view in spite of the visceral urge to respond to present crises. Individual programs may have more flexibility and therefore might perform the mesoallocation that removes some decision-making from the front lines. Poverty law offices may also want to explore the prospect of representing *groups* more often. Within groups the rescue mission is at least diffused, and the long view may be more attainable.

Finally, the question of the role of the "client voice" theme needs to be addressed. The discussion above points out the need for some separation between the individual clients in need and the imposition of long view lawyering. The client voice theme argues for much greater connection between those in need and the lawyer who responds to that need. To the extent rebellious lawyering does not seek deferral of gain, such greater connectedness would be nothing but a blessing. But to the extent rebelliousness takes the long view, increased connectedness would only make that view more difficult to sustain. The "value-rational" is apt to conflict deeply with the "goal-rational" and some means of resolving that tension will need to be devised.

Conclusion. Writers have been imploring poverty lawyers to pursue empowerment and collective mobilization for [decades]. Yet rebelliousness remains the exception, and not the norm. In my opinion this is not due to a lack of power or force in the argument for rebelliousness. I have tried to show that psychological factors, most notably the visceral attraction to the here-and-now, and institutional factors, including the failure of existing programs to remove allocative decisionmaking from street-level lawyers, account for the prominence of regnant ideology. Unless and until progressive theorists can counteract the inherent rescue preference in neighborhood legal services offices with something more than exhortation, poverty lawyering will remain more or less conservative.

Selected References

Anthony V. Alfieri, Reconstructive Poverty Law Practice: Learning Lessons of Client Narrative, 100 Yale Law Journal 2107 (1991).

Steve Bachmann, Lawyers, Law, and Social Change, 13 NYU Review of Law and Social Change 1 (1984–85).

Gary Bellow & Jeanne Kettleso, From Ethics to Politics: Confronting Scarcity and Fairness in Public Interest Practice, 58 Boston University Law Review 337 (1978).

Edgar S. Cahn & Jean C. Cahn, The War on Poverty: A Civilian Perspective, 73 Yale Law Journal 1317 (1964).

Jerome E. Carlin & Jan Howard, Legal Representation and Class Justice, 12 UCLA Law Review 381 (1965).

James F. Childress & Tom L. Beauchamp, Principles of Biomedical Ethics (3d ed. 1989).

Roger C. Cramton, Crisis in Legal Services for the Poor, 26 Villanova Law Review 521 (1980–81).

Charles Fried, An Anatomy of Values: Problems of Personal and Social Choice (1970).

Raanon Gillon, Philosophical Medical Ethics (1986).

Joel F. Handler, Dependent People, the State, and the Modern/Postmodern Search for the Dialogic Community, 35 UCLA Law Review 999 (1988).

Robert J. Levine, Ethics and Regulation of Clinical Research (2d ed. 1986).

Gerald P. Lopez, Reconceiving Civil Rights Practice: Seven Weeks in the Life of a Rebellious Collaboration, 77 Georgetown Law Journal 1603 (1989).

Robert L. Nelson, Ideology, Practice, and Professional Autonomy: Social Values and Client Relationships in the Large Law Firm, 37 Stanford Law Review 503 (1985).

Edmund Pellegrino & David C. Thomasma, The Philosophical Basis of Medical Practice (1981), quoted in Robert M. Veatch, Justice in Health Care: The Contribution of Edmund Pellegrino, 15 Journal of Medicine and Philosophy 269 (1990).

Ian Robinson, Clinical Trials and the Collective Ethic: The Case of Hyperbaric Oxygen Therapy and the Treatment of Multiple Sclerosis, in Social Science Perspectives on Medical Ethics (George Weisz ed., 1990).

William H. Simon, Visions of Practice in Legal Thought, 36 Stanford Law Review 469 (1984).

Mark Spiegel, Lawyers and Professional Autonomy: Reflections on Corporate Lawyering and the Doctrine of Informed Consent, 9 Western New England Law Review 139 (1987).

Lucie E. White, Mobilization on the Margins of the Lawsuit: Making Space for Clients to Speak, 16 NYU Review of Law and Social Change 535 (1987–88).

Further Reading (selected work by Paul R. Tremblay)

Moral Activism Manqué, 44 South Texas Law Review 127 (2002).

Shared Norms, Bad Lawyers, and the Virtues of Casuistry, 36 San Francisco Law Review 659 (2002).

The New Casuistry, 12 Georgetown Journal of Legal Ethics 489 (1999).

Acting "A Very Moral Type of God": Triage Among Poor Clients, 67 Fordham Law Review 2475 (1999).

The Role of Casuistry in Legal Ethics: A Tentative Inquiry, 1 Clinical Law Review 493 (1994).

Toward a Community-Based Ethic for Legal Services Practice, 37 UCLA Law Review 1101 (1990).

CHAPTER TWELVE

MULTICULTURAL LAWYERING*

… Lawyers are professionals because they are trained in an area that requires intellectual skill and specialized knowledge. This training creates a power imbalance in the lawyer-client relationship: the client supposedly goes to the lawyer for assistance because the lawyer has expertise the client lacks. Thus, in a traditional model of lawyering, the lawyer controls: she is the one who knows the law and uses this knowledge to make predictions about the best legal outcomes and to set legal strategy.

But the traditional model of lawyering is in many respects unsatisfactory. Crafting a good solution to a client's problem could require familiarity with more than just the relevant legal facts; indeed, familiarity with more facts about the client's situation could determine whether the lawyer even is thinking about the right legal claim. Clients too might be dissatisfied with directive lawyering: humanized lawyering accords them more respect and allows them greater control over the process. So, client-centered models of lawyering have developed. The first model, promulgated by Binder and Price, (hereinafter the Binder-Price model) recognizes that the client has superior knowledge about her values, goals and situation, which will enable her to better choose a satisfactory resolution. Thus, client-centered lawyering attempts to shift the power imbalance by engaging the client as a participant in the lawyering process.

However, the original formulation of client-centered lawyering was often inapt, at least as applied to clients many students encounter in clinical and legal services practice. Critics noted that the Binder-Price model conceptualized the client as a copy of the lawyer, minus the legal know-how. This copy shared the lawyer's socioeconomic status, perspective, organizational modes, etc.—for example, related his situation in clear, chronological order—and thus was ready, willing, and able to participate in the lawyering model promulgated by Binder and Price. Other clients, who might ramble, evince reluc-

---

* **Carwina Weng**, *Multicultural Lawyering: Teaching Psychology to Develop Cultural Self-Awareness*, 11 CLINICAL LAW REVIEW 369 (2005), http://papers.ssrn.com/abstract_id= 704023.

tance to discuss certain topics or to commence an interview, lie, or display anger or hostility were, in the Binder-Price parlance, "difficult" and "atypical."

The early Binder-Price model does offer some explanation as to why clients might be "difficult," but the reasons do not take into account culture, whether based on race, socioeconomic status, or other factors, except age. The model thus ignores the fact that culture and other power and privilege differences also affect the client's participation in the lawyering relationship.…

In *Constructions of the Client within Legal Education*, Anne Shalleck points out that this undifferentiated model of client-centered lawyering in fact maintains the lawyer as the dominant player. She notes that the model favors a chronological narrative over other forms of storytelling, depends on the lawyer to determine the importance of both legal and nonlegal concerns, assumes a standardized client, and ignores power imbalances. Thus, the Binder-Price model "uses the lawyer-client relationship to construct the interests and motivations of clients through criteria the law controls."

Concerns about a "one-size-fits-all" training model arose among mental health professionals before they arose among law clinicians. Derald and David Sue warned that an "ethnocentric" model of counseling teaches students to practice in a way that can harm their clients. The model views the experiences of clients of color "from the 'White, European-American perspective' … [and] the focus tends to be on their pathological lifestyles and/or a maintenance of false stereotypes." For example, a counselor might view a patient's reluctance to self-disclose as paranoia, when in fact that reluctance might be "a healthy reaction to racism" from the counselor. The counselor might also "overshadow" a client's job-related problems with personal ones, resulting in an underdiagnosis of psychopathology. Thus, mental health professionals also clearly recognized that an ethnocentric model of practice, combined with a power imbalance in favor of the professional, creates a system that permits replication of societal discrimination.

Small wonder, then, that Michelle Jacobs should find the Binder-Price client-centered model troubling when applied to the primary consumer at her clinic, namely poor, black clients. Jacobs reminds us that clients labeled difficult by textbooks espousing client-centered lawyering might be resisting the lawyer's invitation to participate in the lawyering process. Rather than dismiss the client as difficult, lawyers need to ask ourselves why the client might be resisting our invitation. Might the client's response be a reaction to behavior by the lawyer who fails to recognize "the real client in her full context—culturally, politically and economically?" Or based on the client's perception of a lawyer who is culturally different from her?

In the legal arena, as Jacobs warned, attorneys who learn an ethnocentric model may be ill-equipped to perceive and understand different values and world views presented by their clients. These blinders—often unconscious and unintentional—can result in a lawyer's misperception of culturally-based behaviors by her client or of her client's reactions to the lawyer's own culturally-based behaviors. They can affect the lawyer's ability to build trust and, therefore, the information the client chooses to share. They also can determine how the lawyer frames the client's legal problem and directs the strategy. We thus end up with lawyers trained to consider clients who do not fit the model to be at best difficult and at worst pathological....

... Jacobs' and Shalleck's critiques raise questions about how well the standard model of client-centered lawyering works with clients who are disenfranchised and often economically and racially/ethnically diverse from their lawyers. Even though client-centered lawyering focuses on respecting and empowering the client, it does not address the dynamics of power and subordination (historical, actual, or perceived) in the attorney-client interaction. Thus, suggestions to improve client-centered lawyering also draw on the theories of rebellious lawyering and theoretics of practice to change the underlying discourse between lawyer and client. With rebellious lawyering, the emphasis is on the client: how the client's life—including her membership in an outsider group and her group's history of subordination—defines the legal problem, generates the solutions, and determines the course of action. With this emphasis, the client might more effectively participate as an equal in the decision-making process.

With theoretics of practice, the emphasis is on the lawyer: how can the lawyer understand the "assumptions, biases, values, and norms embedded in the law's workings in order to heighten awareness of the political and moral choices made by lawyers and the legal system"? How can the lawyer "listen[] to and describ[e] clients in a way that does not impose upon them categories constructed by lawyers"?

Both rebellious lawyering and theoretics of practice describe approaches to bridging the gap—cultural and power-based—between lawyers and clients who are different from each other. Building this bridge is not an easy task. Empathy and active listening may elicit more details from the client, and questioning the premises of the American legal system may help the lawyer consciously to avoid its biases. But the lawyer's cultural lens will operate automatically to filter this information and to create expectations about the lawyer-client interaction. So, unless the lawyer understands her own culture and the ways it affects her interactions with others, she risks perpetuating the status quo of discrimination.

More recently, concerns about the human impact of lawyering [have] led to developments in "the comprehensive law movement," which have implications for addressing the culture gap between lawyer and client. The movement has not developed specifically as a response to this gap, but rather out of a concern that law exacts a heavy price on lawyers, clients, and others involved in litigation. Overall, the comprehensive law movement utilizes humanistic and interdisciplinary approaches to reconceptualize the lawyer's and the legal system's interactions with the client in ways that consider explicitly the client's context.

This concern can lead to a focus on client context, which encompasses a client's cultural and other group membership. Because the movement seeks in part to improve contextualized outcomes for clients, it draws on generalist social work methods to improve lawyer-client relationships and the effectiveness and reputation of legal systems. A generalist social work model trains the professional to interact with clients at the individual, small group, and agency or community levels so that the "organizational context" of the client is integral to any interaction. As part of that contextual interaction, the client's culture is vital, and the professional must learn to interact in a client-centered, culturally competent manner.

Training in multicultural lawyering brings together the approaches championed by rebellious lawyering, theoretics of practice, and the comprehensive law movement by "combin[ing] personal growth with content learning and skill development." As a starting point, multiculturalists focus on a broad understanding of culture as "unstated assumptions, shared values, and characteristic ways of perceiving the world that are normally taken for granted by its members." Multicultural lawyering training teaches the student to be aware of the cultural basis for his own behavior and champions using "a 'cultural lens' as a central focus of professional behavior ... recogniz[ing] that all individuals including themselves are influenced by different contexts, including the historical, ecological, sociopolitical, and disciplinary." Thus, the student develops a " 'personal-cultural orientation' " toward lawyering in which she considers how her and others' behavior is guided by culturally learned expectations and values. With such knowledge and regular practice, the student is better equipped to develop more accurate decision making that is less biased by the cultural backgrounds of either the lawyer or the client or by the complexity of the problem presented.

Current Methods of Teaching Multicultural Lawyering. To develop this personal-cultural orientation, multicultural counseling trainers recommend a three-fold approach: developing awareness and knowledge of one's own culture; developing awareness of the client's culture; and learning specific skills to minimize the impact of one's own biases and prejudices toward the multicultural interaction. Within each of these domains, students focus on becoming competent cognitively, affectively, and behaviorally.

By contrast, some of the literature of multicultural lawyering emphasizes developing awareness of the client's culture, without delving into developing cultural self-awareness. For example, Stefan Krieger and Richard Neumann urge that students acquire "an instinct for situations where another person's cultural assumptions may be very different from yours." To develop this instinct, they suggest a three-step process: (1) learn about the other cultures an attorney is most likely to encounter; (2) anticipate situations in which taking culture into account will improve lawyering and plan non-stereotyped, non-offensive behavior; and (3) apologize in a prompt and straightforward manner if a mistake occurs. Thus awareness of the other, rather than of the self, takes precedence.

Paul Tremblay, like Krieger and Neumann, urges lawyers to anticipate the most likely areas of cultural differences and the way these differences affect the multicultural interaction. But whereas Krieger and Neumann do not detail cultural differences, Tremblay identifies six areas in which differences are most likely to occur—proxemics, kinesics, time and priority considerations, narrative preferences, relational perspectives, and scientific orientation. Tremblay posits that knowledge of cultural differences in these areas will assist the lawyer in avoiding cultural blunders.

… A 1992 study by Stephan and Stephan [and drawn upon by Professor Michelle Jacobs] reveals that one risk of a narrow focus is anxiety about difference affecting interaction. In this study, the authors followed a group of American students going to Morocco, to consider how the students handled immersion in a new culture. The students received lectures on cultural differences and classes on the history and culture of Morocco prior to their arrival. However, upon their arrival in Morocco, this instruction did not improve the students' interactions. Instead, the study determined that the students' increased awareness of the differences between the cultures, of their own cultural incompetence, and of the pitfalls in navigating the culture increased the students' anxiety. Stephan and Stephan hypothesize in part that a better instructional method, namely a combination of lectures and simulation, would more effectively help students to interact with a culture different from their own by allowing the students to practice using the substantive cultural knowledge they had acquired.

Many students react to a culturally different client with an anxiety similar to that of the students' in the Stephan and Stephan study. That anxiety then can manifest in multiple ways: as unconscious avoidance—the student who postpones meeting with a disability client diagnosed with Post-Traumatic Stress Disorder for fear of asking questions about the illness and having to cope with the client's responses; or tentativeness during the interaction—the student who self-consciously shies away from eye contact with an Asian-American client; or over-eagerness—the student who recalls her repertoire of high-school Spanish to greet a Guatemalan client. These reactions are counterproductive; they overemphasize the cultural differences between lawyer and client and, therefore, interfere with the creation of a secure, nonjudgmental environment in which the lawyer and client can interact.

A second risk is that a focus on cultural knowledge can give students "a false sense of accomplishment" that the acquisition alone of such knowledge enables them to work with members of that particular culture. This sense can cause students to resist exploring their own cultures and attitudes toward other cultural groups and can reinforce the notion of the client as "the other." If, however, a student understands her relationship to her own culture and the ways that culture creates or reinforces stereotypes, she might not presume that information on cultural differences is accurate for a given client, and she might alter her lawyering to fit the actual client, not the essentialized one....

A third risk is that the student who is unaware of his own culture may not examine his reactions to information about a different culture for unconscious biases or prejudices that impair cultural competence.... [W]e must be vigilant in confronting our own biases and prejudices and beware stereotyping the individual client with whom we are working. As Sue Bryant admonishes, the culturally competent lawyer must acknowledge her own cultural persona, analyze how it affects the client relationship, acquire knowledge about the client's culture but apply it accurately, and interact based on the actual details of the client's circumstances. By starting with cultural self-awareness, the lawyer is better able to understand the client's culture and the interaction of the two cultures. Thus, the key to developing multicultural competence is cultural self-awareness....

Because of their concreteness, the habits for cross-cultural lawyering and Tremblay's related heuristics add depth to the process espoused by Krieger and Neumann and are particularly valuable in clinical teaching. Their use helps students to change behavior to foster better lawyering for the individual client; the culturally-aware lawyer might hear the client's narrative more accurately and relay it to the legal decision maker with less distortion or engage the client more fully in a decision to exploit a cultural stereotype. In addition, Krieger and Neumann's reminder to apologize can help to repair respect, trust, and open communication when mistakes in multicultural interactions occur....

The Psychological Underpinnings of Multicultural Lawyering Training. Why is some understanding of cognitive and social psychology necessary? Because, currently in our society, we typically do not discriminate intentionally against people who differ from ourselves. So, lawyers treat clients in culturally insensitive ways due to "unconscious or aversive racism," which can stem from categorization errors that characterize cognitive functioning and from unconscious tendencies to favor members of social groups similar to themselves over members of other groups. Learning more about these psychological processes provides a basis for understanding how lawyers behave in ways that cause discrimination and, therefore, how to assess their own beliefs and lawyering practices.

A lawyer who understands that he has subconscious cognitive categories—called schemas—and that the way he automatically employs them can cause subordinating treatment might be less defensive about acknowledging that his *behavior* is discriminatory. In addition, awareness of how a schema is created might enable a dominant-culture lawyer to understand how that culture influences the contents of his schemas and to make conscious efforts to diversify his interactions and to question the contents of his schemas in an effort to act with more accuracy regarding members of different cultures. Such a change could more easily allow the client's life, including her membership in an outsider group and that group's history of subordination, to define the legal problem, generate the solutions, and determine the course of action.

Let us consider then, how schemas are created and how they affect our behavior: A lawyer meeting a client automatically places the client into a cognitive category or schema. The schema itself is not inherently bad. Rather, it is simply a means of organizing information "to identify objects, make predictions about the future, infer the existence of unobservable traits or properties, and attribute the causation of events." A schema thus enables people to process information quickly and largely automatically. We create our schemas through the experience of our daily lives, from personal encounters, second-hand information, the media, etc. Behavior becomes associated with race, gender, age, roles, and character traits, and event scripts develop through repetition. With regard to people, physical characteristics like skin color, gender, and age are readily perceived and therefore are more likely to become salient features in our cognitive categories. Each category then becomes a prototype or reference point for the people we meet, and we interact with others based on the category that is activated. If we do not question the expectations evoked by the activated category, insensitive behavior can result....

[S]ocial categorization operates on an automatic level. Based on one's own characteristics, a person sorts others into "in-groups" sharing characteristics with the perceiver and "out-groups" that do not. The separation of others into in-groups and out-groups further influences the way in which the perceiver views others. So, if a lawyer has limited experience with members of different cultures, then the behavior of those few members of the out-group culture becomes more salient and may be seen as representative of that culture. In addition, the perceiver may use her in-group as a reference point for interpreting her own behavior as well as that of others. On a subconscious level, she may exaggerate differences among groups and favor members of her in-group over members of out-groups....

A problem with schemas is that they are susceptible to unconscious biases and stereotyping.... Because a stereotype can become ingrained in a schema, the stereotype can create an unconscious expectation that a specific individual will behave in conformity with the stereotype. If the expectation is distorted or illusory ... then the perceiver might unconsciously be biased in the way she interacts with the client.

When the client comes from a culture different from the lawyer's, the risk of stereotyping is greater. Experience with members of the client's culture that was seen as negative is more readily recalled, and thus the lawyer runs the risk of expecting negative behavior and finding it, whether or not it actually occurred. In addition, the lawyer is more likely to attribute behaviors of the out-group client to character traits if the behaviors fit the expectation and to situational factors if the behavior seems aberrant. Then, the lawyer might start to label the client who does not return phone calls as rude or uncaring instead of considering that work, personal, child-related, or other factors might cause the delay.

Given these problems with cognitive schemas, one might become discouraged, wondering whether we could ever become culturally competent. Explicit discussion of the schemas and stereotypes we hold, however, might enable us to uncover the hidden assumptions. Thus, the teaching of nonracist behaviors, coupled with cognitive and social psychology, can help lawyers to examine their values, biases, and prejudices and therefore to change their behaviors and attitudes....

Selected References

Anthony A. Alfieri, Stances, 77 Cornell Law Review 1233 (1992).

David A. Binder & Susan C. Price, Legal Interviewing and Counseling: A Client-Centered Approach (1977).

David A. Binder et al., Lawyers as Counselors: A Client-Centered Approach 4 (2nd ed 2004).

Susan Bryant, The Five Habits: Building Cross-Cultural Competence in Lawyering, 8 Clinical Law Review 33 (2001).

Susan Daicoff, The Comprehensive Law Movement, 19 Touro Law Review 825 (2004).

Phyllis Goldfarb, Beyond Cut Flowers: Developing a Clinical Perspective on Critical Legal Theory, 43 Hastings Law Journal 717 (1992).

Michelle S. Jacobs, People from the Footnotes: the Missing Element in Client-Centered Counseling, 27 Golden Gate Law Review 345 (1997).

Stefan H. Krieger & Richard K. Neumann, Jr., Essential Lawyering Skills (2nd ed. 2003).

Gerald P. Lopez, Preconceiving Civil Rights Practice: Seven Weeks in the Life of a Rebellious Collaboration, 77 Georgetown Law Journal 1603 (1989).

Jean Koh Peters, Access to Justice: The Social Responsibility of Lawyers: Habit, Story, and Delight, Essential Tools for the Public Service Advocate, 7 Washington University Journal of Law & Policy 17 (2001).

Charles R. Ridley, Overcoming Unintentional Racism in Counseling and Therapy: A Practitioner's Guide to Intentional Intervention (1995).

Anne Shalleck, Constructions of the Client within Legal Education, 45 Stanford Law Review 1731 (1993).

Derald W. Sue & David Sue, Counseling the Culturally Different: Theory and Practice (3d ed. 1999).

Paul R. Tremblay, Interviewing and Counseling across Cultures: Heuristics and Biases, 9 Clinical Law Review 373 (2002).

Part II

Institutions and Legitimacy

A. Separation of Powers

CHAPTER THIRTEEN

STATUTORY VIOLATIONS AND EQUITABLE DISCRETION[*]

Equity, that ancient and amiable dowager of Anglo-American law, often appears to have ambled through the twentieth century free of the stress and strains that have belabored the common law. A closer analysis of the practice and logic of equity in the modern statutory context, however, undercuts that appearance of immutability. The resulting recasting of equitable doctrines has important implications, not only for equity theory, but also for contemporary legal analysis of administrative law, the relationship between courts and legislatures, and modern pluralistic democracy.

Today's equity treatises nevertheless remain largely grounded in the classic common law litigation setting. In part, no doubt, this is because equity, unlike the common law, has rarely been subjected to direct, specific reforms. While the common law has absorbed major dislocations in its settled doctrines—through judge-made revolutions like those in products liability and modern landlord-tenant law and statutory retoolings like the Uniform Commercial Code—equity, as a peculiarly procedural assemblage of remedy doctrines, has sustained few basic changes. To be sure, modern statutes and ... conditions have cast equity's substantive jurisdictions in the areas of divorce, trusts, and decedent's estates into new forms, but even there the judicial flexibility that is the essence of equity lies relatively undisturbed. When judges seek precedential authority for modern tort, contract, and property cases, they only rarely find it relevant to cite cases from a hundred or even fifty years ago. For equity cases, however, the nineteenth century is still thought to provide relevant guidance.

In larger part, however, the equity treatises' non-statutory focus is attributable to a simple failure to take full account of modern governmental

* **Zygmunt J.B. Plater**, *Statutory Violations and Equitable Discretion*, 70 California Law Review 524 (1982), http://papers.ssrn.com/abstract_id=760379.

processes. Modern times—the vast complexities and consequences of a corporate economy, ... technology, the legislative and administrative processes of the regulatory state—have altered the workings of equity in modern court practice even if the rhetoric of courts and scholars remains largely unchanged. It is time that our analysis and understanding of equitable doctrines be conformed to their reality, especially in the context of modern statutory law.

To analyze equity in the modern statutory setting is to tread on the toes of one of the most venerable formulas of equitable jurisprudence: that an appeal to equity is always an appeal to a court's discretion to balance the equities. But this maxim, an accurate description of the role of equity in the classic common law cases, is simply not an accurate description of its role in the face of statutory commands.

This Article examines the role of equitable discretion in the modern statutory context. It begins ... with a proposition that can be as unsettling to trained legal minds as it is self-evident to those without the benefit of a legal education: that a court has no discretion or authority to exercise equitable powers so as to permit violations of statutes to continue.... [It] explores the traditional forms of equitable discretion as they exist in the classic common law context. Properly viewed in this context, equity has three distinct and separable balancing components: a threshold balance, a balance on the question of abatement or required conduct, and finally a balance in tailoring equitable remedies to effectuate the second determination.... Viewed in light of the three separate elements of equitable balancing, the holdings in statutory cases reveal a consistent pattern. Courts defer to the legislature's statutory commands and proscriptions—the second stage of equitable balancing. On the other hand, they generally retain discretion in making the threshold determinations and in tailoring remedies, and statutes only rarely take over these two equitable functions. Over the years, however, the courts have demonstrated confusion and vagueness in their discussions of equity and statutory violations....

A Modern Equity Proposition. The problems of traditional equitable discretion in the modern context are most dramatically presented by the difficult but illuminating case of a defendant found violating a specific statutory term, especially where the trial judge considers the violation trivial or a mere anachronism. The judge may also be convinced that the defendant is committing the violation while engaged in an enterprise of overriding public importance. If the same defendant were involved in purely non-statutory litigation, the court could simply weigh the public importance of the defendant's activity against the plaintiff's interest. As a result of this classic balancing of the equities, the court could permit the defendant's otherwise tortious or illegal conduct to continue. But what happens in the statutory context? A review of old and new equity cases and a consideration of the tripartite nature of the modern state leads to a contrary proposition: When a court in equity is confronted on the merits with a continuing violation of statutory law, it has no discretion or authority to balance the equities so as to permit that violation to continue.

This conclusion may upset generally accepted notions of equity jurisdiction, however outdated or unrealistic they may be. Yet this proposition is far less disturbing than the contrary assertion that courts, balancing equities, have the power to permit particular defendants to continue to violate statutes with impunity. This alternative would constitute a remarkably direct extension of the judicial function into the process of amending legislation.

When the classic doctrines of equitable discretion confront the reality of clear statutory violations, the time-honored dogma of balancing cannot survive without some sympathetic analytical retooling. Far from stripping the courts of their traditional powers of equitable discretion, however, the analysis advanced here draws distinctions that preserve a discretionary role for equity courts even where statutes are involved....

The restriction of statutory balancing to the legislature will, no doubt, be disturbing to many who share our profession's longstanding suspicion of absolutist principles that cannot be compromised and balanced by a court. The initial instinctive reaction of most attorneys and jurists is to assume that when Congress authorized injunctive relief for statutory violations, it must have intended to incorporate the full discretion of equity as well. Courts must always be able to compromise statutory violations; they do so all the time.

Beyond the constitutional implications of the contention that courts have the power to override statutes, one response to reactions against limitations of equitable discretion is to point to the remarkable absence over the years of equity cases permitting statutory violations to continue. It is difficult, if not impossible, to find cases in which courts have permitted proved statutory violations to continue unabated. There have, of course, been literally hundreds of statutory violation cases in which injunctions have not been issued. Those cases, however, all fit into one or another category that is consistent with the present proposition.

By far the largest category of statutory violation cases where injunctions have been denied involves past violations where the courts find that statutory compliance will henceforth be achieved without injunctive relief. A second category involves preliminary proceedings seeking temporary restraining orders or preliminary injunctions. Because such proceedings occur prior to a full hearing on the merits, it is understandable that these cases do not always result in enforcement orders against putative violators. In another class of

cases, estoppel or other threshold questions may preclude statutory enforcement, especially with regard to criminal statutes. In these cases the courts bar
the question of the need for injunctive relief from being heard, so here too
they never reach the merits of the alleged violations. Nor do cases in which
federal courts decline to issue injunctions when state proceedings are underway or available contradict the proposition, for again the courts never reach
the merits of the claimed violations.

Other major categories where injunctions have been refused include cases
of procedural violations where substantial compliance has occurred prior to
the resolution of the suit; cases where the courts have simply concluded that
the defendant's actions do not violate the statute at issue; and cases in which
a statute gives a court discretion to permit continued noncompliance, vests
the court with authority to determine what constitutes a violation in particular circumstances, or provides for exemptions. There is also a category of cases
in which it is not perfectly clear what the district court actually held with regard to a particular statutory violation. And in cases where the alleged violation is based on a constitutional rather than a statutory mandate, courts paradoxically possess more discretionary authority to permit delayed or lessened
compliance, for example "with all deliberate speed."

Finally, it is both logical and consistent with the proposition of judicial
deference to statutes to recognize that equity courts can refuse to issue injunctions where compliance is impossible. Like King Canute, equity courts
would accomplish nothing (beyond humbling themselves and diminishing
popular respect for their powers) if they attempted to order the ocean to
hold back its waves or rivers to run uphill. Futility is properly a limitation
of equitable discretion, since equity will not command the doing of a vain
thing.

In sum, these assorted variations on a theme demonstrate a variety of adjustments to a basic principle, not the undercutting of the essential proposition that equity must defer to statutory commands. The case law reflects a remarkable, though unheralded, consistency over the past fifty years: cases hold
that statutes dispositively define the nature of prohibited and permitted conduct, thereby removing one entire area of discretion from the courts.

Recognition of an equitable power to override statutes would represent a
significant expansion of judicial authority beyond its existing limits; it would
also require extremely sensitive definitions of limits and standards to the open-
ended discretion thereby unleashed. But there is no apparent need to let that
judicial genie out of the bottle. Analysis of equitable theory indicates that such
an extension of equitable discretion is as unnecessary as it would be conceptually difficult.

Historical Origins. It should not be very controversial to discern a principle in American jurisprudence that courts cannot permit a statutory violation, once proven, to continue unrestrained. Discretion, however, has always lain at the heart of equity jurisdiction, and courts have always had the right and duty to "balance the equities" when requested to issue injunctions. The present analysis circumscribes the traditional definitions of equitable discretion in a manner that may seem extreme. It would hold that a court has no discretion to allow statutorily proscribed conduct to continue. Where a defendant is intransigent, an injunction abating the defendant's conduct must issue.

The consternation this proposition engenders may be a tribute to the cloudiness with which the subtleties and character of equitable jurisprudence are understood. Equity springs from ancient sources, and in many regards retains the principles of its past. It is also, however, a component part of our vastly evolved modern legal system. It should not be surprising that equity has developed applications and nuances that add to and differ from those of past centuries, nor that modern statutes have made a major difference.

Traditional notions of equitable discretion have their origins in the earliest roots of equity. Aristotle's concept of equity was first and foremost the power of the tribunal to override specific rules where particular circumstances seemed to require such dispensation.... Equity as translated into the jurisprudence of the English chancellors was likewise an appeal to the conscience of the tribunal, an articulation of principles of fairness or morality that were specifically designed to exempt defendants from compliance with the harshness of rigid legal rules.

Equity grew far beyond its dispensation function, of course, developing the special remedies that today are its most visible attribute. Still, however, equity was dedicated to the implementation of an over-arching law of morally-tinged fairness and ethics to be applied when legal rules fell short. The injunctive order, issued by the church-based equity courts, was an extraordinary remedy. It was reserved, at least in theory, for those cases where courts operating under rules of law would not adequately protect plaintiffs from being unfairly had by defendants. At that point, equity would step in and go beyond the law.

A special perspective of balance and relativity has characterized the development of equity law. In Aristotelian terms it was a balance between the citizen violating a particular rule and the more general societal context in which other facts or norms might excuse the violation. Principles of relativity also governed application of the injunction as it developed over the years. If plaintiffs could prove a cause of action at common law, yet felt that the common law would inadequately redress their injuries, an appeal to equity was still available. But before the injunction would be issued, plaintiffs, in response to affirmative defenses, had to satisfy tests of relativity between themselves and defendants that were not required at law: a reasonable alacrity in suing, relatively clean hands, a favorable balance of convenience, and the like. Out of these principles of relativity came the touchstone phrase "balancing the equities" that has so characterized and beclouded debates over equity both in the past and present.

A vast array of discretionary equitable concepts has been included over the years in the concept of balancing the equities: laches, estoppel, balance of hardships, clean hands, balancing of comparative utilities, consideration of the public interest, weighing the adequacy of legal remedies, irreparability, the balance of convenience, and the tailoring of remedies. All of these principles require equitable relativity and discretion in their application—a comparison of the circumstances of plaintiffs, defendants, and frequently of society at large.

Often, however, the term "balance of equities" is used to denote only a balancing of private and public interests, thereby obscuring all the other balances of the parties' relativity. The inconsistency and vagueness with which the term is sometimes used argue for acknowledgment of the term's all-inclusive scope or its rejection in favor of the more straightforward concept of discretion. The imprecision of terminology is of more than academic concern. When courts and commentators fail to specify what particular aspects of the elements available for balancing they are including within the comprehensive term "balancing the equities," they set the stage for significant misunderstanding and conflict: any constraint on a single element of the equitable balance appears to endanger the heart of the equity jurisdiction....

"Balancing the Equities". Equity's relationship to the common law over the centuries provides the analytical filter through which most commentators describe and dissect equitable jurisdiction. Understandably, then, the common law colors the analysis of equity when statutes are involved. In fact, the present analysis of judicial discretion limited by statute fits comfortably into the traditional law of equity. It is based upon distinctions found in the old law itself.

When equity's application in traditional common law cases is subjected to careful analysis, some basic clarifications emerge. Analytically it can be argued that the umbrella terms "balancing the equities" and "equitable discretion" obscure what are really three separate areas of balancing, three different functions fulfilled by three different types of equitable relativism. The three areas are:

Threshold Balancing, based in both law and equity, which tests whether plaintiffs can maintain their actions. This stage includes questions of laches, clean hands, other estoppels, the lack of an adequate remedy at law, proof of irreparable harm, and similar issues.

The *Determination of Contending Conducts* ascertains which conduct will be permitted to continue and which will be subordinated. It often involves the question of abatement, a separate issue from the question of liability for past injuries to protected interests.

Discretion in Fashioning Remedies involves a process of tailoring remedies to implement the second stage determination of contending conducts.

Consider, for example, the relatively simple field of private nuisance torts where equity has traditionally played an active role. The classic *Ducktown Copper* case demonstrates all three of equity's distinctly different roles. In that turn-of-the-century case, the court had to deal with an early example of an environmental tradeoff. The smelting industry was getting underway in the foothills of southeastern Tennessee and northern Georgia.

It was likely to provide sizable revenues for the entrepreneurs of Atlanta and Chattanooga, jobs for local residents, and copper and other materials for the nation's industrial economy. The copper ore was mined in nearby hills, then smelted in large open-air piles layered with firewood and coal. This firing process, however, produced acidic "sulphurectic" air emissions that eventually turned nearly a hundred square miles of hills into a remarkably stark, denuded desert, its topsoil slowing washing away down sterile, chemical-laden streams. The plaintiffs were farmers whose fields and orchards began to die as the smelting got underway.

The Tennessee high court held that the smelting was a continuing private nuisance, but after long and careful deliberation allowed the defendant industries to continue operations despite their drastic impact upon the plaintiffs' land and livelihood. The court required only that the mills compensate the plaintiffs for their losses. In common parlance, it awarded legal compensatory damages but denied any injunctive remedy, based on a balancing of equities. The *Ducktown* court certainly balanced the equities. Analytically, however, it did so not once but thrice.

1. *Threshold Balancing.* The first type of balancing addresses threshold questions which plaintiffs must survive if a cause of action is to be heard. Some issues appear in the guise of affirmative legal defenses: laches and coming to the nuisance, for example, are legal defenses grounded in principles of equitable estoppel. Other issues—clean hands, additional estoppel principles, proof of irreparable harm, and the inadequacy of legal remedies—are more specifically equitable, brought to bear only where the plaintiff seeks equitable remedies. Each of these threshold issues involves comparisons and balances that are part of the longstanding discretionary processes of equity. The *Ducktown* court made several such determinations, excluding some plaintiffs on laches grounds as to certain defendants, confirming their rights to sue as to

others, and noting injuries to land that analytically made equitable remedies potentially available on grounds of irreparability.

2. *The Determination of Contending Conducts.* After plaintiffs survive equity's threshold gauntlet, nonstatutory litigation moves to the application of rules of conduct. The major discretionary function of the equity court of this second stage is the determination of whether the defendant's conduct will be permitted to continue. To reach this abatement determination, however, courts must first consider issues of liability.

The initial question is whether defendants are liable at all, whether their conduct is "illegal" under the common law. In this question equity may play a part, though not a cardinal role. The basic common law definition of liability for past conduct may itself be infiltrated by equitable balancing in those jurisdictions that retain some notion of comparative utilities as an element of the substantive tort, and not just as part of the remedy question.

There has been a long-running incestuous relationship between law and equity. Equity, it is true, has generally kept a separate identity as to the availability and issuance of remedies—a heritage traceable to the dispensations of Greek philosophy, the fairness principles of canon law, and the flexibility of orders in chancery. This separate identity has continued despite the merger of law and equity in England in 1873 and in the United States in the 1930's. As early as the 1600's, however, an interchange of substantive principles between law and equity began. Some equitable defenses became legal defenses by osmosis.

In the field of nuisance law, equity invaded the common law by introducing a comparative weighing of public values in trespass actions. Instead of merely viewing a case as a contest between an injured plaintiff and a causative defendant, an equitable balance came to be incorporated in the cause of action. Thus, in a famous early English air pollution tort case [*Ranketts Case*], the injury caused to plaintiff's nose and habitation by a nearby candlemaker's malodorous establishment was ignored by the court of law, which found no tort to exist because "*le utilitie del chose excusera le noisomeness del stink*," a quintessentially equitable distinction.

When courts of law allowed proof of preponderant public utility to nullify a nuisance cause of action, plaintiffs were effectively non-suited from even a legal remedy because of an essentially equitable balancing. Similarly, the tort definitions of substantial injury and unreasonable action also have turned to some extent on a balancing that resembles an equitable rather than a legal standard. Thus, in some common law actions equitable balancing negated liability where it would otherwise lie. No matter how substantial plaintiff's injuries, if the public benefits of defendant's operation were greater, there would be no liability.

This draconian approach is being replaced by theories that separate the questions of liability and consequent damages from those of abatement in intentional tort. Under this approach, if a suit seeks compensatory damages alone, no further equity issues arise beyond the threshold stage. More typically, however, plaintiffs in private nuisance cases and in other common law areas seek equitable remedies—particularly injunctions—as well as damages. In such cases, once tort liability is found, the court turns to the different question of whether defendant's conduct will be abated.

Perhaps the grandest pitfall of equity jurisprudence is the tendency for lawyers and judges to equate the judicial decision to abate a defendant's conduct (the second type of equity balancing) with the judicial choice of an injunction remedy (the third type of equity balancing). But the abatement decision and the choice of remedy are not the same. Abatement, whether total or partial, is a functional term referring to the decision to restrict the defendant's activity. It is this functional decision that is taken over when a statute declares a mandatory rule of conduct. Injunctions, in their multiple variety, are merely remedial directives designed to implement the court's determinations on threshold questions, substantive liability, and future conduct, which may or may not include abatement. In fact, of course, the vast majority of abatements are implemented by injunction, and the vast majority of injunctions issued in the private law field are abatements.

The mistaken but understandable confusion of the abatement decision with the choice of remedy reflects the modern acceptance of injunctions as the normal remedy of choice. But lumping the two together obscures the fact that they constitute two separate judicial decisions. While most judges, attorneys, and commentators discuss equity cases in terms of whether an injunction will issue, the functional result apparently concerns them more than the particular design of the remedy: Will defendant's conduct be permitted to continue? Which form of conduct will be affirmed for the future and which subordinated? Will the court establish a rule for future conduct that prevents further tort injuries to the plaintiffs or relegate them to sequential damage actions?

The second type of equitable inquiry—the determination of contending conducts—was the heart of the *Ducktown* case. Since they could not coexist, would the court permit the farms or the mills to continue? The question presented both a legal and an equitable aspect. First, it had to be established that the mills were subject to tort liability as a private nuisance. The outcome of that inquiry determined the question of compensation for past injuries suffered by plaintiffs. A negative determination would have eliminated further equity questions. But the court found that the smelters constituted a tort, and that triggered the balance of equities on the abatement question.

The *Ducktown* abatement question focused on the desirability and consequences of the competing forms of conduct, considering relative hardship between the parties, the balance of comparative social utility between the two
competing conducts, and the public interest (which usually amounts to the
same thing). The court declared:

> A judgment for damages in this class of cases is a matter of absolute
> right, where injury is shown. A decree for an injunction is a matter
> of sound legal discretion, to be granted or withheld as that discretion
> shall dictate, after a full and careful consideration of every element
> appertaining to the injury.

Citing a series of equity cases in which the utility of defendant's enterprises
weighed against injunctions, the court's "careful consideration" began with a
question that virtually answered itself:

> Shall the complainants be granted, by way of damages, the full meas-
> ure of relief to which their injuries entitle them or shall we go fur-
> ther, and grant their request to blot out two great mining and man-
> ufacturing enterprises, destroy half of the taxable values of a county,
> and drive more than 10,000 people from their homes?

The *Ducktown* decision launched a modern trend in private nuisance cases,
clearly separating the questions of liability and abatement and requiring defendants whose continued operations serve public welfare nevertheless to ab-
sorb the cost of injuries imposed on neighbors as a cost of doing business. It
also stands as a paradigm of equitable balancing in determining the abatement
of future conduct. In determining that defendants' conduct could continue
despite inevitable future injury to plaintiffs, the court compared the parties'
private interests and balanced their interests against the court's own view of
public welfare. True, a more modern court might well have brought more
public and private values such as health, water quality, and aesthetics into the
balance. Yet the *Ducktown* court opened the equitable balance to a wide-ranging review of competing values and made its decision based upon its own subjective judgment of the relative intrinsic values of competing conducts.

Thus, the non-statutory setting provides an inclusive model of equitable
discretion in the determination of contending conducts. In traditional common law cases, the court-made rules of conduct which determined damage
liability were more or less rigidified in the evolved tort doctrines, while the
equitable question of abatement was decided anew in each case. The tort debts
owed by one party to the other might be decided by uniformly applicable substantive tort principles, but questions of the life and death of farms and smelt-

ing plants—of who must stop and who may go on—were left in the flexible hands and heart of equity. In short, courts have used equity to define and exercise a separate judicial role, grounded upon a rational discretion and working beyond the rigid rules of the law.

3. *Tailoring the Remedies.* Having defined and distinguished the first two kinds of discretionary balancing, the third role of equity becomes anticlimactic, though important. At this point in a lawsuit, law and equity have determined all the substantive issues, and only the equitable function of implementation remains. If the court had decided in the second stage balance that defendant's conduct may continue, the award of legal damages for past injuries ends the question of remedy. In that situation no equitable remedy is necessary unless required to enforce payment of damages.

When the court determines that defendant's conduct may not continue, on the other hand, a full array of equitable options exists. If defendants agree to abate their activity voluntarily, the court has the option of not issuing any formal equitable remedy at all.... [A]n injunction need not issue if the court finds that the abatement decision will be implemented without it, but will usually issue where there is any doubt on the matter. Between these two extremes lies the declaratory judgment, a remedy slightly more formal and more assertive than the no-injunction option but similarly unenforceable through contempt proceedings. Yet in the case of good faith defendants, a declaratory judgment or less may be all that is necessary to implement the court's abatement decision.

The strength and flexibility of injunctions, however, makes them attractive as the remedy of choice in many cases. Equity courts shape injunctions in multifarious forms: injunctions to halt an enterprise completely, to shut down a particular component activity, to scale down overall activity by a certain percentage, to halt a specific offensive effect, to abate after a lapse of a specific term if certain performance standards are not achieved—these are but a few. Injunctions also serve different tactical ends. They can be wielded to drag a rambunctiously recalcitrant defendant into compliance, to tighten the reins on slipshod defendants whose compliance efforts may be sloppy, or merely to add a final reassuring level of certainty to a good faith defendant's compliance....

Analytically, the third stage remedy decision involves a weighing of the comparative efficacy of available remedies rather than a comparative weighing of interests. Since the tailoring of remedies involves choices between options, shaped by the court's judgment about the practicalities and relative effectiveness of those options, it does no violence to the term "balance of equities" to include this latter balance within it.

Recognizing that courts sitting in equity do compare the available alternatives in deciding what remedy to issue to effectuate the prior decision on the merits clarifies the fact that the remedy choice is a separate decision. Separating the role of equity into its three components also establishes a useful analytical framework for the modern statutory injunction....

Conclusion. To most nonlawyers the analysis advanced here—that a court confronted with a violation of statutory law cannot permit that violation to continue—is self-evident. If a legislature prohibits an action, it is prohibited. To judges and attorneys steeped in the common law tradition of judicial flexibility, however, it is initially a discomfiting proposition.

Nevertheless, if equitable discretion in traditional non-statutory litigation is separated analytically into its three component functions, the statutory cases reveal a remarkable consistency with the proposition of limited discretion. Over the years, without recognizing the principle clearly, courts have uniformly refused to substitute their own judgment for the legislature's on the question of which conduct is to be permitted and which abated. Equitable discretion remains in the threshold balances which admit parties to the equity forum, and in the balancing which helps fashion particular remedies, but statutory compliance there must be.

By consistently drawing this line in practice, the courts have avoided the difficulties inherent in any attempt to define an equitable power to override legislative commands, a process that would be both unnecessary and constitutionally hazardous. This equitable discretion, moreover, with its fundamental deference to the legislature, has practical consequences that accord well with our nation's evolving theories of pluralistic democracy.

Selected References

Guido Calabresi, A Common Law for the Age of Statutes (1982).
Winston Churchill, A History of the English-Speaking Peoples (1956).
Dan B. Dobbs, Remedies (1973).
Owen Fiss, Injunctions (1972).
Henry M. Hart, Jr. & Albert M. Sacks, The Legal Process: Basic Problems in the Making and Application of Law (1958).
W. Hawkins, Pleas of the Crown (1787).
William Holdsworth, A History of English Law (1927).
Theodore F.T. Plucknett, A Concise History of the Common Law (5th ed. 1956).
John N. Pomeroy, Equity Jurisprudence (5th ed. 1941).
J. Sax, Defending the Environment (1971).
J. Stephen, A General View of the Criminal Law of England (1890).
Richard Stewart, The Reformation of American Administrative Law, 88 Harvard Law Review 1667 (1975)

Cases

Madison v. Ducktown Sulphur, Copper & Iron Co., 113 Tenn. 331, 83 S.W. 658 (1904).
Rankets Case (K.B. 1606), reported in 2 H. Rolle, Rolle's Abridgement (1668).

Further Reading (selected work by Zygmunt J.B. Plater)

Environmental Law and Policy (Aspen 3rd ed. 2004) (with David A. Wirth and others).
Endangered Species Act Lessons Over 30 Years, and the Legacy of the Snail Darter, a
    Small Fish in a Pork Barrel, 34 Environmental Law 289 (2004).
Environmental Law and Three Economies: Navigating a Sprawling Field of Study,
    Practice, and Societal Governance in which Everything is Connected to Everything
    Else, 23 Harvard Environmental Law Review 359 (1999).
The Three Economies: An Essay in Honor of Joseph Sax, 25 Ecology Law Quarterly
    411 (1998).

CHAPTER FOURTEEN

JUDGES V. LEGISLATORS AS SOURCES OF LAW*

Much substantive law in the United States is created not through the legislative process but, rather, by the common law courts of the various states and, to a lesser extent, the federal courts. During the Nineteenth Century, when American society was challenged by the development of new technologies such as the railroad and the telegraph, it was the common law courts of the various states that crafted legal responses attempting to balance the various interests involved. The justices of the state supreme courts worked together in developing a new body of common law to govern these new technologies. They wrote opinions in which they claimed to be drawing their norms from basic values already recognized in past common law decisions in both America and England and to be applying those norms to the facts of the cases before them. The Supreme Judicial Court of Massachusetts was one of the leading courts in this effort. The Court's Chief Justice, Lemuel Shaw, came to be called "America's Greatest Magistrate" in recognition of his contribution to the framing of law in this area. But justices from many courts, building on each other's decisions, contributed to the establishment of these legal norms on a case-by-case basis.

In much the same way, the Twentieth Century has seen the common law courts of the several American states serve as an important source—perhaps the most important source—of legal norms responding to the technological challenges of our times. This is particularly true in the field law regulating what has come to be called "the right to die." When, in 1976, Karen Quinlan's father sought approval from the Supreme Court of New Jersey for removing his daughter from artificial ventilation in order to end her meaningless existence in a persistent vegetative state (PVS), no legal norms directly on point

---

* **Charles H. Baron**, *Life and Death Decision Making: Judges v. Legislators as Sources of Law in Bioethics*, 1 JOURNAL OF HEALTH & BIOMEDICAL LAW 107 (2004), http://papers.ssrn. com/abstract_id=425460.

for deciding the case were available to the court. The New Jersey statutes most nearly relevant were those dealing with homicide and assisting suicide. However, the court could see that such criminal statutes were inadequate tools for dealing with the problems of modern high-technology medicine. Therefore, the court set out on a process of crafting new common law that would achieve an appropriate balance of the interests at stake. In doing so, it drew upon state and federal case law that it saw as providing helpful sources of societal values that could inform its judgment. But, it drew also upon a great many non-legal sources of norms. The most influential of these were statements of existing or proposed norms of medical practice respecting care of terminally-ill and comatose patients.

There are, of course, obvious tensions that the phenomenon of law-making by judges has with the ideal of political democracy in a republic such as the United States. In a political democracy, it is typically assumed that law-making power ultimately rests with the elected representatives of the people—the legislature. The value choices that are to be made in the process of law-making are supposed to be those of the majority of the people—not those of an elite professional class such as judges. Judges are, after all, graduates of colleges and law schools. They are among the top stratum of the country from a socio-economic perspective. They typically do not have to face frequent elections in which they may be defeated at the polls on the basis of the choices they make as the people's representatives.

There are also tensions that exist between the phenomenon of law-making by judges and notions of fairness and the rule of law. Whereas, legislative acts typically apply only prospectively, and after citizens have been given fair notice of the law's import by publication in some written form, judge-made law is typically applied retroactively to the parties to the very case in which the rule is announced. When the legislature acts, the United States Constitution prohibits passage of ex post facto laws—laws enacted by the legislature after the commission of the acts that are made illegal by the law. Although the *ex post facto* clause has been held to apply only to criminal laws, civil laws that are applied retroactively may well be held to violate the Due Process clauses of the fifth and fourteenth amendments to the United States Constitution.

Moreover, judge-made rules are developed in circumstances where the judge knows the identities of the persons who will benefit by the rule and those of the persons who will be burdened by it. This is the opposite of the ideal of justice proposed by philosophers such as John Rawls—the notion that the just rules are those that are made behind a "veil of ignorance" so that the lawmaker does not know in advance whether he himself, his family, his friends, or his class will be winners or losers under the new rule.

Nonetheless, there are many things to be said for the operation of judge-made law, in even a political democracy dedicated to due process of law. And many of the defects of law-making by judges are also, paradoxically, its advantages as well. The fact that judges are not immediately answerable to the public for the law that they make works to the advantage of the public in many instances. Likewise, the fact that the law judges make will be applied retroactively to the actions that were taken in the case before it provides an important safeguard in the process of the development of common law. And, the fact that the judge knows the identities of the parties and the full facts of the situation that calls for the development of the law to be applied to it so as to provide relief—these qualities of judge-made law also have the capacity to make the law more just rather than less. To see how this is so, let us try to make a list of those characteristics of law-making by judges that arguably make it superior to law-making by legislatures.

1) The first, and most important, of these characteristics is the requirement that judges, when they make law, must write opinions that attempt to justify the law that is there announced. The judge who writes such an opinion knows that his audience will include not only other judges and practicing lawyers, but also law professors and law students—who will make such opinions grist for their teaching mills in "Socratic Method" law school classes where the questions will be "What does this case mean?" "Is it consistent with earlier case law?" "Is it good law?" "Does it make any sense whatsoever?" In many cases, it will also be read by journalists and reported on (and maybe published) and criticized in the media. And of course, the opinion is open to being criticized by the other judges sitting on the case, who may write concurring or even dissenting opinions.

The legislature, when it passes a law, need give no argument for the law's validity beyond the fact that a majority of the legislature voted in its favor on a particular day at a particular time. Not a word need be said about its quality in order to justify it. In contrast, the judge cannot rely merely on the fact that a majority of elected representatives voted for the law that he makes. He must convince the reader that the rule announced follows on precedent and that it is good law.

2) A second characteristic to note is that the burden on the judge of proving "rightness" of his decision is reinforced by the fact that the rule announced is to be applied retroactively to the case before it. Not only must the judge convince the reader of his opinion that the rule applied is the "right one," he must convince everyone, including the losing party in the case, that it is "so right" that the losing party should have anticipated the fact that it would be applied in the case. The model is of Solomon the Wise. The losing party

should be able to walk away feeling: "Such a wise judge." "I should have known." "In any event, now we all know." ·

3) A third characteristic is the fact that, because the court must justify the rules it develops by convincing the reader of their "rightness," judges typically are not required to justify them by standing for election on the basis of whether they have properly applied the public will. This frees the court to do what it believes to be right rather than what will keep it from being voted out of office. Even in those American jurisdictions where judges are elected, the public does not expect them to produce rules of law on the ground that they are the rules that the public would vote for. It expects them to exercise legal reasoning to produce the "just rule" based upon prior case law. This insulation from direct political accountability frees the court to do the right thing in a way that a legislature may be fearful to do.

These advantages of courts in making law over legislatures as law-makers begin to explain why it was that Mr. Quinlan sought out the courts of New Jersey—rather than its legislature—when he looked to find release for his daughter from her living death in a persistent vegetative state.

4) This is especially true when we combine the above three characteristics with a fourth: Yet another of the qualities of common law courts that was critical for Mr. Quinlan is the fact that the courts of common law are held to be open to all at any time for the rendering of justice. Unlike a legislature, they cannot decide merely not to consider a matter once it has been brought to their attention. Indeed, many state constitutions contain provisions drawn from Chapter 40 of *Magna Carta* "requiring that justice shall be administered without sale, denial, or delay" that are interpreted by state supreme courts to require that the courts render a legal decision in any case brought before them. It is the rare instance in which a lower court can just "decide not to decide."

Mr. Quinlan knew that it was unlikely that he would get the relief that he needed for his daughter from the New Jersey State Legislature if he applied to it for a change in the laws regarding homicide and assisted suicide. Unlike a common law court, the state legislature was not bound to rule one way or another on a legal problem placed before it. And it was clear, in the wake of *Roe v. Wade* and the "right to life" political activism that the decision spawned in the United States, that any legislator who voted in favor of amending homicide or assisted-suicide laws in a way that seemed to relax bans on euthanasia risked political suicide. The fact that the legislature much preferred to have this problem taken from its hands and solved by the courts is made very clear by the fact that it took some fifteen years from Quinlan for the New Jersey State legislature to pass any sort of "right to die" legislation—despite repeated calls from the New Jersey Supreme Court to do so. And then it responded only with legislation regulating some of the procedures for the handling of cases involving incompetent patients.

Thus, the courts were a better body in which to look for relief because they could not, like the legislature, simply duck the issue, and, being forced to decide it, they could also feel relatively immune from political retribution if they decided to find a means for avoiding the laws regarding homicide and assisted suicide.

5) Yet another reason why the courts might feel "safer" dealing with these issues is provided by a fifth advantage of law-making by common law courts. When legislatures amend laws or pass new laws, they do so in sweeping general fashion. When the law is changed in such a way, the law maker must worry about what sort of Pandora's Box is being opened that later may be difficult to shut without undue harm to society. Thus, in creating loopholes in existing criminal laws for patients in a persistent vegetative state, the legislature would have to draft in advance a law that attempted to cover all and only those cases where it thought that society could tolerate allowing death to be hastened by the intentional acts of family members and attending physicians. But when a common law court creates law, it does so in incremental fashion—case by case—on the facts of those cases—in a way that allows it to take one step at a time and with room for it to take steps back if need be. This process produces several related advantages of the common law process.

6) A sixth advantage stems from the fact that the law made by the judge on the facts of the case responds to the specific problem before the court and the judge sees the beneficial consequences in that case. It may well be that human beings are much better at deciding what is the best solution in a particular case than they are in developing sweeping general rules that will apply without exception in a large class of cases not before them at the moment.

7) A seventh advantage stems from the fact that the judge not only gets to determine the rule with the facts and the consequences of the ruling before him in the case, he also must face the losing party and tell him or her that he or she is being asked to bear the consequences of the ruling. In this respect, the legislature is like the B-52 pilot who drops bombs in Afghanistan and then returns to his base in the United States. The judge is like the infantryman who must look his enemy in the eyes if he is to shoot him.

8) An eighth advantage, and the final one I will address today, is the on-going dialectic context in which judge-made law is developed. In his law-making, the judge is assisted by the adversarial process conducted by counsel who make the best arguments for their clients regarding the law that the court should develop to apply to their clients' cases. He is also assisted by the opinions of other judges from his own and other jurisdictions who have consid-

ered the same or similar questions, by scholars who have discussed these cases and these issues in published articles, and by attorneys for various interested groups who may file briefs *amicus curiae*....

All of these advantages can be shown at work in the *Quinlan* decision and its aftermath. It was clear to the New Jersey courts that Mr. Quinlan, his daughter, and all the attending medical personnel found themselves caught in a very painful situation. Although Karen Quinlan could not herself feel any pain, her family, after many years of holding out hope for her recovery and struggling for what they believed to be best for Karen, came to the conclusion that everyone would be better off if she were allowed to die a natural death. Karen's physicians were sympathetic to the request, but were fearful of legal and professional sanctions if they acceded to it. The court realized that it had to decide the case. Not to decide would also be a decision. It would leave the Quinlan family and the medical profession to continue to suffer in confusion. Thus, the court realized it had to make a decision.

The court also realized that it had to write an opinion in which it justified that decision—and with a level of persuasion that would convince even those who might have originally opposed the court's decision that the rule it applied in reaching it was sufficiently just that it could govern the case before it.

In doing so, however, the court knew that it could decide just the case before it on the facts and merits that it presented. Unlike the legislature, it did not have to devise a sweeping general rule of law that would apply to a vast range of cases in the future. (Its members also did not have to worry about losing an election because of the positions they took in the case. New Jersey's judges are among those in the US that are appointed to serve on good behavior until a specified retirement age.) Of course, it was not enough just to decide the case before it. In its opinion, the court needed to draw upon and state general rules that would give the reader a fair idea of how the present decision was justified in past opinions and how similar cases would be decided in the future. But the rules did not need to be too general. They could always be extended in future cases. And, if it was decided that they were too sweeping—or even that the decision taken in the *Quinlan* case was wrong in some way—there was always the possibility of limiting too sweeping principles in later cases or even overruling the earlier case.

Moreover, if the state legislature were truly unhappy with the result reached by the court, it could always overrule what the court had done (assuming that the case was not decided on the basis of constitutional principles) and set the court on a new course of development in the future. Thus, in *Quinlan*, the court ultimately decided the questions brought to it by Mr. Quinlan and Karen's attending medical personnel. They did so by giving legal authority to

Mr. Quinlan and Karen's attending physicians to end Karen's vegetative existence by terminating her artificial ventilation—so long as a hospital "ethics committee" agreed with the decision. And, in writing the opinion in which they justified that decision, they attempted to set out a preliminary set of legal rules for governing the case before them and tentatively governing future cases as well. They also explicitly called upon the legislature to help them in this process—but they realized that, until the legislature did act, the courts had to make the best decisions that they could in the cases before them.

Of course, *Quinlan* was just one part of a process of common law development of principles in this area. Decisions of courts in other states, and later decisions of the Supreme Court of New Jersey as well, conducted a process of adjusting and refining the principles of *Quinlan* that is ongoing. I will here only sketch a few highlights of that process.

The decision in *Quinlan*, it is important to observe, did not rest upon recognition of a patient's absolute right to refuse treatment. Indeed, as the New Jersey court notes in its opinion, recognition of such a right would have been inconsistent with decisions it had rendered only a decade before in which it had authorized physicians to force blood transfusions upon Jehovah's Witness patients who objected to such treatment on religious grounds. The court's holding in *Quinlan* was restricted to cases like Karen's where medical treatment offered no hope of being restored to a meaningful "quality of life." Her case was different from that of the Jehovah's Witnesses, said the court, in that the latter were "most importantly [patients] apparently salvable to long life and vibrant health;—a situation not at all like the present case." The driving factor in the *Quinlan* case appeared to be the fact that allowing a PVS patient to die was the reasonable and humane thing to do. In the end, the court did not even require that Karen Quinlan's wishes be taken into consideration in deciding whether or not she should be removed from life support. Testimony that had been offered at trial of what she had told friends she would want if she were ever permanently on life support was rejected by the court as being "without sufficient probative weight." Instead of attempting to establish Karen's wishes, the court gave discretion to her physicians to decide whether or not life support should be withdrawn—so long as that decision was agreed to by her guardian, her family, and a hospital ethics committee.

Quinlan, in many ways, represented an effort on the part of the medical profession to take back a freedom from regulation it had enjoyed prior to the advent of modern high-technology medicine. When patients died at home, under the care of family physicians, and in a context that did not afford seemingly-unlimited options for prolonging life, attending physicians regularly made decisions for patients and families that "enough was enough." But by the 1960's and 1970's, hospital staff was being confronted with the need to make increasingly stark life and death decisions in a frighteningly public environment. The very recent history of legal treatment of abortion decision-making was not such as to inspire confidence that doctors could consider themselves immune from legal prosecution. In the wake of the Thalidomide abortion controversy in the United States, professional practices regarding abortion had come under public scrutiny and legal control had been tightened in many jurisdictions. The solution to this problem had come with the 1973 decision of the Supreme Court of the United States in *Roe v. Wade*. On the basis of a "right to privacy" it had previously found in the Due Process Clause of the Fourteenth Amendment to the United States Constitution, the *Roe* Court had delegated to the pregnant woman's attending physician almost all aspects of the determination of whether or not an abortion could be performed.

In *Quinlan*, the New Jersey Supreme Court essentially followed the lead of *Roe*. Where *Roe* had used the federal constitutional right to privacy to protect professional autonomy at the beginning of life, *Quinlan* used that right (and a right to privacy that the court found in the New Jersey Constitution as well) to protect professional autonomy at the end of life. Because the patient was in a persistent vegetative state, and there was no reasonable chance that medical treatment could restore her to a higher "quality of life," the patient's right to life was outweighed by her right to privacy. Thus, her physician could lawfully hasten her death by removing her from her ventilator so long as this was agreed to by her guardian, her family, and an appropriate hospital ethics committee.

In 1977, the year following *Quinlan*, the Supreme Judicial Court of Massachusetts rendered a decision in a case that was very like *Quinlan* in many ways but unlike it in significant respects as well, and the Massachusetts court extended the principles of *Quinlan* in some ways and restricted them in others. The case was *Saikewicz v. Superintendent of Belchertown State Hospital*. It was brought by physicians at a state hospital for the mentally retarded who were seeking permission to withhold chemotherapy treatment from a 67-year old, profoundly mentally retarded inmate who was terminally-ill with cancer. Without chemotherapy, the patient would die of his cancer within weeks or months. With the treatment, the patient might live for as much as a year, but at the cost of the serious side effects of chemotherapy. A decision to treat him was complicated by the fact that his profound state of mental retardation would prevent him from understanding why he was being subjected to the discomforts of chemotherapy. It would also prevent him from enjoying the sense of hope that a competent patient might obtain from the sense that every effort was being made to defeat the disease.

The Massachusetts court, like the New Jersey court in *Quinlan*, provided the physicians with legal permission to withhold treatment. Like the *Quinlan* court, the *Saikewicz* court based its decision on the right to privacy (which it, like the New Jersey court, found in its state constitution as well as in the federal constitution), and it held that this right outweighed interests in preserving life in circumstances, like those in the case before it, where treatment could not significantly improve the patient's "quality of life." Thus, *Saikewicz* followed *Quinlan* and even extended its holding to apply to patients who were being treated for a terminal illness—not just to patients in a persistent vegetative state....

While ... legal developments were taking place in the courts of New Jersey and Massachusetts, there was, for many years, no action taken by the legislatures of those states. This was unfortunate. Just as there are advantages to lawmaking by courts, there are, of course, advantages to law-making by legislatures. Such advantages are typically the correlatives of the advantages of law-making by courts. There are, for example, the obvious advantages of lawmaking by an elected body that can give the people what they want rather than what a court thinks they should want. There are the advantages of having general rules laid out in advance of the occurrence of problems so that the problems may be avoided. There are the advantages that stem from not having to justify law-making on the basis of principles of "reason."

When law-making calls for the establishment of essentially arbitrary rules, *e.g.*, rules of the road regarding right of way, speed limits, minimum requirements of age and competence for a driver's license, etc., the job cannot easily be performed by a court. There are many other advantages as well. In *Conroy*, the New Jersey Supreme Court explicitly noted some of these advantages. "Perhaps it would be best," said the court, "if the Legislature formulated clear standards for resolving requests to terminate life-sustaining treatment for incompetent patients. As an elected body, the Legislature is better able than any other single institution to reflect the social values at stake. In addition, it has the resources and ability to synthesize vast quantities of data and opinions from a variety of fields and to formulate general guidelines that may be applicable to a broad range of situations."

By 1987, in the face of a continuing absence of "right to die" legislation in New Jersey, the state court felt obliged to take steps that might have been better left to the legislature. In the case of *In re Peter*, the court noted with regret the absence of legislation providing for the execution of a "living will"—a "a written statement that specifically explains the patient's preferences about life-sustaining treatment." Many other states, the court observed, had passed statutes recognizing the validity of "living wills" and prescribing procedures for their execution. "Unfortunately," said the court, "the New Jersey Legislature hás not enacted such a law." New Jersey also had not enacted a health care proxy law—a type of statute, passed in many other states, that enabled patients to appoint health care agents empowered to make life-sustaining treatment decisions if the patients became mentally-incompetent. Despite the lack of such statutory authority, Hilda Peter, the patient in the case before the court, had executed a document purporting to appoint a friend as her agent to make health care decisions for her. The court decided to grant legal authority to the document. It did so by providing a strained construction to New Jersey's general statute providing for the appointment of agents. "Although the statute does not specifically authorize conveyance of durable authority to make medical decisions," said the court, "it should be interpreted that way."

But, the court continued to make clear that it would prefer that the legislature play its proper role in law-making. In an effort to encourage action from the state legislature, the New Jersey court gave evidence of backing away from its reliance upon the right to privacy as its principal basis for the "right to die." In 1985, in *Conroy*, the court held that the right to refuse artificial nutrition and hydration could be justified entirely upon common law principles of informed consent and refusal. There was no need, the court thought, to consider whether Ms. Conroy's rights were protected as well by the federal and state constitutions. In 1987, in *In re Farrell*, the court held that a patient's right to refuse treatment rested "primarily" on the common law....

American legislatures have the power to overrule common law, but they do not have the power to override constitutional rights. Massachusetts and some other states that had earlier relied upon the right to privacy followed the New Jersey lead. In 1991, the New Jersey legislature finally enacted legislation providing for "advance directives for health care." Earlier, the Massachusetts legislature had passed legislation providing for the appointment of "health care proxies." In doing so, the two state legislatures brought their jurisdictions in step with the vast majority of American states. By 1994, 47 states had enacted some form of living will legislation, and all but two states had passed some form of health care agency act. These statutes achieved progress of a sort that is difficult to work out on a case-by-case, common law basis. They laid out clear and precise general procedures for establishing the validity of living wills and for appointing health care proxy decision-makers. And, to deal with situations where patients failed to take advantage of living will or health care proxy laws before becoming incompetent, a growing number of jurisdictions also began to warn patients that, failing a choice on their part, health care proxies would be selected for them on the basis of criteria chosen by the legislature.

Some of the state statutes went beyond merely prescribing procedures for formalizing expressions of patient will. In such instances, tension could be generated between the courts and legislatures of the states. For example, in *McConnell v. Beverly Enterprises*, the Supreme Court of Connecticut found itself confronted with a statute in which the legislature seemed clearly to have eliminated a patient's right to refuse artificial nutrition and hydration. Mrs. McConnell, the patient in the case before the court, was a 57 year-old woman who had worked as a nurse in emergency medicine up until the time of an accident that had rendered her comatose. On the basis of her professional experience, she had communicated to her friends and family her firm wish never to be kept on any sort of life support in the event of permanent incapacity. Despite the clear language of statute, all of the judges of the Connecticut court held that Mrs. McConnell had a right to have artificial nutrition and hydration stopped.

At least one of the justices would have decided the case on the basis of either the right to privacy (which would have overridden the statute) or the common law (which he argued had not been explicitly supplanted by the statute). A majority of the justices felt obliged to decide the case under the statute, but they did so only after giving the statute a strained interpretation that would avoid questions regarding the statute's constitutionality. The court first noted how often it, like the Supreme Court of New Jersey, had called upon the state legislature to take action in this area of the law.... The court then interpreted the statute to prohibit only cessation of spoon feeding and water provided by mouth. This interpretation, said the court, permitted a decision employing the statute and, at the same time, avoided the possibility that the statute might be found unconstitutional. Subsequently, the Connecticut legislature amended the language of the statute, not to overrule the *McConnell* decision, but rather to bring it into explicit conformity with the interpretation that the court had given it in that case.

In the end, legislatures and courts both play important roles in the process of developing principles governing bioethics in the United States. In many instances, courts will take the initiative, making new law on the basis of new problems that are brought to them for resolution. The legislature may then supplement the common law or it may modify or overrule it. In reaction, the courts may then reinterpret the law or find it unconstitutional. Then the legislature may, yet again, react by passing more explicit legislation or by attempting to have the constitution amended. The driving force in this process is the fact that, in the American legal system, neither branch of the government feels truly institutionally subservient to the other. Thus, in the process of law-making, the branches may well struggle with each other in crafting what the public will ultimately accept as the better law.

Selected References

Sir Edward Coke, Commentary upon Littleton (1628).
Alan Meisel, The Right to Die (1989 & 1994 supp.).
John Rawls, A Theory of Justice (1971).

Cases and Statutes

Brophy v. New England Sinai Hospital, 497 N.E.2d 626 (Mass. 1986).
Commissioner of Correction v. Myers, 399 N.E.2d 452 (Mass. 1979).
In re Conroy, 486 A.2d 1209 (N.J. 1985).
Cruzan v. Dir. Mo. Dep't. of Pub. Health, 497 U.S. 261 (1990).
In re Farrell, 529 A.2d 404 (N.J. 1987).
In Re Hughes, 611 A. 2d 1148 (N.J. 1992).
Lane v. Candura, 376 N.E.2d 1232 (Mass. App. Ct. 1978).
McConnell v. Beverly Enterprises, 553 A.2d 596 (Conn. 1989).
In re Peter, 529 A.2d 419 (N.J. 1987).
In re Quinlan, 355 A.2d 647 (N.J. 1976).
Roe v. Wade, 410 U.S. 113 (1973).
Saikewicz v. Superintendent of Belchertown State Hospital, 370 N.E.2d 417 (Mass. 1977).
In re Spring, 405 N.E.2d 115 (Mass. 1980).
Advance Directives for Health Care, N.J. Statutes Annotated, §§26:2H-53 to -78 (West 1996).
Health Care Proxies, Massachusetts General Laws, ch. 201D (1996).
Connecticut General Statutes Annotated, §§19a-570 to -580d (West. Supp. 1977).

Further Reading (selected work by Charles H. Baron)

Pleading for Physician-Assisted Suicide in the Courts, 19 Western New England Law Review 371 (1997).
A Model State Act to Authorize and Regulate Physician-Assisted Suicide, 33 Harvard Journal on Legislation 1 (1996) (with co-authors).

B. Federalism

CHAPTER FIFTEEN

FEDERAL PROSECUTION OF STATE AND LOCAL OFFICIALS*

… The Federal Government prosecutes state and local officials all the time, sometimes in politically charged contexts. Totally apart from possible political dimensions, these prosecutions raise serious questions of constitutional federalism. In *Sabri v. United States* the Supreme Court managed to avoid almost every one of them, while upholding federal prosecution of a routine local bribery scheme. In the process, it issued a unanimous decision that seems both to confirm the national role in policing state and local officials and to cast doubt on the depth of the Court's commitment to any "New Federalism." One explanation for this apparent paradox is that the Court's commitment to the precept is far from firm. An alternative perspective emphasizes the fact that the defendant was convicted under a statute passed pursuant to the spending power—the federal program bribery statute. The Court has suggested that spending power statutes are exempt from whatever strictures the New Federalism imposes.

In this Article, I offer a third perspective. *Sabri* confirms the high priority that the Court places on the National Government's authority to fight corruption at any level in order to protect the democratic process and public confidence in it. The key Supreme Court decision for understanding *Sabri* is one issued the same Term: *McConnell v. FEC*—the "Campaign Finance Reform" decision. There, the Court held that the governmental interest in combating corruption outweighs the powerful First Amendment interests at play in the political process. In *Sabri*, the Court could be seen as holding that this same governmental interest outweighs powerful federalism arguments in favor of letting state and local governments prosecute their own officials. In a sense, the 2003 Term was the Anti-Corruption Term. The Court showed sensitivity

---

* **George D. Brown**, *Carte Blanche: Federal Prosecution of State and Local Officials After Sabri,* 54 CATHOLIC UNIVERSITY LAW REVIEW 403 (2005), http://papers.ssrn.com/abstract_id=600595.

to the national mood of concern over abuse of power, and distrust of politicians and their susceptibility to corruptive influences.

True, the contexts of the two cases are different. So are their contents. *McConnell* dealt at length with constitutional arguments against an array of restrictions on campaign-related activity and its financing. There were definite splits among the justices. *Sabri* is the product of a unanimous Court. The analysis barely touches on the constitutional problems raised by the particular statutory issue presented. Indeed, the reasoning seems almost simplistic, as developed below. What unites the two cases, however, is a concern for integrity, both in the political process itself and the governmental process that follows it.

Sabri looks like a run-of-the-mill bribery prosecution. The defendant, a developer, had allegedly offered kickbacks and other inducements to a city councilor to facilitate a proposed project. However, like many other prosecutions of state and local officials, *Sabri* was brought by federal officials in a federal court. The statute which authorized this criminal proceeding is 18 U.S.C. §666: the federal program bribery statute—sometimes referred to as the "Stealth Statute," or the "Beast in the Federal Criminal Arsenal." It applies to any entity, including governments, that receives more than $10,000 a year in federal benefits. Within such an entity, numerous acts are made federal crimes. This case involved the portion of the statute that imposes federal criminal liability on anyone who

> corruptly gives, offers, or agrees to give anything of value to any person, with intent to influence or reward an agent of an organization or of a State, local or Indian tribal government, or any agency thereof, in connection with any business, transaction, or series of transactions of such organization, government or agency involving anything of value of $5,000 or more.

Under this language, it makes no difference whether any federal funds are involved in or connected to the proscribed transaction. Once an entity is covered, the specified corrupt acts within it are federal crimes. In *Sabri*, the Supreme Court considered, and rejected, arguments that some nexus to federal funds ought to be required. This issue had divided the lower courts. For the Court, however, the crucial determinant was the National Government's ability to protect funds it had disbursed under the spending power by ensuring the integrity of the recipient of those funds.

The broad sweep of §666 did not bother the Court at all. Indeed, this breadth turns §666 into something of a national anti-corruption statute. Such a statute has long been the holy grail of federal prosecutors. Perhaps they already have it. Still, if *Sabri* has, in fact, irrevocably tilted the debate on federal anti-corruption efforts in a nationalist direction, there may be more plausible and direct methods to reach this result, other than the rationale of somehow protecting federal funds. If fighting corruption at all levels of government is part of the National Government's role in the American federal system, why not come out and say so? ...

Corruption at the National Level. Whatever the definition of corruption, one can postulate several reasons why the National Government might want to proscribe such behavior in its own ranks. The basic argument can be seen in the President's oath to "preserve, protect and defend the Constitution of the United States." A democratic government has the inherent power, indeed the duty, to preserve the democratic system and the line it establishes between public and private "markets" for allocating goods and services. Closely related to this argument is the contention that preventing corruption is essential to preserving public confidence and participation in the democratic process. One finds this contention in numerous Supreme Court cases, primarily in the area of Campaign Finance Reform, where the anti-corruption imperative has been dominant. The contention has also played a key role in upholding conflict of interest legislation. In each context, the concept of the mere appearance of corruption or impropriety plays a large role in attempting to assess the impact of behavior on public attitudes towards the system as a whole....

Prosecuting state and local government is thus only another example of the fundamental national role of acting to preserve the democratic system. The argument has an intuitive appeal but seems short on empirical justification, although it is true that in other societies public perceptions of corruption have undermined confidence in basic governmental institutions. Nonetheless, the anti-corruption imperative present in both *McConnell* and *Sabri* may reflect the Court's sense of a need for a response to a widespread public perception that "they are all crooks." ...

Bribery, and similar attempts at distorting outcomes reached through political processes, may present a special justification for federal intervention. If corruption leads to inequality in the provision of public goods and services, a national role somewhat similar to the protection of civil rights may be justified. At some level, extreme state and local corruption might lead to a breakdown in particular governmental units....

(New) Federalism Concerns.... The essence of the New Federalism is twofold: an emphasis on the Constitution's enumeration of powers as limiting the powers of the National Government; and, the concept of states as quasi-sovereign, largely autonomous entities owed great respect by the coequal National Government. For that government to usurp from another government entity

the quintessentially sovereign task of controlling its own officials seems totally at variance with what the Court has been saying. [T]he logic of federalism, old and new, seems to cut sharply against the practice of widespread prosecution of sub-national officials....

The Constitution as a Direct Prohibition.... The national government has a very restricted authority to interfere in the administration of the state governments, triggered only by systemic misuse of state authority that undermines the legitimacy of the exercise of official power. The federal concern is that abuse of authority should not reach a level that would result in the destruction of the state government by a tyrannical leader.

The existence of ... an "anti-corruption legacy" would play an important, perhaps dispositive, role in analyzing many of the questions raised by federal prosecutions of state and local officials.... However, the premise of any such legacy, particularly one that rises to the level of a guide to constitutional interpretation, seems questionable on several counts. As an initial matter, if the Framers felt that strongly about state and local corruption, one might ask why they did not place in the document more specific prohibitions on corruption as well as national authority to deal with it.... Far more than, say, the provision for Diversity Jurisdiction, the Guarantee Clause can be interpreted as touching upon the overall quality of government within the states, through a broad construction of the concept of a "Republican Form of Government."....

[There are also] nagging doubts about why federal prosecution of state and local officials maintains the federal balance.... The prosecutions can be seen as usurping state and local governments' inherent authority to police their own ranks as their political processes deem appropriate. Moreover, to the extent that they enhance the role of national actors, particularly the U.S. attorney, within the sub-national political process, federal prosecutions disturb equilibrium and alter balance....

Reliance on the Guarantee Clause is [another possibility].... [T]he Guarantee Clause ... provides in part that "the United States shall guarantee to every State in this Union a Republican Form of Government." The language certainly points in the direction of some authority over state and local government, and perhaps even to the quality of that government.... The Framers cared about "public virtue" as an essential element of republican government....

[This source of power has] the advantage of placing the federal prosecutorial role within the logic of the federal system as a whole. Reconciling the prosecutions with federalism is thus not a problem.... The main advantage of [this] thesis is that it represents a plausible basis for dealing directly with the problem of the prosecutions: validation under a general statute, of those prosecutions. However, Congress has never taken such a broad view of its power.... More importantly, recent Supreme Court invocations of the Guarantee Clause seem to view it more as a source of state autonomy than a font of federal power.

The Enumerated Powers. Suppose, however, that one rejects the thesis that the Constitution addresses the issue of state and local corruption, either through a direct prohibition or through provisions strong enough to create a background understanding about this corruption. That is not the end of the matter in terms of finding federal power to bring the prosecutions. Congress may well be able to make the basic value judgment, as it has in so many other areas, through exercise of the enumerated powers. In fact, three of these powers are the bases on which most federal anti-corruption law rests. The postal power is the source of the mail fraud statute, an important tool in the federal prosecutor's arsenal. As a textual matter, this outcome requires a series of leaps.... If we limit our search to the text of the postal power and a reasonable construction of it, this power does not seem to be the basis of a general anti-corruption statute.

The Commerce Clause presents more complex questions. We are used to a legal universe in which this Clause is the basis for a range of moral judgments about practices Congress wishes to condemn. While *United States v. Lopez* reminds us that the Commerce Clause has limits, the Clause has nonetheless played a key anti-corruption role. The Hobbs Act is the major example. The Act requires an effect on commerce as a jurisdictional predicate for prosecuting crimes prohibited under the Act, including extortion under color of official right. It is, indeed, possible to imagine specific instances of corruption that have such an effect.... Taking the language of the Hobbs Act and its case-by-case emphasis, as representative of current approaches to the Commerce Clause, the leap from commerce to any general anti-corruption statute requires some effort.

The third source of congressional power, the one endorsed in *Sabri v. United States*, is the spending power. Congress can "lay and collect Taxes, Duties, Imposts and Excises to pay the Debts and provide for the common Defense and general Welfare of the United States." It is not a leap to conclude that the general welfare includes governments free from corruption, especially given a history of deference to Congress's determination of what the general welfare means. Congress could, for example, enact a grant program to fund state and local anti-corruption efforts. It could probably attach anti-corruption "strings" to federal grant programs for those units of government. *Sabri*, however, involves a statute that does neither. [18 U.S.C. §666] is a criminal statute, apparently designed to protect federal funds from diversion and other dishonest practices. After *Sabri*, the statute has become the closest thing our system has to a general federal anti-corruption law. The fact that the Court took this extraordinary step, and did so almost casually, merits close examination.

Section 666 and Sabri—No Limits? The major debate surrounding the statute has … involved the issue of a possible "nexus" requirement within the statute. That is, should courts require that the prosecution not only prove the corrupt acts and the receipt of the funds, but should a connection between the federal funds and the corruption be present in the case as well? Opinions have differed as to whether any such requirement should be read into the statute as an element to be proved in each case, or whether it is the ultimate test of the statute's validity if applied to situations where no such connection exists.…

The ultimate question posed by the statute is what the federal role should be in policing state and local corruption through creation of a federal criminal offense. It seems clear from the legislative history that the drafters had no such lofty ambitions in mind as creating a general anti-corruption statute and did not view an enactment concerning " 'theft or bribery concerning programs receiving Federal funds' " as presenting these fundamental issues.…

The Court first dealt with the statute in the 1997 case of *Salinas v. United States*. The unanimous decision upheld a broad construction of the statute against the contention that it might require that "the Government … prove the bribe in some way affected federal funds, for instance[,] by diverting or misappropriating them, before the bribe violates [it]." The Court rejected any "interpretation that federal funds must be affected." It relied primarily on the broad language of the statute. The opinion does not stand for the proposition that §666 raises no constitutional issues. The Court emphasized that there was "no serious doubt about the constitutionality" of the statute "as applied to the facts of this case." Indeed, the Court concluded that "the statute is constitutional as applied in this case." The opinion did not reject a nexus requirement, holding only that the Government did not have to prove federal funds were "involved" in the bribery at issue. Thus, while hospitable to the statute, *Salinas* contains tantalizing suggestions that serious constitutional questions do, indeed, lurk beneath the surface.

The Court continued its hospitable construction of §666 in *Fischer v. United States*. At issue was whether hospitals participating in the Medicare program received "benefits" under §666(b), thus triggering its criminal provisions. The Court concluded that participation in the program resulted in receipt of benefits, turning to *Salinas* for support of a construction of §666 that could be described as " 'expansive,' both as to the [conduct] forbidden and the entities covered.'" Again, the Court showed awareness of and concern for the potential federalism issues raised by the breadth of the statute and the need to limit it. The majority stated that it did not wish to "turn almost every act of fraud or bribery into a federal offense, upsetting the proper federal balance." Indeed, Justices Thomas and Scalia dissented, relying in part on federalism considerations such as those enunciated in *Lopez*. For the dissenters, "without a jurisdictional provision that would ensure that in each case the exercise of federal power is related to the federal interest in a federal program, §666 would criminalize routine acts of fraud or bribery, which, as the Court admits, would upset the proper federal balance.'" Their dissent, as well as the cautionary notes sounded by the entire Court in *Salinas*, appeared to indicate a continuing awareness of the federalism issues and constitutional questions referred to above. However, in *Sabri*, caution disappeared.

Sabri involved the indictment of a Minneapolis developer for the following corrupt acts: offering a $5,000 kickback to a city councilor for obtaining regulatory approvals; offering a $10,000 bribe to the councilor to set up a meeting with objecting abutters; and, a ten percent commission on community economic development grants that the defendant sought from the city and its funding entity for housing and economic development. The proposed prosecution easily met the requisites of §666. In the year of the acts at issue, the Minneapolis City Council had administered twenty-nine million dollars in federal funds. Moreover, the housing and economic development entity from which the defendant sought aid was, itself, a substantial recipient of federal funds. Defendant Sabri challenged the "indictment on the ground that §666(a)(2) is unconstitutional on its face for failure to require proof of a connection between the federal funds and the alleged bribe, as an element of liability." ...

... The Supreme Court stated that its reason for granting certiorari was to resolve this circuit conflict. The Court had no problem in resolving the issue in favor of a broad construction of the statute dispensing altogether with any nexus requirement, and "readily disposed" of the contention that this broad construction posed any constitutional problem. Indeed, although there were two separate concurring opinions, no justice seemed to see any problem with the constitutionality of §666 as a general anti-corruption statute.

The Court's opinion is a model of simplicity. First of all, Congress had unquestioned authority to appropriate federal grant funds to further the general welfare. Although the Court did not refer to the facts at hand on this point, the housing and other grants received by Minneapolis are typical examples of the spending power in action. Second, Congress has "corresponding authority under the Necessary and Proper Clause, to see to it that taxpayer dollars appropriated under [the spending] power are in fact spent for the general welfare, and not frittered away." Congress could well be concerned that dishonest public officers who are "untrustworthy stewards" or who "do not deliver dollar-for-dollar value" will not distinguish according to the source of funds when committing their corrupt acts. Furthermore, the fungibility of federal funds is an additional reason for not requiring proof of their presence in any particular corrupt activity. The Court invoked Justice Marshall's venerable hypothetical in *McCulloch* to the effect that the "power to establish post-offices and post-roads entails authority to punish those who steal letters."

The Court's short and simple analysis almost masks the fact that it adopted one of the major contending arguments in the ongoing debate over the constitutionality of §666: the integrity rationale. The rationale proceeds on the assumption that measures directed solely at transactions involving federal funds will often be insufficient to protect those funds. What is needed is a broad net that achieves protection through sweeping up all corrupt transactions in order to guarantee the integrity of the recipient entity. However, this rationale can readily extend to treating the concern for state and local integrity as the major federal interest, with the protection of federal funds operating almost as a pretext.

Federalism concerns were barely mentioned in *Sabri*. The Court relegated any problems stemming from "federal prosecution in an area historically of state concern" to a footnote. It found *Lopez* and *United States v. Morrison* totally inapplicable because those Commerce Clause cases involved activity that had little relation to economic conduct that Congress could regulate. Here, there was no need to "'pile inference upon inference'" since the spending power was directly involved. In sum, whatever constitutional reservations the debate over §666 had previously engendered and had come to light in *Salinas* were summarily rejected. After *Sabri*, §666 seems free to roam the political landscape as long as the sub-national entity where it comes into play receives more than $10,000 in federal funds "'in any one year,'" and the corrupt transaction involves more than $5,000 or, in the Court's words, "goes well beyond liquor and cigars." …

The central constitutional aspect of *Sabri* is its acceptance of the integrity rationale, that is, that the Federal Government can act "to safeguard the integrity" of grant recipients in order to protect the disbursed funds. Obviously, integrity might have several meanings. The term might be limited to the federal funds themselves or to the broader manner in which a particular federally funded program is administered. For example, in *Salinas*, correction officials took bribes to permit conjugal visits to federal prisoners housed in a state jail. Integrity might mean the fiscal honesty of a recipient unit as a whole.

Again, one can see a tie, albeit less direct, to the federal funds. However, integrity will certainly bear a much broader reading: the general quality of a recipient unit, in the case of a governmental one, whether or not it practices "good government."

One could surely find a lack of integrity in a governmental unit in which nepotism and patronage are rampant, "no-show" jobs exist, opposition parties are squelched by entrenched officeholders and there is a general sense of helplessness on the part of excluded groups. Would the *Sabri* rationale permit the Federal Government to regulate these practices directly, for example, by penalizing the awarding of patronage jobs? Ultimately there could be a relation back to some federal funds (in the sense that administrative positions with control over those funds might not be awarded on merit), but the goal of federal intervention seems to be the use of the spending power to achieve broader federal public policy ends of good government....

In the end, [this] is the lesson and the question that we must take from *Sabri*: to what extent does a perceived national anti-corruption imperative, whatever its source, overcome considerations of federalism? [True,] perceived extreme cases of intervention can be curbed, but the general phenomenon persists. Certainly the widespread prosecution of state and local officials for the manner in which they govern raises serious questions. Holding those officials accountable for their style of governance ought to be as much a matter of constitutional concern as the policies they adopt....

At this point, it is instructive to compare *Sabri* with *McConnell. McConnell* upheld restrictions on campaign finance practices and related activities, restrictions that could be enforced through the criminal law. The restrictions were imposed by Congress in the Bipartisan Campaign Reform Act of 2002 (BCRA). BCRA increased the level of regulation of federal campaigns in two primary ways. It sharply curtailed the role of soft money—contributions to political parties for purposes other than the direct influencing of a national election.

BCRA also imposed substantial limits on "issue ads," defined by the Court as ads "specifically intended to affect election results," but omitting "'magic words' such as Elect John Smith,' or Vote against Jane Doe.'" Opponents mounted a substantial First Amendment challenge to BCRA, but a majority of the Court built upon the line of cases beginning with *Buckley v. Valeo*, and amplified in later precedent such as *Nixon v. Shrink Missouri Government PAC*, to formulate a set of anti-corruption governmental interests that met the Government's burden to justify incursions on the First Amendment....

One can, of course, identify differences between the two cases. In *McConnell*, the statute regulated the electoral process. In *Sabri*, the statute regulated the functioning of government. McConnell involved the regulation of activities primarily at the federal level. *Sabri* involved the regulation of activities at the local level. In *McConnell*, the regulated activities were essentially political advocacy and political contributions. In *Sabri*, the regulated activity was bribery. In *McConnell*, the principal constitutional defense against the challenged statute was the First Amendment. In *Sabri*, the challenge was based on federalism. Finally, *McConnell* relied substantially on notions of public confidence and the appearance of impropriety. *Sabri* focused substantially on the integrity of governmental operations.

Despite these differences, I see the two cases united by a broad anti-corruption imperative that justifies Congress's role as the guardian of the democratic process at all stages and at all levels. Each case focused on the importance of integrity in government. The integrity of recipient governments is the key to *Sabri's* protection of federal funds rationale. *McConnell* invoked prior precedents as demonstrating a congressional intent in protecting "'the integrity of our system of representative democracy.'" As in *Sabri*, the notion of "integrity" is central to the analysis. Indeed, parts of *McConnell* point in a "good government" direction. Beyond a similar approach to recognizing Congress's role in achieving good government, each case demonstrates considerable deference to Congress in determining how to achieve that goal, even in the face of serious constitutional objection.

Section 666 After Sabri. Sabri certainly looks like a sweeping victory for proponents of national anti-corruption efforts. Before further examination of how best to vindicate that position, it may be useful to consider whether the decision completely forecloses any consideration of the constitutionality of §666 in a case where there is little if any perceptible nexus between federal funds and the corrupt act charged. At first blush, the answer would seem to be yes, given the Court's adoption of the no-nexus construction of the statute and its equally strong adoption of the integrity rationale for that conclusion. However, ... the *Sabri* Court [also] stated that, at best, the petitioner could assert that the statute would be unconstitutional as applied to someone else, but refused to let him make that person's hypothetical challenge. What happens now if such a person comes before the Court armed with a challenge that Sabri, who was clearly attempting to tamper with federal funds, could not make?

... We now have something very close to a general anti-corruption statute in the form of §666. How far it extends will then depend, not on any judicial oversight, but on the restraint and/or creativity of federal prosecutors. There will be some direct supervision from Washington, whether through specific interventions ... or through the general guidance of the United States Attorneys' Manual. But individual discretion will be extensive....

Conclusion. During the 2003 Term, the Supreme Court issued two important decisions aimed at keeping corruption out of government: *McConnell v. FEC* and *Sabri v. United States. McConnell* got all the publicity, but *Sabri* is just as significant. *Sabri* not only validated a sweeping reading of the federal program bribery statute (18 U.S.C. §666), but it also focused on protecting the integrity of state and local governments as the means of protecting federal funds. The case thus stands as an affirmation of the federal role in prosecuting state and local officials for political corruption.

In this Article, I have raised the recurring question whether the prosecutions are consistent with the Supreme Court's New Federalism. A strong argument can be made that they are not, but the Court has established that its anti-corruption imperative trumps federalism. If *Sabri* represents a victory for the nationalist view on corruption prosecution, the question remains whether the spending power—coupled with the notion of protecting federal funds—is the best route to get there. There are alternative constitutional and statutory possibilities for a general anti-corruption statute. *Sabri's* greatest strength may be that it takes us to the point where we can deal with the matter openly.

Selected References

Susan-Rose Ackerman, Corruption: A Study in Political Economy (1978) & Corruption and Government: Cases, Consequences, and Reforms (1999).

Lynn A. Baker, Conditional Federal Spending After Lopez, 95 Columbia Law Review 1911 (1995).

Richard W. Garnett, The New Federalism, the Spending Power, and Federal Criminal Law, 89 Cornell Law Review 1 (2003).

Peter J. Henning, Federalism and the Federal Prosecution of State and Local Corruption, 92 Kentucky Law Journal 75 (2003).

Roderick M. Hills, Jr., Corruption and Federalism: (When) Do Federal Criminal Prosecutions Improve Non-Federal Democracy?, 6 Theoretical Inquiries in Law 113 (2005).

Adam H. Kurland, The Guarantee Clause as a Basis for Federal Prosecutions of State and Local Officials, 62 USC Law Review 367 (1989).

Calvin Massey, Federalism and the Rehnquist Court, 53 Hastings Law Journal 431 (2002).

Paul Salvatoriello, The Practical Necessity of Federal Intervention Versus the Ideal of Federalism: An Expansive View of Section 666 in the Prosecution of State and Local Corruption, 89 Georgetown Law Journal 2393 (2001).

Robert G. Vaughn, Ethics in Government and the Vision of Public Service, 58 George Washington University Law Review 417 (1990).

Gregory Howard Williams, Good Government by Prosecutorial Decree: The Use and Abuse of Mail Fraud, 32 Arizona Law Review 137 (1990).

Cases and Statutes

Buckley v. Valeo, 424 U.S. 1 (1976).
Fischer v. United States, 529 U.S. 667 (2000).
McConnell v. FEC, 124 S. Ct. 619 (2003).
Nixon v. Shrink Missouri Government PAC, 528 U.S. 377 (2000).
Sabri v. United States, 124 S. Ct. 1941 (2004).
Salinas v. United States, 522 U.S. 52 (1997).
South Dakota v. Dole, 483 U.S. 203 (1987).
United States v. Lopez, 514 U.S. 549 (1995).
United States v. Morrison, 529 U.S. 598 (2000).
Hobbs Act, 18 U.S.C. §1951 (2000).
18 U.S.C. §666 (2000).
Bipartisan Campaign Reform Act of 2002, Pub. L. No. 107-55, 116 Stat. 81.

Further Reading (selected work by George D. Brown)

New Federalism's Unanswered Question: Who Should Prosecute State and Local Officials for Political Corruption? 60 Washington and Lee Law Review 417 (2003).

Constitutionalizing the Federal Criminal Law Debate: Morrison, Jones, and the ABA, 2001 Illinois Law Review 983.

Putting Watergate Behind Us—*Salinas, Sun-Diamond*, and Two Views of the Anti-corruption Model, 74 Tulane Law Review 747 (2000).

Stealth Statute—Corruption, the Spending Power, and the Rise of 18 U.S.C. §666, 73 Notre Dame Law Review 247 (1998).

Should Federalism Shield Corruption?—Mail Fraud, State Law and Post-*Lopez* Analysis, 82 Cornell Law Review 225 (1997).

The Constitution as an Obstacle to Government Ethics—Reformist Legislation after *National Treasury Employees Union*, 37 William & Mary Law Review 979 (1996).

Chapter Sixteen

Corporate Federalism[*]

The longstanding academic debate about whether competition among states for corporate charters has led to a "race-to-the-bottom" or a "race-to-the-top" in corporate law, exaggerates the true extent of competition among states for corporate charters. Instead, recent scholarship suggests no race exists at all. That is, when a corporation considers a state other than its home state in which to incorporate, it almost invariably chooses Delaware. These same commentators have observed that other states do not actively compete with Delaware for charters. Neither the statutes, the court systems, nor the corporate franchise tax structures of these states appear designed to allow the states to generate additional revenue by attracting out-of-state incorporations.

For years, scholars have argued that competition among states leads to greater innovation and experimentation in the development of corporate law rules. The recent assertion that no meaningful interstate competition exists for out-of-state incorporations detracts from the market-based arguments these scholars invoke to refute the prescriptions of others who advocate national standards of corporate conduct. The dearth of competition also weakens these same scholars' arguments that the federal system of corporate law has led to the development of efficient or optimal corporate law rules.

For regulatory competition actually to impact the development of corporate law in a manner that properly balances management and shareholder interests, Delaware must have a rival. Only the federal government can offer an alternative regulatory scheme that can compete with Delaware for the public's acceptance. This Article's vision of regulatory competition departs sharply from the model of horizontal competition that dominates corporate law scholarship. In this view, regulatory competition is not driven by the pursuit of additional corporate charters or franchise fees. Instead, the rival regulators compete for the public's confidence and concomitant regulatory authority and power.

[*] **Reneé M. Jones**, *Rethinking Corporate Federalism in the Era of Corporate Reform*, 29 Iowa Journal of Corporation Law 625 (2004), http://papers.ssrn.com/abstract_id=459400.

In this paradigm, voters play the primary role in achieving a desirable balance between federal and state power in corporate regulation. If the public disapproves of the actions of federal regulators in a substantive area, voters can elect representatives at the national level who will defer to states on such issues. In the context of corporate regulation, if Delaware, the dominant state for corporate law, regulates corporate affairs competently, then Delaware and other states should continue to enjoy broad regulatory authority. Conversely, if the public loses confidence in the existing regulatory regime, voters would be expected to pressure Congress to adopt laws that impose more appropriate standards. Such public pressure might lead Congress to preempt certain provisions of state corporate law. Such pressure may also lead states to take measures to forestall preemption by modifying state law to more closely comport with the demands of the voting public.

Delaware's response to the enactment of Sarbanes-Oxley suggests that Congress has the ability to prod Delaware to adopt corporate law rules preferred by voters, without resorting to wholesale replacement of state law with federal law. The Act has been described as "the most far-reaching reforms of American corporate practices since the time of Franklin Delano Roosevelt." Unlike the reforms of the Roosevelt era, the Act departs from the securities laws' traditional model of disclosure regulation and mandates corporate governance reforms that previously had been the exclusive province of the states. Among other interventions, the Act forbids all corporate loans to directors and executive officers and dictates the composition and responsibilities of the audit committee of the board of directors. With these provisions, the Act displaces some of the basic tenets of state corporate law....

[R]enewed federal engagement in corporate law issues should be welcomed and sustained. However, in contrast to other proposals, I do not advocate wholesale federal preemption or the development of an optional federal regulatory scheme. Instead, I urge a sustained vigilance from Congress and a willingness to take limited preemptive measures when state corporate law rules fall short in providing adequate protection for investors....

The Modern Debate. For almost thirty years, academics have debated about whether competition among states for corporate charters has precipitated a race to the top or a race to the bottom in corporate law. The debate is central to corporate legal scholarship, for at its essence it is a debate about the proper substance of corporate law rules. In our federal system of corporate law, state governments set the rules governing the relationships among the primary participants in the corporate enterprise: directors, officers and investors. Each state has its own corporate statute and a corporation may incorporate under the laws of any state, regardless of whether it owns assets or conducts operations in that state. Under the "internal affairs doctrine," it is the law of the se-lected state that governs all disputes regarding a corporation's internal affairs, regardless of the forum in which such disputes are litigated. Although the fed-eral securities laws and other federal laws impose significant limitations on corporate operations, the U.S. has no federal corporate statute....

Race-to-the-bottom theorists argue that regulatory competition has had a negative impact on the development of corporate law. William Cary most forcefully articulated this view. Cary argued that Delaware, in its zeal to maintain its primacy as the favored state of incorporation, adopted legal rules that favor managers at the expense of shareholders. He asserted that because corporate managers enjoy exclusive power to select or change the state of in-corporation, Delaware had declared it to be the "public policy of the State" to adopt legal rules that managers desired. Implicit in Cary's argument is the premise that government regulation is necessary to prevent corporate man-agers from exploiting shareholders who exercise little meaningful control over the modern corporate enterprise. Having concluded that the federal system discourages such active regulation, Cary urged Congressional legislation as the only means to effect the regulatory regime he viewed as essential to main-tain the proper balance of power among managers, shareholders and other corporate constituents. He thus proposed the establishment of federal min-imum standards of corporate conduct that would apply to large American corporations.

Defenders of the corporate federal system (referred to here as corporate fed-eralists) argue that the very interstate competition that Cary so excoriated, has led instead to a "race-to-the-top" in corporate law. These theorists, led by Ralph Winter, agree with Cary that the federal system discourages active reg-ulation of corporations, but they embrace this deregulatory bias as the legit-imate result of the corporate law race. Race-to-the-top theorists maintain that market forces are sufficient to prevent excessive managerial self-dealing and opportunism. They take the market-based defense of the federal system a step further by arguing that not only do conventional market forces rein in man-agement excess, but that a competitive market for corporate law works to en-sure that states will adopt legal rules that appeal to managers and sharehold-ers alike....

The Reality. Despite the longevity of the race debate, recent empirical stud-ies demonstrate the fallacy of the fundamental assumption upon which the great debate rests—that states actively compete for corporate charters. In sep-arate studies, Lucian Bebchuk and Assaf Hamdani, and Marcel Kahan and Ehud Kamar have asserted that the interstate competition which has been credited with fueling the corporate law race is largely illusory. These com-

mentators show that not only is Delaware the clear leader in chartering pub-
licly-traded corporations, but that no other state serves as a credible rival to
Delaware in attracting charters from out-of-state corporations.…

By persuasively demonstrating the absence of interstate competition in the
development of corporate law, these recent studies detract from the standard
arguments of corporate federalists who advance and defend the free-market
approach to corporate law embodied in the states' enabling corporate law
codes. Because there is no meaningful interstate competition for corporate
charters, competition could not have affected the development of corporate
law in the way that corporate federalists posit. Thus, corporate federalists' defense of the states' enabling corporate codes must rest on other grounds.

The absence of vigorous competition among states for corporate charters
does not by itself establish that fundamental problems exist in the corporate
law rules that states created. It is one thing to refute the assertion that interstate competition exists, and has led to optimal corporate law rules, and quite
another to demonstrate that the existing rules are flawed. Nonetheless, there
are valid reasons to suspect that certain problems will persist in corporate law
when the rules are established through a political process that managerial interests dominate.…

Horizontal Competition. Traditional corporate law theory has focused almost exclusively on the purported benefits of horizontal regulatory competition while ignoring another important federalist ideal: that state governments
would compete with the federal government for regulatory power. A core argument of corporate federalists is that the federal (state-based) system enhances the development of corporate law through reliance on competitive
mechanisms that federal intervention would hamper. These theorists argue
that the fifty states and the District of Columbia function as regulatory labo-
ratories that facilitate innovation in the development of rules that improve the
substance of corporate law. When competing states observe successful experiments in innovative states, they adopt similar rules which lead to the optimal
corporate legal rules prevailing throughout the nation.

Corporate federalists also argue that national regulation as advanced by
Cary and others would disrupt this ideal competitive process because the federal government would enjoy monopoly power, nullifying the ability of competitive forces to advance optimal legal rules. Finally, opponents of national-
level regulation argue that such regulation would not likely do better than state
law in protecting shareholders as Congress is just as susceptible to business
lobbying as state legislatures.

Some scholars have challenged the corporate federalists' unvarnished view
of the superiority of state-level regulation in corporate law. William Bratton

and Joseph McCahery assert that the economic theory that underlies the corporate federalist model has been significantly qualified by economists. They point out that Charles Tiebout's model of horizontal regulatory competition sought only to demonstrate the superiority of local level determination of government expenditures on public goods and services, such as police protection, public schools, and swimming pools. Legal scholars subsequently integrated Tiebout's model into legal literature as they sought to expand the model to apply to the "production" of government regulation. The Tiebout model thus became a basis for the defense of current system state-based corporate regulation. However, most public economists now concur that the Tiebout model is burdened by too many unrealistic assumptions to predict reliably the superiority of local level regulation over national regulation....

Vertical Competition. Despite its curious absence from the debate on corporate law competition, the concept of vertical competition was central to the framers' vision of the federalist system. The dual regulatory authority of federal and local governments was part of the framers' design. They anticipated that such a system would enable the public to "give most of their confidence where they may discover it to be most due." Thus, the original federalists envisioned that state and federal governments would compete to persuade the public as to which was better suited to regulate in a particular field. The public would observe which level of government exercised regulatory authority in a field and could evaluate that regulator's performance. If dissatisfied with the dominant regulator's performance, voters could lobby for intervention from an alternative regulator and thereby shift regulatory authority from the states to the federal government or vice versa.

In contrast to modern federalists' unyielding attacks on federal regulation, the original federalists were more circumspect about the proper limits of federal power. In James Madison's view, any expansion of federal power in response to voters' demands would bear legitimacy....

In the modern context, the model of vertical regulatory competition predicts that if states regulate corporations competently, federal deference to state authorities would be politically popular and national politicians who eschewed extensive federal regulation would be elected to federal office. Conversely, if states failed to regulate adequately or permitted a regulatory void, the federal government could step in and win public confidence by filling the existing void with regulation that voters demand. In such a context, federal regulation would become politically expedient and politicians who supported such regulation could expect to be re-elected.

In a contemporaneous work, Mark Roe also argues that the federal government is Delaware's main competitor in the corporate law realm. Roe argues that the federal government reserves for itself those areas of corporate law that it wishes to regulate, leaving the states to regulate the remainder of the field. Whenever the federal government disapproves of state policy, it may, and often does, preempt state law. Roe also observes that the federal government can influence Delaware law through many mechanisms that fall short of preemption.

Roe's arguments are consonant with this Article's description of federal corporate reform legislation provoking reform at the state level. However, Roe refrains from offering a normative evaluation of the proper role of national regulation in the development of corporate law. In contrast to Roe's agnosticism, this Article asserts that adherence to basic democratic principles justifies federal intervention, particularly when such intervention represents a legislative response to public demands for significant legal reform.

Toward A New Model of Vertical Regulatory Competition. Recent scholarship demonstrates a lack of interstate competition for corporate charters, exposing a gap in modern theories of regulatory competition in corporate law. This Article's proposed model of vertical competition attempts to fill that gap. Vertical regulatory competition is not driven by a regulator's desire to maximize revenues, but by the quest for popular legitimacy and its attendant authority to regulate. The rival regulators (the state and federal governments) compete with one another for the confidence of voters who will reward, with their votes, those politicians whom they perceive as protecting their interests, and penalize those who do not. This model of regulatory competition better explains recent developments in corporate law, in which the Delaware judiciary is apparently seeking to regain public confidence by reforming its law as part of a bid to prevent further federal preemption.

Advantages. The vertical model has normative appeal because it recognizes the need for policymakers to consider a broader range of interests than the horizontal competition model deems important. As Cary and others have observed, a policymaking process characterized by horizontal competition encourages policy makers to appeal to management interests, to the exclusion of the interests of all other corporate constituents, because management initiates the selection of the state of incorporation and retains control over any reincorporation decision.

The race-to-the-top paradigm advanced by Winter and others relegates investors to a reactive role and accepts their exclusion from participation in the policy debate when legal rules are crafted. In Winter's paradigm, the only role for shareholders in the regulatory process is that of ratifying or rejecting management's choice by choosing whether or not to invest in a corporation chartered in a particular state. Under this model, investors face a "take it or leave it" proposition. Because of the convergence of modern corporate law rules, the law of all states is essentially the same and investors are deprived of any meaningful choice.

In contrast, the presence of vertical competition pushes policy-makers at both the state and federal level to give greater consideration to the interests of investors and broader societal issues. Nationally dispersed shareholders lack direct political influence in Delaware, while management interests are well-represented. At the national level, in contrast, representatives of shareholder interests, can participate directly in policy debates. Sophisticated and organized aggregations of shareholders can and do lobby Congress and the SEC to ensure that shareholder interests are considered. Labor unions, public pension funds, and trade groups such as the Council for Institutional Investors have the wherewithal to make a persuasive case to Congress and the SEC.

As a policy matter, encouraging vertical competition is preferable to promoting horizontal competition among states. Federal engagement provides voters throughout the country an opportunity to persuade Congress to pre-empt those state law provisions that lack popular support. This dynamic allows investors to influence state corporate law, if only indirectly. A posture of absolute federal deference to state regulators would deprive citizens of this power, enhancing management's dominance of the state regulatory process.

Objection: The Federal Constraint is too Weak. Several commentators have acknowledged the preemptive threat's disciplining effect on Delaware. Yet, they generally conclude that the federal constraint is too weak and sporadic to be relied upon to affect state law significantly. For example, Bebchuk and Hamdani argue that the federal constraint is "hardly a tight one" and that it requires the federal government to identify corporate governance arrangements that harm shareholders and seek to correct them. Bratton and McCahery similarly argue that political barriers make it difficult for shareholder groups to influence national policy, and that Delaware, when threatened, easily defuses the federal threat through minimal concessions to shareholders.

The vertical competition model emphasizes Congress's ability, through incremental action, to impact law significantly at the state level. Indeed, recent developments in Delaware corporate law show that commentators may have underestimated the latent power of the preemptive threat and misgauged the limited precision with which Congress must act to evoke a significant state-level response. By engaging in quite limited preemption, the Act, along with other national reform proposals, has significantly influenced the development of state law. Congress did not need to precisely identify all of the flaws in state corporate law and systematically address them. To effect state-level reform, Congress merely needed to demonstrate that it was willing to exercise its constitutional authority to preempt state corporate law. Even though as a matter the exercise of federal preemptive power in the corporate realm has been episodic, it need not remain so. By continuing to scrutinize and evaluate corporate affairs, the federal government can maintain its disciplinary role.

To sustain vertical competition, federal regulators must remain willing to intervene when the public becomes dissatisfied with the state regulatory regime. Prior to Sarbanes-Oxley, the federal government eschewed dictating corporate governance standards and instead sought to regulate corporate conduct through an awkward amalgamation of tax policy and securities law disclosure requirements. The corporate scandals sparked public outrage which forced the federal government into a mode of direct regulation. This development disrupted the stagnant environment in which modern corporate rules had evolved.

Objection: Delaware's Dominance Lacks Legitimacy. A stronger critique of the advocacy for constrained and limited federal preemption rests on the argument that scant justification exists for allowing a small state such as Delaware to dictate the law on issues having a significant impact on the national economy. Thus, a complete shift of regulatory authority from the states to the federal government is preferable to the limited preemption advanced here. Although there is some appeal to this argument, several factors caution against replacing state law with a federal incorporation scheme.

Because of the states' historical role in the development of corporate law, considerable expertise and experience in grappling with corporate law issues is vested in state authorities. State-based law and jurisprudence have considerable value to businesses and lawyers representing sunk costs that may be squandered if federal law entirely replaced state law. Furthermore, there are some advantages to local-level regulation even in the absence of horizontal regulatory competition. Local chartering offers advantages in terms of cost and convenience that a federal regime could not match. States may be more responsive to citizen concerns than the federal government, and opportunities for experimentation afforded by the state-centered system should be preserved where possible. Although this attribute has been oversold by corporate federalists, some useful corporate reforms are made possible because of the ability of multiple jurisdictions to experiment with changes in the law.

More importantly, the state regulatory regime can continue to serve as a regulatory "safety valve." If federal regulation fails due to corruption or regulatory capture, the state-centered system provides an alternative venue for addressing future problems. The importance of this safety valve can be shown by analogy to the securities enforcement regime....

Sarbanes-Oxley: The Federal Preemptive Threat. Examining the Sarbanes-Oxley Act's impact on the development of state corporate law offers an opportunity to evaluate whether the threat of federal preemption actually works the way the vertical model of regulatory competition would predict. [P]ublic dissatisfaction with state-based corporate regulation prodded Congress to adopt Sarbanes-Oxley which preempts certain provisions of state law....

Sarbanes-Oxley represents an amalgamation of corporate reform proposals that had drifted through the halls of Congress since the Enron debacle first came to light. The Act reformed regulation of the accounting industry, enhanced securities law disclosure requirements, created a number of new white-collar crimes, and enhanced criminal and civil penalties for corporate fraud. In a marked departure from the securities laws' traditional mode of disclosure regulation, the Act directly regulates corporate governance. In reaction to reports of abuse at Enron, WorldCom, Adelphia, and others, the Act bans all corporate loans to officers and directors. In contrast to Congress' bright line rule, most states permit such loans, subject only to vague standards embodied in the duty of loyalty.

The Act also encroaches on state law by specifying requirements for the composition and conduct of the audit committee of the board of directors. The Act requires each public corporation to have an audit committee comprised solely of "independent" directors. The Act's definition of independence is more stringent than that embodied in Delaware common law. To qualify as independent under the Act, a director cannot accept payment of any consulting, advisory, or other compensatory fees other than director fees.

In addition, the Act reallocates many key responsibilities from corporate management to the audit committee. It specifies that the audit committee must retain responsibility for appointing, compensating, and overseeing the work of the company's independent auditor, and that the auditors must report directly to the committee. The Act also demands that the audit committee have the authority to hire independent advisers, such as lawyers and accountants, and that companies must provide the committee with the necessary funding to fulfill its newly-designated duties. Finally, the Act requires the audit committee to establish a reporting system for the receipt of confidential, anonymous reports from employees concerning questionable accounting or auditing matters. In contrast to the Act's requirements, Delaware law affords the full board the authority to designate committees, with discretion to determine committee composition and to delegate (or withhold) authority to committees as it wishes.

Critiques of Sarbanes-Oxley. A first wave of academic commentary has criticized the Act generally for the haste with which it was adopted, and more specifically for what some say is the ill-advised step across the well-respected lines established by the internal affairs doctrine. These substantive critiques, however valid, gloss over an important point. The Act's very adoption triggered an important reaction and initiated legal reforms with impact beyond its limited substantive provisions. When analyzed as part of the complex dynamic of vertical competition, the Act is properly viewed as a critical political response to public dissatisfaction with the states' performance as virtually exclusive regulators of internal corporate affairs.

Delaware's Response: The Perceived Threat. As the model of vertical regulatory competition would predict, the public outrage over the corporate scandals appears to have affected the Delaware judiciary, which is ever mindful of Congress' preemptive power. In response, Delaware's judiciary has taken the initiative to reform its state's corporate law in an effort to forestall further federal preemption. This reform effort has been facilitated by the state's open-ended, standards-based jurisprudence which allows judges to adjust the law in response to external forces without having to explicitly acknowledge such efforts....

Reflecting the tenor behind judicial pronouncements about the risk of federal preemption, recent Delaware decisions suggest a trend toward stricter judicial scrutiny of director decision-making. Since June of 2002, the Delaware Supreme Court has reversed chancery court decisions in favor of defendant directors, and ruled for the shareholder-plaintiffs six times. This series of reversals represents a sharp departure from earlier patterns, in both the number of reversals and the number of pro-shareholder decisions. Moreover, the supreme court's jurisprudential shift has trickled down to the court of chancery, which apparently has taken heed of the supreme court's message after such an unusual string of reversals....

It is possible that Delaware would have proceeded on a path of reform absent the national debate that led to Sarbanes-Oxley. It is also possible that the recent jurisprudential shifts are simply a part of the natural norm evolution that characterizes the common law. Despite these possibilities, judicial comments expressing concern that Congress might displace Delaware's sovereignty provide a reason to explore other factors that might have contributed to this apparent shift.

Admittedly, the small number of cases [since Sarbanes-Oxley is a limited basis] for making ultimate conclusions about the proper role of federal and state governments in shaping corporate law rules. Nonetheless, a fundamental shift in Delaware corporate jurisprudence does seem to have occurred. Two Delaware judges (including the chief justice) have publicly stated their belief in the necessity of legal reforms in light of the scandals and the federal preemptive threat. In addition, corporate practitioners have taken notice of the courts' trend toward higher scrutiny of board decision-making. These lawyers' advice to their clients in light of these decisions further supports the inference that a shift in jurisprudence has occurred....

Looking Forward.... There is reason to suspect that if the federal threat recedes, Delaware will revert to its more lax jurisprudence. The history of Delaware law is replete with examples of the imposition of strict judicial standards, followed by prolonged periods of deference. The same indeterminacy that permits judges to impose more restrictive standards of director conduct can be used to relax such standards when the political climate changes. Though perhaps inescapable, this possibility only bolsters arguments for sustained federal engagement in corporate governance issues to prevent such retrenchment. Congress must continue to monitor corporate conduct, remaining apprised of developments in state corporate codes and jurisprudence. In addition, Congress must be willing to preempt objectionable state law rules.

Congress can maintain a credible preemptive threat by demonstrating a sustained interest in corporate governance issues. The SEC, through its enforcement and rule-making functions, should remain at the forefront of this vigilance. Congress can demonstrate its continued engagement by holding hearings on governance issues, investigating corporate misconduct, and actively overseeing the SEC's enforcement of federal securities laws, including the Sarbanes-Oxley Act.

Conclusion. The response in Congress and in Delaware to the recent corporate scandals demonstrates that the model of vertical regulatory competition framed in the Federalist Papers endures. This political dynamic also reveals flaws in modern federalist arguments denouncing national-level regulation. Unreflective allegiance to the internal affairs doctrine and the economic theories invoked in its defense should no longer serve to dissuade Congress from preempting objectionable provisions of state corporate law. Instead, the threat of federal preemption remains a necessary predicate to the ability of the national citizenry to pressure the state of Delaware to shape its corporate law to reflect national rather than parochial interests.

Selected References

Lucian A. Bebchuk & Assaf Hamdani, Vigorous Race or Leisurely Walk: Reconsidering the Competition over Corporate Charters, 112 Yale Law Journal 553 (2002).

William W. Bratton & Joseph A. McCahery, The New Economics of Jurisdictional Competition: Devolutionary Federalism in a Second-Best World, 86 Georgetown Law Journal 201 (1997).

George D. Brown, New Federalism's Unanswered Question: Who Should Prosecute State and Local Officials for Political Corruption?, 60 Washington & Lee Law Review 417 (2003).

Victor Brudney, Contract and Fiduciary Duty in Corporate Law, 38 Boston College Law Review 595 (1997).

William L. Cary, Federalism and Corporate Law: Reflections Upon Delaware, 83 Yale Law Journal 663 (1974).

John C. Coffee, Jr., What Caused Enron? A Capsule Social and Economic History of the 1990's, 89 Cornell Law Review 269 (2004).

Lawrence A. Cunningham, The Sarbanes-Oxley Yawn: Heavy Rhetoric, Light Reform (And It Just Might Work), 35 Connecticut Law Review 915 (2003).

Frank H. Easterbrook & Daniel R. Fischel, The Economic Structure of Corporate Law (1991).

Marcel Kahan & Ehud Kamar, The Myth of State Competition in Corporate Law, 55 Stanford Law Review 679 (2002).

Jonathan R. Macey & Geoffrey P. Miller, Toward an Interest Group Theory of Delaware Corporate Law, 65 Texas Law Review 469 (1987).

Michael A. Perino, Enron's Legislative Aftermath: Some Reflections on the Deterrence Aspects of the Sarbanes-Oxley Act of 2002, 76 St. John's Law Review 671 (2002).

Todd E. Pettys, Competing for the People's Affection: Federalism's Forgotten Marketplace, 56 Vanderbilt Law Review 329, 338–45 (2003).

Mark J. Roe, Delaware's Competition, 117 Harvard Law Review 588 (2003).

Roberta Romano, The Genius of American Corporate Law (1993).

Larry E. Ribstein, Market vs. Regulatory Responses to Corporate Fraud: A Critique of the Sarbanes-Oxley Act of 2002, 28 Iowa Journal of Corporation Law 1 (2002).

Leo E. Strine, Jr., Derivative Impact? Some Early Reflections on Corporate Law Implications of the Enron Debacle, 57 Business Lawyer 1371 (2002).

Charles M. Tiebout, A Pure Theory of Local Expenditures, 64 Journal of Political Economy 416 (1956).

Ralph K. Winter, Jr., State Law, Shareholder Protection and the Theory of the Corporation, 6 Journal of Legal Studies 251 (1977).

Further Reading (selected work by Reneé M. Jones)

Dynamic Federalism: Competition, Cooperation, and Securities Enforcement, 11 Connecticut Insurance Law Journal 108 (2004).

C. Contemporary Lawmaking

Chapter Seventeen

Private Standards in Public Law[*]

Government increasingly leverages its regulatory function by embodying in law standards that are promulgated and copyrighted by non-governmental organizations. Departures from such standards expose citizens to criminal, civil and administrative sanctions, yet private actors generate, control and limit access to them. Despite governmental ambitions, no one is responsible for evaluating the legitimacy of this approach *ex ante* and no framework exists to facilitate analysis. This Article contributes an analytical framework and proposes institutional mechanisms to implement it.

The lack of a comprehensive framework for evaluating copyright to standards embodied in law is surprising because the range of standards potentially affected is large and growing. It includes standards relating to accounting, consumer product safety, energy, government contracting, insurance, medicine, and telecommunications; codes for buildings, corporations and legal ethics; and manuals for stock exchange listings and scores of others.

To illustrate, it is a violation of federal law for any person to file required financial statements with the Securities and Exchange Commission (SEC) that are not in conformity with generally accepted accounting principles (GAAP) or for auditors to attest to such financial statements unless audited in accordance with generally accepted auditing standards (GAAS). The SEC has enforced these laws in thousands of administrative proceedings and hundreds of federal court cases asserting violations of GAAP and/or GAAS. Yet these accounting standards are not freely available to the public or to prosecuted persons. Instead they are claimed to be copyrighted by the so-called "private" standard-setters the SEC and/or Congress anoint to establish them.

---

  [*] **Lawrence A. Cunningham**, *Private Standards in Public Law: Copyright, Lawmaking and the Case of Accounting*, 104 Michigan Law Review 291 (2005), http://papers.ssrn.com/abstract_id=677647.

This Article develops a three-part classification scheme to facilitate analysis of the copyright-eligibility of such works based on how privately-generated standards are embodied in public law. Otherwise copyright-eligible works can assume attributes of law potentially ineligible for copyright through three routes: by passing reference in legal materials (weak form), by incorporation into law after creation (semi-strong form), or by *ex ante* governmental-designation of the standard setter as an officially-recognized body (strong form). This Article's framework facilitates analysis of all private standards embodied in public law; its case study of accounting standards is especially useful because their complex generation process provides illustrations of each class in this scheme.

Specifically (a) contemporary auditing standards are generated by a recent Congressionally-created and publicly-funded body (the Public Company Accounting Oversight Board, PCAOB) (strong form route); (b) contemporary accounting principles are generated by a single SEC-recognized and publicly-funded body (the Financial Accounting Standards Board, FASB) whose standards for three decades have been incorporated by the SEC (semi-strong form route); and (c) auditing and accounting standards were set before these bodies were created by a private not-for-profit professional association (the American Institute of Certified Public Accountants, AICPA) whose standards were given the SEC's imprimatur by reference (weak form route).

Generally, under the framework this Article proposes, copyright is (a) not recognized in the strong form route; (b) recognized and generally continued in the weak form route (subject to qualifying conventions such as compulsory licensing and broadened fair use); and (c) derecognized in the semi-strong form route when factors concerning the author, the work, the copier and the governmental relation to each bear features more akin to the strong form than to the weak form. For accounting standards, this means that PCAOB work cannot be copyrighted; AICPA work retains copyright, subject to some qualifying conventions; and most FASB work becomes ineligible for copyright.

These copyright adjustments are necessary to provide requisite access to standards. Otherwise, persons seeking access face considerable obstacles. In the case of accounting standards, only the most straightforward portions are available without charge on the Internet; others must be purchased from standard setters. Those wishing to copy materials must apply for permission and pay fees, which can require numerous inquiries of the standard setters and consume months of diligent effort. Copiers must pay or risk lawsuits, with nothing to rely upon but notoriously uncertain defenses to copyright infringement claims....

Two matters of administrative law arise that this Article's framework also helps to analyze. First, embodying private standards in public law can amount to abdication of lawmaking functions, violating traditional principles limiting lawmaker power to delegate this function to private parties. Delegation risks should be insignificant in the weak form route because embodiment is limited and insignificant in the strong form route because the promulgator is a recognized lawmaker. They may be considerable in the semi-strong form route, however. Second, federal governmental agencies may incorporate by reference private standards in public law without following requisite rulemaking procedures or publication requirements, likely posing issues in semi-strong form cases but not in weak or strong form circumstances.

For the federal government, this Article proposes to require the Director of the *Federal Register* to classify standards embodied in law according to this Article's three-part framework and to administer related copyright effects. It also contemplates that the Director would police impermissible delegation of lawmaking functions to private actors and assure agency compliance with publication requirements. The proposed regulatory approach to copyright consequences is necessary because of institutional limitations on the federal judiciary's competence to provide a comprehensive *ex ante* framework. Short of the regulatory solution, however, guidance developed in this Article should aid courts in resolving disputes....

Ancient Concepts. Since Roman times, a central feature of a law-based civilization is public access to legal materials. The ancient concepts were adopted early in United States history when the Supreme Court announced in the classic cases of *Wheaton v. Peters* and *Banks v. Manchester* that judicial opinions cannot be protected by copyright. A critical rationale is that these opinions bind all citizens and so must be "free for publication to all" (what might somewhat simply be called the public domain rationale). A related rationale is that judges need no incentives to generate written legal opinions because this production function is an essential component of their work assignment (call this the incentives rationale). The same rationales apply to legislative enactments, making these likewise ineligible for copyright. These principles apply to all judicial opinions and statutes constituting law, both federal and state. They encompass regulations and rules of administrative bodies and local governmental entities.

In the Copyright Act of 1976, Congress furthered these ancient concepts by extending relinquishment of claims to copyright for any work of the United States government. Relinquishment does not reach works of other governmental entities nor does it automatically extend to work that federal agencies commission from independent contractors. In the latter context, the Copyright Act's legislative history provides guidance to federal agencies. It suggests that copyright would be (a) inappropriate when the independent contractor produces work the agency could produce itself but (b) appropriate when denying it "would be unfair or would hamper the production and publication of important works." The issue is balancing the need for free access to the work with the need of the private author to secure a copyright. Thus where government would be incapable of inducing the work's production except through copyright protection, copyright may be justified.

Modern Standards. Contemporary production of legal materials relies significantly and increasingly on private-sector standard setters, whose products are embodied in law by legislatures, regulators, courts, and other governmental authorities. Fitting these standards into the ancient concepts making law ineligible for copyright is not as easy as declaring that legislative and judicial pronouncements are ineligible for copyright. Apart from ambiguity as to whether they constitute law in the way legislation and court decisions do, neither public domain concerns (of due process and free access) nor inherent incentives of lawmakers to produce law are as obvious. Even the somewhat more involved balancing inquiry used to assess suitability of copyright to government works prepared by independent contractors does not readily resolve such cases.

A prominent illustration is the Fifth Circuit's divided *en banc* opinion in a 2002 case concerning municipalities adopting as law a privately-generated building code (*Veeck v. Southern Bldg. Code Congress Int'l, Inc.*). The eight-member *en banc* majority emphasized that legislative adoption rendered the code law and this, *ipso facto*, put it in the public domain, ineligible for copyright. The six-member *en banc* dissent (through two separate opinions) emphasized the need to consider incentive effects of such a conclusion on future production of kindred materials. Each side recognized the legitimacy of the other's argument: the dissenters observed that the case raised no due process or free access issues (the copier was neither charged with nor prosecuted for any violation of law) and the majority observed that no incentives were upset because the private standard-setter in question promulgated standards principally for the purpose of getting them enacted into law.

Dividing the majority and dissents in *Veeck* was also disagreement as to the proper role of intermediate federal appellate courts in resolving such a profound issue of public policy (not merely of law, but posing novel legal issues in a complex public policy context). Thus while all the court's judges appeared to accept the basic policy stakes as pitting public domain concerns against incentive effects on production, they emphasized different aspects of these competing policy objectives.

What makes *Veeck* a difficult case is that the standards at issue were adopted (a) formally rather than in passing and (b) in full and after the fact. Point (a) made it difficult for the majority to shrug off adoption as one might a passing judicial reference to a professional standard in a negligence case; point (b) made it difficult for the dissents to accept the impaired incentives entailed by copyright vitiation upon the code's adoption as law. This combination of points marks relatively easier cases at each end of the spectrum: (1) passing reference in legal materials to standards does not make standards law with copyright-destroying effects (even *Veeck's* majority makes this clear) and (2) formal *ex ante* anointment of an organization to prepare standards bearing binding legal effects can destroy copyright (even *Veeck's* dissents appear to accept this, certainly when due process issues arise).

Three-Part Classification. A three-part classification scheme thus emerges, as both a descriptive and normative matter. The classes within the threefold classification scheme by which standards become embodied in law may be called for convenience: weak form, semi-strong form and strong form. Descriptively, this framework derives from reconciling judicial opinions in cases like *Veeck*; normatively, it enables capturing the important factors relevant to conducting requisite public policy balancing inquiries: the author's identity, the nature of the work, the identity and nature of the copier, and the relation of the governmental entity to the author, work and copier. Consider some illustrations.

Standards take the weak form route into law by reference, as when courts admit authoritative materials into evidence to evaluate a defendant's potential liability. Judicial references to *Gray's Anatomy* to help define a physician's standard of care do not destroy copyright in that work. The author and the work are autonomous from any governmental action and the governmental use arises in a discrete context. Derecognizing copyright is not necessary as a due process matter because the referenced text does not formally bind all or a class of citizens *ex ante* but is used in a particular judicial evaluation; letting such judicial use vitiate copyright in particular works would destroy copyright altogether, eliminating all incentives copyright offers.

This class is as widespread as the legal regime it ultimately but indirectly serves—and is growing in size as more standards are embodied in law. Critical to traditional jurisprudential recognition of such references, however, is both their authoritative status and their accessibility. As this class of standards embodied in law grows, these attributes assume greater social significance, requiring more formal assurance that the standards are widely available to affected persons.

The semi-strong form route occurs through adoption when, as in *Veeck*, a legislative body formally enacts a standard as law. As the split court in *Veeck* attests, this context poses considerable difficulties. The author may or may not seek to contribute its work to the fabric of law, the work itself may or may not assume characteristics of a law-like codification, and the governmental interest in it may be expressed by wholesale adoption or cut-and-paste adaptation. Difficult issues arise from these differences in the exercise of balancing free access and due process on the one hand with the incentive effects on prospective producers of such standards on the other. This class can be sizable, including, for example, the American Bar Association's *Model Code of Professional Responsibility* adopted by many state supreme courts and promulgations of the Gas Industry Standards Board embodied in regulations of the Federal Energy Regulatory Commission.

The strong form route of standards-into-law arises by ordainment, as where a governmental authority anoints a designated standard-setter to produce materials the authority itself could produce. This is the functional equivalent of legislative enactment. In contrast to weak form adoption, this is an outright assignment of the task and comprehensive embrace of the work to bind all those to whom the legal, regulatory and standard-setting framework speaks; in contrast to semi-strong form adoption, those features negate incentive concerns. This class appears likely to have few members at present, but could become an increasingly appealing governmental policy option.

A distinguishing feature of this class of strong form standards-into-law is how standards form the *corpus* of the law governing those addressed. They do not merely inform the legal basis for negligence and other transgressions to which passing references (weak form adoption) may be applied, but constitute the fabric of that law. As a result, covered persons need knowledge of these standards to comply with law, as do lawyers advising them. In these respects, such materials are *de facto* law. The source of this distinguishing feature is formal legislative and administrative anointment of the body as an official legal standard-setter, needing none of the incentives that copyright provides.

These descriptive illustrations can be summarized abstractly. Component variables reveal the ultimate policy tension as balancing incentive needs with access needs. Conceptually, the framework relates trade-off relativity as follows: weak form embodiment circumstances are characterized by greater incentive needs for producers and lesser access needs for users while strong form embodiment circumstances are characterized by lesser incentive needs for producers and greater access needs for users (semi-strong embodiment circumstances are characterized by needs of intermediate orders). The following summarizes:

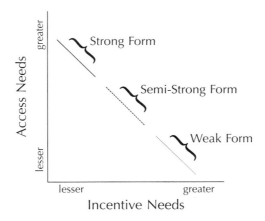

As to author identity and the nature of a work, private actors producing materials for purposes other than embodiment in law epitomize the weak form route (non-copyright incentives may be low), while officially anointed actors creating standards for embodiment in law epitomize the strong form route (non-copyright incentives suffice). As to user identify, persons who are members of a class affected by a standard embodied in law signal the strong form route (class access is critical), while randomly affected persons associate with the weak form route (*public* access is not compelling). The governmental relation to each likewise drives towards the strong form route when government's role is consciously a lawmaking function and towards the weak form route in opposite cases....

Governmental Strategy. All governmental uses of privately-promulgated standards are intended, in part, to conserve governmental resources. Government seeks to leverage its regulatory effectiveness and oversight by piggybacking on costs expended in the private sector. At least in the case of the federal government, it simultaneously seeks to preserve copyright in those privately-promulgated standards.

This two-fold policy is at war with itself.... Optimizing leverage necessarily entails reduced copyright protection. While these competing objectives cannot easily be reconciled, trade-offs can be crystallized using this Article's three-class scheme to relate the leverage function to its copyright consequences.

Optimal leverage from using private standard-setters occurs by the strategy that minimizes use of governmental resources while maximizing achievement of regulatory objectives. Resource conservation is maximized when private standards are used by passing reference, incorporating benefits of privately-produced standards without associated costs. But while this weak form route maximizes resource conservation, it may not maximize regulatory objectives. Maximizing regulatory objectives is achieved through the strong form route standards take into law, by formal designation of a statutory standard-setter; optimization is achieved when costs are met by a governmentally-directed function, but not from governmental revenues. Intermediate leveraging occurs through the semi-strong form route.

Apart from leverage, governmental strategy of embodying private standards in public law using the semi-strong form route confronts two administrative law constraints. First, constitutional principles nearly as old as those prohibiting copyrighting judicial opinions limit governmental delegation of lawmaking functions to private parties. There may be some legitimate room for permitting private parties to perform lawmaking functions. But the assignment poses considerable questions of legitimacy and implicates transcendent issues of democracy. Second, a powerful norm pulsing through the administrative lawmaking function requires publication of regulatory promulgations in the spirit of open government and public access to law. Federal lawmakers respect these animating themes by comporting with due process footings upon which such laws are founded. Steps include publication of adopted laws....

Strong Form. When a governmental authority promulgates standards for embodiment in law, no question of copyright arises, either because the standards assume the status of legislative enactment *per se* as a matter of due process (constitutional law) or because of the government works doctrine (the Copyright Act). Hundreds of federal agencies promulgate standards of various kinds routinely. A prominent example is the National Institute of Standards and Technology, created in 1901 as a non-regulatory federal agency within the Commerce Department to promote standards in a broad cross-section of fields. The National Institute of Standards and Technology makes its Web site and its content widely accessible, noting that most "information presented on these pages is considered public information and may be distributed or copied."

In turn, federal law requires copies of governmentally-generated standards to be deposited with the National Technical Information Service. This Service is the federal government's clearinghouse for scientific, technical information produced by or for federal agencies. Information includes results from scientific and engineering research, as well as economic and market information relevant to business and industry. This Service catalogues, organizes, and disseminates resulting materials (totaling some 3 million items) to business, industry, academia and the general public. According to its Web site, the Service "receives no appropriations and sustains its operations through the sale of such documents to the public and by providing related information-dissemination services to other Federal agencies."

One step removed from direct governmental production of standards is the anointment of a designated standard-setter to produce standards embodied in law using the strong-form route. To date, PCAOB appears to be the sole example of a governmental standard-setter Congress designates as residing outside the formal boundaries of the federal government. Internal federal standard-setters abound and numerous federal corporations exist, but the latter do not generally produce standards embodied in law as PCAOB does. PCAOB's public-body characteristics, moreover, alleviate concerns that Congressional delegations of lawmaking power to it are unconstitutional or illegitimate and PCAOB follows to a tee the publication and other requirements necessary to the legitimacy of administrative agency lawmaking.

Despite absence of federal PCAOB-equivalents, the PCAOB model may be appealing to governmental agencies.... [F]ederal agencies may elicit superior standard-setting from private organizations by threatening to persuade Congress to follow a similar route in their regulatory domain. If necessary funding sources can be obtained outside the federal budget as with PCAOB, this can be an ideal way to generate standards while retaining regulatory control. Such an approach would also substantially eliminate difficulties associated with copyright to standards embodied in law.

Weak Form. While Dr. Samuel Johnson quipped that no one but a blockhead writes, except for money, the volumes of materials published suggest the cynicism in this hyperbole. The vast majority of such materials likely would be produced even absent copyright incentives to do so (so long as attribution norms are maintained). Nevertheless, copyright is designed to provide incrementally requisite incentives—not quite rewards—for this labor and its utilitarian underpinnings justify preserving such incentives, if only to promote production of the minority of materials for which copyright is an inducement. Thus passing references to these materials, even to contribute significantly to deciding a judicial case or prescribing a legislative or regulatory policy, should respect such copyright....

[G]overnmental leverage is exploited by avoiding costs to generate standards. Preserving copyright promotes incentives for numerous standard setters to vie for regulatory recognition, helping the regulator to a menu of alternatives. Provided materials are sufficiently available and recognized to justify such invocation, public domain concerns of due process and access diminish to the vanishing point....

... Thus copyright is not vitiated by: (1) federal court rules requiring attorneys to follow *The Bluebook: A Uniform System of Citation*, published by a group of law school journals; (2) an agency limiting reimbursable dental benefits to those listed in the reference work *Current Dental Terminology*, published by the American Dental Association; or (3) an agency limiting reimbursement for medical costs associated with mental disorders listed in *Diagnostic & Statistical Manual of Mental Disorders*, published by the American Psychiatric Association. In each case, constitutional and prudential limitations assure related access. Such materials would not be entitled to such recognition unless they were readily available for access.

When such materials supply a more general basis of legal obligations, additional qualifying conventions are necessary.... Weak form references to these standards may not justify vitiating related copyright, but as sources of functional law, qualifying doctrines of fair use, compulsory licensing, or regulations mandating access are necessary to meet due process requirements. Attention to the role of rights to create derivative works can also be important. At present, however, no mechanism exists for establishing these administrative necessities, except on an *ad hoc* basis through federal adjudication.

Semi-Strong Form. Between the relatively easy classes of cases arising under the strong and weak form routes standards take into law are the more difficult cases following the semi-strong form route. In this context, a private-sector cottage industry promulgates standards, to which copyright's incentive structures may or may not contribute. Participants include organizations pursuing broad-gauged standard-setting and dissemination efforts and specialized industry standard setters.

How lawmakers embody standards produced by such organizations into public law varies. Some governmental authorities affirmatively encourage agencies to adopt private standards. Congress did so for the federal government in the National Technology and Transfer Act, directing agencies to adopt private sector standards whenever practicable and appropriate; executive branch implementing guidance directed agencies to preserve copyright in such standards when embodied in law. Agencies follow a regulated and routine process when doing so. This process differs somewhat from traditional administrative rulemaking, particularly as to publication requirements.

In traditional administrative rulemaking, agencies are required to publish resulting promulgations in the *Federal Register*. When embodying private standards in public law, however, Congress authorizes agencies to sidestep the publication requirement using an exception known as incorporation by reference. In particular, the Freedom of Information Act and implementing regulations direct that agencies incorporate copyrighted standards by reference into agency regulations. Rather than publish embodied standards in the *Federal Register* in full, agencies simply refer to them.

To be eligible for incorporation by reference under the statute, an agency must determine that standards are reasonably available to the class of persons affected by the publication. Agencies must then submit proposed regulations to the Office of the Federal Register, and regulations only become effective when published in the *Federal Register*. The Director of the Federal Register is charged with reviewing such submissions for approval or disapproval. The Director's review includes a determination that materials incorporated by reference are reasonably available.

Reasonable availability does not require that materials be free. In fact, while some standard setters do not require payment for reproduction, it is common for them to charge fees to defray associated publication and overhead costs. They tend to follow the approach the National Technical Information Service uses by charging fees to recoup associated production costs (likely to be far more essential than copyright royalties to generate production). However, nothing prevents standard setters from charging the monopoly rates that copyright law facilitates ... or limiting third-party creation of derivative works. Nor does the process require lawmakers to publish resulting standards according to usual administrative practice.

The same process — with associated infirmities — applies when federal statutes direct agencies to incorporate private standards. To illustrate, the Consumer Product Safety Act directs the Consumer Product Safety Commission (CPSC) to use private standards when possible and consistent with regulatory objectives. CPSC adopted regulations governing testing bicycle helmets that incorporated by reference standards promulgated by private organizations. Regulations indicate that the Director of the Federal Register approved incorporation by reference. Following the Director's guidelines, CPSC states the name and addresses of the standards organizations from which copies of these standards are available and that they are available for copying from the Secretary of the CPSC. They are not published in the *Federal Register....*

Administration. Alternative institutional arrangements may be designed to facilitate classifying standards embodied in law for copyright and lawmaking purposes. For the federal government, an existing central participant in the embodiment process is the Director of the Federal Register, who oversees the process and can be assigned the additional task of classification. State and local governmental authorities would follow similar procedures in conformity with respective administrative and legal infrastructures.

The Director of the Federal Register would be charged with evaluating the route taken, as weak, semi-strong or strong. The Director would determine the copyright effect of embodiment, applying the factors discussed in this Article. In all strong form cases, no copyright may be granted. In other cases, classification analysis and copyright effects would proceed as follows.

In weak form cases, copyright may be maintained, so long as the Director confirms that designated materials are widely available (this is an evaluation the Director makes under existing practice). If not, the Director should suggest to the submitting agency that it require access by regulation. Failing this, the Director must determine whether compulsory licensing is necessary. In this determination, the Director would coordinate with the Librarian of Congress, the Copyright Office and Copyright Royalty Judges. These bodies are currently required to participate in administering the Copyright Act's existing compulsory licensing arrangements. All possess expertise to guide the Director in making necessary determinations.

In semi-strong form cases, the Director should make two procedural determinations, likely already required but worth emphasizing. First, to police delegation, agencies must exercise judgment and reach an independent determination of appropriateness as to private standards they embody in public law, to respect basic concepts reposing lawmaking functions in lawmakers. Second, to promote legitimacy, the Director should scrutinize incorporation by reference practices to concord with due process norms pervading traditional administrative processes, particularly concerning publication. In certain circumstances, the agency mandate to make materials publicly available may not be met by incorporation by reference but may require publication in the *Federal Register*.

In semi-strong form cases, the Director must make substantive determinations as to whether copyright is derecognized. If so, the government must determine whether, and to what extent, embodiment constitutes a taking under the Constitution. Not all embodiments constitute takings, particularly for standards whose authors intend them for this purpose. Such standard setters effectively grant an implied license to governmental entities to embody the standards in law. License scope includes permitting citizens to use such works, negating takings claims. Many embodiments that are takings will amount to taking a relatively modest property interest. After all, under copyright doctrine, the scope of protection provided to standards is thin, even before embodiment in law.

For such evaluations, the Director would follow existing procedures governing governmental takings, specifically those denominated as regulatory takings. Under existing law, administrative agencies are empowered to exercise judgments concerning takings rights, claims and proceedings, subject to judicial oversight. In the proposed framework, the Director would require each agency to make such a determination but would also have *de novo* review over agency judgments. Similar to weak form cases, the Director of the Federal Register would consult with the Librarian of Congress, the Copyright Office and Copyright Royalty Judges in reaching determinations. Directorial decisions would remain subject to judicial review for adequacy and constitutionality, as under existing law....

Selected References

Will Durant, Caesar and Christ: The Story of Civilization (1944).

Dennis S. Karjala, Distinguishing Patent and Copyright Subject Matter, 35 Connecticut Law Review 439 (2003).

William M. Landes & Richard A. Posner, The Economic Structure of Intellectual Property Law (2003).

Joseph P. Liu, Regulatory Copyright, 83 North Carolina Law Review 87 (2004).

L. Ray Patterson & Craig Joyce, Monopolizing the Law: The Scope of Copyright Protection for Law Reports and Statutory Compilations, 36 UCLA Law Review 719 (1989).

Richard J. Pierce, Jr., et al., Administrative Law and Process (3d ed. 1999).

Sidney A. Shapiro, Outsourcing Government Regulation, 53 Duke Law Journal 389 (2003).

Alfred C. Yen, Restoring the Natural Law: Copyright as Labor and Possession, 51 Ohio State Law Journal 517 (1990).

Cases, Statutes, Regulations

Banks v. Manchester, 128 U.S. 244 (1888).

Carter v. Carter Coal Co., 298 U.S. 238 (1936).

Nash v. Lathrop, 6 N.E. 559 (Mass. 1886).

Veeck v. Southern Bldg. Code Congress Int'l, Inc., 293 F.3d 791 (5th Cir. 2002) (*en banc*), *cert. denied* 539 U.S. 969 (2003).

Wheaton v. Peters, 33 U.S. (8 Pet.) 591, 668 (1834).

Administrative Procedure Act, §552(a)(1)(D).

Federal Advisory Committee Act, Pub. L. No. 92-463, 86 Stat. 770 (1972).

Federal Register Act, 44 U.S.C. §1507.

National Technology and Transfer Act of 1995, Public Law 104-113, §12(d), 110 Stat. 783 (1996).

OMB Circular A-119, 63 Fed. Reg. 8545, 8555 (Feb. 19, 1998).

Sarbanes-Oxley Act of 2002, Pub. L. No. 107-204, §109.

Further Reading
(selected work by Lawrence A. Cunningham)

Law and Accounting: Cases and Materials (West 2005).

Introductory Accounting, Finance and Auditing for Lawyers (West 4th ed. 2004).

Choosing Gatekeepers: The Financial Statement Insurance Alternative to Auditor Liability, 52 UCLA Law Review 413 (2004).

Sharing Accounting's Burden: Business Lawyers in Enron's Dark Shadows, 57 Business
    Lawyer 1421 (2002).

CHAPTER EIGHTEEN

UNCERTAIN RISK[*]

… [I]nquiring about the risks of placing mercury in one's mouth, in the form of a dental filling, is likely to meet with resounding assurances of safety from the dental profession. According to the American Dental Association, "dental amalgam has been studied and reviewed extensively, and has established an extensively reviewed record of safety and effectiveness." While such comforting disclaimers are meant to ease patient concerns, many continue to worry about the safety of dental mercury.…

Despite [a] long and contentious history, there has been very little case law or clinical research dealing directly with mercury amalgams.… [I]t remains unclear exactly how much mercury enters the body from fillings, as well as at exactly what levels mercury becomes harmful to humans. While the debate over the scientific validity of mercury's perceived health risks continues, patient concerns about amalgams are quite genuine. And, because such patients view mercury risks as material to their decisions regarding treatment options, the doctrine of informed consent should apply. Nevertheless, the dental profession has basically ignored its duty to disclose material risks and has taken overt measures to ban its members from discussing potential risks with patients.…

[W]hile a patient's legal right to information concerning the risks and benefits of amalgams should be straightforward, the interplay of professional regulation with state statutory and tort law, FDA regulations, and the shadow of federal preemption add to the uncertainties and worries of dental patients. Only by disentangling conflicting concerns and competing strategies can a dental patient's right to informed and autonomous decision-making be effectuated.…

Professional Regulation: ADA Hostility to the Anti-Amalgam Position. An amalgam is a mixture of metals, and dental mercury amalgams are comprised of approximately 50% mercury, 35% silver, 9% tin, 6% copper, and trace amounts of zinc. Although the mixture is soft at first, it eventually hardens

---

[*] **Mary Ann Chirba-Martin**, *An Uncertain Risk and an Uncertain Future: Assessing the Legal Implications of Mercury Amalgam Fillings*, 14 HEALTH MATRIX 293 (2004) (co-authored with Carolyn M. Welshhans), http://papers.ssrn.com/abstract_id=780325.

and the mercury is bound within it. [S]mall amounts of mercury are released slowly from the filling into the body due to factors such as corrosion, chewing, and grinding of the teeth.... Among the purported advantages are mercury amalgam's lower costs, easier use, and greater durability as compared to alternative materials. The ADA therefore lends its dentists' seal of approval to a variety of amalgam products, an action that some challenge as a conflict of interest because the ADA allegedly is paid for such endorsements....

... [T]he United States government, acting primarily through the FDA, has largely deferred to the ADA's position that mercury amalgams are highly beneficial and pose only slight risks in rare cases. Nevertheless, the FDA does acknowledge that it lacks the information necessary to state with certainty that mercury amalgam is entirely safe. In response to growing pressures from consumer safety advocates, the FDA decided in 2002 to reclassify dental amalgam from a Class I to a Class II device. This change requires dental amalgam manufacturers to list all ingredients on the product's label and encourages dentists and patients to report side effects as "adverse events." ... Nevertheless, the FDA continues to share the ADA's position on mercury amalgam safety, justifying the new classification as protecting those few individuals who may be allergic to mercury.

Despite the assurances of the FDA and ADA, many continue to question the safety of mercury amalgam and the wisdom behind placing mercury in one's mouth. The growing concern about long-term exposure to even small amounts of mercury is demonstrated by changing practice patterns in the dental profession. In 2001, 24% of dentists used no mercury fillings at all. This figure represented an increase of almost 15% in just four years of dentists who refused to use mercury amalgams....

The ADA's ethical rules, which typically are adopted in similar form by state dental boards, reflect the ADA's suspicions about dentists who advocate mercury removal. Rule 5.A states that "dentists shall not represent the care being rendered to their patients in a false or misleading manner." An advisory opinion on this rule explains that:

> Based on current scientific data, the ADA has determined that the removal of amalgam restorations from the non-allergic patient for the alleged purpose of removing toxic substances from the body, when such treatment is performed solely at the recommendation or suggestion of the dentist, is improper and unethical. The same principle of veracity applies to the dentist's recommendation concerning the removal of any dental restorative material.

A dentist who is found guilty of violating the ADA Code of Ethics may be sentenced, censured, suspended, or expelled from the ADA....

One early example of professional discipline in this context is the 1990 case of *Board of Dental Examiners v. Hufford*, which involved a dentist who advised a full mouth extraction of his patient's mercury-filled teeth in order to arrest the progression of her multiple sclerosis. Iowa's state dental board suspended Dr. Hufford's license for five years on the grounds that extracting all of his patient's teeth was fraudulent and violated numerous statutes and professional rules pertaining to the practice of dentistry. Dr. Hufford appealed the board's ruling, emphasizing that the patient affirmatively sought him out specifically because of his anti-amalgam position.

Although the court acknowledged this fact, it focused on Dr. Hufford's failure to explicitly discuss the majority position on mercury amalgam safety. Of even greater concern to the court, however, were the prohibitive costs of alternative treatments, which led the patient to choose the less expensive, but riskier, full mouth extraction. In the court's view, these price figures indicated that Dr. Hufford did not believe his amalgam position, but rather was interested in the personal profit he could obtain from the removal procedure. In this regard, the court referred to the dentistry board's findings that Dr. Hufford did not extract the teeth for dental reasons—but, again, that board was not about to recognize reducing mercury exposure as a valid reason for treatment.

While the *Hufford* facts raise issues of informed consent and duty of care, the disciplinary board and court minimized the significance of the patient's wishes. Instead, both the state dental board and the affirming court unequivocally embraced the ADA's position on mercury amalgam's unconditional safety. What is even more troubling, however, was their endorsement of the ADA's view that critics of its viewpoint must be motivated by more sinister concerns than patient health and respect for patient autonomy. As the 1990s continued, dentists who advocated against mercury amalgams were subjected to further state dental association disciplinary proceedings. Although brought before state commissions, these actions and their later court appeals continued to involve the ADA and its position on several levels. State dental associations and disciplinary boards not only adopted the ADA's position as a matter of routine, but the board members themselves often belonged to the ADA as well.

This deeply entrenched reluctance to countenance open discourse on the risks of mercury amalgam was further stoked by the courts, which were bound to employ deferential standards of appellate review on such matters. *Breiner v. State Dental Commission* illustrates the strong ties between the ADA and state dental commissions. It therefore demonstrates the obstacles facing anti-amalgam dentists, which have led some to charge the ADA with engaging in a "witch-hunt" of anti-amalgam dentists. In *Breiner*, a dentist was brought before the state dental commission for "incompetent or fraudulent conduct by claiming that the removal of mercury amalgam fillings could alleviate symptoms of various medical conditions." These charges, which attacked the dentist's views and advice rather than a concrete episode of actual treatment, were brought not by his patients, but by other dentists. Thus, *Breiner* evidences the willingness of the ADA and state boards to discipline dentists for their viewpoints, even when those beliefs may not translate into harmful dental procedures....

[T]he ADA no longer relies solely on its influence over professional discipline to effectuate its views on mercury amalgam. The ADA has recently entered into a new type of discipline: litigation aimed at defending its reputation and discouraging further lawsuits by patient-plaintiffs against mercury amalgam. For example, [in *American Dental Association v. Khorrami*] after a Los Angeles attorney sued the ADA on behalf of patient-plaintiffs claiming that mercury amalgam caused autism in children, the Association countersued the attorney on the grounds of defamation. The ADA allege[d] that the lawyer falsely accused it "of defrauding and endangering the lives of the American public by promoting allegedly unsafe dental practices—specifically the use of dental amalgam fillings—and of exerting 'undue and unfair pressure' on dentists as a result of a purported 'vested economic interest' of the ADA in amalgam." ... The ADA has also intervened in mercury amalgam suits brought by patient-plaintiffs in which the ADA argues in favor of mercury amalgam's safety.

While undoubtedly designed to quash the debate over amalgam safety, the ADA's litigation strategy seems to have achieved the very opposite result. It has angered some dentists, generated bad press for the ADA, and exacerbated the already deep divide between pro- and anti-amalgamists. It has also placed those dentists who would fall into the "middle" in an increasingly difficult "Catch 22." ...

Informed Consent: Litigation Alone Cannot Protect Patient Safety or Autonomy. Despite—or perhaps because of—the ADA's efforts to extinguish the amalgam controversy, the anti-amalgam movement continues to grow, with patient-plaintiffs taking the lead in a new wave of personal injury litigation. These cases do not involve actions for negligent mercury amalgam removal but, rather, allege negligent non-removal of mercury fillings and/or lack of informed consent involving their original insertion. Like most claims of professional negligence and/or product liability, plaintiffs need to rely upon expert testimony to prove that mercury amalgam generally causes adverse health effects and specifically caused the health problems in the individual plaintiff's case. While such litigation in the amalgam context is embryonic at best, lessons gleaned from these cases to date as well as from other product liability cases predict that any barriers erected by the ADA are likely to pale in comparison with the difficulties in overcoming *Daubert* requirements for evidentiary admissibility.

As they do in all forms of product safety and medical malpractice litigation, the *Daubert* standards are likely to vex the mercury amalgam issue and generate pages of conflicting judicial opinions about the viability of such claims. In *Daubert v. Merrell Dow Pharmaceuticals, Inc.*, the United States Supreme Court enunciated a standard by which the judge is required to have a gate-keeping role, in which "the trial judge must ensure that any and all scientific testimony or evidence admitted is not only relevant, but reliable." While *Daubert* seemed to suggest that expert testimony that had the potential for "misleading the jury" could be addressed through Federal Rule of Evidence 403, later courts have concluded that the purpose behind *Daubert's* gate-keeping function is to preserve the integrity and efficacy of a trial's fact-finding function by keeping "unreliable and irrelevant information" from the jury.

[*Daubert* directs attention to the following special factors]: (1) whether the theory or technique can be tested; (2) whether it has been subjected to peer review; (3) whether the technique has a high known or potential rate of error; and (4) whether the theory has attained general acceptance within the scientific community. Although the *Daubert* factors were intended to function as a nonexclusive set of guidelines rather than a closed set of inflexible requirements, their application in practice has served to preclude much expert testimony, particularly in the absence of supporting epidemiology. In the context of dental mercury, the ADA's and amalgam manufacturers' investment in the status quo provides no incentive to conduct epidemiological studies. Even under optimal circumstances, conclusive epidemiological results would be difficult to obtain given the diverse nature, potentially low prevalence, and under-reporting of adverse health effects....

For these reasons, mercury amalgam plaintiffs are likely to encounter formidable barriers to reaching the merits of their claims due to a lack of admissible scientific evidence of causation, particularly in the form of epidemiological studies conducted on human subjects. Studies conducted on sheep, monkeys and rats have demonstrated the correlation between mercury and adverse health effects such as immune suppression, neurotoxicity, renal impairments, and multiple sclerosis, as well as adverse health effects passed from mother to fetus, including brain damage, incoordination, blindness, and seizures. They also indicate that mercury can be transmitted across the placenta and through breast-feeding, a link further acknowledged by the United States Department of Health and Human Services. While they are only animal studies, they still cast doubt on the ADA's findings of no statistically significant effects in humans....

Since patient personal injury litigation is likely to be so hindered by *Daubert* problems, the ADA's confidence in its pro-amalgam position will surely endure. Perhaps, however, such litigation may finally force the ADA to substantiate its own claims of amalgam safety instead of relying so heavily on such tactics as challenging the gaps in plaintiffs' evidence or gagging candid discourse among its own members. Dental professionals allegedly have hesitated to fund and participate in in-depth studies of the effects of mercury amalgam. The ADA itself cannot point to any large scale epidemiological studies to substantiate its conclusion that amalgam fillings pose no greater health risks than non-metallic composites....

State Statutes: The Best Protection for Patients. While the ADA has succeeded in maintaining the dominance of its position on amalgams through its use of professional discipline and the successful defense against personal injury and consumer protection litigation, anti-amalgam advocates have made significant inroads at the state legislative level.... [A] growing number of state legislatures are at least considering the imposition of a duty upon dentists to discuss the risks of mercury amalgam with their patients. These statutes should directly affect both the practice of dentistry and the discipline of that profession. It may also have the indirect but no less dramatic impact of opening an alternative route of litigation for patients and consumer safety advocates under a theory of statutory violation.

The earliest statute to address mercury amalgam risks appeared in California. Popularly known as Proposition 65, the statute was enacted by statewide initiative in 1986. Proposition 65 is not specific to dental amalgams; rather, it requires users of identified reproductive toxins, including mercury and mercury amalgams, to warn employees and patients of the risks of exposure to these products.... Proposition 65 has been used successfully to compel dentists to warn their patients of mercury's potential toxicity. Maine ... enacted an even more specific statute that requires any dentist who uses mercury amalgam in any dental procedure to display a poster in the waiting area and provide each patient with a brochure about mercury amalgam....

Despite the early promise of the state statutory movement in fostering consumer choice while side-stepping *Daubert's* hurdles, it is not without problems. In addition to the countless difficulties in getting a law passed and enforced, the ADA and amalgam producers will argue that such statutes are preempted by federal law. While they have yet to succeed on this point, current Supreme Court opinions create enough loopholes and ambiguities to ensure that vulnerability to preemption is a serious concern.

In *Committee of Dental Amalgam Manufacturers and Distributors v. Stratton,* for example, amalgam manufactures sought a declaratory judgment that California's Proposition 65 was preempted by the Medical Device Amendments ("MDA") to the Food, Drug, and Cosmetics Act ("FDCA"). Both the district and appellate courts found that dental amalgam did constitute a medical device, thereby bringing it within the purviews of the MDA. The issue thus became whether Proposition 65's warning requirements were preempted by the MDA. Section 360(k) of the MDA provides:

> No state or political subdivision of a state may establish or continue in effect with respect to a device intended for human use any requirement: "(1) which is different from, or in addition to, any requirement applicable under this chapter to the device, and (2) which relates to the safety or effectiveness of the device or to any other matter included in a requirement applicable to the device under this chapter."

The district court held that the FDA affirmatively chose not to impose any reproductive toxicity warning requirements on dental amalgam. Accordingly, Proposition 65 was different from, and in addition to, the FDA's requirements and therefore was preempted. The Court of Appeals for the Ninth Circuit reversed, relying heavily upon the Supreme Court's holding in *Medtronic, Inc. v. Lohr,* which dealt with the same MDA preemption provision as in *Stratton.* In *Medtronic,* the Court held that the MDA did not preempt Lohr's common law claims against a defective pacemaker. Preemption would conceivably occur where the statute was specific as to a particular device, but because the MDA requirements, however, dealt with regulation generally and not with specific devices, they were "not the sort of concerns regarding a specific device or field of device regulation that the statute or regulations were designed to protect from potentially contradictory state requirements." Moreover, the Florida common law requirements at issue were general and not developed "with respect to a medical device[]." Such non-specificity allowed the state law to evade federal preemption.

If, on the other hand, the state statute and/or federal regulation specifically concerned a particular medical device, the plurality in *Medtronic* would seemingly find preemption. Justice Breyer was more explicit in stating that state common law claims could sometimes be preempted by the MDA when its application created a "requirement … which is different from, or in addition to, any federal requirement." Justice Breyer also suggested that preemption could be extended to the corresponding standards of care for common law claims. The dissent would go even further, reasoning that state common law claims were in fact "requirements" under the MDA and, therefore, preempted when they impose something different from the FDCA's requirements. Justice O'-Connor contended that some of the common law claims dealt with the labeling and warning of Medronic's pacemaker device, compelling requirements different from those imposed under the FDCA and resulting in preemption under the extensive labeling requirements already imposed by federal law.

In applying these principles of *Medtronic*, the Ninth Circuit in *Stratton* interpreted the MDA's provisions to mean that preemption occurs only if a specific requirement or regulation exists in reference to a particular device. It found no such preemption of Proposition 65 since it was a general state law that was not enacted with respect to medical devices specifically. Rather, Proposition 65 applies to all products and services that meet the definition of a reproductive toxin. Mercury is listed as one of many reproductive toxins, and thereby requires certain warnings, but no specific regulation or requirement is aimed solely at mercury or mercury amalgam.

Based on *Stratton* and *Medtronic*, it is not certain that mercury amalgam warning statutes will always survive preemption. The dissenting opinion in *Medtronic* certainly envisions that state common law warning requirements are different from and in addition to the FDCA provisions, and can trigger preemption. It is likely that these Justices would therefore find explicit product-specific labeling or warning requirements even more obviously deserving of preemption. The plurality opinion, moreover, suggests that in certain circumstances, a state statute could be preempted....

Conclusion. The mercury amalgam debate allows for a fascinating examination of the intersection of law and science and the allocation of decision-making authority in matters of risk and uncertainty. Despite the ADA's enduring endorsement of mercury amalgams, science has yet to: (1) state with certainty that mercury amalgam is safe, (2) identify at what levels it becomes harmful to humans, or (3) ascertain how much mercury is released into the body from mercury fillings. Although a patient is legally entitled to information regarding the risks and benefits of proposed and alternative treatments, the ADA and state dental boards have vehemently resisted informing patients about the risks of mercury amalgams. Instead, professional regulation has been aimed at disciplining dentists who advocate against mercury amalgams or simply want to inform the patient about both sides of the controversy.

An increase in litigation by patients against dentists and the ADA for failure to warn or for non-removal of mercury amalgams may inspire additional scientific research. However, in the short-term, *Daubert* issues portend limited successes for these patient-plaintiffs. For this reason, state statutes offer the best method of protecting patients and effectuating their autonomy. Statutory violation suits largely avoid the obstacles posed by *Daubert*, while protecting the patient's right to be informed about mercury's potential risks. Additionally, enacting and enforcing such statutes will raise public awareness about the risks of mercury amalgam and the need for further study. These laws, however, must be drafted with care in order to avoid federal preemption....

Selected References

American Dental Association, Statement on Dental Amalgam.
American Dental Association, Principles of Ethics and Code of Professional Conduct (2003).
Consumer Reports, The Mercury in Your Mouth (May 1991).
Lynn R. Goldman *et al.*, Technical Report: Mercury in the Environment: Implications for Pediatricians, 108 American Academy of Pediatrics 197 (2001).

Legislative Materials

Dental Devices: Classification of Encapsulated Amalgam Alloy and Dental Mercury and Reclassification of Dental Mercury; Issuance of Special Controls for Amalgam Alloy, 67 Fed. Reg. 7620, 7622 (proposed February 20, 2002) (codified at 21 C.F.R. pt. 872).
Safe Drinking Water and Toxic Enforcement Act of 1986 ("Proposition 65"), California Health & Safety Code, §§ 25249.5–.13 (West 1999).
Maine Revised Statutes Annotated, 32 §1094-C(1) (Supp. 2002).
Mercury in Dental Filling Disclosure and Prohibition Act, H.R. 4163, 107th Cong. (2002).
Medical Device Amendments of 1976 (MDA), 21 U.S.C. §§ 360(c)–(k).

Cases

Am. Dental Ass'n v. Khorrami, No. 02-3852, (C.D. Cal. petitioner's complaint, filed May 14, 2002).
Bd. of Dental Exam'rs v. Hufford, 461 N.W.2d 194 (Iowa 1990).
Breiner v. State Dental Comm'n, 750 A.2d 1111, 1115 (Conn. App. 2000).
Committee of Dental Amalgam Manufacturers and Distributors v. Stratton, 92 F.3d 807 (9th Cir. 1996).
Daubert v. Merrell Dow Pharm., Inc., 509 U.S. 579 (1993).
Medtronic, Inc. v. Lohr, 518 U.S. 470 (1996).

CHAPTER NINETEEN

THIRD WORLD ENVIRONMENTAL ISSUES*

... [There is] need for a new approach to guide public interest advocacy for decisions taken in the United States that may have significant environmental consequences in the Third World. However, to date, there has been little effort to define the characteristics of responsible environmental reform efforts by private citizens and organizations in the United States on foreign environmental problems, such as the quality of foreign aid. Moreover, there have been virtually no attempts to identify a principled role for American lawyers in Third World environmental issues. This Essay ... respond[s] to these lacunae by articulating a new approach to advocacy based on a partnership model.

Given the limitations of existing international structures, a partnership model of advocacy can be an effective tool for domestic and Third World public interest organizations to achieve responsible environmental policies in developing nations. Moreover, past successes with such a model show that it can provide a basis for substantially improving access by individuals and public interest organizations in the Third World to international decision-making processes in the future....

The Need for a Partnership.... [T]he environmental integrity of foreign aid, whether of bilateral or multilateral origin, has been the subject of significant concern. Partnerships ... are not only desirable, but, in many cases, necessary to improve the environmental integrity of development assistance, both generally as well as on a case-by-case basis. A partnership benefits from both the Third World group's stake in environmental issues directly affecting it and the American organization's leverage in international decision-making bodies. Combining the elements of legitimacy and leverage synergistically augment each group's ability to advance the partnership's agenda.

---

* **David A. Wirth**, *Legitimacy, Accountability, and Partnership: A Model for Advocacy on Third World Environmental Issues*, 100 YALE LAW JOURNAL 2645 (1991), http://papers.ssrn.com/abstract_id=753572.

Joining Legitimacy and Leverage Through Partnership. The model of the public interest law firm, designed to advocate aggressively the needs of underrepresented constituencies such as the poor and victims of racial discrimination, has existed in the United States for some time. [A good example is the Natural Resources Defense Council (NRDC), one of a number of American public interest environmental law firms that work to improve the environmental quality of foreign aid, including through loans provided by the World Bank.] This structure has been adopted abroad as well. For example, [the Environmental Foundation, Ltd. (EFL), a Sri Lankan organization concerned about World Bank funding to implement custodial plans for tropic forests of Sri Lanka] consciously modeled its structure in part on American public interest law firms like the Sierra Club Legal Defense Fund and NRDC.

A number of public interest law firms are membership organizations whose members are the underrepresented interests to which the organization is ultimately accountable. Implicit in the model of a membership-based public interest law firm is a minimum connection between the issues the organization takes on and its members' interests. For domestic membership organizations engaged in public policy advocacy in American judicial, legislative, or administrative *fora* on domestic environmental and public health issues, establishing that nexus is relatively straightforward. In the domestic context, the legal and policymaking system also ensures a minimum level of accountability to the interests an advocate purports to represent. For instance, the doctrine of "associational" or "organizational" standing articulates an analysis for substantiating the connection between an organization and the interests on whose behalf it acts. If this inquiry reveals such a connection, then the organization can bring suit in its own name on behalf of its members.

The question of an advocacy group's legitimacy becomes considerably more problematic if any component of this formula is missing, especially if the locus of the problem the group seeks to address is in a foreign country. If there is inadequate linkage between, on the one hand, a domestic organization and its constituent members and, on the other, the foreign interests it purports to represent, serious questions arise about the organization's authority to represent those interests. This principle applies regardless of how meritorious the underlying issue seems. [As an example, while] it is credible to assert that forest preservation interests in Sri Lanka are underrepresented, that does not, in itself, legitimize NRDC's representation of those interests before the World Bank....

The question of legitimacy aside, American environmental organizations like NRDC potentially exercise a great deal of leverage over issues such as forest preservation in Sri Lanka. Over time, these organizations have built up reputations for expertise on domestic environmental issues with the United States government. Their influence on United States policymaking extends easily to the area of international relations, such as bilateral foreign aid. In addition, the United States is typically a significant, if not the predominant, player in intergovernmental organizations. Among the 155 members of the World Bank, the United States government currently holds over fifteen percent of the voting power, nearly twice as much as any other country. The physical presence of the Bank in Washington further magnifies the importance of the United States government within the institution. Ironically, American environmental organizations often have far greater leverage than the real stakeholders, members of the public in developing countries....

Overcoming Obstacles at Multilateral Institutions.... Public interest organizations like EFL and NRDC find multilateral institutions like the World Bank significantly more difficult to monitor and influence than bilateral assistance agencies. The latter are ultimately accountable to national legislatures that are able to exercise legislative and oversight power to ensure the environmental integrity of those agencies' projects, policies, and programs. In the United States, additional domestic legal requirements, like the procedural and substantive guarantees of the Administrative Procedure Act and the Privacy Act of 1974 (Freedom of Information Act), give the public additional safeguards and remedies it can use to hold bilateral assistance organizations accountable.

By contrast, the multilateral development banks are considerably more intractable and less accountable to the public. For more than a decade, one of the World Bank's primary mandates has been to help alleviate poverty. Nonetheless, Bank management has repeatedly asserted that the institution's professional staff is accountable principally, if not exclusively, to the institution's member governments. As a result, there is virtually no role in the institution's governance or policymaking processes for members of the public in borrowing countries, the intended beneficiaries of Bank lending. Progress toward greater public participation in the institution's decision-making procedures has been slow and ad hoc at best. In addition, the institution's highly secret decision-making procedures routinely shield its actions from public scrutiny in borrowing and donor nations alike. This means that members of the public in borrowing countries may have little or no notice of crucial decisions that will affect the very world in which they live.

Even World Bank member nations have only highly attenuated control over Bank management. Twenty-two Executive Directors, appointed or elected by member country governments, represent member nations in Washington on a day-to-day basis. The authority of member country governments, acting through the Executive Directors, over the Bank's operations and its management and professional staff is cloudy....

As a practical matter, for many member country governments the Bank's system of representation results in a highly diluted presence at the institution. For instance, one executive director represents the unlikely configuration of the Netherlands, Romania, Yugoslavia, Israel, and Cyprus. Another, often referred to as the "Canadian" Executive Director, also represents most of the Caribbean countries. Such odd juxtapositions of donor and borrowing countries—whose interests at the institution are unlikely to converge—can create serious conflicts for executive directors.

Sri Lanka is represented on the Board of Executive Directors by a national of India, a country whose relationship with Sri Lanka has been characterized by considerable tension over the past several years because of Sri Lankan fears of Indian hegemony. In addition, executive directors often receive background documents as little as ten days in advance of a vote on a proposed loan, demonstrating that the central governments of member countries, particularly those that do not appoint their own executive director, are likely to have virtually no opportunity to examine proposed loans before Board action.

The worldwide campaign for environmental reform of the World Bank compellingly demonstrates a new approach to advocacy on Third World environmental issues. As concern for the environment has intensified worldwide, the number of private environmental organizations in the developing world has exploded. The relationship between the environment and development assistance from industrialized country governments and multilateral financial institutions has been a principal concern for many of these organizations. At the same time, the limitations on public policy advocacy on Third World issues by public interest law firms based in the United States have become abundantly clear. The resulting *ad hoc* working relationships between Third World and American organizations provide background for articulating a new model for advocacy in this largely unexplored realm....

Understanding Advocacy through Partnership. With the growing concern about the environmental effects on Third World countries of capital infusions from international financial institutions like the World Bank, a partnership model of advocacy has begun to coalesce. A developing country group first establishes a relationship with an American organization, which then communicates the developing country group's concerns to the United States government. Next, the United States, which has identified as a foreign policy goal improving the environmental quality of multilateral development bank lending, intervenes with the World Bank, which, in turn, makes representations to the developing country's government. Incredibly, this circuitous method of partnership advocacy is often more effective in achieving environmental improvement than direct communication between a foreign public interest group and its own government. These partnerships also create significant additional benefits, such as empowerment of Third World organizations and long-term linkages between nongovernmental advocacy groups in developing and industrialized countries.

The Benefits of Partnership. Typically, a policymaking nexus in both the developing country in question and the United States is part of a successful cooperative advocacy relationship. For instance, American citizens are ordinarily more effective advocates with their own government, through which they can indirectly exert pressure over multilateral institutions like the World Bank. By contrast, at the Bank itself, Americans are often perceived as lacking an immediate connection to problems in foreign countries; nationals of borrowing countries usually have a greater impact. A joint undertaking with Third World activists fills this lacuna by providing legitimacy for American advocates when they deal directly with the Bank. In addition, judging the merits of a particular advocacy goal or strategy in its own legal, social, political, and economic context requires the perspective provided by a foreign counterpart. In other words, cooperation with those who hold a direct stake in the outcome is necessary to identify the public interest in any particular situation.

When working effectively, collaborations ... synergistically magnify the strengths of the individual participants many times. The empowerment of citizens' organizations in developing countries is a particularly important benefit from this interdependent relationship. Partnership advocacy creates new opportunities for these organizations to overcome barriers to effectiveness in their own countries. Paradoxically, the indirect route by which Washington-based organizations act as interlocutor with the United States government and the World Bank is often a more effective mechanism for Third World activists to achieve their goals than dialogue with their own governments. Ideally, there should be channels for individuals and organizations in the Third World to obtain remedies directly for environmental harm anticipated from or caused by Bank-financed projects....

American public interest groups also benefit from partnership with developing country groups. A close relationship with those who hold a direct stake in policy decisions gives the United States-based organization stature and credibility that it would not have if it were representing purely American interests. The American group can then effectively use its preferential access to factual information of accuracy, depth, and breadth from the foreign organization to make a unique contribution to the public policy debate within the United States and on the international level.... Moreover, interaction with Third World groups provides American nongovernmental organizations with a more

nuanced perspective on related international questions similar to the particular issue for which the partnership was formed.

The Responsibilities of Partnership. Although, on its face, collaboration between Third World and American public interest organizations has some elements of an attorney-client relationship, closer inspection reveals that this
analogy is imperfect. First, more than just the needs of the foreign "clients"
shapes the priorities of the American "attorneys" in these joint undertakings.
American organizations like NRDC are players in their own capacity in their
domestic political and legal system. Their success as advocates for Third World
environmental concerns derives from the leverage they use not only for their
"clients"—foreign organizations like EFL—but for themselves as well.

American organizations working in cooperative relationships with Third
World groups ordinarily have their own constituencies to which they are accountable as well as their own substantive stake in international issues. Consequently, they cannot, as a "real" attorney would, act purely as agents or instrumentalities of interests distinct from those domestic constituencies....

The attorney-client analogy might appear somewhat more appropriate in
an international forum, such as at the World Bank. In this context, American
advocacy groups use superior information and other resources to introduce
the concerns of Third World groups into international decision-making
processes. However, even on the international level the parallel breaks down.
Most of an American organization's access to and leverage at the World Bank
stems from its influence with the United States government, which wields disproportionate influence in most multilateral financial institutions. The American organization's duty to its domestic constituency requires that it preserve
its ability to influence American policymaking and, accordingly, can restrict
its ability to represent the interests of its foreign "client." The American partner faces additional limitations on generic policy issues, like energy lending
priorities or Bank document disclosure, where it may represent a multitude
of "clients" whose interests are not identical.

The conflicts between an American organization's various constituencies
can render extremely difficult the identification of the "public interest" that
the American advocate seeks to advance. For example, the greenhouse effect
engages issues of the global commons, of which the United States is a part.
The United States contributes, directly through AID and indirectly through
the World Bank and other multilateral organizations, to the formulation of
energy policies in foreign countries. An American organization can quite cred-
ibly argue that it, as distinct from Third World organizations, has its own interest in assuring that public funds do not exacerbate the threat of global
warming. In such a situation, there may be tension between an American or-

ganization's strictly domestic agenda, grafted onto an international issue, and the needs of a foreign organization that expects to realize its goals in part through a relationship with the American organization.

Even if American environmental advocates can assert some interest in Third World environmental issues because of their connection to problems of the global commons, they cannot ignore parties with a considerably greater stake in those issues and fail to give those voices the commensurately greater deference and weight they deserve. Even when an American organization claims a stake in a geographically remote problem, it needs a foreign counterpart's on-the-spot perspective in order to craft a credible and effective remedy.

This analogy demonstrates that collaborative relationships between American and foreign environmental organizations are best characterized as partnerships, with the terms of each relationship defined on a case-by-case basis to meet the needs of the participants in a particular context. This conclusion, however, does not imply the absence of ethical considerations. In advocacy on the international level, there is no court to police a standing requirement. It is entirely possible for well-intentioned, but poorly informed American advocates to urge reform with little or no accountability to those in the Third World who will be affected, perhaps adversely, by those changes. Without the legitimacy and perspective that come from an alliance with a Third World partner, there is a sizeable risk that American environmental organizations will operate as unaccountably as, for example, the World Bank. This suggests, at a minimum, the necessity for an American group to locate those with a significant stake in a problem and to create a partnership with, and joint strategy acceptable to, those interest groups before undertaking public policy advocacy on that issue.

Once the American advocate has recognized the need for a partnership and identified a prospective partner, the terms of the relationship are up to the participants. The purposes for which a partnership may be formed, the goals of the partnership, and the needs of the participants are so context-specific that it is difficult to make generalizations about the content of the partnership relationship. However, common aspects of most successful partnerships include the open sharing of information, consultation in the formulation of joint strategies, and consensus decision-making.

Beyond Partnership.... [T]he partnership advocacy model still provides strictly ad hoc remedies. From the point of view of Third World environmentalists, the necessity to speak through the mouth of a foreign organization to resolve important questions of environmental and public health policy in their own countries may be unsatisfying in practice and unsatisfactory in principle. These makeshift arrangements are not a substitute for direct access to meaningful remedies by those with a direct stake in the problem.

Limitations of the Partnership Model. The roundabout partnership strategy, while acquiring greater resilience with increasing use, can break down at any step along the way for reasons that have nothing to do with environmental quality. First, non-environmental factors may color the United States' reaction to allegations of environmental shortcomings in a World Bank loan. In January 1989, for example, environmental and economic concerns motivated the World Bank to defer indefinitely consideration of a proposed $500 million electric sector loan to Brazil that would have supported that country's nuclear energy program and a power expansion agenda involving up to seventy-nine dams in the Amazon basin.

The fact that $600 million in additional lending by private American banks was contingent on approval of the World Bank proposal significantly complicated the position of the United States government. While sympathetic to environmental concerns about the World Bank loan, the Department of the Treasury also had an interest in assuring approval of the proposal as a component of the executive branch's policy for alleviating the Third World debt crisis. Moreover, even when it is sympathetic to the partnership's goals, the United States may be wary of adverse reactions from other member countries at the Bank.

Among Bank staff, the likelihood of conflicting goals is at least as great. Enumerated policies, such as the new operational directive on environmental assessment, govern the design of Bank-financed loans and projects. But many of these standards, such as the Bank's environmental assessment procedures, are hortatory rather than binding. The day-to-day dynamics within the institution tend to discourage the stringent enforcement of environmental conditions after loan approval. A strong institutional imperative, reinforced by career incentives to professional staff, encourages the Bank's management to move large amounts of capital out the door and into the hands of borrowing country governments. Environmental concerns may delay or impede this objective. These same staffers, who have often invested months or years in the development of a particular loan, are the same individuals who respond to environmental concerns from member country governments, citizens organizations in the United States and abroad, and members of the public both before and after loan approval. The extreme difficulty of obtaining access to both the Bank's decision-making process and the documents it generates exacerbates these problems.

Adjudicatory Mechanisms. Loan agreements between the World Bank and a member country government are analogous to treaties and contain enforceable obligations. The Bank also has internal operating procedures and requirements that reflect evolving international standards in the areas in which the Bank operates. At present, however, the remedies for failures by borrowing countries to observe loan conditions and for deviations by Bank professional staffers from their own operating procedures are discretionary and largely within the hands of the World Bank's staff, who are often the very same individuals who negotiate and implement the loan agreement with the borrowing country.

A neutral adjudicatory mechanism would fill this gaping inadequacy in the existing international structure. In addition to creating a remedy for individual grievances, the adoption of a "private attorney general" model of citizen enforcement would advance the public interest by encouraging compliance with applicable standards. Moreover, the creation of an adjudicatory mechanism to resolve grievances arising from the development assistance process would further the goals of accountability and empowerment at least as well as, and probably better than, the stopgap partnership model.

There are several precedents for access by private parties to multilaterally-established mechanisms to adjudicate violations of treaty obligations by states and failures to observe internal operating procedures by the staff of multilateral organizations. The International Labor Organization (ILO) grants members of the public—in that case workers' and employers' organizations—access to a number of mechanisms to adjudicate nonobservance of binding standards established under ILO auspices. These procedures have been highly successful in encouraging ILO member states' adherence to binding treaty obligations like those in World Bank loan agreements. In one of the most celebrated cases, after the Polish government declared martial law in December 1981 and dissolved all existing trade unions, two workers' delegates initiated a successful proceeding against the Polish government under the ILO's constitution and ILO conventions guaranteeing the right to organize and bargain collectively. Similar mechanisms at institutions such as the UN Human Rights Committee, the UN Commission on Human Rights, and regional courts and commissions have been highly successful in responding to both individuals' and organizations' complaints concerning human rights violations.

Likewise, there are precedents for adjudicatory mechanisms which are available to individuals to remedy infringements of the internal procedures of international organizations. Most international organizations, such as the UN and the ILO, have an administrative tribunal for adjudicating disputes, primarily employee grievances, between officials of the organization and the organization itself. In 1980, the World Bank ... created an administrative tribunal along the lines of the UN and ILO precedents.... Creating causes of action for those with a direct stake in Third World environmental issues would enable them uniformly to seek effective remedies for their injuries. Unlike the partnership model, which leaves developing country groups dependent on American advocates, such new adjudicatory mechanisms would directly empower members of the public in Third World countries.

Conclusion. Until the international community creates adjudicatory mechanisms to give aggrieved members of the public in developing countries direct access to the foreign aid decision-making process, the partnership model of public policy advocacy is the best prospect for improving the environmental quality of development assistance. While passions in the United States about tropical forests, energy policy, and other Third World environmental issues run high, our ability effectively to craft public policy that is responsive to local needs overseas often does not. With an attenuated or nonexistent stake in the outcome, we can find ourselves doing more harm than good. The American role in public policy advocacy on Third World issues comes into clear focus only when seen in relation to those who hold a direct stake in the outcome: the public in the developing world. Partnerships with overseas counterparts enhance the legitimacy, efficacy, and accuracy of American environmental activism on these issues. Over time, and with continued successes, such partnerships may pave the way for greater accountability in development assistance and, ultimately, international legal processes generally.

Selected References

Chittharanjan Felix Amerasinghe, The World Bank Administrative Tribunal, 31 International and Comparative Law Quarterly 748 (1982).

Nan Aron, Liberty and Justice for All: Public Interest Law in the 1980s and Beyond (1989).

Pat Aufderheide & Bruce Rich, Environmental Reform and the Multilateral Banks, 5 World Policy Journal 301 (1988).

Robert L. Ayres, Banking on the Poor: The World Bank and World Poverty (1983).

John A. Horberry, The Accountability of Development Assistance Agencies: The Case of Environmental Policy, 12 Ecology Law Quarterly 817 (1985).

Ernest A. Landy, The Effectiveness of International Supervision (1966).

Zygmunt J.B. Plater, Multilateral Development Banks, Environmental Diseconomies, and International Reform Pressures on the Lending Process, 9 Boston College Third World Law Journal 169 (1989).

Bruce Rich, The Emperor's New Clothes: The World Bank and Environmental Reform, 7 World Policy Journal 305 (1990).

Ibrahim Shihata, The World Bank and Human Rights: An Analysis of the Legal Issues and the Record of Achievements, 17 Denver Journal of International Law & Policy 39 (1988).

William H. Timbers & David A. Wirth, Private Rights of Action and Judicial Review in Federal Environmental Law, 70 Cornell Law Review 403 (1985).

Further Reading (selected work by David A. Wirth)

Environmental Law and Policy (Aspen 3rd ed. 2004) (with Zygmunt J.B. Plater and others).

Teaching and Research in International Environmental Law, 23 Harvard Environmental Law Review 423 (1999).

Globalizing the Environment, 22 William & Mary Environmental Law and Policy Review 353 (1998).

At War With the Environment, 84 Virginia Law Review 315 (1998).

Reexamining Decision-Making Processes in International Environmental Law, 79 Iowa Law Review 769 (1994).

PART III

LAW AND SOCIETY

A. DEMOCRATIC ORDER

Chapter Twenty

Democracy, Taxes and Wealth[*]

... This Article explores two important issues arising from the increased concentration [of] wealth [in the United States that began in the early 1980s]. First, is ... concern about the adverse impact of wealth concentration legitimate? What social harms might arise from the concentration of wealth in the same family from generation to generation? Second, should the tax system be used to decrease wealth concentration by taxing wealth transfers? ...

Worldly Philosophers' Views of Wealth Transfers. For centuries, philosophers and economists have debated whether governments should curtail inherited wealth. Philosophers have struggled with the question whether the social contract between citizens and the state requires protection of a decedent's property rights after death. John Locke, for example, argued that natural law required that parents be permitted to bequeath property to their children. He viewed the ability to transfer property at death as a fundamental property right that the state should not abridge.

Other philosophers, however, weighed social concerns more heavily than postmortem property rights. Jeremy Bentham, for example, placed less importance on the entitlement of the property owner and more importance on the interests of society.... John Stuart Mill similarly favored taxing legacies heavily.... William Blackstone also asserted that there was no natural right to bequeath property at death, and, therefore, that the government could control transfers of property from the dead to the living.

The debate among philosophers continues.... The modern philosopher John Rawls has advocated inheritance and gift taxes in order "gradually and continually to correct the distribution of wealth and to prevent concentrations of power detrimental to the fair value of political liberty and fair equality of

[*] **James R. Repetti**, *Democracy, Taxes and Wealth*, 76 NYU Law Review 825 (2001), http://papers.ssrn.com/abstract_id=271264.

opportunity." In contrast, [others] argue[] that taxing bequests violates a major tenet of [prevailing] norms because [it] discourages saving.

While philosophers debated the right to tax wealth transfers, economists examined the efficiency effects of restricting wealth transfers. Portending the argument of some present economists, Adam Smith asserted that death taxes transfer productive capital from private citizens to the government.... Similarly, David Ricardo argued that death taxes prevented the efficient use of capital. Some economists today, who argue that the estate tax discourages investment and saving, advance this argument. Another strain of argument against death taxes can be found in the work of economist Leon Faucher, who argued that inheritance maximizes utility because it confers benefits on the transferor and transferee. Presently, some have suggested that there is a net gain of social welfare in a system which does not tax wealth transfers.

Finally, early political scientists expressed concerns about the effect that the transfer of wealth from generation to generation may have on political institutions. Alexis de Tocqueville [held] this concern [shared by] Thomas Jefferson and Thomas Paine.... Jefferson wrote in a 1789 letter to James Madison: "The earth belongs in usufruct to the living; ... the dead have neither powers nor rights over it. The portion occupied by any individual ceases to be his when [he] ceases to be[,] and [it] reverts to the society." Similarly, Paine wrote: "[No] generation [has] a property in the generations which are to follow.... It is the living, and not the dead, that are to be accommodated. When man ceases to be, his power ceases with him...."

Many state legislatures in the United States disfavored devices which had been utilized in Great Britain to transfer family estates from generation to generation—trusts, primogeniture, and entail.... For its first 150 years, however, the United States federal government only used an inheritance tax to raise revenue during times of war. It was not until President Theodore Roosevelt proposed adopting a heavily progressive income tax in 1906 that national focus shifted to using the tax to prevent concentrations of wealth as well as to raise revenues. He proposed a tax to prevent "the owner of one of these enormous fortunes to hand more than [a] certain amount to any one individual." The estate tax was not actually adopted until 1916. At that time, the economist Irving Fisher urged an estate tax to address the "danger of an hereditary plutocracy" to "democratic ideals." ...

The Macroeconomic Effects of Wealth Concentration. Economic studies are remarkably unanimous in suggesting that high concentrations of wealth correlate with poor economic performance in the long run.... Because data about wealth concentration are often difficult to obtain for extended periods in some countries, many studies use concentrations of income as a proxy for wealth.

Economists believe that this does not alter the results, because concentrations of income follow the same patterns as concentrations of wealth in those countries for which both sets of data are available....

[Numerous] studies clearly suggest that over a long period of time, wealth concentration hurts economic growth. All the published studies that have examined periods of twenty-five years have concluded that inequality at the start of the period correlates with poor economic growth during the period. Similarly, most of the studies that have examined periods of at least ten years have found that high levels of inequality correlate with poor economic growth. In contrast, the results of studies using periods of five years or less are mixed....

[C]onventional wisdom was that inequality should contribute to increased growth because: (1) the wealthy had a higher marginal propensity to save than the poor; (2) only the wealthy could make the large capital commitments necessary for industrial growth; and (3) the poor would be motivated to work harder than the wealthy. However, the long-term studies suggest that other, more powerful forces may be involved. As a result, new explanations have been offered for why inequality corresponds with poor economic growth....

One of the early theories attempting to link inequality to growth was developed by the economist Simon Kuznets. He theorized that as a society develops from a rural to an industrial economy, inequality initially should increase because industrial workers earn higher incomes compared to rural workers. Inequality subsequently should decrease, however, as more rural workers transition into industrial jobs. The findings ... that link inequality to slow growth, therefore, may reflect merely the process of transition from a rural to an industrial economy. The difficulty with this explanation, however, is that inequality actually has increased in industrial countries, contrary to Kuznets's hypothesis, leading many to question its validity.

Dissatisfaction with the Kuznets hypothesis has caused some researchers to look for alternative explanations. Some scholars argue that countries with concentrated wealth experience poor growth rates because those countries seek to redistribute wealth by taxing income from capital and by applying higher rates to higher amounts of income. The theory is that in a democracy, the majority of voters will derive small amounts of income from labor and capital and, therefore, will favor higher tax rates on higher amounts of income. The higher tax rates will, in turn, discourage capital investment and thus impair growth.

Initially, this explanation seemed to be supported by the findings of Alberto Alesina and Dani Rodrik that countries with high concentrations of wealth have low investment in capital as a percentage of their gross domestic product. However, studies that directly have included tax rates in their regression models have found that high tax rates do not play a negative role in growth. A study of sixty-three countries (forty-five low-income and eighteen industrial) by Charles Garrison and Feng-Yao Lee found no support for the hypothesis that increases in tax rates adversely affect economic activity. Similarly, Roberto Perotti found no empirical support for an adverse effect of taxes on the growth rate of the sixty-seven countries in his sample. To the contrary, using the average marginal tax rate as the tax variable in his regression models, Perotti found that the coefficient for tax was positive and highly significant, suggesting that higher tax rates correlate with higher growth.

There are many potential explanations for Perotti's findings. Perotti proposes that countries with higher tax rates may have adopted policies that increase investment in education, which promotes productivity. Many others also advance the failure to invest adequately in education as a likely cause of the correlation between concentrated wealth and poor productivity growth. Alternatively, Perotti notes that countries with higher tax rates may have adopted redistributive policies that enhance social consensus and thereby increase productivity....

Many studies demonstrate the importance of education ... [and how] the deprivations suffered by one generation have a long-term impact on the next generation. Studies of intergenerational income mobility find a significant correlation between parents' and children's incomes for life. Thus, to the extent that the adverse effect of wealth concentration on economic growth is linked to a failure to invest adequately in education, the effects should appear over a long period of time.

The explanation for the link between wealth concentration and inadequate investment in education by the poor takes two forms. First, some suggest that where the poor have a difficult time borrowing, a family that is poor is constrained from investing in education. The inability to invest in human capital traps many families in inter-generational poverty, thus slowing the nation's economic growth. Alternatively, some suggest that there may be a more complex link between wealth, investment in education, and fertility. An increase in family wealth leads to lower fertility rates and to higher investment in human capital. When wealth is highly concentrated, higher fertility rates may result in lower investment in education, and as a result, lower productivity growth. Perotti found direct statistical support for both versions of the explanations involving education, *i.e.*, the borrowing constraint and the fertility models....

Perotti also has found strong support for the theory that large disparities of wealth cause sociopolitical instability, which impedes growth. Instability discourages investment because it creates uncertainty and disrupts market activities and labor relations. Using measures of instability such as the number of political assassinations, successful coups, unsuccessful coups, and violent deaths per million, the study found a significant negative impact on economic growth. One need only look to the effect of social unrest in some American urban areas to appreciate the impact of such unrest on investment in those areas. Moreover, the long-lasting difficulties in attracting investment to those urban areas clearly cause a long-term waste of human capital.

The Political Impact of Wealth. In addition to having an adverse economic effect in the long run, concentrations of wealth have a harmful impact on the effectiveness of democracies to the extent that an objective of democracy is to give all participants an equal voice. To understand the adverse effects of concentrations of wealth on the political system, it is helpful to review briefly the various descriptive models for democracies. Theorists propose three models to describe the manner in which a democracy may function. The first, the "majoritarian" model, describes a parliamentary system in which voters can express their will quickly in national elections in which major policy changes are debated. The second, the "elite" model, posits that a "small political and socioeconomic elite controls our government." The third model is a "pluralistic" democracy in which persons and entities with common interests organize into groups to influence government.

According to Anthony Gierzynski, most political scientists agree that the U.S. system does not fit the majoritarian model. It is "rare that elections can bring about wholesale changes in government in the United States because the executive and legislative branches of the national and state governments (both of which hold power in the system) are elected from separate constituencies, at separate times." Similarly, most believe that it is unlikely that the "elite" control our government or constantly win political battles. Instead, the majority of political scientists view the "pluralistic" model as the most descriptive one.

However, it is not necessary to decide which model is correct. Concentration of wealth can have a significant impact on the operation of a democracy described in any of the three foregoing models because it gives the wealthy disproportionate power and influence.

The famous studies of Muncie, Indiana in the books *Middletown* and *Middletown In Transition* support the notion that wealthy individuals exercise disproportionate local influence on their communities. *Middletown* commented upon the [powerful] effect that wealthy business owners have on the media through their placement of advertisements.... *Middletown* also noted that the affluent exerted control over the news content of the local newspapers.... Subsequently, *Middletown in Transition* discussed the political pressure which the affluent applied not only through the press but also through their employees....

While analysis of the influence of wealthy individuals on their employees and on the media has been anecdotal, analysis of the effect of wealth on the electoral process and conduct of public officials has been based upon statistical analysis. The analysis shows that nearly half of all contributors making large donations (at least $200) are individuals who have incomes over $250,000 per year, and that they wield significant influence.... [The effects of] campaign finance law in the United States.... [are that] individuals (as opposed to corporations and unions) make most of the contributions to candidates and their parties. [A] majority of the individuals making contributions are well-to-do.... The contributions clearly influence election results and, as a result, cause the wealthy to have a disproportionate voice.

Wealth Concentration and The Role of Dynasties. [T]he weight of evidence [thus] strongly supports worries about the concentration of wealth. Wealth concentration correlates with poor economic growth in the long run because of educational disadvantages for the poor and because of sociopolitical malaise generated by disparities in wealth. Moreover, concentrations of wealth enable wealthy individuals to influence disproportionately the elective and legislative process, as well as their communities. Indeed, such influence probably accounts for the difficulty Congress has adopting significant campaign finance reform that effectively limits wealthy donors' political power.

A large portion of wealth in the United States is dynastic. [A]pproximately fifty percent of wealth in the United States is inherited. In 1984, 241 of the wealthiest 400 individuals in the United States started with a significant inherited fortune. In 1999, 149 of the 400 wealthiest individuals in the United States started with a significant inherited fortune.

The harmful effects of wealth on the media and the political process are likely stronger in the case of dynastic wealth, as compared to wealth held by different families each generation. Where different families hold wealth each generation, it is likely that each new family will bring new perspectives, life experiences, and concerns to the political process and the media. Moreover, since the wealth will have been created by those that possess it, it is likely that such wealth-holders also will have significant talents. In contrast, where wealth simply is transmitted from a generation that created it to subsequent generations in the same family, it is less certain that the subsequent generations will have new perspectives, life experiences, or great talent....

Moreover, wealth passed from generation to generation magnifies political power. It is one thing to deal with a more powerful person than yourself; it is another to consider that your children will have to deal with the children of the powerful person, and that your grandchildren will have to deal with her grandchildren. Families seeking to preserve their power may exercise it to prevent others from acquiring wealth. This would decrease diverse views and ideas which help create a vibrant society. In its worst form, of course, this creates a royalty....

Using Taxes to Prevent Concentration of Wealth and Family Dynasties. Because of the concerns about dynastic wealth, society legitimately could decide to use the tax system to curb the transfer of wealth to those who did not create it. The tax system should do more, however, than merely help check wealth concentration. The macroeconomic literature ... on the effect of wealth concentration has emphasized the need for investment in human capital. This suggests that another objective of a tax system seeking to curb dynastic wealth should be to raise revenues to fund such investment. Also, it is important that the tax not create other problems that outweigh the foregoing benefits....

Revenues. An important goal of a tax to prevent wealth concentration should be to raise revenues to fund education and build an infrastructure (including communications and transportation) that will increase opportunities for all citizens. The increased investment in education could occur either by the government increasing its investment or by individuals increasing their investments with grants received from the government. Despite its many imperfections, our current wealth transfer tax appears to raise revenues that could be used for this purpose....

As economist B. Douglas Bernheim has argued, however, the estate tax actually may reduce revenues when the income tax and estate tax are viewed together. He suggests that this occurs because the estate tax causes taxpayers to engage in transactions that decrease the amount of income taxes collected by more than the amount of estate and gift taxes collected. The decline in revenue, Bernheim states, occurs in two ways. First, he argues that tax revenues are lost because high-income-tax-bracket taxpayers make gifts of income-producing property to low-bracket taxpayers. To support this, he makes several critical assumptions. He estimates that, in any given year, the value of inter vivos gifts equals approximately 52.7% of the value of bequests in that year. He further assumes that the maximum income tax rate applies to income of the donors and that lower tax rates apply to income of the donees.

Subsequent studies suggest that these assumptions are wrong. For example, data about the value of gifts occurring each year appear to contradict Bernheim's assumption that annual *inter vivos* gifts equal 52.7% of annual bequests. An examination of estate tax returns for decedents who died in 1992 shows that during the period 1977 through 1992, decedents made aggregate taxable gifts equal to only two percent of their terminal wealth. Similarly, for all taxable estate returns filed in 1995, taxable gifts comprised only 3.8% of the value of estates. It is possible that taxpayers are making more nontaxable gifts (annual gifts of $10,000 or less per donee). However, James Poterba reviewed the 1995 Survey of Consumer Finances and found that the probability of a household making nontaxable gifts was only modestly greater than the probability of making taxable gifts.

Also, it is unlikely that Bernheim's assumption that the donees of such gifts are in lower income tax brackets than the donors is correct. The adult children of wealthy donors are usually in high-income tax brackets themselves. Moreover, investment income of donees under age fourteen, such as the donors' grandchildren, is subject to income tax at their parents' maximum rate to the extent such income exceeds a minimal amount ($1,400 in 2000). Lastly, if the gifts are in trusts that may accumulate income, the income tax brackets applicable to such income are highly compressed. The maximum rate of 39.6% applied to undistributed taxable income of a trust in excess of $8650 in 2000.

Bernheim's second explanation for why the estate tax results in a revenue loss is that it encourages contributions to tax-exempt charitable entities. Bernheim assumes that charitable bequests would fall by about 79.3% without an estate tax. Based on an assumption that income tax would have been paid at the maximum statutory rate on income generated by the bequeathed assets if the decedent's family had kept the assets, he estimates that the loss of revenue is $.80 per dollar contributed to charities where the maximum individual statutory tax rate is 28% and $1.25 per dollar contributed where the maximum statutory rate is 50%.

Bernheim's estimate of the revenue loss, however, is too large. Income from the transferred property would not have been taxable to the donor at the maximum statutory rate. Since taxpayers can defer recognition of capital gains, it is likely that the effective tax rate on such gains is only one-third to one-quarter the statutory rate, ignoring inflation. Moreover, it is likely that one-half of accrued gains are held until death and escape income taxation entirely. Also, many theorists argue that other portfolio adjustments may allow sophisticated investors to escape taxation on most of their return from capital. The data suggest that sophisticated investors are able to reduce their taxable income. David Joulfaian examined the 1981 income tax returns for decedents who died in 1982. He found that wealthier individuals tended to have lower taxable income from capital as a percentage of their wealth ...

Does Taxation Affect Wealth Concentration and Dynasties? The fact that the concentration of wealth in the United States has stayed relatively constant since 1989, after significant increases that occurred in the 1980s, does not mean that the estate tax has failed to affect wealth concentration and family dynasties. [In fact,] eliminating the estate and gift tax would increase the percentage of national wealth held by the top one percent from a conservative estimate of a ten percent increase to an aggressive estimate of a twofold increase.

Indirect evidence also suggests that the amount of wealth transferred from one generation to the next would have been larger without an estate tax. The amounts of estate tax paid by decedents with respect to taxable returns filed in 1997 represented twenty-four percent of the aggregate taxable estates reported in those returns. Moreover, the estate tax reduces wealth transferred within a family, not only because of the amount of taxes paid, but also because it encourages charitable contributions. Most studies have concluded that the estate tax encourages charitable contributions....

The combination of the estate tax liability and charitable contributions significantly reduces the amount of wealth transferred within a family.... [T]ax returns for persons who died in 1982 found that the combination of charitable bequests, estate expenses, and taxes accounted on average for forty-one percent of the net worth (gross estate less debt) of decedents with gross estates over $10 million. [This suggests] that taxing wealth transfers does not impose hardship on decedents' children. The study found that the average income of children of decedents with gross estates over $10 million at the time the decedents died was $271,254, measured in 1981 dollars. The children of decedents who died in 1982 with more modest estates, between $2.5 million and $10 million, had an average adjusted gross income of $123,452 the year before their parent's death, again measured in 1981 dollars.

The difficulty with a wealth transfer tax is that it is a blunt instrument to curb wealth concentration. The tax is based upon the amount of wealth transferred by the transferor, not the amount received by the transferee. Thus, the transferor pays the same tax whether the transfer is to one person or several persons. A device such as an accessions tax could be much more focused, because it determines liability based upon amounts received by each transferee. Despite the blunt nature of the estate tax, however, it is helping to check wealth concentration.

Effect on Savings. The major criticism of taxing wealth transfers is that it reduces social welfare because it discourages savings. The effect of our current estate tax on savings is an important issue since, as stated earlier, bequests and gifts account for approximately fifty percent of all wealth accumulation in the United States.... [H]owever, this assertion is not supported by theory or by the empirical evidence. Theory does not predict the effect of a tax on savings, and the majority of the statistical studies indicate that taxes have little or no impact.

Economic theory proposes two opposite effects about how savings may respond to taxes. The first, the income effect, occurs where taxpayers increase savings to offset the effect of the tax. The second, the substitution effect, occurs where taxpayers reduce savings and increase current consumption in response to a tax. The result of these opposing theories is that it is difficult to predict a priori what the effect of a tax will be on savings and investment.

Further complicating the analysis is uncertainty about what motivates taxpayers to make bequests and gifts. There are several potential explanations that likely apply to some taxpayers some of the time. In the accident bequest model, taxpayers save for retirement and to meet unexpected contingencies. Only unexpended amounts which remain because of the uncertainties of life result in bequests. In the altruistic model, parents make bequests solely to help their children. Alternatively, in the strategic bequest model, parents make bequests and gifts as rewards for service obtained from their children. Lastly, some have argued that individuals save, not to make bequests, but to obtain the power associated with wealth. In that model, the transfer of wealth at death is merely a consequence of the decedent's unwillingness to give up this power.

If bequests merely represent amounts left over because the decedent expected to live longer or because the decedent was saving for contingencies, estate taxes will have minimal impact on savings. Alternatively, if a taxpayer is accumulating wealth in order to exercise the power that wealth confers during his life, or if the decedent is saving to confer some form of benefit on heirs or to reward them for services, the estate tax may have an impact. But it is not clear whether that tax will cause taxpayers to increase savings to counteract the tax or decrease savings in response to the tax.

… What is the effect on aggregate savings if the transferee is also included in the analysis? Some economists have developed models indicating that in situations where transferors reduce bequests in response to taxes, the transferees may increase savings to offset the shortfall. The result is that [estate tax changes create offsetting effects to donors and recipients] and, therefore, will not harm savings.

Finally, it is important to recall that the tax is being collected to fund governmental activities. Even if there is a net decrease in saving when the responses of the transferor and transferee are considered together, there may not be a decline in aggregate saving if the government uses the tax revenues to invest in a public good such as education or, alternatively, transfers the revenues to low-income individuals who in turn invest in education.…

Selected References

Henry J. Aaron & Alicia H. Munnell, Reassessing the Role for Wealth Transfer Taxes, 45 National Tax Journal 119 (1992).

Alberto Alesina & Dani Rodrik, Distribution, Political Conflict and Economic Growth: A Simple Theory and Some Empirical Evidence, in Political Economy, Growth, and Business Cycles (Alex Cukierman et al. eds., 1992).

Alberto Alesina & Dani Rodrik, Distributive Politics and Economic Growth, 109 Quarterly Journal of Economics 465 (1994).

Jeremy Bentham, Principles of the Civil Code, in The Theory of Legislation (1802).

B. Douglas Bernheim, Does the Estate Tax Raise Revenues?, in 1 Tax Policy and the Economy 113 (Lawrence H. Summers ed., 1987).

2 William Blackstone, Commentaries (1899).

Charles Garrison & Feng-Yao Lee, Taxation, Aggregate Activity and Economic Growth: Further Cross-Country Evidence on Some Supply-Side Hypotheses, 30 Economic Inquiry 172 (1992).

Anthony Gierzynski, Money Rules: Financing Elections in America (2000).

Letter from Thomas Jefferson to James Madison (Sept. 6, 1789), in 5 The Writings Of Thomas Jefferson (Paul Leicester Ford ed., 1895).

David Joulfaian, The Federal Estate and Gift Tax: Description, Profile of Taxpayers, and Economic Consequences 21 (Off. of Tax Analysis, U.S. Dept. of the Treasury, Paper No. 80, Dec. 1998).

Simon Kuznets, Economic Growth and Income Inequality, 45 American Economic Review 1 (1955).

Robert S. Lynd & Helen Merrell Lynd, Middletown: A Study in American Culture (1929) & Middletown In Transition: A Study in Cultural Conflicts (1937).

John Stuart Mill, Principles of Political Economy (1848).

1 The Complete Writings of Thomas Paine (Philip S. Foner ed., 1969).

Roberto Perotti, Growth, Income Distribution, and Democracy: What the Data Say, 1 Journal of Economic Growth 149 (1996).

Roberto Perotti, Political Equilibrium, Income Distribution, and Growth, 60 Review of Economic Studies 755 (1993).

James Poterba, Estate and Gift Taxes and Incentives for Inter Vivos Giving in the United States 10 (NBRE Dec. 1998).

David Ricardo, Principles of Political Economy and Taxation (1817).

Theodore Roosevelt, Speech at the House of Representatives Office Site (April 14, 1906).

Adam Smith, An Inquiry into the Nature and Causes of the Wealth of Nations (1776).

Alexis de Tocqueville, 1 Democracy in America (1835).

Further Reading (selected work by James R. Repetti)

Introduction to United States International Taxation (Aspen 2005) (with Paul R. McDaniel and Hugh J. Ault).

Partnership Income Taxation (Foundation 4th ed. 2005) (with Alan Gunn).

Federal Wealth Transfer Taxation: Cases and Materials (Foundation 5th ed. 2003) (with Paul R. McDaniel & Paul L. Caron).

Textualism and Tax Shelters, 24 Virginia Tax Review 1 (2004) (with Noël B. Cunningham).

The Misuse of Tax Incentives to Align Management-Shareholder Interests, 19 Cardozo Law Review 697 (1997).

CHAPTER TWENTY-ONE

THE OVERLOOKED MIDDLE[*]

Humans can ignore anything, G.K. Chesterton observed, as long as the thing being ignored is big enough. The contemporary discussion swirling about the issue of labor law reform well illustrates the curious truth of Chesterton's remark. Despite the intensity with which this debate has been conducted and the air of scientific objectivity and certainty that frequently permeates it, we have managed to overlook some pretty big things. For example, we completely have failed to appreciate the fact that the better than thirty-year long decline of unions is not an isolated occurrence. Instead, it is part of a much broader and deeply troubling trend that has affected every sort of mediating group in our society. Our blinkered insistence on treating the deterioration of autonomous employee associations as a solitary phenomenon has precluded us from comprehending either the complexity of its causes or the full extent of its implications. We similarly are inclined to look past the significance of collective bargaining as a social institution as well as the conditions necessary to stable and ongoing cooperation, whether in the workplace or anywhere else.

The unifying theme in all this is our pronounced tendency to overlook the importance of the middle. By middle, I mean families, religious congregations, service and fraternal groups, grassroots political clubs, unions and like institutions that mediate the relation between individuals and the large institutions of market and state that characterize so much of public life today. The healthy functioning of these mediating bodies—which Edmund Burke described as the "little platoons" of society—is of crucial concern. For it is through these bodies that we literally learn and practice the habits necessary for self-rule at both the individual and social level. This fact explains why Tocqueville placed such stress on the importance of associations and mediating groups and their potential to act as "schools for democracy." As he so clearly

---

* **Thomas C. Kohler**, *The Overlooked Middle*, 69 CHICAGO-KENT LAW REVIEW 229 (1993), http://papers.ssrn.com/abstract_id=782024.

understood, individuals and societies alike become self-governing only by repeatedly and regularly engaging in acts of self-government. It is the habit that sustains the condition.

[W]e cannot learn toleration and respect for others in a vacuum. Nor can we learn or practice self-rule in isolation. As humans, we are not self-sufficient beings. We only learn who we are, and gain some sense of the fullness of our human character, through dealing with others. Hence, it is the small associations and mediating bodies, where society is realized, that act as the seedbeds for the civic virtues. For it is in them that we learn the habits necessary to sustain democratic political life. To leave these seedbeds untended is to put the entire project of self-rule at grave risk. Our tendency to overlook the middle grows out of our curious propensity to ignore the biggest thing of all: what we are as human beings and the intrinsically social character of our personhood. By so doing, we sell ourselves short and trade over our full status for a pot of message. While we—and, more importantly, those who come after us—are bound by such exchanges, we cannot help ultimately but to be both disappointed and injured by them.

[T]he well-being of these various mediating bodies is deeply interdependent. Their existence is mutually conditioning, and the health of any one of them has an impact on the rest. [T]here is more involved and more at stake in labor law reform than we may think. What follows is a brief outline of a few of the things I believe are too big to ignore in considering the shape labor law reform may take.

Does the Employment Order Matter? Does It Matter in the Way We Typically Think It Does? Just as we have sold the character of our personhood short, so do we tend to understate the significance of the order that shapes the employment relationship. It is tempting to ascribe this restraint to modesty, but that is one characteristic for which lawyers and academics generally are not well-known. Rather, we tend to understate the function and importance of this order because we understate or misconstrue the character of our personhood. There may be a further reason as well. Perhaps none of us really want to own-up to the responsibility that comes with suggesting and promoting a framework of norms by which peoples' lives should be conducted.

As Aristotle, Montesquieu, and Tocqueville (among others) are at pains to point out, people's habits are of more significance than their law. Yet, as they also make clear, law performs a pedagogical function. It thereby plays a direct role in shaping and developing the habits that undergird the legal order. In short, the law and the culture stand in a reflexive, mutually conditioning relationship. To understand the meaning of either, or their long-term effects and direction, one must take account of both.

The big problem with taking labor and employment law as seriously as we ought is that it is basically, well, a bit scruffy. Like family law (from which it developed), labor law deals with messy things like personal relationships and seemingly mundane day-to-day issues. It lacks the cool hauteur of constitutional law and the sort of cachet that attaches to model building and theory spinning. Consequently, it is relatively easy to assign the law governing employment a low status in the legal hierarchy.

Nevertheless, it is precisely its impact on the daily, the concrete, the particular, that marks the real significance of the law governing work. People are self-constituting beings. We make ourselves to be what we are through the activities in which we habitually are engaged. Consequently, it is the seemingly insignificant routines and actions of everyday life that make all the difference. For it is through them that we literally are forming ourselves as individuals and as a society.

As David Feller pointed out [decades] ago, the law governing the work relationship touches employees more directly and frequently than virtually any other aspect of the public ordering regime. That statement remains true. But it is now true of far more people, and of a far greater proportion of our populace. Indeed, the overall increase in labor force participation is one of the most striking social developments of the past forty years.

A few statistics help to illustrate the point. Currently, about ninety-three percent of adult males are in the labor force—a figure that has remained roughly steady for some decades. Since 1950, however, women's participation in the workforce has climbed by more than two hundred percent. Presently, seventy-four percent of women aged twenty-five to fifty-four are employed, the overwhelming proportion of them full-time. Not surprisingly, working hours for women have been increasing steadily over the past twenty years. Additionally, one recently published major study shows that after years of gradual decline, the normal work week for Americans has increased to the point where the average employee now works the equivalent of an additional month more than was worked in 1970.

… Working for pay now occupies more of the time of more of our populace than ever. The job has become a central part of most adults' lives and being employed (by one or more employers) is the way people spend the major share of their waking hours. Consequently, anyone with serious concerns about the kind of people we are making ourselves to be over the long run, and whether we can sustain the sorts of habits necessary to the well-being of a democracy, must pay close and critical attention to employment and the way that relationship is ordered. Briefly stated, the employment order involves far more than simply wage rates, power relationships, productivity, quality, or workplace voice. It quite literally involves the constitution of human beings.

... The term collective bargaining virtually is synonymous with the Wagner Act. The core goal of that statute is the protection and enhancement of individuals' status through the defense and maintenance of freely-formed employee groups. This feature defines the statute and the unique position that the Wagner Act holds in American law. It represents the only place in our otherwise highly individualistically-oriented jurisprudence where the law has encouraged the formation of mediating groups that foster individual empowerment and promote self-determination.

It may be old news to observe that collective bargaining can provide an unmatched opportunity to involve people in making and administering the law that most directly determines the details of their daily lives. It may be slightly more novel, or at least more important, to point out that in contemporary society, work has become a — and perhaps for many the — primary source of common life for adults. As Durkheim understood, work creates a moral environment, and its influence extends to nearly every sphere of life. Similarly, work is the chief — and again for many the only — place outside the family where people are engaged in a common undertaking.

These points highlight one of the key aspects of collective bargaining. Unions are autonomous bodies. They stand independently both of the state as well as the organizations that employ their members. They come into being as a result of employee self-organization, and their well-being depends on the ability of the members to maintain solidarity. Winner-takes-all attitudes don't produce enduring relationships or democracies. Healthy and well-functioning employee associations can provide a place where people learn to lose a point without resentment, prevail on an argument without triumphalism, and most importantly of all, practice the art of reasonable compromise.

[T]he town meeting, the neighborhood ward, grassroots political organizations, and many of the other places where these sorts of skills might be learned and practiced are withering or absent altogether. Given the degree to which people now are tied to the market, employee associations would seem to be the natural thing to stand in the place of these other institutions. The fact that unions themselves virtually have disappeared turns us to consider briefly why this is so.

Unions and the Vanishing Middle. Accounting for the decline in union membership has become something of a cottage industry for academics during the past several years. Theories abound.... Prominent explanations ... include structural changes in the economy; peculiar characteristics of American labor law, combined with its weak or unsympathetic enforcement; and stiff but sophisticated employer opposition to worker self-organization. Added to these is the undoubted fact that incidents of corruption, mob influence, and wrongdoing of various sorts by union officials have had a marked and lasting impact on our attitudes toward unions.

All of the reasons offered to explain union decline have some force. But none of them, either singly or in combination, adequately account for the long and steady decline in union membership that has occurred in the United States since the late 1950s. They don't because once again, we have overlooked the significance of the middle. Scholars and commentators seem invariably to neglect the point. Yet the plain fact of the matter is that unions went into decline in the United States at roughly the same time that all other sorts of mediating institutions began to unravel, and for strikingly similar reasons. As Americans, we are deeply and increasingly ambivalent toward association in almost any form. The decline of unions is but part of a much larger story.

… A brief comparison of union decline with the steady withering of mainline religious denominations may help to illuminate my point. As has been frequently observed, Americans are among the most religious people on Earth. Over nine in ten Americans claim they believe in the existence of God, and a huge proportion states that religion is "very important" (fifty-four percent) or "fairly important" (thirty-two percent) in their lives. Likewise, about six in ten Americans "believe that religion can answer all or most of today's problems." Despite this, George Gallup and Jim Castelli report that "while Americans attach great importance to religion, they do not equate religion with church membership or attendance." Gallup and Castelli also found that a vast majority of Americans believe that one can be a good Christian or Jew without being part of a religious congregation.

These figures take on great interest for our purposes when they are compared with American attitudes toward unions. As Seymour Martin Lipset points out, extensive survey data repeatedly show that "the majority of Americans believe that unions are essential and do more good than harm, [and] that without unions employers would maltreat workers." Most Americans— six in ten in the most recent poll—also indicate that they "approve" of unions and an overwhelming proportion of the population believes that "workers should have the right to join unions." Despite all this, only about three in ten workforce participants indicated that they would join a union if given the opportunity.

[N]otions of self-sovereignty and misgivings about reliance on a mediator of whatever character are pervasive. For example, ninety percent of Americans say that they pray. Nevertheless, Americans also state that they rely on themselves "rather than an outside power such as God," to resolve life's problems. Similarly, while a substantial majority of Americans approve of the functions unions perform in society and think unions are necessary to protect em-

ployees and to give them a voice in the workplace, nearly the same proportion believe that they don't need a union to get fair treatment. [W]e think
unions, churches, and the other mediating institutions that compose civil society are great—but, for somebody else.

We should not be surprised that union decline has occurred at the same
time that families, churches, fraternal and service groups, local political clubs,
and similar mediating institutions began to deteriorate. No single mediating
structure of whatever description is likely to survive in the absence of others.
All require and can ingrain the same sorts of habits: decision, commitment,
self-rule, and direct responsibility. No single institution alone can inculcate
or restore these habits. The existence and decline of all these bodies is mutually conditioning. The collapse or deformation of any one of them threatens
the rest.

Indeed, it seems likely that the correlation between the decline of unions
and religious congregations is stronger than it may first appear. For example,
Catholics and Jews traditionally have been thought to be more hospitable to
union organization than other portions of the populace, and persons from
Catholic or Jewish backgrounds still tend to be predominant in union leadership positions. There undoubtedly are a great many reasons for this, one of
the most obvious being that as members of immigrant groups, many Catholics
and Jews had strong financial incentives to become active in and to support
unions.

But, I think there is more involved in all this than simple economic interest alone. For instance, Southern workers have had similar financial reasons
to join unions, yet they traditionally have been resistant to organization. To
condense a lot into a sparse description: Habits of thought related to these two
religious traditions may have had rather a lot to do with the general willingness of Catholics and Jews to become involved in or to support unions. Both
traditions, for instance, place an enormous emphasis on community. Similarly, neither would tend to understand community—at least in its most profound forms—simply in terms of a voluntary association of like-minded individuals. Accordingly, neither tradition emphasizes the supremacy of
individual conscience over the norms authoritatively transmitted through the
community. As Tocqueville observes, "Catholicism may dispose the faithful to
obedience, but it does not prepare them for inequality." In contrast, however,
"Protestantism in general orients men much less toward equality than toward
independence."

One can add to this the fact that since the issuance of the first "social en-
cyclical" in 1891, the Catholic Church officially and continuously both has
sanctioned and encouraged the formation of unions. [W]hether they them-

selves were in any sense "religious," unions and the sorts of habits they require to sustain themselves may have been particularly intelligible to persons of Jewish or Catholic backgrounds. As both groups have become more assimilated, so has the special intelligibility of unions (and other mediating bodies) faded.

The accuracy of this thesis notwithstanding, it seems likely that for the foreseeable future, we can expect a continued decline in mediating groups generally. As a nation, we fast are losing the habit of participating in organizations that require more than dropping a check in the mail. Moreover, we increasingly no longer see the need for or the significance of these mediating bodies. What we characteristically do and the sorts of things we are open to understanding—indeed the very sorts of questions that are likely to occur to us—go hand-in-hand. Since we increasingly don't participate in them, mediating bodies have lost their meaning for us. We won't make a commitment to what we don't understand. And increasingly, we don't understand what things like unions, churches, Lions' Clubs, or the Lower West Side Democratic Club have to do with anything.

Of course, the problem is that we cannot sustain a healthy democracy or polity without these bodies. So, the question is how we can intelligently and effectively work toward setting the conditions for their restoration. I do not mean to suggest that if unions were somehow magically restored, everything else would follow. Moreover, whatever form they take, autonomous employee associations will have to take on different, or at least additional, forms and function in somewhat different ways than they have during the past fifty years.

What is clear is that any sort of responsible labor law reform will have to take into account the centrality of employment, its function in inculcating habits, and its role in creating a moral environment. In short, responsible reform will have to take the middle into account, and the intrinsic interdependence of mediating groups upon one another. The costs of overlooking the role and contributions of autonomous employee associations to grounding the conditions for authentic self-rule are simply too high.

Alternatives to Autonomy: New Forms of Representation. We must live in the world as it is. And as it is, unions currently constitute a fading presence on the American scene. What sort of promise do alternative forms of worker representation hold for us? What can we do for the unorganized? …

Perhaps we first should consider some of the central features of the scheme we may be reforming. Contrary to others, I see little in the essence of the Wagner Act that is tied to, or a direct result of, the patterns of economic organization of the nation in the mid-1930s. It is true enough that unions historically represent a response to changes in social organization that occurred through the rise of liberal economies. And, it is also true that the patterns of union organization and bargaining reflect the shape of industrial arrangements.

Nevertheless, little about these patterns is compelled by the statute or important to the Wagner Act's central scheme.... In enacting the Wagner Act, and in sharp contrast to the course taken by the rest of the industrialized world, Congress deliberately opted for a law-making system that would involve minimal state intervention in the employment relationship. The Act stands as an example of what Gunther Tuebner calls a "reflexive" legal scheme. In this sort of regime, the state establishes and sanctions a voluntary ordering system, but leaves the outcomes achieved through the process to be determined by the parties themselves, free of state influence. The goal of reflexive law, Tuebner suggests is "regulated autonomy," or structured self-regulation. As such, reflexive schemes represent a sharp departure from statist ordering regimes.

The Act also represents an attempt to apply the principle of subsidiarity. [S]ubsidiarity is an organizational norm. It recommends that institutions of all sorts be ordered so that decision making can occur at the lowest capable level. The principle rests on the idea that the state and all other forms of association exist for the individual. Thus, organized bodies should not take up what individuals can do, nor should larger groups assume what smaller associations can accomplish. Conversely, the state and other large institutions have the positive responsibility to undertake those activities that neither individuals nor smaller associations are capable of performing. In this perspective, associations and social relationships exist to supply help (subsidium) to individuals in assuming self-responsibility. Hence, the subsidiary function of associations of any sort consists not in displacing but in setting the conditions for authentic self-rule. A key feature of the subsidiarity principle rests in its emphasis on the middle, *i.e.*, the fostering of autonomous mediating groups in which civil society exists and through which individual self-realization can occur. Not incidentally, the principle's development has stressed the importance of work, beginning with the inherent dignity of the human who performs it, as well as the social function of autonomous employee associations.

In brief, the Act sought to establish a private ordering system for developing and administering the law that governs one of the most important of relationships in modern times: employment. This was a far bolder move than it may first appear to us, the inhabitants of the modern regulatory state. It must be remembered that there was relatively little employment law in the United States in 1935. In the sixty or so years preceding passage of the Act, the ordering of the relationship had been increasingly left to the market. Other industrialized states had responded to the call for the reformation of this sort of system by legal regimes that involved rather heavy state intrusion into and regulation of the employment relationship. As noted, we went in precisely the opposite direction. The Wagner Act held out the promise of a highly flexible scheme that would permit the parties directly affected to come up with an order appropriate to their circumstances. To paraphrase the late, great Harry Shulman, this was a system that was intended to keep the state out, and ("mind you") to keep the lawyers' role in it properly understood. That properly apprehended role for lawyers would be as counselors and problem-solvers, not as litigators and appellate advocates. Ultimate responsibility was to rest with reasonable and responsible actors at the ground level, not with agents of the state.

In sum, the Act's central scheme avoids what Max Weber called the "iron cage" in which we imprison ourselves when we see bureaucracies or the market as the sole available ordering solutions. It should come as no surprise that the piecemeal and ad hoc regulation of the employment relationship has grown markedly in direct correlation with the decline of the practice of private ordering through collective bargaining. The past seventy-five years, and particularly the past twenty, have taught us a clear lesson concerning employment: If ordering does not occur through the organs of civil society, it will occur through the state—whose guarantees may be more formal than effective, and whose methods will be far less supple and adaptive than privately arrived at solutions.

Our experience with the development of common law wrongful termination doctrines is illustrative.... A recent study conducted by the Rand Corporation shows that as a result of a jury trial of a wrongful discharge claim in California, "the majority of employees can expect a payment that, in present value dollars, is the equivalent of a half year of work." The same study found that because of the high transaction costs associated with a trial, "95 percent of all cases settle for an average of about $25,000."

These findings are eerily reminiscent of the common law order that obtained generally in England and in some American jurisdictions through the middle part of the Nineteenth Century. Broadly speaking, in this regime, an employer could discharge an employee only upon proper notice, save in those cases where good cause existed for not giving such notice. The amount of notice required turned on the character of the plaintiff's position, *e.g.*, one month's notice for household help, up to six months for more highly compensated employees. The reported cases from this period appear not to inquire into the question of cause, but instead deal with the nature of the plaintiff's job and whether the parties intended for their relationship to be on terms other than those established by the general rules. The remedy for discharge in the absence of proper notice was the income the plaintiff would have received had that person worked through the end of the notice period.

Because they turn on the question of the existence of good cause, modern trials over wrongful discharge may be more involved, more expensive, and more intrusive upon the employer-employee relationship than their Nineteenth Century predecessors. Taken as a whole, however, (and assuming that California is any guide) the modern doctrines seem to have developed a sort of de facto common law rule that permits plaintiffs roughly half a year's pay in cases where some question exists about whether they were discharged with just cause. Given the costs and uncertainties associated with litigation, and the results that litigation on average produces for plaintiffs, perhaps we eventually will see a statutory regime that would require that persons to be discharged receive notice of some stated period (*e.g.*, six months), and in its absence, "severance pay" in the amount of a half year's salary, or some combination of the two, save in a presumably narrow band of cases (which would be statutorily defined) where "good cause" exists to give neither. I am not urging the desirability of such a scheme. But, I think it does typify the sorts of limited results one can expect from reliance upon a public ordering regime. And indeed, it is just the sort of regime that exists in jurisdictions that do not rely upon collective bargaining systems.

In sharp contrast to bureaucratically oriented regimes, the whole scheme of the Act revolves around the formation and maintenance of autonomous employee associations. [It]was intended to do far more than settle a longstanding squabble about how employees might achieve voice in managerial decision making. It would also serve to anchor what was supposed to be a comprehensive system for ordering all aspects of the employment relationship.... Given the importance of the work-life sphere in contemporary culture, the promotion of employee self-organization could serve as a buffer against the sort of fragmentation of the polity that Tocqueville understood would deform and pervert a democracy. This fragmentation results when people lose the ability to settle on and engage in undertaking a common purpose.

The rise of this sort of fragmentation is as insidious as it is pernicious. As the circles within which they act shrink, people literally lose touch with one another, and thereby the commonality of understandings, sentiments, judgments, and goals that sustain willing cooperation and a healthy polity dissipate. The idea of some common good is replaced by factional interest, and worse, a sense of individual helplessness vis-a-vis the state or the large institutions of the market. With the habits of self-action weak or in desuetude, and the sentiments necessary to sustain commonality lax, people drift into a state of atomistic isolation and effective dependency on the state or other large institutions. Common action comes to appear at best a romantic yearning "for a simpler era" and self-government another way of saying every man or women for him or herself. Interest groups narrowly described replace the middle, and increasingly, only the institutions of market or state are seen as credible.

Whatever else they may do, alternative forms of "worker representation" will not truly take the place of those anchored by and developed through free-standing employee associations. The alternatives will (or, do) not represent the product of self-organizational activity. They are not autonomous. As such, they do not constitute a part of the crucial middle that I have been describing.

Nor, of course, are the alternatives intended to perform the same functions as the autonomous employee association. As George Strauss and Eliezer Rosenstein pointed out [decades] ago, participative management theory springs from entirely different sources and assumptions, and is intended to serve a rather different and far more restricted set of goals, than is the so-called collective bargaining model. [T]hose goals are organizational effectiveness (as bureaucratically defined), not private ordering or employee self-determination.

These differences raise many issues. One of them is this: Do participative schemes unanchored by an autonomous employee association promise more than they deliver? There is much reason to believe that this is the case. As is frequently pointed out, "participation" is a managerial ethic. The ethic rests on the creation of an atmosphere of trust between the parties that will set the grounds for the willing and intelligent cooperation by employees with organizational goals, which ultimately are established and controlled by management.

A relationship of trust implies a selflessness among the parties, for the one trusted must be constantly willing to put the others' good before his or her own. In short, trust involves a sort of self-transcendence and, as Aristotle observes, it is a hallmark of the most authentic sort of friendship. [P]articipative management theories make self-transcendence easy. For they rest on the idea that there are no inherent conflicts of interest among people in work organizations that demand structural accommodation. Thus, *pace* Adam Smith, the interests of employer and employed are identical.

Trust as selflessness thus involves no real moral or intellectual conversion in the sense suggested by traditional religious thought or classical political philosophy. People, including those with ultimate decisional authority, simply will act in a trustworthy (*i.e.*, selfless) manner once they understand that they should. In other words, being "good" is a matter of education, because people will do the "right" thing once they know what it is. To use Etienne Gilson's description, such ideas represent a species of "angelism." But, of course, as James Madison points out, men are not angels, and hence attention must be paid to structures that can accommodate conflicting interests and to limit the *libido dominandi* that is so much a part of all of us. It comes as no surprise that participative schemes like TQM (Total Quality Management) are spoken of by their proponents as a new religion. But, like the new religion proclaimed by the boy prophet in Flannery O'Connor's *Wise Blood*—the Church of Christ without Christ—it seems to be missing something.

Participative management theories have another deeply troubling aspect as well. Corporate bodies of whatever description, whether they be business organizations, political communities, voluntary groups, etc., all face a common issue: How we can be both one and many, or to put the matter just slightly differently, how each person can be a distinct and unique individual, yet be related to and operate cooperatively with other distinct and unique individuals. Participative management techniques attempt to resolve this problem by seeking to create a state of complete identity between the individual and the group. In other words, they reify the group as the sole individual. They do this by seeking to replace individual attitude and conscience with a group conscience, which in turn is given its shape and orientation by corporate leadership. In short, this is why participative theory techniques represent a bureaucratic adjunct. They are intended to achieve a mass that will act efficiently and as one. To use Tatsuo Inoue's term, such schemes can produce a form of "companyism" that may deny individual status altogether. In the theoretical perspective from which these schemes tend to proceed, individuals exist only in and through the group; they have no separate character outside it.

I do not mean to suggest that there is nothing whatever of value to participative management schemes. That is plainly not the case. As a managerial ethic, participative schemes can enhance the scope of the individual workers to make workplace decisions vis-a-vis other styles of managing. By increasing the organization's reliance upon the good sense of the man or woman on the spot best to figure out how to accomplish a task, such schemes also are intelligent. But, given the foregoing, perhaps it is no surprise that the data show that participation plans function best, and have the best chance for survival, when they are anchored by an autonomous employee association. Our domestic experience is confirmed by the experience of other nations, which shows that devices like works councils only function well, and achieve significant results for employees, when they exist in an organized context....

Conclusion. Wholes cohere about a middle. But, even as they described the crucial role mediating institutions play in a liberal democratic order, the farseeing amongst us continually have warned about the destructive pressures that the institutions constituting the middle would face. At first glance, these sorts of issues would seem far removed from labor law and the employment order. The more one looks into the matter, however, the more clear it becomes how deeply interrelated the problems of the middle are with the seemingly mundane world of work....

[O]ur ability to "compete" is not a mere matter of technology, of selecting and properly employing the right management techniques. Maintaining a liberal political and economic order is truly hard work. It requires that people possess a certain sort of discipline. However inconvenient, the plain fact remains that there is no replacement for individual goodness, intelligence, reasonableness, and responsibility. But, these characteristics are virtues. A virtue is an operative habit, and habits require inculcation and practice. In short, the health and competitiveness of our polity and our economy depend on the existence of functioning schemes that can regularly and recurrently assist people in obtaining the sorts of habits on which a liberal order depends. We must never forget that we do not just trade in time, but we constantly are trading across time as well. What we have is not solely our creation, and the effects of the order we are establishing will be felt less by us than by those who come after us.

Labor law reform confronts us with some enormously difficult and complex problems. It is tempting to ignore them, but pretending they aren't there won't make them go away. Looking past our difficulties only makes them more acute. If we are to deal with these problems in an effective and responsible way, however, we must go beyond our well-worn, comfortable because familiar, but all-too-narrow analytical boundaries and habits of thought. The employment order involves much more than we typically think.

… Institutional orders inconsistent with our character as humans will not survive. Consequently, the most pressing question we face is whether and to what degree our notions of ourselves as human actors is accurate. Everything turns on the answers to this query. Bluntly stated, try as we might, in the final analysis, we can't get past ourselves. We're simply too big to ignore.

Selected References

Bureau of Labor Statistics, U.S. Dep't of Labor, Bull. No. 2385, Working Women: A Chartbook 48 (1991).

Gallup Org., August 3, 1991 (telephone poll conducted July 18–21, 1991 of 1002 respondents).

Adam Smith, The Wealth of Nations (1776).

Aristotle, Nicomachean Ethics (Books 8, 9).

Peter L. Berger & Richard John Neuhaus, To Empower People: The Role of Mediating Structures in Public Policy (1977).

Edmund Burke, Reflections on the Revolution in France (Thomas Mahoney ed. 1955).

Emile Durkheim, Suicide (1897).

David E. Feller, A General Theory of the Collective Bargaining Agreement, 61 California Law Review 663 (1973).

George Gallup, Jr. & Jim Castelli, The People's Religion: American Faith in the 90's (1989).

Mary Ann Glendon, The New Family and the New Property (1981).

Andrew M. Greeley, Religious Change in America (1989).

Theodore N. Greenstein, Marital Disruption and the Employment of Married Women, 52 J. Marriage & Fam. 657, 658 (1990).

Tatsuo Inoue, The Poverty of Rights-Blind Communality: Looking Through the Window at Japan, 1993 BYU Law Review 517.

Benton Johnson et al., Vanishing Boundaries: The Religion of Mainline Protestant Baby Boomers (1994).

Pope Leo XIII, Rerum Novarum on the Condition of Labor (1939).

James Madison, The Federalist No. 51, at 322 (Clinton Rossiter ed., 1961).

Seymour Martin Lipset, Unions in Transition: Entering the Second Century (1986).

Rand Corporation Study: James N. Dertouzos & Lynn A. Karoly, Inst. for Civ. Just., Labor-Market Responses to Employer Liability 36 (1992).

Juliet B. Schor, The Overworked American: The Unexpected Decline of Leisure (1991).

Harry Shulman, Reason, Contract, and Law in Labor Relations, 68 Harvard Law Review 999 (1955).

George Strauss & Eliezer Rosenstein, Workers Participation: A Critical View, 9 Industrial Relations 197 (1969).

Gunther Teubner, Substantive and Reflexive Elements in Modern Law, 17 Law & Society Review 239 (1983).

Alexis de Tocqueville, Democracy in America (1850).

Max Weber, The Protestant Ethic and the Spirit of Capitalism (Talcott Parsons trans., 1930).

Further Reading (selected work by Thomas C. Kohler)

Lessons from the Social Charter: State, Corporation, and the Meaning of Subsidiarity, 43 Toronto Law Journal 607 (1993).

Individualism and Communitarianism at Work, 1993 BYU Law Review 727.

Setting the Conditions for Self-Rule: Unions, Associations, Our First Amendment Discourse and the Problem of *DeBartolo*, 1990 Wisconsin Law Review 149.

Models of Worker Participation: The Uncertain Significance of Section 8(a)(2), 27 Boston College Law Review 499 (1986).

Chapter Twenty-Two

Federal Fraud Protection in the Labor Market[*]

... Federal law provides a high level of protection against fraud in the capital market but offers a comparatively low level of such protection in the labor market.... Federal protection against fraud in the capital markets grew out of the common law, and numerous federal statutory provisions give animation to the core idea that market participants should not lie in a market transaction in order to take value from others....

The requirements that corporate communications be truthful and complete are premised on the belief that an increase in the quantity, and an improvement in the quality, of information available to investors will facilitate intelligent investment decisions and improve the efficiency of securities markets in pricing securities and in allocating financial capital to real capital. The mechanism through which this occurs is relatively straightforward. When fraud is not penalized, the price of a company's security is not likely to reflect accurately the underlying ability of the firm to create wealth. Financial capital then moves from higher-valuing to lower-valuing users. But if fraud is illegal and accurate information about firms is otherwise available to people looking to invest, the market prices of the securities of those firms will better reflect the relevant characteristics of those firms. If the securities are priced below (or above) what informed investors are willing to pay, the informed investor will purchase (or sell) the securities until the price rises (or falls) to the price the informed investor is willing to pay. Thus, when information—untainted by fraud—is available, the market price will automatically adjust as a result of the activity of the informed investors....

Like investors, workers contribute an essential input to companies' creation of wealth through the production of goods and services. Also like investors,

* **H. Kent Greenfield**, *The Unjustified Absence of Federal Fraud Protection in the Labor Market*, 107 Yale Law Journal 715 (1997), http://papers.ssrn.com/abstract_id=41900.

workers have a difficult time acquiring and evaluating the information necessary for them to decide whether and how they should make their contribution. Like investors who have to evaluate factors including the complexity of financial documents, market risk, and expected returns, workers have to analyze the financial strength of employers, market risk, working conditions, benefits, wages, termination policies, promotion practices, grievance procedures, and hours. Moreover, the decisions workers make in choosing employers tend to have long-term implications, probably to a greater extent than for investors choosing among investment vehicles. Unlike investors, however, workers are not protected by a federal statute comparable to those protecting capital investors. No generally applicable federal protection exists, even for statements that would seemingly be at the core of antifraud protection.

To be sure, workers enjoy a range of federal protection in the workplace, and some federal statutes require employers to disclose information. For example, the Worker Adjustment and Retraining Notification (WARN) Act generally obliges employers of one hundred or more employees to give employees or their union sixty days notice of a plant closing or mass layoff. An employer who violates the notice provisions is liable for penalties equal to back pay for each day of the violation, up to sixty days. In addition, certain statutes require employers to disclose information about workplace risks to which employees are exposed, and federal labor law requires that companies negotiating with unions hand over certain relevant information. Moreover, to the extent that much of the need for protection from employer fraud arises in the context of possible plant closings, the National Labor Relations Act provides some protection by allowing unions to bring charges against an employer before the National Labor Relations Board for unfair labor practices. Unfair labor practices may include the refusal to bargain about the effects of a plant closing. To the extent that the need for fraud protection arises in the context of employee benefits, the Employee Retirement Income Security Act of 1974 (ERISA) may provide some limited protection.

None of these statutes, however, provides a general remedy to protect workers from employer fraud. Indeed, not only are employees afforded fewer statutory protections than shareholders, but federal law also makes it more likely that employers will not be held liable for any untrue statements to their employees. It does so by making it more difficult for employees to take advantage of fraud remedies they might have otherwise received under the common law. Section 301 of the Labor Management Relations Act (LMRA) grants federal jurisdiction over suits for violations of collective bargaining agreements. Under section 301, courts must determine whether the collective bargaining agreement preempts claims an employee has brought under other statutes or the common law. Because this preemption doctrine is interpreted quite broadly, it often stands as a significant obstacle to unionized employees seeking to sue their employers over putative misstatements pertaining to plant closings or job security. ERISA similarly includes a broad preemption doctrine. If the employee fraud suit pertains to alleged misstatements about employee benefits, a number of courts have held that federal law preempts such claims. In addition, the remedies that ERISA provides are less protective of workers than those offered by the common law. Thus, not only do workers have less federal statutory protection from fraud than capital investors, they also face obstacles in pursuing common law fraud claims that equity investors do not....

One possible justification for the lack of federal fraud protection for workers is that information is not important, or not as important, in the labor market as in the securities market. This part responds to that possible justification by outlining the basic economic importance of information in ensuring efficient markets and by applying these insights to the labor market. This part then highlights why some of the costs of fraud are even greater in the labor market. Because of this, one must reject the idea that the reason for the absence of an antifraud law protecting workers is a reduced need for information in this sphere.

The Basic Model.... In the labor market, jobs differ from one another in many characteristics: the prestige of the position, the dangerousness of the work, the pleasantness of the surroundings, the security of the job, and the level of the wages, to name just a few. Workers do not choose which job to accept on the basis of wages alone but on the whole package of attributes, both good and bad. For equilibrium to occur in the labor market, the wage rate in jobs with more desirable attributes must fall, and the wages in the less desirable jobs must rise, until the total of advantages and disadvantages are equalized across jobs available to a particular worker. Differences in rates of pay— "compensating wage differentials"—equalize the net attractiveness of jobs that offer different sets of attributes.

For the sake of simplicity, it is useful to isolate two attributes of work that are likely to be important to workers choosing among possible jobs—wages and job security. Job security is important to workers because a worker is not likely to make her choice between jobs on the basis of which firm has the highest present wage rate but rather on which provides the best future income stream. If one company offers employment that is seasonal or less secure for some other reason, the worker may choose to accept a position with a firm that pays less but provides more security....

... Those employees working for the insecure employment firm have to run the risk that they will suffer the costs of job discontinuity. These costs will depend on such factors as the expected length of time between jobs, the availability of information about other jobs, the location (and indeed existence) of other work, and whether a replacement job will pay the same. The difference between the wages offered by the secure employment firm and the wages offered by the insecure one will therefore differ greatly in different markets....

It is important to recognize that it is [efficient] from society's point of view that insecure employment firms must offer higher wages to fill their jobs than secure ones because different individuals have various tastes for security and risk. Some workers will prefer to have a secure job rather than an insecure one that offers a wage that is fully compensatory of the expected financial losses arising from any future job loss. Others will prefer the riskier job with a higher possible payoff. Even if the expected financial benefit of both jobs were the same (that is, if the probability of the payoff multiplied by the amount of the payoff were equal in both firms) and even if everything else were equal, some people would still prefer the risky job and others would prefer the secure job.

That different people have different preferences for risk and security is an important part of this story because it helps explain why a competitive, fully informed market makes everybody better off. If a worker prefers job security more than her fellow workers (that is, if she is risk averse), she can choose to work for a company that offers more secure employment, though with lower wages. In effect, she can purchase job security with a portion of her wages. If a worker does not need or want job security as much as her fellow workers, she is free to accept a job with the firm with less security but with higher wages. In effect, she can sell her preference for risk (or lack of desire for job security) in exchange for a higher wage. Both workers are able to maximize their job satisfaction, or utility, by giving up what they value less (for example, the extra dollar in wage) for what they value more (the extra amount of job security). The workers have achieved allocational efficiency; they have allocated their labor in such a way as to maximize their utility, within the constraints of the market.

Not only is this result better for workers, but firms also become more efficient when a competitive market requires truthful information. Secure employment firms will want to sell their security in the labor market by offering lower wages, and insecure employment firms will need to purchase (through higher wages) workers' willingness to be subject to job discontinuities. If workers can learn which firms provide secure employment and which do not, the operation of the competitive labor market will mean that risk preferrers will end up in the firms providing risky employment and risk avoiders will end up in the firms offering secure employment. The market ensures that each firm satisfies its needs at minimum cost. Because secure employment firms can sell their security to risk-averse workers, they will be able to decrease their labor costs more than they would if workers did not know which firms were risky and which were secure. Similarly, because insecure employment firms can purchase a willingness to be subject to risk from risk preferrers, their labor costs will be less than if they had to purchase the same amount of risk bearing from a cross section of workers....

The analogy to capital markets is straightforward. With accurate information, risk-averse investors can place their investment funds in financial vehicles that offer a secure return and low volatility. Businesses in secure, low-volatility market sectors can entice capital investment at lower cost from these risk-averse investors than they can from a broader group of investors because the risk-averse investors will pay a portion of their returns in exchange for security. Risk-prone investors will similarly be able to find investment vehicles that offer their preferred mix of expected return and risk. Businesses in highly volatile industry sectors will have a lower cost of capital than they would if they had to seek capital from a larger group of investors. Without accurate information, the market price will not reflect the value of the underlying securities....

... [W]hen workers know which firms offer secure employment and which offer insecure employment, the market induces wage adjustments so that each firm is able to hire the number and type of workers it demands. These equilibrium points are seen as optimal from a societal point of view because any movement away from them imposes more costs than benefits. For example, if employment in the insecure employment firm is forced up artificially, the social costs of providing the extra work are greater than the social benefits gained through the extra work. Analogously, if the employment levels in the firm providing secure employment are held artificially low, society is losing potential benefits. At any point below the equilibrium amount of hours worked, the benefits of employing a worker for an additional hour are greater than the costs of providing the extra hour.

Fraudulent information in the labor market tends to cause this very effect. Consider what happens when firms are able to lie about the security of the employment they offer. When lying is allowed, workers will not be able to tell the difference between a secure firm that is telling the truth and an insecure firm that is lying. Hence workers will be unable to demand a wage differential from insecure firms because they will not know from which firms to demand it. Similarly, secure firms will be unable to offer lower wages than insecure firms because workers will not be able to tell if the secure firms are telling the truth about the security of the jobs offered. Instead, workers will be forced to calculate their willingness to work based on assumptions about the relative proportion of secure versus insecure jobs in the marketplace. In other words, they will view all firms as average and make their decisions about where to work accordingly. The supply of labor for both firms will be somewhere between what would have been the supply for the secure and the insecure employment firms and would reflect the workers' beliefs about the probability that the firm they work for is secure or insecure. Moreover, one would expect that the cost of labor for the economy as a whole would rise because workers would have to be compensated for being subject to fraud by their employers.

False information thus has serious consequences. Firms that offer insecure employment are able to decrease the wages they pay their employees, even though the underlying insecurity of the employment they offer has not changed. Also, because they no longer have to pay a wage differential, insecure employment firms will demand more workers. Secure employment firms, on the other hand, are forced to pay a higher wage, even though the underlying security of the employment they offer has not changed. Because they are forced to pay a higher wage, the secure employment firms will tend to employ fewer workers.... [T]oo many people (from the societal perspective) are working for the insecure employment firm, and too few are working at the secure employment firm; the wages at the secure employment firm are too high, and the wages at the insecure employment firm are too low.

Of course, while this scenario is inefficient overall, the skewing of the information available in the market is favorable to some. The workers who retain their jobs in secure employment firms will be making a higher wage. The shareholders of insecure employment firms, or more precisely, the shareholders of insecure employment firms that lie about the riskiness of the employment they offer, will benefit from the opportunity to employ more workers at a lower wage. But people suffer in this scenario as well. Because wages at secure employment firms will be (artificially) increased, they will not be able to employ as many workers. Some of their employees will be thrown out of their jobs. If these laid-off workers find jobs at untruthful, insecure employment firms, they will be working for less than they would demand if they knew about the insecurity of their employment. Workers at untruthful, insecure employment firms will have their wages cut. Quite a number of investors will lose as well. Truthful, insecure employment firms will suffer financially because they bear an unfair competitive disadvantage *vis-a-vis* untruthful, insecure employment firms. Shareholders of secure employment firms will also lose because those firms will no longer be able to offer lower wages because of the security of the employment they offer. Although this scenario creates some "winners," the losers have lost more than the winners have won. Incomplete information has moved us away from the socially optimal equilibrium.

Over time, the harmful effects multiply. Because the profits of secure employment firms will tend to fall and the profits of (untruthful) insecure employment firms will tend to rise, some secure employment firms will go out of business (or, said another way, will become insecure employment firms). The market will begin to be dominated by insecure employment firms. The lies of the insecure employment firms not only will have hurt their own workers but will have dragged down the market as a whole.

Lack of accurate information about job security (or, for that matter, about any other employment condition valued by employees) will cause workers to allocate their labor to inefficient uses and will force employers offering secure employment to pay more in wages than they would need to if workers had correct information. Fewer workers will be employed by firms offering secure employment, and more workers will be employed by firms offering insecure employment. The story thus far is sufficient to show that, as in the capital market, the need for correct information is important to ensure allocative efficiency in the labor market.

Job Security as an Endogenous Variable. There is an additional reason that the law should seek to ensure accurate information in the labor market by prohibiting fraud against employees. Up to this point, this analysis has assumed that the level of risk of job discontinuity is a fixed, exogenous variable, something which each firm accepts as given and which is unaffected by company policy or practices. This assumption is certainly correct in many respects because companies are subject to market forces they cannot control and some industries are inherently more risky in this sense than others. Yet this assumption is incorrect in other ways because the incidence of job discontinuity is partially a function of planning, company policy, management, capital investment, and marketing.

Thus the amount of job security that a company provides is something that the company can affect. Some efforts to reduce the incidence of job discontinuities will impose costs on the firm. But they need not be large costs; indeed, the company may be able to decrease the incidence of job discontinuity cheaply by, for example, planning production schedules more carefully or buying more advertisements. But it is to be expected that the cost of reducing job discontinuities will increase as the rate of job discontinuities falls and it becomes increasingly difficult to find simple and low-cost methods of reducing job risk. In other words, a firm faces increasing marginal costs of preventing job discontinuities.

Significantly, however, a firm does not only incur additional costs with improvements in job security. It also realizes the monetary benefit based on the wage differential for secure employment firms. When a company decreases the incidence of job discontinuity its workers must suffer, it will be able to attract a work force at a lower wage rate.... [T]he threat of job discontinuity is something that, other things being equal, workers would rather avoid. As the incidence of job discontinuity increases, informed workers demand a higher risk premium for each additional amount of risk. Thus, as the rate of job discontinuity increases, firms will have to pay a higher and higher wage premium. As they decrease the risk of job discontinuity, they receive a benefit by way of the lower wages they can pay to attract workers.

When deciding how much to spend on preventing job discontinuities, a firm must consider both the monetary cost and monetary benefit of reducing such discontinuities. The optimal level of expenditures is at the level where the cost of prevention and the marginal cost of discontinuity are equivalent. Consider the possibility that firms will mislead workers about the security of their employment. If firms can lie with impunity, all firms will have incentives to mislead their workers into believing that their jobs are more secure than they are. With such widespread mendacity, workers likely would not demand a fully compensatory risk premium in wages. They will probably assume that their jobs are more secure than they are in fact and thereby demand less of a wage differential to compensate them for that additional risk.

In such a case, the company's marginal cost of job discontinuity would be falsely deflated. Because the costs of job discontinuity would be held falsely low, a firm would tend to spend less on the prevention of job discontinuities. The false equilibrium brought about by fraud would thus tend to involve a higher level of job insecurity than if fraud were not present. Incomplete information, therefore, not only takes us away from allocational efficiency but plausibly results in a greater number of job discontinuities such as layoffs and plant closings. Allowing fraud in the labor market decreases the benefits firms gain from offering security and decreases the costs firms bear from providing insecurity, which makes insecurity more likely.

Some Additional Costs of Fraud in the Labor Market.... [T]he capital market's greater national scope and efficiency might appear to argue for greater protection than in the labor market. The national exchanges facilitate a highly efficient and very important system for security sales and purchases. If a company issues stock using misleading statements, the fraud will be incorporated into the prices of the company's stock, wherever the purchaser might be. Moreover, if fraud is not punished effectively, investors will eventually lose confidence in the securities market and will tend to shift to alternative methods of investing. Because the health of, and confidence in, national exchanges is vital to a strong national economy, fraud protection for such markets is seen as essential.

Labor markets, on the other hand, are less efficient and less national. If a company fraudulently assures workers in Ohio that their jobs are secure, such fraud is unlikely to affect workers in California greatly. Labor fraud is likely to have local, or perhaps regional effects, rather than national ones. In addition, one might argue, confidence in the labor market is less essential to the health of the national economy. Labor markets do not depend on a national labor "exchange," the success of which turns on the confidence of workers that it is not tainted by fraud. While investors have more alternatives and could throw the markets into a tailspin if fraud were quotidian, workers have to work. It is more important, one would say, to erect national fraud protection for the capital market than for the labor market.

This argument goes too far. Because it is less efficient and fluid, the labor market certainly is less sensitive to changes in worker "confidence" than the capital market is to investor confidence. But the sensitivity of the capital market also makes it more likely that fraud will be found out without the intervention of legal rules, as the incentives for monitoring the validity of company statements are quite high. Much money can be made by sniffing out fraud and either using such information to inform one's own trades or selling the information to other investors. It is less likely that private monitors for fraud will spring up in the labor market; the opportunities for arbitrage do not exist.

Furthermore, even if the labor market is less national than the capital market, it is certainly national enough to provide the basis for federal fraud protection. Employer fraud often creates an interstate effect, more obviously at some times than at others. Its national effect would be at least as high as other aspects of the employment relation subject to federal control. Indeed, the Supreme Court [in *Local 174, Teamsters v. Lucas Flour Co.*] has noted that the law surrounding labor agreements and collective bargaining "is "peculiarly one that calls for uniform law' " because "the possibility that individual contract terms might have different meanings under state and federal law would inevitably exert a disruptive influence upon both the negotiation and administration of collective agreements." The concern that words—the terms of understanding between employers and employees—be allowed to have a consistent meaning across jurisdictional boundaries would argue for a national fraud law just as strongly as for a national collective bargaining law.

One basis for concluding that the need for fraud protection is particularly strong in the labor market is that, from a macroeconomic perspective, fraud in the labor market arguably creates more allocative inefficiency than much of the fraud that occurs in the capital market.... [T]he securities laws make actionable not only the deceit that occurs in the initial distribution of securities, but also fraud that affects trades in the secondary market. As Paul Mahoney has explained, "Lies told in secondary markets have smaller allocative effects than those told in primary markets." Deceit in the secondary market does not cause the misdirection of financial capital to the issuer but rather the misdirection of shares among traders. Because the shares are not themselves the productive asset, "the overall efficiency consequences of putting noncontrolling shares of stock in the hands of one investor rather than another [are] small."

In contrast, the fraud of concern in the labor market—employers misleading employees to entice them to stay in or accept a job—is in the primary market. The workers' labor is itself the productive asset, and a misallocation of that asset from a higher-value use to a lower-value use inflicts deadweight loss on society in every case. This deadweight loss can be severe....

That financial capital is more fluid than human capital means that fraud in the labor market hurts workers in ways that capital investors need not suffer. As Daniel Fischel has observed, "Investors in capital markets are protected by the virtually infinite number of investment substitutes." Companies compete for capital investment, and if an investor is dissatisfied with the performance of a particular investment, she can usually sell it with little difficulty and at little cost. If a firm has misled capital investors with regard to, say, potential for investment gains, investors can generally find substitute investment vehicles in short order. They will have suffered loss, to be sure, but their loss can be minimized by rapidly transferring the funds from the defrauding firm to a truthful firm.

On the other hand, as Fischel states, "fewer substitutes exist for labor opportunities." Being unemployed or even self-employed is a less efficient substitute for a steel worker who loses her job than placing money in the bank is for an investor who must sell her stock in the steel company. An investor can find a multitude of alternative uses for disposable cash; a steel worker has many fewer alternatives for her skills. Cash does not need to be "retrained" before it can be used profitably again, but an unemployed steelworker might need such retraining.

Moreover, while investors in the securities markets typically can leave the market completely at little cost, the "exit option" is much more costly for workers. Workers simply cannot move as quickly as capital.... The exit option may in fact become more costly the longer the employee stays in her job. To the extent that the worker develops firm-specific skills or develops other links to a particular job or place, she becomes more dependent on the firm for continued employment. Thus, workers' ability to leave firms tends to become more constrained the longer they work for particular employers. The costs of employer fraud will therefore tend to be quite high when the employees affected are long-term employees.

There is yet another way in which fraud in the labor market is more costly than in the capital market. Capital investors can protect themselves *ex ante* from fraud by placing their funds in a number of different investment vehicles. From the standpoint of the individual investor, the risk of fraud can be seen as simply another risk of the market. While one firm might commit fraud on its investors, it is unlikely that many will do so at any one time. The costs of being victimized by fraud will be less when only a portion of one's investments are in the defrauding firm. Workers are much less able to protect themselves *ex ante* through diversification. Investors can put their eggs in many different baskets; full-time workers have only one egg and must place it in only one basket. In more economic terms, human capital is difficult to diversify because employees are unable to divide their labor resources—efforts and knowledge and skill—among a large number of firms. Employees are thus especially vulnerable to fraud by their employers because any cost they suffer is felt across their human capital "portfolio" rather than merely in one portion of it.

There is one final way in which fraud in the labor market is particularly costly. By definition, capital investors use savings to purchase stock. In addition, for most investors the income and capital gains from investments are not typically necessary for subsistence. A job, on the other hand, is much more closely tied to survival. For most, work is the method by which one gathers the necessities of life. One could generalize, then, and say that when a company defrauds an investor about an investment, the damage is to savings. When a company defrauds a worker about her work, the damage is to subsistence.

In the labor market as in the capital market, information matters. The damage of false or incorrect information is severe to workers, employers, and society in general. In addition, costs are present in the labor context that are absent from the securities one. Thus, unless some other factor is present, the conclusion that statutory protection is a good thing in the securities market is sufficient to demonstrate that it should exist in the labor market....

The Possibility of Market Self-Correction.... Government regulation of fraud may be unnecessary because the market will self-correct; perhaps competitive pressures will penalize fraud sufficiently that a rule against it is unnecessary. This argument is based on the insight that sellers of a good cannot lie costlessly about the qualities of the good. Some purchasers will seek to verify the representations before purchase, and, to the extent the representations were misleading, the potential purchaser will likely go elsewhere. Even if the purchaser fails to verify the seller's statements at the time of purchase, any misrepresentation will decrease the probability of repeat purchases. Moreover [as Easterbrook and Fischel explain] "[m]any sellers have competitors anxious to expose misstatements." Finally, firms that genuinely offer superior products will seek ways to bond their statements (with warranties, for example), to provide purchasers the opportunity to verify the seller's representations (through inspection or trial use periods, for example), or to allow third parties (outside accounting firms or consumers' groups) to check the truthfulness of the sellers' statements.

But, as Easterbrook and Fischel remind us, these market corrections will not work perfectly. Sellers of low-quality products can partly frustrate verification by "mimicking the disclosure of ascertainable facts while making bogus statements about things buyers cannot verify." Some sellers will not care about repeat transactions. Itinerant vendors, for example, "have no brand name to protect and seldom engage in multiple transactions with the same buyer, so they have strong incentives to misrepresent the quality of their wares in order to obtain a higher price." Even with the possibility of repeat purchases, sellers of low-quality items may often find that, as Easterbrook and Fischel put it, "the gains from one-shot deception [are] greater than the reputational loss"; that is, "some firms will find fraud to be the project with the highest net present value." In addition, certain products are simply not subject to accurate verification. Many securities, for example, constitute an interest in unique projects; in such case, "neither competitors' statements nor the prospect of repeat purchases will impose restraints, and it is very hard for a buyer to verify statements before the sale."

Market corrections are difficult in the labor market as well. Many workers will find it difficult, if not impossible, to verify employers' or potential employers' statements with regard to the safety of the workplace, job security, or certain employment benefits. Moreover, the labor market enjoys less protection from private monitors than does the capital market. While the capital market could rely on a number of private mechanisms to monitor fraud, unions are labor's best hope for ferreting out employers' misstatements. Unions, however, are in a period of historical weakness.

Even when verification and bonding are possible, they impose costs on the market transactions, and these costs are not always borne by the fraudulent party. These costs decrease the aggregate amount of commercial activity—if a widget purchaser has to spend five percent of the purchase price to verify the quality of the widgets she buys, she can purchase fewer widgets. If the high-quality supplier of widgets has to offer a warranty that adds five percent to the cost of providing the widget, then she too will sell fewer widgets. Moreover, to the extent that these verification and bonding devices are imperfect, sellers will begin to lose confidence in the market as a whole; they will tend to discount the quality of all the widgets in the market. Buyers will no longer be willing to spend as much as previously, even on good widgets, because they will be less sure that they are in fact buying good widgets. The makers of good widgets will tend to exit the market because they cannot get a fair price for their product. The market will then come to be dominated by makers of poor widgets.

One would expect that this effect would also occur in the labor market. Honest employers will have to expend resources to bond their statements, making it more expensive for them to hire any given amount of labor. To the extent that bonding and verification are imperfect, employees will tend to lose confidence in the labor market as a whole, making them less likely to enter the labor market in the first place and to demand higher wages if they do.

A rule against fraud can mitigate these effects. As Easterbrook and Fischel explain, a penalty for fraud makes it more costly for firms providing low-quality products (or employment, one might add) to use false disclosures to mimic firms providing high-quality products or employment; the fraud penalty, meanwhile, imposes no or low costs on honest firms providing high-quality products or employment. In fact, the rule against fraud decreases the costs that firms providing high-quality products or employment need to expend to certify their products. The costs of providing high-quality products or employment will fall while the costs of passing off low-quality products or employment will increase.

Of course, antifraud rules will themselves not operate perfectly, and they will impose costs of their own. To the extent that they are underenforced, or that the penalties imposed are too low to deter fraudulent conduct, firms providing high-quality products or employment may still need to use some additional certification devices. In order to enforce the rule, the government will have to dedicate resources to investigating, prosecuting, adjudicating, and punishing fraudulent activity. If the rule is overenforced or enforced inaccurately, honest firms will incur expenses protecting themselves from possible liability. Without a detailed empirical analysis, it is difficult to prove conclusively that the costs of a rule against fraud outweigh the benefits. But rules against fraud are indeed ubiquitous. They have been a concern of the common law for centuries, and they are presently found in the laws of all fifty states and of the federal government. If the costs of such rules outweighed their benefits, one would expect to see at least some jurisdictions without such rules....

Selected References

George A. Akerlof, The Market for "Lemons:" Quality Uncertainty and the Market Mechanism, 84 Quarterly Journal of Economics 488 (1970).

Sissela Bok, Lying (1978).

Stephen Breyer, Regulation and Its Reform (1982).

Victor Brudney, A Note on Materiality and Soft Information Under the Federal Securities Laws, 75 Virginia Law Review 723 (1989).

David Charny, The Employee Welfare State in Transition, 74 Texas Law Review 1601 (1996).

Frank H. Easterbrook & Daniel R. Fischel, The Economic Structure of Corporate Law (1991).

Daniel R. Fischel, Labor Markets and Labor Law Compared with Capital Markets and Corporate Law, 51 Chicago Law Review 1061 (1984).

Bruce E. Kaufman, The Economics of Labor Markets (4th ed. 1994).

Paul G. Mahoney, Precaution Costs and the Law of Fraud in Impersonal Markets, 78 Virginia Law Review 623 (1992).

Katherine Van Wezel Stone, Labor and the Corporate Structure: Changing Conceptions and Emerging Possibilities, 55 Chicago Law Review 73 (1988).

Case

Local 174, Teamsters v. Lucas Flour Co., 369 U.S. 95 (1962) (quoting *Pennsylvania R.R. v. Public Serv. Comm'n*, 250 U.S. 566 (1919)).

Further Reading (selected work by H. Kent Greenfield)

New Principles for Corporate Law, 1 Hastings Business Law Journal 87 (2005).

Using Behavioral Economics to Show the Power and Efficiency of Corporate Law as Regulatory Tool, 35 U.C. Davis Law Review 581 (2002).

Ultra Vires Lives! A Stakeholder Analysis of Corporate Illegality, 87 Virginia Law Review 1279 (2001).

The Place of Workers in Corporate Law, 39 Boston College Law Review 283 (1998).

CHAPTER TWENTY-THREE

THE PUBLIC'S RIGHT TO KNOW*

Since the September 11 attacks, the government has used nontraditional methods to detain, process, and prosecute individuals allegedly engaged in terrorist activities. One clear benefit of these nontraditional procedures has been that the government has been able to control the flow of information concerning its counterterrorism efforts by relying on the processes to which the public's constitutional and statutory "right to know" is at least arguably inapplicable. In addition, the government has capitalized on the judiciary's hesitation to force the disclosure of any information that will allegedly harm national security.

The judiciary's general unwillingness to enforce the "right to know" in a time of crisis is not surprising given the relatively short and tortured history of this right under the Freedom of Information Act (FOIA) and the First Amendment.... This Article suggests that the courts must keep in mind the interest in effective self-government that drove FOIA's passage in 1966 and the recognition of the First Amendment right of access in 1980. The right to know is more, not less, important in a time of crisis....

The History of the Right to Know.... The public's statutory and constitutional rights to access federal government information and proceedings are relatively new. Before the FOIA was passed in 1966, the executive branch agencies could, in essence, deny access to information at will.... Although the common law provided a limited right of access to judicial documents, it was only in 1980 that the Supreme Court held [in *Richmond Newspapers*] that the First Amendment guaranteed the public a right of access to criminal trials.

FOIA and the First Amendment right of access are powerful mechanisms by which the press and public alike can force the disclosure of and obtain ac-

---

* **Mary-Rose Papandrea**, *Under Attack: The Public's Right to Know and the War on Terror*, 25 BOSTON COLLEGE THIRD WORLD LAW JOURNAL 35 (2005), http://papers.ssrn.com/abstract_id=651402.

cess to government documents and proceedings. Even before September 11, 2001, however, the judiciary struggled to apply these rights. Courts reviewing FOIA claims have always been extremely reluctant to question the government's assertion that releasing the requested information would threaten national security. Likewise, courts have struggled to make sense of how to apply the constitutional right of access outside the context of criminal trials....

First Amendment Right of Access.... Early First Amendment cases recognized the right of private entities to impart—and of the public to receive—information.... These decisions recognized that the government cannot interfere with an individual's constitutional right to receive information from a willing speaker. Although these cases emphasized the importance of an informed public in a democracy, none addressed whether the First Amendment gave the public the right to force the government to disclose information.... In the 1970s, the Court decided a trio of prison access cases that seemed to sound the death knell for any First Amendment right of access to government information. [These included dissenting opinions generally emphasizing] political theory arguments that would later become the foundation for *Richmond Newspapers* ... [For example, in *Houchins*, Justice] Stevens argued that "the preservation of a full and free flow of information to the general public has long been recognized as a core objective of the First Amendment to the Constitution." ... Citing Alexander Meiklejohn and James Madison, he explained that the right to receive information is based on the need for an informed citizenry, which is essential for self-government.... Although none of the Court's pre-1980 decisions ever squarely determined whether the public enjoyed a First Amendment right of access or right to information, the dicta of the majority and plurality opinions in these cases certainly made the Court's eventual recognition of such a right appear implausible at best.

The Revolutionary Richmond Newspapers Decision. Richmond Newspapers, Inc. v. Virginia marked a seismic shift in the Court's interpretation of the First Amendment. In this case the Court recognized, for the first time, that the First Amendment played a structural role in requiring an open government.... Chief Justice Burger ... explained, like the rights of association and of privacy, the right of access is "implicit" in the enumerated rights. Underlying this implicit right, Burger elaborated, is the long history of open criminal trials in both England and colonial America. Citing scholars such as Jeremy Bentham and William Blackstone, who had argued that public scrutiny is the best "check" on perjury, bias, and other misconduct by trial participants, Burger noted the "significant community therapeutic value" of public trials by "providing an outlet for community concern, hostility, and emotion." ...

Burger [also] stated that openness is essential for the proper functioning of government itself, as it increases "respect for the law" and knowledge of "the methods of government," while also securing strong confidence in judicial remedies that "could never be inspired by a system of secrecy." Public attendance at trials enables citizens to understand the judicial process both generally and in a particular case. Burger remarked that "people in an open society do not demand infallibility from their institutions, but it is difficult for them to accept what they are prohibited from observing." ... In a concurring opinion joined by Justice Marshall, Justice Brennan explicitly emphasized that the right of access plays a structural role "in securing and fostering our republican system of self-government." ...

... [In] subsequent cases the Court adopted a two-prong history-and-logic test derived from Justice Brennan's *Richmond Newspapers* concurrence. This inquiry requires the consideration of two factors: (1) whether the proceeding has traditionally been open to the public, and (2) whether public access to the proceeding at issue would play a positive role. If the right of access attaches, the proceeding can only be closed only if the court makes specific findings that a "compelling governmental interest" necessitates closure, and that the closure is "narrowly tailored" to serve that interest. By applying a strict scrutiny standard, the Court made clear that the public's First Amendment right of access rises to the same level as the right to communicate....

The Freedom of Information Act. Although some courts and commentators have argued that the First Amendment right of access logically extends to government documents, most courts have rejected this view outside the context of judicial records. Instead, the public's right to obtain government documents and information is based largely on the Freedom of Information Act, or FOIA. The passage of FOIA in 1966 revolutionized the public's ability to force the government to release information. In the almost four decades since its creation, however, courts have been extremely reluctant to question government assertions that national security demands the continued confidentiality of the requested information. This has not changed despite congressional efforts to amend FOIA in order to encourage greater judicial scrutiny of these national security claims....

[For example, in] 1958, Congress tried to constrain the executive branch's right to withhold information from the public with an amendment to the Housekeeping Statute, which declared that the statute "does not authorize withholding information from the public or limiting the availability of records to the public." Although the House and Senate both passed this amendment unanimously, agencies continued to withhold documents from the public by relying on the limitations of section 3 of the [Administrative Procedure Act (APA)]. By the end of the 1960s, it was clear that amendments to section 3 were required to foster openness in government activities. Recognizing that comprehensive standards for disclosure and the right of judicial review were necessary in order to provide public access to government records, Congress replaced section 3 with FOIA in 1966.

Under FOIA, the public need not demonstrate a "need to know" to gain access to government documents; instead, FOIA creates a statutory "right to know." A person requesting documents also need not show any particular interest in or need for them; FOIA protects an individual's right to obtain documents for any purpose. Unlike its precursor, section 3, FOIA also provides for de novo judicial review of an agency's decision to withhold documents.

Recognizing the need to strike a balance between the right to know and the often compelling need to keep information private, Congress structured nine exemptions to FOIA's mandatory disclosure provisions. FOIA itself does not contain a broad "national security" exemption, but addresses national security directly only in Exemption 1, which exempts from disclosure information that has been classified pursuant to an Executive order.

In an effort to limit the amount of information that could be withheld under the vague pre-FOIA "public interest" standard, and to force the Executive to be more specific about its reasons for withholding information, Exemption 1 excuses from disclosure matters that are "specifically required by Executive order to be kept secret in the interest of the national defense or foreign policy." ...

Congress [further] amended the national security exemption of FOIA in 1974 to make clear that the judiciary should not simply rubber-stamp the Executive's classification decisions. Congress specifically designed the amendments to Exemption 1 to empower courts to exercise "meaningful judicial review of classification decisions" in order to rectify the "widespread over-classification abuses in the use of classification stamps." The 1974 amendments clearly authorized courts to review classified documents in camera for a de novo determination of their classification....

Although the plain language of FOIA allows courts to review *de novo* the Executive's decision to withhold information on the basis of Exemption 1, and nothing in FOIA requires judicial deference to the Executive's classification decisions, courts nevertheless have uniformly deferred to the government's classification determinations....

The Right of Access After September 11. Since September 11, the government has used administrative or military proceedings to detain and process individuals allegedly involved in terrorist activities. By proceeding in this way, the government has ... been able to conduct its counterterrorism efforts largely outside of public view....

Administrative Proceedings. Within seven weeks after the September 11 attacks, the government had detained over a thousand aliens as part of its counterterrorism investigation. In an effort to keep information about these detainees secret, Chief Immigration Judge Michael Creppy issued a directive to all U.S. immigration judges ordering heightened security measures in "special interest" cases. The Creppy Directive offered no definition of this "special interest" category, but the Department of Justice indicated in litigation that the category included removal proceedings for aliens who "might have connections with, or possess information pertaining to, terrorist activities against the United States." In practice, the government applied this category to all aliens rounded up during the post-September 11 investigation, regardless of whether actual evidence existed that they had been involved in terrorist activities. The Creppy Directive required judges to close the hearings to the public, with "no visitors, no family, and no press," and to neither confirm nor deny whether a particular case was even on the docket....

Various media and public interest groups attempted to obtain information about those noncitizens living in the United States who were detained in the aftermath of September 11. In one set of cases, they sought access to the detainees' immigration hearings, arguing that the Creppy Directive violated the First Amendment right of access. In another case, parties challenged the government's refusal to honor their FOIA request for basic information about the post-September 11 detainees, including their names, date of arrest, and place of detention. Appellate courts reviewing the government's national security secrecy claims reached mixed results, and the Supreme Court declined to review the issue. As a consequence, the public still has very little information about the identity and processing of these individuals.

Challenges to Closure of "Special Interest" Immigration Hearings. Two federal appellate courts—the Third and the Sixth Circuits—examined the First Amendment challenges to the Creppy Directive and reached opposite results. Although both courts agreed that the *Richmond Newspapers* history-and-logic test applied to the removal proceedings, the Sixth Circuit applied the test and concluded that the presumptive right of access attached, while the Third Circuit concluded that it did not.

In response to the First Amendment challenges to the Creppy Directive, the government argued that the "closure of removal proceedings in special interest cases is necessary to protect national security by safeguarding the Government's investigation of the September 11 terrorist attack and other terrorist conspiracies." Specifically, the government maintained that disclosing the names of the "special interest" detainees would enable possible terrorists to compile seemingly innocuous information and create a "mosaic" that would reveal the direction, patterns, and progress of the investigation; this mosaic would thus reveal which terrorist cells had been compromised and which ports of entry were most dangerous.

Both the Third and Sixth Circuits agreed that the two-pronged history-and-logic test dictated the relevant inquiry for determining whether there is a constitutional right of access to deportation hearings. The courts rejected the government's argument that the Executive's plenary power over immigration required deference on "all facets of immigration law" as long as they are "facially legitimate and *bona fide*," noting that this deference was appropriate only to the Executive's promulgation of substantive immigration laws, not rules of procedure implicating constitutional rights. The courts also rejected the government's contention that *Richmond Newspapers* applied only to criminal proceedings, emphasizing that a removal proceeding is an adversarial process that closely resembles a judicial trial.

It was in the application of the *Richmond Newspapers* test, however, where the courts' agreement ended. The Sixth Circuit applied the history-and-logic test and concluded that there was a constitutional right of access to the deportation hearings, and that the government had not met its burden of showing the closure order was narrowly tailored to address the government's compelling interest in national security. In contrast, the Third Circuit determined that there was not even a presumptive right of access to "special interest" deportation hearings because they failed both prongs of the history-and-logic inquiry.

The courts' disagreement first centered on whether removal proceedings had a sufficient tradition of openness to satisfy the history prong. The Sixth Circuit found that "although exceptions may have been allowed, the general policy has been one of openness." The court noted that no immigration statute had ever required closure, and that since 1965, INS regulations have provided explicitly for presumptively open proceedings. The court took notice of historical evidence that some deportation hearings were conducted in prisons, hospitals, and homes, but discounted these hearings as rare exceptions. The Third Circuit, in contrast, placed much more emphasis on these exceptions, and concluded that the history of openness of deportation hearings "has neither the pedigree nor uniformity necessary to satisfy *Richmond Newspapers'* first prong."

Although the Third Circuit's conclusion concerning the history of openness of deportation proceedings is debatable…, its analysis of the logic prong was truly unprecedented. The Sixth Circuit approached the logic inquiry in a traditional manner and concluded that its requirements were met in the context of deportation hearings. The court emphasized that public scrutiny was particularly important in immigration proceedings because in that area "the government has nearly unlimited authority, [and] the press and the public serve as perhaps the only check on abusive government practices." In addition, after September 11, openness has particularly significant "cathartic" effect by serving as an outlet for the hostility and high emotions resulting from the terrorist attacks.

The Third Circuit, in contrast, voiced frustration that the "logic" prong did not do much "work," noting that it could not identify a case where the proceedings passed the history test but failed the logic test. The court concluded that the logic prong therefore must require consideration of not only whether openness can play a positive role, but also whether openness could "impair the public good." The court emphasized that "in the wake of September 11, 2001, a day on which American life changed drastically and dramatically ... the primary national policy must be self-preservation." The Third Circuit summarized the reasons the government gave for closing all "special interest" deportation hearings—with no discussion of whether the government assertions were reasonable or credible—and held that the government had met its burden of presenting substantial evidence that a presumption of open hearings could threaten national security. The Third Circuit conceded that the government's showing of national security risk was "to some degree speculative," but concluded that "we are quite hesitant to conduct a judicial inquiry into the credibility of these security concerns, as national security is an area where courts have traditionally extended great deference to Executive expertise."

The Sixth Circuit was far more skeptical of the government's national security argument. First, the court considered whether government had met its burden of rebutting the presumption that the right of access applied. To meet its burden, the government was required to show that not only its compelling interest in closure, but also that the broad Creppy Directive was narrowly tailored to serve this interest. The Sixth Circuit accepted that the government had a compelling interest in preventing terrorism, and that the government's "mosaic" argument had possible merit—that is, that terrorists could take "bits and pieces of information that may appear innocuous in isolation" and piece them together "to help form a bigger picture' of the government's terrorism investigation." The court concluded, however, that the government had not demonstrated that the Creppy order was narrowly tailored to serve its national security interests, or that "no less restrictive alternative would serve the government's purpose." ...

Request for Detainee Information Under FOIA. [Numerous] public interest organizations committed to human rights and civil liberties issues filed a FOIA request to make public the identities of the detainees and their attorneys, dates of arrest and release, locations of arrest and detention, and the reasons for detention. To support their request, the plaintiffs submitted press reports that "raised serious questions about deprivations of fundamental due process, including imprisonment without probable cause, interference with the right to counsel, and threats of serious bodily injury." In response, the government indicated that the detainees fell into three categories: (1) individuals criminally charged; (2) individuals held on immigration charges; and (3) material witnesses. The Department of Justice agreed to release a small portion of the requested information concerning the few detainees who had been criminally charged. With respect to the immigration detainees, however, the government refused to reveal their names, the names of their counsel, the dates of arrest, any filed charges, or the dates on which any of the detainees had been released. The government refused to disclose any information at all about the material witnesses. The requesters filed suit in federal district court in the District of Columbia challenging the Department's withholding decision.

In opposing the lawsuit, the government claimed that the detainee information was exempt from disclosure under FOIA because its release would interfere with the government's counterterrorism efforts. Throughout its brief, the government emphasized that the court must defer to the Executive's determination that releasing the information would pose a threat to national security. Like the Creppy Directive, which applied indiscriminately to post-September 11 detainees, the Department of Justice's response to the FOIA request did not distinguish between the detainees who had been found to have terrorist connections and those who did not; instead, the Department asserted that the information needed to be protected under a "mosaic" theory.

Although the government claimed that "national security" concerns required the nondisclosure of detainee information, the government did not claim that this information was exempt from disclosure under Exemption 1.... Exemption 1 applies only to information that has been properly classified pursuant to an Executive order. Because information about the post-September 11 detainees had not been classified, the government could not invoke that exemption. Instead, the government claimed that the detainee information was exempt from disclosure under [other] FOIA ... exemptions that permit the withholding of information "compiled for law enforcement proceedings" when disclosure "(A) could reasonably be expected to constitute an unwarranted invasion of personal privacy, ... (C) could reasonably be expected to constitute an unwarranted invasion of personal privacy, [or] ... (F) could reasonably be expected to endanger the life or physical safety of any individual.

The D.C. Circuit rejected the request for detainee information. Just as the Third Circuit created an exemption to the First Amendment right of access for national security matters, the D.C. Circuit essentially created a "national security" exception to FOIA. The court explained that the appropriateness of judicial deference to the Executive "depends on the substance of the danger posed by disclosure—that is, harm to the national security—not the FOIA exemption invoked." At several points throughout its opinion, the D.C. Circuit reiterated the importance of judicial deference to the Executive when national security matters are at issue. The court appeared concerned, as the government repeatedly warned in its brief, that grave consequences would result if the court released the requested information about the detainees. The majority noted that "the need for deference in this case is just as strong as in earlier cases. America faces an enemy just as real as its former Cold War foes, with capabilities beyond the capacity of the judiciary to explore." Just as the Third Circuit [had done], the D.C. Circuit concluded that when national security matters are implicated, it would be "unwise to undertake searching judicial review."

Applying this extremely deferential mode of analysis, the court accepted as "reasonable" the government's argument that releasing the names of all the post-September 11 detainees would enable potential terrorists to map the counterterrorism investigation and develop ways to impede it. The court rejected the plaintiffs' argument that terrorist organizations most likely know which of its members have been detained, stating that it had "no way of assessing that likelihood" and that even if it did, "a complete list of detainees could still have great value in confirming the status of their members." A terrorist group might not know that one of its members had been detained briefly and released, and if it learned that information, "this detainee could be irreparably compromised as a source of information." In addition, the court explained, a released detainee might not be a member of a terrorist group but merely have information about terrorists who are members of their mosques or community groups. These individuals will be less likely to cooperate with officials if their names are released, and terrorist groups might attempt to intimidate these individuals or feed them false or misleading information. The Court also noted that future potential informants are less likely to come forward if they believe their identities will be revealed.

At a pivotal moment in its opinion, the majority seized on the vague assertion in a government declaration that "concerns remained" about the detainees' links to terrorism to leap to the conclusion that in fact "many of the detainees have links to terrorism." The court added that "this comes as no surprise given that the detainees were apprehended during the course of a terrorism investigation, and given that several detainees have been charged with federal terrorism crimes or held as enemy combatants." The court disregarded the fact that, as of the time the FOIA suit was filed, only one detainee out of 1,182 had been criminally charged in connection with the September 11 attacks, and ignored as well the government's concession that many of the detainees included individuals proven to have no connection with terrorist activity and "no information useful to the investigation."

The majority also agreed with the government's contention that disclosing the names of the detainees' attorneys, or the dates and locations of arrest, detention, and release for each would have the same potentially "disastrous" consequences as releasing the names of the detainees themselves. The court predicted that the press would talk to the attorneys to compile information about the detainees, and that the remaining information concerning the date and place of their arrest, detention, and release "would provide a chronological and geographical picture of the government investigation," allowing terrorists to "derive conclusions as to how to more adequately secure their clandestine operations in future terrorist undertakings." ...

The D.C. Circuit opinion ... exacerbates a longstanding tendency of the courts to defer to the Executive's classification decisions. Even before the terrorist attacks of September 11, courts and commentators had lamented the judiciary's excessive deference to the Executive's classification decisions. The text of FOIA makes clear that all decisions to withhold information from the public must be reviewed "de novo." Affording broad, almost conclusive deference to the Executive's decisions regarding the disclosure of information whenever the Executive asserts a "national security" need for secrecy—whether for classified information subject to Exemption 1 or not—is contrary to Congress's clear intention, and returns the public's right of access to its unfortunate status before FOIA, when the Executive could withhold information on the basis of his unreviewable determination that it was "in the public interest" to do so.

The Threat to the Right to Know. Although the Third and D.C. Circuits were evaluating different claims—respectively, the First Amendment right of access and FOIA—the cases are remarkably similar in a number of ways. Most obviously, the two courts considered whether the public should be given access to essentially the same information about the post-9/11 detainees, and in doing so, both courts had to evaluate the government claims that such access would threaten national security. Beneath the surface, the two decisions also reflected deeper misgivings as to the value of the right of access, particularly when the government alleges that releasing the information could harm national security, and even more so when that information concerns noncitizens, a group historically suspect in times of war....

Failure to Recognize the Value of the Public's Right to Know.... Both the D.C. and Third Circuits failed to recognize the importance of an open government for the democratic process. When determining whether the public's interest in openness proceedings outweighed the government's interest in national security, the Third Circuit gave virtually no weight to the democratic importance of openness and the checking function that informed public debate can have on government actors. Instead, the court disparaged the value of openness as merely providing a "community benefit of emotional catharsis."

With this limited view of the value of the right of access, the court not surprisingly concluded that it was "impossible" to weigh this interest "against the security risk of disclosing the United States' methods of investigation and the extent of its knowledge." Indeed, the Third Circuit went so far as to state that "the reality" was that "the persons most directly affected by the Creppy Directive are the media." Both the Third and D.C. Circuits accepted the government's assurances that it had respected the civil liberties of the detainees by protecting their due process rights and providing them access to counsel. The D.C. Circuit explained that press access was unnecessary because the detainees "had access to counsel, access to the courts, and freedom to contact the press or the public at large." ...

[T]he courts' focus on the underlying rights of the detainees ignores the broader purposes of the right of access. It is not simply the media that benefits from openness, but the public that they serve. It is through the press—and increasingly watchdog groups—that the public learn about the government's processes and see for themselves whether those processes are fair. It is not merely about the "emotional catharsis" value of openness, but the democratic values this openness serves. If the government released information about the detainees and it turned out that the detainees were treated properly, this fact would increase the public's confidence in the government. Instead, by concealing detainee information, the government only gives credence to the suspicion that the government has something to hide.

The Sixth Circuit had no trouble identifying the public's interest in presumptively open removal proceedings, particularly in a time of crisis. It closed its opinion by noting that the open proceedings best served the public's interest, particularly after September 11, in order to "ensure that our government is held accountable to the people and that First Amendment rights are not impermissibly compromised." Noting that "democracies die behind closed doors," the court said that:

> it would be ironic, indeed, to allow the Government's assertion of plenary power to transform the First Amendment from the great instrument of open democracy to a safe harbor from public scrutiny ... Even though the political branches may have unfettered discretion to deport and exclude certain people, requiring the Government to account for their choices assures an informed public—a foundational principle of democracy.

It is difficult to comprehend how public pressure can begin to be effective if the public does not even have sufficient information by which to judge its government....

Conclusion. The Freedom of Information Act and the First Amendment right of access have served as poor tools for ensuring the public's ability to obtain information about the government's detention of individuals as part of its counterterrorism efforts. As demonstrated above, a variety of factors contribute to this problem. FOIA is riddled with large, undefined exceptions. When information arguably involves national security, courts are too timid to force the executive branch to provide a thorough explanation for continued secrecy. The First Amendment right of access likewise has significant limitations. Although the scope of the right has expanded significantly since the Supreme Court first recognized it in the *Richmond Newspapers* decision, its scope remains severely limited....

Selected References

Harold L. Cross, The People's Right to Know (1954).
John Hart Ely, Democracy and Distrust: A Theory of Judicial Review (1980).
David Mitchell Ivester, The Constitutional Right to Know, 4 Hastings Constitutional Law Quarterly 109 (1977).
Heidi Kitrosser, Secrecy in the Immigration Courts and Beyond: Considering the Right to Know in the Administrative State, 39 Harvard Civil Rights-Civil Liberties Law Review 95 (2004).
Potter Stewart, Or of the Press, 26 Hastings Law Journal 631 (1975).

Cases and Statutes

Ctr. for Nat'l Sec. Studies v. U.S. Department of Justice, 331 F.3d 918 (D.C. Cir. 2003).
Detroit Free Press v. Ashcroft, 303 F.3d 681 (6th Cir. 2002).
Houchins v. KQED, Inc. 438 U.S. 1 (1978).
New Jersey Media Group, Inc. v. Ashcroft, 308 F.3d 198 (3rd Cir. 2002), *cert. denied*, 538 U.S. 1056 (2003).
Nixon v. Warner Communications, Inc. 435 U.S. 589 (1978).
Pell v. Procunier, 417 U.S. 817 (1974).

Richmond Newspapers, Inc. v. Virginia, 448 U.S. 555 (1980).
Saxbe v. Washington Post Co., 417 U.S. 843 (1974).
Freedom of Information Act, 5 U.S.C. §552 (2000).

B. Equality and Difference

CHAPTER TWENTY-FOUR

DEPORTATION, SOCIAL CONTROL, AND PUNISHMENT*

We live in a time of unusual vigor, efficiency, and strictness in the deportation of long-term permanent resident aliens convicted of crimes. This situation is the result of some fifteen years of relatively sustained attention to this issue, which culminated in two exceptionally harsh laws: the Antiterrorism and Effective Death Penalty Act of 1996 (AEDPA) and the Illegal Immigration Reform and Immigrant Responsibility Act of 1996 (IIRIRA). In many cases, these laws have brought about a rather complete convergence between the criminal justice and deportation systems. Deportation is now often a virtually automatic consequence of criminal conviction. This convergence, and the harshness of these laws—their retroactivity, their use of mandatory detention, the automatic and often disproportionate nature of the deportation sanction, and the lack of statutes of limitation—raise two related questions: First, why are we doing this? Second, what could be the consequences of this approach for the constitutional legitimacy of deportation proceedings?

The answer to the first question seems not necessarily to be that we have abandoned our traditional openness to immigration. Indeed, the United States presents the rather paradoxical picture of a nation-state that has expanded both the number of people whom it admits and the number of people whom it expels. The concern, it seems, is not so much with the quantity of immigrants as with their personal qualities. Deportation policy, in particular, has aimed increasingly at permanently "cleansing" our society of those with undesirable qualities, especially criminal behavior.

This trend prompts the second question—that of constitutional legitimacy. The justifications that proponents commonly offer for current deportation policies are simple, compelling, and frequently (although not always) devoid

---

* **Daniel Kanstroom**, *Deportation, Social Control, and Punishment: Some Thoughts About Why Hard Laws Make Bad Cases*, 113 HARVARD LAW REVIEW 1889 (2000), http://papers.ssrn.com/abstract_id= 715208.

of any obvious anti-immigrant or racist sentiment. First, we deport people as part of our efforts to control serious crime in our communities. Second, we deport people to maintain the credibility and legitimacy of our immigration laws. These two justifications, although easily conflated, are quite distinct and raise rather different conceptual and doctrinal problems. This Essay, which deals mostly with the first, suggests that the ascendancy of the crime control justification, together with the increasing real-world convergence between our criminal justice and deportation systems, compels a rethinking of the foundational principles underlying the constitutional status of deportation. In particular, the constitutional norms applicable to criminal cases should inform our approach to deportation far more specifically than they have in the past.

My argument is one of logic, consistency, and justice; it is not aimed at achieving greater efficiency. Locally, and in the short term, deportation as a crime control strategy is efficient. If criminal aliens are no longer here, and if they are prevented from returning, they are *ipso facto* no longer part of our crime problem. They are now somebody else's problem.... Despite the likely international costs of such a policy, its propriety seems so self-evident that much of the recent scholarly literature on the subject has focused more on critiques of the INS for its alleged failure to deport enough criminal aliens than on why we have such a policy in the first place and what its constitutional implications are. Indeed, the latter two questions are rarely, if ever, asked by commentators. As [Peter Schuck and John Williams] put it: "It is hard to think of any public policy that is less controversial than the removal of criminal aliens.... No policymakers or significant interest groups have argued that aliens who commit serious crimes after IIRIRA's effective date should not be removed."

But even were this assessment true, consensus is no proof of coherence, and efficiency is not justice. It does not require much analysis to see that the dramatic increase in deportation of long-term permanent residents, who may have lived in the United States since early childhood, for increasingly minor post-entry criminal conduct raises profound humanitarian and constitutional concerns.

The basic doctrinal problem is not new, but the increasing convergence of deportation and crime control warrants a fresh look at it. In brief, the problem is this: In the language of criminal law theory, whether consequentialist and utilitarian or nonconsequentialist and based on "desert," deportation of long-term lawful permanent residents for post-entry criminal conduct seems in most respects to be a form of punishment. It serves an incapacitating function to the deported and a deterrent function to others. It may also, of course, be understood as a form of retribution.

Because each of these justifications—incapacitation, deterrence, and ret-ribution—is traditionally accepted as part of our criminal law, as opposed to our civil law, one might well assume that persons subject to these types of pro-ceedings would at least have the most basic constitutional rights accorded to criminal defendants. That such proceedings are initiated by a government en-forcement agency, are directly based on criminal conduct, involve incarcera-tion and forced movement of persons, and may result in lifetime banishment supports the logic of this assumption. Still, our courts have long held that de-portation proceedings are civil rather than criminal, and that deportation, however harsh it may be in practice, is not punishment. Indeed, as Justice Scalia's ... majority opinion in *Reno v. American-Arab Anti-Discrimination Committee* determined, "while the consequences of deportation may assuredly be grave, they are not imposed as a punishment." This principle reduces to the basic idea that non-citizens have no substantive claim to remain in the United States and are therefore subject to whatever rules Congress chooses to make, even if they are retroactive. They are not being punished; they are simply being regulated.

However, this argument is tautological: deportation is not punishment be-cause we do not view it as punishment. The argument is also counterintuitive: most people undoubtedly do see deportation as punishment. Furthermore, the argument is difficult to reconcile with another important aspect of U.S. legal history. Governmental power over non-citizens, particularly legal per-manent residents, has never been absolute. There are limits, which have been expressed as the line between regulation and punishment. The task of draw-ing that elusive line in deportation cases cannot be as easily avoided as it might at first appear from the broad language of some Supreme Court cases. Al-though the Court has repeatedly distinguished deportation from punishment and has characterized deportation as civil, this does not mean that every de-portation law is immune from constitutional scrutiny. Nor does it mean that the nature of that scrutiny is immutable.

Nearly a century ago, the Supreme Court's decision in *Yamataya v. Fisher* established the basic procedural norms to be applied to deportation cases: non-citizens within the United States who face deportation, whether for crime or for other reasons, are protected only by the procedural requirements of the Due Process Clause. If non-citizens should happen to have any of the rights accorded to criminal defendants, it is primarily because of statutory or regu-latory protections or because the courts have read such rights to be implicit components of due process.

The fluidity of this constitutional method—as contrasted to one more grounded in specific textual rights—has had a wide range of negative implications for non-citizens in many areas of law, including the law of retroactivity, the right to appointed counsel, the Fourth Amendment exclusionary rule, the privilege against self-incrimination, and the right against cruel and unusual punishment.

For a court to reconsider all of this would be portentous, if not, as Justice White once put it [in *Hicks v. Feiock*] infectious. So it is hardly surprising that courts have historically declined to do so, despite a chorus of scholarly opinion in support of the proposition that much of the edifice of deportation law rests on a shaky doctrinal foundation.

But hard times warrant hard thinking. This Essay therefore seeks to reinvigorate the discussion of how best to understand the constitutional doctrine of deportation law, particularly as it relates to post-entry conduct of lawful permanent residents. To do this, we must first disaggregate deportation from the formalistic generalities that have governed U.S. immigration law for more than a century. We should view deportation functionally and treat it as subject to the type of constitutional limitations placed on analogous government control of individual behavior. We may then determine whether current deportation laws relating to legal permanent residents warrant a basic reevaluation of some venerable, but increasingly untenable, ideas....

... [T]he foundational cases of U.S. immigration law [reveal] a basic contradiction among three approaches. *Fong Yue Ting v. United States*, the first case to determine that the source of federal deportation power was the same as the source of the power to exclude, implied that the deportation power is essentially limitless. The Court modified this view in *Yamataya v. Fisher* to the extent that it applied a flexible notion of procedural due process. But another case from the same era, *Wong Wing v. United States*, apparently endorsed substantive constitutional limits under certain circumstances. *Wong Wing* expressly distinguished deportation *per se* from imprisonment of deportable non-citizens at hard labor, holding that the latter required the constitutional protections applicable to criminal cases. Though this dichotomy masks some complexity, *Wong Wing* provides a very different model from that of *Yamataya*: if particular aspects of deportation are punitive, then particular constitutional protections are required....

Two Models of Deportation Law. The powerful convergence of racial, ideological, cultural, and doctrinal factors led the late nineteenth-century Supreme Court ... to make sweeping statements in support of the immigration control power of government and against the rights of immigrants. It is therefore easy to understand why the Court exhibited little interest in the existence of a subtle distinction between two basic types of deportation laws: those that constitute extended border control and those that involve general social control of alleged post-entry misconduct (or even danger based on mere status) of legally resident noncitizens. It is somewhat harder to explain why the current Court overlooked this point in *Reno v. American-Arab Anti-Discrimination Committee*, although the issue was not squarely presented by the facts of the particular deportation proceedings. Still, Justice Scalia's remarkably short discussion of why a selective prosecution defense should not be available to a person facing deportation proceedings seems to reflect a view of those proceedings as essentially related to border control. But the distinction between border control and social control deserves a more substantial analysis if the constitutional implications of *Wong Wing's* line between regulatory and punitive deportation laws are to be taken seriously. Moreover, it makes good theoretical sense to view these processes differently.

Extended border control deportation laws, viewed functionally, have three possible variants, each of which has been a part of U.S. law for many years. First are laws that prescribe the deportation of persons who have evaded border controls, either physically (that is, by surreptitious entry into the United States) or by fraud or misrepresentation. Second are laws that permit the deportation of persons who violate an affirmative condition on which they were permitted to enter. For example, a person who enters the United States as a student may be required to maintain a full course load. Third, and concededly more problematic within a regulatory/punitive framework, are laws that seek to address the violation of an express prohibition of which a noncitizen was informed at the time of admission into the United States. Thus, an immigrant may be informed when she arrives or during her application process that she should not receive public benefits within five years. The enforcement of such conditions may be viewed as essentially contractual, though if the provisions are too broad, either substantively or temporally, the contract metaphor becomes more tenuous. Still, this third type forms a bridge to a different category of deportation laws.

Pure social control deportation laws are not necessarily tied to the border or to the admission process at all. They follow what might best be termed an "eternal probation" or, perhaps, an "eternal guest" model. The strongest version of this model would suggest that noncitizens, including long-term lawful permanent residents, are harbored subject to the whim of the government and may be deported whenever the government so desires. A more constitutionally refined variant of this model would impose some structural limits on this power, perhaps requiring that deportation decisions be made pursuant to a statutory authority. Traditionally, however, U.S. courts have imposed virtually no substantive limits on deportation power. The basic idea has been that noncitizens, even lawful permanent residents, may be subject to a shifting, even retroactive, regime of deportation sanctions.

Constitutional deportation doctrine developed in the late nineteenth century in relation to laws that were primarily a form of extended border control. Though often quite harsh in their practical effects, these sorts of deportation laws generally fit well within traditional civil and regulatory models. For one thing, as noted, such laws seem essentially contractual. A condition is imposed at entry. If the condition is violated, the remedy fits the contract model: the primary goal of an extended border control law is to return the government and the individual to the status quo ante. There is no necessary link to wrongful conduct beyond the breach of the condition. Indeed, even an innocent violation of an entry requirement may result in the nullification of one's status....

The Civil/Criminal and Regulation/Punishment Distinctions. The Supreme Court ... has repeatedly asserted that deportation is, in general, neither a criminal process nor a punishment. This conclusion is based primarily on a view of the status of a lawful resident alien as akin to that of a guest or a probationer, even if the alien is a lawful "permanent" resident. But the Court has never held that alien status renders a person subject to whatever treatment the government cares to authorize. Indeed, *Wong Wing* made clear that the nature of the proceeding, not the status of the individual, matters most. There must be limits, but how are these to be determined?

... [T]he concept of procedural due process has done much of this work. Still, questions such as whether a lawful permanent resident may be subject to retroactive deportation, incarcerated indefinitely, deported for minor offenses or even no offense, or given a right to appointed counsel may directly implicate both the distinction between civil and criminal law and the shifting idea of which government conduct qualifies as "punishment."

Unfortunately, the courts have not taken a consistent approach to either the civil/criminal line or the definition of punishment for constitutional purposes. This inconsistency derives from the inherent ambiguity of the terms themselves, to the profound consequences that may flow from particular interpretations of them, and perhaps, to increasing numbers and types of government activities that do not fit well into either of the two traditional categories. As [Susan Klein puts it:] "To maintain a system that grants special procedural protections only to defendants in criminal proceedings, we must be able to distinguish the criminal from the civil. This task has become impossible...." Still, an attempt to bring doctrinal coherence to these issues provides a framework (if not a precise model) within which deportation statutes may be analyzed. Despite its vacillations, this approach is analytically superior to the formalist shroud applied to the subject by *Fong Yue Ting* and the amorphous due process calculus of *Yamataya* and its progeny because it most directly grapples with the intent, nature, and consequences of government action....

Though obscured by the invocation of precedent, the conflation of two types of deportation, and the ideological forces at work in the twentieth-century cases, the modern Court's ambivalence toward the civil/criminal distinction also may cause unwillingness to grapple seriously with the argument that deportation is punishment in the constitutional sense. The multivalence of the civil/criminal problem and the uncertainty of possible implications of each particular approach have led to extraordinary doctrinal volatility between functionalist and formalist approaches. A model that seems to work adequately in one context breaks down as its implications become too obviously pro-defendant in another. This instability recently became clear when the Court, which had expanded the scope of certain double jeopardy protections in *United States v. Halper*, very soon thereafter radically restricted its prior functionalist understanding of the punitive nature of certain civil forfeiture cases.

The general rule that forfeiture was a quasi-criminal proceeding, established in 1886 in [*Boyd v. United States*], lasted for nearly a century, although the exact nature of the constitutional protections that flowed from this approach was never completely clarified. The Warren Court extended this rather open-ended attitude toward the civil/criminal distinction, indicating a willingness in various contexts to look beyond legislative labeling and to consider the nature and effects of "civil" or "remedial" laws. The most relevant of these cases was *Kennedy v. Mendoza-Martinez*, in which the Court invalidated a statute that revoked the U.S. citizenship of persons found to have evaded the draft. The *Mendoza-Martinez* Court developed a functional, multi-part test to determine whether the law was civil or punitive in nature. The Court concluded that the law was essentially criminal and that "this punishment cannot be imposed without a prior criminal trial and all its incidents."

It might at first seem to be a relatively small logical step to move from *Mendoza*-Martinez to a functional analysis of deportation laws, especially as they pertain to long-term legal residents. But there are problems with this move. First, deprivation of citizenship strikes many as a more severe sanction than deportation. Indeed, a significant part of the *Mendoza-Martinez* opinion deals with the fact that a person deprived of U.S. citizenship would likely be rendered stateless. Second, the *Mendoza-Martinez* Court went to some pains to distinguish the problem it was considering from that presented in *Trop v. Dulles*. *Trop* involved an individual's loss of U.S. citizenship as a result of a conviction by court-martial for wartime desertion. Five members of the *Trop* Court agreed that the statute at issue was invalid, but disagreed as to why.

The fractured approach of the Warren Court toward citizenship questions may explain why the *Mendoza-Martinez* Court did not view *Trop* as directly controlling. Indeed, the *Mendoza-Martinez* Court distinguished *Trop* on the ground that the latter case had "required conviction by court-martial for desertion before forfeiture of citizenship could be inflicted." This distinction is somewhat puzzling, however, because Mendoza-Martinez had been criminally convicted of draft evasion, which might well have seemed a sufficient factual predicate for expatriation. The Court dismissed this problem in a footnote as "of no relevance," noting that "the fact is that the 'crime' created by [the relevant sections of the Nationality Act of 1949 and the Immigration and Nationality Act of 1952] includes an element not necessary to conviction for [draft evasion]."

Thus, for the *Mendoza-Martinez* functional analysis to be applied at all to deportation for crime, one would apparently have to show that the deportation requires proof of something in addition to the crime itself. Such a showing may be possible, however, as deportation cases invariably require at least proof of alienage, and often other elements such as whether a crime is one of "moral turpitude." This is not the sole ambiguity present in *Mendoza-Martinez*, however. The majority opinion alternatively emphasized the quasi-criminal model and the argument that "it is fundamental that the great powers of Congress to conduct war and to regulate the Nation's foreign relations are subject to the constitutional requirements of due process." When the holding was stated plainly, it was grounded in both the Fifth and the Sixth Amendments.

In any case, the Warren Court did not extend the holding of *Mendoza-Martinez* to deportation. And the post-Warren Court moved more generally in the opposite direction as it began to disavow *Boyd*—the implicit underpinning of the *Mendoza-Martinez* method. In *United States v. Ward*, the Court expressly distanced itself from *Boyd* and developed a two-part test that emphasized the use of legislative intent for determining whether a penalty is civil or criminal. This development effectively sounded the death knell for the multi-functional type of analysis endorsed by the *Mendoza-Martinez* Court. A legislative decision to label a sanction as a "civil penalty" was now given deference, unless the defendant could offer "clear proof" that the proceeding was "so punitive either in purpose or effect as to negate [legislative] intention."

This analysis was not immediately used in the context of double jeopardy, however. In *United States v. Halper*, ... the Court held that a monetary civil sanction imposed by the government for the same offense for which a defendant had been convicted constituted a second punishment and was therefore unconstitutional under the Double Jeopardy Clause. Declining to defer to the legislative label, the Court concluded that "a civil sanction that cannot fairly be said solely to serve a remedial purpose, but rather can only be explained as also serving either retributive or deterrent purposes, is punishment." ...

The Court's recent disinclination to view harsh government action as punishment [extends to many circumstances]. Thus, life imprisonment based on a finding of mental abnormality and future dangerousness, confiscation of property owned by the innocent wife of a man who used it during the commission of a crime without her knowledge or consent, and permanent deprivation of the ability to work in a chosen profession are not punishments. There is significant methodological turmoil here....

... [R]ecognition of the need for some significant level of protection is an important thread throughout this meandering line of cases. The Court, it seems, cannot completely ignore the functional strain in civil/criminal jurisprudence, even as it seeks to avoid the dramatic effect of too easy an invocation of the Double Jeopardy Clause. This tension becomes especially clear in contexts such as long-term civil commitment, in which the sanction is the same as that imposed after a criminal trial. We have simply come too far to rely completely on legislative labeling or a priori formalist categories. Constitutional revulsion at excessively disproportionate fines or excessively facile procedures leading to incarceration remains a powerful value. How, then, might this understanding apply to deportation?

Two Models. Much scholarly effort has been devoted to critiquing the plenary power doctrine and reconciling the divergence between immigration law and what some have termed "alienage jurisprudence." Although many strands run through this body of work, there is virtual consensus among commentators that whatever the justifications may be for plenary power at the national border, the justifications are considerably weaker when applied to the deportation of permanent residents. As Nancy Morawetz ... asked: "How can it be that a permanent resident has a right to establish a laundry business, but no right to any protection as to the criteria governing deportation?" Courts today, as has long been the case, are generally unwilling to extend serious consideration to claims of rights by undocumented non-citizens.... If such claims were to succeed in importing criminal law protections to social control deportations, they would likely follow one of two basic models: substantive due process or analogical extension.

The Substantive Due Process Model. Some scholars and some courts, struck by certain harsh aspects of the new deportation laws, have suggested that the laws violate substantive due process. Since 1996, this approach seems to have been most resonant in the contexts of retroactivity and long-term detention, especially of legal permanent residents, and even, in some cases, after a final order of deportation has been rendered. Few circuit courts have squarely addressed these issues, however, and district courts have split over challenges to the mandatory detention aspects of the 1996 laws.

The Supreme Court has said [in *Foucha v. Louisiana*] that "freedom from bodily restraint has always been at the core of the liberty protected by the Due Process Clause from arbitrary governmental action." And the fiction that deportation is not punishment is especially hard to maintain when a person is incarcerated for a long period of time as part of the process....

To my knowledge, no substantive due process claims against the new deportation laws have prevailed outside the contexts of long-term detention and retroactivity. And the prospect of any application by the Supreme Court of substantive due process to deportation is not promising. Indeed, suggesting that a particular law violates substantive due process is a good way to start an argument with some Supreme Court Justices. Few doctrinal subjects more directly implicate normative values. The Court is sharply divided on how even to approach the question. A conservative majority supports a strict methodological limitation on what sorts of rights might qualify for due process protection, with two requirements, each of which might cut against the invocation of substantive due process rights in deportation cases. First, these Justices limit substantive due process protection to those fundamental rights and liberties that are, objectively, "deeply rooted in this Nation's history and tradition." Second, the Court requires a "careful description" of the asserted fundamental liberty interest.

Conversely, in a somewhat more promising formulation for deportation purposes, Justice Souter [in *Washington v. Glucksberg*] articulated an approach to substantive due process based on Justice Harlan's dissent in *Poe v. Ullman*. This approach seeks to reject the "deviant economic due process cases" while reaffirming the Court's "obligation to conduct arbitrariness review." Justice Souter cited Justice Harlan's *Poe* dissent in support of "three things that point to our responsibilities today." The first is respect for the tradition of substantive due process review itself. The second is a reminder that the purpose of such review is "not the identification of extratextual absolutes but scrutiny of a legislative resolution (perhaps unconscious) of clashing principles, each quite possibly worthy in and of itself, but each to be weighed within the history of our values as a people." In other words, it is "a comparison of the relative strengths of opposing claims that informs the judicial task, not a deduction from some first premise." The third is the need for the explicit attention to detail that "is no less essential to the intellectual discipline of substantive due process review than an understanding of the basic need to account for the two sides in the controversy and to respect legislation within the zone of reasonableness." This formula arguably leaves the door open to substantive due process claims against retroactivity, indefinite detention, and perhaps extremely disproportionate deportations of long-term legal residents for minor offenses.

To be sure, Justice Souter, like Justice Harlan, would limit protection to values truly deserving of constitutional stature—either those expressed in constitutional text (such as, perhaps, the Ex Post Facto Clauses) or those exemplified by "the traditions from which [the Nation] developed" or revealed by contrast with "the traditions from which it broke." Justice Souter also emphasized that "constitutional review, not judicial lawmaking, is a court's business here." The "weighing or valuing of contending interests" is only the first step—it is "no justification for judicial intervention merely to identify a reasonable resolution of contending values that differs from the terms of the legislation under review." Rather, "it is only when the legislation's justifying principle, critically valued, is so far from being commensurate with the individual interest as to be arbitrarily or pointlessly applied that the statute must give way." This is far from a radical doctrine, but it does seem powerfully antagonistic to the retroactive deportation of long-term legal residents for minor crimes.

General Analogical Extension.... [P]romising analogies might also be derived from arenas in which arguably civil proceedings have been recognized as criminal or quasi-criminal in nature. Juvenile delinquency is one obvious example. The Supreme Court held in *In re Gault* that juveniles in delinquency proceedings have a right to notice of charges, to counsel, to confrontation and cross-examination of witnesses, and to the privilege against self-incrimination. Although the Court set out the historical reasons that the juvenile justice system was created as a civil system, it noted that the unbridled discretion of juvenile courts, however "benevolently motivated," was "frequently a poor substitute for principle and procedure." Justice Fortas reasoned that whatever the historic rationale behind the juvenile justice system, the reality of Gault's situation called for procedural safeguards and "the exercise of care implied in the phrase "due process.' " The Court then turned to an assessment of Gault's particular situation and found that, although he was sent to an "industrial school" for juveniles, the "school" basically served as a way in which to incarcerate him. In view of the extreme loss of liberty at stake, the majority concluded that "[a] proceeding where the issue is whether the child will be found to be "delinquent' and subjected to the loss of his liberty for years is comparable in seriousness to a felony prosecution." Thus, due process required the provision of assistance of counsel. Similarly, the Court noted that "it would indeed be surprising if the privilege against self-incrimination were available to hardened criminals but not to children." Thus, the Court regarded juvenile delinquency proceedings, which could lead to commitment to a state institution, as criminal proceedings for purposes of the privilege.

The *Gault* Court, as noted, invoked the language of due process and did not rely directly on the Sixth Amendment, but the protections applied to criminal cases formed the model for the Court's determination of what due process required. The decision embodied a due process analysis that was powerfully informed by criminal law constitutional protections, as illustrated by the specific application of the Fifth Amendment privilege against self-incrimination. If the Court took such an approach to deportation proceedings, the results would likely be similar: at a minimum, there would be a constitutional right to counsel and a proscription of retroactivity.

The argument against this approach to due process, however, was also powerfully articulated in *Gault*. Justice Harlan, concurring in part and dissenting in part, was troubled by his inability to "determine with any certainty by what standards the Court decides that Arizona's juvenile courts do not satisfy the obligations of due process." He did not believe that the content of due process should be determined "by resort to any classification of juvenile proceedings either as criminal or as civil," because such an approach is "too imprecise to permit reasoned analysis of these difficult constitutional issues." Rather, Justice Harlan proposed considering "the settled usages and modes of proceeding," the "fundamental principles of liberty and justice which lie at the base of all our civil and political institutions," and "the character and requirements of the circumstances presented in each situation." This analysis, of course, is redolent of his dissent in Poe v. Ullman, discussed above, and the results would not necessarily be much different from the analysis employed by the Gault Court. In *Gault*, for example, Justice Harlan concluded that due process required timely notice, a right to appointed counsel (at least for those who are confined in an institution), and a written record for purposes of appellate review.

Conclusion. A unified field theory of constitutional punishment remains unwritten and elusive. This has led to odd results, such as periods when forfeiture garners greater protections than civil commitment, and when parents have a right to counsel if the state seeks to take their children, but no such right if they or their children face separation as a result of one or the other's deportation.

In the field of immigration law in general, and deportation law in particular, the lack of a comprehensive theoretical approach has been even more problematic. Classifying the proceedings as "civil" has simply subjected questions of fairness and rights to decisions based on a muddle of models. Historically, in order to avoid confronting directly the functional nature of deportation, the courts have relied on [a hodgepodge of] techniques.... The continuation of such approaches would not necessarily mandate complete acquiescence to the 1996 deportation statutes. But it would mean that the judicial system would have missed a unique opportunity to rectify some of the harm caused by *Fong Yue Ting* and to highlight the dubious legitimacy of its progeny....

Selected References

Louis Henkin, The Constitution and United States Sovereignty: A Century of Chinese Exclusion and Its Progeny, 100 Harvard Law Review 853 (1987)

Siegfried Hesse, The Constitutional Status of the Lawfully Admitted Permanent Resident Alien: The Inherent Limits of the Power to Expel, 69 Yale Law Journal 262 (1959).

Susan R. Klein, Redrawing the Criminal-Civil Boundary, 2 Buffalo Criminal Law Review 679 (1999).

Kenneth Mann, Punitive Civil Sanctions: The Middleground Between Criminal and Civil Law, 101 Yale Law Journal 1795 (1992).

Nancy Morawetz, Rethinking Retroactive Deportation Laws and the Due Process Clause, 73 NYU Law Review 97 (1998).

Gerald L. Neuman, Strangers to the Constitution: Immigrants, Borders, and Fundamental Law (1996).

Jim Rosenfeld, Deportation Proceedings and Due Process of Law, 26 Columbia Human Rights Law Review 713 (1995).

Peter H. Schuck & John Williams, Removing Criminal Aliens: The Pitfalls and Promises of Federalism, 22 Harvard Journal of Law & Public Policy 367 (1999).

Cases and Statutes

Boyd v. United States, 116 U.S. 616 (1886).
Cooper v. Telfair, 4 U.S. (4 Dall.) 14 (1800).
Fong Yue Ting v. United States, 149 U.S. 698 (1893).
Foucha v. Louisiana, 504 U.S. 71 (1992).
In re Gault, 387 U.S. 1 (1967).
Hicks v. Feiock, 485 U.S. 624 (1988).
Kennedy v. Mendoza-Martinez, 372 U.S. 144 (1963).
Mathews v. Eldridge, 424 U.S. 319 (1976).
Poe v. Ullman, 367 U.S. 497, 543 (1961) (Harlan, J., dissenting).
Reno v. American-Arab Anti-Discrimination Committee, 525 U.S. 471 (1999).
Trop v. Dulles, 356 U.S. 86 (1958).
Untied States v. Halper, 490 U.S. 435 (1989).
United States v. Ward, 448 U.S. 242 (1980).
Washington v. Glucksberg, 521 U.S. 702, 720–21 (1997) (Souter, J., concurring in the judgment).
Wong Wong v. United States, 163 U.S. 228 (1896).
Yamataya v. Fisher, 189 U.S. 86 (1903).

AEDPA, Pub. L. No. 104-132, 110 Stat. 1214 (codified as amended in scattered sections of 8, 18, 22, 28, 40, and 42 U.S.C.).

IIRIRA, Pub. L. No. 104-208, div. C, 110 Stat. 3009-546 (codified in scattered sections of 8 and 18 U.S.C.).

Further Reading (selected work by Daniel Kanstroom)

Criminalizing the Undocumented: Ironic Boundaries of the Post-September 11th 'Pale of Law,' 29 North Carolina Journal of International Law and Commercial Regulation 639 (2004).

From the Reign of Terror to Reining in the Terrorists: Defining the Rights of Non-citizens in the Nation of Immigrants, New England Journal of Comparative and International Law 47 (2003).

St. Cyr or Insincere: The Strange Quality of Supreme Court Victory, 16 Georgetown Immigration Law Journal 413 (2002).

Deportation and Punishment: A Constitutional Dialogue, 41 Boston College Law Review 771 (2000).

Crying Wolf or a Dying Canary?, 25 NYU Review of Law & Social Change 477 (1999).

CHAPTER TWENTY-FIVE

GIRLS IN THE JUVENILE JUSTICE SYSTEM*

As girls have entered the juvenile justice system in ever-increasing numbers, the limitations of a system built on the profiles of young male offenders have become manifest. The influx of girls has not only stretched the resources of this system, but it has also challenged all who work in the juvenile justice system to pay heed to their special needs—needs that may or may not be addressed by programs focused on, and driven by, boys' experiences and backgrounds. Girls deserve programs and services that allow them to flourish as individuals, freed from generalizations about what girls can or cannot, and should or should not, do.... [T]he disparities girls face in the juvenile justice system can be remedied by employing an equal rights analysis, including the federal Equal Protection Clause, state Equal Rights Amendments (ERAs) and Title IX of the Education Amendments of 1972....

Girls in the Juvenile Justice System: Who Are They? Promoting the rights of girls in the juvenile justice system requires an understanding of who these girls are. While boys and girls entering the system share many characteristics, research confirms that girls overwhelmingly have childhood histories of trauma and abuse, mental health disorders, and family separation. In addition, girls are more likely to be involved in prostitution or prostitution-related offenses. Finally, girls in the system, like boys, have experienced significant school failure....

[A] portrait of girls in the juvenile justice system shows a pattern of pre-delinquent trauma that runs deeper than that experienced by many of their male counterparts. Moreover, while there has been a marked increase in the arrest rates of girls for violent crimes such as aggravated assault, girls are still

---

* **Francine T. Sherman**, *When Individual Differences Demand Equal Treatment: An Equal Rights Approach to the Special Needs of Girls in the Juvenile Justice System*, 18 WISCONSIN WOMEN'S LAW JOURNAL 9 (2003) (co-authored with Marsha L. Levick), http://papers.ssrn.com/abstract_id=410368.

more likely than boys to be arrested for status offenses such as running away, curfew violations, and underage drinking, as well as prostitution and related offenses....

The Right to Individualized Treatment: The Enduring Purpose and Philosophy of the Juvenile Justice System.... Treatment rather than punishment has been central to the philosophy of the juvenile court.... .In its landmark decision *In re Gault*, the [Supreme] Court expressly noted the historical purpose of the court to treat and rehabilitate, rather than punish. Justice White, in his oft-quoted concurrence in *McKeiver v. Pennsylvania*, decided a few years after *Gault*, captured the fundamental differences between the juvenile and adult criminal justice systems:

> Reprehensible acts by juveniles are not deemed the consequence of mature and malevolent choice but of environmental pressures (or lack of them) or of other forces beyond their control. Hence the state legislative judgment not to stigmatize the juvenile delinquent by branding him a criminal; his conduct is not deemed so blameworthy that punishment is required to deter him or others. Coercive measures, where employed, are considered neither retribution nor punishment. Supervision or confinement is aimed at rehabilitation, not at convincing the juvenile of his error simply by imposing pains and penalties. Nor is the purpose to make the juvenile delinquent an object lesson for others, whatever his own merits or demerits may be. A typical disposition in the juvenile court where delinquency is established may authorize confinement until age 21, but it will last no longer and within that period will last only so long as his behavior demonstrates that he remains an unacceptable risk if returned to his family. Nor is the authorization for custody until 21 any measure of the seriousness of the particular act that the juvenile has performed.

This philosophy of the juvenile court emanates from the belief that youth are less blameworthy and more capable of reform than adults. It is believed that parents, society, and the state have a caretaking and custodial role to play with respect to minors that they do not have with adults. Unlike criminal courts, juvenile courts exercise jurisdiction as *parens patriae*. A "medical model" has therefore predominated in which behavioral ills have been identified and diagnosed, with treatment and therapy the focus of disposition. [As explained by Holland and Mlyniec, even] where "punishment" has recently been included by some jurisdictions as a component of disposition, the juvenile court retains its obligation "to insure that manifest rehabilitation accompanies the inevitable punishment." ...

As a direct consequence of the juvenile justice system's commitment to individualized treatment and rehabilitation, disposition is driven by the needs of the offender rather than the offense. In situations where the punishment is determined by statutory guidelines calibrated to the type and seriousness of the offense committed, a significant number of the juvenile justice statutes also require that dispositions be based on the youth's individual needs....

[C]ourts have repeatedly referenced the juvenile court's historic and continuing commitment to individualized treatment and rehabilitation, while highlighting the distinctions between the juvenile and adult justice systems.... Further underscoring the central rehabilitative purpose of the juvenile justice system, courts have also repeatedly recognized a "right to treatment" for juveniles who have been adjudicated delinquent. The legal underpinnings of this right have evolved over the course of the last three decades. In the 1970s, courts relied on the Eighth and Fourteenth Amendments to the U.S. Constitution to find a constitutional right to treatment for adjudicated youth. In particular, courts generally found the right to treatment in the due process guarantees of the Fourteenth Amendment....

Equal Rights Analysis on Behalf of Women and Girl Offenders: Comparing Apples and Oranges? Having established that girls in the juvenile justice system often have distinct needs from boys, and that the juvenile court is statutorily required to meet these individual needs, we turn to a discussion of equal rights strategies to enforce this mandate. The three strategies we discuss, the Equal Protection Clause of the Fourteenth Amendment, state Equal Rights Amendments and Title IX of the Education Amendments of 1972, all hold promise, and a note of caution.

Female prisoners challenging gender-based disparate conditions, policies and practices under the Equal Protection Clause of the Fourteenth Amendment and Title IX have met mixed success. Furthermore, state Equal Rights Amendment jurisprudence is quite limited with respect to prison conditions and practices. Yet Title IX's protection of equality in educational programming and activities is particularly applicable to alleged discrimination in juvenile justice programming and services. This is especially true where juvenile residential programs must serve a dual role as residential schools for their school-age residents who retain their state-created rights to basic and special education even while in placement....

Federal Equal Protection Analysis. The Equal Protection Clause of the Fourteenth Amendment "commands that no State shall 'deny to any person within its jurisdiction the equal protection of the laws,' which is essentially a direction that all persons similarly situated should be treated alike." When addressing equal protection claims, courts review the challenged law or policy under three standards of review: strict scrutiny, intermediate or heightened scrutiny, or rational basis. Usually, the court applies rational basis review. [As stated in *City of Cleburne*, this] means a governmental policy "is presumed to be valid and will be sustained if the classification drawn by the statute [or policy] is rationally related to a legitimate state interest." But, where suspect or quasi-suspect classifications or fundamental rights are at issue, the court will apply strict scrutiny to the classification. Under strict scrutiny, the classification must be narrowly tailored to meet a substantial or compelling governmental interest....

Despite ... substantial constitutional skepticism regarding official gender-based policies and practices, equal protection challenges under the Fourteenth Amendment to disparate treatment and conditions asserted by adult women offenders have faced significant obstacles. First, courts have not viewed men and women prisoners as similarly situated. Adult men and women are theoretically incarcerated for similar purposes: punishment, public safety, deterrence, retribution and, lastly, rehabilitation. However, women are most often incarcerated in different facilities for shorter time periods, with lower security ratings, for less serious or violent crimes than men. Also, they can get pregnant or are more likely to be parents than their male counterparts. Courts have therefore concluded that men and women prisoners are not similarly situated for the purposes of equal protection analysis. While some dissenting judges have noted the circular reasoning of this analysis—the more disparate the treatment of men and women prisoners the less such disparities may be subjected to constitutional scrutiny—the majority view remains that the inquiry fails at this threshold level....

The second stumbling block female prisoners have encountered is that courts tend to apply rational basis scrutiny to their challenges despite contemporary equal protection jurisprudence requiring heightened scrutiny of gender-based classifications. In applying a lower level of scrutiny to claims of gender-based discrimination by women prisoners, these courts have relied principally on the U.S. Supreme Court's decisions in *Turner v. Safleyn* and *O'Lone v. Estate of Shabazz*. The Court found in these cases that prison regulations challenged as burdening or interfering with the exercise of constitutional rights are subject to only minimum constitutional scrutiny....

In applying *Turner*, courts have drawn a distinction between equal protection challenges that allege discrimination between prison programs themselves, and challenges to the process by which programming decisions are made. [Some courts have] held that challenges aimed at the programs themselves do not implicate a facial challenge to gender-based statutes, polices or procedures, and accordingly are both subject to only rational basis scrutiny and require proof of invidious discrimination. On the other hand, prison policies may be subject to a heightened scrutiny review in an equal protection analysis of the decision making process.... As a consequence, when courts have viewed the female prisoners' challenges as targeting gender-neutral programming differences, the courts have upheld the challenged practices or policies as reasonable under ... *Turner* ... [While such cases] cloud the prospects for equal protection challenges to discriminatory prison practices based on gender, the landscape is not entirely bleak. Other circuits have found in favor of the female prisoners....

Women's cases offer guidance for lawyers raising federal equal protection challenges to unequal conditions on behalf of girls in the juvenile justice system.... [S]everal questions [arise]: Are the plaintiffs similarly situated to their male counterparts? What is the appropriate standard of review? What constitutes a facially discriminatory, as compared to gender-neutral, classification? What governmental interests may be held to support the maintenance of disparate policies or practices?

With respect to the threshold question of whether the litigants are similarly situated, the juvenile justice system's promise of individualized treatment and rehabilitation places girls on a stronger footing than women, who are limited by the traditional criminal law objectives that drive the adult corrections system.... [T]he juvenile justice system was built upon the philosophy that the individual needs and characteristics of adjudicated youth must be identified and met. Accordingly, juveniles' dissimilarities as offenders or inmates are precisely what make them similar for the purpose of equal protection analysis. In other words, both male and female juvenile offenders are similarly situated in their shared right to an individualized disposition once they are adjudicated delinquent.

The standard of review of gender-based claims in the adult correctional context is clearly unsettled. Some of the more recent cases have favored the rational basis test of *Turner* and *O'Lone*. Even these cases, however, have drawn a distinction between challenges to the process by which program decisions are made and challenges to differences in the programs themselves. Thus, there remains the opportunity to frame challenges to disparities in the juvenile justice system in terms of the "process" exception [which notes] that male and female inmates are similarly situated at the beginning of the decision-making process. Under this rationale, claims that a court or agency has taken boys' but not girls' needs into account in designing or offering a particular program or service, may warrant the higher level of scrutiny....

State Equal Rights Amendments. Most state Equal Rights Amendments (ERAs) are modeled after the proposed federal Equal Rights Amendment.

They typically provide that, "Equality of rights under the law shall not be denied or abridged ... because of the sex of the individual." Nineteen states currently have ERAs, which were enacted in the late 1970s and early 1980s. Though not used frequently, they present a potentially powerful litigation tool for girls....

However, as with federal equal protection analysis, there are hurdles to overcome. First, under state ERAs there must be a determination that the males and females in question are similarly situated. Second, in applying state ERAs to prison regulations, at least two courts have adopted the reasoning from *Turner* and *O'Lone* that inmates' constitutional rights are limited in the prison environment....

Another critical difference between federal equal protection analysis and analysis under state ERAs is the standard of review.... [A]lthough claims of unconstitutional gender discrimination are accorded, at best, an intermediate standard of review under federal equal protection law, at least ten of the nineteen ERA states require higher justification for gender-based classifications under the state ERA.... Eight other states clearly apply a strict scrutiny standard to sex-based classifications under their states' ERAs.... Under the strict scrutiny standard, courts presume sex-based classifications in statutes, regulations, policies, or practices invalid unless they serve a compelling state interest, are narrowly drawn to protect that interest, and the interest cannot be adequately protected by alternative means....

Equal rights challenges on behalf of girls should be more successful in court than equal protection challenges for three reasons. First, whether or not adult women and men prisoners are similarly situated, the juvenile court's focus on the individual offender's needs minimizes the risk that individual differences will trump equality of treatment in challenges brought by girls. Second, the higher standard of review afforded sex-based classifications by most of the state equal rights provisions should elevate judicial review of sex-based claims in the juvenile justice system above the rational relationship test currently applied to most constitutional challenges in the adult prison context. Third, the adoption of the rational relationship test for adult offenders was motivated by penological concerns that favor deference to prison administrators, whereas the juvenile court's emphasis on rehabilitation makes these concerns less compelling in the face of similar claims by girls....

Title IX of the Education Amendments of 1972. Another potential tool for achieving equality in the programs and services offered to girls in the juvenile justice system is through Title IX of the Education Amendments of 1972. Title IX provides, in relevant part, that "no person in the United States shall, on the basis of sex, be excluded from participation in, be denied the benefits of, or be subjected to discrimination under any education program or activity receiving federal financial assistance." Policies and practices that disadvantage girls in the juvenile justice system clearly fit within the intended objectives of Title IX. As articulated by the United States Supreme Court [in *Cannon v. University of Chicago*], the purpose of Title IX is "to avoid the use of federal resources to support discriminatory practices" and "to provide individual citizens effective protection against those practices."

Discrimination on the basis of gender is flatly prohibited by Title IX in juvenile justice facilities where the programming is provided in accordance with state educational requirements. Virtually all youth in the juvenile justice system are school-age, and many remain subject to state compulsory school attendance laws. Accordingly, incarcerated youth possess the same state-created rights to basic and special education as their non-incarcerated peers. In this respect, juvenile correctional facilities are more analogous to residential schools than they are to adult prisons. Furthermore, a juvenile's right to treatment encompasses not only a right to rehabilitation, but also a right to education.

... Title IX applies to all correctional facilities that receive federal assistance. Women prisoners challenging discriminatory practices or conditions have therefore also looked to Title IX for relief. However, similar to challenges brought under the federal Equal Protection Clause—and despite this clear statutory applicability—Title IX challenges to discriminatory programming in adult prisons have found little success, and yielded contradictory analyses....

... Like the federal equal protection and state ERA cases, [the cases] suggest hurdles for girls looking to bring similar claims in the juvenile justice system. These cases also leave some questions unresolved. Must plaintiffs demonstrate that they are "similarly situated" to male prisoners under equal protection standards in order to seek relief from discriminatory practices? What programs and activities fall within the commands of Title IX? And finally, when mounting a Title IX challenge, must plaintiffs allege that the discrimination occurs throughout the entire system, or may a claim be successfully pursued by comparing the programming at two individual facilities, or even one facility housing both men and women, or boys and girls?

Despite the contradictory and narrow decisions in the adult system, Title IX should be an effective tool for improving access to programs and services for girls in the juvenile justice system. Given the distinctions between adult and juvenile corrections..., the obstacles encountered by women prisoners should not discourage Title IX litigation on behalf of adjudicated girls. The strong wording and intent of the statute, coupled with its aggressive enforcement in the high school and college athletic context—where gender-segregated programming is common but inequality is not tolerated—should provide a powerful litigation tool for girls.

Additionally, because most juveniles are school-age and must be provided the opportunity to earn high school credits, a high school degree, or a GED even while incarcerated, Title IX is particularly relevant to charges of gender-based discrimination in juvenile facilities' programming. While courts may be hesitant to characterize discrimination in adult vocational, recreational, or counseling programs as discrimination in educational opportunities for Title IX purposes, these same services are an integral part of the educational programming typically offered to school-age youth, delinquent or otherwise. Discrimination in their availability to juvenile offenders should fall squarely within the parameters of Title IX....

Conclusion. Girls in the juvenile justice system are like unexpected guests who arrive too late to find a seat at the table. The door is wide open to them, but there is little to sustain them once they enter. The qualitative and quantitative deficiencies in gender appropriate services for adjudicated girls that we have described in this article require prompt and thoughtful attention from public officials, policymakers, administrators and providers, judges, and lawyers.... [W]e have offered a suggested blueprint for legal challenges that may be brought to remedy some of the disparities and disadvantages that girls face. But as lawyers, we occupy only a few seats at this table. We urge all of the individuals who share the responsibility for meeting the needs of these young women to also look behind them, and make room.

Selected References

Janet E. Ainsworth, Re-Imagining Childhood and Reconstructing the Legal Order: The Case for Abolishing the Juvenile Court, 69 North Carolina Law Review 1083 (1991).

Georgia Department of Juvenile Justice, Painting It Pink Is Not Enough (2002).

Paul Holland & Wallace J. Mlyniec, Whatever Happened to the Right to Treatment? The Modern Quest for a Historical Promise, 68 Temple Law Review 1791 (1995).

Peter Kratcoski & Lucille D. Kratcoski, Juvenile Delinquency (1996).

National Mental Health Association, Factsheet: Mental Health and Adolescent Girls in the Justice System (1999).

Howard Snyder, Law Enforcement and Juvenile Crime (2002).

Cases and Statutes

Cannon v. University of Chicago, 441 U.S. 677 (1979).

City of Cleburne v. Cleburne Living Ctr., 473 U.S. 432 (1985).

In re Gault, 387 U.S. 1 (1967).

Klinger v. Dep't of Corr., 31 F.3d 727 (8th Cir. 1994).

McKeiver v. Pennsylvania, 403 U.S. 528 (1971).

O'Lone v. Estate of Shabazz, 482 U.S. 342 (1987).

Pargo v. Elliot, 894 F. Supp. 1243, 1264 (S.D. Iowa 1995).

Turner v. Safleyn and, 482 U.S. 78 (1987).

Women Prisoners of the D.C. Dep't of Corr. v. District of Columbia, 93 F.3d 910 (D.C. Cir. 1996).

20 U.S.C. 1681-1688 (2003) ("Title IX").

CHAPTER TWENTY-SIX

PATIENTS' BILL OF RIGHTS*

... In the 2000 presidential election campaign, Republican and Democratic candidates alike recognized the great importance of health care reform and expressed specific support for [a] patients' bill of rights.... [This essay] offers a vision of a patients' bill of rights that bases its reform on principles of both equality and due process. Empirical research demonstrates that although managed care systems appear to provide roughly adequate health care for the general public, they may not be providing equal treatment for the poor and elderly. Furthermore, empirical research also indicates that race accounts for the largest disparities in treatments....

The [term] "patients' bill of rights" analogously refers to the U.S. Constitution's Bill of Rights. This terminology highlights the perceived importance of ... proposed reform. This reform establishes procedural protections of patients' choices of treatment within managed care systems. The proposed rights for patients bear a striking similarity to rights guaranteed by the Due Process Clause of the U.S. Constitution. Just as the Due Process Clause guarantees criminal [defendants] a right to a fair trial and to appeal jury verdicts, the proposed patients' bill of rights gives patients the right to external reviews of medical decisions and to sue HMOs. Similarly, just as police must read criminal suspects their *Miranda* rights while under custody, the patients' bill of rights would require health plans to disclose certain information about coverage and ban gag clauses in physicians' contracts.

Moreover, the proposed reform's emphasis on protecting particular kinds of patients' choices bears some similarity to a different aspect of the Due Process Clause that involves "substantive" due process rights. The Supreme Court in *Roe v. Wade* established that the Due Process Clause guaranteed a woman's right of access to a particular medical procedure, an abortion, that cannot be interfered with by the government or even by her spouse. Similarly,

---

* **Dean M. Hashimoto,** *The Proposed Patients' Bill of Rights: The Case of the Missing Equal Protection Clause,* 1 YALE JOURNAL OF HEALTH POLICY, LAW AND ETHICS 77 (2001), http://papers.ssrn.com/abstract_id=271715.

[politicians] contemplate[] establishing a patient's right to access specialists and emergency rooms without approval by his or her primary care physician.

Abortion rights and the proposed patients' rights share yet another similarity. Those who are financially unable to afford to exercise these rights cannot benefit from the existing rules. In *Harris v. McRae*, the Supreme Court held that the government is not required to provide financial support to the indigent who seek abortions under Medicaid even if medically necessary. Similarly, the proposed patients' bill of rights would not extend its protections to the indigent who receive their medical care through Medicaid managed care plans. The government remains committed in both cases to enforcing the due process guarantees for the majority who can afford to exercise their rights in the private realm. On the other hand, the government does guarantee a right of equal access by the poor who constitute a minority in the community. Thus, the real challenge is to make this "equal" access truly meaningful.

While proponents of the patients' bill of rights rely on due process as the main framework for reforming managed care, they neglect an important perspective within the U.S. Constitution—our society's commitment to equality.... [Proposals] for reforming managed care systems consist[] of a bill of rights that lacks an equal protection clause....

Researchers in health care services have identified substantial disparities in health care delivery involving racial/ethnic minorities, the poor, and the elderly. Dr. Jack Geiger, an expert in this field, stated in an editorial in *The New England Journal of Medicine* that "race was the overriding determinant of disparities in care" and that "these issues are all the more urgent because of the risk that managed competition and capitated payment systems may increase the likelihood of discriminatory judgments, not least in the urban teaching hospitals that are essential resources for inner-city populations."

The emphasis by the patients' bill of rights on individual choice, due process protections, and limiting its jurisdiction to private health plans will result in an important regulation that largely benefits the employed middle class. This essay critiques the proposed reform and then advocates the addition of a complementary perspective based on equality of choices, equal protection, and responsiveness to socioeconomic diversity. The patients' bill of rights should promote health care delivery that is inclusive in its application, not just its conception. Reformers should extend the reform's application to Medicaid managed care plans.

[Politicians] propose to extend the patients' bill of rights to privately insured health care plans, thus covering only those that are self-insured and possibly those that are employer-sponsored. This ... reform will not extend to Medicaid managed care plans, which have become the dominant delivery model for low-income beneficiaries. Medicaid managed care plans include more than seventeen million beneficiaries—more than half of the Medicaid-eligible population.

The federal government encouraged the development of Medicaid managed care programs by establishing a waiver process in 1993 that allowed states to enroll Medicaid recipients in managed care programs. Medicaid enrollments in managed care programs have skyrocketed since the initiation of the waiver process. States have substantially increased their reliance on Medicaid managed care systems in the absence of strong empirical evidence that they result in any substantial improvements in care. On the other hand, state Medicaid programs estimate that the rates of savings range from 5–34%. Thus, the current benefits of managed care may lie in their financial benefits, not their direct health effects.

It is unfair to guarantee special legal protections to members of private managed care plans while failing to provide these same guarantees to members of publicly financed managed care programs including Medicaid. The U.S. Supreme Court recently described in *Pegram v. Herdrich* how HMOs must engage in rationing medical care to reduce medical costs. The Court noted that this "rationing necessarily raises some risks while reducing others (ruptured appendixes are more likely; unnecessary appendectomies are less so)." The Court also indicated that this decision-making involves "judgments of social value, such as optimum treatment levels and health care expenditure." The patients' bill of rights is premised on the belief that health care has a high social value that warrants special protections to encourage these optimum treatment levels and expenditures. By not making the patients' bill of rights applicable to Medicaid, we are further segregating the health care system of the lower socioeconomic class and increasing differences in the quality of health care provided.

The poor and the elderly may have a greater need to be protected by a system that safeguards patients' rights. Dr. John Ware and other Boston area physicians analyzed differences in health outcomes of chronically ill adults treated in HMOs and fee-for-service systems over a four-year period, and they published their results in the *Journal of the American Medical Association* in 1996. After conducting this observational study of 2,235 patients, they found that the average patient's physical and mental health outcomes did not differ between managed care and fee-for-service systems. The elderly and poor in HMOs, however, were nearly twice and more than twice, respectively, as likely to decline in health compared to other patients in fee-for-service systems.

While the application of the patients' bill of rights to Medicaid would increase expenses, it is not an impractical concept. Many of the proposed reforms are similar to rights that have been established for publicly funded managed care plans associated with Medicare. Under Medicare regulations, patient protections include the right to external reviews, prohibitions of certain financial incentives for physicians, and standards establishing consumers' rights to access specialists and other services. Moreover, some states have similar protections for their Medicaid managed care plans. States may establish these patient protections through their contracts with MCOs. Reformers should examine these state contracts and choose those patient protections that have proven effective for uniform application across states.

The [debated] patients' bill of rights establishes appellate review for patient challenges to denials of treatment by MCOs. While the procedural due process protections—including internal and external review procedures—are important in individual cases, they will only benefit a small percentage of managed care enrollees. Among those patients who are denied a treatment request, few seek external reviews. While the procedural rights of review are important patient protections, reform that is based on the principle of equality should have more expansive effects. In particular, the reforms currently proposed will not broadly impact the daily decisions and the important conversations that occur between physicians and patients. Empirical studies have pointed out that physicians, not MCOs, may be offering less care, even if medically necessary, to patients in managed care plans compared to those in fee-for-service arrangements. The advice and recommendations offered by physicians to patients ultimately impacts care to a greater extent than MCO policies or treatment denials.

Researchers at Harvard Medical School recently published a study regarding the preeminent importance of doctor-patient communications on health care in *The New England Journal of Medicine*. They compared the use of coronary angiography after acute heart attacks among Medicare beneficiaries in managed care plans and fee-for-service arrangements. They analyzed data from more than 50,000 beneficiaries and evaluated patient care based on guidelines proposed by the American College of Cardiology and the American Heart Association. Among those patients for whom angiography is useful and effective, 46% of fee-for-service beneficiaries underwent angiography compared to 37% of managed care beneficiaries. Thus, in situations where angiography is believed to be medically useful, physicians order it less often for those enrolled in managed care programs than for those in fee-for-service arrangements.

The study offered two other important conclusions. In both managed care and fee-for-service arrangements, the level of angiography use was much higher among patients initially admitted to a hospital with angiography facilities than among those admitted to a hospital without such facilities. Thus, the physical infrastructure of health care delivery may have a decisive impact on what is offered to patients. The most striking conclusion, however, is that physicians in both groups ordered angiography for less than half of those patients for whom it would have been medically useful.

Physicians have a greater impact on patient choices than MCOs. MCOs deny physician recommendations in just 3% of cases overall and in only 1% of cases involving hospitalization and surgical requests. In cases where angiography is believed to be medically useful, physicians ordered it in less than half of the cases, whether or not their patients were in managed care or fee-for-service plans. If we are serious about protecting the choices of patients, we must focus reform on finding ways to profoundly influence physician-patient relationships and what physicians are recommending to their patients.

Dr. Jay Katz described in his book, *The Silent World of Doctor and Patient*, the need in an age of medical science and sophisticated technology for more honest and complete conversations between physicians and patients. Although his book was published more than fifteen years ago, its message remains important in today's managed care settings. To achieve effective physician-patient relationships, we need to go beyond the banning of gag clauses in physician contracts or simply requiring MCOs to add more fine print in managed care contracts with patients. Managed care plans may provide an important infrastructure for educating physicians, identifying health priorities, and monitoring data to ensure that adequate treatments are more universally provided.

In addition, MCOs should make their treatment guidelines more accessible to patients through their physicians. For example, when a patient suffers from a heart attack, a physician should discuss the evaluation and treatment options (including obtaining an angiogram) with the patient and his or her family. The physician should also disclose if the managed care plan's guidelines differ from national recommended guidelines, and should discuss the availability of angiography facilities. In short, to make the patients' bill of rights truly effective, reformers should move in the direction of enhancing physician-patient relationships in ways such as these.

The proposed patients' bill of rights does not address disparities in health care treatments and outcomes of racial/ethnic minorities. Physicians tend to pursue less aggressive therapies for African-American patients compared to white patients. Researchers affiliated with the Health Care Financing Administration (HCFA) [including Marian Gornick] analyzed Medicare administrative data from 1993 to study the relationship between race and the utilization of health care services. These data demonstrated that physicians performed certain procedures—including mammography, coronary angioplasty, coronary artery bypass surgery, and hip repair surgery—less frequently on African-American patients. Many other research studies have confirmed some of these findings and have also shown that black patients receive fewer nephrology referrals, less frequent surgeries for lung cancer, and have generally poorer health outcomes. Because managed care places increased economic pressures on physician judgments, there may be an increased likelihood of discriminatory results in treatments and health outcomes.

The results of [a study by Ashish K. Jha and others] offered surprising and controversial results. The study included 147 Veterans Administration (VA) hospitals for six common medical diagnoses (pneumonia, angina, congestive heart failure, chronic obstructive pulmonary disease, diabetes, and chronic renal failure). Prior studies of VA hospitals have indicated that there are racial differences in the treatment of specific diseases. The more recent study found that African-American patients had lower mortality rates than whites for each of the six diagnoses.

Critics of this study pointed out that it is difficult to know if the empirical results are "real." It may be that the differences in outcomes between African-American and white patients were due to differences in the severity of their illnesses and other co-morbidities at the time of admission. Even the authors of the VA study conclude that the outcomes may be attributable to the nature of the VA system as an equal-access health care system. The VA system has few financial barriers and may therefore offer better access to care for African-American patients.

Obviously, further research needs to be done to better understand racial differences in treatments and outcomes. Researchers should study managed care systems where the financial pressures may be more pressing than fee-for-service systems. For example, researchers should conduct more empirical research on the effects of deductibles and co-payments, the quality of translational services, the presence of minority physicians, and the geographic proximity of health care delivery to minority groups.

[Debate over a] patients' bill of rights is an example of what Professor Mary Ann Glendon calls "rights talk." It tends to lead to discussions that ignore our responsibilities and "regularly promotes the short-run over the long-term, crisis intervention over preventive measures, and particular interests over the common good." Managed care plans should increase their collaboration with local and state agencies to improve access to health care programs by racial/ethnic minorities and the indigent. Public health programs include immunizations, injury prevention, diabetes detection and treatment, cancer screening, heart disease risk management, and protection from environmental hazards. Racial/ethnic minorities and the indigent are among the chief beneficiaries of public health programs because of the higher disease incidences, reduced access, and poorer health outcomes in their populations. Managed care plans may provide an important structure for collecting data, identifying priorities, supporting outreach programs, and promoting incentives to improve the success of public health activities.

Reformers should base their reforms on programs that have promoted public health through health care financing systems. An example of a successful Medicaid program is early periodic screening, diagnosis, and treatment (EPSDT) for children under twenty-one years of age. This program entitles children to vision, dental, hearing, and screening services. Studies have demonstrated that EPSDT programs can improve children's health, although their implementation has been limited to less than 40% of poor children.

It is ironic that Congress has analogized ... reform in health care to the Bill of Rights in the U.S. Constitution and yet appears to create a patients' bill of rights that is missing an equal protection clause. After all, the most renowned civil rights case is *Brown v. Board of Education.* Declaring that "education is perhaps the most important function of state and local governments," the U.S. Supreme Court held that the segregation of public elementary schools based on race violated the equal protection of laws guaranteed by the Fourteenth Amendment. In its opinion, the Court rationalized its holding based, in part, on empirical studies of children taught in segregated schools that purportedly showed that their educational and mental development was retarded because of segregation.

The Court also issued a companion case, *Bolling v. Sharpe,* on the same day as *Brown.* In *Bolling* the Court considered whether racial segregation in the District of Columbia public schools violated the Bill of Rights. Because these schools received federal funding, the Court could not, as it had in *Brown,* rely on the Fourteenth Amendment's equal protection clause that applies to state action. The Court had to interpret the Fifth Amendment that restricts federal action. Unlike the Fourteenth Amendment that contains both equal protection and due process clauses, the Fifth Amendment only has a due process clause. In *Bolling,* the Court thus considered the case of a missing equal protection clause. The Court nevertheless declared that "it would be unthinkable that the same Constitution would impose a lesser duty on the Federal Government," and required, therefore, that the District of Columbia public schools must be desegregated just as in *Brown.* The Court believed that segregation in public education should no longer be tolerated. Equality, in that context, was too important a principle to ignore.

[F]ew would contend that the *Brown* or *Bowling* cases were incorrectly decided. Yet, we have learned that desegregating public school systems did not lead to true equality in education. Our ongoing struggle to provide adequate education and health care remain parallel and require our full commitment to promoting adequate quality in both public and private domains....

Selected References

H. Jack Geiger, Race and Health Care—An American Dilemma?, 335 New England Journal of Medicine 815 (1996).

Mary Ann Glendon, Rights Talk: The Impoverishment of Political Discourse (1991).

Marian E. Gornick et al., Effects of Race and Income on Mortality and Use of Services Among Medicare Beneficiaries, 335 New England Journal of Medicine 791 (1996).

Edward Guadagnoli et al., Appropriateness of Coronary Angiography After Myocardial Infarction Among Medicare Beneficiaries: Managed Care Versus Fee for Service, 343 New England Journal of Medicine 1460 (2000).

Ashish K. Jha et al., Racial Differences in Mortality Among Men Hospitalized in the Veterans Affairs Health Care System, 285 Journal of the American Medical Association 297 (2001).

Jay Katz, The Silent World of Doctor and Patient (1984).

Peter R. Kongstvedt, editor, Essentials of Managed Health Care (2001).

Jeffrey P. Koplan & Jeffrey R. Harris, Not-So-Strange Bedfellows: Public Health and Managed Care, 90 American Journal of Public Health 1824 (2000).

David H. Mark, Race and the Limits of Administrative Data, 285 Journal of the American Medical Association 337 (2001).

Barbara Noah, Racial Disparities in the Delivery of Health Care, 35 San Diego Law Review 135 (1998).

Note, The Impact of Medicaid Managed Care on the Uninsured, 110 Harvard Law Review 751 (1997).

Alycia C. Regan, Regulating the Business of Medicine: Models for Integrating Ethics and Managed Care, 30 Columbia Journal of Law and Social Problems 635 (1997).

John E. Ware et al., Differences in 4-Year Health Outcomes for Elderly and Poor, Chronically Ill Patients Treated in HMO and Fee-for-Service Systems, 276 Journal of the American Medical Association 1039 (1996).

Stefan C. Weiss, Defining a "Patients' Bill of Rights" for the Next Century, 9 Journal of the American Medical Association 856 (1999).

Cases

Bolling v. Sharpe, 347 U.S. 497 (1954).

Brown v. Board of Education, 347 U.S. 483 (1954).

Harris v. McRae, 448 U.S. 297 (1980).

Pegram v. Herdrich, 530 U.S. 211 (2000).

Roe v. Wade, 410 U.S. 113 (1973).

Further Reading (selected work by Dean M. Hashimoto)

Science as Mythology in Constitutional Law, 76 Oregon Law Review 111 (1997).

The Legacy of *Korematsu v. United States*: A Dangerous Narrative Retold, 4 UCLA Asian Pacific American Law Journal 72 (1996).

The Future Role of Managed Care and Capitation in Workers' Compensation, 22 American Journal of Law & Medicine 233 (1996).

CHAPTER TWENTY-SEVEN

TRANSRACIAL ADOPTION*

Trans-racial adoption is a sensitive topic, evoking acrimonious debate.... Efforts to declare race-matching preference policies or statutory schemes unconstitutional are intensifying. Some legal writers assert that such a prohibition is needed in order to avoid or minimize harm to Black youngsters in the foster care system....

Race and color continue to be unresolved issues in our society—inextricably tied and merged with issues of power, status, and inequality—that mock American claims of being a democratic land of equal opportunity. Race and color profoundly influence the lives of all within our society, governing the choices one makes and the choices one believes she has. Issues of race and poverty in American society directly contribute to the disproportionate numbers of Black children remaining in the foster care system for longer periods of time than other children, due to a shortage of approved Black adoptive homes.

I believe that race cannot be ignored. The key to successful living as a minority person in a discriminating, denigrating society is to have positive affiliations with others like oneself, from whom one can gain support and affirmation, and can learn coping skills. Most individuals are not "colorblind"; skin color and perceptions of racial difference trigger within the beholder unconscious stereotypical expectations and assumptions which then often govern any ensuing social interactions. Thus, to promote and protect a child's "best interests," race is an important factor to be considered when evaluating the appropriateness of prospective adoptive parents. Does the person have the awareness, capacity, and sensitivity to prepare the nonwhite child to handle the challenges that will be encountered because of the child's racial appearance? Advocates for trans-racial adoption who naively espouse a "Love conquers all" philosophy may represent an assault on the Black family and Black

---

* **Ruth-Arlene W. Howe**, *Redefining the Transracial Adoption Controversy*, 2 DUKE JOURNAL OF GENDER LAW & POLICY 131 (1995), http://papers.ssrn.com/abstract_id=772807.

community that is as dangerous as some recent Supreme Court decisions that seem to herald an end to the gains of the Civil Rights Movement of the 1960s....

Whose interests would be served if consideration of race were completely eliminated from adoptive placement decision-making? What really drives the growing momentum to eliminate race considerations from all adoptive placement decisions? What would be the consequences of eliminating same-race placement preferences for a particular Black adoptee, for the status and integrity of the Black family and Black community, and for American society generally? ...

From my perspective, the trans-racial adoption debate is about establishing a new right or entitlement for certain white adults who wish to become parents by any means they select. Proponents of trans-racial adoption who claim that same-race placement preferences are victimizing the increasing numbers of Black children in foster care are employing a diversionary "smokescreen" strategy. This smokescreen obfuscates important systemic problems and creates additional barriers to meeting the needs of Black children, Black families, and the Black community. The focus of attention should be shifted from the illusory debate about the merits of trans-racial adoption to the real issue: whether it is appropriate to establish new rights for adults seeking to adopt children....

The realization that the focus of the trans-racial adoption controversy is not the needs and interests of Black children, but instead the interests of prospective adoptive parents, has an important implication. The needs of Black children will not be better served until our society honestly and publicly acknowledges race and color as defining influences. Stated another way, Black children will not benefit until we reverse the current "retreat from race" and commit ourselves to addressing and redressing past and present inequities. Action is needed, not just at the level of individual morality, but rather at the institutional, community, and societal levels. We must commit ourselves to developing, implementing, and supporting policies and programs that enhance successful continuation of a democratic society in which all citizens enjoy equal opportunities to reap the rewards of "life, liberty and the pursuit of happiness."

The basis for my position that the trans-racial adoption controversy is not about the needs and interests of Black children requires further explanation. I have based this position on data and on inferences drawn from various materials reviewed: available statistics on adoption, reported developments and trends in the adoption field, and demographic data and surveys, including statistics compiled by the U.S. Bureau of the Census. Since 1972, statistics demonstrate that the total pool of American children readily available for adoption has changed significantly, both in size and composition. Furthermore, if one looks back over four decades of adoption practices to the early 1950s, one discovers that there have been notable changes in how adoptions are arranged. These changes raise interesting questions about how best to allocate roles and responsibilities between child welfare and legal professionals.

Adoption Statistics. Although exact numbers are not known, it is generally agreed that annual finalized adoptions in the United States—in contrast to "informal" arrangements that are never legalized—peaked at about 175,000 in 1970, dropped to about 104,088 in 1986, and rose to a reported 118,529 in 1990. Formal adoptions include both related adoptions and unrelated adoptions. Related adoptions refer to step-parent adoptions and adoptions by a non-parent relative. In an unrelated adoption, a non-relative adopts the child.

Related adoptions totaled 91,141 in 1982, but were down to 52,931 by 1986. This drop probably reflects a decrease in the number of step-parent adoptions following re-marriage, which in turn simply may mean that fewer step-parent families chose to formalize their parenting arrangements through legal adoption. Unrelated adoptions, after reaching a high of 89,200 in 1971 and dropping to about 49,700 in 1974, have remained at or near 50,000 a year. Since 1971, unrelated adoptions have comprised less than half of all adoptions.

Factors Affecting Unrelated Adoptions. Children become available for adoption in one of two ways. Generally, new-borns and infants are available because birth parents voluntarily relinquish them to an adoption agency for placement or specifically consent to another person's petition to adopt their child. Other children, mostly older, become available for adoption because the parental rights of their parents are involuntarily terminated by a court on grounds of abandonment or parental unfitness.

The most dramatic development affecting the size and composition of the domestic pool of children available for adoption, and hence the total number of annual domestic adoptions, is the drastic decline in recent years in the rate of unmarried mothers' voluntary relinquishments of their infants. Before 1973, nine percent (approximately 36,000 annually) of all children born to never-married women were relinquished for adoption; however, during 1982–1988, voluntary relinquishments had dropped to two percent (approximately 16,500 annually) of all non-marital births. Most of this decline is the result of a drastic drop in the rate of relinquishments by white, unmarried women.

Before 1973, 19% of children born to never-married white women [approximately 33,269 each year] were placed for adoption, compared with 8% [roughly 25,600 annually] in 1973–1981 and 3% [or approximately 13,000] in 1982–1988. Among never-married black women, fewer than 2% of children were relinquished before 1973, and the rates do not appear to have changed much since then.

Moreover, the National Council for Adoption (NCFA), formerly the National Committee for Adoption, indicates that nearly all infants born to unmarried women are not relinquished. As a result of the lack of available infants, foreign adoptions have become more attractive to many prospective adoptive parents.

The impact of the decline in the rate of relinquishments of white babies is emphasized when two other phenomena are noted. First, the overall birth rate for unmarried mothers rose through the 1970s and most of the 1980s.... Second, in the mid-1990s with few healthy, white new-borns being voluntarily relinquished, the children legally free for adoption through public and many private agencies are often either older youngsters with "special needs," or infants who are born HIV positive or drug exposed. In all parts of the country, the total population of Black children in foster care continues to grow at an alarming rate. Not all of these children, however, are legally free for adoption. In some instances, the case plan may not call for adoption, but rather a reunion with the birth family. Many of those who are legally free are both older and disabled.

Not only is the size of the adoption pool smaller because of fewer relinquishments, the characteristics of the children now waiting for adoption has changed.... Perhaps because these children may be challenging to parent, special needs adoptions constituted just over a quarter of all unrelated domestic adoptions during most of the 1980s.... Unfortunately, the families waiting to adopt "do not match up" with these children.

Changing Placement Arrangements. Finally, if one looks back to the 1950s and compares adoptive placements then and now, one discovers some important structural changes.... In 1951, more than half of all unrelated adoptions were arranged privately. These independent arrangements were either brokered by a third party—doctor, attorney, member of the clergy, or other person—or involved a direct placement by the birth mother with the adopters. Only eighteen percent of unrelated adoptions were through public agencies; private agencies handled less than a third of all adoptions.

After 1951, public agency placements slowly increased from eighteen percent until they stabilized at about thirty-eight percent in 1972; private agency unrelated adoptions peaked at forty percent in 1973. The type of placement arrangement that shifted most dramatically is the independent private adoption. These dropped to a low of twenty-one percent in the early 1970s.... By1986, private independent adoptions accounted for 31.4% of all domestic unrelated adoptions (approximately 16,040), whereas thirty-nine percent of unrelated adoptions (about 20,064) were through public agencies, and private agencies handled just under thirty percent (or 15,063).

Given the changes in relinquishment patterns and the characteristics of children waiting for adoption in the foster care system, it should not be a surprise that more new-borns are placed each year through independent adoptions than through agencies, either private or public. Because there is no current comprehensive collection of annual adoption data at the national level, the number of independent private adoptions may be significantly undercounted. Despite the lack of comprehensive data, three trends stand out. First, new-borns and infants are the strong preference of first time adoptive parents, especially the infertile, leading many to pursue an international adoption. Second, there is no strong demand for the growing numbers of older children with special needs. Whether these children are white or Black, it is difficult to find appropriate homes for them because of the challenges they pose for any prospective parent. Third, the decline in voluntary relinquishments since 1973 is almost exclusively the result of a drastic drop in relinquishments among white, never-married women.

A New Phenomenon: Rise in Biracial Births. In addition to the above data, other recent demographic trends provide a different backdrop for understanding the current drive to eliminate the factor of race from all adoptive placement considerations. There is a growing potential new source of infants, if the racial designation of "Black" is not attached to biracial infants. Many Americans are refusing to fit themselves into one of the Census Bureau's four official racial categories. In the 1990 census, almost ten million people refused to classify themselves as white, Black, Asian, or American Indian.... America may be poised to experience some new patterns of interracial mixing, especially among young people....

Between 1970 and 1993, the number of interracial married couples almost quadrupled, growing from 310,000 in 1970 to almost 1.2 million in 1993. This represented an increase from less than one percent to more than two percent of all reported married couples. Among interracial married couples, the largest number, 920,000, were white/other race couples; Black/white couples were only 242,000, or less than one out of five interracial couples. In contrast to the incidence of Black/white married couples, forty percent of all multiracial births in 1990 (excluding births for which the race of mother or father was unknown) were mixed Black and white, up from thirty-two percent in 1970. According to the National Center for Health Statistics (NCHS), which has tracked mixed race births since 1968, "birth rates of children with one black and one white parent have been climbing. In 1991, 52,232 such births were recorded, compared to 26,968 in 1981, and 8,758 in 1968."

In short, ... the rate of Black/white births far exceeds the number of Black/white marriages. Given the reported increase in the adoption of mixed-race babies, it is reasonable to infer that many of these babies are children born to unmarried couples who might be relinquished for adoption. Until such time as the Census Bureau amends its rules and adds new racial categories, many of this growing group of mixed babies will be deemed to be "Black." Thus, I view the push to eliminate race from placement considerations as a maneuver to enable whites who seek to adopt infants to gain access to the growing number of non-marital, mixed-race children who may be relinquished for adoption, free of the constraints imposed by same-race or same-culture placement preferences. Hence, I assert that the trans-racial adoption controversy is not about addressing the needs of the many older Black children who enter the foster care system; rather, it is about giving preferences to certain white adults who seek to adopt infants. [T]his trend could be characterized as an attempt to garner the market in infants.

Adoption Paradigm Shifts: A New Focus and New Key Professionals.... Two crucial paradigm shifts have occurred in the field of adoption. First, the adoption process formerly focused on the interests of children, serving as a specialized welfare service for the child in need of a permanent home. Today, the focus has shifted to serving adults who seek to parent. Second, adoption professionals are no longer predominantly social workers. Now-lawyers are often the key players, asserting that their clients have a legal right to adopt.

Historical Review of Adoption Practices. For nearly 150 years, adoption in the United States has been governed by state statutes.... A guardian might be named in a will, or petitions of adoption and name changes were filed as special state legislative bills. In 1851, Massachusetts enacted the first "modern" state adoption statute, rendering public what had been a private arrangement by requiring judicial supervision and approval of adoptions.

From 1851 until the 1950s, adoption evolved both as a statutory process and as a child welfare service. By 1929, all states had enacted some form of adoption legislation. Typically, these statutes required: (1) consent of the birth parent or guardian (and of the child, over age twelve to fourteen); (2) an investigation (or social study) conducted by the placing agency to determine the suitability of the prospective home; (3) a probationary trial period in the adoptive home under appropriate supervision; (4) issuance of a final decree, withheld until a court received evidence of satisfactory adjustment of adoptive parents and child to each other; and (5) secrecy of the legal proceedings and provision for alteration of the child's birth certificate. This adoption process was thought to protect [children against being adopted by unsuitable persons]. The dominant professionals in the adoption process were social workers—the staffs of public and private licensed child welfare agencies, many of which were church-related. As trained child welfare specialists, they conducted investigatory home studies and supervised probationary trial placements.

By the mid-1950s, intake policies of many agencies effectively limited adoption to the "perfect" or "near perfect" baby. The perfect baby typically was a healthy white infant, born out-of-wedlock, and relinquished at birth or shortly thereafter by a mother reluctant to face the disapproval of family and community by attempting to rear the child as a single parent. Agencies placed great emphasis on matching an infant with an adoptive family in terms of appearance, religion, ethnicity, and presumed IQ potential. The typical, "perfect" prospective adoptive couple was infertile, well-adjusted, well-established in their community and careers, and financially stable; in other words, they were solid, middle-class, and white. These agency practices, coupled with a decline in births during and immediately after World War II, led to the development of very high-priced "black markets" in independent or private adoption—the focus of 1955 Senate hearings chaired by Senator Kefauver.

The Pendulum Swings Back. For decades now, the demand for healthy, white infants has consistently exceeded the numbers available for adoption. As the shortage of infants increased, some infertile couples turned to nontraditional sources, such as trans-racial and international adoptions. Others entered into surrogate parenting arrangements or attempted to use some form of alternative means of reproduction, such as artificial insemination, in vitro fertilization, embryo transfer, or ovum donation.

[A] new generation of private services and networks has sprung up to help bring together a relinquishing parent or willing surrogate with a prospective adopter. Often these placements are deemed to be "open" rather than "closed" because the parties know each other and many expect to maintain ongoing relationships. The key professionals involved are typically lawyers, doctors, or other intermediaries, who seek to help an adult client achieve the goal of becoming a parent. The primary task of these new services is to find adoptable babies for childless adults, rather than to find homes for dependent, mistreated, and abused children. Less "desirable" children remain the charges of public agencies and private agencies servicing children in publicly-financed foster care.

The National Conference of Commissioners on Uniform State Laws (NC-CUSL) Uniform Adoption Act, finalized at the Conference's August 1994 Annual Meeting, is viewed by some as a triumph for the assertive private adoption bar. In my opinion, adoption lawyers have been relentlessly attempting to establish dominance in the adoption field for more than a decade in order to meet the desires of adult clients seeking to adopt healthy infants.

New Questions Regarding a Constitutional Right to Adopt. What does this paradigm shift in focus from meeting a child's need for an adoptive home to an adult's desire to parent mean for legal practitioners and theorists? Advocates of trans-racial adoption question the constitutionality of statutory same-race preference schemes and agency practices. But do adult prospective adopters have a constitutional "right to adopt" any child—including a child whose racial and ethnic heritage is different from their own?

Currently, no such constitutional right to adopt exists. Although the U.S. Constitution does not explicitly mention parents or families, courts have expansively interpreted substantive rights protected by the Due Process Clause of the Fourteenth Amendment. For more than seventy years, the Supreme Court has defined "liberty" to include the right "to marry, establish a home and bring up children" [as the Court put in the 1923 case of *Meyer v. Nebraska*]. The Court [in *May v. Anderson*, in 1953,] described the custody rights of parents to be "far more precious ... than property rights." In its 1972 landmark *Stanley* decision, the Court stated: "it is plain that the interest of a parent in the companionship, care, custody, and management of his or her children 'come(s) to this Court with a momentum for respect lacking when appeal is made to liberties which derive merely from shifting economic arrangements.'"

Nevertheless, under the common-law concept of *parens patriae*, parents' substantive rights to the custody and control of their child may be subordinated to the state's interest in the child's welfare. In resolving conflicts between parental rights and the state's interest in the welfare of a child, courts apply a "best interest of the child" standard.

With respect to proceedings concerning a parent-child relationship, the procedural aspect of the Due Process Clause of the Fourteenth Amendment, at a bare minimum, has been held to prohibit a state from denying notice and an opportunity to be heard to someone who has a liberty interest in the relationship. With respect to procedural matters, the Supreme Court applies the balancing approach articulated in *Mathews v. Eldridge*. The Court, depending on the time, place, and circumstances of the particular case before it, has reached seemingly conflicting conclusions....

Practice Ethics and Knowledge-Based Skills. In my opinion, there are also professional and ethical challenges for an attorney who elects to aid an adult client seeking to become a parent. The adult may be the paying client, but does the attorney, as an officer of the court and as a public citizen, have any obligation to promote and protect the "best interests" of the adoptee? These questions require close consideration, as a new network of private services and agencies springs up, one in which lawyers play dominant roles in bringing together relinquishing parents and prospective adopters. Given the importance of the "best interests of the child" standard in adoption, are there not potential conflicts of interest or professional malpractice problems lurking in the background? Also, does the lawyer possess the requisite skills to counsel and advise his or her client competently? What does the lawyer need to know in order to help the client make an informed decision that appropriately recognizes and balances the unique individual needs of a prospective adoptee and the client's desires to parent? Should the attorney be concerned about whether the adult client possesses the appropriate skills to meet the needs of the individual child? ...

[S]ocial work agencies—public and private—have not responded well to the increasing number of Black children in foster care. They largely have failed to employ Black professionals to help address the special problems that Black children confront in our society. At the same time, as the private sector moved into making trans-racial placements, most private agencies have ignored the needs of the Black community and have not worked in concert with it. Not only has the private sector ignored the Black community, private agencies and independent professionals have ignored other important issues as well, such as properly identifying who their clients are and to whom they owe their loyalties.

Repudiating the Myth of a "Shortage in Black Adoptive Families." ... To address these issues of cultural insensitivity and fee-driven practices, social work agencies should recognize and remove the barriers that exist between them and the Black community. Agencies should employ different strategies and methods to increase the identification and processing of appropriate same-race homes for children of color. For example, state and private agencies could forge more partnerships with minority agencies, churches, and other community-based organizations. Definitions of family may need to be enlarged to accommodate the Black family kinship structure which recognizes both blood and non-blood relatives. Financial obstacles to grandparent, kinship care, guardianship, and adoption may need to be removed or eased. No appropriate individual should be excluded from adopting because of an inability to pay a private agency fee if a church or civic group were willing and able to cover the fee on behalf of the individual.

Just Love Is Not Enough.... An emerging body of clinical literature, to some extent drawing on the study of biracial adults and teens, is beginning to recognize and address the additional problems and pain these individuals encounter as they move into adulthood. It would appear that "a loving home" and "loving parents" may not be enough within a society such as ours where diversity and difference are not honored, but denigrated. More care, not less, needs to be given to assessing the appropriateness of placing a Black child with parents of another race. The way a child is reared and socialized can ensure that the child, as an adult, is either in or out of touch with his or her social and racial reality. To ignore this fact is irresponsible. Much more needs to be understood about challenges or dilemmas encountered by the person who, because of physical appearance, is deemed by others to be Black, but who, if reared by whites without any close or intimate affiliations with Blacks, is socialized to be white....

Interracial marriages are increasing and attitudes among the younger generations are changing. Yet, it is one thing for an adult to choose to enter into an interracial or inter-religious marriage or relationship, or even to elect deliberately not to identify with one's racial or ethnic group. Those are adult decisions. The biracial child of an intact family has the opportunity to be connected through each parent to her mixed heritage without any cloud of uncertainty or feelings of abandonment so frequently a part of the adoptive experience. The question I find most troubling is whether it is appropriate, fair, and equitable virtually to eliminate a full range of future choices and to create difficult obstacles for the Black child adoptee who, as an adult, may have to cope with ... social experience and psychic incongruity....

Conclusion. The trans-racial adoption controversy needs to be redefined. I urge others to reexamine the discourse about trans-racial adoption and to consider closely what is currently happening as a consequence of the general shift in focus from meeting the needs of children for permanent homes to satisfying the desires of adults to become parents. The needs and interests of Black children, Black families, and Black communities are being ignored. The stage cannot truly be set to meet and advance these needs or interests if a constitutional "right to adopt" were to be recognized.... To set the stage for meeting the needs of Black children and advancing the interests of Black families and communities, the problem must be accurately assessed. A range of possible responses must be identified and considered, followed by the selection and implementation of an agreed strategy which can be evaluated and modified as necessary.

Trans-racial adoption, as a response to the disproportionate numbers of Black children who enter and remain in the foster care system longer than white children, is a classic example of embracing and promoting a solution without accurately defining the problem. The true history of adoption in the United States, as a specialized child welfare service, includes the development of agencies and private intermediaries who primarily placed white infants with white, infertile parents. The standards and protocols adopted were meant to be exclusive—to screen more applicants out than in. The aim was to match the "perfect" infant with the "perfect" white, infertile couple.

During the 1960s and 1970s, public and private agencies moved incrementally into Black adoptions when various social phenomena created changes in the pool of children available for adoption. Often, these placements were made without the benefit of any changes in staff, policies, or protocols for recruiting and approving applicants. Generally, no meaningful use was made of existing organizational resources in Black communities. In my opinion, it is deceitful to assert that not enough appropriate Black homes exist. This myth covers up the incompetence or disinterest of the child welfare community which initially accepted trans-racial adoption as the appropriate solution, given the large numbers of approved white applicants for whom no infants existed.

Regrettably, there was and has been little aggressive movement to fashion culturally sensitive services and strategies to meet the needs of the growing number of Black children in foster care. Public and private agencies have formed few working partnerships with organizations and institutions within the Black community. Such partnerships, predicated on respect for the expertise of Black child development professionals and the overall integrity and dignity of the Black community, would accord opportunities for participation in a thoughtful process of problem definition, identification, and brainstorming to generate viable alternative strategies and selection of models to be trial-tested....

Trans-racial adoption raises many issues that highlight the continuing American societal dilemma of unresolved problems of race and inequality. The differing perspectives identified by Perry of colorblind individualism and color and community consciousness are like responses to an "indivisible problem" that mask the full complexity of the situation and prevent any meaningful solution from being achieved. If race were completely eliminated from all adoptive decision-making, the critical question would then be how to assure all approved applicants—Black, white, or "other"—equal access to all children—Black, white, or "other." ...

During the height of the Civil Rights movement, much attention was given to issues of voting, education, jobs, and housing. These were all areas in which Blacks suffered grievous discrimination. But denial of opportunities in these areas did not threaten the continued integrity of the Black community as directly as does a policy endorsing wholesale, unregulated, trans-racial placements. Such a policy today is an assault that dis-empowers Black families, undermines the future viability of Blacks to participate in our pluralistic democracy, and runs the further risk of creating effete individuals.

I acknowledge that in some instances a trans-racial adoption may be an appropriate placement for a specific child. Also, I do not argue that a family of another race could never successfully rear a Black child. Instead, it is my hope that from continued open dialogue and discussion, new understandings can be achieved. Efforts must be undertaken to develop mechanisms for identifying and selecting the most appropriate adults to parent Black children in need of families....

To feel comfortable with one's racial heritage and at peace with one's adopted family, a person should be positively socialized and supported by family members who were consciously "culturally competent" about the racial realities of life in the United States at the end of the twentieth century. The child should have opportunities for institutional affiliations within the Black community. A successful trans-racial adoption should permit the adoptee an array of choices as an adult regarding the identifications and affiliations he or she elects to pursue. This will only be possible if the child is reared in a supportive environment, has positive, accepting experiences with both Black and diverse persons and groups, and truly feels comfortable with all.

Note

Extensive data are drawn from the following sources, among others: (a) *primary*: National Committee for Adoption, 1989 Adoption Factbook: United States Data, Issues, Regulations and Resources (1989); Bureau of the Census (1994); Select Comm. on Children, Youth, and Families, No Place to Call Home: Discarded Children in America, H.R. Rep. No. 395, 101st Cong., 2d Sess. (1990); (b) *secondary*: Christine A. Bachrach et al., Relinquishment of Premarital Births: Evidence from National Survey Data, 24 Family Planning Perspectives 27 (1992); Kathy S. Stolley, Statistics on Adoption in the United States, The Future of Children, Spring 1993; Nattional Legal Resource Center for Child Advocacy & Protection, American Bar Association, Adoption Of Children With Special Needs: Issues in Law and Policy (Ellen C. Segal ed., 1985); Symposium, Adoption, 72 Child Welfare 195 (1993).

Selected References

Elizabeth Bartholet, Where Do Black Children Belong? The Politics of Race Matching in Adoption, 139 Pennsylvania Law Review 1163 (1991).

Comment, Moppets on the Market: The Problem of Unregulated Adoptions, 59 Yale Law Journal 715 (1950).

Zanita E. Fenton, In A World Not Their Own: The Adoption Of Black Children, 10 Harvard Blackletter Journal 39 (1993).

Owen Gil & Barbara Jackson, Adoption and Race: Black, Asian and Mixed Race Children in White Families (1983).

Lucille J. Grow & Deborah Shapiro, Black Children, White Parents: A Study of Transracial Adoption (1974).

A. Leon Higginbotham, Jr. et al., *Shaw v. Reno*: A Mirage Of Good Intentions With Devastating Racial Consequences, 62 Fordham L. Rev. 1593 (1994).

Margaret Howard, Transracial Adoption: Analysis of the Best Interests Standard, 59 Notre Dame Law Review 503 (1984).

David S. Rosettenstein, Trans-racial Adoption and the Statutory Preference Schemes: Before the "Best Interests" and After the "Melting Pot," 68 St. John's Law Review 137 (1994).

Rita J. Simon & Howard Altstein, Transracial Adoptees and Their Families: A Study of Identity and Commitment (1987).

Jacinda T. Townsend, Reclaiming Self-Determination: A Call for Intraracial Adoption, 2 Duke Journal of Gender, Law and Policy 173 (1995).

Dana Y. Takagi, The Retreat From Race: Asian-American Admissions and Racial Politics (1992).

Cases and Statutes

Mathews v. Eldridge, 424 U.S. 319 (1976).

May v. Anderson, 345 U.S. 528, 533 (1953).

Meyer v. Nebraska, 262 U.S. 390, 399 (1923).

Stanley v. Illinois, 405 U.S. 645, 651 (1972).

Multiethnic Placement Act of 1994, Pub. L. No. 103-382, sections 551–54, 108 Stat. 3518, 4056–57 (1994) (to be codified at 42 U.S.C. section 5115a).

Further Reading (selected work by Ruth-Arlene W. Howe)

Adoption Law and Practice in 2000: In Whose Best Interests? 33 Family Law Quarterly 677 (1999).

Transracial Adoption (TRA): Old Prejudices and Discrimination Float Under a New Halo, 6 Boston University Public Interest Law Journal 409 (1997).

Who Speaketh For The Child? 23 New England Law Review 421 (1988).

PART IV

CONVENTION AND CRITIQUE

A. ASPIRATIONS

Chapter Twenty-Eight

Situated Decisionmaking[*]

Increasingly, legal theorists are interested in problems of perspective. The idea that it is possible to make legal decisions in an atmosphere of judicial detachment has seemed less compelling in the face of an increasingly complex and diverse society. As this reality has sunk deeper into the collective unconscious, scholars have begun a reexamination of the phenomena of legal reasoning and legal judgment with a view towards understanding their "situated" character. These theorists reject the notion that there is a universal, rational foundation for legal judgment. Judges do not, in their view, inhabit a lofty perspective that yields an objective vision of the case and its correct disposition. Instead, these scholars understand the role of judging more pragmatically; they recognize that all judges bring their own situated perspective to the case and do the best they can, under all the circumstances, to reach a fair and just disposition.

These differing theoretical perspectives correspond roughly to the roles of agent and spectator as they are invoked in contemporary ethics and epistemology. How we think about questions like "What should I believe?" and "What should I do?" depends in part upon whether we confront them as an agent or as a spectator—as a real participant in the flow of human activity or as a philosopher. This consideration has led many philosophers to adopt agent-centered theories that are "situated" in the sense that the philosopher assesses the rationality of certain beliefs and values with reference not to an abstractly conceived philosophical foundation, but rather to a contingent web of experience and location that provides individual agents with their own particular point of view. These philosophers describe themselves as "pragmatic" and find comfort in Wittgenstein's famous phrase: "I have reached bedrock and this is where my spade is turned."

When we turn from ethics and epistemology to the rendering of legal judgments, there seems to be an equally helpful distinction to be made between

---

* **Catharine Wells**, *Situated Decisionmaking*, 63 USC Law Review 1727 (1990), http://papers.ssrn.com/abstract_id=780447.

agents and spectators. Common sense tells us that those who are engaged in a controversy will judge its merits differently from those who stand apart. The law recognizes this distinction by requiring that judges recuse themselves from adjudicating any matter in which they have a significant interest. But this requirement does not eliminate the problems that arise from judicial engagement. Judges are not spectators. The judicial role requires that they locate themselves within the situated sphere of activity if only to fulfill their function of rendering judgment. Thus, judging must be viewed as a second-order activity that is distinct from, and logically posterior to, the first-order activities that are the subject of judgment. With respect to first-order activities, judges are supposed to be spectators; with respect to the second-order activity of judging, they are agents. Judges are agents not only because they render particular judgments in particular cases, but also because they participate in the larger task of shaping the development of an adjudicatory tradition.

If we apply the roles of "agent" and "spectator" to the second-order activity of judging, we get two very different images of the judicial role. When we picture judges as "spectators," we expect that they will base their decisions upon a rational foundation of law; when we picture them as "agents," we recognize that they inevitably bring their own distinctive perspective to their consideration of the case. The argument between these two conceptions of the judicial role occupies a central place in the history of American legal theory. Langdell, who conceived of a spectator-judge utilizing rational first principles and deductive logic, has served as a lightning rod for attacks against the possibility of rational foundations. The naive realist, on the other hand, has been accused of undermining the legitimacy of the legal system by introducing the agent-judge as an element of corruption and cynicism. For reasons that have been amply stated in the ensuing debate, neither judicial stance gives an entirely satisfactory account of legal judgment. The notion of a rational foundation for law is attractive but intractably elusive; the notion of situated judgment is accessible but offends fundamental ideals of justice and fairness. In a diverse society, the agent-judge runs afoul of such important aspirations as treating like cases alike and making official decisions that are a product of laws rather than persons.

The renewed interest in pragmatism among legal theorists must be viewed in the context of these concerns about situated judging. Pragmatic legal theories reject traditional notions of judicial detachment and emphasize the situated character of legal judgments. They therefore encounter the same dilemma that challenged the realists—being a realist about judging seems to entail being a cynic or a skeptic about justice. The purpose of this Article is to examine the concerns that surround situated judging and the central question to which they give rise: How can a situated judge render a just decision? On its face, the question appears to be both decisive and unanswerable. Upon deeper examination, however, we can see that the question relies upon a doubtful set of presuppositions about situated decisionmaking. It presupposes, for example, that situated decisionmaking is an entirely ad hoc and intuitive process. Further, it presupposes that there is an alternative method of decisionmaking that is capable of producing just and principled outcomes. Finally, the objection assumes that pragmatic judges engage in the first manner of decisionmaking and that non-pragmatic judges engage in the second....

Two Models of Normative Decisionmaking. Normative decisions require complex interactions of beliefs, attitudes and feelings. Deliberative styles are highly personal and, even in a specialized context like law, there are no standard protocols for making a decision. In this section, I will describe two distinct approaches to normative decisionmaking that define opposite ends of a continuum. At one end of the continuum is a highly structured procedure of investigation and interpretation that aims at resolving specific cases in accordance with previously established norms of judgment. At the other end is a less structured, more contextual exploration of the case that aims at prompting sound intuitive recommendations concerning its resolution. The first, in effect, transforms the case into an instance of a more general rule; the second recreates the case as an individual narrative that requires an outcome satisfactory to our sense of justice in this particular context. The first places legal structure in the foreground as a central organizing theme; the second brings background to foreground by focusing directly upon the "facts" of the case as they are experienced by the participants.

Structured Decisionmaking. Structured decisionmaking treats each individual normative problem as a token that is to be understood in terms of its type. The facts of the case are compared to a general hypothetical type of situation, and the solution to the case is found by applying a rule, standard, or value that is generally recognized as the appropriate touchstone for resolving cases of this type. Factual inquiries are rigorously controlled by conceptions of relevancy that are built into the recognized classifications. Controversy about the case centers not upon the merits of the proposed solution in this particular case, but upon the appropriateness of the case's characterization as an instance of the chosen type. In short, normative questions are resolved by fitting the case into a preexisting classificatory scheme. Structured deliberations include the following steps.

Deliberation begins with a decision as to what kinds of arguments should count in evaluating the circumstances presented by the case. For example, the decisionmaker might select a utilitarian theory and thereby decree that arguments will have weight to the extent that they demonstrate that the parties' conduct tends to the net benefit or detriment of society as a whole. The selection of such a background theory will often be tacit or will be seen as given by the nature of enterprise.

The decisionmaker will investigate the case by paying particular attention to the factual issues that seem relevant under the normative theory (s)he has selected. (S)he will thus treat certain details of the situation as central to the normative problem and marginalize or disregard the remainder. For example, suppose the situation involves a deceptive representation made to a member of the green team by a member of the blue team. The decisionmaker could focus on the case either as an instance of a deception or as an instance of blue/green interaction. If the chosen normative theory permits clear conclusions about the utility of deceptive practices but does not speak clearly about the effects of favoring one team over the other, a structured approach requires treating the case as an instance of deceptive conduct rather than as a question of blue/green interaction.

The decisionmaker might consider how to define the general circumstances under which deceptive conduct would promote or subvert the chosen normative goals. For example, (s)he could decide that a certain amount of "puffing" is beneficial (perhaps it lubricates commerce), but that deceptive claims that are specific enough to induce reliance are detrimental (perhaps they subvert the gains that can be made by informed bargaining).

The decisionmaker might formulate rules of general application that identify practical criteria by which good or benign cases could be separated from undesirable cases. For example, (s)he might use a distinction between misrepresentations as to matters of opinion and misrepresentations as to matters of fact to condemn harmful deceptions while maintaining a lawful place for harmless puffing.

The decisionmaker might reexamine the original case to determine whether its facts fit the categories established in the formal rule. For example, (s)he could decide that the claim "goes from zero to sixty in thirty-five seconds" is a misstatement of fact whereas the claim "a speedy little sports car" is a matter of opinion. If there is no controversy concerning the actual words used by the salesperson and if these words fall neatly into one category or the other, then there is, under this approach, a clearly correct outcome for the case.

Contextual Decisionmaking. Contextual decisionmaking treats a case as an individual set of circumstances that requires resolution upon its own terms. Rather than fitting the facts to preconceived categories of legal significance, the decisionmaker focuses upon the parties' own characterizations of what happened. Inconsistent responses will prompt deeper inquiries concerning viewpoint and perspective. Solution of the problem requires a reconstruction of the underlying circumstances in such a way that differing accounts form a coherent whole. Once the controversy is understood as a coherent whole, it prompts an intuitive response that specifies the appropriate outcome. Understanding a controversy in this way requires that it be experienced from several different perspectives as a developing drama that moves towards its own unique resolution.

A contextual decisionmaker undertakes a number of separate tasks. Typically, these tasks are not performed in any determinate order but are done and redone as the process unfolds. Contextual decisionmaking involves the following steps.

The decisionmaker begins by becoming familiar with the general outlines of the controversy. (S)he may speak to participants, to experts, and to anyone who has useful insights or information. (S)he may inspect the site, read documents, or consider extrinsic evidence. The object of this activity is to recreate in the decisionmaker's mind as much of the context and detail as possible.

The decisionmaker imagines the event as it may have appeared from the vantage point of each participant. By successively standing in the shoes of all the various players, (s)he seeks to reconstruct subjective appearances and motivations.

The decisionmaker constructs a story that is consistent with all the known details and accounts for each character's subjective experience and known motivations. The story aims at plausibility; the actions of every character must be sufficiently supported by his or her goals, state of mind, and perception of the unfolding event.

At any given point, the decisionmaker will have a point of view with respect to the relative praiseworthiness and blameworthiness of the various participants in the incident. Questions of relevancy will not be determined by a pre-selected normative theory. Instead, as the decisionmaker thinks about the case, some details will begin to emerge as particularly salient. (S)he will base tentative conclusions not only upon an emerging grasp of the situation but also upon prior experience of similar matters and perhaps even upon certain preconceptions. Normative intuitions may be affected by all these items whether we regard them as consciously relevant or not.

Having formed an initial response, the decisionmaker may entertain doubts about its correctness. These doubts arise by reflection upon the limitations that may be inherent in her point of view. Whether these doubts can be adequately or even partially resolved is open to question, but it is nevertheless clear, as a descriptive matter, that some process of self-criticism is frequently an important step in coming to a final judgment.

Structured and Contextual Justification. Just as the structured and contextual models describe two very different conceptions of normative decision-making, they each suggest two distinct forms of justification. With a structured decision, issues of justification center upon the normative theory that has been utilized in the deliberative process: Is the theory the appropriate basis for resolving disputes of this kind? Has it been properly applied to the facts of this case? A contextual decisionmaker, on the other hand, focuses upon the particular circumstances that have created the controversy. Thus, justification for her decision is less abstract and more circumstantial. For example, (s)he might describe her or his deliberative process as a way of showing that (s)he has reached a decision in a conscientious way. In effect, (s)he proclaims: "This is the best I could do under all the circumstances of this case." Such justification is inherently "pragmatic" in the sense that it recognizes that even good decisions are subject to the limitations of perspective and viewpoint.

In the context of legal decisionmaking, the problem of justification is complicated by the demand that cases should be decided in accordance with law. Many structured judges, for example, justify their decisions by a two-step process: first, does the outcome result from a correct application of a correct legal rule and, second, is the legal rule justified by a larger normative theory. Under this approach, legal theory seems to require increasingly abstract statements of "the law" and correspondingly abstract theories of justification. Contextual judges, on the other hand, resort to less universal forms of justification that may seem problematic in a legal context. While they rely upon their intuitions in reaching a decision, they justify their decisions by writing opinions that appeal to traditional sources of legal authority. This has led many legal scholars to question the authenticity of contextual justification. Some scholars argue that it is inappropriate for a judge to cite reasons that (s)he does not herself find persuasive. Others simply point out that nearly every legal outcome could be justified by this kind of ex post justification. Since the end of the realist movement, these arguments have been widely viewed as decisive with the vast majority of legal scholars, one group of legal scholars believing that legal decisions require structured justification and another group believing that all legal decisions are inherently arbitrary.

In the context of this analysis, the pragmatist seems to embrace several contradictory positions. First, (s)he concedes that ex post facto justifications are not adequate justifications for legal outcomes. On the other hand, (s)he also believes that structured theories fail to provide the kind of timeless and universal justification that the theories themselves seem to require. But, despite the fact that the pragmatist rejects these two major forms of justification, (s)he also believes that justification for legal decisionmaking is both necessary and possible. In the remainder of this Article, I will suggest that this position is not so contradictory as it seems. Rather, the contradiction seems fatal only in the context of a vastly oversimplified model of normative decisionmaking. By developing a more complex model of normative decisionmaking, we can begin to develop a notion of justification that has both structured and contextual elements.

Legal Adjudication. As a descriptive matter, it seems clear that legal decisionmaking has both structured and contextual elements. The structured elements are highly visible in the simplest reconstructions of legal method. The contextual elements are less visible but can be seen in the common law preference for case-by-case adjudication, in relaxed standards of evidential relevance, and in the use of juries to resolve legal controversies. In this section, I will develop the distinction between structured and contextual decisionmaking with a view towards showing that neither can operate independently of the other. Thus, the fact that legal adjudication displays elements of both models should not surprise us.

The Two Models Compared. The two models of normative decisionmaking are sometimes contrasted by using words like "abstract," "rational," "universal," and "rule-bound" to characterize structured decisionmaking and opposing words like "concrete," "intuitive," "particular," and "case-specific" to characterize contextual decisionmaking. But these characteristics are misleading in several ways.

First, the difference between structured and contextual decisionmaking is not in the type of mental operations that they employ; both models require the use of abstraction, reason, and intuition. We cannot, for example, engage in contextual decisionmaking as I have described it without recreating the central events from several different viewpoints. This step requires the use of both abstraction and reason. On the other hand, structured theorists frequently appeal to intuition as a justification for certain parts of their analysis.

Second, the two models are not adequately characterized by contrasting pairs of terms such as "general" and "particular" or "universal" and "concrete." These are relative terms. A case may be described as "an auto accident," "a hit and run," "an accident on Main Street on December 3rd," "an accident between Mr. Smith and Ms. Jones," or even as "an accident between Mr. Smith and Ms. Jones on Main Street on December 3rd," and it will still be a general description. Descriptions are always general and general terms are always necessary to describe "particular" facts. The "facts" of a legal case are inevitably only descriptions of fact, and these descriptions are not identical with the concrete circumstances that gave rise to the case. On the one hand, we are able to talk about a "case" only if the descriptions are specific enough to pick out a unique set of circumstances. On the other hand, the "case" is not a specific occurrence but an amalgam of descriptions of the circumstances surrounding the occurrence. In thinking about contextual decisionmaking, it is important not to confuse the legal "case" with the concrete circumstances that generate it. Contextual decisionmakers may be more concerned with factual detail and complexity, but they are nevertheless entirely dependent upon general descriptions. Even a wealth of description will not recreate, except in a metaphorical way, the actual event being investigated.

Third, the use of terms like "rule-centered" and "case-specific" to describe these models is also misleading. On the one hand, it is true that the structured model focuses on categories and criteria while the contextual model focuses on specific circumstances. On the other hand, the conception of rule-centeredness itself is open to widely varying interpretations. Several generations of legal theorists have analyzed the role of legal rules in resolving individual cases. This considerable body of literature has generated a diverse array of understandings about what it means to decide a case in accordance with a legal rule. Are rules prescriptive statements of the form, "If x and y are true, rule in favor of the plaintiff"? Or are they to be understood as a particular hierarchy of values? Because there is no consensus surrounding the use of the word "rule," its meaning is often imprecise and it is therefore not very helpful in analyzing normative decisionmaking. Furthermore, the designation "rule-centered" is deceptive in overlooking the diversity of legal theories that could be considered structured theories. It is true that structured theories invoke rules, standards, or values as a part of their procedure, but that is not a full description of the strategy. For example, Dworkin clearly does not believe that legal decisions result from applying a formal rule to the facts of a controversy; nevertheless, he pursues a structured approach to normative questions. His Hercules begins with a political theory, a theory of legislation, and a theory of precedent, then, with "superhuman skill, learning, patience and acumen," fashions a result that accords with those theories. In short, Hercules need never retreat to his own contextual judgment of the concrete case because "his theory identifies a particular conception of community morality as decisive of legal issues." Dworkin's Hercules may not be a simple rule follower, but his approach is clearly structured in the way outlined above.

The Interdependence of Structured and Contextual Analysis. For the reasons discussed above, it is an oversimplification to think of the structured and contextual models as two separate ways of making a decision. Instead, we can understand each model as describing a set of activities that are essential to normative decisionmaking. In this respect, an analogy will be helpful.

Imagine that a traveler is lost in the middle of nowhere and that it is imperative that (s)he get home. The structured approach resembles the approach we would use if (s)he could give us a signal that would locate her on a giant map. In order to locate her specific position and direct her to her destination, it would be necessary to zero in on her by employing a series of maps that cover successively smaller territories. The location on the large map would give us coordinates that we could use to select a more detailed but less extensive map that also contained the specific location. The location would then be extrapolated onto the second map and new, more exact coordinates would be obtained. The process would be repeated until a map was found with sufficient detail that we could identify the road on which our traveler stood and the exact location of her home. The use of a structured approach to solve normative problems presupposes that we have a very large map (*i.e.*, a reason to prefer one normative theory to another) and that we are able to locate the traveler (define the problem) within the map (in terms of the theory) by means of coordinates (*i.e.*, morally relevant features) that are contained on the map (in the theory) itself. It assumes that both the maps and the signal that places the traveler on the map are accurate.

The contextual approach is the approach we would use if we could locate the traveler but had no map. We would join the traveler and begin to explore. We would try various roads, ask any people we met, and begin to construct our own tentative map of the immediate vicinity. In short, we would look for any clues that we could find until we were able to lead the traveler home. This process could be very time consuming or, with some luck, we might complete it relatively quickly. The use of a contextual method to solve normative problems presupposes that we have no map or only a partial one. The only means of investigating the problem is to exploit our potential connection with it. We can put ourselves in the traveler's shoes, but we can not locate her in the larger universe.

The two approaches represent the difference between zeroing in on a spot from afar or starting with the spot and working our way outward. The virtue of the first approach is that it removes us from the traveler's subjective situation into an objective but abstract conception of her terrain. The strength of the second approach is that it brings us closer to the problem by placing us "on the spot." Despite these apparent differences, it is clear that the two approaches are strongly interrelated. The objectivity of the mapmaker's space is achieved by abstraction and reason, but abstraction and reason, by themselves, are not effective tools. Their usefulness depends upon the accuracy of the information that they analyze. Thus, making a map requires keen "on-the-spot" observation of real geographic areas. Similarly, the "situated" rescuer cannot rely solely upon observation. To be effective, (s)he must make at least some effort to map out, i.e., to record and interpret, what (s)he sees.

It is tempting to draw a distinction between maps and observations that is based on the idea that individual observations are situated while maps are not. On the one hand, individual observations are "situated" in the sense that they are each made relative to an individual viewpoint. On the other hand, maps seem to be less situated in that they are constructed from observations that have been obtained from more than one viewpoint. Even so, maps can never be entirely free of perspective. Consider two different maps: One is drawn by a giant who is hunting tigers; the other is drawn by a Lilliputian who is seeking a sunny place for a nap. Will these two maps look the same? Which one is more objective? Are footprints or rays of sunshine the objective features of this terrain?

The analogy between mapmaking and legal adjudication suggests two things about structured and contextual decisionmaking. First, it suggests that we should not view the structured and contextual analyses of legal adjudication as an either/or proposition. Instead, we should recognize that decisionmakers cannot create a particular structure unless there is a willingness independent of the structure to commit themselves to the correctness of some individual decisions in some individual cases. Thus, even the most abstract forms of deliberation ultimately rely upon contextual decisions. Second, the analogy suggests that even the structured elements of legal decisionmaking are themselves situated. Legal rules do not necessarily begin with first principles; they may begin, like mapmaking, with observations of what seems to be an appropriate response to an individual case. Thus, a legal analysis cannot be perspective free if the categories it uses arise from a decisionmaker's (or a group of decisionmakers') experience in adjudicating cases. Inevitably, what these decisionmakers come to regard as salient and objective features of the decisional terrain will depend upon their own particular situation. This means that the structures that are used to analyze cases are themselves situated in a particular history of adjudicating cases and in a particular set of purposes for engaging in adjudicatory activity.

The Interdependence of Factual and Normative Judgments. Many theorists would deny that there is a useful analogy between the traveler's dilemma and the decision of a legal case. Their objection centers upon the nature of evaluative judgments. The traveler's problem, in their view, is factual and is therefore most readily solved by a combination of particular observation and accumulated knowledge. An evaluative judgment, on the other hand, differs from a factual one in that observations of, or intuitions about, concrete circumstances are inherently untrustworthy. It is clear, they argue, that individual normative responses undergo significant variations as a result of such subjective factors as mood, prejudice, and self-interest. Because of this variation, the argument continues, normative theory should be based upon rational arguments rather than contextual intuitions. Or, to put the point in terms of the mapmaking analogy, normative decisionmakers who place themselves "on the spot" are sure to lose their way in a tangle of unreliable and subjective impressions. Thus, the argument continues, reliable "maps" of normative terrain can be drawn only from a detached and objective stance.

The alternative to "on-the-spot" moral judgments are detached normative theories that begin with first principles and lead to conclusions about particular cases. Examples include the utilitarianism of Bentham and Mill, Kantian theories of deontic obligation, and Rawlsian conceptions of justice and fairness. These theories solve the problem of value by appealing either to self-evident principles such as the value of human utility or to principles that are derived from such worthy conceptions as personhood or justice. The consequent distinction between fact and value excludes the possibility that legitimate judgments of value can be made intuitively by simple observation of an individual case.

Despite the analytical clarity of this distinction between facts and values, the distinction is extremely problematic when we attempt to apply it to the normative decisionmaking of ordinary life. Intuitive normative judgments are an essential and pervasive feature of human experience. For example, we choose a particular route to get to work; we decide to spend more time with our children; we call a questionable tennis serve in or out; we work late so that we can do a better job; or we take time to help a person find something (s)he has lost. We are confronted hourly with demands upon our attention that we can ignore or to which we can respond. Sometimes we decide in accordance with previously articulated principles; most of the time we simply have a "feeling" about such situations. On the basis of this feeling, we believe that certain things ought to happen; under certain circumstances, we are even moved to try to make them happen. This feeling rarely comes to us as the result of conscious application of previously enunciated standards of judgment. Rather, it is a response to a situation taken as a whole—a signal of our "individual stance" with respect to that situation. In responding, we see not only that certain things have been done but also that we favor or oppose those things. In short, we not only perceive an event but we develop an attitude towards the event that, in turn, focuses our attention and colors further perceptions.

When we examine experience in this way, it is clear that a sharp distinction between factual observations and normative judgments cannot be maintained. What we see and hear is filtered and interpreted within a cognitive framework that is constructed largely from our own individual temperament and prior experience. Normative judgments in particular cases are strongly influenced by perceptions about the nature of the controversy within this larger framework. Thus, reality is not something that can be easily or naturally reported as a series of simple observations. Instead, we are enmeshed in scores of overlapping dramas, and our experience of the facts is shaped, in part, by the dramatic roles we play.

It is possible, of course, to make conscious efforts to cleanse our perceptions of their more obvious evaluative elements. We might, for example, say "John approached the group" rather than "John approached the group like a mean son-of-a-gun." But the most scrupulous efforts at impartiality will not restore the details lost as a result of selective attention nor will they permit us to come to a neutral judgment about the facts. I might recognize, for example, that my belief in X's truthfulness is a product of my bias. Nevertheless, this recognition will not necessarily lead to a less partisan view of "the facts." When I discount my estimate of X's credibility, I can't simply conclude that X is lying. Nor is it possible to measure the effect of my bias on the strength of my feelings and to reduce those feelings accordingly; I cannot simply order up a new and corrected sense of the situation. While recognition of bias may be an important step in improving our understanding of a situation, it will not necessarily provide us with a sanitized version of the facts of a case. This does not mean that we cannot make, under some circumstances, factual observations that are relatively untainted by our normative attitudes. We can, for example, make efforts to ensure that scientific observations in a controlled experimental setting are relatively factual. But there is a natural limit to these kinds of efforts, and this is especially true when they are taken outside the laboratory.

In the legal context, the rules governing admissibility of testimony attempt to exclude the most obvious evaluative statements. Nevertheless, witnesses do not observe events under experimental conditions, and trials do not resemble scientific experiments. Controlled observation is not the experience of daily life nor is it the experience that legal testimony describes. Legal testimony is "histrionic" in the sense that it is the telling of a story by one who is a part of the story. Witnesses may be minor characters, but they are nevertheless a part of the story; their view of the facts is as dependent upon their normative position as it is upon their physical viewpoint.

Considerations like these suggest that legal decisionmaking may well be like mapmaking after all. It is true that intuitive normative responses are somewhat unreliable, but it is equally true that they cannot be easily discarded in favor of rational first principles. It is also true that there can be no unbiased and sanitized version of the facts of a case to which such principles can be applied. Instead, the legal enterprise is a complicated endeavor that aims at reaching a considered normative judgment in the face of a confusing array of participant accounts. Such judgments are relative to a perspective; they are situated in prior experience and affected by normative attitudes. They are based upon complex, if not fully conscious, estimates of the relative soundness of each party's case....

Selected References

1 William Blackstone, Commentaries (4th ed. 1899).

Patricia A. Cain, Good and Bad Bias: A Comment on Feminist Theory and Judging, 61 USC Law Review 1945 (1988).

Benjamin N. Cardozo, The Nature of the Judicial Process (1921).

Jules L. Coleman & Jody Kraus, Rethinking the Theory of Legal Rights, 93 Yale Law Journal 1335 (1986).

Arthur Linton Corbin, The Law and the Judges, 3 Yale Review 234 (1913).

Robert M. Cover, The Supreme Court, 1982 Term-Foreword: *Nomos* and Narrative, 97 Harvard Law Review 4 (1983).

Ronald Dworkin, Taking Rights Seriously (1978).

Owen M. Fiss, The Death of the Law?, 72 Cornell Law Review 1 (1986).

George P. Fletcher, Fairness and Utility in Tort Theory, 85 Harvard Law Review 537 (1972).

Thomas C. Grey, Langdell's Orthodoxy, 45 Pittsburgh Law Review 1 (1983).

Duncan Kennedy, Freedom and Constraint in Adjudication: A Critical Phenomenology, 36 Journal of Legal Education 518 (1986).

Max Lerner, The Shadow World of Thurman Arnold, 47 Yale Law Journal 687 (1938).

Francis E. Lucey, S.J., Natural Law and American Legal Realism, 30 Georgetown Law Journal 493 (1942).

Catharine A. MacKinnon, Sexual Harassment of Working Women (1979).

Mari J. Matsuda, Looking to the Bottom: Critical Legal Studies and Reparations, 22 Harvard Civil Rights-Civil Liberties Law Review 323 (1987).

Frank I. Michelman, The Supreme Court, 1985 Term-Foreword: Traces of Self Government, 100 Harvard Law Review 4 (1986).

Martha Minow, The Supreme Court, 1986 Term-Foreword: Justice Engendered, 101 Harvard Law Review 10 (1987).

Hilary Putnam, The Many Faces of Realism (1987) (quoting Ludwig Wittgenstein, Philosophical Investigations, 1953).

Margaret Jane Radin, Reconsidering the Rule of Law, 69 Boston University Law Review 781 (1989).

John Rawls, Two Concepts of Rules, 64 Philosophy Review 3 (1955).

Judith Resnik, On the Bias: Feminist Reconsiderations of the Aspirations for Our Judges, 61 USC Law Review 1877 (1988).

Roger J. Traynor, Some Open Questions on the Work of State Appellate Courts, 24 Chicago Law Review 211 (1957).

David Wiggins, Deliberation and Practical Reason, in Essays on Aristotle's Ethics (1980).

Further Reading (selected work by Catharine Wells)

A Pragmatic Approach to Improving Tort Law, 54 Vanderbilt Law Review 1447 (2001).

Why Pragmatism Works For Me, 74 USC Law Review 347 (2000).

The Perils of Race and Gender in a World of Legal Abstraction, 24 San Francisco Law Review 523 (2000).

Old Fashioned Postmodernism and the Legal Theories of Oliver Wendell Holmes, Jr., 63 Brooklyn Law Review 59 (1997).

Pragmatism, Feminism, and the Problem of Bad Coherence, 93 Michigan Law Review 1645 (1995).

CHAPTER TWENTY-NINE

TRADE AND INEQUALITY*

Economic inequality among states ... is a problem in moral philosophy as well as trade law. Moral and political philosophy are concerned with the order we bring to our social relations, both on the level of individual decisions and relationships, and in terms of the basic structure of our social institutions. The problem of inequality in the distribution of wealth and resources is a basic, yet troublesome, aspect of social life which theorists have struggled with since the beginning of political thought.... [T]he impact of international trade on the fact of inequality is not neutral: the smaller economies characteristic of developing countries are uniquely vulnerable in trade because of such inequalities. In other words, international trade exacerbates existing problems in the distribution of resources, and creates new ones—the rich can get richer, and the poor poorer.

Since international trade seems destined to serve as the cornerstone of global economic and social policy, then developed and developing countries alike must be prepared to evaluate the structure and effects of international economic law in terms of its basic justice. If the developed world's economic relationship to the developing world is in fact governed by moral obligation, and not simply by the instrumental calculations of the moment, then there must be a normative framework within which to articulate the implications of this inequality. Within such a framework, basic doctrines and policies of international economic law can be designed and evaluated in terms of their effectiveness in discharging basic obligations of justice, thereby serving both the normative and pragmatic interests of the developed and the developing world alike....

Justice and Trade Among Unequal Economies. The problem of trade and inequality is a paradigmatic case of the link between trade and justice. The distribution of social goods among the richer and the poorer members of a so-

---

* Frank J. Garcia, *Trade and Inequality: Economic Justice and the Developing World*, 21 MICHIGAN JOURNAL OF INTERNATIONAL LAW 975 (2000), http://papers.ssrn.com/abstract_id=240611.

ciety is a central concern of domestic theories of justice. One of course finds rich and poor individuals outside of one's own society, and one can speak in aggregate terms of richer and poorer states as well. Following Brilmayer, this Article takes the "vertical" approach to the moral issues these facts raise, namely that transnational relations involving inequality, indeed all aspects of transnational relations, require justification in terms of "domestic" political theory. Thus we look to what has been considered traditionally as simply domestic political theory, for the normative justification of distributive patterns in which the richer and the poorer are individuals considered together as states, and not individuals within a state.... Because this Article is aimed at clarifying the moral obligations of wealthier states, and the preponderance of such states consider themselves Western-style liberal democracies, this Article will work within the general framework of liberalism, the dominant philosophical approach to matters of government and society in the West since the Enlightenment....

Liberalism as a Theory of Justice. Liberalism is a notoriously difficult term to define. This article adopts the approach suggested by Michael Sandel and Jeremy Waldron and focuses on liberalism as a theory of justice, a view about the justification of social arrangements. What is most characteristically "liberal" about liberalism as a form of justification is its assertion that the consent of each individual under a system of political order is necessary for that order to have legitimacy. This insight can be said to unite the disparate liberalisms of theorists such as Kant, Mill and Nozick. The form which that consent takes, and the principles consented to, differ according to the particular strand of liberalism to be considered. This Article considers three: egalitarianism, and to a lesser extent utilitarianism and libertarianism.

A further unifying theme in the discussion of liberalism is the liberal commitment to "equality," to treating people as equals. Following Dworkin, Waldron has argued that liberalism is more deeply committed to the ideal of equality than of liberty, rejecting the common view that liberalism is characterized by an attempt to strike a balance between these competing ideals. Kymlicka further develops this point into an approach to liberal theories of justice as attempts to work out, in different ways and to different conclusions, the precise content of the term "equal treatment." If Waldron, Dworkin and Kymlicka are right, then liberalism can also be analyzed comprehensively as a theory of justice as equality, and any individual liberal theory can be critiqued on the basis of how well it achieves this equality.

Egalitarian Liberalism: Rawls' Theory of Justice. If equality is central to liberalism, then the natural starting point in considering liberal theories of justice is the leading egalitarian theory of justice: John Rawls' *"Justice as Fairness."*

The problem of inequality is at the heart of Rawls' theoretical enterprise. The principal work in which Rawls sets forth his response to inequality, the theory of Justice as Fairness, is *A Theory of Justice,* and it is the theory as set forth in that seminal work which shall be the basis for the treatment which follows.

Rawls is concerned with the inequalities that arise with respect to the distribution of primary goods, or goods "that every rational man [sic] is presumed to want," goods that "normally have a use whatever a person's rational plan of life." Primary goods come in two basic varieties. Social primary goods, such as "rights and liberties, powers and opportunities, income and wealth," are distributed by "the basic structure of society," namely its principal social institutions. In contrast, natural primary goods, such as "health and vigor, intelligence and imagination," are by definition not subject to distribution by the basic structure—they are, in other words, "natural"—although their possession is "influenced by the basic structure."

In particular, Rawls is concerned with inequalities that arise in the distribution of social primary goods. Inequalities in the natural distribution of natural primary goods, while they deeply affect people's life chances, are not themselves the subject of justice; rather, it is how a society responds to such inequalities that forms the basic subject of justice. The central problematic of justice is that inequalities in natural primary goods often lead, through the operation of social institutions, to inequalities in the social distribution of social primary goods.

The central moral intuition underlying Rawls' treatment of inequality is that the inequalities in social primary goods that result from such social operations are not deserved, since they are deeply influenced by an underlying natural inequality untouchable by categories of moral responsibility and entitlement. Rawls' primary concern is, therefore, to elaborate a theory which "nullifies the accidents of natural endowment." Put another way, Rawls requires that a liberal theory of justice be "endowment-insensitive," in order to capture our intuition that we do not deserve in any meaningful moral sense the advantages or disadvantages that we enjoy as a consequence of the physical and social circumstances of our birth.

Rawls argues that as a result, the basic structure of society must be arranged "so that these contingencies work for the good of the least fortunate." The distribution of natural talents is to be considered a common asset, and society structured so that this asset works for the good of the least well off. In so doing, Rawls considers this society to meet the basic Kantian obligation of mutual respect, to treat each other as ends and not as means. Elaborating and defending this view is the chief task of *A Theory of Justice.*

... In *A Theory of Justice,* Rawls articulates the principles that would be chosen by "free and rational persons concerned to further their own interests" in an "initial position of equality" to define the fundamental terms of their association. The "general conception" of justice as fairness consists of a single central idea: "All social primary goods—liberty and opportunity, income and wealth, and the bases of self-respect—are to be distributed equally unless an unequal distribution of any or all of these goods is to the advantage of the least favored."

Justice is therefore tied to the notion of an equal share in social goods. People are treated as equals, however, not by removing all inequalities in social distribution, but by removing only "unjust" inequalities, those inequalities that cannot be justified in terms of their benefit to the least advantaged. Rawls contends that a given inequality, in income distribution for example, is nevertheless just if it can serve the interests of the least advantaged by, for example, drawing out a socially useful talent such as entrepreneurial ability, such that jobs and other opportunities are created for the least favored. Such an allocative scheme, however, entails making a myriad of difficult decisions involving competing principles of distribution, such as efficiency, merit and need.

This general conception is further developed into a system of principles and priorities intended to help resolve such conflicts. The resulting "special conception" of justice consists of two principles:

> *First Principle*: Each person is to have an equal right to the most extensive total system of equal basic liberties compatible with a similar system of liberty for all.
> *Second Principle*: Social and economic inequalities are to be arranged so that they are both (a) to the greatest benefit of the least advantaged ... and (b) attached to offices and positions open to all under conditions of fair equality of opportunity.

It is Rawls' contention that the application of these two principles would be adequate to assure the implementation of a just overall system of allocation of social primary goods.

Rawls' argument for justice as fairness depends on a key procedural device, the so-called "original position." As Rawls intends it, the original position is a hypothetical, carefully defined state in which people with certain stipulated attributes make a single, joint decision regarding the principles of justice for their future association. The resulting theory of justice is fair, so the argument goes, because the conditions under which the original choice is made are "fair." The constitution of the original position, therefore, becomes of the first importance for the cogency of the resulting theory.

Key elements of the original position are, first, that it is hypothetical— Rawls is not positing an actual state of nature, nor is he positing an actual, quasi-Edenic pre-constitutional convention. Second, the principles are chosen behind a veil of ignorance; that is, the parties in the original position are ignorant as to the contingent social facts that, afterwards, will determine their relative position in society, with its attendant advantages and disadvantages. They do not know, for example, their social status, wealth, natural endowments, or even their individual conception of the good. Third, those in the original position possess certain qualities. They are moral, in the narrow sense that they have ends that they value; they are rational, i.e., capable of reasoning in the narrow sense of judging the means which best suit their ends; they are mutually disinterested, in that they do not take an interest in each other's interests (or, put another way, they are not moved by empathy or altruism), and they have a sense of justice. Any decision reached under these circumstances is fair, according to Rawls, because all are similarly situated and none can design principles that will favor his or her situation beyond the original position.

Out of this original position comes the choice of the two basic principles of justice which form the bedrock of Rawls' theory. Since, in attempting to work out a system of basic liberties, each person in the original position does not know under what circumstances they will find themselves beyond the veil of ignorance, it would be irrational to choose a system of liberty that gave some a permanent advantage in liberty at the risk of a permanent loss of liberty, or permitted some to increase their wealth, for example, at the risk of less liberty. Each person will therefore choose the maximum degree of liberty consistent with an equal system of liberty for all, *i.e.*, Rawls' First Principle of Justice, and a priority rule that does not permit liberty to be sacrificed for other social goods.

Similarly, when faced with a risk of unknown probability that they will find themselves the most disadvantaged in the natural lottery, those in the Original Position will maximize the minimum share allocated under the system of primary social goods. The resulting difference principle, argues Rawls, best expresses this "maximin" strategy, in that any justifiable inequality must therefore work to the advantage of the least well-endowed.

Inequality and the Debate Within Liberalism. Liberalism offers at least two other basic approaches to the problem of inequality: utilitarian and libertarian theories of justice. While utilitarianism and libertarianism are both liberal theories, they differ fundamentally from egalitarianism in their approach to the problem of inequality. For the reasons set forth below, this Article suggests that when contrasted to egalitarianism, both positions fall short of developing an adequate justification for the economic inequalities that plague developing countries.

Utilitarianism. Utilitarianism is a particular form of consequentialism or, as it is also known, the teleological approach to ethical theory. In general terms, utilitarianism determines the morality of an act according to its consequences for the aggregate of individual utility. Utilitarianisms can be distinguished on the basis of their particular theory of utility, or value. Historically, utility was defined generally in terms of individual happiness. In classical utilitarian theory, human happiness is identified as the good to be sought in all actions. If morality consists of exhortations to do good for people, then an essential characteristic of moral acts is that they in fact do good for people. The greatest good for people, to paraphrase Bentham, is to be happy.

"Happiness" has since been generalized into the concept of "welfare" or "utility," variously conceived of as hedonic satisfaction, desirable mental states, simple preference satisfaction, or rational preference satisfaction. Modern utilitarians are more likely to define utility in terms of the satisfaction of interests or "preferences," which are understood to include a wide range of desired activities, objects and states. For economists, preference satisfaction generally takes the form of welfarism, in which the sum or average of resulting individual welfare levels determines the correctness of an act, principle or policy. Essentially, utilitarianism claims that the principle of utility maximization follows naturally and compellingly from the simple fact that people have such preferences, and will thus be happier to the extent to which such preferences are satisfied.

Historically utilitarian theory was concerned with the problem of inequality. Both Bentham and Mill considered utilitarian theory to be a liberal theory precisely because it distributes public voice equally across social and economic inequalities—each counts for one, and no one for more than one. Utilitarianism as a theory of justice directs that social ordering acts and decisions be arranged so as to satisfy as many rational preferences as possible. Because resources are limited, however, not everyone's preferences will be satisfied. Utilitarianism therefore counsels that the just social ordering is one in which utility, however defined, is maximized. Moreover, in determining the utility effects of particular arrangements, each person's preferences count equally. As reformers, both Mill and Bentham therefore expected utilitarianism to justify changes to the existing social, political and economic systems that would favor the least well-off.

At first blush, therefore, a utilitarian approach to the problem of inequality would seem well-suited to the socioeconomic claims of the developing world. When one considers the levels and distribution of wealth across both the developing and the developed world, it seems quite likely that utility maximization will require wealth-transfers to developing countries. There are, after all, many more people in developing countries than in developed countries, and differences in marginal utility will weigh in heavily in such a calculation.

As a theory of international distributive justice, however, utilitarianism runs into trouble. The central problem for a utilitarian theory of international distributive justice is the problem of standing. When determining the utility effects of a given act, whose utility counts? This problem has both a formal and a political dimension. Formally, it has been argued in the cost-benefit literature that the choice of whose preferences to count is underdetermined by utilitarian economic theory, leaving the matter open to the discretion of the analyst. In such cases, cost-benefit decisions involving cross-border externalities may be analyzed without taking into consideration the preferences of those outside the social unit of the decision-makers, since the basis for any right on their part to have their preferences counted may be unclear.

While there may be arguments against this view on a theoretical level, there are strong political reasons why the restricted preference approach may be favored in practice. Utilitarian economists and philosophers are free to adopt a global point of view with regard to utility maximization, but national decision-makers are not likely to do so. If decision-makers in developed countries consider wealth redistribution policies along utilitarian lines, they are far more likely to restrict their analysis to the utility effects on their national constituency. After all, in a system of nation-states and representative government, national constituencies are the party to whom such leaders are accountable.

This restriction dramatically alters the utility calculus and makes it far less likely that any wealth redistribution will occur, despite the overwhelming numerical superiority of the world's poor and the undeniably welfare-enhancing effects of such redistribution. The same social facts supporting redistribution on global utility grounds drastically undercut the argument for redistribution when standing is limited to the national sphere. The theory of comparative advantage does suggest that not all transfers from developed to developing countries will constitute a zero-sum game. Nevertheless, there will almost certainly be a relative, if not absolute, decrease in the welfare of developed countries in order that the welfare of all states may increase. In such a scenario it is unlikely that national decision-makers will argue for policies resulting in decreases in national welfare, whether absolute or relative, by appealing to the welfare increases in poorer states and the resulting overall welfare increase.

In such cases, utilitarians would have to marshal a variety of domestic utility-based justifications for various types of assistance to poorer states in order for individuals in richer states to find utilitarian-based redistribution compelling. Such justifications might include an appeal to increased stability in international relations or to the creation of larger and stronger markets of consumers for developed country exports. While these arguments may have merit in their own right, the degree of redistribution they justify is likely to fall short of the redistribution justifiable on global utility lines. Moreover, the moral rationale for addressing the problem of inequality now smacks of egoism, a questionable moral philosophy even among individuals, let alone among nations.

The utilitarian approach to the problem of inequality is also hampered by the fact that inequality for utilitarians is not a special or unique problem. Inequality is a social fact among many other social facts. In contrast, the problem of inequality is a central, if not paradigmatic concern for egalitarian liberalism. The goal and standard for any egalitarian theory of distributive justice will be a principle of justice by which social organization can be adequately justified in the face of inequality, even if this involves the redistribution of wealth towards, if not absolute equality of outcomes, then justifiable inequality.

Libertarianism. As with egalitarianism, the problem of inequality is central to libertarians—however, they draw opposite moral conclusions from the same social facts. The classic libertarian-egalitarian conflict involves a fundamental disagreement over the moral legitimacy of state-effected wealth redistribution, based on a contrary view of the moral implications of natural inequality. While egalitarians see in the arbitrariness of natural inequality a justification for the difference principle as a condition of moral equality, libertarians see moral equality as equality of rights, in particular rights to unequal endowments and their fruits. For libertarians, this results in a system of social inequalities that, while perhaps regrettable, can justly be addressed only by some minimal notion of procedural fairness or fairness of opportunity on the part of the less advantaged.

Libertarian theory asserts the fundamental primacy of individual rights, in particular rights to property broadly conceived. Taking Nozick as an example, the starting point of his theory, strongly stated at the very outset of *Anarchy, State and Utopia*, is that "individuals have rights, and there are things no person or group may do to them without violating their rights." For Nozick, the central core of a property right in X is the right to determine what shall be done with X, constrained only by the negative rights of others. Each person has ownership rights over themselves and their abilities. Therefore, each person has the right to freely dispose of themselves and their abilities.

This strong Lockean statement of the priority of individual rights leads libertarians such as Nozick to approach the problem of distributive justice in negative terms: "So strong and far-reaching are these rights that they raise the question of what, if anything, the state and its officials may do. How much room do individual rights leave for the state?" Nozick concludes that in fact there is very little room for anything beyond a minimal state enforcing negative rights: "any more extensive state will violate persons' rights not to be forced to do certain things, and is unjustified." In particular, there is no room for the sort of distributive project Rawls sees as central to the role of the state: "the state may not use its coercive apparatus for the purpose of getting some citizens to aid others."

The basis of Nozick's theory of [no-]distributive justice is his entitlement theory, which is a theory about "justice in holdings." A just society is one in which everyone is entitled to the holdings they possess. Nozick divides the question of justice in holdings into three major topics: justice in the original acquisition of holdings, justice in the transfer of holdings from one person to another, and the rectification of injustice in holdings. Justice in acquisition is a theory of how unheld things come to be held. Justice in transfer is a theory of the permissible and impermissible manners of transferring our holdings to others, and thereby acquiring the previously held holdings of another. Distributive justice, for Nozick, therefore, is "simply that a distribution is just if everyone is entitled to the holdings they possess under the distribution."

The entitlement theory is fairly open and underdeveloped. In fact, the operative core of Nozick's theory is not the general theory of entitlement, but the assumptions underlying the outlines of his theory of justice in acquisition. Key to Nozick's theory of justice is that natural endowments are not, in contrast to Rawls, morally arbitrary. Natural endowments are, in fact, morally significant, in that each person acquires rights in their natural endowments and in the fruits of those endowments. In other words, the theory of justice in acquisition includes acquisition through natural endowment as a form of just acquisition.

As a theory of liberal justice, libertarianism runs into several difficulties. One can object, as does Rawls, on the ground that our intuitions run counter to the entitlement theory on the key issue of the moral significance of our endowments. Libertarianism depends on an individual's moral claim to their talents and the fruits of such talents—if this claim indeed runs counter to our intuitions, then libertarianism is in deep trouble. Rawls in effect makes such an argument by asserting that in the Original Position, libertarian principles would not be chosen, since they would not under the veil of ignorance be a rational choice.

One can also argue that this inconsistency is revealed in the relationship between inequality in resources and effective equality of liberty and moral status. The central distributive mechanism for libertarians is the market, since it is in the market that self-owning individuals can parlay their talents and abilities into title over other resources. However, even if one grants that the free market is the best mechanism for basic distribution questions, the moral basis for this approach when applied to all distributive questions is substantially undermined by the reality of inequality in natural endowments. Access to social resources, which enable one to effectively exercise one's liberty and realize one's life plans, will be skewed by natural endowments, whose distribution the individual had no control over.

For this reason egalitarians consider such endowments arbitrary, and therefore open to redistributive mechanisms. Nozick's primary objection to egalitarian redistribution, however, is that it undercuts formal self-ownership. Libertarianism, however, fails to address the fact that purely formal self-ownership without adequate resources to realize one's life projects undercuts the substance of self-ownership, namely the ability to get on with one's life projects. In Nozick's world, only some individuals are substantively equal, in that they have a reasonably equal chance in fact of acting on their conceptions of themselves. Such a restriction is fundamentally illiberal.

This same difficulty arises in the international distributive context: libertarianism fails to adequately confront the problem of inequality of resources in the international economic plane. The reality of gross inequalities in international endowments undercuts the possibility of effective equality of rights among states (sovereignty), which is the centerpiece of libertarianism.

A system of purely formal equality between states, equivalent in the trade context to a simple system of free open-market exchanges, will further undercut the possibility of substantive equality between states.... If liberalism is to be conceived as a theory of equality, then a libertarian system of "natural liberty" among states, a purely formal equality of opportunity, will be inadequate to achieve liberal justice absent some mechanism for addressing the problem of inequality in resources.

Justice as Fairness in International Economic Relations.... [T]he socioeconomic predicate underlying the need for a domestic theory of justice (social cooperation yielding new benefits and burdens) is present in international economic relations. Moreover, ... the problem of inequality in natural endowments is as present internationally between states as it is domestically between individuals, and leads in a similar fashion to inequalities in the distribution of resulting social goods such as wealth, knowledge and power.... [Accordingly,] the international problem of inequality should be treated in the same manner as the domestic problem, and with similar results....

Understanding the problem of trade and inequality as a problem of justice has several implications for both discourse and policy.... [U]nderstanding the trade and inequality link as a justice issue implies that we are not free to govern our economic relationships with developing countries solely with regard to the politics of the moment. It becomes incumbent on those seeking to establish an economic order that does not fully address the claims of less developed states, to articulate a normative basis for this position. In other words, they must explain why such an order would be just.

Moreover, viewing the trade and inequality link as a justice matter renders it problematic to adopt the stance of an egalitarian liberal at home, and a libertarian or political realist abroad. If one is an egalitarian liberal on domestic issues of justice, then the logic of one's position would dictate that one commit to some form of distributive justice on an international plane as well. This conclusion is reinforced by the degree to which trade with poorer countries has in fact been part of the wealth-creation that sustains the domestic economy's success....

Finally, analyzing the problem of inequality as a problem of justice means that international trade law must continue to incorporate a robust form of the difference principle. The key to a Rawlsian justification of international trade law is to see the disparities in market power and expertise between states as manifestations of the problem of inequality. International trade law must therefore be structured so as to put the power of developed country markets and knowledge at the service of the least developed countries....

Selected References

Charles R. Beitz, Political Theory and International Relations (1979).

Lea Brilmayer, Justifying International Acts (1989).

Ronald Dworkin, Liberalism in A Matter of Principle (1985).

R.G. Frey, Utility and Rights (1984).

Ethan B. Kapstein, Distributive Justice and International Trade, 13 Ethics and International Affairs 175 (1999).

Will Kymlicka, Contemporary Political Philosophy (1990).

John Madeley, Trade and the Poor (1992).

John Stuart Mill, Chapters on Socialism, in 5 Collected Works of J.S. Mill (1967).

Robert Nozick, Anarchy, State, and Utopia (1974).

Thomas W. Pogge, Realizing Rawls (1989).

John Rawls, A Theory of Justice (1971).

John Rawls, Political Liberalism (1993).

John Rawls, The Law of Peoples (1999).

David Ricardo, Principles of Political Economy and Taxation (1819).

Michael J. Sandel, Liberalism and the Limits of Justice (1998).

Adam Smith, An Inquiry into the Nature and Causes of the Wealth of Nations (Kathryn Sutherland ed., 1993).

Jeremy Waldron, Theoretical Foundations of Liberalism, 37 Philosophical Questions 127 (1987).

Further Reading (selected work by Frank J. Garcia)

Trade, Inequality, and Justice: Toward a Liberal Theory of Just Trade (Transnational 2003).

Beyond Special and Differential Treatment, 27 Boston College International and Comparative Law Review 291 (2004).

Building a Just Trade Order for a New Millennium, 33 George Washington International Law Review 1015 (2001).

Review of The Law of Peoples by John Rawls, 23 Houston Journal of International Law 659 (2001).

Trade and Justice: Linking the Trade Linkage Debates, 19 University of Pennsylvania Journal of International Economic Law 391 (1998).

CHAPTER THIRTY

THE APOGEE OF THE COMMODITY[*]

The black is the apogee of the commodity. It is the point—in time as well as in space—at which the commodity becomes flesh. And, for the system of capital, the black is both the instrument of its demise and the vehicle of its ensoulment. Provisionally, let us call the time and space of ensoulment Virginia, 1619 A.D. It begins with a document:

> About the latter end of August, a Dutch man of Warr of the burden of 160 tuñes arriued at Point-Comfort, the Cammando[rs] name Capt Jope, his Pilott for the West Indies one Mr Marmaduke an Englishman.... He brought not anything but 20. and odd Negroews, wch the Governo[r] and Cape Marchant bought for victuale (whereof he was in great need as he pretended) at the best and easyest rate they could.

A legal relationship emerges ("20. and odd Negroews ... bought for victuale ..."). There is a field of knowledge, a science of right, within which that relation is said to exist. It all comes to an end with the question of reparations.

What is a legal relation? The question brings us back to the commodity that reaches its apogee in the black. What connects a document to a body of rules and to the bodies governed by its rules?

Capital becomes a system of right in and through the voice of the commodity. Commodities do speak. Commodities speak of rights (the science of right is the study of the use of words in the language of the commodity). The commodity might like to be human, but humanity, within the system of capital, is ownership. Human rights, then, are precisely what the commodity cannot possess and yet precisely what it perpetually prays to receive. The question of reparations is the expression of this contradiction. The commodity dreams

---

[*] **Anthony Paul Farley**, *The Apogee of the Commodity*, 53 DePaul Law Review 1229 (2004), http://papers.ssrn.com/abstract_id=789744.

of equality. The commodity is that which dreams of equality; the dream of equality, in other words, is the without which not of the commodity.

The dream is a disguised wish. The commodity hides its desire from itself through dreams and prayers for rights. The commodity dreams of equal rights, of being human, and that dream-surface of rights hides the secret shame of the commodity. The commodity's dream of equal rights is a disguise for its secret and shameful desire to remain a commodity. The commodity has been trained to be a commodity and it follows that training all the way to the end. The end is the question of reparations, but before the end is the beginning.

There are objects and there are owners. When there are owners, one is either object or owner. Objects capable of ownership and exchange are commodities. One owns or does not own. The one that owns is an owner and the one that does not own is either owned or lost. Of the lost, nothing can be said. Of the owned, nothing need be said; they speak with the voice of their owners, they speak of rights. What is the origin of the commodity?

The one who would own must first create a world of objects capable of being owned. This requires, before all else, a marking of bodies. The otherwise common flesh of the human must be divided into the bodies of the owner and the owned. Race and sex, for example, are marks.

No one has the power to bind others to respecting a mark made on the earth or anything in it. One person cannot force another to respect or with respect to anything at all, at least not for long and not for life. One person may temporarily overpower another but the one must sleep sometime and during that time the other may depart, become stronger than the one, or find an ally. With each night's dreaming, the rule and the rules of the one melt into the sea like castles made of sand. The rule of the one, then, does not allow for the reduction of the other to an object capable of being owned. The one who would own must, therefore, first find others who would own and then jointly devise a "system of marks."

These marks must be written on the body so that those who would own can recognize each other as owners and others as owned. Those who would own author a system of marks so that they can organize themselves into a single body powerful enough to force others to respect their will. The powerful group, which shares a common mark, can bind others to its will. The will of the powerful ones, the would-be owners, becomes, through force and habit and force of habit, the system of marks. The powerful group marks itself and marks its others and then forces its less powerful others to respect the system of marks, to accept its will. The mark is forced upon the others and that force is the force of law and the system of property.

The powerful group of would-be owners soon mark the earth and all that is in it. These marks place everything in or out of a system of exchange. This secondary marking is seen as the birth of property. Property comes only after the system of marks has been written on the body. We are divided into owners and owned before there is property, before there can be property. The owners are the ones who bear the mark of the powerful group on their bodies. The mark is white-over-black. ("20. and odd Negroews, ... bought for victualle....") The owned are all the others, white-over-black. The others are commodities, white-over-black. The commodity acquires the rules of its rulers, white-over-black. This acquisition or capture is seen as the rule of law. The rule of law is seen as necessary to the system of exchange, a system in which the owners seem to meet each other as equals.

There is nothing in the rule of law, save that which has been placed there by training. And there is no there there, only bodies and pleasures. There is a body of rules, these rules are pleasures. The body of rules, the body of the law, is, literally, the desire of the rulers to rule and the desire of the ruled to be ruled. The body of the law is the desire of the owners to own and the desire of the owned to be owned. These desires, sadistic and masochistic, and perfectly complementary in non-revolutionary situations, are experienced as the body of the law and in the bodies marked as owner and owned.

The rule seems to point in a certain direction. We follow the rule when we move in the generally accepted direction. But there is nothing in the rule itself (or in any rule for rule interpretation or in any rule for interpretation of a rule for rule interpretation and so on ...) that points us in any direction whatsoever. The rule only seems to point. The direction in which it seems to point is the direction of our training. We move in the direction that we are trained to move and we call it the rule of law. We have been trained to see, and do in fact see, the rules as if they determine the circumstances of their own application. This is legal fetishism.

Legal concepts seem, somehow, to have relations with each other. Legal rules seem, somehow, to apply themselves to circumstances and, before so doing, make arrangements with each other regarding each rule's role in the entire process. It seems, somehow, to those who bow before the rule of law, that legal rules have a way of determining the circumstances of their own application. How is this possible? Legal relations, relations between legal concepts, are our own social relations viewed as if they were not our own social relations but were instead rational or natural relations between rules of law that seemingly organize themselves and then, uncannily, determine the circumstances of their own application.

... Our lived relations with each other are repressed through law. We describe our relations with each other as if they were relations between Rawlsian points of light, as if we were all glittering and windowless monads, as if we were all sparks floating up to heaven and lighting the world. Our worldly relations, our worldly pleasures, are beneath notice, we repress. Legal method is the instrument of repression and, therefore, the vehicle of return. When the repressed desire returns, its vehicle is the repressing instrument itself. Our lived relations bear, therefore, an uncanny resemblance to the structure of our laws. Our legal concepts, our legal relations, arrange themselves in white-over-black.

The system of marks is the system of training. The system of property is the system of training. The system of law is the system of training. There are no systems. There is only training. We go in the direction of our training. We go in the direction of our marks. We go in the direction of our pleasure, however much that pleasure is secreted from ourselves. We move property as we move bodies, in the direction of our training, in the direction of our marks, and in the direction of our pleasure. That direction is seen as the rule of law. We live our training as our future and endlessly repeat the past. We repeat the system of marks in the system of property and we repeat the system of property in the system of law. All systems—the system of marks, the system of property, and the system of law—are repetitions of training. We live our training as our future. Every way of life is itself a form of training in following that way of life. White-over-black, for example, is a form of training, a way of life:

> The everyday activity of slaves reproduces slavery. Through their daily activities, slaves do not merely reproduce themselves and their masters physically; they also reproduce the instruments with which their master represses them, and their own habits of submission to the master's authority. To [those] who live in a slave society, the master-slave relation seems like a natural and eternal relation. However, [people] are not born masters or slaves.

… We are trained in the things our trainers find useful. In this way we acquire a value, a pleasure, and an orientation within the system of marks, the system of property, and the system of law. There is a pleasure in hierarchy, in white-over-black. The pleasure of white-over-black is experienced through the system of marks. The pleasure of white-over-black is experienced through the system of property. The pleasure of white-over-black is experienced through the system of law. These systems—of marks, of property, of law—are surfaces. The pleasure of white-over-black is beneath.

The sum of our training is the sum of our hierarchies. The color-line divides the entire field of vision. The field is the world. The system of marks is all there is, white-over-black supercedes whatever it was that nature might or might not have created. The system of property is white-over-black. The system of law is also white-over-black, white-over-black only, and that continually....

If white-over-black is the general order of things, then training will generally be in the direction of white-over-black. We acquire a white-over-black orientation through training and are thus ourselves acquired by the system of marks. Once acquired, we orient ourselves within institutional spaces using our sense of white-over-black (our sense of pleasure in the white-over-black position). Thus, we repeat the system of marks in the system of property, and the system of property in the system of law. We see white-over-black; this is a pleasure and a form of training in itself. We distribute goods and services and fashion a system of exchange according to white-over-black; this too is a pleasure and a form of training. We respect laws respecting the distribution of goods and services and the system of exchange according to white-over-black; this is yet another form of pleasure and training. This last pleasure, the rule of law, is infinite and infinitely perverse and perversely requires the participation of the commodities themselves.

The rule of law is the secret of the commodity and its fetish. There is no rule of law. Laws do not and cannot rule anything. There are the rulers and there are the ruled and that is all, except the secret thing that goes on between the rulers and the ruled in non-revolutionary situations. The secret thing is the pleasure of hierarchy: a pleasure experienced in the system of marks, in the system of property, and in the system of law. The pleasure of hierarchy is sadistic for those on top and masochistic for those on the bottom....

With every move, with every turn of the page, there is the risk that one might lose one's way. In the space between the lines we fear not because we have the ability to find our place. We find our place, we orient ourselves by following our pleasure. Training gives us the ability to know where we are in the system of marks; we are oriented in the direction of white-over-black. Through training, we always know where we are in the system of property; we are oriented in the direction of white-over-black. And because of our training we always know where we are in the system of law; we are oriented in the direction of white-over-black. We live our training as our future. We point eternally in the direction of white-over-black. We point eternally in the direction of our training.

A fetish is an artifact that is treated as if it were not the product of human work. The fetishist forgets the creation of the artifact and then absurdly bows down before his or her own work. Law, looked upon as if it were something other than the force of the system of marks and the system of property, is a fetish. Law, looked upon as if it were something other than white-over-black, is a fetish. Law is white-over-black, white-over-black only, and that continually.

Law only appears after the system of marks and the system of property. Law is the way that awareness of the system of marks and the system of property is banished from consciousness. Law is always repression and so only appears in the form of the fetish. There is no need, therefore, to critique or expose legal fetishism. Law cannot be anything other than fetish. Law is the most important fetish. The desire for the rule of law is the unconscious desire for white-over-black. Law is the way we make ourselves unconscious of our pleasure in white-over-black.

Law begins to look like a system when those who are placed at the bottom begin to dream of equal rights. The dream of equal rights requires a system of law and a science of right in which the legal relation of equality can exist and make sense. The dreamers dream for the entire system, they dream the system into being. Without the dreamers and their dream there is no system of law, there are only chaotic statements accompanying the fact of movement in the direction of our hierarchies. With the dreamers and within their dream, there appears a system that seems coherent, even beautiful, but for a few changes, but for equality of right. It is in this way that the commodity gives up the ghost.

Equality of right leads to questions of redress and reparations, and the question of reparations for slavery leads to the end of the dreamers, and thus to the end of the dream. When the commodity prays for reparations and redress it prays for reparations and redress for having been made a commodity. To repair slavery is to end inequality and the end of inequality is the end of right altogether.

The question of reparations forces the commodity to confront the rule of law and its own role in maintaining the system of white-over-black.... The question of reparations is uncanny because it marks the place and time that the commodity experiences its estrangement from itself.... The somnambulant path of the law leads to the question of reparations because the law promises a remedy for every wrong. The commodity dreams of equality and, therefore, of reparations. Rights are the manifest content of the commodity's dreams and all the commodity ever speaks of. Below the surface of the commodity's dreams of equal rights, however, there is the latent desire for white-over-black. It is in this way that the system of capital acquires its spirit.

Only the injured dream of rights. The injury occurs when and where the mark is attached to the body. The system of marks, then, is a systematic injury; white-over-black. That injury can be understood by examining the system of property and the way property is organized as white-over-black. Pleasure is a many-splendored thing. Everything can be made a pleasure. There are no limits to desire. Even injuries can become desired pleasures. White-over-black is the injury that begins the dream of rights. The injury, however, seems to fade from consciousness when one turns to the system of law. This is the secret of the commodity and its fetish.

The commodity is made to desire equality. The commodity has less and so it seeks to balance an equation. The commodity has been marked as less, as white-over-black. The commodity has also been marked for less; property flows in the direction of white-over-black. The commodity desires equality. The commodity presents its suffering, its non-ownership, as a prayer for legal relief from the inequality that it experiences as its injury. The commodity prays for equal rights but rights cannot be equal.

Rules are endlessly interpretable. Desire sorts them out. Desire is cultivated and educated in a way that leads us in certain directions, directions that those who cultivate and educate us find useful. Interpretation comes to an end when we move in the generally accepted way. We move in the generally accepted way when our training, made possible by and through the cultivation and education of our desire, has proceeded in the generally accepted way. We interpret and follow a rule correctly when we move in the generally accepted way. We move in the generally accepted way when our training has resulted in the acquisition of the usual orientation, white-over-black....

A right will always be interpreted and followed in the direction of white-over-black and so rights cannot be equal. We pursue our pleasure; that is what we have been trained to do. If our training is white-over-black and we have been successfully trained, then we will move in the direction of white-over-black and equal will always end in white-over-black. The sum of our institutions is the sum of our training. The sum of our training reveals the totality of our pleasures. We follow our pleasure to infinity and thus endlessly repeat our training. Our institutions are white-over-black. All of them. Our training is white-over-black. Our pleasure is white-over-black. Our desire is white-over-black. We follow white-over-black and thus endlessly project our past into our future. We do this through rights.

To request equality is to surrender before one begins. To request equality is to grant one's owners the power to grant or deny one's request. To grant one's owners such a power is to surrender oneself to one's owners entirely and completely. To grant such a power is to accept one's status as a commodity, a thing the future of which is rightly left to the persons granted the power to grant or deny the request for equality. To grant such a power is to accept one's future, and therefore oneself, as owned by the ones granted the power to grant or withhold one's request for equality. To pray for legal redress is to bow before the authority of law. There is no mystery in the authority of law. Law's authority is only the surrender-and-training of the commodity. Law is only the relation of white-over-black to white-over-black to white-over-black. When we follow a legal rule we follow only the track that we have ourselves laid down. In other words, we ourselves are the track, we become the track when we lay down, and we follow that track white-over-black into the future that lasts forever.

Sometimes training goes awry and things fall apart. Sometimes the "caged anger within" escapes. The words of J.G. Fichte, although written in another context, are nonetheless helpful in understanding such moments:

> I would be sorry if they understood me. Until now it has gone according to my wishes with these people; and I hope even now that this exordium will so bewilder them that from now on they see nothing but letters on the page, while what passes for mind in them is torn hither and thither by the caged anger within.

… A passage in a letter penned by political prisoner Afeni Shakur during the conspiracy trial of the *Black Panther 21* is an open window the moment that the commodity realizes and refuses its role:

> We know that the 13th, 14th and 15th amendments did not liberate us—that they only legalized slavery and expanded the *Dred Scott* decision to include the Indians, Spanish speaking and poor whites. We know that things have not gotten any better—but only progressively worse. We know that it is the rich man's courts, laws, and justice. It is his skies and air—we can only look at it and breathe it if he says so.… We know that the Almighty dollar which everyone is taught to revere is only guaranteed by slavery and exploitation. We know that we live in a world inhuman in its poverty.

The question of poverty concerns the relation between persons and property. There is no relation between persons and property. Nature does not produce property. Property, considered as a natural object, does not exist. The line drawn by the law from persons to property, therefore, connects nothing, because there is nothing to connect. Relations between persons and property do not exist. What does exist is a relation between persons that is treated as if it were a relation between objects. The laws we lay down do not connect persons to property. We ourselves connect persons to property when we lay down before the law.

The act of laying down before the law occurs before there is law, before there is anything before which to lay down. A person lays down and becomes a thing, a thing that lays down, a commodity. The commodity lays down and thus makes itself a thing-that-can-be-owned. Ownership, then, is a relation between persons that is disguised as a relation between objects of property. And those objects of property are themselves disguised as legal relations.

Ambiguity always exists. Everything has its ambiguities. The ambiguities are too many to be named, counted, or categorized. The ambiguities are endlessly available for interpretation. To be oppressed is to have the ambiguities, which are infinite as well as indefinable, interpreted in a way that oppresses. A right is always ambiguous and, therefore, available to be interpreted. An equal right or a right to equality is, likewise, always ambiguous and interpretable. Equality can be anything at all. To be oppressed is to have one's rights interpreted oppressively. The ubiquity of ambiguity means that equality and right are both available for oppressive interpretations. The ambiguities are where desire prepares its endless strategies and masquerades. Equality is the most covert hiding place for, and the most effective mask of, oppression. Oppressive interpretations marshal the ambiguities against the oppressed.

When the commodity prays for legal rights it bows down before the rule of law. If the ambiguities were not always read as white-over-black, then the commodity would have no need to pray for equal rights. The rule of law, like everything, is filled with ambiguities. The ambiguities are resolved into white-over-black. The rule of law is nothing other than the ambiguities and the ambiguities are nothing other than white-over-black. Prayers for relief will be answered with white-over-black when relief is granted and when it is not. A rule granting an equal right is as available for a white-over-black interpretation as is a rule mandating an unequal right. Equality is as available for white-over-black as is inequality.... Law is the ambiguity that pretends most intensely not to be. Law is white-over-black.

Prayers for relief can only be answered in the form of white-over-black. These prayers are acts of state worship (and ecstatic exhibitions of the commodity's death-drive). The state is the desire for white-over-black. Rule fetishism (fundamentalism and fealty to the "system") is always simultaneously the hiding place and stronghold of the will to oppress....

The question of reparations reveals the state for what it is and presents the commodity with a choice. Reparation for slavery requires the undoing of white-over-black and that requires the end of the system of marks, the end of the system of property, and the end of the system of law. The state will not grant the prayer for reparations; it cannot without destroying itself. Without white-over-black the state withers away. The commodity's choice is to remain awake and force the undoing of white-over-black and all its reifications or remain asleep and continue to dream of equal rights.

The commodity has been trained to be the commodity, to be white-over-black. The commodity that prays for relief, as has been shown, prays, as it has been trained to pray, for white-over-black. The commodity prays in the ec-stasy of total surrender, of infinite masochism or inverted sadism. The white-over-black that the commodity receives, whether in the form of equal rights or in the form of the denial of equal rights, is the secret face of its own desire for white-over-black.

White-over-black is the form of the situation that leads the commodity to pray. White-over-black, being the form of our institutional situations, is the form of our training and, therefore, the form of our desire. White-over-black fills the ever-present ambiguities and all is resolved into the pleasure of white-over-black, the words are simply the sweet nothings of a relief that serves only to prolong the agonizing pleasure of white-over-black. The ambiguities are everywhere. Without the commodities' dream-work, the system would have no coherence, no consistency, no foundation. Indeed, it would not be a sys-tem, it would only be an obvious and insane and random war of all against all. The feeling that the "system" is a "system" is produced by the commodi-ties themselves through their dream-work, through their dreams of equal rights. And if they left off dreaming of equal rights?

The system is a desire for death. Freedom from ambiguity comes only with death. Death balances every equation. An essay by Black Panther Linda Har-rison, written in 1969, is another open window into the moment the com-modity realizes and refuses its role:

> All [people] can die, and this is the only thing that equalizes them. Under many systems those with money die less often. Any con-frontation which gives [people], no matter what their social or eco-nomic position, an equal chance to die under equal conditions is up-lifting for those who consider themselves at the bottom and degrading and toppling for those who are at the top.

Death is what happens when the commodity realizes and refuses its role. The commodity is the system's repressed death-drive. And the repressed always re-turns. And when it returns it returns through the vehicle of the instrument of the repression itself. The commodity dons black flesh and then it begins. There is a specter haunting the United States, the specter of the commodity, the spectral return of the repressed, the specter of servile insurrection. Black Panther Connie Matthews, in a speech delivered at the Vietnam Moratorium demonstration at San Jose State College on October 15, 1969, spoke with an awareness of the death that comes with the refusal of the commodity form:

> Get with it and educate your people because the Black Panther party is out there in the front but we can't stay out there in the front forever. We

will stay until everyone of us is killed or imprisoned by these racist pigs, but then someone will have to take over. So don't let us all die in vain.

Matthews was prophetic. The Black Panther Party could not remain "out there" in front forever. A war was waged against them and all who refused the commodity form that they had been assigned. Those who realized and refused the commodity form were killed or imprisoned. But the system of marks that is the system of property that is the system of law continues to produce, every now and then, commodities that realize and refuse their role. The question of reparations can only be answered with the end of the system of marks, the end of the system of property, and the end of the system of law. The wide-awake world of the former commodity is the end of marks, the end of property, and the end of law:

> [Afeni Shakur spoke:] We realize that freedom is a duty and it is our duty to get this freedom for our people and to yield to no one in ob-taining it. We will be beggars no longer. You brought the nigger into existence and now finally, we are destroying him. We know that your economic system is a chain around our necks and we are breaking all of your chains.

The question of reparations can only be answered by the commodity that wakes up from the dream of equal rights. The Black Panther Party understood that the system of law would not commit suicide:

> [Afeni Shakur continued:] You are the state and we say "All Power to the People" and the people will have the power. But you will try to stop us. You will oppress us until we stop you and we will stop you. History shows that wars against oppression are always successful. And there will be a war—a true revolutionary war—a bloody war. No one not you nor us nor anyone in this country can stop it from occurring now. And we will win. We admit all of this.

The question of reparations is produced by the system of marks. The ques-tion of reparations is produced by the system of property. The question of reparations is produced by the system of law. The answer to the question re-quires the end of law, the end of property, and the end of marks. The answer to the question of reparations is the end of white-over-black. Of an earlier waking moment in the life of the commodity, C.L.R. James wrote:

> The slaves destroyed tirelessly.... They were seeking their salvation in the most obvious way, the destruction of what they knew was the cause of their sufferings; and if they destroyed much it was because

they had suffered much. They knew that as long as these plantations stood their lot would be to labour on them until they dropped. The only thing was to destroy them.

The commodity that realizes and refuses its commodity form is the end of the system of marks, the system of property, and the system of law.

Every mark is an attack. Every claim of ownership is an attack. Every law is an attack. Rule of law is a lie, perhaps the longest lie. The Earth, and all that is in it, belongs to everyone. There is as much and as good for everyone. There is as much and as good for all of us to have and to give as fits our infinitely varied needs and incalculably diverse abilities.

Quoted Sources

The opening document is a letter from John Rolfe to Sir Edwin Sandys, January 1619, reprinted in 3 *The Records of the Virginia Company of London* 243 (Susan Myra Kingsbury ed., 1906).

J.G. FICHTE, THE SCIENCE OF KNOWLEDGE (1794).

The quotation concerning slavery reproducing slavery is from Fredy Perlman, The Reproduction of Daily Life, in ANYTHING CAN HAPPEN (1992).

Selections from members of the Black Panthers appear in THE BLACK PANTHERS SPEAK (Philip S. Foner ed., 1995): Afeni Shakur, "We Will Win: Letter from Prison;" Linda Harrison, "On Cultural Nationalism;" and Connie Matthews, "The Struggle Is a World Struggle."

C.L.R. JAMES, THE BLACK JACOBINS: TOUSSAINT L'OUVERTURE AND THE SAN DOMINGO REVOLUTION (1963).

Other Selected References

James H. Cone, Black Theology & Black Power (1969).

George Fitzhugh, Cannibals All! Or Slaves Without Masters (1856).

Jean Genet, Prisoner of Love (Barbara Bray trans., 1992).

Maria Grahn-Farley, The Law Room: Hyperrealist Jurisprudence & Postmodern Politics, 36 New England Law Review 29 (2001)

Maria Grahn-Farley, A Theory of Child Rights, 57 Miami Law Review 867 (2003).

Colette Guillaumin, Race and Nature: The System of Marks, in Racism, Sexism, Power and Ideology (Mary Jo Lakeland trans., 1995).

Saidiya V. Hartman, Scenes of Subjection: Terror, Slavery, and Self-Making in Nineteenth-Century America (1997).

Richard Hildreth, Despotism in America: An Inquiry into the Nature, Results and Legal Basis of the Slave-Holding System in the United States (1854).

Winthrop D. Jordan, White Over Black: American Attitudes Toward the Negro 1550–1812 (1995).

Huey P. Newton, War Against the Panthers: A Study of Repression in America (1996).

Further Reading (selected work by Anthony Paul Farley)

Perfecting Slavery, 36 Loyola University Chicago Law Journal 221 (2004).
Cassiopeia, 9 Cardozo Women's Law Journal 423 (2003).
The Dream of Interpretation, 57 Miami Law Review 685 (2003).
Amusing Monsters, 23 Cardozo Law Review 1493 (2002).
Lacan & Voting Rights, 13 Yale Journal of Law & Humanities 283 (2001).
The Black Body as Fetish Object, 76 Oregon Law Review 457 (1997).

B. Affiliations

Chapter Thirty-One

Fiduciary Relationships[*]

We ought to call one province of the law "affiliations" or perhaps "relationships." Contract law is one of its parts. Another is fiduciary law — the law governing attorneys, trustees, guardians, corporate directors, and partners. Fiduciary law delineates the ways in which such relationships arise and identifies the standards of conduct to which a fiduciary must conform, including requirements of loyalty, zeal, and self-sacrifice.

A fundamental change in the jurisprudence and ethics of affiliations is underway, or at least several prominent writers are attempting to work such a change. An insurgent theory asserts that fiduciary relationships are really contractual in nature. Judge Easterbrook and Professor Fischel tell us: "Fiduciary duties are not special duties; they have no moral footing; they are the same sort of obligations, derived and enforced in the same way, as other contractual undertakings."

Of course, fiduciary relationships do have an important feature in common with loan transactions, purchases and sales of goods and the like: namely, that they are (usually) entered into and perpetuated voluntarily. Having this important feature in common, these sorts of relationships and others as well — marriage, for example — can reasonably be organized together as part of a genus. Perhaps some contractualist thinkers intend no more than to point this out, and to propose that we use the word "contract" as the name for this genus. (Usage sometimes supports such an approach, as in the terms "marriage contract" and "partnership contract.") ...

But fiduciary relationships also have important features which differ from those of loan transactions and agreements for the purchase and sale of goods. Though fiduciary relationships may, like marriage relationships, be part of the same genus, they are, like marriage relationships, members of a different species. They differ in doctrinal structure. They differ in ethical basis. Some

---

[*] **Scott T. FitzGibbon**, *Fiduciary Relationships are not Contracts*, 82 Marquette Law Review 303 (1999), http://papers.ssrn.com/abstract_id=780384.

contractualist writing, going beyond suggestions as to lexical definition, denies one or the other of these two propositions. This [essay] aims to establish that both are true....

A fiduciary must be beneficent. He must be zealous to serve the interests of the beneficiary. He has an especially high duty of disclosure: He must go beyond avoiding fraud and false statements; he is obliged to "volunteer" information. He must treat beneficiary confidences with the highest respect. His duty of "good faith" is especially strong—stronger than that which applies in commercial arrangements generally. He is sometimes required to refrain from competing with the beneficiary, from taking the beneficiary's "opportunities," from profiting from transactions with the beneficiary, from developing other adverse interests, and even from profiting for himself in other ways, at least in matters related to the fiduciary relationship. His dealings with a potential beneficiary—even preliminary dealings—readily put him under fiduciary obligations, and he is restricted in his right to terminate the relationship....

The classic statement is that of Justice Cardozo [in *Meinhard v. Salmon*]:

> Joint adventurers, like copartners, owe to one another, while the enterprise continues, the duty of the finest loyalty. Many forms of conduct permissible in a workaday world for those acting at arm's length, are forbidden to those bound by fiduciary ties. A trustee is held to something stricter than the morals of the market place. Not honesty alone, but the punctilio of an honor the most sensitive, is then the standard of behavior. As to this there has developed a tradition that is unbending and inveterate. Uncompromising rigidity has been the attitude of courts of equity when petitioned to undermine the rule of undivided loyalty by the "disintegrating erosion" of particular exceptions ... Only thus has the level of conduct for fiduciaries been kept at a level higher than that trodden by the crowd. It will not consciously be lowered by any judgment of this court ... Salmon had put himself in a position in which thought of self was to be renounced, however hard the abnegation....

[In contrast,] Judge Easterbrook and Professor Fischel state: "The fiduciary principle is fundamentally a standard term in a contract." [They opine that] "[f]iduciary duties are not special duties; they have no moral footing; they are the same sort of obligations, derived and enforced in the same way, as other contractual undertakings." The objective of fiduciary law is the same as that of contract law, they say: namely, to "promote the parties' own perception of their joint welfare." Judge Posner agrees [as he made clear in *Jordan v. Duff & Phelps, Inc.*].

Let us uncover the elements underlying this argument. Utilitarianism in some form underlies economic analysis of the law, including in the works of Judge Posner. In its classic form, [John Stuart Mill's work, *Utilitarianism*, defines it as]:

> the creed which accepts as the foundation of morals "utility" or the "greatest happiness principle" … [It] holds that actions are right in proportion as they tend to promote happiness; wrong as they tend to produce the reverse of happiness. By happiness is intended pleasure and the absence of pain; by unhappiness, pain and the privation of pleasure.

Different definitions of "utility" can be constructed which leave out the experiential element and refer only to "preferences" or "choices." Economists sometimes speak this way without meaning to embrace any theory of ethics; they aim merely to relate choices and preferences to supply, price, or some other factor. But when economists go beyond prediction to recommend changes in the law, they are committed to advancing some theory of the good. So there is a theory of ethics which takes a similar form. John Harsanyi, for example, states that we should:

> follow the economists in defining social utility in terms of the preferences … of the individual members of society … We should help [other people] to obtain pleasure or to avoid pain, or to attain "mental states of intrinsic worth," or to achieve any other objective, only as far as they want to achieve it.

Professor Harsanyi calls his version "Preference Utilitarianism."

Many writers in the utilitarian tradition embrace not only an account of the good but also an account of the person; not only an ethic but also an anthropology: They describe a utilitarian or economic person. He is out for himself; he is interested in other people insofar as they can benefit Number One. As George Stigler says: "We live in a world of reasonable well-informed people acting intelligently in pursuit of their self-interests." Amartya Sen [in his book *On Ethics and Economics*] states: "In the usual economic literature a person is seen as maximizing his utility function, which determines all his choices."

Classic writers describe him as "out for himself" in the sense of "out to satisfy his appetites"; but as with ethics, so with anthropology: In recent decades economists have attempted to develop a theory which is "bleached" of appetites and of almost all psychological content. A "canonical formulation" [stated in the essay *Formulation of Rational Choice*] by Professor Sen indicates that we assume that each player's objective is to maximize the expected value of his own payoff, which is measured in some utility scale." The payoff function is a real-valued representation of the person's preferences over the outcomes. Rationality is seen as intelligently maximizing such a payoff function, using all the available instruments, subject to feasibility.

This anthropology describes a man who is "rational" in the sense of internal consistency; the theory does not specify what goal he consistently pursues.

The ethics tells us that affiliations are good insofar as they enhance utility. The anthropology tells us that people affiliate each for his own utility. Putting the ethics and the anthropology together leads to the conclusion that where conditions are conducive to each party's pursuit of his purposes and when under those conditions the parties elect to affiliate, the affiliation is good.

A relationship of friendship of kinship may enhance utility; and a transfer of goods or services within such a relationship—an anniversary present; a helping hand in time of trouble—may contribute to this good. The gift or service enhances not only the utility of the donee, but also that of the donor because of the phenomenon of "interdependent utilities." The donor is better off because he takes pleasure in the pleasures of the friend, or because the satisfactions of the friend are high on his preference scale. Where his utilities are interdependent, one party looks out for the interests of both.

A relationship where there are no interdependent utilities may also enhance utility. Sales, barters, exchanges of goods or services: these may enhance the utility of both parties even though neither may care much what happens to the other. A sale, we can be reasonably sure, enhances the utility of both the seller and the buyer because each looks out for his own interests. With gifts between friends, it is something special about the two parties and the way they have related to one another above and beyond the transfer which establishes the gift's utility; with sales and exchanges, there need be no such special personal feature—the parties may be strangers. The parties focus not on one another but on the goods, the services, and the price.

This latter type of affiliation is the paradigmatic one for contractualists. [John Stuart Mill, in *Elements of Political Economy*, states]:

> When a man possesses a certain commodity, he cannot benefit himself by giving it away. It seems to be implied, therefore, in the very fact of his parting with it for another commodity, that he is benefited by what he receives. His own commodity he might have kept, if it had been valued by him more than that for which he exchanges it. The fact of his choosing to have the other commodity rather than his own, is proof that the other is to him more valuable than his own.

And here is Judge Posner to similar effect [in *Economic Analysis of Law*]: "Where resources are shifted pursuant to [a voluntary transaction], we can be reasonably sure that the shift involves an increase in efficiency." Let us call this sort of affiliation a Utility Contract.

An aggressive claim can be advanced about Utility Contracts for optimal market conditions: Here Utility Contracts not only enhance utility, they may enhance it to the maximum. When a commodity is sold in a well functioning market, it not only goes to some user who will be better off for it; it may go to the most efficient user. The interests of the seller lead him to demand the best price he can get. A more efficient user will pay more than an inefficient one. Here is an advantage of the Utility Contract over an affiliation of donation, according to this line of thought. There is no assurance that a gift goes to a recipient who can use it best.

All of this suggests that the guide for the law is this: "Look for a Utility Contract and enforce it appropriately." This mandate contains [the following] five elements.

An appropriate process is one involving self-interested parties, as charitable donors do not form Utility Contracts; and capacities and conditions conducive to utility calculations, because incapacity, duress, or other circumstances which cast doubt on the occurrence of competent utility calculations undermine the case for enforcement.

The law should fix on the outcome of the utility calculations, and not on hypotheses or preliminary determinations. "Both parties," not just one, for reasons which are obvious from what has been said. The law should look for a moment—the "moment of formation"—when the parties concur on a firm and final set of terms.

The law should, according to this line of analysis, give preference to norms which trace their pedigrees to the final determination referred to above. It should reflect the view that "contractual obligations are by definition self-imposed." (A good name for this is "positivism.").

So—the flip side of positivism—the law should be reluctant to undertake to create duties for contracting parties; it should stick to what they have settled (together, perhaps, with what they would have settled....). It should eschew norms which lie off the charts of normal Utility Contract anthropology: obligations of self-sacrifice; any duty to "renounce thought of self."

What, though, about those recurrent situations in which the determinations of the parties are incomplete or fuzzy? Some contractualist writings seem to say that fiduciary doctrines can be explained as the fillers for this sort of gap.... The academic literature contains two principal lines of approach to incomplete contracts. One recommends that the judge in some such situations apply the terms that the parties themselves would have applied had they reached a bargain under optimal conditions and agreed upon terms for the "gap." (Judge Posner seems to recommend this approach, and Judge Easterbrook and Professor Fischel seem to think it leads to fiduciary duties.). The other recommends that the judges look beyond the specific bargain and its parties and apply the rule that would be best from the point of view of its effects on contracting generally (or on contracts of that "type"). Neither approach leads to fiduciary law, for two reasons.

First, as proponents of both approaches candidly admit, judges can easily get it wrong. To quote Judge Posner [in *Economic Analysis of Law*]:

> the people who make a transaction—thus putting their money where their mouths are—ordinarily are more trustworthy judges of their self-interest than a judge (or jury), who has neither a personal stake in nor first-hand acquaintance with the venture on which the parties embarked when they signed the contract.

If the good of contracting is entirely a matter of pleasures, satisfactions, and preferences; if it lies entirely in *foro interno*; if parties always rationally seek it, then little can be achieved by a judge who undertakes to revise their determinations (for example by making "intersubjective comparisons of utility"). He can only engage in judicial guesswork, unreliable because of the idiosyncratic nature of the parties' appetites and preference scales....

Because judges can easily go wrong, they should be parsimonious; reluctant to adopt aggressive and sweeping doctrines like those found in fiduciary law. Being parsimonious will sometimes mean refusing to give any legal effect to the agreement because of its failure of specificity. This can be justified as a "penalty default" which gives subsequent contracting parties an incentive to be specific and complete.

Second, any inferences made by judges who accept utilitarian ethics and anthropology is for obvious reasons unlikely to attribute to parties the self-sacrificing motives prominent in fiduciary law....

Fiduciary relationships are not creatures only of law and lawyers. Fiduciary relationships and fiduciary duties reflect the precepts of social morality and practice. Alasdair MacIntyre illustrates this idea with a description of a fishing crew:

> Consider ... a crew whose members ... have acquired ... an understanding of and devotion to excellence in fishing and to excellence in playing one's part as a member of such a crew. The dependence of each member on the qualities of character and skills of others will be

accompanied by a recognition that from time to time one's own life will be in danger and that whether one drowns or not may depend upon someone else's courage. And the consequent concern of each member of the crew … will characteristically have to extend to those for whom those others care: the members of their immediate families … and perhaps beyond them to the whole society of a fishing village. When someone dies at sea, fellow crew members, their families and the rest of the fishing community will share a common affliction and common responsibilities.

These fishermen are fiduciaries for one another—not in the eyes of the law, but in their own eyes; in one another's eyes; socially; as a matter of social morality. That is, they are bound, through social morality, by standards of conduct similar to those which traditional fiduciary law recognizes. Their obligations to one another evolve and cannot be traced to an act of the will jointly made at the moment of formation. They are expected to be self-sacrificing and zealous in one another's service. They renounce exclusive thought of self.

Some fiduciary relationships arose primarily as social institutions. This was the case, for example, with the etymologically primal fiduciary, the Roman *fiduciarius*. Under Roman law certain classes of persons—most unmarried adults—were disqualified to receive property by inheritance.

In order to circumvent these … restrictions … the practice had grown up … of requesting a validly appointed heir … to make over the whole or some part of what he received to the person whom the testator wished to benefit. Such a request was without legal effect: its fulfillment was "committed to the faith of" the heir …

This entrusted heir was called *fiduciarius*. The root is *fides*—meaning faith, confidence, reliance, trust, and belief.

Today as well, many fiduciary relationships are structured outside the positive law: by custom, for example, and by authorities on professional ethics. Social fiduciary relationships are supported by traditional social virtues such as loyalty, civility, self-sacrifice, vocational excellence, and high standards of honesty. Even many business institutions, such as the corporation and the investment company, are a composite of contractual relationships and social fiduciary ones: a fiduciary element is involved in their relationships with lawyers, investment bankers, directors, and officers. It is not only from the Utility Contract with the butcher and the baker that we expect our dinner.

Professor Coleman notes in his book *Markets, Morals and The Law*:

> Traditional economic analysis is consequentialist ... Moreover, it believes that what is to be justified are particular events or rules, in isolation ... Constitutionalists, in contrast, believe that individual events—policies, market transactions, political decisions or the like—can be given content or meaning only within an institutional framework. In the constitutionalist view, the proper object of justification is not an event or rule in isolation but the network of rules that gives it life and substance. Moreover, these institutions are to be measured not by their effect on the pursuit of some socially desirable end state, for example, their capacity to increase social wealth; rather, their measure is the acceptance they secure within a given population or community.

This suggests an institutional constitutionalist objection to contractualism. The fiduciary nature of the professional, and the fiduciary structure of institutions such as hospitals, residential care facilities, charitable trusts, educational institutions, and some of the great law firms is important not only to the participants but to outside parties—to the public generally and to the honor and stability of the social order. If the law were to change the conduct of lawyers and of the officers, directors and trustees of business and charitable institutions in a contractualist direction, it might undermine their acceptability to the public. An attitude of hard-nosed self-seeking on the part of some lawyers, including partners at prominent law firms, has surely contributed to the decline in respect for the legal profession.

A large canvas for disutility arguments is spread by Professor Francis Fukuyama in his recent book *Trust: The Social Virtues and the Creation of Prosperity*. This book advances the thesis that "trust"—bonding beyond the family—is an important contributor to economic development. A legal system which neglected commitments of loyalty would probably undermine this social characteristic.

A more fundamental objection to prescriptive contractualism looks beyond legitimacy-based and utility-based arguments and asserts that fiduciary affiliations serve different purposes than those known to utilitarianism. Different purposes call for different structures; in many instances, fiduciary law fits better.

Are there goods other than utility? In another context [addressed in *Economic Analysis of Law*] Judge Posner concedes that "the term efficiency, when used as in this book to denote that allocation of resources in which value is maximized, has limitations as an ethical criterion of social decision making. Utility in the utilitarian sense also has grave limitations.... There is more to justice than economics, a point the reader should keep in mind in evaluating normative statements in this book." But Judge Posner dismisses any systematic analysis with the airy comment that "other familiar ethical criteria have their own serious problems."

Are there motives other than the pursuit of utility? Prominent economists accept that there are (although some forget this once they get down to grinding out the theoretical sausages). Thus Professor Amartya Sen writes [in *The Formulation of Rational Choice*]: "A divergence between choice and well-being can easily arise when behavior is influenced by some motivation other than the pursuit of one's own interest or welfare (*e.g.*, through a sense of commitment, or respect for duty)."

Some classic economists including Adam Smith embraced similar views: Although people often do pursue each his own utility (especially, [as F.Y. Edgeworth noted], in special situations such as "war and trade"), not everyone acts that way all the time.

A "thought experiment" based on Robert Nozick's *Anarchy, State and Utopia* supports these views:

> Suppose there were an experience machine that would give you any experience you desired. Superduper neuropsychologists could stimulate your brain so that you would think and feel you were writing a great novel, or making a friend, or reading an interesting book. All the time you would be floating in a tank, with electrodes attached to your brain. Should you plug into this machine for life, preprogramming your life's experiences? ... Of course, while in the tank you won't know that you're there; you'll think it's all actually happening.... Would you plug in? What else can matter to us, other than how our lives feel from the inside?

Several years' worth of asking this question of students confirms what common sense in any event suggests: most people would not get in the machine, and thus most people do not make pleasure or any other experience the point of it all. Utility is not the only motive. If you would not get into the machine, you accept the guidance of goods other than pleasure or any other experience.

Another argument to this effect is advanced by Professor Sen [in *On Ethics and Economics*]:

> The hopeless beggar, the precarious landless labourer, the dominated housewife, the hardened unemployed or the over-exhausted coolie may all take pleasures in small mercies, and manage to suppress intense suffering for the necessity of continuing survival, but it would be ethically deeply mistaken to attach a correspondingly small value to the loss of their well-being because of this survival strategy.

There is something bad about the conditions in which such people find themselves, one must agree, that goes beyond the suffering. If there are goods beyond that identified by preference utilitarianism, then you have a reason to live and your neighbor has a reason to refrain from rubbing the lamp. And surely there may be.

Justice requires some allocations and forbids others. It forbids giving a fatal disease to an innocent person. It forbids hanging him. It forbids enslaving subject peoples. It forbids allocating the art treasures of Europe to Hitler. Precepts like these are not just rules of thumb about how to maximize utility. Better free the slaves than offer them the machine; liberate Europe and defeat the Reich rather than give all the victims a drug against pain; the justice done by Lincoln and Churchill was a good beyond its affective consequences.

The same can be said about less dramatic instances. Justice demands the return of stolen property, the payment of debts, and the performance of obligations under partnership agreements. You should stay out of the machine for the purpose of paying your debts, for example, and for purposes of sticking with your marriage. (It would be no substitute to put your creditor into the machine, or your spouse.).

Utilitarianism makes no sufficient place for justice. Judge Posner generously admits something like this: "Since economics does not answer the question whether the existing distribution of income and wealth is good or bad, just or unjust ... neither does it answer the ultimate question whether an efficient allocation of resources would be socially or ethically desirable."

Utility will sometimes be enhanced by unjust projects. For example, secretly inducing cancer in order to do medical research on the victim may be utile. Hanging an innocent man to avert a riot may be utile. Enriching the undeserving is utile if they take a disproportionate pleasure in wealth. Utilitarianism cannot recommend a permanent grasp on rules and principles of justice: it makes rules of justice into rules of thumb, to be disregarded when circumstances require.

The relationship of the representative with the class in class-action litigation is a good example. He has a duty to be fair in distributing benefits and burdens. His affiliation, in other words, serves justice, not merely utility. His obligations look backwards in time, not forwards; and they do not rest on an assessment of the pleasure one or another members of the class may take in compensation nor on the ordering of their preferences. The same can be said of a trustee in bankruptcy when he determines how assets should be distributed among creditors and of a corporate director when he decides how to distribute dividends among classes of stock....

Professor Nozick's thought experiment may suggest that it is mainly for the sake of activities that we would stay out of the machine. But surely not only activities, but attributes of character as well. Suppose the machine was structured so as to require the sacrifice not only of our activities and projects—not only of what we might do—suppose it deprived us of much of what we are. Suppose that a lifetime inside incurs the loss of the capacities of the mind and the coherence of the personality. Suppose your memory deteriorates, your logic slips, your reason clouds over, and your judgment wobbles. Suppose the effects of the machine are like those of alcoholism. Is it all worth it for the pleasure it buys? These hypotheticals indicate that there is a good in virtue—the virtues, taking that word to mean worthwhile attributes of the character—that there is a good in virtue beyond its utility.

Utilitarianism cannot accept the good of the virtues except as instruments for pleasure. Posnerian analysis is to the same effect: "Honesty, trustworthiness, and love reduce the cost of transactions." Therefore, utilitarianism will sometimes recommend decisions which distort the personality. An individual seeking to enhance his own utility under Stalinism would be best advised to jettison habits of courageous speech and independent analysis. Utilitarianism cannot recommend a permanent grasp on virtue: A virtue should be discarded when it is no longer serviceable to utility. If the regime changes and Stalinism is replaced by Thatcherism utility is served by a change of character. An individual seeking to enhance his own utility in a modern liberal social order might be well advised to abandon those virtues which demand too much in the way of loyalty to friends and family.

The fiduciary duties of the guardian are a good example. They include the duty to educate and "to maximize opportunities for the ward's personal growth." The guardian of a minor is a substitute parent: he should help educate the child not only vocationally but also morally; not only to earn a good living but also to lead a good life.

The responsibilities of attorneys are to some extent similar. Assisting in the development of the virtues—especially the civic virtues—is one important aspect of the attorney-client relationship. Especially in business practice and other non-litigation situations, good lawyering involves more than seeing to it that the client wins; it has an educational side: It involves helping him fit himself to live well in his moral and social culture.

In the Utility Contract each party acts for the sake of what he may get from the other and each would just as soon avoid giving much in exchange. In many fiduciary relationships, however, the fiduciary rightly regards the conferral of fiduciary benefits as a good for himself as well as for the beneficiary. The lawyer may not practice only for the fee, nor the doctor or guardian for a stipend. Their roles involve the development of their own characters; growth in maturity; enhancement of wisdom; and attainment, even, of some degree of nobility.

Prominent writers tell us that freedom is something bestowed on mankind by nature (Aquinas), "our most precious possession" (Cicero), "God's most precious gift to human nature, for by it we are made happy here as men, and happy as gods in the beyond" (Dante), "the natural condition of the human race" (Lincoln), "our unalterable destiny" (Schiller), "an inalienable ingredient in what makes human beings human" (Berlin), something "of which a human being cannot divest himself or be deprived without temporarily or permanently ceasing to be human" (Oakeshott), and the source of love (Schiller).

Utilitarianism suggests that freedom is an instrumental good; free markets, for example, maximize utility. But surely freedom is more than instrumentally good. Merely instrumental goods are dispensable, once their objects are achieved, but who would agree to give up his freedom once it had been employed in producing enough wealth? Similarly, merely instrumental goods need not be afforded people who cannot or will not use them to pursue the relevant object, but who would approve of a government which deprived people of freedom on grounds of incompetence or unwillingness to compete in the marketplace?

Freedom seems to be a noninstrumental ("final") good in at least two principal ways. First, freedom relates to the moral standing of good action. When an action is a good one; when the objective, *foro externo* aspects of the action are commendable—then not only the act but also the person himself—the actor—may deserve credit. Freedom is a necessary condition for this. Only when he exercises freedom in acting is he fully the author of the act and only then does he fully deserve credit for it.

Second, freedom is a component of learning, self-development, and self-realization. Doing good things and participating in good projects is a way to develop one's knowledge of their goodness. Doing good things and participating in good projects is a way of bringing their goodness into yourself and making it a part of yourself....

... Relational positivism makes sense when the goal of a relationship is subjective—known best to the parties and likely to be peculiar to them—and when the parties are well motivated and well equipped to pursue it. Fiduciary law and discourse is "relational semi-positivism": The parties' wills play an important role but the law also applies its own views of what is appropriate. Relational semi-positivism seems to be appropriate when the good of the relationship is not entirely subjective or peculiar to the parties; when the parties are only imperfectly positioned and motivated to pursue that good. [R]elations of mutual good faith involve the greatest goods. Mutual good faith and similar fiduciary characteristics lead a relationship to justice and virtue and they enhance freedom....

Selected References

Dante Alighieri, Monarchy, Book One, XII, in Monarchy and Three Political Letters (Donald Nicholl trans., Garland Library ed., 1947).

Thomas Aquinas, On the Sentences II (The Pocket Aquinas, Vernon J. Bourke trans., 1960).

Isaiah Berlin, Four Essays on Liberty (1969).

Victor Brudney, Contract and Fiduciary Duty in Corporate Law, 38 Boston College Law Review 595 (1997).

Bruce Catton, The Coming Fury (1961) (quoting L.E. Chittenden, Recollections of President Lincoln and His Administration (quoting Abraham Lincoln)).

Marcus Tulius Cicero, Letter to Atticus of October 25, 44 B.C., in 3 Letters to Atticus (E.O. Winstedt trans., 1918).

Cicero, De Officiis II, IX (Walter Miller trans., 1943).

Jules L. Coleman, Markets, Morals and the Law (1988).

Frank H. Easterbrook & Daniel R. Fischel, Contract and Fiduciary Duty, 36 Journal of Law and Economics 425 (1993) & The Economic Structure of Corporate Law (1991).

F.Y. Edgeworth, Mathematical Psychics: An Essay on the Application of Mathematics to the Moral Sciences (1881).

Philippa Foot, Utilitarianism and the Virtues, in Consequentialism and its Critics (Samuel Scheffler ed., 1988).

Francis Fukuyama, Trust: The Social Virtues and the Creation of Prosperity (1995).

Robin Grant, Judge Richard Posner's Wealth Maximization Principle: Another Form of Utilitarianism?, 10 Cardozo Law Review 875 (1989).

John C. Harsanyi, Rule Utilitarianism and Decision Theory, 11 Erkenntnis 25 (1977).

Martin Hollis & Robert Sugden, Rationality in Action, 102 Mind 1 (1993).

A Partial Response to My Critics, in After MacIntyre: Critical Perspectives on the Work of Alasdair MacIntyre (J. Horton & S. Mendes eds., 1994).

John Stuart Mill, Elements of Political Economy (3d ed. 1844) & Utilitarianism (Samuel Gorovitz ed., 1971) (1863).

R.D. Miller, Schiller and the Ideal of Freedom (1970).

B. Nicholas, An Introduction to Roman Law (1962).

Robert Nozick, Anarchy, State and Utopia (1974).

Martha C. Nussbaum, Flawed Foundations: The Philosophical Critique of a Particular Type of Economics, 64 Chicago Law Review 1197 (1997).

Michael Oakeshott, A Place of Learning, in The Colorado College Studies, No. 12, at 7 (Jan. 1975).

Richard A. Posner, Economic Analysis of Law (4th ed. 1992) & The Problems of Jurisprudence (1990) & Gratuitous Promises in Economics and Law, 6 Journal of Legal Studies 411 (1977).

Amartya Sen, On Ethics and Economics (1987) & The Formulation of Rational Choice, 84 American Economic Review 385 (1994).

George Stigler, Economics or Ethics?, in 2 Tanner Lectures on Human Values (Sterling M. McMurrin ed., 1981).

Cases

Jordan v. Duff & Phelps, Inc., 815 F.2d 429, 446–47 (7th Cir. 1987) (Posner, dissenting).
Meinhard v. Salmon, 164 N.E. 545, 546–48 (N.Y. 1928) (Cardozo).

Further Reading (selected work by Scott T. FitzGibbon)

Marriage and the Ethics of Office. 18 Notre Dame Journal of Law, Ethics & Public Policy 89 (2004).

Marriage and the Good of Obligation, 47 The American Journal of Jurisprudence 41 (2002).

"True Human Community:" Catholic Social Thought, Aristotelean Ethics, and the Moral Order of the Business Company, 45 St. Louis University Law Journal 1243 (2001).

CHAPTER THIRTY-TWO

MARRIAGE AS PARTNERSHIP[*]

... Marriage in American law has ordinarily been thought of as a status entered into for life and regulated by the state. The American legal source of this concept is the nineteenth century United States Supreme Court case of *Maynard v. Hill*. In that case, the Court held that the legislative assembly of the territory of Oregon had the authority to dissolve the "bonds of matrimony" between David Maynard and his wife Lydia. It was in that case that Justice Field wrote what has perhaps become the most famous quotation about marriage in American appellate court opinions:

> Marriage, as creating the most important relation in life, as having more to do with the morals and civilization of a people than any other institution, has always been subject to the control of the legislature. That body prescribes the age at which parties may contract to marry, the procedure or form essential to constitute marriage, the duties and obligations it creates, its effects upon the property rights of both, present and prospective, and the acts which may constitute grounds for its dissolution.

Thirty-seven years before *Maynard* was decided, the Supreme Court of Florida stated in *Ponder v. Graham* that marriage was a contract. This concept was, of course, not new, having its roots in common law, incorporated in colonial practice, and is consistent with what Professor Grossberg has described as a "displacement of patriarchalism by contractualism" in the nineteenth century. However, the Florida court's labeling of marriage as a contract in the context of the case did not mean that parties were completely free to set their own terms. It meant that the Florida legislature had no power to dissolve a marriage contract, for by so doing it would be impairing the right to contract.

Yet Justice Semmes' words in *Ponder* help to define marriage as contract. He wrote, "I know of no reason why the word contract, as used in the Con-

---

* **Sanford N. Katz**, *Marriage as Partnership*, 73 NOTRE DAME LAW REVIEW 1251 (1998), http://papers.ssrn.com/abstract_id=715502.

stitution, should be restricted to those of pecuniary nature, and not embrace that of marriage, involving as it does, considerations of the most interesting character and vital importance to society, to government, and the contracting parties." The two concepts of marriage, that of status and that of a special kind of contract, seemingly contradictory, have co-existed throughout the nineteenth century and are still referred to today.

In contemporary times, however, it is difficult to fit marriage neatly into the legal construct called contract. Normally contract law assumes freedom of contract, party autonomy, and equal bargaining power. The marriage contract is not totally free of governmental regulation, and therefore parties have limited freedom of choice. Party autonomy and equal bargaining power may not be present in marriage. Perhaps the most that can be said is that while in the past the marital relationship was wholly defined by the state, now certain aspects of the relationship can be negotiated by the parties. Also, by including the marriage contract within the world of contract, one effect is a change in the attitudes of the couple and the courts. Presumptions that actions are motivated by a donative intent are less difficult to overcome. Vocabulary changes from words of intimacy to the language of commerce (for example, profit and investment) and self-interest. Spouses become parties, participation becomes contribution, and divorce becomes dissolution.

Antenuptial Agreements. If the terms of the marriage relationship were completely state-regulated with no opportunity for couples to set their own terms for their relationship, like a contract of adhesion, or the economic consequences of the termination of that relationship, antenuptial agreements could not exist to the extent they do now. In other words, the concept of marriage as partnership contract provides the legal foundation for antenuptial agreements. Professor [Mary Ann] Glendon believes that the movement toward discretionary distribution in the assignment of property under equitable distribution statutes in divorce necessitates the agreement for couples with significant, or potentially significant, financial resources.

Historically, antenuptial agreements were entered into by wealthy people in their desire to preserve their estate plan, which was drafted before their marriage. Or the agreements were used by older people, usually after they had already been married at least once, who wanted an agreement that would order the distribution of assets upon death. They might do so to protect the financial interests of children from a previous marriage. If litigation over agreements arose, courts would interpret them against the background of the then contemporary social conditions and community values. If a term in an antenuptial agreement was written in contemplation of divorce, either the term or the entire agreement would have been unenforceable, due to the strong belief in the permanence of marriage and the possibility that enforcement could leave a spouse (probably the wife, given the social and economic reality of the time) destitute.

In 1970 the Supreme Court of Florida broke with tradition and, in *Posner v. Posner*, decided that in light of changes in social conditions in which divorce was a fact of life, an antenuptial agreement that settled alimony and property rights upon divorce was not contrary to public policy and ought to be enforced. Although the facts in *Posner* concerned the couple's successful attempt to order privately their economic relationship should they divorce, the case's holding has had much broader significance. It provided the opportunity for couples to define their marital relationship, delineating the roles each person will play, who will make what decisions, and how children will be raised. Professor [Walter O.] Weyrauch has suggested that even though some of these matters are legally unenforceable, "they function in a manner comparable to the traditional requirement of legal consideration or form in the law of contracts by safeguarding deliberation and determining the intent of the parties."

The major question about antenuptial agreements is whether they really are contracts governed by conventional contract law doctrine or whether they are a special kind of contract peculiar to family law.... [I]f one takes seriously that stability and predictability are two of the fundamental principles of contract law, their absence is a fatal flaw. What seems to be becoming more clear is that contracts dealing with domestic relations—antenuptial agreements being an example—present a special contract model in which certain kinds of questions are posed. Whereas in commercial contracts, questions about industry practices and the impact on the economic relations of the parties—for example, maximizing profits—may be relevant to deciding a result, different questions, including family policy considerations..., are posed as to whether an antenuptial agreement should be enforced.

Two theoretical questions asked when enforcement of a commercial contract is at issue concern process and substance. The same questions are relevant in antenuptial agreements but the basis for responding to them is quite different. A special body of law has developed to test the validity of antenuptial agreements, and it can be divided into matters dealing with process and substance.

In commercial contracts, other than adhesion contracts, courts are ordinarily not concerned with whether the terms of a contract are fair if true equal bargaining exists. What is of concern is that the process by which the contract was entered into is free from misrepresentation, coercion, and duress. In antenuptial agreements both the process and the terms must be fair. A fair process includes a full disclosure of each person's financial worth, something totally foreign to the enforcement of commercial contracts where a confidential relationship does not exist, and in some instances representation by counsel....

The issue of unfair or unjust antentuptial agreements may become less frequent as more and more women (in the past usually the economically disadvantaged person) obtain positions of equal importance and pay as their male counterparts and are able to accumulate wealth not through inheritance, but by their own efforts. At the present time, because of the uncertainty of the enforcement of antenuptial agreements as written, even with procedural safeguards in place (for example, representation by counsel), some lawyers refuse to draft them for fear of malpractice actions brought by their clients after their antenuptial agreements have been made ineffective.

Contract Cohabitation. Long before the three *Marvin* cases were decided, cohabitation arrangements had been enforced using legal theories such as implied partnership or joint venture, constructive or resulting trust, or express or implied contract. Yet the *Marvin* cases are perhaps one of the most important set of cases in family law during the last quarter century, because the California Supreme Court placed its judicial imprimatur on the legality of two persons (nowhere in the opinion is the relationship limited to heterosexuals) living together in a non-common law marriage jurisdiction in a sexual relationship. It is even worth noting that the relationship began while one (in this case the male) was still married. *Marvin* provided disappointed cohabitants with a variety of legal theories for compensation upon break-up. No longer was it necessary for lawyers or courts to create legal fictions or try to interpret the facts to have them conform to some pre-existing legal construct. Couples themselves could create an express cohabitation agreement.

The initial reaction to the *Marvin* cases was by no means totally positive. Illinois, a jurisdiction that seems particularly moralistic where marital relationships are concerned, and which has held that a divorced woman who lived with a man to whom she was not married was unfit to care for her child, rejected the *Marvin* approach in 1979. In *Hewitt v. Hewitt*, the Supreme Court of Illinois refused to provide a remedy to a woman, Victoria Hewitt, who had lived in a marriage-like relationship for fifteen years, and in which she had three children. Taking a particularly inflexible approach, the Illinois court was unwilling to affirm the appellate court's decision, which had been sympathetic to the woman's argument that she and her "companion," with whom she shared the same last name, had lived a "conventional married life," not as a formally married couple but as parties to an express oral contract.

The court would not enforce the woman's contractual claim, holding that to do so would contravene Illinois' public policy. That policy was reflected in the state's abolition of common law marriage in 1905 and its 1977 enactment of its marriage and divorce law, which had rejected "no-fault" divorce. The Supreme Court of Illinois seemed to be concerned about how enforcement of the Hewitt arrangement could be justified in a state that had recently reaffirmed "the traditional doctrine that marriage is a civil contract between three parties—the husband, the wife and the State." The court also stated that Illinois had a strong interest in maintaining the marriage contract as one that cannot be terminated at will. To the court, the Hewitt arrangement was a "private contractual alternative to marriage." In other words, the court seemed to be saying that enforcement of a cohabitation contract reflected values the Illinois court did not choose to advance. To do so would send the wrong message to Illinois citizens....

Hewitt is a particularly troublesome decision from a woman's point of view. Victoria Hewitt relied on Robert Hewitt's statement that a formal marriage ceremony was not necessary for the couple to be considered married in Iowa, a common law marriage jurisdiction, where their relationship began while they attended college. He gave her every indication that theirs would be a shared relationship. Since the support of the Hewitt children was not a part of the case, the loser was Victoria Hewitt. She not only cared for the couple's children and the house, but also assisted Robert Hewitt financially in securing his professional degree so that he could establish a pedodontia practice, again with her money. If ever there was a case to which the *Marvin* remedies should have applied, it was Hewitt.

In *Morone v. Morone*, the highest court in New York refused to imply a contract from the conduct of the parties, but would have enforced an express contract. Like "Mrs." Hewitt, "Mrs." Morone had given birth to children fathered by Mr. Morone. She and Mr. Morone lived together for eight years, while holding themselves out to the community as a married couple. Their long term relationship based on a contract was both for domestic and business purposes.

"Mrs." Morone sought, among other claims, to have Mr. Morone account for the moneys he had received during their contract of partnership. In dismissing "Mrs." Morone's complaint in the lower court, the judge interpreted her claim as an attempt to recover for "housewifely" duties within a marriage-type relationship. The Appellate Division affirmed the trial court because of "Mrs." Morone's failure to assert an express agreement.

In writing for the majority of the court, Judge Meyer pointed out that he was following precedent by requiring an express contract between a non-married couple that did not include illicit sexual relations as part of the consideration. He alluded to the fact that to enforce an implied-in-fact contract would be tantamount to resurrecting common law marriage, which the state had abolished. In addition, Judge Meyer listed a series of questions that he felt made a court-imposed contract (implied-in-fact) problematical.

The trial court's statement that "Mrs." Morone's claim was for compensation for "housewifely" duties and therefore without merit illustrates the confusion about recovery in cohabitation relationships. The old common law view was that a wife performs household duties, not with the expectation of payment, but out of a legal obligation: a wife owes her husband the duty to perform household services. Also, a common law presumption exists that spouses act not for individual profit or advancement, but for altruistic motives. Yet the New York trial court applied the presumption to a marriage-like relationship. Thus, "Mrs." Morone was in a "no win" situation.

What should recovery be in termination of cohabitation contracts? If there is to be a meaningful distinction between formal or informal marriage and cohabitation contracts, then there ought to be distinct recoveries upon termination. Implied or express cohabitation contracts should be enforced, but the divorce model should not be used for fashioning the remedy. Surely one who terminates a cohabitation arrangement should not be required to support the other person in the same sense as alimony is used (based on need unless clear expectations have been expressed in a contract). "Palimony," the word that has been coined to relate to a cohabitation contract remedy, is misleading since it implies alimony, which is a support obligation only awarded upon a divorce.

Professor Glendon makes a strong case in her opposition to applying the same discretionary rules for property distribution upon divorce to termination of cohabitation contracts. She has written [in *The Transformation of Family Law*] that in [states] where courts distribute cohabitants' property as they do in divorce cases, cohabitants share with married couples the "same degree of uncertainty about their economic rights as the legislatures in their unfathomable wisdom have granted to married couples." However, applying the divorce model of equitable distribution of property to a cohabiting couple does make sense where property has been acquired jointly with the expectation that it would be jointly enjoyed.

Couples living under a contract of cohabitation have not received the same kind of legal protection that exists in an informal or formal marriage. And except in limited circumstances, there does not seem to be any legislative movement to extend such protection. The cohabitation relationship is not considered confidential, and therefore an individual cannot claim any privilege to prevent a conversation with his or her companion from being revealed in court. Wherever status, rather than dependency, is the basis for obtaining financial benefits, cohabitants do not qualify.

There is a limit to which cohabiting couples enjoy the economic advantages of marriage. Perhaps the most important restriction is that unless the survivor of the relationship has left a valid will, he or she has no statutory rights in the decedent's estate. Cases have held that a cohabitant cannot recover for loss of consortium or wrongful death. Nor can a cohabitant recover social security benefits. Judicial responses to attempts by cohabitants to recover for work-men's compensation benefits have not been uniform.

At least two jurisdictions have allowed a same sex cohabitation couple to adopt a child who was the biological offspring of one of the cohabitants. This may be an important development in legally recognizing a cohabitation arrangement as establishing the first step in the formation of a family unit.

Without the legal sanction of cohabitation contracts, it does not seem possible that the current trend of municipalities enacting domestic partnership laws could have occurred. These domestic partnership laws are a successful attempt to regulate cohabitation contracts. Not only do they set down formal requirements for the establishment of the relationship (regardless of the sexual orientation of the couple), but they also provide the formal requirements for termination of the relationship. In a certain sense the domestic partnership laws define what some may say is the ideal marriage: an intimate relationship based on mutual trust and support.

For the most part, municipal domestic partnership laws are designed to provide cohabiting couples who have fulfilled the requirements of the registration law with employment benefits, most notably health care and sick leave. Objections to passing municipal domestic partnership laws have been based on economic reasons: enacting such laws will increase municipal budgets because of the need for more money to pay for additional employee benefits. Whether these arguments mask moral objections is not at all clear....

Divorce. [In *The Transformation of Family Law*] Professor Glendon has lamented the "withering away of marriage as a legal institution" and the ease in which married couples can terminate their relationship. She is particularly critical of those jurisdictions which blur the distinction between spousal support and marital property. She questions the assumptions courts make about spousal self-sufficiency after divorce when awarding alimony or assigning property. And she believes equitable distribution statutes are an invitation to judges to use their discretion—in other words, personal values—in deciding the economic post-divorce life of the couple.

Professor Glendon has posed the question as to whether the discretionary distribution of marital assets in any way reflects either the intent or the behavior of a marital couple. She thinks not. Nor does she believe that couples in an ongoing marital relationship either intend or practice a partnership-like relationship or would like to subject their property, no matter how acquired, to be split according to the discretion of a judge. She reserves her severest criticism for the legal assumption, manifested either in statutes or by judicial action, that marriage is a "partnership of two equal individuals who may have been economically interdependent in marriage, but who are at least potentially independent upon divorce."

Treating a marriage as a partnership contract does not necessarily have to result in devastating economic consequences. If one were to consider marriage as a true partnership, certain benefits would accrue. What is the modern marriage? It is a contract in the sense that has already been described. It is also a partnership in that it is a fiduciary relationship of two individuals who retain their individuality, who love each other, and who share in and expect to reach mutual aspirations. Marital partners lead their lives with the hope that their conjugal and financial partnership will last. To that end each makes his or her contribution. Like some commercial partnerships, one person may contribute capital, the other may contribute human resources.

But the modern marriage partnership deviates from the commercial partnership in that, in making a contribution, one of the partners may have to make certain sacrifices, such as abandoning a career entirely or suspending one's plans for an uncertain future. Consistent with partnership law, however, is the principle that a partner cannot benefit himself by using partnership assets to advance his self interest. If he does, the benefit accrues to the partnership. This is consistent with the emphasis that current laws dealing with equitable distribution place on contribution. One spouse may invest in the other spouse as part of the plans for the partnership. This investment may include contributing financially and emotionally to the spouse's education, career advancement, or business. It is unrealistic to think that any person entering into a partnership would expect to leave the partnership less economically secure than when she entered it.

How should assets be distributed following marital failure? Should there be a fifty-fifty split or should each case be examined on an individual basis? Professor Glendon recommends an equal distribution, and that spousal support remain distinct from the assignment of marital property. She also urges judges to be mindful of the lives post-divorce women lead. In the main, the burden falls on them to provide a home and comfort for the children of the divorcing parents. Also, given the current economic conditions, they suffer from employment inequalities. They are the ones who become impoverished upon divorce.

Before the adoption of equitable distribution in non-community property states, the title theory dominated. The old adage, "He who owns the property, gets the property," was followed. This unfair method of allocating property upon divorce allowed for no inquiry into the time of purchase, the use to which the property was put, or the identity of the person who was responsible for the appreciation of the property (not necessarily the same person who made the initial financial investment). Basically, in many instances the title theory masked a reality favoring men.

A fifty-fifty split in property may be an easy formula for a termination of a commercial partnership, and may underscore the sense of community in a marriage. But it may result in unfairness in a marriage. There are too many variables in a marriage to support a mechanical formula. One of the most important variables is the length of the marriage. The key is the contribution of the individual to the marriage. If equitable distribution laws, like those modeled after Section 307 of the Uniform Marriage and Divorce Act, are applied with attention to current case law, they provide a fair method for distributing assets upon divorce. Rather than a mechanical formula or unlimited judicial discretion, they require a judge to consider certain factors. If a judge is required to make a finding for each factor, abuse of discretion can be checked on appeal. Also, the statutory factors provide attorneys with a checklist and a way of organizing their evidence for litigation. Legal scholarship may have a function here to keep watch that neither judges nor legislators continue to apply dated societal values.

The new property ... is now part of both equitable distribution statutes and case law. Now, a wife who puts her husband through professional school can acquire a return on that investment by having an interest in his professional degree or license. She can receive a share of his pension and an interest in his business. The husband who helps to build the career of his wife who becomes a celebrity may expect to obtain an interest in that career. A homemaker who stays home to care for children may be compensated for her services by considering those services as a human capital contribution to the partnership. Consideration of, or recovery for, any of these contributions would have been unthinkable before equitable distribution became law. Today, divorce need not result in looking at the marriage partnership as an investment that did not pay off at all.

Conclusion. ... The tension between adhering to traditional rules of contract or partnership law, and considering the unique social policy considerations in marriage, causes a certain amount of distortion. How can private ordering be respected or even encouraged if legal recognition is in doubt? Is family law, ordinarily classified as private law, moving toward being considered as public law? Will the questions posed in matters dealing with antenuptial agreements, cohabitation contracts, and property settlement agreements be similar to those asked when legislation is being interpreted? Must those kinds of private agreements serve the public interest to be enforced?

If we move away from the protection of the individual in family law matters, and toward communal values, we shall be breaking with fundamental traditions in this country. In the case of marriage, for example, communal values and public policy considerations may treat that relationship as a vehicle to enforce national concerns, for example in regard to national morality. The concept of privacy and individual assertion of rights, if only within a contractual context [is] in flux....

Selected References

Grace C. Blumberg, Cohabitation Without Marriage: A Different Perspective, 28 UCLA Law Review 1125 (1981).

Victor Brudney, Contract and Fiduciary Duty in Corporate Law, 38 Boston College Law Review 595 (1997).

Ira Ellman, The Theory of Alimony, 77 California Law Review 1 (1989).

Mary Ann Glendon, The New Family and the New Property (1981) & The Transformation of Family Law (1996) & Family Law Reform in the 1980's, 44 Louisiana Law Review 1553 (1984) & Abortion and Divorce in Western Law (1987).

Joseph Goldstein & Jay Katz, The Family and the Law (1965).

Michael Grossberg, Governing the Hearth (1985).

Thomas C. Kohler, Individualism and Communitarianism at Work, 1993 BYU Law Review 727 (1993).

Thomas C. Kohler & Matthew W. Finkin, Bonding and Flexibility: Employment Ordering in a Relationless Age, 46 American Journal of Comparative Law 1101 (1998).

Frances E. Olsen, The Family and the Market: A Study of Ideology and Legal Reform, 96 Harvard Law Review 1497 (1983).

Walter O. Weyrauch, Informal and Formal Marriage—An Appraisal of Trends in Family Organization, 28 Chicago Law Review 88 (1960) & Metamorphoses of Marriage, 13 Family Law Quarterly 415 (1980).

Cases

Hewitt v. Hewitt 394 N.E.2d 1204 (Ill. 1979).

Marvin v. Marvin, 557 P.2d 106 (Cal. 1976).

Marvin v. Marvin, 176 Cal. Rptr. 555 (Cal. Ct. App. 1981).

Marvin v. Marvin, 5 Fam. L. Rep. 3077 (1979).

Maynard v. Hill, 125 U.S. 190 (1888).

Morone v. Morone 413 N.E.2d 1154 (N.Y. 1980).

Ponder v. Graham, 4 Fla. 23 (1851).

Posner v. Posner, 233 So.2d 381 (Fla. 1970).

Further Reading (selected work by Sanford N. Katz)

Family Law in America (Oxford 2003).

Cases and Materials on Family Law (West 1994) (with Walter O. Weyrauch & Frances Olsen).

American Family Law in Transition (1983) (with Walter O. Weyrauch).

CHAPTER THIRTY-THREE

CONSENSUAL AMOROUS RELATIONSHIPS*

... Growing awareness of the magnitude, dimensions, and effects of sexual harassment at educational institutions and the potential for institutional liability have prompted educators to adopt policies to avert such problems. Many private and public colleges and universities include these policies in their faculty and student handbooks. The policies typically prohibit sexual harassment of employees and students and alert the university community to the serious effects of sexual harassment and the potential for student exploitation....

Some universities have gone beyond establishing regulations directed at the widely litigated problems of sexual harassment and have promulgated policies addressing the problematic issues surrounding consensual amorous relationships between faculty and students.... Institutions which have included statements regarding amorous relationships in their sexual harassment policies acknowledge the difficulty of drawing a line between sexual harassment and intimate consensual relationships. Therefore, consenting relationships and sexual harassment cannot be dealt with as entirely distinct concerns....

Courts may view the asymmetry of power between faculty and students as analogous to the power differential existing between a supervisor and an employee. Students are keenly aware of their vulnerability to the broad discretionary power of faculty. Regardless of faculty intention, potential coercion can influence students to consent to sexual involvement with faculty. Students may consent to unwanted sexual liaisons because of uncertainty regarding the academic consequences of noncompliance.... [W]hat may appear to be an adult, consensual, private relationship may be the product of implicit or explicit duress and thus may constitute the basis for individual or institutional

---

* **Elisabeth A. Keller**, *Consensual Relationships Between Faculty and Students: The Constitutional Right to Privacy*, 15 JOURNAL OF COLLEGE AND UNIVERSITY LAW 21 (1988), http://papers.ssrn.com/abstract_id=871705.

liability. Additionally, truly consensual relationships may change and lead to rancor, disappointment and retaliatory claims of sexual harassment.

Concern for protecting students and faculty and avoiding potential liability may encourage colleges and universities to consider a total ban on all amorous relationships between faculty and students. Such a ban, however, raises other legal issues unrelated to those concerning sexual harassment, and may, depending upon the public or private identity of the institution, raise constitutional issues as well.... Actions by private colleges and universities to prohibit consensual intimate relationships between faculty and students would be treated similarly to private company rules prohibiting such relationships between managerial and non-managerial personnel. Court challenges to such rules have been unsuccessful, even though employees dismissed for violation of so-called "non-fraternization" rules have usually alleged wrongful discharge and tortious invasion of privacy....

While employer-employee relationships in private institutions are governed by contract principles and state constitutional provisions, generally such institutions are not subject to the federal constitutional provisions, which require state action. However, public institutions with policies banning amorous relationships must consider the principles which protect an individual's constitutional rights, since a public institution's enforcement of administrative policies constitutes state action.

Freedom of Association. The constitutional guarantees of freedom of association would appear to apply to policies which improperly prohibit consensual amorous relationships between faculty and students in public institutions.... [F]irst amendment cases ... recognize[] that freedom of association may apply to relationships which promote social and personal ties, rather than just those that advance political and religious beliefs.... [T]he right of a public employee to date falls under the protection of the first amendment.... Although the constitutional rights at issue in consensual amorous relationships may be thought to be first amendment rights of association, they are more properly considered as protected under the penumbral right to privacy.... Intimate association, an intrinsic element of personal liberty, is not grounded solely in the first amendment but is secured generally by the Bill of Rights and the fourteenth amendment.... [U]niversities contemplating restrictions on the personal associations of faculty and students must consider the constitutional right to privacy.

Right to Privacy. While the right to privacy is not explicitly mentioned in the Constitution, numerous Supreme Court decisions rest on this principle and explore its scope. One of the earliest statements of the fundamental right to privacy appears in the dissenting opinion of justice Brandeis in *Olmstead v.*

United States. In *Olmstead,* the Court considered the government's gathering of criminal evidence through unauthorized wiretapping. The majority found that no violation of the defendant's fourth or fifth amendment rights resulted from this conduct. Brandeis' dissent stated that "[t]he makers of our Constitution ... conferred, as against the government, the right to be let alone—the most comprehensive of rights and the right most valued by civilized men." This dissent was later relied upon to overrule the case....

Not until 1965, in *Griswold v. Connecticut,* was the privacy concept identified as an independent constitutional right. In *Griswold,* the Court declared unconstitutional a Connecticut statute forbidding the use of contraceptives by married persons. Justice Douglas, writing the majority opinion, considered the constitutional right to privacy to have roots in the penumbras of the first, third, fourth, fifth, and ninth amendments. Other justices believed that the right to privacy emanated from the ninth amendment or the concept of personal liberty in the fourteenth amendment. Although the specific textual source of the constitutional right to privacy may still be debated, a line of Supreme Court decisions, beginning with *Griswold,* clearly established an independent constitutional right to privacy, the scope of which is still being explored and defined. In *Griswold,* Justice Douglas asserted that marriage is a relationship that lies within the zone of privacy created by the emanations of several fundamental constitutional guarantees ...

Given the emphasis placed by the Court on the interrelationship among the right to privacy, marriage and child-bearing, the formation of consensual intimate relationships, viewed as natural precursors to the more formal bond of marriage, should similarly be protected by the right to privacy. Otherwise, one might argue, the specific rights of privacy previously announced by the Court are hollow.

[Professor Karst has] suggested that the right to privacy may be the "least stable terrain of modern constitutional doctrine." There is little doubt, however, that Americans believe that their civil rights include the right to engage in highly personal relationships free from governmental intrusion. In our daily lives, [in Karst's words] "the values of intimate association loom larger than the value of freedom of expression or political association." Many faculty have immediately deemed university policies prohibiting faculty-student dating, violative of their civil rights, thus reflecting the "natural law" quality of the right to privacy....

The right of privacy, however, is not absolute. As with any constitutionally guaranteed individual right, a compelling state interest permits certain infringements of that right. Laws which limit the fundamental freedoms of an individual must serve a compelling state interest and also must be narrowly drawn to serve only that interest. The context of an educational institution may reveal such a compelling interest. Case law, however, has not been very helpful in this regard since courts have not properly addressed these issues or have avoided them by focusing on the particular facts or egregious behaviors before them....

... Cases involving consensual sexual relationships between faculty and students in institutions of higher education may also involve allegations of sexual harassment or other such egregious behavior on the part of faculty compelling schools to take action. Because court decisions often focus on such behavior, it is difficult to discern the limits of permissible infringement on the rights of faculty and students to private relationships....

The inherent asymmetry in faculty-student power is manifest primarily in the instructional context, which includes course work, advisorships, student evaluation, recommendations, and similar processes. When amorous involvement and academic responsibilities intersect, a student's meaningful consent to an intimate relationship is suspect. The voluntary nature of the association cannot be assured. Even when the faculty member intends no coercion, these concerns are still valid. However, when a faculty member does not academically supervise a student, these concerns cannot be entirely substantiated....

Limits.... In the landmark abortion case, *Roe v. Wade*, the Court deemed it appropriate for states to interfere with the mother's right to abortion for only a limited time during the pregnancy. The Court utilized a time line to delineate the boundary of permissible state regulation in areas otherwise protected by the mother's right to privacy. The timeline in *Roe v. Wade* illustrates when it is appropriate for the state to regulate areas protected by the right to privacy. This approach could be adapted to establish the permissible limits of university authority to regulate intimate consensual relationships between faculty and students. In the university setting, however, a situational paradigm would be more appropriate than a temporal one.

The overall university setting should be viewed as a large circle encompassing all its activities and interrelationships. Within the larger circle, a smaller circle sets off the activities and interrelationships that fall within the "instructional" context that could appropriately be regulated. Intimate associations between faculty and students arising within the "zone of instruction" carry the presumption of coercion and render the consensual nature of the relationships suspect. Here the university has a compelling interest in preserving academic integrity and safeguarding students from duress and exploitation.

Within the instructional context, students fearing adverse consequences from noncompliance may feel compelled to enter or to continue undesired intimate relationships with faculty members, even when such duress is not intended by the faculty member. Other students may also assume that such relationships result in unfair academic advantage. Since such perceptions damage the academic climate and the exact nature of such relationships is difficult to determine, the university may legitimately proscribe all such associations.

Outside the instructional context, the presumption that an intimate faculty-student relationship results from coercion cannot be justified. Since the faculty member does not academically supervise the student, the university has no reason to question the consensual nature of the association. The faculty person cannot use the threat of reprisal or the promise of reward to manipulate the student. Also little reason would exist for others to suspect academic favoritism. Consequently, proscribing such relationships would serve no compelling interest.

A bright-line test can thus be formulated for public universities, defining the area of permissible state intrusion into constitutionally protected private relationships: the university may proscribe the formation of intimate faculty-student relationships within the instructional context, namely, when the faculty member academically supervises the student. Intimate consensual relationships falling outside the instructional context are constitutionally protected from university interference….

The bright-line test suggests the constitutional minimum which public institutions should incorporate into a policy. However, universities may need to address other concerns before adopting a policy on amorous relationships. Frances Hoffman, writing in the *Harvard Educational Review*, discussed some of the implications of such policies. Hoffman believes that amorous relationships between faculty and students are generally inappropriate and risky. She labels all such relationships inappropriate when there is an abuse of power. However, Hoffman suggests that policies should not "reinforce status hierarchies and ignore or deny the right of individuals to establish relationships when, with whom, and where they choose." The paternalistic attitude of policies on amorous relationships runs counter to higher education's abandonment of the *in loco parentis* role….

The entire definition of amorous relationships is fraught with ambiguity, which may result in a further chilling effect on mentorship and the social interactions that are part of a nurturing academic environment. Therefore, policymakers should carefully delineate the realm of unacceptable behavior, which is a difficult task. Consequently, some institutions may choose to have no explicit policy and others may prefer to articulate a very general statement with no mention of sanctions.

The freedom to decline or resist intimate association is inextricably bound up with the freedom to form intimate association. Upholding both these freedoms in the university setting generates inherent conflict.... [T]he right to form adult consensual intimate relationships is a fundamental personal freedom. A strong and effective university policy against sexual harassment, together with the recognition of the right to privacy of faculty and students, will, within the parameters of constitutional guarantees, serve both the interests of the university and those of the individual.

Selected References

Frances Hoffman, Sexual Harassment in Academia: Feminist Theory and Institutional Practice, 50 *Harvard Education Review* 105 (1986).

Kenneth L. Karst, The Freedom of Intimate Association, 89 Yale Law Journal 624 (1980).

Amy Somers, Sexual Harassment in Academe: Legal Issues and Definitions, 38 Journal of Social Issues 21 (1982).

Nancy Tuana, Sexual Harassment in Academe: Issues of Power and Coercion, 33 College Teaching 53 (1985).

Cases and Statutes

Griswold v. Connecticut, 381 U.S. 479 (1965).

Olmstead v. United States 277 U.S. 438 (1928) (*overruled* in *Katz v. United States* 389 U.S. 347, 88 S. Ct. 507 (1967)).

Roe v. Wade, 410 U.S. 113 (1973).

Title IX of the Educational Amendments of 1972, 20 U.S.C. §1681 (1982).

Title VII of the Civil Rights Act of 196442 U.S.C. §§2000e–2000e-17 (1982).

C. Lawmakers

CHAPTER THIRTY-FOUR

THE ARTICLE 2
MERCHANT RULES*

In 1949, Karl Llewellyn and his all-star drafting crew publicly unveiled the Uniform Commercial Code. Article 2 of the Code, the sales article, did something that prior sales law had not: it sometimes stated two rules regarding a legal issue, one for merchants, another for nonmerchants. Section 2-509(2), for instance, provided that a merchant-seller bore the risk of loss until the buyer actually received the goods, while a nonmerchant seller assumed the risk only until he tendered delivery. Article 2 defined the term "merchant" to establish who was subject to the special merchant rules....

... Believing the merchant rules to be faithful reflections of business practices, courts have concluded that the Article 2 merchant rules apply only to those familiar with business practices or to those who have previously engaged in similar transactions because only they would know the relevant trade customs and business practices codified by the merchant rules. As a consequence, courts have never entertained the possibility of applying the Article 2 merchant rules to nonmerchants....

... Llewellyn, the principal draftsman of Article 2, invented the merchant rules. The necessity that mothered his invention was his passionate desire to make "commercial law and practice clear, sane, and safe." The merchant rules are statutory expressions of Llewellyn's drafting creed that "[s]impler, clearer, and better adjusted rules, built to make sense and to protect good faith, make for more foreseeable and more satisfactory results both in court and out." Llewellyn sculpted the merchant rules to bring "the beautiful" to commercial law and commercial practice. To Llewellyn's eye, legal beauty lay in functional rules—rules that could guide businessmen in conducting their business affairs, rules that could assist them in their "trouble shooting, trouble evasion

_____

* **Ingrid Michelsen Hillinger**, *The Article 2 Merchant Rules: Karl Llewellyn's Attempt to Archive The Good, The True, The Beautiful in Commercial Law*, 73 GEORGETOWN LAW JOURNAL 1141 (1985), http://papers.ssrn.com/abstract_id=781044.

and forward planning." Llewellyn drafted the merchant rules to apprise businessmen, attorneys, and courts of the peculiar obligations of businessmen. Their clarity, rationality and certainty in application would protect decent businessmen and promote sound, reasonable, and decent business practices.

The idea of separate merchant rules for businessmen sprang from Llewellyn's pragmatism. Llewellyn believed businessmen needed rules on which they could rely, rules that would produce predictable results. The existence of predictable rules would make commercial activity more rational and would thereby encourage its expansion. Moreover, Llewellyn believed the policies and considerations involved in a mercantile situation differed from those in a nonmercantile situation, and that a unitary approach to sales rules would inevitably muddle policies and rationales. This result would jeopardize the predictability he so wanted to create for businessmen. Under a single rule, governing both businessmen and nonbusinessmen, a court trying to protect Aunt Tilly might manipulate, distort, or misconstrue the rule, making uncertain its later interpretation or application to Tilly, Inc. Rules fashioned specifically for a commercial setting, and insulated from nonmercantile considerations, would thus protect the rules' predictability for businessmen. One set of sales rules for businessmen and another for Aunt Tilly would eliminate the possibility of undermining the commercial rule to do justice to Aunt Tilly.

Yet Llewellyn did not intend to preclude judicial application of the merchant rules to nonmerchants in every instance. If application to a nonmerchant would not jeopardize the rule's certainty and predictability, Llewellyn wanted the courts to apply the merchant rule to nonmerchants. Indeed, a provision in the 1949 draft expressly so provided....

The Myth. Many scholars have assumed the Article 2 merchant rules merely codified preexisting commercial practices. In recommending the Code's enactment, no less a stalwart than Professor Arthur Corbin, a Code advisor, wrote that "[t]he Commercial Code has taken notice of the developing law merchant and in a comparatively small number of sections has constructed rules based on merchant custom, applicable to those who regularly deal within its coverage and to others who know or have reason to know it." In 1954, Professor Lattin maintained [that] "The strongest argument in favor of the adoption of the Sales Article (and and remainder of the Uniform Commercial Code for that matter) is that this is merchants', and not lawyers' law.... Even Grant Gilmore, a Llewellyn disciple who helped draft the Code, noted [in his *Ages of American Law*] that Article 2 reflected Llewellyn's attempt to draft "a statute which would reflect (as the Sales Act did not) the actual practices of businesses in the twentieth century."

The Code helps create the impression that the merchant rules embody trade custom. In its first substantive provision, it announces that one underlying purpose of the Act is "to permit the continued expansion of commercial practices, through custom, usage and agreement of the parties." If the Code intends to foster commercial practices, the special merchant provisions logically might embody the business customs and usages which the Code seeks to promote. Indeed, the overall tone of Article 2 suggests a clear respect for, if not deference to, commercial practices. Its rules speak in terms of commercial reasonableness, commercial standards, trade customs, and commercial understanding, all of which require courts to refer to actual commercial practice and understanding to resolve legal disputes. It seems reasonable to conclude that the merchant rules similarly respect commercial realities....

Llewellyn's testimony to the New York Law Revision Commission appears to confirm the spiritual link between the old "law merchant" and the new Article 2 merchant rules. In defending the Code generally, Llewellyn stated that the Code sought "to remake the sales law of New York ... in order that the law may be made to conform to commercial practice and may be read and make sense." Rallying specifically to the cause of his merchant concept, he argued that the House of Lords, by thinking a single rule was needed for everyone, "slowed and delayed for a century the development of the admirable and needed law of letters of credit." Article 2's statement of one rule for merchants and another for nonmerchants would presumably avoid the English error and, like the "law merchant," facilitate the development of the law regarding commercial practices generally.For Llewellyn, "this line of spotting and fulfilling mercantile need, without confusing it by including people and factors which would blur or distract, was a major achievement of Article 2." ...

The Reality. The Article 2 merchant rules represented Llewellyn's attempt to create simpler, clearer, and better adjusted rules for commercial transactions. The rules incorporated actual business practice, however, only to the extent that such practice comported with Llewellyn's view of sound and reasonable commercial conduct. This finds its clearest expression in section 2-205 [which] provides:

> An offer by a merchant to buy or sell goods in a signed writing which by its terms gives assurance that it will be held open is not revocable, for lack of consideration, during the time stated or if no time is stated for a reasonable time, but in no event may such period of irrevocability exceed three months.

Comment 1 explained that the section was "intended to modify the former rule which required that 'firm offers' be sustained by consideration in order to bind, and to require instead that they must merely be characterized as such and expressed in signed writings." Comment 2 noted that section 2-205 was designed "to give effect to the deliberate intention of a merchant to make a current firm offer binding." Thus, section 2-205 has the smell and feel of "merchants' law," or at least law which was not "lawyers' law." In rejecting the common law requirement of consideration as the earmark of irrevocability, the section removed a legal obstacle to judicial protection of the offeree's reasonable expectations arising from the merchant's firm offer.

Heady from section 2-205's gracious accommodation to merchant mores, one comes upon the last sentence of comment 2: "However, despite settled courses of dealing or usages of trade whereby firm offers are made by oral communication and relied upon without more evidence, such offers remain revocable under this Article since authentication by a writing is the essence of this section." Quite clearly, section 2-205 was not going to accommodate any trade custom or mercantile understanding regarding firm offers that departed from the section 2-205 manner of expressing them. Section 2-205 did not state merchant custom; it stated Llewellyn's law of irrevocable offers with respect to merchants.

The Article 2 merchant firm offer rule reflects Llewellyn's statutory response to a concern he discussed as early as 1931. Generally, Llewellyn approved of the common law doctrine of consideration, and was convinced that it "comfortably cared for the great bulk of business promises." Consideration was a helpful tool to identify the enforceable promise because "the existence of bargain equivalency does indeed commonly evidence positively that the promise was deliberate—considered—meant." Furthermore, bargain equivalency afforded a reasonable basis "for believing that some promise was in fact made." Still, although it answered problems more often than not, the doctrine of consideration troubled Llewellyn in four cases, the first of which was "business promises such as 'firm offers,' understood to be good for a fixed time, but revoked before. They are frequent; they are and should be relied on. As to them our consideration doctrine is badly out of joint." Llewellyn drafted section 2-205 to "realign" the law of business offers and give effect to those firm offers that Llewellyn thought should be enforced.

Llewellyn's discussion of the problems of enforcing business offers explains the thinking that prompted him to draft section 2-205. It also reveals something about Llewellyn's basic attitude with respect to writings, a requirement shared by three provisions containing a special merchant rule. Llewellyn felt "the handing over of a signed promise in writing [*i.e.*, the firm offer] would go far to assure the values and functions which the doctrine of consideration had previously served." A writing would suggest the promise was "deliberate—considered—meant." It would also provide objective evidence that an offer was actually made, thereby reducing the possibility of perjury. Finally, it would be "an excellent objective indication not only of the creation of expectation in the promisee, but of the reasonableness of there being expectation and of its being related to the promise."

For Llewellyn, a signed writing would advance all the policies served by consideration. He believed nothing more was required to recognize an irrevocable offer, and if the law required more, for example, consideration, the law would deny effect to some firm offers that he thought should be effective. By making a signed writing "the essence" of an irrevocable offer, Llewellyn simply recast the legal requirements to state what he considered a more rational rule. Section 2-205 represented a "better adjusted rule, built to make sense" because it would produce what Llewellyn thought to be more reasonable commercial results.

Along with making commercial law more rational, Llewellyn also sought to make it clearer. Businessmen, knowing the rule of section 2-205, could quickly determine when their own offers would be binding and, more importantly, when they could safely rely on the 'firm offer' of another. If the firm offer were oral, industry-wide reliance notwithstanding, section 2-205 would not recognize it as binding.

The story of the Article 2 statute of frauds provision is the story of section 2-205 retold. Throughout the drafting process, the basic ingredients of the statute of frauds never changed. For contracts exceeding $500, section 2-201(1) required "some writing sufficient to indicate that a contract for sale has been made between the parties ... signed by the party against whom enforcement is sought." ...

Llewellyn knew that businessmen occasionally indulge in informal, oral deals. He also knew that a legal system could survive without a statute of frauds because he himself had observed that ten or more states had "found it unnecessary to have any Statute of Frauds in regard to the sales of goods," and "the entire continent of Europe ha[d] also handled mercantile dealings for a few hundred years without that necessity." Yet section 2-201 left businessmen operating in this manner to their own extrajudicial devices. Measured against the rality of business practice, the requirement of a writing seems far from accommodating.

Llewellyn's insistence on formality as a prerequisite to the enforcement of contracts is also confusing in light of Professor Corbin's attitude toward the statute of frauds. Corbin was Llewellyn's mentor, his "father-in-the-law," as Llewellyn once described him. Yet, in his 1950 article urging adoption of the Code, Professor Corbin had criticized the basic concept of a statute of frauds as inconsistent with what people actually do....

Surely, Llewellyn's inspiration for the merchant provision of the statute of frauds did not come from business reality. In fact, as Corbin intimated, a requirement of formality would thwart many a businessman's contractual expectations. Rather than paying homage to actual mercantile practice, section 2-201, like section 2-205, codified what Llewellyn thought should be the law regarding commercial transactions. At most, section 2-201(2) codified the best practice of some businessmen, but at its core section 2-201 represented Llewellyn's considered policy judgment reflecting his view of the statute of frauds and his vision of the proper role of law in commercial transactions.

In the same 1931 article in which he discussed the problem of "business offers," Llewellyn spoke approvingly of the statute of frauds. He described it as "an amazing product" in which "de Leon might have found his secret of perpetual youth" because two and a half centuries after its enactment, it stood "in essence better adapted to our needs than when it first was passed." Without doubt, Llewellyn believed in writings. No system could "ignore the value of forms as records"; forms provided "permanent and reckonable evidence of what was agreed upon." Llewellyn declared that "contracts are transactions, not mere events; and, as deliberate transactions, are capable of prophylactic regulation." Section 2-201, subsections (1) and (2), illustrate Llewellyn's prophylactic regulation in action....

Llewellyn never hid the fact that he was creating business duties—here, a duty to send out a confirmation letter after the conclusion of an oral deal and a duty to read a confirmation letter received. Moreover, Llewellyn maintained that his proclamation of business duties only followed venerable legal tradition: "The fact is, and the cases show, that different responsibilities have been imposed both by explicit law and by the cases upon persons who have professional responsibilities as contrasted with other persons. To bring this to explicit attention is to clarify the law, not change it."

Section 2-201(2) states law that embraced Llewellyn's view of what constituted decent and sound business practice. Admittedly, it was law sensitive to the needs and realities of business life, but very clearly it was law and not business custom. Llewellyn acknowledged that "neither the existing law nor the Code has managed a wholly satisfactory solution.... [T]he difference is that the existing law is utterly unsafe and unsatisfactory." As far as Llewellyn was concerned, his modifications of sales law were at least correctly aimed because they made the situation safer and more rational for businessmen.

With section 2-603, Llewellyn strengthened his architectural design for a sound commercial law that would induce reasonable commercial behavior. Section 2-603 details a merchant buyer's duties when he rightfully rejects goods and the seller has neither an agent nor "place of business at the market of rejection." Section 2-603(1) requires a merchant buyer to follow his seller's reasonable instructions regarding the goods. For Llewellyn, this duty arose from simple business decency ...

Comment 1 to section 2-603 suggests a common law genesis of the rule: "This section recognizes the duty imposed upon the merchant buyer by good faith and commercial practice to follow any reasonable instructions of the seller as to reshipping, storing, delivery to a third party, reselling or the like." But in fact section 2-603 had no basis in the common law. The comment's reference to "commercial practice" did not refer to actual commercial practice, but the commercial practice Llewellyn wanted to institute. Llewellyn thought it both reasonable and decent to require a merchant buyer to follow his seller's reasonable instructions when a distant seller had no available means to retrieve and redirect the goods....

Through the Article 2 merchant rules regarding firm offers, satisfaction of the statute of frauds, and a buyer's duties upon rightful rejection, Llewellyn sought to make commercial law rational, or to use his own term, "sane." Sane rules would promote sane commercial law and conduct.... Following Lord Mansfield's lead, Llewellyn used the merchant rules to articulate Llewellyn's law of merchants' peculiar obligations. The merchant rules did not codify merchant reality, but rather Llewellyn's view of what that reality should be. They were one part of Llewellyn's overall goal to make "commercial law and practice clear, sane and safe."

The Mystery. There is something extremely peculiar about Llewellyn's law of merchants' peculiar obligations. Since the merchant rules are so sensible and reasonable, one feels compelled to ask, why limit these rules to merchants? Certainly the reasons behind the merchant rules provide no clue as to their limitation to merchants. If a signed writing is an acceptable substitute for consideration, why are only merchant firm offers binding without consideration? If a confirmation letter is acceptable objective proof of the existence of a contract, and the sending of one is a sound business practice, why does the nonmerchant who sends one to a merchant or other nonmerchant not have the benefit of section 2-201(2)? If decency and common sense require a buyer to follow his seller's reasonable instructions regarding rejected goods, why do the dictates of reasonableness and common decency suddenly disappear when the buyer is a nonmerchant?

When pressed on this last question, ... Llewellyn's response [was] singularly unresponsive. Section 2-603 only imposes a duty to follow a seller's reasonable instructions and to require a householder to reship three tons of coal would be unreasonable. The question posed was why not require all buyers to follow their seller's reasonable instructions? Llewellyn's answer suggest[ed] that he felt it was inappropriate to impose such a duty on nonbusinessmen.

Llewellyn's reply also suggest[ed] that the nonmerchant rules may simply have been the product of a vision limited by an all-consuming passion for business law and issues. Llewellyn rarely strayed far from business and mercantile considerations in his writings on sales. He confined one article's discussion to the "mercantile phases of sales" and another "to the initiation of business deals." In the preface to his 1930 casebook on sales, Llewellyn acknowledged his commercial orientation: "The book errs, I think, in too happily assuming the needs of buyers and sellers to be the needs of the community, and in rarely reaching beyond business practice in evaluation of legal rules." He apologized that "time for building a wider foundation for judgment has been lacking." Lacking expertise in noncommercial matters, Llewellyn may have chosen to leave essentially unaltered the prior Uniform Sales Act's treatment of such matters. Alternatively, Llewellyn's business orientation may have caused him to confuse good business sense with just plain good sense.

Although these theories may explain Article 2's merchant distinction, they are unsatisfying, both intellectually and emotionally, with respect to Llewellyn. By 1941, one would assume Llewellyn would have corrected this deficiency, especially when he was crafting a law rather than writing an article or casebook. In fact, Llewellyn's writings and statements before the New York Law Revision Commission suggest another theory, far more appealing to "Llewellyn-watchers," as an explanation of Article 2's merchant and nonmerchant rules. Along with explaining what Llewellyn was doing, and why, they lead to the conclusion that Llewellyn never intended to limit the Article 2 merchant rules to merchants.

The Merchant Rules, Legal Realist's Law, or, How to Build a Beautiful Commercial Law. Professor Danzig once observed that Article 2 presented a rare opportunity to study a statute "drafted by a self-conscious jurisprude." Preoccupied with the more immediate struggle of figuring out what an Article 2 provision means or was intended to accomplish, we forget to consider that Llewellyn was "at least as reflective about the role of law in society and the relation of lawmaking institutions to each other as he was about the particular law-making task at hand." It is Karl Llewellyn's jurisprudence that explains why he limited rules of seeming universal application to merchants.

Llewellyn planned to create beautiful law for businessmen. Such law would be beautiful because it was functional. For Llewellyn, legal esthetics were in essence functional esthetics. Article 2 would create law businessmen could use, law which would guide them in their affairs.... Legal rules could be functional only if they were clear, certain and predictable. Predictability, in turn, would be insured only if the rules protected good faith and did not require misconstruction to produce good results. In drafting Article 2, Llewellyn sought to create "a body of sales law which is clear, guidesome, which it is almost impossible to misconstrue." Llewellyn wanted his rules to protect good faith and provide predictable and satisfactory results, both in court and out. That aim, determined by Llewellyn's theory of what legal rules should accomplish, explains why he stated separate merchant rules in Article 2.

Gilmore observed that regardless of whether in fact there was such a thing as a "Realist School" or a "Realist Movement," "the academic theorists who emerged after World War I agreed ... that the traditional or Langdellian way of achieving doctrinal unity on the level of case law or Restatement was absurd." The merchant rules reveal Llewellyn's approach to the creation of doctrinal unity in commercial law....

Llewellyn believed proper results required "suitable explicit intellectual equipment." He felt "the getting of such stock equipment is a struggle [and until] the case-results get themselves a prophet and a suitable doctrine, there is unpredictability, high, wide and handsome." Llewellyn's merchant was the prophet, his merchant rules the suitable doctrine. In statements before the New York Law Revision Commission, Llewellyn argued the Code would "produce intelligent and workable commercial law," "make commercial law and practice clear, sane and safe," and "hugely increase not only speed and flexibility, but safety and certainty in this area." It was, he modestly remarked, "a rather amazing piece of legal engineering."

Llewellyn's repeated emphasis on the Code's safety, certainty and clarity might lead one to conclude that pre-Code law was unsafe, uncertain and unclear. No doubt Llewellyn perceived it that way, but others believed differently.... [T]he most probable [explanation for disagreement] lies in the debaters' differing perceptions of "the law." Those occupying the "law-is-well-settled" camp viewed "the law" as doctrinal statements. Llewellyn conceived of "the law" as what courts do. In saying the law was uncertain and unsettled, Llewellyn meant that under the pre-Code rules no one could safely predict what a court would do in any given instance. If you could not predict a court's behavior, you could not adjust your own. Since unpredictable rules could not guide action, Llewellyn considered the situation intolerable for businessmen who needed to plan and act rationally....

To provide the predictable, functional commercial law he so dearly wanted, Llewellyn believed there was a "vital need for distinguishing merchants from housewives and from farmers and from mere lawyers." Presumably, the issues and considerations inherent in a commercial context differed from those in a noncommercial context, requiring separate treatment for each. Predictable commercial law required rules specially crafted for a commercial context. A court would not need to distort a sensible legal rule fashioned for a commercial context in order to produce a good result in a commercial dispute. If honest application of a rule would produce satisfactory results, the rule would be reliable and it could guide action. Llewellyn stated separate commercial rules to preserve the integrity and reliability of his commercial rules. Such soundly classified, special commercial rules would achieve doctrinal unity in commercial law....

Llewellyn was "clarifying" the law by stating rules that would require all courts to adopt a mercantile approach to the legal issues addressed by the merchant rules. Llewellyn's claim of "clarification" is somewhat misleading. In fact, he was codifying a mercantile approach to commercial disputes, an approach that he believed distinguished the good commercial judges and good commercial decisions from the bad. He was mandating all courts to follow the approach he believed to be proper and necessary with respect to commercial sales issues.

Llewellyn's spirited defense of Article 2's unconscionability provision provides further insight into his Article 2 merchant approach. Llewellyn did not like the judicial torture, manipulation and misconstruction of contractual language or intent to which courts resorted to achieve their desired result. He referred to these exercises in judicial gymnastics as "covert tools" of intentional and creative misconstruction, which were unacceptable to businessmen for three different reasons. First, businessmen, relying on what a court had said, would "recur to the attack" by attempting to draft contract language that better expressed their contractual intent.... Judicial reliance on covert tools led businessmen down the primrose path: the problem was not one of better drafting, but of objectionable commercial intent. Second, judicial subterfuge failed to tell businessmen what was and was not permissible. Third, judicial use of covert tools would "seriously embarrass later efforts at true construction."...

Article 2 gave a devastatingly simple solution to the covert tool problem and its attendant unsettling effect on the planning and transacting of business. Section 2-302, the unconscionability provision, gave courts an overt tool that would eliminate any need for covert activity. Rather than misconstruing contractual language to mean what it clearly did not, a court could deny effect to a clause it disliked by holding it unconscionable. The unconscionability provision was good for businessmen. They could rely on courts to interpret contractual language as it was intended. They could also assume opinions meant what they appeared to mean. Most importantly, the accumulation of opinions over time would provide businessmen with explicit guidelines as to what was and was not beyond the pale. The unconscionability provision, amorphous as it was, would give concrete direction to businessmen in the future drafting of their contracts....

The Article 2 merchant rules recognize that businessmen "have skills and knowledge whose use is properly to be relied on." Llewellyn's rules expected the knowledge and guaranteed the reliability. Clarity, rationality, and predictability in the rules governing business transactions would create the legal certainty necessary to enable businessmen to prosper. The commercial rules would let businessmen know where they were, so they could know what to do. For Llewellyn, a major achievement of the Article 2 merchant rules was that they spotted and fulfilled mercantile need "without confusing it by including people and factors which would blur or distract." By stating separate commercial rules, noncommercial factors could not jeopardize the predictability or integrity of Llewellyn's rules for businessmen.

Who is a Merchant? A Question of Sound and Fury, Probably Signifying Little. In concluding that good commercial law and practice required special commercial rules, Llewellyn was not concluding that the commercial rules could have no application to a noncommercial context. Section 1-102(3) of the 1949 draft makes that clear: "A provision of this Act which is stated to be applicable 'between merchants' or otherwise to be of limited application need not be so limited when the circumstances and underlying reasons justify extending its application."

According to Article 2 as originally planned, the merchant rules would be invoked in a nonmercantile context if the purpose and reasoning behind a merchant rule applied. Llewellyn did not codify the special merchant rules to shut out nonmerchants. Rather, he sought to insulate his bedrock commercial rules from creeping, noncommercial considerations that might blur or distort the predictability of his commercial rules....

Llewellyn had every good reason to apply section 2-205 to nonmerchants. Aside from the preprinted, unintelligible, firm offer form supplied by an offeree, what offeror (absent duress, fraud, mistake, etc.) would not fully understand the nature and effect of a writing that he composed and signed which expressed his offer as firm?

Yet, section 2-205's limitation of the firm offer rule to merchants reflected Llewellyn's drafting caution. Had section 2-205 not been limited to merchants, a court, confronting a nonbusinessman and wanting to find his offer revocable, might twist and distort the unitary rule to do so. Llewellyn feared that nonmercantile considerations might seep in and ultimately undermine the certainty of his commercial rules. At all costs, Llewellyn wanted to protect the clarity, meaning and predictability of his commercial rules. However, if the predictability of the rule would not be sacrificed through its application to a nonmerchant, there was no reason to limit its application to merchants. In fact, there was good reason not to, because an arbitrary limitation could result in individual injustice. Llewellyn's drafting solution was masterful. A rule for merchants, stated as an absolute, gave businessmen the predictability and certainty they needed. Liberal extension of the rule to nonmerchants when "the circumstances and underlying reasons" justified such an extension would avoid arbitrariness, but never at the expense of the predictability of the commercial rule.

Had the 1949 provision authorizing liberal application of the merchant rules to nonmerchants survived and been enacted, the question of merchant status would not have assumed its current importance. Courts could have sidestepped many status questions by concluding that merchant status was ultimately irrelevant, and the reasons underlying the merchant rule—reasonableness, soundness, and decency—would justify its application to the nonmerchant. Unfortunately, the drafters finally bowed to merchant critics and eliminated section 1-102(3), apparently as a political concession to save the embattled Article 2 merchant distinction itself....

Section 1-102(3)'s demise has clearly created a problem. Llewellyn, were he alive, would find the present situation ironic. He would see his merchant definition become one of the covert tools he fought so hard against. He would see some courts misconstruing his intended merchant definition in order to achieve a just result through application of the merchant rule. He would see other courts reach an unreasonable, unjust result by correctly construing his merchant definition and blindly applying the nonmerchant rule....

The loss of section 1-102(3) and a basic misunderstanding about the underlying purpose of the Article 2 merchant rules have created a flaw in Article 2's bifurcated system. Courts assume the existence of an Article 2 barrier, which precludes application of the merchant rules to situations involving only one merchant or only nonmerchants. Courts either respect the barrier, often reaching poor results, or surmount it by various means to reach the proper results. Those who are unquestionably nonmerchants suffer most. They can never find refuge in the Article 2 merchant rules. This situation is especially ridiculous because there does not appear to be anything intrinsically commercial about most of the Article 2 merchant rules. The merchant rules for firm offers, the statute of frauds, risk of loss, and so on, are edicts issuing forth from the temple of reason, not the marketplace. The merchant rules embody good sense, not just good commercial sense.

Compared with the nonmerchant rules, the merchant rules seem enlightened. The merchant rules impose only the mildest, most modest of responsibilities, such as the duty to open one's mail and respond to it promptly. The merchant's failure to abide by these duties often results in equally innocuous conseqences. For example, the businessman who fails to reply to a confirmation letter simply loses his statute of frauds defense against contract enforcement. The businessman who fails to read or respond to the offeree's letter of acceptance is bound by minor additional contract terms contained in the acceptance. These are rules which, in most instances, could apply to the common man with little fear of judicial distortion or doctrinal confusion. In fact, it may be said that what's good for businessmen in Article 2 is good for the rest of us....

Selected References

David W. Carroll, Harpooning Whales, Of Which Karl N. Llewellyn Is the Hero of The Piece; Or Searching For More Expansion Joints In Karl's Crumbling Cathedral, 12 Boston College Industrial & Commercial Law Review 139 (1970).

Arthur L. Corbin, The Uniform Commercial Code—Sales: Should It Be Enacted?, 59 Yale Law Journal 821 (1950).

Richard Danzig, A Comment on the Jurisprudence of the Uniform Commercial Code, 27 Stanford Law Review 621 (1975).

Jerome Frank, Words and Music: Some Remarks on Statutory Interpretation, 47 Columbia Law Review 1259 (1947).

Grant Gilmore, The Ages of American Law (1977).

Grant Gilmore, The Good Faith Purchase Idea and the Uniform Commercial Code: Confessions of a Repentant Draftsman, 15 Georgia Law Review 605 (1981).

Grant Gilmore, The Commercial Doctrine of Good Faith Purchase, 63 Yale Law Journal 1057 (1954).

Norman D. Lattin, The Law of Sales in the Uniform Commercial Code, 15 Ohio State Law Journal 12 (1954).

Karl Llewellyn, Memorandum Replying to the Report and Memorandum of Task Group 1 of the Special Committee of the Commerce and Industry Association of New York, Inc. on the Uniform Commercial Code (August 16, 1954), reprinted in 1 State of New York Law Revision Committee Report, Hearings on the Uniform Commercial Code 108 (1954)

Karl Llewellyn (Books): Cases and Materials on the Law of Sales (1930); The Common Law Tradition (1960).

Karl Llewellyn (Articles): What Price Contract? An Essay in Perspective, 40 Yale Law Journal 704 (1931); On Warranty of Quality, and Society, 36 Columbia Law Review 699 (1936); Our Case-Law of Contract: Offer and Acceptance, II, 48 Yale Law Journal 779 (1939); Across Sales on Horseback, 52 Harvard Law Review 725 (1939); On the Good, the True, The Beautiful, in Law, 9 Chicago Law Review 224 (1942); The Modern Approach to Counseling and Advocacy—Especially in Commercial Transactions, 46 Columbia Law Review 167 (1946); On Law and Our Commerce, 1949 Wisconsin Law Review 625.

William Schnade, A Short History of the Preparation and Enactment of the Uniform Commercial Code, 22 Miami Law Review 1 (1967).

Philip W. Thayer, Comparative Law and the Law Merchant, 6 Brooklyn Law Review 139 (1963).

William Twining, Karl Llewellyn and the Realist Movement (1973).

Further Reading
(selected work by Ingrid Michelsen Hillinger)

Commercial Transactions/Secured Financing: Cases, Materials, Problems (LEXIS 3rd ed. 2003) (with Raymond T. Nimmer & Michael G. Hillinger).
The Merchant of Section 2-314: Who Needs Him? 34 Hastings Law Journal 747 (1983).

CHAPTER THIRTY-FIVE

LESSONS FROM THE ARTICLE 8 REVISION[*]

When locomotives were developed in the early part of the nineteenth century, they were called "iron horses." When automobiles were developed at the end of the nineteenth century, they were called "horseless carriages." Today, those metaphors sound quaint. It is amusing that the people of the nineteenth century could not think of these marvelous new devices in any way other than by commenting on their "horseness" or lack thereof. But were the terms really all that odd? At the time, horseness was not an incidental characteristic of modes of land transportation. From the dawn of civilization, the legs of animals—whether human or non-human—provided the only means of land transportation, and for many centuries the horse had been the animal of choice.

In a very real sense, horseness was a key concept in land transport, so any new means of land transport could quite sensibly be regarded as some variant on the horse. If the automobile had remained a plaything for the rich and our air remained pungent with the odor of manure rather than petroleum fumes, no adjective would need be added to the word "carriage" to express the assumed "horse drawn"; and an automobile still would be, in a sense more literal than metaphoric, a horseless carriage. But that's not what happened. Horses and carriages are now the curiosities; cars and trucks are the ordinary modes of land transport. Not surprisingly, then, the "horseless carriage" metaphor has become archaic. As practices change, so too must language and concepts. That, in a nutshell, is the lesson to be drawn from the past few decades' work on the commercial law of investment securities.

Article 8 has the distinction of being the first article of the Uniform Commercial Code to reach the third generation. We have the original version, the

---

[*] **James Steven Rogers**, *An Essay on Horseless Carriages and Paperless Negotiable Instruments: Some Lessons from the Article 8 Revision*, 31 IDAHO LAW REVIEW 689 (1995), http://papers.ssrn.com/abstract_id=771630.

1978 version, and now the 1994 version. The original version of Article 8 was based on the traditional system in which transfer of securities was effected by physical delivery of certificates from seller to buyer. The 1978 version added new provisions dealing with "uncertificated securities." The most recent revision effort recast the law to deal more adequately with the system of securities holding through intermediaries.

For those interested in the study of the process of legal response to technological change, the somewhat checkered career of the 1978 revision of Article 8 is an extremely instructive episode. What was done in that revision project was so obviously sensible that it is hard to imagine how one could have done anything else. Indeed, there are probably many projects exactly like the 1978 revision that are currently either being considered or undertaken. We had a commercial system based on paper and a law written in terms of paper. The paper was being replaced by electronic media, so the law had to be revised to reflect that change. How do you do that? Simple; you just take the paper part out. If we had a law of paper security certificates, we add a law of paperless "uncertificated securities."

So today we hear a good deal of discussion of the need for a law of electronic negotiable promissory notes, or electronic bills of lading. Or, to use current jargon, we consider rewriting the law in "media neutral" terms, so that it will not matter whether the thing in question is represented by carved stone, ink on paper, or electronic pulses. But there's the rub. Are we really so sure that the world is media neutral? To define, and hence limit, law revision projects by the effort to devise electronic equivalents of the familiar paper-based representations, such as security certificates, promissory notes, or bills of lading, is to assume that technological change will have no significant ontological consequences. We'll still have the same old things, they'll just look (or not look) a little different.

The lesson from Article 8 is that it doesn't always work that way. By the late 1960s it was clear that the traditional certificate based system of securities transfers was not going to work any longer. The securities markets were quite literally grinding to a halt because the back-office operations needed for settlement by physical delivery could not keep pace with increasing trading volume. At the time of the "paper crunch" in the late 1960s, the trading volume on the New York Stock Exchange that so seriously strained the capacities of the clearance and settlement system was in the range of 10 million shares per day.

Today, the system can easily handle daily trading volume on routine days of hundreds of million shares. Even during the October 1987 market break, when daily trading volume reached [a] record level of 608 million shares, the clearance and settlement system functioned relatively smoothly. Obviously this processing capacity could have been achieved only by the application of modern electronic information processing systems, and that is the case. Physical delivery of certificates plays only a minor role in the settlement system that processes this enormous volume of securities trading. Yet the legal rules under which the system operates are not the uncertificated securities provisions of Article 8 that were drafted in response to the obvious fact that the paper-based system had to be replaced by an electronic system.

Displaying the usual perverse tendency of the world to behave in a fashion other than that which seems most logical to a law professor, the operations people in the securities clearance and settlement system solved the problem in a different way. They have kept the paper certificates, they just don't do anything with them. The certificates are surrendered to a securities depository, such as the Depository Trust Company, which holds the certificates on behalf of its member banks and broker, who in turn hold on behalf of themselves and their customers. Settlement of securities trades can then be effected merely by entries on the books of these intermediaries.

The most significant step in the Revised Article 8 project was the realization that the system of securities holding through intermediaries was sufficiently different from the traditional system in which an investor's right to the underlying security was represented by a definitive paper certificate, or from a system of the sort contemplated by the 1978 revision, where the investor's interest would be recorded electronically on the issuer's shareholder registry, that it required a different set of commercial law concepts and rules. Thus, the basic organizational principle of the 1994 revision is the distinction between the direct holding system, whether certificated or not, and the indirect holding system. The 1994 revision uses the new term "security entitlement" to describe the interest of a person who holds a security through a securities intermediary, and the new term "entitlement holder" to refer to a person who has a security entitlement.

A new Part 5 of Article 8 specifies the basic rights of those who hold security entitlements, subject to any applicable regulatory law such as the federal securities laws. The term "security entitlement" is defined in section 8-102(a)(17) as the package of rights that a person who holds a security through a securities intermediary has against that securities intermediary and the property held by that securities intermediary. Like many legal concepts, however, the meaning of "security entitlement" is to be found less in any specific definition than in the matrix of rules that use the term.

The Part 5 rules provide that a securities intermediary must itself maintain a sufficient quantity of securities, however held, to satisfy all of its entitlement holders, and that the positions held by the intermediary for the entitlement holders are not subject to claims of the intermediary's general creditors. Thus, a security entitlement is not merely an *in personam* claim against the intermediary, but a property interest consisting of a pro-rata claim to the fungible pool of underlying securities held by the intermediary.

The concept of a security entitlement does, however, include a package of rights against the intermediary. The indirect holding system rules cover such basic matters as the duty of the securities intermediary to pass through to entitlement holder the economic and legal rights of ownership of the security, including the right to receive payments and distributions, and the right to exercise any voting rights. The rules also specify that the securities intermediary has a duty to comply with authorized orders from the entitlement holder and to convert the entitlement holder's securities position into any other available form of securities holding that the customer requests, such as delivering a certificate or transferring the position to an account with another firm.

To see the difference between the basic concepts of the new indirect holding system rules and those of the traditional Article 8 system, consider how settlement of a typical securities trade is analyzed under the old law and the new. Suppose that Able places an order through Broker One to sell 10,000 shares of ABC Co. stock, and that Baker places an order through Broker Two to buy 10,000 shares of ABC Co. stock. Through the trading facilities of the exchange or market on which that security is traded, Able's sell order is matched with Baker's buy order, so that a contract is formed for the purchase and sale of 10,000 shares of ABC Co. stock.

By the custom and rules of the exchange or market, that contract calls for settlement five days after trade date ([now] three days). Settlement requires that Able cause it to occur that Baker acquire a 10,000 share position in ABC stock. On the settlement date, entries are made on the records of Broker One, Broker Two, and the central securities depository so that Able's account with Broker One is debited for 10,000 shares, Baker's account with Broker Two is credited for 10,000 shares, and appropriate entries are made on the records of the depository to reflect the changes in the positions of Broker One and Broker Two.

The traditional Article 8 rules on security certificates were based on the idea that the paper certificates could be regarded as complete reifications of the underlying rights, so that the rules on transfer of securities could be written using the same basic concepts as the rules for physical goods. The ordinary mechanism for transferring property interests in chattels is physical delivery; so too, physical delivery of a security certificate was the basic method of dealing with interests in securities. The old Article 8 rules used the same conceptual structure securities transactions implemented through the indirect holding system.

By virtue of the rather complex and obscure provisions in section 8-313 of the 1978 version, specifically, section 8-313(1)(d)(iii), one could conclude that once all of the entries were made on the records of Broker One, Broker Two and the depository, this resulted in the "transfer" to Baker of "a security."

The concept of transfer is so familiar that its use in the analysis of settlement of securities trades seems entirely natural, whatever the details of the particular settlement system. Yet if one looks a bit more closely at the operation of the modern clearance and settlement system, one begins to see some difficulties with the continued use of the transfer concept. Any two major broker-dealers may have executed hundreds or even thousands of trades with each other in a given security on a single day. It would be extremely inefficient if each transaction had to be settled by making a corresponding individual entry on the records of the depository.

Significant processing efficiency can be achieved by netting all of the transactions among the major players that occur each day, so that entries need be made on the depository's books only for the net changes in the positions of each participant at the end of each day. Thus, in our example, although Broker One will debit Able's account for 10,000 shares of ABC stock and Broker Two will credit Baker's account for 10,000 shares, one would not be able to identify any specific entry on the records of the depository as reflecting the transfer of those 10,000 shares from Broker One to Broker Two. Indeed, it might well turn out that Broker One had a net receive position and Broker Two a net deliver position for that settlement date. How, then, is one to give coherent meaning to the concept that settlement of the trade between Able and Baker occurs by transfer of 10,000 shares of ABC stock from Able to Baker?

Actually, current Article 8 finesses this question. Though current section 8-313 permits one to conclude that a transfer occurred to Baker, it never actually says that this was a transfer from Able to Baker; indeed, it never says anything about who the transferor was. To be sure, there are ways of tidying up the transfer analysis. One could analyze the steps in the settlement process one by one, so that however the positions between Broker One and Broker Two may have been adjusted, the final step in which an entry was made on Broker Two's records crediting Baker's account for 10,000 shares could be described as a transfer from Broker Two to Baker. The key point, however, is that the only reason that one would need to trace the path of an individual item of property through the settlement process is to enable one, by the technique made famous by Procrustes, to squeeze the analysis into the same conceptual structure used for simple face to face deliveries of discrete identifiable physical objects.

Revised Article 8 takes a different approach to the analysis of settlement of securities transactions through the indirect holding system. Section 8-501(b) provides that "a person acquires a security entitlement if a securities interme-diary ... indicates by book entry that a financial asset has been credited to the person's securities account." Thus, when Broker Two credits Baker's account for 10,000 shares of ABC stock, Baker acquires a security entitlement to 10,000 shares of ABC stock. That security entitlement is a package of rights against Broker Two and the property held by Broker Two, but the step by which Baker acquired that package of rights and interest is not described by Revised Article 8 as a "transfer" of something from Broker Two to Baker.

Traditionally, one of the principal objectives of the commercial law of investment securities was to assure that the title of a purchaser was secure even though the transaction in which the purchaser acquired its interest may have been wrongful against someone else. Negotiability rules accomplished that objective by providing that a purchaser who took delivery of a security certificate in proper form acquires it free from any adverse claims if the purchaser gave value and acted without notice of any adverse claim. If we think of the task of law revision in this area in terms of finding electronic equivalents for the traditional paper-based negotiable security certificates, the redescription of the property interest of a person whose interest in a security is reflected in electronic records would seem to call for finding an electronic equivalent of negotiability.

Viewed most narrowly, the question would seem to be "Are security entitlements negotiable?" That, however, is not a particularly helpful way of framing the question. The specific rules and concepts associated with negotiability are inextricably entwined with the system in which abstract rights are reified in pieces of paper which are then transferred from person to person. If we shift away from a commercial law analysis of settlement of securities trades based on the concept of a transfer of a discrete thing from person to person, there is no need or occasion to ask the traditional questions posed by negotiability doctrines.

Asking whether a purchaser takes an item of property free from, or subject to, property claims presupposes that the purchaser has the same thing that someone else used to have. Thus, asking whether an electronic representation of a security or other financial right is "negotiable" is a bit like asking whether a car with a flat tire is a lame horseless carriage. There is, to be sure, an important question to be addressed here. But, to continue the metaphor, the question is not whether the horseless carriage needs to be reshod or has to be shot, the question is whether we can keep the vehicle running. So too with the commercial law of the securities settlement system. Rather than asking whether security entitlements are, or could be, "negotiable," we need to ask whether the questions for which negotiability rules were the answer will also arise in an electronic environment, and if so, we need to provide appropriate solutions.

The real question, then, is what legal rules need be established in order to ensure that a person who holds securities through a securities intermediary does not face the risk of losing her position if someone else contends that the transaction which resulted in the person having that position was wrongful. For example, suppose that Able in the example described above had been holding the 10,000 shares of ABC stock as trustee for Claimant, and that Able acted in violation of her obligations as trustee in selling the stock. Could Claimant assert an adverse claim to the 10,000 share position that Baker now holds through the account with Broker Two? The answer might well be no, simply because the item of property that Baker holds is not the "same thing" as the item that Able previously held as trustee for Claimant. There might however, be a plausible argument, via equity tracing rules and constructive trust doctrines, that Claimant's interest followed through the steps in the transaction so that it could be asserted against the property in Baker's hands.

In any event, from the perspective of the design of commercial law rules, a system of rules for securities settlement would obviously be incomplete if it did not deal directly with this problem. Revised Article 8 does just that—it deals directly with the issue. Section 8-502 provides that "An action based on an adverse claim to a financial asset, whether framed in conversion, replevin, constructive trust, equitable lien, or other theory, may not be asserted against a person who acquires a security entitlement under Section 8-501 for value and without notice of the adverse claim." There is no need to ask whether a security entitlement is or is not "negotiable;" nor is there is there any need to answer the metaphysical question whether the security entitlement that Baker has is the "same thing" that Able previously had. All that is necessary it to state the issue directly and provide a clear answer.

Much the same story can be told with respect to the other major concern in the commercial law of securities—providing a simple and certain structure for the creation of security interests in investment securities. The traditional rules concerning security interests in investment securities were based on the common law pledge. A secured party who wished to obtain the fullest measure of protection would take physical possession of the certificate representing the security, with any necessary indorsement. This physical delivery sufficed to give the secured party "possession" of the collateral and thereby establish an effective common law pledge. Moreover the pledgee could qualify as a "bona fide purchaser" who took free from adverse claims and thereby assure priority over any other claimants, including holders of conflicting security interests.

Revised Article 8, and related provisions of Article 9, set out a new structure of rules that deal directly with the requirements for attachment, perfection, and priorities of security interests in investment securities. The new rules are based on the concept of "control." The formal definition of control, set out in section 8-106, is somewhat complex, but the basic point is simple. A secured party obtains control if the secured party has done whatever is necessary, given the way that the security is held, to assure itself that it can have the collateral sold off without further consent or action by the debtor. Thus, as with respect to issues of adverse claim protection, it is neither necessary nor useful to ask what it would mean to obtain "possession" or "constructive possession" of something which by definition is not a physical object capable of possession. Rather, the task is to accomplish the objectives that the old rules accomplished through physical concepts, but do so without reliance on physical concepts.

In one of my earliest essays on the Article 8 revision project, I described the modern indirect holding system in language which at the time struck me a rather clever: "For most, if not all, of the securities held through DTC, physical certificates representing DTC's total position do exist. These 'jumbo certificates,' however, are never delivered from person to person. Rather they are stored in carefully guarded vaults, where they live out their wholly uneventful lives as testaments to the difficulties of adapting legal structures to rapidly changing commercial practices."

When I first learned about this system, the only word I could think of to describe it was "silly." Indeed, during the most enjoyable part of my job as Reporter—going on "field trips" to see how the system worked—I insisted that someone pull out one of these certificates so that I could actually see and touch it, mostly because I couldn't help but feel a bit skeptical about whether there really were any such certificates. But as I reflect upon the phenomenon now, a few years later, I see it somewhat differently. The fact that the certificates in an immobilized securities depository system are essentially irrelevant points to some rather important things about the task of adapting law to technological change. In this setting—and I suspect in many others—the movement from a paper to an electronic environment has not simply been a matter of changing predicates of unchanging legal objects; the significant objects themselves have changed.

In the traditional securities holding system, the key relationship for commercial law was that between the investor and the issuer, and that relationship could be analyzed by application of property concepts to a physical embodiment of the underlying rights. In the modern indirect holding system, it remains just as true that for most purposes the key relationship is that between the investor and the issuer, but for purposes of the commercial law rules concerning the mechanics of settlement the key relationship is that between an investor and its securities intermediary. That relationship is neither represented by any physical or metaphysical object, nor capable of analysis in terms drawn from the property law of physical objects. As the significant legal objects change, so too must the legal language. A car is not really a horseless carriage, and a securities position recorded electronically is not really an electronic certificate.

Selected References

Except in the specific cases noted, references to the Uniform Commercial Code, the "Code" or to "Sections" refer to the 1994 official version of the Uniform Commercial Code.

Further Reading (selected work by James Steven Rogers)

An Overview of the Current Project to Revise U.C.C. Article 8, U.C.C. Bulletin (May 1992).

Negotiability, Property, and Identity, 12 Cardozo Law Review 471 (1990).

The Myth of Negotiability, 31 Boston College Law Review 265 (1990).

The Irrelevance of Negotiable Instruments Concepts in the Law of the Check-Based Payment System. 65 Texas Law Review 929 (1987).

Negotiability as a System of Title Recognition, 48 Ohio State Law Journal 197 (1987).

CHAPTER THIRTY-SIX

COPYRIGHT OPINIONS[*]

[J]udges should be conscious of aesthetics when deciding copyright cases. Intuitively, this proposition ought to be uncontroversial. Copyright exists "[t]o promote the Progress of Science and useful Arts." Judges therefore need an overall understanding of art to make intelligent decisions about this progress. Deciding copyright cases without knowledge of aesthetics seems as implausible as deciding antitrust cases without knowledge of economics.

However, orthodox interpretations of copyright law leave little, if any, room for aesthetics. The reasons for this seem entirely plausible. First, the inherent ambiguity of aesthetics is considered incompatible with the supposedly objective rules and principles that govern judicial opinions. Judges run an unacceptably high risk of being arbitrary or wrong if aesthetic choices influence their decisions. Second, even if judges could make "objectively correct" aesthetic choices, judges should not impose these choices on society because such action suggests government censorship.

Consider how copyright promotes the creation of art. If copyright did not exist, authors might not create for fear of appropriation by others. Copyright overcomes these fears by giving authors limited legal rights to prevent others from copying or borrowing copyrighted material. The possibility of censorship arises because copyright does not protect all works, nor does it prohibit all borrowing from copyrighted works. Thus, when courts interpret the contours of copyrightable subject matter, they single out certain works for a special economic subsidy.

Additionally, since copyright suits are often brought against defendants who have mixed their own creative labor with borrowed material, judges wind up suppressing certain types of future creativity by declaring certain artistic practices infringement. If judges used their aesthetic tastes to make these determinations, they would presumably influence the kinds of art created in the

---

[*] **Alfred C. Yen**, *Copyright Options and Aesthetic Theory*, 71 USC LAW REVIEW 247 (1998), http://papers.ssrn. com/abstract_id=770768.

future. Artists would prefer creating works that meet the aesthetic preference of judges because other works would either not get the benefits of copyright protection or wind up being suppressed. People whose aesthetic sensibilities differ from the aesthetic sensibilities of judges might have difficulty finding or creating art that they prefer.

Because of these concerns, the general irrelevance of aesthetics has become a cornerstone of copyright jurisprudence. Courts implicitly assume a sharp divide between aesthetic reasoning and legal reasoning. Aesthetic reasoning is subjective and indeterminate, while legal reasoning is objective and rigorous. The elimination of aesthetics from copyright therefore serves two related goals. If judges avoid considering aesthetics in copyright cases, aesthetic censorship seems logically impossible. Moreover, judges can now make copyright law appear objective by firmly establishing legal reasoning as the only legitimate basis for deciding copyright cases. This would make it impossible for aesthetics to affect future copyright cases because the objective, rigorous nature of legal reasoning would discipline courts away from the subjectivity of aesthetics. Copyright would become an objective, aesthetically neutral method of promoting all forms of art.

However ... the distinction between aesthetic reasoning and legal reasoning is illusory. To be sure, copyright opinions do not openly adopt specific aesthetic perspectives to justify case outcomes. Judges seem quite conscious of the dangers identified with aesthetic reasoning and therefore use legal reasoning to derive their conclusions. Nevertheless, the analytical premises of copyright opinions are practically identical to those of major aesthetic theories. Copyright law develops as judges change the premises governing interpretation of the law. In fact, those changes often seem necessary because existing precedent embroils the courts in aesthetic controversy. The new premises seemingly eliminate the controversy by directing judicial attention away from the aesthetically troubling determinations existing precedent requires. Unfortunately, these efforts ultimately fail because the move to a new analytical perspective is itself a decision of aesthetic significance. It is simply a matter of time until the unanticipated nuances of future cases draw the courts back into aesthetic controversy.

Th[is] phenomenon leaves copyright in a most peculiar state. Judges do not overrule existing precedent when they adopt new analytical perspectives. Analytically inconsistent cases therefore exist simultaneously as "good law." This means that the precedent which governs new cases may be inconsistent, and that the outcome of a case could depend on the precedent a judge chooses to apply. To the extent that these inconsistencies parallel differences in aesthetic theories, the judicial selection of controlling precedent in a given case effectively becomes a choice among competing aesthetic theories. In short, judges necessarily show a preference for certain aesthetic perspectives when they decide cases because copyright law simply requires aesthetic choices.

The realization that judges necessarily make decisions of aesthetic significance in copyright casts doubt upon the orthodox belief that legal reasoning avoids discrimination among artistic practices. Since no aesthetic perspective can be neutral and all-encompassing, aesthetic bias becomes inherent in copyright decision-making because an aesthetic perspective must necessarily be chosen. An allegedly different method of reasoning such as legal reasoning cannot eliminate the problem of aesthetic bias in copyright. The inevitable aesthetic bias of copyright decision-making can only be controlled if those who exercise bias are aware of it and take affirmative steps to counter it. A truly open-minded copyright jurisprudence therefore requires explicit consciousness of aesthetics....

Some Major Themes from Aesthetics. Aesthetics is a branch of philosophy dedicated to the study of art. [It provides] contrasting answers to two basic aesthetic questions: What is art, and how should art be interpreted? [S]tandard answers to these questions are practically the same as those given by courts when asked to define the existence and scope of copyright protection. Moreover, as in copyright law, the search for clarity and objectivity motivates many of the intellectual changes which have occurred in aesthetics. Aestheticians constantly propose new theories in response to problems with other theories, and evaluate them on the basis of whether they provide clear, unbiased descriptions of art and its interpretation.

What is Art? The question "What is art?" is important because the failure to define art leaves aesthetics completely open-ended. Aestheticians have therefore spilled a fair amount of ink on the subject, but their efforts have not created a uniformly accepted definition of art. However, three contrasting approaches to defining art are particularly relevant....

Formalist Definitions of Art. Clive Bell's *Art* provides a good example of a formalist definition of art. According to Bell, "[a]ll sensitive people agree that there is a peculiar emotion provoked by works of art." The key to defining art is the identification of the peculiar qualities that enable certain objects, but not others, to provoke this "aesthetic emotion." Bell then asserts that "certain unknown and mysterious laws" govern whether humans react aesthetically when they look at an object. Objects that cause aesthetic emotions must have literal formal qualities that conform to these laws. Bell labels these formal qualities "significant form" and claims that "[it] is the one quality common to all works of visual art."

Bell's definition of art implies a disciplined, narrow focus. One identifies a work of art solely by specifying which formal properties provoke an aesthetic reaction. Other things such as the creator's state of mind or things a work depicts are irrelevant....

There are many reasons to find Bell's definition of art persuasive. If nothing else, Bell describes a process for identifying art that roughly parallels the things a layperson might do: Look at the object and identify its aspects that move her aesthetically. Moreover, Bell's emphasis on the object itself means that the lay observer can make informed aesthetic judgments without an expert's knowledge. For example, viewers often know little about an artist when they see a work. If aesthetic judgment depends on knowing an artist's life and thoughts, "uninformed" viewers would frequently be unable to appreciate a work properly.

However, many aestheticians believe that formalists like Bell err in emphasizing significant form to the exclusion of everything else. This mistake renders formalist definitions of art both over- and underinclusive....

Intentionalist Definitions of Art. Monroe C. Beardsley's *An Aesthetic Definition of Art* offers a good example of an intentionalist definition of art. In contrast to Bell, Beardsley does not believe that "certain unknown and mysterious laws" naturally provide the distinction between art and other objects. Instead, Beardsley considers art one of many cultural activities in which people participate. The cultural genesis of art means that the laws hypothesized by Bell cannot control whether a given activity is artistic. Activity becomes artistic only if those who participate in it perceive it that way.... Beardsley therefore adopts the following definition of art: "An artwork is something produced with the intention of giving it the capacity to satisfy the aesthetic interest."

Beardsley's emphasis on intent implies a focus that is as narrow as Bell's. Even if a person creates an extremely aesthetic work, it is not art unless she had the state of mind required by Beardsley during creation. Accidents, no matter how beautiful, cannot be art. "Paint may be spilled and pottery cracked unintentionally, and the pattern of paint or of the cracks may be capable of satisfying the aesthetic interest; but that alone does not make an artwork." Although some might find this result unduly restrictive, Beardsley apparently believed that his narrow focus was precisely what made his definition valuable....

Institutional Definitions of Art. George Dickie's *Art and the Aesthetic: An Institutional Analysis* ... represent[s] a clear reaction to the problems associated with formalist and intentionalist definitions of art. He recognizes the difficulties aestheticians have faced when defining art, but rejects the growing sense that art cannot be defined.... Dickie considers formal properties and the creator's intent unimportant when deciding if an object is art. He turns instead to an examination of "what we do with certain objects." Borrowing from a seminal article by Arthur Danto, Dickie proclaims the existence of the "artworld": "the broad social institution in which works of art have their place." This artworld is comprised of artists and viewers who participate in a traditional social practice of creating, presenting, and appreciating art.

Dickie then defines art as: "(1) an artifact (2) a set of the aspects of which has had conferred upon it the status of candidate for appreciation by some person or persons acting on behalf of a certain social institution (the artworld)." This means that objects become art when someone who believes that he is a member of the artworld invites others to view the object aesthetically. If a museum displays something, Dickie would consider it art. Indeed, artists may confer the necessary status on their own works.

Formalism, intentionalism, and institutionalism all provide plausible approaches to defining art, but each theory has significant weaknesses that the others address. Formalism parallels the way many laypersons might identify art, but it has difficulty explaining trends in modern art and fakes. Intentionalism does a better job of handling fakes, but it still has trouble with some aspects of modern art. Institutionalism has no trouble with modern art, but its definition of art is so broad that it loses the discriminating sensitivity that formalism and intentionalism provide. This overlapping pattern of strengths and weakness practically guarantees that none of these theories will emerge as the comprehensive, authoritative definition of art....

How Should a Work Be Interpreted? The definition of art represents only the first step in aesthetic inquiry. Once a work of art has been identified, how should it be appreciated? How should its meaning be fixed? For some people, this question may seem a bit absurd because they think that viewers should appreciate art in whatever way they want. Lay expressions for this attitude might include "beauty is in the eye of the beholder" or "different strokes for different folks." Many aestheticians, however, take a different view. For them, it is important to identify correct interpretations of works because failure to do so may bring about chaos....

Formalist Theories of Interpretation. Formalist theories of interpretation have assumptions similar to formalist definitions of art. Meaning exists entirely in the work itself. A work has a single, objective meaning and "correct" statements about art can therefore be made. Like formalist definitions of art, formalist theories of interpretation bear a rough resemblance to the interpretive approach that many laypersons might take. The work causes ideas, thoughts, and feelings to arise in the viewer's mind. Object-oriented theorists, however, take this approach one step further by holding that the viewer ought to bring nothing to the interpretation of art. Knowledge of the author's intention, history, or personal experience is not only irrelevant, it is positively harmful to an objective understanding of the work....

Formalism superficially solves the problem of subjectivity in interpretation. If meaning is contained in an object or text, then the viewer or reader simply discovers meaning. Interpretation becomes an objective empirical inquiry devoid of personal views. Of course, sophisticated viewers of art know that the search for meaning seldom works out this way. To take a crude example used by William Tolhurst, consider the sentence "Nixon is the best President since Lincoln." Is this a serious statement of fact, or is it a humorous statement? According to critics of formalism, problems like this demonstrate that texts do not have meanings that can be discovered by formalist methods, and that other interpretive theories are better.

Intentionalist Theories of Interpretation. The most obvious "solution" to the problems of formalism is intentionalism. If one does not know the meaning of "Nixon is the best President since Lincoln," it makes sense to ask what the person who made the statement intended. Intentionalists contend that this method of interpretation is correct for two reasons. First, art is the product of deliberate behavior, so it must be understood that way.... Second, reference to a creator's intention realizes the formalist dream of making interpretation objective because the creator's state of mind is a real thing that can be discovered, at least in theory.

Intentionalism is certainly a valuable interpretive strategy. However, it is not as comprehensive or objective as its proponents claim. First, as formalists have been quick to point out, meaning and intention are not always linked. Texts sometimes have unintended meanings. All meanings of "Nixon is the best President since Lincoln" are worth studying, even if unintended. Even typographical errors can have meaning. Furthermore, how can intentionalists explain the fact that words themselves apparently change meaning over time? Second, even if one concedes that intention is worth considering, evidence of an author's intention is often missing or unclear. In those situations, personal biases again creep into the process of interpretation.

Copyright Opinions and Aesthetic Theory.... Judges apparently recognize that copyright adjudication can easily slip into the subjectivity of aesthetic taste, and the opinions considered here appear to interpret copyright law so that courts can make objective legal determinations instead of subjective aesthetic ones. However, familiarity with aesthetic theory leads to the conclusion that these legal interpretations amount to the judicial adoption of formalist, intentionalist [or] institutionalist ... aesthetic theories.

Originality. Originality provides the basic definition of copyrightable subject matter.... One of the first major cases to address the issue of originality was *Burrow-Giles Lithographic Company v. Sarony*…. Sarony claimed copyright in a photograph entitled "Oscar Wilde No. 18." The defendant Burrow-Giles, which had made 85,000 copies of the photograph for sale, defended by arguing that Congress did not have the power to protect photographs under copyright…. The Supreme Court unanimously … held that the photograph was copyrightable….

[T]he findings on which the Court relied establish two different perspectives from which to analyze originality. First, calling the photograph "useful, new, harmonious, characteristic and graceful" is basically an elaborate statement of the work's beauty. This implies that originality depends on whether the work's intrinsic form has aesthetic merit. Second, the Court's reference to the plaintiff's selection and arrangement of the photograph's features implies that originality depends on the operation of a putative author's mind, and not the features of the work itself. However, this interpretation of originality is not the only one that courts have adopted.

In *Bleistein v. Donaldson Lithographing Co.*, the Supreme Court moved away from the interpretation of originality laid down in *Sarony*. At issue was the plaintiff Bleistein's claim to copyright in three chromolithographs that he had prepared to advertise a circus. Each chromolithograph depicted scenes and people from the circus. Bleistein argued that the defendant Donaldson had infringed copyright in the chromolithographs by making reduced size reproductions. Donaldson argued that the chromolithographs were not copyrightable….

… The Court dealt with the possibility that the works were uncopyrightable because they lacked aesthetic merit or were not "connected with the fine arts." The Court found that Bleistein's works contained sufficient merit to meet any statutory or constitutional restrictions on copyrightable subject matter. With respect to [the statutory requirement] that works be "connected with the fine arts," the Court reached its conclusion by defining "fine arts" in a somewhat surprising way. Instead of analyzing Bleistein's works to show their connection to fine art, Justice Holmes simply defined the problem away, stating that "[t]he antithesis to "illustrations or works connected with the fine arts' is not works of little merit or of humble degree, or illustrations addressed to the less educated classes; it is "prints or labels designed to be used for any other articles of manufacture.'" …

In *Sarony*, the Court found aesthetic merit in the plaintiff's photograph by evaluating its physical form and deeming it "useful, new, harmonious, characteristic, and graceful." This implied that future courts would have to make similar evaluations of new works if controversy over copyrightability should arise. However, the prospect of such an analysis made Justice Holmes uneasy.

He therefore changed the test for aesthetic merit from an evaluation of a work's formal properties to a practically tautological observation about public reaction to a work....

... To the extent that *Sarony* left open the possibility that "ordinary photographs" might not be copyrightable, *Bleistein* clearly stated the Supreme Court's view that copyright protected even humble art. Originality is therefore an easily met standard that is not a serious bar to copyright for most works. However, the fact that originality is a low standard does not necessarily make it any easier to identify the few works which still do not meet the test. For example, Holmes stated that "personal reactions upon nature" are copyrightable when embodied in a work. Those reactions would ordinarily be conscious and therefore purposely included in an author's work. However, in some cases a reaction might be unconscious. If that unconscious reaction found its way into a work, would it also be copyrightable?

The Second Circuit answered this question affirmatively in *Alfred Bell & Co. v. Catalda Fine Arts, Inc.* In that case, the plaintiff claimed copyright in reproductions of public domain paintings. The reproductions were made by hand-engraving the image of the public domain work onto a plate which was then used to print out the reproductions. The defendant claimed that these reproductions could not support copyright because they were copies of other works, and hence not original. This assertion made a fair amount of sense because the plaintiff was trying to reproduce already existing works. How then could there be the sort of purposeful selection and arrangement of shapes and objects that supported copyright in *Sarony* and *Bleistein*?

... If it had wanted to, the *Catalda* court could have decided in the plaintiff's favor while following the *Bleistein* analysis. When a conventional artist tries to paint an entirely faithful representation of a tree, that depiction surely receives copyright protection. In *Catalda*, the engraver was simply trying to faithfully represent an existing painting. If, as *Bleistein* suggests, the personal reaction inherent in depicting an existing object supports copyright, it should not matter whether the object depicted is natural or man-made. In either case, the mental process of creating the work would be the same. Copyright would therefore protect both the painting of a tree and the engravings of *Catalda*.

The problem, of course, is that many people distinguish "copying" a tree from copying an existing painting. The former is generally considered "real art" while the latter carries a stigma related to plagiarism. Accordingly, the *Catalda* court could not use the *Bleistein* analysis to support the plaintiff without entering a controversy about what it means to create a work of art—the very sort of aesthetic determination that *Bleistein* admonished courts to avoid. It therefore made sense for the Second Circuit to fashion a less obviously controversial analysis to support its conclusion. The court did this by ignoring the intent of the alleged author in favor of the physical form of the plaintiff's work. According to the Second Circuit, copyright existed simply because the plaintiff's works were physically distinguishable from other works. To the extent that *Sarony* and *Bleistein* required human intent to support copyright, *Catalda* reduced that requirement to one of mere human agency....

... *Sarony*, *Bleistein*, and *Catalda* ... illustrate how subtle changes in legal interpretation initially appear to keep aesthetics out of copyright law.... *Sarony* based originality on ... the physical form of the plaintiff's photograph [having] aesthetic merit [and that] plaintiff created the work by purposefully selecting and arranging the objects and shapes represented in the photograph. By contrast, *Bleistein* rested originality almost entirely on the fact that the plaintiff created the work. To be sure, *Bleistein* did address the issue of aesthetic merit. However, *Bleistein* abandoned any effort to follow *Sarony's* aesthetic evaluation of the formal properties of the plaintiff's work because Holmes considered it inappropriate for judges to make aesthetic determinations. Instead, *Bleistein* analyzed the way that others, including the defendant, reacted to the plaintiff's work. If others found the work meritorious, the Court would simply agree.

Like *Bleistein*, *Catalda* also reinterpreted the originality standard to keep ambiguous, controversial, and ultimately aesthetic judgments out of copyright. *Catalda's* emphasis on the form of a work avoided problematic assertions about whether judgments made by the plaintiff's engravers were equivalent to those of someone painting a tree. Indeed, the distinguishable variation standard itself appears to make originality an easy issue to analyze. If a court can identify a variation between the plaintiff's work and any others, a distinguishable variation must exist. No qualitative assessment about the aesthetic significance of the variation is necessary.

Of course, familiarity with aesthetic theory shows that neither *Bleistein* nor *Catalda* actually kept aesthetic issues out of copyright. Instead, courts resolved each of the cases analyzed here by adopting interpretations of copyright that correspond to major aesthetic theories about the definition of art. *Sarony's* emphasis on the "useful, new, harmonious, characteristic and graceful" nature of the photograph is simply a formalist interpretation of originality, and its attention to the photographer's purposeful selection and arrangement is intentionalist.

In *Bleistein*, the Court considered the plaintiff's circus posters copyrightable, but *Sarony* arguably supported the opposite result because the posters were aesthetically pedestrian reproductions of circus scenes. If the Court decided for the plaintiff, it might appear as if the Court were imposing its own aesthetic tastes on the case. The Court avoided this problem by avoiding formalist aesthetics in favor of intentionalism and institutionalism. The Court declared aesthetic evaluation of the work's form irrelevant, and instead relied primarily on analysis of the creator's behavior. To the extent that copyright still required a showing of aesthetic merit, the Court adopted an institutionalist stance, stating that the public's appetite for the plaintiff's works was sufficient.

The effort to avoid aesthetic controversy took a somewhat different turn in *Catalda*. In that case, the Second Circuit believed that copyright protected the plaintiff's reproductions of public domain paintings. However, the court would have had great difficulty supporting its conclusion with a *Bleistein* or *Sarony* type analysis of the creator's behavior because the plaintiff's works were made for the express purpose of faithfully reproducing already existing paintings. This made it difficult for the court to conclude that the engraver had either engaged in creative selection and arrangement or expressed personal reactions upon nature. The Second Circuit solved this problem by directing its analysis away from the creator's mental processes to the very thing that *Bleistein* ignored—the form of the work. In fact, the Second Circuit concentrated on the same things as formalists do when they confront forgeries of great works—the minute differences between the authentic work and the reproduction. This emphasis allowed the court to find "distinguishable variations" between the plaintiff's reproductions and the originals, differences that the court considered significant because of copyright's low standard of originality....

Conclusion. [J]udicial application of legal reasoning has not kept aesthetic determinations out of copyright law. Leading cases adopt analytical perspectives that are equivalent to major branches of aesthetic theory. In fact, the very effort to avoid aesthetics has led courts to adopt these varying perspectives because the facts of individual cases often make one analytical perspective seem more or less subjective and aesthetically controversial than others. To those not familiar with aesthetic theory, it looks as if copyright is being refined through the process of legal reasoning. Courts seemingly recognize the pitfalls of aesthetic reasoning, and then adopt legal interpretations of copyright designed to avoid those pitfalls. However, familiarity with aesthetic theory shows that courts are essentially swapping one set of aesthetic premises for others in response to the facts of particular cases. Copyright opinions therefore amount to the judicial declaration of preference for one aesthetic perspective over others. Indeed, copyright opinions rendered today necessarily require the judicial declaration of such preference.

Consider how the cases considered above affect copyright law. In one sense, each case ostensibly clarifies copyright by installing a particular set of analytical perspectives as the latest interpretation of the law. However, none of these cases actually overrules prior inconsistent precedent. In fact, many of the opinions do not even hint at inconsistency with prior precedent. When courts look for guidance in new cases, they will find analytically inconsistent cases that are still good law. Selecting precedent to govern new cases therefore requires a judge to choose one set of premises over others. Courts have to declare their preference of aesthetic perspective when they decide copyright cases. This raises interesting questions about the state of copyright jurisprudence and the fair treatment of varying artistic practices.

[A]esthetics are supposed to be largely irrelevant to copyright for two reasons. First, aesthetic determinations are inherently subjective. Second, even if judges could make aesthetic determinations objectively, it would still be bad public policy for them to do so because official pronouncements about aesthetic matters run perilously close to censorship. However, if judges necessarily declare their aesthetic preferences when deciding copyright cases, objectivity or neutrality in copyright decision-making cannot be achieved because the crucial distinction between aesthetic reasoning and legal reasoning has collapsed.

One possible response to this challenge might be the creation of new doctrines that have nothing to do with aesthetics. However, such efforts make little sense because the aesthetic premises in question are so deeply ingrained in our culture that we cannot help but think about art in these ways. New copyright doctrines and concepts would almost certainly reincorporate aesthetics into copyright law. Even if successful, these efforts would prove undesirable because copyright doctrines that differ greatly from cultural intuitions about art will be unintelligible to artists, audiences, judges, or juries. Imagine the chaos that would ensue if the existence of copyright or its scope of protection depended on thoughts that no serious observer of art had ever entertained.

Another possible response would be a reduction in the number of aesthetic choices judges make. For example, the Supreme Court could explicitly consider all of the existing interpretations of originality, the useful article doctrine, or substantial similarity and eliminate the ones that result in analytic confusion. Future courts would not have to choose among aesthetic theories because binding precedent would control. This might sound appealing, but it would actually defeat the very purpose for avoiding aesthetic determinations in the first place, namely, the accommodation and promotion of diverse philosophies about art.

The declaration of binding precedent would reduce aesthetic diversity because it implies the adoption of a single set of aesthetic perspectives. If courts always use the same aesthetic premises, then there really would be an officially sponsored and enforced authoritative perspective on art. By contrast, if copyright law is left in its presently ambiguous state, different judges will continue to make different aesthetic choices in different cases. Uniformity and objectivity in copyright law might suffer, but diversity in legal thinking about art would be preserved. It is better for many small subjective decisions to be made than for a few extremely significant ones to control the outcome of all future cases.

If this is the case, however, what is to become of the principle of aesthetic neutrality? Are we truly subject to copyright law that simply imposes numerous acts of judicial fiat? At a certain level, the answer is yes. Judges have and will continue to have the power and ability to decide copyright cases on the basis of their personal aesthetic sensibilities.

At another level, however, judges can take steps that will diminish (but not eliminate) the importance of their personal aesthetic biases. A judge must realize that he is not an objective, disinterested observer of the works under consideration. His initial intuitions inevitably come from the peculiar set of circumstances that make up his life. These intuitions may fortuitously be "ordinary" or similar to those held by other people. However, a judge must realize that this fortuity does not make, and cannot make, his intuitions correct in the strongest sense of the word. At best, his intuitions can be correct in a culturally relative way. In short, a judge must know that his intuition which "seems right" probably stands on highly contestable intellectual premises. Reflexive rejection of other possibilities represents the very sort of subjective censorship that Holmes warned against.

A judge who is conscious of this problem can guard against it by being particularly open-minded to alternate aesthetic sensibilities. For example, a dedicated formalist should listen particularly carefully to arguments based in intentionalism.... Traditionally oriented judges should listen carefully to avant-garde arguments. By doing this, a judge will gain perspective on works that she would never have realized by simply rejecting alternate interpretations as "mistaken" or "wrong." In some cases, these alternate arguments will convince the judge to change her mind and decide a case differently than she initially had thought she might. In other cases, the alternate arguments will prove unpersuasive and the judge's initial intuition will stand. The net result is that courts will wind up embracing a broader set of aesthetic conventions by openly thinking about aesthetics than they would by simply applying doctrine that embodies existing dogma.

Of course, some may complain that the solution to aesthetic bias proposed here is in fact no solution at all. In each case, a judge eventually makes a subjective decision about which argument she finds more persuasive. Judicial subjectivity and aesthetic bias remain completely unconstrained. These critics have a point. The solution proposed here expects and permits a large degree of subjective judicial decision-making. However, if this … analysis is correct, that objection must be considered a weak one because aesthetically subjective decision-making is the only possible approach in copyright cases. The point here is not to eliminate aesthetic subjectivity. Rather, the goal is to manage it so that subjectivity is exercised under relatively desirable conditions. The proposal simply states that it is better for judges to make subjective decisions about the persuasiveness of competing arguments when they consciously recognize their aesthetic biases and therefore take opposing arguments a bit more seriously than they otherwise might.

Whether we like it or not, the existence of copyright makes subjective judicial pronouncements of aesthetic taste necessary. It will therefore always be possible that copyright selectively chokes off certain types of artistic expression because they do not conform to culturally popular aesthetic sensibilities. Nothing we do can ensure that all forms of art flourish or even survive under copyright. The challenge, then, is to decide how to make sure that as many types of art flourish as is possible. Hopefully, this Article's suggestions represent a step in that direction. Our culture and the judges who live in it will always have biases. However, as long as all concerned remain open-minded, anything remains possible, and that is precisely what our society should desire in art.

Selected References

Keith Aoki, Contradiction and Context in American Copyright Law, 9 Cardozo Arts & Entertainment Law Journal 303 (1991).

Monroe C. Beardsley, An Aesthetic Definition of Art, in What is Art? (Hugh Cutler ed., 1983).

Clive Bell, Art (1958).

Noel Carroll, Anglo-American Aesthetics and Contemporary Criticism: Intention and the Hermeneutics of Suspicion, 51 Journal of Aesthetics & Art Criticism 245 (1993).

Amy B. Cohen, Copyright Law and the Myth of Objectivity: The Idea-Expression Dichotomy and the Inevitability of Artistic Value Judgments, 66 Indiana Law Journal 175 (1990).

R.G. Collingwood, Principles of Art (1938).

Rosemary J. Coombe, Objects of Property and Subjects of Politics: Intellectual Property Laws and Democratic Dialogue, 69 Texas Law Review 1853 (1991).

Arthur C. Danto, The Artworld, 61 Journal of Philosophy 571 (1964).

Arthur C. Danto, Artwork and Real Things, 39 Theoria 1 (1973).

John Dewey, Art as Experience (1934).

George Dickie, Art and the Aesthetic: An Institutional Analysis (1974).

Marcia Mueder Eaton, Basic Issues in Aesthetics (1988).

Owen M. Fiss, Objectivity and Interpretation, 34 Stanford Law Review 739 (1982).
Nelson Goodman, Languages of Art: An Approach to a Theory of Symbols (2d ed. 1976)
Horst Waldemar Janson, History of Art (2d ed. 1977).
W.E. Kennick, Art and Philosophy (2d ed. 1979).
Harold Rosenberg, The De-definition of Art: Action Art to Pop to Earthworks (1972).
Pierre Schlag, The Problem of the Subject, 69 Texas Law Review 1627 (1991).

Cases

Alfred Bell & Co. v. Catalda Fine Arts, Inc., 191 F.2d 99 (2d Cir. 1951).
Bleistein v. Donaldson Lithographing Co., 188 U.S. 239 (1903).
Burrow-Giles Lithographic Co. v Sarony, 111 U.S. 53 (1884).

Further Reading (selected work by Alfred C. Yen)

What Federal Gun Control Can Teach Us About the DMCA's Anti-Trafficking Provi-
sions, 2003 Wisconsin Law Review 649.
Western Frontier or Feudal Society? Metaphors and Perceptions of Cyberspace, 17
Berkeley Technology Law Journal 1207 (2002).
A Personal Injury Law Perspective on Copyright in an Internet Age, 52 Hastings Law
Journal 929 (2001).
Internet Service Provider Liability for Subscriber Copyright Infringement, Enterprise
Liability, and the First Amendment, 88 Georgetown Law Journal 1833 (2000).
The Legacy of *Feist*: The Consequences of a Weak Connection Between Copyright and
the Economics of Public Goods, 52 Ohio State Law Journal 1343 (1991).
Restoring the Natural Law: Copyright as Labor and Possession, 51 Ohio State Law
Journal 517 (1990).

CHAPTER THIRTY-SEVEN

COPYRIGHT AND TIME*

This Article makes a very specific and concrete proposal: it argues that courts should adjust the scope of copyright protection to account for the passage of time by expressly considering time as a factor in fair use analysis. More specifically, this Article argues that the older a copyrighted work is, the greater the scope of fair use should be—that is, the greater the ability of others to reuse, critique, transform, and adapt the copyrighted work without permission of the copyright owner. Conversely, the newer the work, the narrower the scope of fair use. Or, even more concretely, this Article argues that fair use should be greater for Mickey Mouse than for *Harry Potter*.

Up to now, most of the debate over the role of time in copyright law has focused on copyright duration and the controversial issue of copyright term extension. Since passage of the first Copyright Act in 1790, Congress has dramatically extended the copyright term from an original maximum term of twenty-eight years to the current term of seventy years after the death of the author. Congress's most recent extension of the term in 1998 touched off a fierce debate over both the propriety and constitutionality of this extension. Those supporting the extension have argued, *inter alia*, that a longer term encourages creative activity, that it is necessary to provide incentives to preserve copyrighted works in the digital age, and that it is necessary to harmonize our copyright laws with those of other countries. Those opposing the extension have argued that it effectively provides no additional incentive for creative activity, that it harms the public by depriving it of free access to works, and that it may well be unconstitutional.

By focusing so narrowly on the end of the copyright term, however, this debate has neglected the significant issue of how time should affect the scope of copyright protection during the copyright term. That is, whether or not the most recent extension is justified or constitutional, the fact remains that

---

* **Joseph P. Liu**, *Copyright and Time: A Proposal*, 101 MICHIGAN LAW REVIEW 409 (2002), http://papers.ssrn.com/abstract_id=305374.

the copyright term is extremely long. Until now, courts and commentators have generally assumed that the scope of protection during this long term is constant or unaffected, at least directly, by the passage of time. Perhaps this assumption made sense when the copyright term was a short twenty-eight years, but does it still hold when the term of protection can span an entire century? Are the policies and justifications underlying copyright law really unaltered by the passage of time? What implications might there be for the appropriate scope of copyright protection? Up to now, these questions have been left largely unaddressed.

[E]xtremely strong justifications exist for considering time expressly in setting the scope of copyright protection, and that fair use provides an ideal vehicle, both doctrinally and theoretically, for such consideration. Indeed, an examination of the theoretical justifications underlying copyright law reveals that the strength and impact of these justifications are quite directly affected by the passage of time. [O]ver the course of the copyright term, the impact of protection on copyright incentives wanes, as does an author's moral claim to the fruits of his or her labor. At the same time, the societal interest in ensuring widespread access to works and in encouraging re-use and adaptation of copyrighted works increases. By considering time in fair use analysis, courts can adjust the scope of copyright protection to respond more dynamically to these changes in copyright interests over the length of the copyright term.

Furthermore, such a result could be achieved quite easily within existing copyright case law. Unlike constitutional challenges to term extension, this result would not require courts to stretch the doctrine or strike down any statutes. Indeed, existing doctrine provides ample support for consideration of time as a factor in fair use analysis. The Copyright Act and its legislative history expressly authorize courts to consider additional factors in fair use analysis, and courts have used this authorization to consider a wide range of additional factors not expressly mentioned in the statute. Given the strong theoretical arguments for considering time, courts should feel quite comfortable incorporating this inquiry into fair use analysis. Consideration of time would thus be a modest doctrinal change that could have significant benefits.

Finally, the proposal advanced in this Article would provide courts with a legitimate way to inject much-needed public-regarding values into the scope of copyright protection. One of the concerns underlying the debate over copyright term extension is the extent to which this extension, like all prior extensions, resulted from a structural imbalance in lobbying power. While the benefits of term extension accrue to a few, highly-focused and well-organized interests, the costs of extension, though significant in the aggregate, are more widely distributed among the population at large. Term extensions are thus

COPYRIGHT AND TIME   447

difficult to oppose, as public choice theory predicts. Indeed, this imbalance has been reflected not only in the struggle over term extension, but also in other Congressional expansions of copyright protection. For those concerned about this structural imbalance, this Article provides a mechanism for courts to legitimately incorporate public-regarding values into the scope of copyright protection. Even for those who are not concerned, however, the general policy justifications underlying copyright law provide strong support for this proposal....

The Proposal in Context: The Debate over Term Extension. For the next sixteen years, not a single published, copyrighted work in the United States will pass into the public domain. That is, from now until December 31, 2018, not one published, copyrighted work will have its term of copyright protection expire. This is because Congress passed the Sonny Bono Copyright Term Extension Act in 1998, extending the term of copyright protection by an additional twenty years. For works authored by individuals, the term now extends until seventy years after the death of the author; for works "authored" by corporate entities, the term is now ninety-five years from the date of publication or 120 years after creation, whichever expires first. Not only does this apply to future works, but Congress also made this extension retroactive, applying it to all existing works still under copyright protection at the time the extension went into effect. As a result of this retroactive extension, no published works will pass into the public domain for twenty years after the Act went into effect.

The impact of this extension on copyright markets is significant. Until passage of the extension, copyrighted works had been passing into the public domain at a steady pace. In 1998, for example, T.S. Eliot's *The Waste Land*, James Joyce's *Ulysses*, and the movie *Blood and Sand* with Rudolph Valentino all passed into the public domain. In 1996 and 1997, F. Scott Fitzgerald's *This Side of Paradise*, D.H. Lawrence's *Women in Love*, Edith Wharton's *The Age of Innocence*, and the song *Over There* by George M. Cohan all passed into the public domain. What this meant was that these works could now be freely copied, distributed, and built upon by others. So if you wanted to print and sell copies of *The Waste Land*, you could freely do so without seeking a license from, or paying a royalty to, the copyright owner. Similarly, if you wanted to write and sell your own sequel of *This Side of Paradise*, or make a movie out of *The Age of Innocence*, you could do so. All of these uses were now freely permitted once the term of copyright protection ended.

The fact that these works passed into the public domain was no accident. Rather, it was an essential part of the design of copyright law. The basic idea behind copyright law is that an author gets a certain number of years during which he or she can prevent unauthorized copying and distribution of the creative work. This exclusive period permits the copyright owner to exploit the work and obtain a return for his or her creative labor, thus providing an incentive to engage in the labor in the first place. This period of exclusive control is limited, however. The Constitution expressly authorizes copyright protection only for "limited Times," and the Copyright Act places precisely such a limit on the duration of copyright. The idea behind the limited grant is that, after an author has been sufficiently compensated for his or her creative labor, the work should pass into the public domain so that all of society can use it freely, so that it can be disseminated more broadly, and so that its expressive elements can be appropriated and built upon. This reflects the balance struck by copyright law between providing incentives for creation and promoting wide dissemination of the fruits of this creation....

... Congress passed the term extension, despite the fact that the substantive policy arguments supporting term extension were not terribly compelling. Although prospective extension of the term could theoretically provide some minimal degree of additional incentive for creative activity, in practice, the added incentive is trivial. Moreover, retroactive extension can find no reasonable incentive-based justification. And the alternative justifications proffered by Congress, though facially plausible, were extremely weak, particularly in light of the costs imposed by the extension. Indeed, the weakness of the arguments in support of term extension is reflected in the fact that the extension was opposed by an unusually wide array of copyright scholars, including many who normally favor broader protection.

Given the lack of strong policy support for term extension, Congress's passage of the Bono Act can ultimately best be understood as resulting, in large part, from the lobbying efforts of the copyright industries (for example, film, music, publishing, software) which had much to gain from an extension, particularly a retroactive one. Companies, such as Disney, with valuable copyrights that were slated to expire within the next twenty years lobbied aggressively for the extension. These companies had much to gain from retroactive extension of their copyrights, since extension permitted them to protect and exploit their copyrights for an additional twenty years. At the same time, the public interest groups and commentators who opposed the extension had no similar lobbying power. And certainly the public at large was not sufficiently exercised about a topic as abstract as copyright term extension to exert any meaningful pressure on Congress to resist industry calls for extension. Thus it is perhaps not surprising that the extension was passed, despite the lack of strong policy justifications in its support.

Initial Responses to Term Extension. Concerned about the negative effects of copyright term extension and Congress's apparent inability to resist calls for expansion from the copyright industries, opponents of term extension turned to constitutional challenges.... Some commentators have argued that recent Congressional expansions, particularly the retroactive extension of the copyright term, violate internal limits imposed by the Constitution's intellectual property clause. Others have argued that such expansions may violate external limits imposed by the First Amendment. In all, a generous amount of scholarship has been produced analyzing the term extension, much of it concluding that the extension, at least the retroactive aspect of it, is constitutionally problematic.

There are limits, however, on the extent to which constitutional arguments can effectively address the many issues raised by term extension and the long period of copyright protection more generally. True, some of these constitutional arguments are reasonably strong. [But apart from the constitutional issues,] many of the effects of a lengthy term will still be felt whether or not future extensions are permitted. Direct attacks on term extension have little to say about what impact the existing length of the term should have on the scope of copyright protection more generally. That is, by focusing so narrowly on the end of the copyright term, these constitutional arguments do not address the broader question of how the passage of time might affect copyright interests during the lengthy existing copyright term. A constitutional challenge is thus a rather blunt, though important, tool for addressing concerns about the length of copyright protection.

The Proposal—An Overview.... The proposal is simple: in deciding whether a given use of a copyrighted work is fair use, courts should take into account how much time has passed since the work was created. The more recent the work, all other things being equal, the narrower the scope of fair use; the older the work, the greater the scope of fair use. So, for example, a book written seventy years ago should be subject to a greater degree of fair use than a book written yesterday. The ability to make sequels, to copy portions of the work, to comment upon it, to transform and re-work it, should be greater than the similar ability to make fair use of a book written only two years ago.

Courts would implement this proposal rather straightforwardly under existing copyright doctrine. The fair use defense in copyright law is a flexible defense, designed to ensure that the entitlements granted to authors not inadvertently hinder copyright's overall purpose of encouraging widespread dissemination of creative works. The defense privileges certain uses of copyrighted works for purposes of comment, criticism, education, research, and news reporting, even if such uses would otherwise be technically infringing. In assessing whether a use is fair, courts consider four statutory factors: the purpose and character of the use, the nature of the copyrighted work, the amount of the original work used, and the effect of the use upon the potential market for the work.

Under the proposal…, courts would simply consider time as an additional factor in fair use analysis. Although the copyright act lists only four factors, the text of the statute and its legislative history clearly indicate that these factors are not meant to be exclusive. Instead, courts are meant to apply fair use in a flexible manner, and indeed courts have considered many additional factors in deciding fair use cases. Consideration of time as an additional factor would thus fit rather easily within existing doctrine. For older works, this additional factor would weigh in favor of fair use, while for younger works this factor would weigh against fair use. There would thus be more "breathing space" for others to use, copy, transform, and comment upon older works….

Theoretical Arguments: Incentives and Access. The primary policy justification for copyright protection in the United States is the incentive justification. The familiar argument goes like this: copyright protection is necessary to provide adequate incentives for authors to engage in creative activity. Without such protection, others could easily copy and distribute an author's works, quickly driving the price of the work down to the marginal cost of producing an additional copy. Authors would thus be unable to recoup the costs of their original creative labor. As a result, authors would not choose to engage in such labor in the first place, and creative works would not be produced in adequate numbers. Copyright law solves this problem by providing incentives to engage in creative labor, thereby harnessing the economic self-interest of authors to the benefit of society at large.

At first blush, the incentive argument would appear to justify further extension of the copyright term. After all, if some incentive is good, why isn't more incentive even better? The familiar answer is that protection comes at a cost. Copyright law provides incentives to authors, but only by enabling authors to restrict dissemination of the work. In economic terms, copyright law permits an author to raise the price of the work above the marginal cost of producing an additional copy. This provides an incentive to the author, but it also means that those who would have purchased the copy at or above the marginal cost but below the higher price cannot get access to the work. Copyright law thus presents a trade-off. Roughly speaking, depending on the strength of the protection, we can have more works with more restricted access, or fewer works with broader access.

Copyright law also presents another trade-off, this one not between authors and consumers, but between authors and other authors. It is a commonplace that new works draw from and build upon old ones. No work is purely and completely new. All works draw upon prior works, to at least some extent.

Thus, by increasing protection for initial works, we may increase the incentives for producing such works, but we also increase the cost of producing works that draw upon these initial works. If protection is too great, we may in fact decrease the number of total works (that is, the sum of both original and follow-on works). If our aim is to provide adequate incentives for both initial and follow-on works, the strength of copyright protection needs to reflect this balance.

The length of the copyright term is one way (among many ways) in which this balance is struck. Too short a term, and the incentives may not be sufficient to spur initial creation, since authors may not have enough time to obtain sufficient compensation for their efforts. Too long a term, and the work may not be widely disseminated or built upon over time. The optimal or ideal copyright term is probably impossible to determine in any meaningful way. Indeed, the academic literature on this point has provided no firm guidance. Different types of works may require different lengths of protection (for example, protecting software for ten years would probably be sufficient, at least under today's market conditions, given how quickly software becomes obsolete). Even within a given category of work, much might depend on how the market is structured at that particular time, what other incentives exist, etc. Thus, a high degree of uncertainty will inevitably attend discussions about the proper term. The precise number chosen will always be, to some extent, arbitrary. Thus Congress should properly be given some degree of discretion in setting the term.

Even conceding a good degree of Congressional discretion, however, there are good reasons to believe that the current period is too long, i.e. that it substantially hinders access without a corresponding benefit in incentives. Under an incentive justification, the reason for the copyright extension is that it will increase the incentives for the creation of new works. As a matter of simple economics, however, additional increases in the copyright term result in ever-decreasing amounts of additional incentive. For the vast majority of works, there will be little demand more than fifty years after the death of the author. Even for those few works that still retain some market value, the present value of any future income streams will be miniscule. This is because of the simple economic phenomenon of the time value of money.

To see this, take the following example. Assume, for simplicity's sake, that an author creates a work in 2000 at age forty and dies in the year 2030 at age seventy. The term of protection under the 1976 Act would have been until the year 2080. Under the term extension, however, the term will now expire in 2100. What was the incentive value of that additional twenty years? Let's assume a discount rate of ten percent. Let's further assume that the author is one of the very fortunate few whose work is still generating some revenue for his estate from 2081 through 2100. If the work generated one dollar each year for the period from 2081 through 2100, the net present value of that cash flow would be about 0.42 cents, or just under half a penny. If the work is successful, generating say $100,000 per year even that far out into the future, the present value of that cash flow would be approximately $420.

Moreover, we have assumed, unrealistically, that the return is absolutely certain. If we instead discount that amount further by the uncertainty associated with receiving any revenue eighty years later, the amount would be even less. If, for example, only one percent of published novels have any kind of staying power fifty years later, the expected value would be $4.20. Thus, in order to accept the incentive justification, one would need to believe that the prospect of an additional $4.20 to the author in 2000 would be sufficient to result in an appreciable increase in creative effort.

Yet one needn't accept this argument, or even believe that the current period is too long, to accept the argument that time should at least have some impact on the level of protection. That is because, if we accept the incentive argument for copyright protection, the value of the additional incentive to the author decreases the further out we go on the copyright term. This is again the result of the time value of money. Revenue from the first ten years of protection is more valuable than revenue from the next (assuming the amounts of revenue are the same), because the revenue from the next ten years is subject to a greater period of discounting. And so on.

Thus, the present value, and therefore incentive impact, of revenue in the last twenty years of a copyright's term is far less than the first. In the example above, assuming the same revenue received in the first twenty years, the net present value of that cash flow, even prior to discounting to account for the probability of continued success, would be more than $850,000 compared to $420 from the last twenty years. The incentive impact of the last twenty years is thus 0.049% of the incentive impact of the first twenty years. And again, even this understates the differential, since it does not adjust for the very likely possibility that revenue streams would significantly be reduced (perhaps to nothing) as the work becomes older. Accordingly, under the incentive view, the further out we go in the term, the less we should be concerned about the incentive effects of finding no or less protection.

Conversely, there may be quite strong reasons to be concerned about ensuring widespread access over time. The more time that elapses from creation, the more difficult it will be for a potential purchaser or licensor to determine who owns the copyright. The problems associated with finding the holders of copyrights have been well-documented. In some cases, a work may no longer be published. In other cases, difficulties may result because the original author is deceased, and the heirs or devisees need to be identified and contacted. Alternatively, the more time has passed, the more likely it is that the copyright has been transferred to other parties, perhaps several times, and the more complicated it is to identify and contact the current holders. There may also be a good deal of uncertainty over who exactly owns the rights, due to the rather complex provisions of the Copyright Act involving renewals, termination of transfer, and inheritance. Finally, complexities about formalities, renewal and copyright term extension may call into doubt whether the work is even still copyrighted. All of these problems become more acute as the time from creation increases and records and memories grow thin, thus making access to the work more problematic as time passes. Indeed, these costs have been viewed by some as the primary policy reason for the limited term....

Thus, even if we cannot say with any certainty what the optimal length of the copyright term should be, we can say with confidence that time should at the very least be relevant under the incentive justification, and that the scope of copyright protection should properly be sensitive to the impact of time on incentives and access. The longer a work has been out, the weaker the incentive claim and the greater the access claim. Thus, one would expect the scope of copyright protection to decrease over time, under the incentive view.

Encouraging Re-Use and Critique. Sometimes one hears a variation of the incentive argument that goes like this: copyrights (and other intellectual property rights) are needed not only to provide incentives for the initial creation of creative works, but also for their orderly exploitation. That is, we give exclusive rights to copyright owners not only so that they have an incentive to write a book as an initial matter, but so they can also have control over sequels, movies based on the book, and other derivative works. Although this "prospect theory" has been most powerful in the field of patents, it has had some impact on copyright as well, particularly in the area of derivative works. The basic idea is that only one party should have control over Mickey Mouse. Imagine if anyone in the world could make their own Mickey Mouse movie. We would soon have different versions of Mickey (for example, evil Mickey, Mickey in space, an Asian Mickey), and the value created by the original author would be dissipated. Thus, copyright law needs to extend protection to works to provide for orderly development and careful preservation of value....

Even within the prospect justification, however, there is ample support for the idea that the scope of copyright should vary with time. It may well be that an author should be given some period of time during which to develop and control variations or derivative works based upon the original work. This could be justified on both a straight incentive rationale and a prospect rationale. Over time, however, that justification weakens, since the author has already had ample opportunity to engage in such development. Thus, it may be fair to give an author at least ten, perhaps twenty or even thirty years to write one or several sequels. But if she hasn't written a sequel after fifty years, perhaps her interest in controlling the orderly development of the work is more attenuated and others should be permitted to build more aggressively on the work. Alternatively, if she has written twenty sequels in the intervening years, then perhaps she has adequately fulfilled that interest and the work should now be subject to interpretation from other perspectives. Either way, her interest, like the incentive interest, grows weaker as time passes....

A number of scholars have focused a good deal of recent attention on developing a richer concept of the public domain to serve as a counterweight to the recent expansionist tendency of intellectual property law. These scholars have been concerned about the apparent lack of any structural mechanisms to counterbalance such expansions. Accordingly, they have begun to work towards concretely articulating the benefits that derive from a robust public domain and the harms associated with granting ever-stronger private rights over information. According to these scholars, the eventual passage of works into the public domain is an essential feature of our existing copyright structure.

What has been less widely acknowledged has been the way in which works begin this passage from private to public even during the term of protection. That is, certain copyrighted works can take on more and more public character over time as they become more entrenched in popular consciousness and culture. Consider, for example, the iconic status of Mickey Mouse. In the early days, the cultural meaning attached to Mickey was probably not much more than the meaning attached to other cartoon characters of the time. Over time, however, Mickey has come to signify much more in our society and become a target for recasting and a focal point for alternate meanings. In many ways, the public's claim on Mickey has increased over time, even during its period of copyright protection. Many authors have thoughtfully analyzed the extent to which certain images, symbols, and characters may be necessary for us to engage in dialogue about popular culture and our surroundings. As time passes, works begin the passage from pure products of creative expression to objects that are part of our collective cultural history....

Rewarding Authors. The incentive argument discussed above is by far the most important and influential justification for copyright under U.S. law. Thus, the arguments above should be sufficient by themselves to give most courts reason to adopt time as a factor in fair use. In recent years, however, other non-economic theories of copyright law have begun to make inroads. Although they do not approach the incentive argument in importance or influence, I will address them here at least briefly and show that they too support the proposal.

The strongest of these alternative theories has been the "author reward" argument. Based in part on the writings of John Locke, this justification holds that copyright law is a reward for the creative labor of authors. Unlike the incentive argument, the author reward argument is not based on the idea that authors should be rewarded in order to provide greater benefits for society more generally. Rather, the argument is that the authors have a moral claim to their creative works, based on natural law. This argument often finds expression not only in specific judicial opinions and particular features of copyright law, but also in common intuitions about fair treatment of authors and creators. That this justification has force can clearly be seen from the fact that copyright law fully protects works that would have been created even without any financial incentive, like research papers, personal letters, and diary entries. Copyright legislation is often influenced by these moral claims from authors.

The author reward justification has come under attack on a number of grounds. In particular, to the extent that this argument is based on the Lockean notion that all are entitled to the fruits of their own labor, some have questioned whether Locke's famous sufficiency proviso is satisfied, that is, whether there is "enough and as good" for others. After an author has asserted rights over a work, are there "enough and as good" other works or ideas out there for others to claim? Others have critiqued the author reward argument for the practical reason that it appears to have few limiting principles. Reward to authors tells us little about how much protection is enough, how much is too much, how much authors deserve. One could, for example, use the author reward argument to justify perpetual copyright ownership in the fruits of an author's labor.

A number of scholars have responded to this last critique by finding ways to limit the potential reach of natural law, thereby rendering it more useful as a practical justification for copyright law. One such limit is based on the recognition that individuals are only entitled to fruits of their labor that are adequately measurable and practically definable. This is based on the observation that creative labor is rarely the product of a single author, working alone. Rather, authors take ideas, thoughts, concepts, and observations from other authors and society at large as the raw material of their work. The final work is not solely the product of one author's labor, but also of the labor of many others. As a result, the rights of the author should properly be limited, not absolute....

Again, these observations tell us little about how long to set the term. They may suggest a limit imposed by time, but do little to indicate what that limit should be. Once again, however, a precise figure is not necessary to support the broader argument that time should matter. Once we accept the view that an author's moral claim to compensation should be limited and that a limit on the term of the copyright is an appropriate mechanism for such a limitation, it also follows that the longer a piece has been out, the weaker the author's moral claim to compensation is. As time passes, difficulties in defining the scope of the entitlement increase. Moreover, the longer the piece has been out, the greater the chance that it has contributed to the stock of ideas to which the original author owes a debt, and upon which other authors will want to build....

Political Economy Arguments. A final set of arguments in support of the proposal can be found in pragmatic considerations relating to the manner in which copyright law is made in the United States. It is widely accepted that copyright legislation responds quite directly to the lobbying efforts of the copyright industries. It is not hard to see why. A narrow group of interests—namely the movie, music, publishing, and software industries—stands to benefit from expansion of intellectual property protection. They have the resources and incentives to lobby for such expansion in Congress. By contrast, consumers individually are largely indifferent to such expansions. Although they bear much of the cost of expansions, and such costs may be significant in the aggregate, each consumer bears only a miniscule share, spread out over time. Thus, as public choice theorists predict, consumers do not band together in sufficient numbers to oppose efforts by the copyright industries to expand protection. The few interested groups that do have some focus and resources—such as libraries and educational institutions—are simply outgunned by the array of countervailing interests. Moreover, to the extent that the interests of narrow, more focused groups are taken into account, they are usually granted a narrow exemption or privilege, leaving the broader expansion intact.

The impact of this set of circumstances on the expansion of copyright protection has been extensively documented. In the substantial revision of the Act that occurred in 1976, the copyright industries were expressly invited to participate in the crafting of the Act, in part due to the complexity of the Act and the difficulty of balancing so many competing interests. Thus, industry lobbyists had a strong hand in setting the scope of protection. Moreover, the consistent expansion of the copyright term through the 1960s and 70s, and most recently in the Sonny Bono extension act, is a clear example of the political economy of copyright protection at work. Despite opposition by many intellectual property scholars and public interest groups, and despite extremely strong arguments against extension, Congress recently extended the term and applied it retroactively, largely in response to heavy lobbying pressure from the copyright industries. Given this, it is difficult to see how repeated extension of the copyright term can be effectively resisted. Existing copyright holders have powerful incentives to keep petitioning Congress for both prospective and retrospective extensions of the copyright term. The public at large will remain largely unresponsive....

Because of the structural obstacles that limit Congress' ability to equitably address the issue of term expansion, judicial action becomes more attractive as a mechanism for ensuring that public-regarding limits on copyright scope are imposed. In recognition of this, many commentators have turned to the limits in the Constitution imposed by the Copyright Clause and the First Amendment. However, such challenges have significant limitations, as already discussed. The proposal ... provides a practical and effective alternative way for courts to ameliorate some of the undesirable effects of copyright expansion and inject some public-regarding values into copyright scope over time. Considering time in fair use may be one of the few remaining ways for such values to find expression. Courts may thus be able to adjust the scope of protection to compensate for the increase in the term of protection....

Doctrinal Arguments. The arguments above establish that there are extremely strong reasons to consider the passage of time in determining the proper scope of copyright protection. All of the existing justifications for copyright law support the view that copyright protection should vary over time. Indeed, after consideration of the above arguments, it seems particularly odd that courts do not consider time. Given the extreme length of the current copyright term and the extent to which markets and incentives change over such a long time period, a copyright scope that is static and fails to consider the passage of time seems highly artificial....

A court could, consistent with the text of the [Copyright] Act, properly consider time in at least two places. First, a court could consider the passage of time under the second fair use factor, the nature of the copyrighted work. Courts have, in considering this factor, generally focused on whether the work was creative as opposed to factual, and whether it was published or not. As a general matter, creative or unpublished works are accorded greater protection than factual or published works. Nothing in the text of the statute, however, prevents a court from also considering the age of the work, since this is certainly a part of its "nature." Indeed, courts—including the Supreme Court— have considered other aspects of a copyrighted work besides the two most common factors in analyzing the nature of the work. A court could thus, in assessing the "nature" of a copyrighted work, consider the age of the work and thus incorporate this consideration into the fair use analysis.

Second, a court could consider time independently as a separate and distinct factor. It is clear from both the text of the statute and the legislative history that the factors in [Section] 107 [of the Copyright Act] are not exclusive. The text expressly states that the factors to be considered "shall include," and nowhere suggests that these factors are an exclusive list. Indeed, the legislative history behind the Act clearly establishes that Congress meant to give courts broad discretion to consider additional factors not on the list....

In the end, then, the doctrinal argument in support of the proposal is remarkably simple and clear-cut. The text, legislative history, and case law on fair use clearly authorize courts to consider time, whether as part of the second factor or as an independent factor. The only real question is whether a court, in exercising its delegated discretion to consider time in fair use analysis, feels that such a consideration is warranted or desirable....

Selected References

J. Buchanan & Gordon Tullock, The Calculus of Consent (1962).

Robert Cooter & Thomas Ulen, Law and Economics (1988).

Jon Garon, Media & Monopoly in the Information Age: Slowing the Convergence at the Marketplace of Ideas, 17 Cardozo Arts & Entertainment Law Journal 491 (1999).

Jane C. Ginsburg, Copyright Legislation for the "Digital Millennium," 23 Columbia-VLA Journal of Law & Arts 137 (1999).

Jane Ginsburg, Authors and Users in Copyright, 45 Journal of the Copyright Society 1 (1997).

Paul Goldstein, Derivative Rights and Derivative Works in Copyright, 30 Journal of the Copyright Society 209 (1983).

Wendy J. Gordon, A Property Right in Self-Expression: Equality and Individualism in the Natural Law of Intellectual Property, 102 Yale Law Journal 1533 (1993).

Marci A. Hamilton, Copyright Duration Extension and the Dark Heart of Copyright, 14 Cardozo Arts & Entertainment Law Journal 655 (1996).

Paul J. Heald & Suzanna Sherry, Implied Limits on the Legislative Power: The Intellectual Property Clause as an Absolute Constraint on Congress, 2000 Illinois Law Review 1119.

Justin Hughes, The Philosophy of Intellectual Property, 77 Georgetown Law Journal 287 (1988).

William M. Landes & Richard A. Posner, An Economic Analysis of Copyright Law, 18 Journal of Legal Studies 325 (1989).

Mark Lemley, The Economics of Improvement in Intellectual Property Law, 75 Texas Law Review 989 (1997).

Lawrence Lessig, Copyright's First Amendment, 48 UCLA Law Review 1057 (2001).

John Locke, Two Treatises of Government (Peter Laslett ed., Cambridge Univ. Press 1988) (1690).

Glynn S. Lunney, Jr., Reexamining Copyright's Incentives-Access Paradigm, 49 Vanderbilt Law Review 483 (1996).

Robert Patrick Merges & Glenn Harlan Reynolds, The Proper Scope of the Copyright and Patent Power, 37 Harvard Journal on Legislation 45 (2000).

Michael J. Meurer, Copyright Law and Price Discrimination, 23 Cardozo Law Review 55 (2001).

Neil Weinstock Netanel, Locating Copyright Within the First Amendment Skein, 54 Stanford Law Review 1 (2001).

David Nimmer, The End of Copyright, 48 Vanderbilt Law Review 1385 (1995).

William F. Patry, The Copyright Term Extension Act of 1995: Or How Publishers Managed to Steal the Bread From Authors, 14 Cardozo Arts & Entertainment Law Journal 661 (1996).

Margaret Jane Radin, Property and Personhood, 34 Stanford Law Review 957 (1982).

Alfred C. Yen, Restoring the Natural Law: Copyright as Labor and Possession, 51 Ohio State Law Journal 517 (1990).

Further Reading (selected work by Joseph P. Liu)

Regulatory Copyright, 83 North Carolina Law Review 87 (2004).

Copyright Law's Theory of the Consumer, 44 Boston College Law Review 397 (2003).

The DMCA and the Regulation of Scientific Research, 18 Berkeley Technology Law Journal 501 (2003).

Part V

Courts and Beyond

A. Supervision

CHAPTER THIRTY-EIGHT

ORIGIN OF THE APPEAL[*]

The word "appeal" haunts American legal culture. We refer to a higher court review of a lower court or administrative agency decision as an "appeal." We call these higher reviewing courts "Courts of Appeal." And we describe our vertical, multi-tiered legal system in which a Supreme Court is the final arbiter of judgment as an "appellate" system. Reviewing courts ask counsel, "Why are you appealing?" Law school professors ask students, "What was the theory of appeal?" And lawyers ask themselves, "Can I appeal?"

But how did the word and concept of "appeal" ever get into American legal culture and discourse? Almost every legal system develops procedures to address grievances about initial judicial determinations. However, as familiar as the word "appeal" is to us today, the appeal was a surprising procedure for the American colonists to have adopted. Three hundred years ago, the term "appeal" referred to a legal procedure which was available only in the separate system of English courts governed by canon and civil law—and not in the common law system with which the Puritan settlers were so enamored. The legal procedure known as "the appeal" did not refer to what we now think of as an "appeal"—the correction by a higher court of errors of law made by a lower court. Instead, the "appeal" referred to a procedure under which a higher tribunal could completely and broadly rehear and re-decide not only the law, but also the entire facts of a case. Moreover, the legal procedure called "the appeal" represented a substantive theory of justice, emphasizing the importance of equity and a particular attitude towards the hierarchy of authority....

Over time, many of the[] American colonies would replace or combine the appeal with the more traditional review procedures of the common law: the writ of error and the writ of certiorari. And by the eighteenth and nineteenth centuries, these more common-law-like procedures had significantly narrowed the possibilities of review-for example, courts only permitted redress for errors

---

[*] Mary Sarah Bilder, *The Origin of the Appeal in America*, 48 HASTINGS LAW JOURNAL 913 (1997), http://papers.ssrn.com/abstract_id=140477.

of law shown in the written record of the case, similar to procedures in England. Yet the word "appeal" and arguably some of its broader jurisprudential connotations never completely vanished from the American legal system.

The appeal and the writ of error thus were two separate paths, and although our modern appellate system seems to owe more today to the narrow theory of redress represented by the writ of error, the fact that we stubbornly continue to use the word "appeal" suggests that some part of the original substantive theory of the appeal remains with us. In a legal world often obsessed with a static view of the rule of law, with a mechanical distinction between law and facts, and with one-bite-at-the-apple theories of review, perhaps the word still survives because we still remember, perhaps still continue to believe in, this early, broader and more flexible and equitable notion of appeal.

Most scholars of early American law have avoided the possibility that the appeal, as it entered early American colonial law, was initially used to mean the type of broad rehearing available in the ecclesiastical system. The conventional story of the origins of the appeal in America remains that advanced by Columbia Law School Professor Julius Goebel and Harvard Law School Professor Roscoe Pound. Both men explained the broad scope of review exercised by certain early colonial courts and the presence of the word "appeal" by locating the appeal within two preexisting stories of common law development. In an influential set of books on the origins of the appellate system written in the 1940s, Roscoe Pound claimed that the presence of the appeal resulted from "confusion and a laxity or liberality, as one may choose to call it" about English common law legal procedures. Influenced by the "frontier thesis," he saw the appeal in the colonies as part of a "simple system" that was natural to the "circumstances of pioneer communities." In 1971, in the popular first volume of the *Holmes Devise History of the Supreme Court*, Goebel argued that the "so-called appeal" was the result of colonial adaptation of English justice-of-the-peace practice. Still in the grasp of his local practices theory of legal transmission, Goebel proclaimed that "ordinary men" from "the backwaters of the mainstream of common law" brought this justice-of-the-peace practice to the colonies.

Why were such eminent scholars as Professors Goebel and Pound so quick to find the appeal's origin in the common law? Perhaps because like many twentieth century legal academics, both men believed that the American judicial system had developed in a progressively enlightened fashion from a common-law core idea of the importance of rule of law. Pound explicitly stated that the purpose of his history was to "make a proper judicial review in proper cases an available remedy." He sought to distinguish "what is behind the abuses we must eliminate, what principles are sound, as shown by experience, and what are but remnants of ideas which came from English procedure." He wanted to abolish any "accompanying crudities and confusions."

In contrast, Goebel's purpose in claiming a common law heritage may have been not so much a desire to promote judicial review as an Anglophilic belief that most of the good in the American system had come from English common law. Goebel stated that the "Sessions appeal consequently seems the most likely source, unless one is prepared to concede a greater degree of inventiveness than is otherwise observable in procedural matters." Incapable of seeing the early colonists as founding a judicial system that was intentionally inventive, Goebel believed that the modern American system owed its debt to subsequent English lawyers who brought with them the common law and court practices to "crowd out the more rudimentary practices and rules first imported and put to use."

As long as fifty years ago, the eminent legal historian Willard Hurst hinted at dissatisfaction with these types of stories of the history of the appeal, noting that, "[n]o part of the history of United States courts presents such a tangle of detail as does the handling of appeals. Nor does the tangled story unwind towards a happy solution." But regrettably the story has remained tangled to the present perhaps because legal historians, currently fascinated by the "law and society" approach, turned away from and became less interested in institutional legal history..... .

This Article tugs the appeal out of histories about the developments of the common law in America. Instead, it begins by studying the appeal as a word and concept that carried a set of particular meanings. By bringing these meanings to the surface, the Article sketches the beginnings of a different story of colonial legal culture—one which locates the colonists within a transnational, transatlantic, Western European legal culture. In this enterprise, I follow a path that perceptive cultural historians such as religious historian David Hall and others have laid, seeking to explore and explicate "how structures of meaning emerge, circulate, and are put to use." According to this perspective, the meanings that people ascribe to their world resides, in part, in the words they use. Hall explains this idea in describing religious culture in seventeenth century New England:

> [Lay people] knew their way around symbolic language. When they talked about their cows, they drew on a stock of precisely descriptive words. But when they talked about things spiritual, they shifted to a language made up out of words like "wilderness" and "pilgrim." ... For many, the meaning of a situation could be expressed in a word or two-a word that may be meaningless to us ... but that resonated with significance in the context of this culture.

Words are therefore not mere "words;" they represent "well-charted scripts" that can reveal deep-founded beliefs and ideologies. Thus when people use particular words, they choose among different cultural scripts—they select and create meaning. Indeed Hall asks, "What else is culture but a set of scripts?"

Through this approach, the appeal emerges, not simply as a legal procedure, but as a cultural script which should cause us to pause over our lingering belief that the colonists possessed only a low-level understanding of English common law. The meaning of the appeals script arose from the long heritage of canon and civil law in which a commitment to equity required that a higher tribunal must be able to rehear and re-decide both the facts and law of an individual's case. The decisions to adopt the appeals script betrayed the colonial leaders' careful knowledge of English corporation law and their agreement with the broader, more flexible, and more equitable theory of review and redress that the appeal reflected. And in the political struggles over the location of supreme authority which haunted the early seventeenth century, the appeals script became an accepted part of the legal culture because it represented the elusive idea of authority as dependent on a reciprocal exchange through a practical, procedural form.

To connote and emphasize these underlying subtleties and complexities of the early colonial concept of "the appeal," I use the phrase, "culture of appeal." I mean by this phrase to suggest that the specialized technical usage of the word in legal spheres was inseparable from its more colloquial usage in the political sphere and that the term, "the appeal," also referred to a set of broader meanings and practices. I also intend the phrase to allude to a culture of understanding about the appeal which transcended national and colonial boundaries. And the phrase should also help readers, for whom the word "appeal" carries modern common law connotations, to remember that the colonists' initial choice of the appeal represented a moment of "deep cultural reorientation" away from English common law culture. Lastly, the phrase should remind us that even the most technical of legal procedures, beneath their surface reflections, are embedded in the rich culture of their time....

The English Culture of Appeal. Although the New England appeal represented a departure from the English common law, it lay neatly within part of the English legal tradition. Since the fourteenth century, England had possessed two legal cultures. One—the common law—saw itself as the product of an indigenous development through custom by common-law practitioners and judges. The other—the civil law—proudly traced its roots to the grand tradition of Roman law as applied in the ecclesiastical and civil law courts by the civilians. Not only did these cultures have different stories of their origin, they had different procedures for redress. Although the word "appeal" actually appeared in both cultures, it referred to very different legal procedures.

The civilian lawyer, John Cowell, explained in his 1607 dictionary, *The Interpreter*, the difference between the understanding of the "appeal" possessed by the civilian students of the Roman and canon law and their common law colleagues. Cowell noted that "appeal is used in our common law divers times, as it is taken in the civil law: which is a removing of a cause from an inferior judge to a superior as appeal to Rome.... But it is more commonly used, for the private accusation, of a murdered by a party...."

As Cowell's phrase "divers times" indicates, the civil and common law worlds were not completely separate and the civil law meaning of the word "appeal" had already begun to drift into the common law. Yet throughout the early seventeenth century, the concept of the "appeal" was recognized as having its origins in the civil and canon law. During the seventeenth century, as the power of the theory of redress represented by the "appeal" began to invade the common law, these differences were not lost on the New England colonists.

The Culture of Redress within the Common Law: The Writ of Error. Good sixteenth and seventeenth century common lawyers, and perhaps an even wider spectrum of English readers, knew that the "appeal" did not refer to common-law redress procedures. In 1628, Coke noted, "Appellatio, is a removing of a cause in any ecclesiastical court to a superior." He emphasized, however, "but of this there needeth no speech in this place." In an earlier widely popular book on English government and law, Queen Elizabeth's Secretary of State, Thomas Smith, similarly pointed out that "as for provocation or appeal which is used so much in other countries, it hath no place in England."

What most common-law lawyers who looked up "appeal" would have found was a discussion of felonies. The entry under "appeal" in the popular 1579 edition of Rastell's *Difficult and Obscure Words and Terms of the Law of this Realm* referred to an indictment by a private citizen for mayhem, rape, robbery, murder, or other felonies. Indeed, Smith acknowledged England's eccentricity: "that which in England is called appeal, [is] in other places [an] accusation."

In the sixteenth and early seventeenth century, English common law had no word to describe the ability to seek redress from an inferior to a superior court. At that time the common law culture did not imagine a world in which "inferior" and "superior" courts were an important distinction. English legal theory tended to see law as "a system of reasoning" working within a "system of remedies." The crucial issue was the availability and applicability of various pleas and writs. The fascination was more with the correctness of the process than the justness of the result. Although during the seventeenth century, Coke and then Hale would develop increasingly elaborate understandings of the common law, the common law remained a system in which pleas to the judiciary required addressing "reason"—[as Alan Cromartie puts it] "the faculty acquired by training that extracted some workable rules from a formless body of immemorial knowledge"—not appealing for what any ordinary person could claim was justice, equity, or mercy.

Within this culture, therefore, disagreeing with the judgment was tricky. If the law was what reason or custom allowed—or, at least, what judges thought was allowed (and they tended to "think" in a funny version of Latin and French)—then how was the lowly litigant to complain about the result? During the medieval period, one possibility for redress involved accusing the jury or judge of giving a false verdict. In essence, the aggrieved party claimed that the judge or jury had lied about what the judge or jury knew to be the correct verdict. Given the realities of socio-economic power, accusing the judge (the writ of false judgment) was unlikely to have seemed fruitful. And although accusing the jury (the writ of attaint) remained an option for longer period of time, by the beginning of the seventeenth century, it had fallen into disuse.

The other possibility for redress was the "writ of error," the claim that an error had been made in the various writs and pleas of the case. Limited to the record, the writ of error permitted only a narrow scope of review. The aggrieved party was not supposed to bring in new evidence; indeed, the only debatable errors about factual matters involved facts that would show that no judgment should have been entered in the first place. One example was to prove that the original plaintiff had been a minor or a woman. Review was, in essence, limited to errors of law. Even the inquiry concerning errors of law was narrow because "errors" had to be in the record and the "record" usually contained only the writ, the pleadings and issue, the jury process and verdict, and judgment. A party who felt that "manifest injustice" had occurred had to find justice by "proof of a technical error (verbal or procedural) in the previous trial."

The common-law culture of law also meant that common-law courts did not operate in a strictly hierarchical fashion. If the law was what judges thought it was, then one particular set of justices had no supreme claim on knowing the law. Consequently, by 1600, the reviewing authorities for the writ of error operated under a horizontal system of "mutual review." Although decisions of local courts of record were reviewed by King's Bench, the three central courts reviewed each other's decisions in a complicated manner. Decisions in King's Bench were reviewed by justices from Common Pleas and the Exchequer. Decisions in Common Pleas were reviewed by justices of King's

Bench. Decisions in the Exchequer were reviewed by justices of King's Bench and Common Pleas. The House of Lords reviewed King's Bench and the Exchequer Chamber. The review did not involve a rehearing of the case, and reviewed cases were returned to the court for further proceedings or new trials. As [Robert J. Martineau] comments, common law "appellate review had nothing to do with whether justice was done."

The Culture of Redress Outside of Common Law: The Appeal. The common law courts, however, were not the only courts in England. Justice on the merits appeared to be the point of redress elsewhere, and redress elsewhere was by the appeal. In the 1607 dictionary, Cowell described the appeal as "a removing of a cause from an inferior judge to a superior as appeal to Rome." His definition once again embodied many of the cultural understandings of the "appeal." Cowell associated the appeal with the civil law and Rome and, indeed, the appeal dominated the ecclesiastical courts and the courts that used the civil law. Within these courts, the appeal served as a flexible form of redress based on an increasingly important understanding of equity advanced by the civilians. Cowell's use of the word "remove" emphasized the power of the appeal to permit a complete rehearing of both law and fact. His description of the removal from an "inferior" to a "superior" judge hinted that the legitimacy of the appeal rested ultimately on a supreme authority—often the authority of God. Moreover, Cowell's casual mention of "Rome" signaled that the appeal carried a set of political memories. First as a symbol of Rome's authority and then as a symbol of the king, the appeal had been entwined into English political history.

Equity, Authority, and the Appeal in Ecclesiastical Courts. As of the seventeenth century, the appeal's origins stretched back as far as the Catholic church could remember. By the time of Justinian, Roman law had developed an appeal. This appeal basically was a rehearing which permitted the production of new evidence. An early instance of this Roman appeal appears in the Bible in Acts, which recounts Paul's journey from Jerusalem to Rome. At a crucial moment, when it appeared that Paul would be sent back from Caesarea to Jerusalem for trial, Paul stated, "I appeal to Caesar." Festus and the Council accepted Paul's appeal and sent him to Rome.

As a legal device, the Roman appeal melded well with Church hierarchy. By the eleventh century, [as John Gilchrist explains] Pope Gregory VII clarified that "the pope stood supreme above all others." Although the pope therefore "had to listen to all complaints," Gregory emphasized the system of appeal to permit the delegation of cases while maintaining papal judicial supremacy. By the end of the twelfth century, [in J. H. Baker's words] "the Church and its legal administrators had constructed a transnational hierarchy of tribunals with the pope at its apex." The appeal was part of this pyramidal hierarchy. Within England, an appeal moved from the local courts in the diocese to the courts of the archbishops, and then to the courts of the Pope. This ecclesiastical appeal had few procedural requirements. Holdsworth noted that there was an "almost unlimited right of appeal to the Pope" and that "the system of appeals and rehearings was, or might be, never ending." Indeed, with a new Pope, cases often could be re-appealed.

The appeal's association with papal power meant that the cultural understanding of the appeal involved far more than simply seeing it as a procedural device. The appeal was at the center of two significant political struggles between the English crown and Rome. The first conflict involved Archbishop Thomas Becket. In 1164, Henry II proposed the Constitutions of Clarendon. The eighth chapter substituted the king for the Pope as the place of appeal in case the archbishop failed to do "justice." Not surprisingly, Becket disagreed and protested the attempt to end the Pope's appellate jurisdiction. Becket maintained the Pope's power of appeal but at a price—his own violent death at the hands of the king's men at Christmas in Canterbury Cathedral.

Almost four hundred years later, the English kings resurrected the struggle in a more successful, if not less bloody fashion. Pressured by the desire for a legitimate male heir and for an end to his marriage with Katherine of Aragon, Henry VIII needed to prevent any future appeal by Katherine to the Pope. The act, For the Restraint of Appeals, passed in 1533, reached beyond Henry's particular situation to end all appeals to the Pope. Drafted by Thomas Cromwell, the act declared the king the supreme head of the church of England. Using language that would become part of the cultural script for anyone complaining about appeals, the act stated that appeals would be restrained because they were often brought for "the delay of justice" and created "great inquietation, vexation, trouble, cost and charges." Moreover, the "great distance" meant that necessary proofs, witnesses, and "true knowledge of the cause" could not be known and therefore the aggrieved party would be "without remedy."

Ending appeals to the Pope did not end the enormous influence of the ecclesiastical courts and the ecclesiastic appeal procedure. The abolition of appeals had [according to R.H. Helmholz] "simply varied the place to which appealed causes finally went." The "omnipresent" courts continued to handle causes involving marriage and separation, probate and intestate estates, slander and defamation, as well as heresy, witchcraft, usury, profanity, and sexual offenses. With only one brief interruption during the reign of Mary, the ecclesiastical appeal continued into the seventeenth century with the crown as head of both spiritual and temporal jurisdictions. And as popular legal writers from Lambarde to Coke noted, appeals now ran from the courts of the archbishop to a new body commissioned by the crown, the Court of Delegates. The Delegates maintained civil law procedures of the ecclesiastical system: the appeal was conducted in writing, in English, with depositions and interrogatories. It was understood as a rehearing of both law and fact.

Beyond serving as the symbol of fundamental political struggles and the vast jurisdiction of the English church over daily life, the appeal also stood as an equitable theory of justice arising from medieval Roman canon law. In the medieval ecclesiastical system, [as Robert E. Rodes, Jr. explains] "the aspiration to do full justice between the parties led to an appellate process in which all questions were open that had been open in the proceeding appealed from." After the Henrician Reformation, ecclesiastical justice was explicitly linked to "equity." One popular writer [Robertus Maranta] noted that "where the ius civile establishes equity and the ius canonicum formality, the ius civile prevails even in the ecclesiastical forum." Similarly, in one of the sixty-one chapters addressing appeals in the proposed revisions to the canon law in England in 1552, thirty-two of England's most prominent common lawyers, civilians, bishops, and divines wrote:

> Appeals are procured not for the sake of oppressing anyone's justice, but so that imposed grievances inflicted may be repaired, and to correct injustice, and the unskillfulness of the judge, and sometimes to come to the aid of the ignorance of the afflicted one himself.... For what has been omitted in the first instance frequently has a place in the second.

The connection between equity and ecclesiastical law lasted into the seventeenth century. In 1607, [as Daniel R. Coquillette has documented] Sir Thomas Ridley's *A View of Civil and Ecclesiastical Law* noted that the study of civil and ecclesiastical law was called "Aequitas Canonica" because of the "cases of Equity and Conscience."

Indeed, in the sixteenth century, the civilians practicing in the ecclesiastical courts had developed an elaborate theory of equity, and its companion, "conscience." "Equity" was an ancient word—Aristotle and Aquinas had discussed epieikeia. "Conscience" had a similar heritage reaching back as far as the fourteenth century. Both words, however, became ubiquitous after 1530 with the civilian writer St. German's publication of *Doctor and Student* in English. This influential work defined equity as "a righteousness that considers all the particular circumstances of the deed the which also is tempered with the sweetness of mercy." According to [J.A. Guy] St. German theorized that "equitable interventions in the name of good conscience, which were sometimes necessary to mitigate the rigor of common law, were designed to reinforce, not to contradict, general legal principles." Unlike Aquinas who thought equity should be reserved for exceptional interventions, under St. German's theories, equity was "a part of the law not something outside of it." Equity "followeth the law in all particular cases where right and Justice requireth." Equity arose from conscience. St. German wrote:

> And as a light is set in a lantern that all that is in the house may be seen thereby so almighty god hath set conscience in the midst of every reasonable soul as a light whereby he may discern and know what he ought to do: and what he ought not to do.

Conscience was more than the distinction between right and wrong, it was a form of "applied knowledge," an "art of translating" the distinction into "specific rules of conduct to be followed in particular situations." Judgments in the ecclesiastical and civil law courts were to be based on equity and conscience.

Into the seventeenth century, these understandings of equity and the appeal remained linked. Even a common lawyer like Coke grasped the essential meaning. In Coke's discussion of ecclesiastical courts, he stated that the "appeal is a natural defence" and cannot be taken away "by any prince or power." He added, if the appeal is "just and lawful, the superior judge ought of right and equity to receive and admit the same, as he ought to do justice to the subjects." As [G.I.O. Duncan] notes, common lawyers and civilians alike knew that the appeal considered "the merits of the whole cause."

The Ripples of Appeal. This understanding of the appeal as equity and justice, as superior and inferior courts, and as rehearings of law and fact rippled into other areas of English legal life. The martial and admiralty courts had long accepted the appeal and its meanings because of their reliance on civil law procedures. During the late sixteenth and early seventeenth century, this meaning of the "appeal" as an equitable rehearing in front of a superior authority began to spread to two new legal areas in England. The gradual association of the "appeal" with these two areas that emphasized the appeal's association with equity and the delegation of authority demonstrates that [in Charles M. Gray's phrase] a "fairly coherent, though hardly articulated" theory of law had grown up around the appeal.

At the beginning of the seventeenth century, the word "appeal" began consistently to appear in conjunction with discussions of the Chancery courts. The Chancery courts, theoretically originating from the crown, did not use common-law procedure. Like the ecclesiastical courts, Chancery emphasized the importance of equity and an examination, in English, into the peculiar circumstances of the party. Indeed, the civilians had so often used "equity" to justify Chancery jurisdiction that by the seventeenth century, the two words seemed interchangeable. The popular *Lambarde's Archeion* (1635), a text on English legal institutions, simply titled one section: "The Court of Equity, or Chancery."

The precise date during the early seventeenth century when the "appeal" became the descriptive word for grievances brought to and taken from the Chancery courts is not clear. The phrase "appeal to the kings court of chancery" appears as early as the Henrician act restraining appeals. According to one contemporary treatise, Chancery heard "appeals" from maritime and martial matters and from the "mayor of the Staple." And in 1591, a petition in Chancery stated that the "appeal" was the proper device when complaining about a difference between the facts and the judgment.

Nevertheless, by the 1620s, the appeal also had become linked to the idea of broad equitable redress in Chancery, as a series of House of Lords' discussions demonstrate. In the 1620s, the Lords began to discuss whether, and with what scope, they could review Chancery decisions. The issue was framed as to whether they could hear "appeals." In 1620, a petition brought to the House of Lords employed the word "appeal," giving rise to a discussion "whether it be a formal appeal for matter of justice or no." Lord Say argued that it was an appeal and that there was "no appeal from the Chancery but hither." The Committee concluded that it could not find "that the word 'appeal' is usual in any petition for any matter to be brought hither." Nonetheless, the House heard the accusation and a "number of members expressed a willingness to consider the substance of the case, as an appeal," that is, to hear the merits of the cause. By the mid-to-late seventeenth century, the "appeal in equity" was well ensconced within Chancery's practice and, in 1675, the House of Lords accepted jurisdiction over "appeals in equity" from Chancery.

The meaning of "appeal" is also revealed as the appeal spread beyond the ecclesiastical courts into the quasi-governmental entities that English legal culture referred to as "franchises." Franchises were "a miscellaneous lot"—the palatine of Durham, the county of Chester, various local warrens, and corporations. These franchises were all "exercises of the king's rights by private persons"; they involved the "delegation of various jura regalia." Crucial to the franchise was the patent or charter, a document that literally was to be kept under lock and key. Subject to the document, however, the franchise could develop its own system of courts. A number of franchise courts had long employed the appeal. The corporate university courts of Oxford and Cambridge had used appeals to review internal cases. Another franchise court—the Stannary Courts of Cornwall and Devon—did not permit reversals by writ of error to the king but only by the appeal. And the islands of

Jersey and Guernsey had appeals to the King in Council. Within these franchises, the appeal represented the hierarchy of authority of the delegated powers.

In the late sixteenth century, franchises like the English trading companies also began to use the appeal to describe the relationship between the crown and the company. The charters of the trading companies delegated to the governor and company the power to do justice and to pass laws not contrary or repugnant to the laws of England. In some cases, the crown acknowledged that the company had complete legal authority by specifically barring appeals beyond the company. John Wheeler's famous *Treatise on Commerce*, published in 1601, described the Merchant Adventurers' power to "end and determine all Civil causes, questions, and controversies ... without Appeal, provocation, or declination." The charter to the King's Merchants of the New Trade stated that there would be no "further appeal or provocation whatever" from the power and authority of the Company and Fellowship. The Levant company's 1615 charter permitted fines for anyone who appealed to Turkish authorities.

Not only was the appeal used to indicate the delegation of power from crown to corporation, but it also began to be used to delegate power within the corporation. The judicial structure of the corporations was governed by internal acts passed by their general court. In at least one known case, that of the Eastland Merchants, a trading company active in the Baltic since the fifteenth century, internal ordinances established the appeal. Their 1579 charter established a Governor, Deputy, and twenty-four assistants. As merchants from all over England joined the company, they demanded local courts. The London Court agreed but retained control over the local courts by regulating the "appeal." The Privy Council approved an appeals ordinance in 1617, although the ordinance may have re-codified a similar older ordinance. The ordinance discussed in "what cases appeals are made," noting that it was intended for the "avoiding of needless and unjust appeals." The ordinance distinguished among appeals on monetary amount. It prohibited appeals from the local courts in amounts below 20 "dollours." Appeals for matters above 40 "dollours" had to provide security and initiate the appeal within six months.

The use of the appeal by the trading company emphasized the delegation aspect of the appeal—that justice lay in the ability to seek redress of decisions in a superior power. The appeal to the Pope and then to the English ecclesiastical authorities had also emphasized this point. With the rise of the Stuarts, the appeal also began to be associated with the king's supreme authority. James I explained the relationship between king and judge in the infamous Star Chamber: "As Kings borrow their power from God, so Judges from Kings: And as Kings are to account to God, so Judges unto God and Kings." And in *Archeion*, Lambarde wrote:

> Let no man in Suit appeal to the King, unless he may not get right at home; but if that right be too heavy for him, go to the King to have it eased. By which it may evidently appear, that even so many years ago there might Appellation be made to the King's Person, whensoever the Cause should enforce it.

The Appeal of the Appeal. What appealed to the king should not have appealed to the Puritan colonists. The Stuart theory of the divine right of kings and of the "king's powers to remedy grievances" rapidly came under attack in the early seventeenth century. The use of the prerogative court of Star Chamber against Puritan opponents called into question the very existence of prerogative courts and their discretionary powers. The increasing use of Chancery to rehear cases decided in common-law courts called into question the legitimacy of a court without juries and the unbounded discretion of the Chancellor. And the continued power of the ecclesiastical courts led Puritan reformers to criticize the courts as "relics of the popish past" and led common-law courts to attempt to restrain the courts' jurisdiction.

Yet these attacks on these courts did not translate into an attack on the legitimacy of equity or the belief that justice should come from the supreme authority in the Commonwealth. Although Puritans disagreed with the origins of equity, they found the idea of equity essential to bring man's "imperfect" laws into line with the "perfect and absolute" laws of God. Although they disagreed on the application of "conscience," it remained a crucial concept in their vocabulary. And although they were concerned about the Stuart notion of a king-centered hierarchy, [as John Dykstra Eusden puts it] the "conviction that there were ultimate authorities ruling through laws determined the function and relationship of all institutions for Puritans and lawyers."

Perhaps most importantly, these attacks never became an attack on the appeal, instead, the "appeal" became an increasingly powerful word in popular culture. From the widely read political tracts to popular plays by William Shakespeare, the "appeal" made its appearance. The popularizer of the perils of Puritanism, Richard Montagu, recalled Paul's appeal in the title of his work defending the divine right of king: *Appello Caesarem: A Just Appeale from two Unjust Informers*. The Puritan John Yates' response to Montagu, *Ibis ad Caesarem*, also embraced the appeal. Yates addressed his pamphlet to the king: "The Supreme and Sovereign Judge over all Causes and Appeals in his Majesty's Dominion." His title, *Ibis ad Caesarem*, quoted Festus' words to Paul: "Hast thou appealed unto Caeser? Unto Caesar shalt thou go." Yet Yates also was eager to go before the king in this literary appeal. Paraphrasing Paul, he wrote, "I think my self happy (o King) because I shall answer this day before thee." To both men, the appeal provided the opportunity to bring all the facts before a new, higher authority. Even Shakespeare chose the device of the appeal in a crucial scene in the play, *Henry VIII*, which seemed an explicit comment on the reigns of Elizabeth and James I. In that scene, Shakespeare retold the story of Katherine of Aragon's appeal to the Pope. To the king and Cardinal Wolsey, Katherine states "that again I do refuse you for my judge; and here, Before you all, appeal unto the Pope, To bring my whole cause 'fore his Holiness, And to be judged by him."

Like all appellants, Katherine knew the appeal would provide a rehearing of her "whole cause" before a judge whose authority she was willing to accept. From Paul to the Puritans, the appeal permitted a second chance to cry injustice.

Selected References

J. H. Baker, An Introduction to English Legal History (3d ed. 1990).

Edward Coke, Institutes of the Laws of England (reprint ed. 1985) (1817).

Daniel R. Coquillette, The Civilian Writers of Doctors' Commons, London, Three Centuries of Juristic Innovation in Comparative Commercial, and International Law (1988).

John Cowell, The Interpreter, Or Booke Containing the Signification of Words (1607).

Alan Cromartie, Sir Matthew Hale, 1609–1676: Law, Religion, and Natural Philosophy (1995).

G.I.O. Duncan, The High Court of Delegates (1971).

John Dykstra Eusden, Puritans, Lawyers, and Politics in Early Seventeenth-Century England (1958).

Christopher St. German, Doctor and Student (T.F.T. Plucknett & J.L. Barton eds., Selden Society 1974).

John Gilchrist, Canon Law Aspects of the Eleventh-Century Gregorian Reform Programme 27, reprinted in Canon Law in the Age of Reform, 11th–12th Centuries (1993).

Julius Goebel Jr., History of the Supreme Court of the United States: Antecedents and Beginnings to 1801 (The Oliver Wendell Holmes Devise History of the Supreme Court of the United States, 1971).

Charles M. Gray, Boundaries of the Equitable Function, 20 American Journal of Legal History 192 (1976).

J.A. Guy, Christopher St. German on Chancery and Statute (1985).

David D. Hall, Worlds of Wonder, Days of Judgment: Popular Religious Belief in Early New England (1990).

R.H. Helmholz, Roman Canon Law in Reformation England (1990).

1 William Holdsworth, A History of English Law (7th ed. 1956) (1903).

James Willard Hurst, The Growth of American Law: The Lawmakers (1950).

William Lambarde, Archeion, or a Discourse upon the High Courts of Justice in England (Charles H. McIlwain & Paul L. Ward eds., 1957) (1635).

Robertus Maranta, Speculum Aureum et Lumen Advocatorum Praxis Civilis, Part III, no. 76 (Venice 1556) (quoted in Helmholz, above).

Robert J. Martineau, Appellate Justice in England and the United States: A Comparative Analysis (1990).

Roscoe Pound, Appellate Procedure in Civil Cases (1941) & Organization of Courts (1940).

John Rastell, An Exposition of Certain Difficult and Obscure Wordes, and Termes of the Lawes of this Realme 19r-20 (reprint ed. 1969) (1579).

Robert E. Rodes, Jr., Ecclesiastical Administration in Medieval England: the Anglo-Saxons to the Reformation (1977).

Thomas Smith, De Republica Anglorum: A Discourse on the Commonwealth of England (L. Alston reprint ed. 1972) (1583).

Further Reading (selected work by Mary Sarah Bilder)

The Transatlantic Constitution: Colonial Legal Culture and the Empire (Harvard 2004).

The Lost Lawyers: Early American Legal Literates and Transatlantic Legal Culture, 11 Yale Journal of Law & the Humanities 47 (1999).

The Struggle Over Immigration: Indentured Servants, Slaves, and Articles of Commerce, 61 Missouri Law Review 743 (1996).

The Shrinking Back: The Law of Biography, 43 Stanford Law Review 299 (1991).

Chapter Thirty-Nine

Judicial Integrity[*]

The concept of judicial integrity may be described as the role of the judiciary in leading by example. A court can invalidate or rectify certain kinds of offensive official action on the grounds of judicial integrity. In this way, judges act as a beacon or a symbol to society for ensuring lawful acts by the forces of government. Thus, a court is wise to be cognizant of how its actions will affect the public perception of the judicial system. A court may not sanction or participate in illegal or unfair acts. There are two underlying goals of judicial integrity. First, on a public relations level, the court wishes to be regarded as a symbol of lawfulness and justice. Second, the court has the closely related concern of not appearing to be allied with bad acts. Stated differently, the judge does not want to appear to be associated with illegal actors....

A leading exposition of the concept of judicial integrity can be found in Justice Brandeis' dissenting opinion in *Olmstead v. United States*. The Government in that case used illegal wiretaps to secure evidence of criminal activity. The majority did not find this activity to be violative of the Fourth Amendment and allowed the evidence to be introduced. Brandeis asked rhetorically, "will this Court by sustaining the judgment below sanction such conduct on the part of the Executive?" Brandeis answered his own question as follows:

> In a government of laws, existence of the government will be imperiled if it fails to observe the law scrupulously. Our Government is the potent, the omnipresent teacher. For good or for ill, it teaches the whole people by its example. Crime is contagious. If the Government becomes a lawbreaker, it breeds contempt for law; it invites every man to become a law unto himself; it invites anarchy. To declare that in the administration of the criminal law the end justifies the means— to declare that the Government may commit crimes in order to se-

---

* **Robert M. Bloom**, *Judicial Integrity: A Call for its Re-Emergence in the Adjudication of Criminal Cases*, 84 Journal of Criminal Law & Criminology 462 (1993), http://papers.ssrn.com/abstract_id=771587.

479

cure the conviction of a private criminal—would bring terrible retribution. Against that pernicious doctrine this Court should resolutely set its face.

Brandeis' major concern was not the right of the individual defendants; rather, he stressed the symbolic protection of the entire government through preservation of "the purity of its courts."....

The Exclusionary Rule. Concerns for the idea of judicial integrity played a large role in the development of the Fourth Amendment exclusionary rule. [Yet] more recent decisions have devalued the importance of judicial integrity and have largely eliminated it as a justification for the rule. Two previously mentioned and interconnected concerns with the concept of judicial integrity can be found by looking at the roots of the exclusionary rule. First, the Court should be a symbol to the public as the guarantor of the rights provided by our laws. Second, the Court should not participate in the sanctioning of illegal acts.

In the early case of *Weeks v. United States*, which barred the use of evidence in federal prosecution if obtained by federal officers in violation of the Fourth Amendment, the Court indicated the symbolic importance of failing to sanction government misdeeds. "The tendency of those who execute the criminal laws of the courts to obtain conviction by means of unlawful seizures ... should find no sanction in the judgment of the courts."

In *Elkins v. United States*, the Court went on to suppress evidence illegally obtained by a state officer when the prosecution sought to introduce the evidence at a federal criminal trial. This practice is known as the "silver platter" doctrine because a state official delivered illegally obtained evidence, on a so-called silver platter, for a federal prosecution and thereby avoided the exclusion remedy which, prior to *Elkins*, only barred evidence obtained by federal officials. In *Elkins*, the Court spoke of "the imperative of judicial integrity" and decried a situation in which the judge was in any way a participant in the willful disobedience of the law. To support this position, the Court cited the dissenting opinion of Justice Holmes in *Olmstead v. United States* for the proposition that the government was still the same government whether it was acting as a prosecutor or as a judge.

With *Weeks* and *Elkins* as precedent, the Court in *Mapp v. Ohio* applied the exclusionary remedy for Fourth Amendment violations to state prosecutions. *Mapp* reiterated the language about judicial integrity in *Elkins* and in *Weeks* to support its holding. But as was said in *Elkins*, "there is another consideration—the imperative of judicial integrity.' The criminal goes free if he must, but it is the law that sets him free. Nothing can destroy a government more quickly than its failure to observe its own laws, or worse, its disregard of the charter of its own existence." The majority in *Mapp* concluded:

Our decision, founded on reason and truth, gives to the individual no more than that which the Constitution guarantees him, to the police officer no less than that to which honest law enforcement is entitled and to the courts, that judicial integrity so necessary in the true administration of justice.

In addition to judicial integrity, the Court relied on deterrence as a separate and distinct justification for the exclusionary rule. The *Mapp* Court, quoting *Elkins*, stated that, "only last year the Court itself recognized that the purpose of the exclusionary rule 'is to deter—to compel respect for the constitutional guaranty in the only effective available way—by removing the incentive to disregard it.'"

The judicial integrity justification for the exclusionary rule was short-lived. In *Linkletter v. Walker*, decided a mere four years after *Mapp*, the Court refused to give retroactive effect to cases decided prior to *Mapp*. The Court announced the prime justification for *Mapp* to be that the exclusionary rule was the only effective way to deter lawless police action. Because the misconduct had already occurred and would not be corrected by releasing the prisoners, the Court refused to apply *Mapp* retroactively. To the extent that the Court bothered to mention judicial integrity, it did so only in the context of the administrative nightmare that would occur if there were to be a rehearing on the exclusion of evidence when the evidence no longer existed and when witnesses were no longer available.

Subsequent decisions further demonstrated that the Supreme Court discounted judicial integrity as a viable justification for the exclusionary rule. In *United States v. Calandra*, for example, the Court explicitly stated "the rule's prime purpose is to deter future unlawful police conduct." Significantly, Justice Brennan's dissent classified this explanation of the exclusionary rule as a "downgrading" of the rule and as inconsistent with the intent of the Framers of the Constitution. He pointed out that, in adopting the Fourth Amendment, the Framers sought to curtail the government from evil conduct, and it followed, Justice Brennan said, that the Framers recognized the need for an enforcement mechanism. This mechanism had to be "capable of administration by judges." This led him to articulate the dual purposes of the concept of judicial integrity discussed above. He viewed these goals as "uppermost in the minds of the framers," namely, to have the Court serve as a symbol to maintain fundamental rights and to avoid any complicity in illegal government conduct.

The next step in the demise of judicial integrity was to redefine it. In *United States v. Janis*, the Court refused to apply the Fourth Amendment exclusionary rule to civil proceedings and lumped judicial integrity concerns with the deterrent rationale. The Court justified this approach by characterizing judicial integrity in the following limited fashion: "the courts must not commit or encourage violations." Because violations already had occurred, there could be no encouragement at the time the evidence was presented to the Court.

Even more forceful criticism of judicial integrity as a justification for the exclusionary rule appeared in *Stone v. Powell*. The *Stone* Court pointed out that if one were to extend the rationale of judicial integrity to its logical conclusion, the court would have to exclude anything illegally obtained even if the defendant did not object. If one were concerned with preventing illegality, why should there be a "standing" restriction on the exclusionary rule? Justice Powell, speaking for the majority, pointed out another way to approach the symbolic or public perception aspect of judicial integrity. Not only could one view judicial integrity as a means to prevent illegality; one also could look at it as a means to prevent the truth from being served (by excluding reliable evidence) with the result of freeing a guilty person....

The final step in the Court's retreat from utilizing judicial integrity as a justification for the exclusionary rule can be found in *United States v. Leon*. For the first time, the Court refused to exclude evidence in the prosecution's case in chief obtained by police who acted in good faith. Following the lead of *Janis*, the majority merged the deterrence and judicial integrity concerns and reasoned that, when there was no deterrent effect, there was not really any judicial participation. Thus, the integrity of the Court was not offended. The Court also redefined the symbolic effect associated with judicial integrity. It asserted that if probative evidence is excluded and thereby a guilty defendant goes free, especially when the police violation is minor or not deliberate, this use of exclusion may well "generate disrespect for the law and administration of justice."

In a separate opinion, Justice Stevens expressed frustration over the diminution of the power asserted by the Court.

> Today for the first time, the Court holds that although the Constitution has been violated, no Court should do anything about it at any time and in any proceeding ... Courts simply cannot escape their responsibility for redressing constitutional violations if they admit evidence obtained through unreasonable searches and seizures.... If such evidence is admitted, then the Court becomes not merely the final and necessary link in an unconstitutional claim of evidence but its actual motivating force.

In sum, use of the judicial integrity concept to support the exclusionary rule has, as of the present day, been totally discounted and supplanted entirely by the deterrence rationale. It has been recharacterized from a proposition that courts should act as a symbol for lawful conduct to a concern that the courts should not become a symbol for guilty people going free as the result of suppression of probative evidence.

Supervisory Powers. The use of supervisory powers is a way in which the federal courts can monitor the administration of criminal justice in the federal courts themselves without reliance on constitutional or statutory authority. The justification for the use of these powers appears to be closely tied to the idea of judicial integrity. A majority of the current Court has decreased the opportunities for federal courts to use supervisory powers and has thereby demonstrated its disenchantment with the concept of judicial integrity.

[T]he federal courts have utilized supervisory powers in two general contexts. First, these powers have been used to exclude evidence obtained in connection with a bad act by law enforcement officials. Such conduct is regarded as having occurred outside the court system. This judicial practice is not dissimilar to the Fourth Amendment exclusionary rule. The federal courts have also utilized their supervisory powers to ensure that proper procedures are utilized by the court system. The conduct examined in the latter type of cases is that which has occurred within the court system.

McNabb v. United States, which dealt with the action of a police official, is generally regarded as the first decision to invoke supervisory powers. In *McNabb*, federal officers obtained statements by interrogating defendants during a detention in violation of a statute that required an arrested individual to be brought immediately before a magistrate. Since Congress did not provide a remedy for violation of the statute, the Supreme Court determined that it had the inherent power to exclude the evidence. The Court avoided the constitutional issue that Congress had not explicitly forbidden the use of evidence procured in violation of the statute by simply indicating that it had power to review action occurring within the federal court system....

Yet the justification for the *McNabb* decision appears to be similar to Brandeis' formulation in *Olmstead*, namely, that the courts should not participate in the wrongdoing by law enforcement and that the courts ought to be monitors of justice.

> We are not concerned with law enforcement practices except in so far as courts themselves become instruments of law enforcement. We hold only that a decent regard for the duty of courts as agencies of justice and custodians of liberty forbids that men should be convicted upon evidence secured under the circumstances revealed here....

The close relationship between judicial integrity and supervisory powers can be found in cases which have sought to ensure proper court procedure.

In *Ballard v. United States*, the Court dealt with the issue of systematic and intentional exclusion of women from the jury pool. The Court refused to consider whether this exclusion would affect an individual case but did look at the injury to the judicial system and social community. "The injury is not limited to the defendant—there is injury to the jury system, to the law as an institution, to the community at large and to the democratic ideal reflected in the processes of our Courts." With this language, the Court was striving to maintain the judiciary as a symbol for the rest of society as a just institution with high ideals.

Whether designed to do justice in a particular fact situation or to establish general standards, the[ ] supervisory-power decisions reflect concern about the degree of fairness in the judicial process. The courts' increased activity in this field well may emanate, at least in part, from the availability of a named doctrine on which to ground decisions, and from the new-found freedom to ignore whether particular litigants were harmed by the asserted error.

Even though there has not been a clear formulation of the rationale behind cases involving supervisory powers, such powers have been utilized to decide a large number of cases. In analyzing the most recent of such cases, one finds that the present Supreme Court has clearly indicated that the use of supervisory powers should be curtailed. The Court has refused to utilize supervisory powers to expand on existing limitations to constitutional power. The rationale for this approach has been the Court's reluctance to suppress reliable evidence. It should be pointed out that this concern for the probative value of the evidence did not exist in *United States v. McNabb*, where there was no indication that the confession was involuntary and therefore unreliable. Thus, the confession in *McNabb* had considerable probative value.

United States v. Payner ... illustrates the Court's refusal to utilize supervisory powers even when the conduct by law enforcement officials was outrageous, because to have done so would have stretched beyond previously decided constitutional limitations. In *Payner*, the IRS illegally broke into a banker's briefcase and copied documents implicating the defendant. Because the defendant did not have standing for Fourth Amendment purposes, the district court utilized its supervisory powers to monitor police power and suppressed a document found in the briefcase. In rejecting the exercise of supervisory powers in this instance, the Supreme Court felt that the societal interest in allowing for the use of probative evidence outweighed the importance of preserving judicial integrity. In addition, the Court was concerned about the use of supervisory powers to circumvent the Fourth Amendment standing requirements. These constitutional limitations had previously been created by the Supreme Court. In dissent, Justice Marshall cited Brandeis' famous words in *Olmstead*, and pointed out the grossness and the deliberateness of the government's misconduct in the case and argued that the utilization of supervisory power was required to protect the judicial integrity of the court. "The court," Justice Marshall reasoned, "should use its supervisory powers in federal criminal cases 'to see that the waters of justice are not polluted.'"

For improprieties occurring within the court system, the use of supervisory powers has also been curtailed by the present Supreme Court. [T]he *Ballard* decision was more concerned with the symbolic importance of maintaining a just system than in ensuring individual rights. In other words, the court was concerned about the impact that a particular procedure would have on the court system and sought to prevent any institutional harm. This concern, however, is no longer predominant. The present Court has tied the use of supervisory powers to the impact that its utilization would have on a particular individual by instituting the "harmless error" standard. In *Bank of Nova Scotia v. United States*, the defendant sought to utilize the supervisory powers of the Court to dismiss an indictment for prosecutorial misconduct occurring during a grand jury investigation. The Court refused to consider the argument unless the defendant actually could demonstrate that he had been prejudiced by the wrongful acts. In order for the Court to utilize supervisory powers, the action had to meet the "harmless error" standard. In quickly discounting the effect this might have on judicial integrity, the Court stated, "we also recognize that where the error is harmless, concerns about the "integrity of the judicial process' will carry less weight."

[L]imiting the use of supervisory power had been criticized by Justice Brennan, who argued in an earlier dissenting opinion that an important public interest in preserving judicial integrity exists and that it outweighs the upholding of the conviction of a particular criminal defendant.

Admittedly, using the supervisory powers to reverse a conviction under these circumstances appears to conflict with the public's interest in upholding otherwise valid convictions that are tainted only by harmless error. But it is certainly arguable that the public's interests in preserving judicial integrity and in insuring that Government prosecutors, as its agents, refrain from intentionally violating defendants' rights are stronger than its interest in upholding the conviction of a particular criminal defendant. Convictions are important, but they should not be protected at any cost.

The most recent statement on supervisory powers by the Court is found in *United States v. Williams*. Justice Scalia, writing for the Court, suggested that there is not much leeway for the Court to utilize its supervisory powers, especially when doing so would create rules not otherwise expressly provided for in the Constitution or by Congress. In *Williams*, the defendant moved to dismiss an indictment because the prosecution had failed to present exculpatory evidence before the grand jury. The Tenth Circuit had instituted such a disclosure rule pursuant to its supervisory powers. According to Justice Scalia, grand jury procedures have historically enjoyed great independence and consequently judges have generally been reluctant to exercise supervisory powers over them. Justice Scalia suggested that the only time supervisory powers would be appropriate to dismiss an indictment would be when specific statutory provisions exist, or when "clear rules ... are carefully drafted and approved by this Court and by Congress to ensure the integrity of the grand jury's functions." This reasoning did not convince Justice Stevens, who argued in dissent that the Court has an obligation to exercise its supervisory powers to redress misconduct, even if the misconduct was not specifically prohibited by a statute or by the Constitution.

> Unlike the Court, I am unwilling to hold that countless forms of prosecutorial misconduct must be tolerated no matter how prejudicial they may be, or how seriously they may distort the legitimate function of the grand jury—simply because they are not proscribed by Rule 6 of the Federal Rules of Criminal Procedure or a statute that is applicable in grand jury proceedings.

Supervisory powers give judges considerable leeway within the federal court system to rectify procedures or executive actions that they find inherently wrong even though such procedures and actions may not violate constitutional or statutory provisions. This leeway to do the right thing is closely tied to the concept of judicial integrity. As just demonstrated, the Supreme Court has recently shown an inclination to curtail sharply the use of supervisory powers. This decline in the use of supervisory powers appears to be closely aligned with the Court's attitude toward the doctrine of judicial integrity.

Due Process. Due process, as found in the Fourteenth Amendment, presents a somewhat ironic situation with regard to our discussion of judicial integrity. Initially, the standard for the exercise of due process was based on a somewhat amorphous standard of fundamental fairness. Although this standard was consistent with the idea of judicial integrity, judges rarely exercised their discretion to utilize it for a criminal defendant's prosecution. As various amendments became incorporated to the states through the Fourteenth Amendment, a more restrictive standard ironically provided greater protection to the defendant. In recent years, however, the Supreme Court has cut back on the substantive protections provided by the Fourth, Fifth, and Sixth Amendments. The restrictions on the use of due process have negatively impacted on the principle of judicial integrity and have reduced individual protection.

Most criminal prosecutions occur in the state judicial systems. The first eight amendments of the Bill of Rights deal with the protections afforded to the individual against the central (federal) government. The Fourteenth Amendment, ratified in 1868, deals with restrictions on the powers of the states. This amendment has become the vehicle to curb the abuse of power by the states in criminal matters. The initial standard for determining whether a particular criminal proceeding violated due process under the Fourteenth Amendment was left to the discretion of the judge, who determined whether the proceeding offended notions of justice implicit in canons of decency and fairness. This approach allowed for a great deal of discretion by the trial judge and implicitly allowed him or her to exercise judicial integrity. One can see from Justice Frankfurter's language in *Rochin v. California* the important symbolic role of judicial integrity discussed previously. "So here, to sanction the brutal conduct which naturally enough was condemned by the court whose judgment is before us, would be to afford brutality the cloak of law. Nothing would be more calculated to discredit law and thereby to brutalize the temper of a society."

Justice Black did not like the Frankfurter contextual approach to the Due Process Clause of the Fourteenth Amendment. [Dissenting in *Adamson v. California*, he] argued that the specific guarantees of the Bill of Rights should be made applicable to the states through the due process clause of the Fourteenth Amendment. This approach came to be known as total incorporation. Justice Black believed that through total incorporation the Court could avoid the vague and subjective standard of "decency and fundamental justice." Although Justice Black's approach did not attract a majority of the Court, as time went by the Court selectively incorporated particular provisions of the Bill of Rights and thereby automatically embraced the entire body of law with regard to those provisions. Once a particular amendment had been incorporated, judges had to follow the existing body of law with regard to that amendment. Thus, through selective incorporation, Justice Black's position ultimately won out in practice. Ironically, however, this restriction of an individual judge's flexibility also limits the judge's ability to consider the principle of judicial integrity in his or her interpretation of due process.

As a result of incorporation, the Court has limited the meaning of due process as an independent provision of the Bill of Rights. For example, in *Moran v. Burbine*, the police did not inform a suspect who was being interrogated of his attorney's efforts to reach him and at the same time falsely assured the attorney that the suspect would not be questioned. The Court was content to analyze the case under Fifth and Sixth Amendment principles. In briefly considering due process, the Court found that the conduct fell short of the kind of "misbehavior that so shocks the sensibilities of civilized society."

Justice Stevens, in dissent, pointed out the dispatch with which the Court dismissed the due process argument. He argued for a "standard of fairness, integrity, and honor" as opposed to a "shock the conscience" test, and he would have considered the conduct in this case to have violated due process. In language reminiscent of the principle of judicial integrity expressing the symbolic importance of lawful actions by the Court, Stevens said, "in my judgment, police interference in the attorney-client relationship is the type of governmental misconduct on a matter of central importance to the administration of justice that the Due Process Clause prohibits."

Herrera v. Collins probably best represents the current state of the judicial integrity debate within a due process context. This case involved a convicted murderer's petition for habeas corpus on the grounds that new evidence discovered eight years after his conviction suggested his innocence. The petitioner argued that an execution without a hearing under the circumstances would violate his Fourteenth Amendment due process rights. Surely the execution of an innocent man would at least violate due process, and the allowance of such a deplorable event by a court system would clearly implicate notions of judicial integrity.

This opinion, however, was not necessarily shared by Justices Scalia and Thomas, who in concurrence found no right under due process not to be executed if newly discovered evidence indicated innocence. They took issue with the dissenting argument, which looked at the situation from a broad substantive due process view and found that the execution of an innocent man is exactly the type of conduct which "shocks the conscience." Justices Scalia and Thomas, finding no historical basis for judicial review of newly discovered evidence, suggested that the dissenting judges were applying nothing but their personal opinions in finding that executing an innocent man shocks the conscience. "If the system that has been in place for 200 years (and remains widely approved) 'shocks' the dissenters' consciences, ... perhaps they should doubt the calibration of their consciences, or, better still, the usefulness of "conscience shocking' as a legal test."

Although Justice Rehnquist, writing for the majority, adopted the Scalia/Thomas approach and found that a request for a new trial was not fundamental because it was not historically required and therefore did not violate due process, he did concede that if a petitioner could meet an "extraordinarily high" standard and show actual innocence, and that there was no adequate state avenue to raise a claim, then the execution might be unconstitutional.

This most recent decision by the Supreme Court graphically demonstrates that a majority of the Court is inclined to restrict the scope of due process.

Such a restriction of due process limits the leeway afforded to judges and therefore reduces their opportunities to exercise judicial integrity.

In analyzing the *habeas corpus* area, it appears that the Court is concerned with the public perception of the court system, especially when dealing with capital cases. The public is concerned with the amount of time it takes to carry out a death sentence. This sentiment has been characterized by the majority of the Court as concern for the finality of state judgments. As a result of this concern, the Court has developed various doctrines to restrict the use of *habeas corpus* petitions. The *Herrera* decision was certainly consistent with this trend....

Summary: An Argument for Reinstituting Judicial Integrity. Insofar as they are used as instrumentalities in the administration of criminal justice, the federal courts have an obligation to set their face against enforcement of the law by lawless means or means that violate rationally vindicated standards of justice, and to refuse to sustain such methods by effectuating them. They do this in the exercise of a recognized jurisdiction [carrying] an obligation that goes beyond the conviction of the particular defendant before the court. Public confidence in the fair and honorable administration of justice, upon which ultimately depends the rule of law, is the transcending value at stake.

This plea for what some might consider judicial activism is not judicial activism at all. It is grounded in the historical role envisioned for our court system. [In *Law's Empire*,] Professor Dworkin defines a judicial activist as a judge "who would ignore the Constitution's text, the history of its enactment, prior decisions of the Supreme Court interpreting it, and long-standing traditions of our political culture." In our political culture, society sees the court as a symbol of justice. The court derives this status from its role as part of the separation of powers because it acts as a check on the proper conduct of the executive and legislative branches. In order to accomplish this task, the court must employ judicial discretion. [T]here is ample precedent for the exercise of judicial integrity. This can be found in the original justification for the exclusionary rule, the utilization of supervisory powers, and the original concept of due process....

Implicit in the demise of judicial integrity is an inherent distrust in the court system to do the right thing in sanctioning official misconduct. It is assumed to be prudent to limit courts' discretionary power because judges cannot be trusted to exercise that power with restraint. This thinking is unfaithful to the guiding principle that the courts are a separate institution within our governmental system. Furthermore, in recent years the Supreme Court has not exhibited the same desire to limit the discretionary power of the executive (the police)....

If one agrees with Justices Frankfurter and Brandeis that the courts should be a symbol of justice for our society, then one has to give judges some discretion so that they can act as this symbol. We are willing to concede that the concept of judicial integrity allows for a great deal of discretion to be exercised pursuant to relatively vague concepts. However, this exercise of discretion is limited to governmental misconduct, an area which the framers entrusted to the judiciary. In addition, historically, the Court has rarely abused this discretion.

Furthermore, if we were to follow the approach implied by Justices Thomas and Scalia in *Herrera v. Collins* and not have the Court intervene (for instance, exercise what we have been calling judicial integrity) when an innocent man is about to be executed, could one dare say that this is the role our founding fathers had in mind for the court system? Surely the courts cannot stand by while the executive executes an innocent man.

Somewhere along the way notions of judicial integrity have been forgotten. These notions have an important role to play and indeed should become more prominent. The court system should correct injustices even if those injustices do not necessarily violate specific laws or rules. Government improprieties should not find an oasis within the court system.

Selected References

Sara S. Beale, Reconsidering Supervisory Power in Criminal Cases: Constitutional and Statutory Limits on the Authority of the Federal Courts, 84 Columbia Law Review 1433 (1984).

William Cohen, Justices Black and Douglas and the "Natural-Law-Due-Process Formula": Some Fragments of Intellectual History, 20 U.C. Davis Law Review 381 (1987).

George E. Dix, Nonconstitutional Exclusionary Rules in Criminal Procedure, 27 American Criminal Law Review 53 (1989).

Yale Kamisar, "Comparative Reprehensibility" and the Fourth Amendment Exclusionary Rule, 86 Michigan Law Review 1 (1987).

John Kaplan, The Limits of the Exclusionary Rule, 26 Stanford Law Review 1027 (1974).

Donald P. Lay, The Writ of *Habeas Corpus*: A Complex Procedure for a Simple Process, 77 Minnesota Law Review 1015 (1993).

Cases

Adamson v. California, 332 U.S. 46 (1947) (Black, J., dissenting).
Ballard v. United States, 329 U.S. 187 (1946).
Bank of Nova Scotia v. United States, 487 U.S. 250 (1988).
Elkins v. United States, 364 U.S. 206 (1960).
Herrera v. Collins, 506 U.S. 390 (1993).

Linkletter v. Walker, 381 U.S. 618 (1965).

Mapp v. Ohio. 367 U.S. 643 (1961).

McNabb v. United States, 318 U.S. 332 (1943).

Moran v. Burbine, 475 U.S. 412 (1986).

Olmstead v. United States, 277 U.S. 438 (1928) (Brandeis, J., dissenting).

Rochin v. California, 342 U.S. 165 (1952).

Stone v. Powell, 428 U.S. 465 (1976).

United States v. Calandra, 414 U.S. 338 (1973).

United States v. Janis, 428 U.S. 433 (1976).

United States v. Leon, 468 U.S. 897 (1984).

United States v. Payner, 447 U.S. 727 (1980).

United States v. Williams, 504 U.S. 36 (1992).

Weeks v. United States, 232 U.S. 383 (1914).

Further Reading (selected work by Robert M. Bloom)

Criminal Procedure: Examples and Explanations (Aspen 4th ed. 2004) (with Mark S. Brodin).

Ratting: The Use and Abuse of Informants in the American Justice System (Praeger 2002).

CHAPTER FORTY

A MORE INDEPENDENT GRAND JURY*

The bromide that "a grand jury would indict a ham sandwich if the prosecutor asked it to" reflects a generally accurate belief that the prosecutor exerts primary control over the flow of information before the grand jury. Notwithstanding this almost universal recognition that a prosecutor wields great power before the grand jury, it would probably surprise most lay persons to learn that in the federal system a prosecutor has no enforceable duty to present before the grand jury evidence which exonerates the target of the investigation. The debate over a prosecutor's grand jury disclosure obligations, apparently laid to rest for the federal courts by the Supreme Court's 1992 decision in *United States v. Williams*, has now been transferred to state courts and bar disciplinary authorities....

Just as at its inception in twelfth century England, the dual functions of a grand jury in criminal cases are both inquisitorial and accusatorial; that is, grand juries both investigate crimes and decide which charges to present to the sovereign for trial.... Despite the historical duality of the grand jury's role, serious questions have been raised as to the ability of the grand jury to perform its shield function.

In many states and the federal court system, the American grand jury is composed of twenty-three lay citizens. Its work is conducted in total secrecy, and the modern grand jury receives guidance and instruction from only one advocate—the prosecutor. The prosecutor is responsible for making an opening statement, examining witnesses, introducing physical evidence, preparing the draft indictment, and instructing the jury on the legal elements of the crimes presented in the proposed charges. In some states, the prosecutor may even remain in the room while the grand jury deliberates, purportedly to assist in the event that any jurors have questions.

---

* R. Michael Cassidy, *Toward a More Independent Grand Jury: Recasting and Enforcing the Prosecutor's Duty to Disclose Exculpatory Evidence*, 13 GEORGETOWN JOURNAL OF LEGAL ETHICS 361 (2000), http://papers.ssrn.com/abstract_id=871746.

In sharp contrast, counsel for a defendant plays no role in the grand jury except silently to advise should the client be called as a witness. Otherwise, defense counsel is not even allowed in the grand jury room. Neither the rules of evidence, nor the constitutional rights of a defendant to be secure from unreasonable searches and seizures, to confront the witnesses against him, and to testify in his own defense apply in grand jury proceedings.

Perhaps because the prosecutor's power at this early stage of criminal proceedings is paramount, grand juries return indictments in an extremely high percentage of cases. Not surprisingly, the status of the grand jury as an independent and quasi-judicial body capable of screening out unmeritorious charges repeatedly has been called into question.... Many commentators in recent years have called for reform of the grand jury and many states have abolished the grand jury altogether in favor of other methods of pre-trial case screening, such as the use of judicial probable cause hearings.

Those jurisdictions that have abandoned the grand jury generally have done so at significant cost, because the inquisitorial function of the grand jury is not easily replaced. In situations where an arrest has not been made and law enforcement officials are seeking to "solve" a crime, the grand jury may play a unique and valuable investigative role; it may subpoena a witness to appear and answer questions under the pains and penalties of perjury; it may request a court to immunize a witness who asserts his right not to incriminate himself; it may command the production of documents and other physical evidence such as handwriting, voice, and blood samples; and, it may assess, in deliberative fashion, the relative credibility of witnesses whose accounts differ from one another. In lieu of an indictment, the grand juries of many states are authorized to publish their findings in the form of a "report" to the court which impaneled them, recommending civil redress or systemic reform. These important pre-charging investigatory tools are not available to prosecutors or police officers in most states unless they are acting through and on behalf of a duly constituted grand jury. Thus, commentators who call for the wholesale abandonment of the grand jury may be trading away important inquisitorial tools in return for a more balanced case screening process....

An Opportunity Lost. Most federal appellate courts considering the issue prior to 1992 ruled that a prosecutor does not have a general duty to present evidence favorable to a defendant to a grand jury. They reasoned that such a duty would transform the grand jury from an accusatory body into a finder of ultimate fact and would impose substantial resource demands on the judiciary by requiring review of grand jury presentations.

Many courts reaching this result relied on the Supreme Court's 1956 decision in *Costello v. United States*, in which the Court ruled that an indictment based solely on hearsay evidence does not violate the Fifth Amendment. Reacting to concerns that allowing challenges to the quality or sufficiency of the evidence before the grand jury would heavily burden judicial resources with preliminary hearings, the *Costello* court stated that "an indictment returned by a legally constituted and unbiased grand jury ... if valid on its face, is enough to call for trial of the charge on the merits." Indeed, the Court continued, "neither the Fifth Amendment nor any other constitutional provision prescribes the kind of evidence upon which grand juries must act." After *Costello*, lower courts had little trouble interpreting this admonition to mean that courts need not entertain claims that a prosecutor had omitted exculpatory evidence from his grand jury presentation.

A more serious and more difficult question was whether prosecutors had a duty to present to the grand jury substantially exculpatory evidence, that is, evidence which directly negated or contradicted evidence of the defendant's guilt. Unlike general exculpatory evidence, which may simply cast some doubt on the credibility of government witnesses (such as impeachment evidence), evidence that affirmatively suggests that the defendant did not commit the crime, or that someone else did, is directly relevant to the grand jury's accusatory function. If believed, it suggests that there is no probable cause to indict. Prior to 1992, the circuits were split on the question of whether prosecutors have an obligation to present to the grand jury substantially exculpatory evidence in their possession.

In 1992, the Supreme Court resolved this issue in *United States v. Williams*. A federal grand jury indicted John Williams, an investor from Tulsa, Oklahoma, on seven counts of bank fraud for knowingly making false statements intended to influence the actions of a federally insured financial institution. Specifically, the indictments alleged that the defendant misstated his financial position on balance sheets provided to the bank in support of his loan application by: 1) listing under "current assets" $6 million in notes receivable from venture capital companies he had an interest in, notwithstanding that these investments were highly speculative and not reducible to cash value in the short term; and 2) reporting under "income" the interest he received on these notes, notwithstanding that such interest was funded entirely by his own loans to the company.

Williams moved to dismiss the indictments, arguing that the government failed to fulfill its obligation to present "substantially exculpatory evidence" to the grand jury. His lawyers argued that the government failed to introduce to the grand jury federal tax returns and Williams' testimony in a contemporaneous bankruptcy proceeding, both of which established that Williams consistently reported these notes (and interest on the notes) as current assets and income. According to Williams, his consistent treatment of these notes in other reporting forums belied an intent to mislead the banks, which was an essential element of the crime charged.

The district court agreed and dismissed the indictments, ruling that the evidence created "a reasonable doubt about [the defendant's] guilt" and "rendered the grand jury's decision to indict gravely suspect." Applying its ruling in *United States v. Page*, the Tenth Circuit Court of Appeals affirmed, holding that the district court's conclusion that the government possessed and withheld substantial exculpatory information from the grand jury was not clearly erroneous.

The Supreme Court granted *certiorari* to resolve the issue of "whether an indictment may be dismissed because the government failed to present exculpatory evidence to the grand jury." The respondent argued both: 1) that imposing such an obligation on prosecutors is necessary to protect the Fifth Amendment's guarantee of indictment by a grand jury for serious crimes; and, 2) that the Tenth Circuit's disclosure rule, independent of the Fifth Amendment, was consistent with and supported by its general supervisory power over the grand jury. In a majority opinion by Justice Scalia, a sharply-divided Court reversed the Tenth Circuit, ruling that dismissal of an indictment for failure to disclose exculpatory evidence to the grand jury was not proper. The opinion is remarkable not for its result, but for its reasoning. The majority ruled that federal courts are without general superintendence power concerning the nature or quality of evidence presented to the grand jury.

Williams argued that the Tenth Circuit's disclosure rule could be justified "as a sort of Fifth Amendment 'common law.'" Rejecting this argument, the Court ruled that the Tenth Circuit's disclosure rule was not a necessary means to assure the defendant's constitutional right to "an independent and informed grand jury." Focusing on the accusatory role of the grand jury, Justice Scalia stated that "the grand jury sits not to determine guilt or innocence, but to assess whether there is an adequate basis for bringing a criminal charge." He added:

> The [disclosure] rule would neither preserve nor enhance the traditional functioning of the institution that the Fifth Amendment demands. To the contrary, requiring the prosecutor to present exculpatory evidence as well as inculpatory evidence would alter the grand jury's historical role, transforming it from an accusatory to an adjudicatory body.

Justice Scalia rejected the notion that the Fifth Amendment assures putative defendants the right to a balanced presentation of evidence before the grand jury, noting that both in England and in the colonies, a person under investigation had no right to appear before the grand jury himself or to present a defense through others. Because the grand jury had no obligation to hear such defense evidence were it to be tendered, Justice Scalia refused to "convert a non-existent duty of the grand jury itself into an obligation of the prosecutor." His opinion reasoned that because the Fifth Amendment common law of the grand jury would not be abridged "if the grand jury itself chooses to hear no more evidence than that which suffices to convince it an indictment is proper," to require a prosecutor to present exculpatory evidence, while denying that the grand jury has an obligation to consider it, "would be quite absurd."

While Justice Scalia is correct that in England a putative defendant had no right to testify or to present a defense before the grand jury, it does not ineluctably follow from this historical fact that the later enacted Fifth Amendment does not require a prosecutor to present such evidence were it to come into his possession. The placement of the right to a grand jury indictment in the Fifth Amendment, along with other key individual liberties such as the right not to be a witness against oneself and the right to due process of law, suggests that the grand jury was viewed as some form of safeguard between the government and its citizens. The prosecutor is an arm of the government, but the grand jury is a body of the people. It is not inconsistent, and surely not absurd, to suggest that the grand jury has no obligation to hear or consider a particular piece of evidence, but also that the prosecutor has some obligation to present it. In the former case, the finder of fact is given the choice of what evidence to consider; in the latter, the government deprives that very deliberative body of the opportunity to make such a choice.

Justice Scalia also undervalued the historical screening function of the grand jury. The majority in *Williams* concluded that requiring a prosecutor to disclose exculpatory evidence to the grand jury would do little to further the grand jury's accusatory function because its duty is simply to charge, not to determine guilt or innocence. But, both in England and in the colonies, one of the roles of the grand jury was to screen out unmeritorious charges. Where exculpatory evidence is so substantial that to introduce it would actually lead the grand jury to conclude that there is no probable cause to believe that the defendant committed the crime, nondisclosure compromises this core screening function.

On the Fifth Amendment issue, the majority in *Williams* clearly felt constrained by the Court's prior mandate in *Costello* not to inquire into the nature or sufficiency of evidence presented to the grand jury. In *Costello*, the Court had observed:

> If indictments were to be held open to challenge on the ground that there was inadequate or incompetent evidence before the grand jury, the resulting delay would be great indeed. The result of such a rule would be that before trial on the merits a defendant could always insist on a kind of preliminary trial to determine the competency and adequacy of the evidence before the grand jury. This is not required by the Fifth Amendment.

Although the express holding in *Costello* dealt only with judicial review of the competence of evidence before the grand jury (hearsay), the above cited dicta expressed the Court's refusal to review the "competency and adequacy" of evidence before the grand jury. This dicta was repeated eighteen years later in *Calandra*, where the Court refused to apply the exclusionary rule in the grand jury to evidence seized in violation of the Fourth Amendment, stating that "the validity of an indictment is not affected by the character of the evidence considered." By the time *Williams* was decided in 1992, the Supreme Court on two separate occasions had stated its disinclination to allow federal courts to review grand jury presentments to determine whether probable cause existed to support the crime charged, without expressly ruling so on facts properly before it.

Having traveled down this road, the Court felt constrained in *Williams* to forestall challenges to the prosecutor's decisions about what evidence to present to the grand jury: "It would make little sense, we think, to abstain from reviewing the evidentiary support for the grand jury's judgment while scrutinizing the sufficiency of the prosecutor's presentation." As a practical matter, the Court simply promoted efficiency over fairness. The Court did not want to commit the judicial resources necessary to review the scope or quality of evidence presented to the grand jury, worrying that the need to rule on such motions would "consume 'valuable judicial time'" and engage the courts in "preliminary trials on the merits."

Because the Court concluded that the common law of the Fifth Amendment had not been violated by the prosecutor's conduct in *Williams*, and because no specific statute or rule of criminal procedure required the prosecutor to present exculpatory evidence to the grand jury, the Court determined that the Tenth Circuit was without power to create a common law disclosure rule by judicial decision. Justice Scalia concluded that federal courts lack any general supervisory power over the grand jury because grand juries are not "judicial" proceedings. He relied on the fact that the grand jury is not mentioned in the body of the Constitution, but only in the Bill of Rights, to support his conclusion that it belongs to none of the three branches of government. He also pointed both to the scope of the grand jury's power, and to the manner in which it was exercised, to distinguish it from Article III courts. Having concluded that the grand jury is not part of the judiciary, the majority in *Williams* ruled that a court's power to regulate grand jury proceedings is not as broad as its supervisory power over its own proceedings. Therefore, the Court proclaimed that the judiciary's supervisory power over the grand jury should be limited to situations where the constitution, a statute, or a rule has been violated.

The Court in *Williams* also understated the extent to which it had allowed judicial oversight of grand jury proceedings in the past. In the forty years preceding *Williams*, for example, the Court was very active in protecting the process of selecting grand jurors from racial and gender discrimination. The Court has also indicated its willingness to limit a grand jury's subpoena power, and to dismiss indictments when a prosecutor intentionally presents perjured testimony to the grand jury. Not all of these forms of misconduct by or before the grand jury is expressly forbidden by Constitution, statute, or rule. As recently as its opinion in *Bank of Nova Scotia*, the Court looked instead to whether the misconduct complained of had so compromised the integrity of the grand jury as to render its proceedings "fundamentally unfair." When it was deemed important enough, the Court was willing to intervene to protect the integrity of the grand jury process. Justice Scalia's newly-minted and exclusive reliance on violations of express constitutional provisions, statutes, or rules as the bellwether of when a court may intervene in grand jury proceedings without violating principles of separation of powers appears simply to have been made up out of whole cloth.

In relying on principles of separation of powers to reach its decision, *Williams* recognized that "the Fifth Amendment's 'constitutional guarantee [of indictment by grand jury] presupposes an investigative body acting independently of either prosecuting attorney or judge.'" Yet total independence from both bodies is impossible. The grand jury cannot act except on the advice and direction of the prosecutor, and prosecutorial misconduct cannot be prevented and deterred except with the aid and intervention of the courts. By refusing to allow courts to exercise supervisory authority over grand juries, the Court may be preserving the grand jury's independence from the judiciary, but only at the cost of maximizing the grand jury's dependence on prosecutors.

Over twenty five years ago, the Supreme Court [in *Wood v. Georgia*] described the function of the grand jury as follows: "It serves the invaluable function in our society of standing between the accuser and the accused, whether the latter be an individual, minority group, or other, to determine whether a charge is founded upon reason or was dictated by an intimidating power or by malice and personal ill will." A prosecutor who knows of evidence that negates the defendant's guilt, and who consciously chooses not to disclose it to the grand jury, either does not personally believe the evidence is credible, or seeks to gain some form of leverage by indicting an innocent defendant. In the former case, he is imposing his "intimidating power" on the grand jury by substituting his will for the collective and informed judgment of that deliberative body. In the latter case, he is acting "maliciously" by pursuing an indictment not supported by probable cause. The Court in *Williams* failed to recognize that either form of motivation is paradigmatically what the drafters of the Fifth Amendment sought to prevent when they placed the grand jury as a shield between the people and the sovereign. Nondisclosure of substantial exculpatory evidence makes the grand jury exclusively a tool of the prosecutor, rather than a bulwark between the prosecutor and the individual....

A New Model. The Supreme Court's reluctance to impose a duty upon prosecutors to disclose exculpatory evidence to the grand jury reflects pragmatic concerns for the enforceability of this duty once created [under state professional responsibility standards]. How exculpatory must the evidence be to mandate disclosure, and how can a court review an indictment without necessarily substituting its view of the evidence for that of the grand jury? Clearly, the Supreme Court found these questions impenetrable and therefore decided in *Williams* to forego the inquiry altogether. Yet those states that have eschewed the *Williams* approach and adopted a limited rule of disclosure for "substantial exculpatory evidence" have fared no better. They have assumed the laborious and costly task of reviewing grand jury presentations without any assurance that their conclusions as to which omissions "tend to negate probable cause" or "explain away the charge" either represents or protects the will of the grand jury. Nor does such speculation provide any meaningful guidance to prosecutors.

Rather than focusing solely on the materiality of the exculpatory evidence and its likely impact on the grand jury, a more workable and meaningful standard of review can be derived from *Franks v. Delaware*. It focuses on whether the prosecutor intended to distort the evidence and mislead the grand jury. For over twenty years, this standard has been applied successfully to omissions by police officers in search and arrest warrant applications, and it would map well to the topic of exculpatory evidence withheld from the grand jury.

The Supreme Court in *Franks* established a three-part test for reviewing an allegation that a search warrant was issued based on a false or misleading affidavit. To warrant a pre-trial hearing, the defendant must make a substantial preliminary showing that: 1) the affidavit contains false statements; 2) these false statements were made knowingly or intentionally, or with reckless disregard for the truth; and 3) these false statements were necessary to a finding of probable cause; that is, without the false statements the affidavit is insufficient to establish probable cause to search or seize. This showing "must be more than conclusory" and must be accompanied by a detailed offer of proof. "Allegations of negligence or innocent mistake are insufficient."

If the defendant makes an adequate threshold showing of each of these three elements, he is entitled under *Franks* to an evidentiary hearing to test the veracity of the search warrant affidavit. Where the defendant establishes by a preponderance of the evidence after an evidentiary hearing that the affidavit was intentionally perjurious or that false statements were made with reckless disregard for the truth, and that with the false statements set to one side the "remaining content is insufficient to establish probable cause," the Fourth and Fourteenth Amendments require that the fruits of the warrant be suppressed to the same extent as if probable cause was lacking on the face of the affidavit entirely.

The *Franks* test for determining when a misstatement in a warrant application violates the Fourth Amendment protection against unreasonable searches and seizures has been applied to omissions in both search and arrest warrant applications, that is, failure by the law enforcement officer to alert the issuing magistrate to exculpatory facts. Where a police officer intentionally or recklessly omits from a warrant application exculpatory facts which are material to a finding of probable cause, courts have interpreted *Franks* to require suppression of evidence in certain narrowly defined circumstances....

[C]ourts have struggled with the issue of what constitutes an intentional omission for purposes of the *Franks* test. In addressing the issue of when omissions should be sufficient grounds for suppressing the fruits of a warrant, some circuits collapsed the "intentionality" and "materiality" prongs of *Franks* into a single test, ruling that intent to present the magistrate with a "deliberate falsehood" can be inferred from the knowing omission of materially exculpatory evidence. That is, if a police officer knowingly withheld evidence which was so critical as to negate probable cause, such an omission must have been an intentional, or deliberate, falsehood.

This approach was roundly criticized by the Fourth Circuit in the 1990 case of *United States v. Colkley*:

> Every decision not to include certain information in the affidavit is "intentional" insofar as it is made knowingly. If, as the district court held, this type of "intentional" omission is all that *Franks* requires, the *Franks* intent prerequisite would be satisfied in almost every case. *Franks* clearly requires defendants to allege more than "intentional" omission in this weak sense. "The mere fact that the affiant does not list every conceivable conclusion does not taint the validity of the affidavit." *Franks* protects against omissions that are designed to mislead, or that are made in reckless disregard of whether they would

> mislead ... the magistrate.... We have doubts about the validity of in-
> ferring bad motive under *Franks* from the fact of omission alone, for
> such an inference collapses into a single inquiry the two elements—
> "intentionality" and "materiality"—which *Franks* states are inde-
> pendently necessary.

The reasoning of *Colkley* has become the prevailing view. Omissions in search and arrest warrant affidavits will be scrutinized to determine whether the challenged omissions made the application misleading; if they did, the warrant application as a whole may be considered a "deliberate falsehood" within the meaning of Franks. Then and only then must the court turn to the question of materiality and determine whether the inclusion of the omitted material in the affidavit would have negated probable cause.

The *Franks* standard for determining when a search is invalid under the Fourth Amendment would map well in determining when an omission before the grand jury should result in dismissal of the indictment. Applying this framework, states should dismiss indictments where the defendant has proven that: 1) substantial exculpatory evidence was in possession of the prosecutor; 2) the prosecutor knowingly or recklessly failed to disclose it to the grand jury in order to distort the grand jury presentation; and 3) reviewing the grand jury transcript, coupled with the improperly omitted material, the court determines that there is no probable cause to support the indictment.

Unlike the situation in which exculpatory evidence is simply withheld, where the evidence presented to the grand jury has been distorted by the prosecutor, or the grand jury has been told a "half truth," the prosecutor may be viewed as affirmatively misleading or deceiving the grand jury. Although not expressly recognizing that it was doing so, Massachusetts has applied a modified *Franks* approach to challenges of grand jury omissions, ruling that an indictment may be dismissed where "the integrity of the grand jury proceeding [is] impaired by an unfair and misleading presentation." ...

One may argue that the *Franks* framework is inapposite to the grand jury context because a court has no power after *Costello* to dismiss a grand jury indictment not supported by probable cause; if the evidence before the grand jury is not reviewed for sufficiency, why should it be reviewed for veracity? First, not all state courts follow the Supreme Court's rule in *Costello* and decline to review the sufficiency of evidence before the grand jury. More importantly, intentional distortion of evidence is more akin to perjury than it is to omission. Notwithstanding *Costello*, a number of federal courts have either ruled or suggested that a prosecutor's knowing use of perjured testimony before the grand jury violates the Fifth Amendment. In the now famous words of Justice Sutherland [in *Berger v. United States*] "while [a prosecutor] may strike hard blows, he is not at liberty to strike foul ones." A prosecutor owes a duty of good faith both to the grand jury and to the defendant. Intentional distortion, unlike mere omission, clearly raises the specter of bad faith, or, in Justice Sutherland's words, a "foul blow."

Whether the omission of a particular piece of exculpatory evidence has a distorting effect will vary from case to case depending on the interrelationship between the nature of the evidence presented and the importance of the evidence omitted. However, certain general conclusions can be drawn from the foregoing analysis. For example, where the prosecutor introduces evidence of forensic tests performed on a weapon found at a crime scene which link the defendant to the crime (*e.g.*, by fingerprints), it would be a distortion to fail to inform the grand jury of other tests performed on the same weapon which were negative or inconclusive (*e.g.*, DNA sampling). Similarly, it would be a distortion to introduce a portion of a defendant's post arrest statement to the police, without including an exculpatory portion of the same statement on the same subject. These omissions render the portion of evidence presented to the grand jury misleading.

Other omissions clearly are not a distortion within the meaning of *Franks*. The government should be under no general obligation to inform the grand jury of general denials of the crime made by the defendant, prior inconsistent statements made by government witnesses, or other evidence reflecting on the credibility of witnesses before the grand jury, such as bias or inducements. None of these types of exculpatory evidence directly and objectively modify the inculpatory evidence presented to the grand jury; that is, the defendant may falsely deny the crime while others honestly insist on his guilt, a witness may have recounted the facts innocently but inaccurately on a prior occasion yet give a correct account before the grand jury, or a witness might have a variety of palpable motivations for lying, yet still testify truthfully.

Where, however, the omitted material directly modifies the evidence presented to the grand jury such that its omission rises to the level of misrepresentation, a prosecutor should produce it. For example, ... a prosecutor should be under no general duty to disclose to the grand jury evidence that a cooperating witness has made a deal with the government, and the details of this plea bargain. However, if this same crucial witness states or implies to the grand jury that he has come forward solely because he wants to "do the right thing," suggesting that his cooperation is the result of moral conviction rather than inducement, it would be a distortion within the meaning of *Franks* not to correct this misstatement and disclose to the grand jury the parameters of the plea bargain.

The question of whether to present alibi evidence to the grand jury presents perhaps one of the most difficult dilemmas faced by a prosecutor. Many prosecutors who are aware that the target of a grand jury investigation has an alibi defense will for strategic reasons call the purported alibi witness to testify at the grand jury, in order to test the witness's memory under oath and discover in advance of trial his strength as a witness. Other prosecutors will do so out of an overriding sense of fairness, consistent with their ethical duty to pursue "justice" rather than merely to advocate for convictions. While there are strong policy reasons for encouraging prosecutors to present alibi witnesses, failure to do so would not constitute "distortion" sufficient to cause the dismissal of the indictment under a Franks test. Imagine an armed robbery case where the store clerk identifies the defendant as the robber, and the defendant's brother provides an alibi. Although it would be impossible for the grand jury to believe both the clerk and the brother, omission of the brother's statement at the grand jury stage would not be distortive of the clerk's presentation under the foregoing analysis; that is, the brother's testimony does not so directly modify or alter the clerk's testimony that to omit one and include the other makes the grand jury presentation misleading.

Nor should the prosecutor be under an obligation to introduce evidence of affirmative defenses which might be available, such as self defense or insanity, so long as he does not distort any evidence which he voluntarily introduces on such issues of intent. Although requiring production of affirmative defenses would aid the grand jury in exercising its screening function, it would do so only at the combined cost of forcing the prosecutor into the role and mindset of a defense attorney and turning the preliminary probable cause determination into a mini-trial on the merits.

This distortion standard should apply only to the intentional omission of evidence supporting the factual, not legal, innocence of the accused. Examples of situations where the defendant may be factually guilty (that is, he committed the proscribed offense with the requisite intent) but legally innocent (the law does not recognize him as guilty) include those cases where a confession was coerced, a search was illegal, the statute of limitations had expired, essential evidence was inadmissible, or some other procedural rule operated to bar a conviction. While some commentators have argued that consideration of legal innocence by the grand jury should be mandatory in order to prevent unwarranted trials, they overlook the public's interest in seeing the guilty brought to justice through an open and visible process. Because the grand jury operates in secrecy, encouraging the grand jury to "no bill" a case where the defendant is factually guilty but legally innocent would bring public disrespect upon the criminal justice system. Where the grand jury declines to return an indictment of a factually guilty person on the basis of legal innocence, the public's ability to comprehend and respect the criminal justice process may have been compromised. For this reason, only those exculpatory facts which support factual innocence of the accused should be the subject of a *Franks* distortion analysis....

Selected References

Peter L. Arenella, Reforming the Federal Grand Jury and the State Preliminary Hearing to Prevent Conviction Without Adjudication, 78 Michigan Law Review 463 (1980).

William J. Campbell, Eliminate the Grand Jury, 64 Journal of Criminal Law and Criminology 174 (1973).

Andrew D. Leipold, Why Grand Juries Do Not (and Cannot) Protect the Accused, 80 Cornell Law Review 260 (1995).

Cases

Ballard v. United States, 329 U.S. 187 (1946).
Bank of Nova Scotia v. United States, 487 U.S. 250 (1988).
Berger v. United States, 295 U.S. 78 (1935).
Costello v. United States, 350 U.S. 359 (1956).
Franks v. Delaware, 438 U.S. 154 (1978).
United States v. Calandra, 414 U.S. 338 (1974).
United States v. Colkley, 899 F.2d 297 (4th Cir. 1990).
United States v. Page, 808 F.2d 723 (10th Cir. 1987).
United States v. Williams, 504 U.S. 36 (1992).
Wood v. Georgia, 370 U.S. 375 (1962).

Further Reading (selected work by R. Michael Cassidy)

Prosecutorial Ethics (West 2005).

"Soft Words of Hope:" *Giglio*, Accomplice Witnesses, and the Problem of Implied Inducements, 98 Northwestern Law Review 1129 (2004).

Sharing Sacred Secrets: Is It (Past) Time for a Dangerous Person Exception to the Clergy-Penitent Privilege?, 44 William & Mary Law Review 1627 (2003).

B. Examination

Chapter Forty-One

Maximum Sentence Enhancements[*]

... A vast difference exists between an accused's rights at trial and a convicted defendant's rights at sentencing. At trial, a criminal defendant is entitled to the full panoply of due process protections: the right to counsel, notice of the charges, to compulsory process, to confront and cross-examine adverse witnesses, to trial by jury, and the right to have the prosecution prove the elements of the offense beyond a reasonable doubt. After conviction, a defendant stands in a radically different position. These due process guarantees vanish except for the right to counsel.

Discretionary Sentencing Regime. A traditional criminal statute defines the elements of a crime and sets out a maximum penalty permitted for its commission. A judge has the discretion to impose any penalty within the maximum the statute prescribes. The statute does not require the judge to make any fact-finding before imposing sentence. The jury's finding that the defendant committed the elements of the crime permits the judge, without more, to impose the maximum penalty, if the judge wishes.

The United States Supreme Court set out the rationale for denying due process claims under discretionary sentencing in *Williams v. New York*.... [A] jury had convicted the defendant of murder and recommended a life sentence. The murder statute permitted a maximum sentence of death, if the judge found it appropriate. At sentencing, the judge considered information the probation department and other sources had supplied.... The information included accusations of other crimes for which the defendant had not been con-

---

* **Frank R. Herrmann, S.J.,** *30=20: "Understanding" Maximum Sentence Enhancements,* 46 Buffalo Law Review 175 (1998), http://papers.ssrn.com/abstract_id=748244. [In a case several years after Professor Herrmann's paper was published, the Supreme Court found the U.S. Sentencing Guidelines violated the Sixth Amendment to the extent that they permitted judicial rather than jury fact-finding as a basis for sentencing. *United States v. Booker,* 543 U.S. 220 (2005).]

victed and an allegation that he had a "morbid sexuality." ... The judge relied on this information to reject the jury's recommendation of life and instead to impose a death sentence....

Williams challenged the New York sentencing scheme arguing due process entitled him to confront and cross-examine the sources used against him at sentencing. The Supreme Court rejected Williams's challenge.... [S]entencing information helps a judge decide whether to do what the conviction already entitles the judge to do.... The *Williams* rationale for denying due process claims at discretionary sentencing fails to address an obvious problem. [It] blinks away any difference between the judge who says, "I sentence you to death for this murder" and the judge who says, "I sentence you to death for this murder because I believe reports that you committed other bad acts and have a morbid sexuality." ... The difference, however, is clear to any defendant....

The engine driving the *Williams* Court's rationale was not logic but experience. Judges need information if they are to exercise their sentencing discretion prudently. The Court feared over-burdening judges with the requirements of full criminal due process for sentencing factors.... Judges could not tailor punishment to the individual criminal if the due process safeguards of a criminal trial had to accompany each additional finding made at sentencing. Williams, therefore, drew the due process line at conviction. A defendant is entitled to full safeguards during trial. Once convicted, the defendant's due process rights under discretionary sentencing are virtually extinct....

Complex Sentencing Scheme.... Colorado's Sexual Offender Act ... permitted a judge to sentence a person convicted of indecent liberties to a term from one day to life as a sexual offender if the judge found the defendant posed a threat of bodily harm or was an habitual offender and mentally ill. These factors were not elements of the crime of indecent liberties. The Sexual Offender Act permitted the judge to make the additional findings without affording the defendant the opportunity to be heard. The defendant had no right to confront or cross-examine witnesses or to present or compel evidence in his behalf.... Upon conviction, he was subject to whatever loss of liberty the legislature prescribed for his crime.

The Supreme Court [held in *Specht* that this] sentencing scheme violated the Due Process Clause. The Court reaffirmed that, in the discretionary sentencing context of *Williams*, the Due Process Clause did not require a sentencing judge to hold a hearing or permit a defendant to participate in it.... However, the Supreme Court refused to extend *Williams* to the facts of Specht. Under the Colorado scheme, Specht received a greater punishment than his conviction for indecent liberties permitted. He was subject to the greater penalty only because the sentencing judge made an additional factual finding that the defendant was a sexual offender. Because at the sexual offender hearing Specht received a "magnified sentence,".... Specht faced a "radically different situation" than the defendant in *Williams*....

Some appellate courts have opined that it was the bifurcated nature of the Colorado sentencing proceedings that made *Specht* radically different from *Williams*. The *Specht* Court noted the Colorado scheme made a conviction for indecent liberties the basis for commencing another proceeding under the Sexual Offenders Act. But, for Specht, dividing the hearings into two was constitutionally significant only because the second hearing required "a new finding of fact that was not an ingredient of the offense charged" in the first hearing. It would elevate form over substance to conclude due process is satisfied if the judge imposes the magnified sentence based on additional fact-finding at one hearing rather than two.

Mandatory Minimum Sentencing Schemes. Mandatory minimum sentencing statutes restrict the sentencing judge's traditionally broad discretion. The statutes typically describe certain aggravating circumstances concerning the crime itself or the defendant's background. They require judges to determine if the designated circumstances were present. If a judge finds such aggravating facts exist, the judge is no longer free to sentence anywhere within the maximum range, as under a discretionary sentencing statute. Rather, the judge must impose at least the minimum sentence prescribed in the statute. The judge retains the discretion to impose a sentence greater than the minimum. The uppermost limit on the sentence remains the maximum term the statute prescribes for the elements of the crime. For example, assume a kidnapping statute imposes a maximum sentence of twenty years. It also lists the use of a weapon as an aggravating factor. It mandates a minimum five-year sentence if the aggravating factor is present. If, at the sentencing hearing, the judge finds the convicted defendant used a gun to commit the offense, the judge's traditional discretion is cabined. The judge must, at a minimum, sentence the defendant to five years.

Must a court afford a defendant the full due process protections of a criminal trial before a judge can impose a mandatory minimum sentence? According to the United States Supreme Court, no. *McMillan v. Pennsylvania* involved a due process challenge to the validity of a state mandatory minimum statute. The Pennsylvania statute punished the commission of certain enumerated felonies with at least five years in prison if the defendant visibly possessed a firearm in the course of the designated felonies. Each of the felony convictions carried possible maximum sentences in excess of five years regardless of aggravating circumstances. The statute expressly stated that visible possession was not an element of any of the offenses. It authorized the sentencing judge to find visible possession and permitted the judge to base his or her finding on a preponderance of the evidence....

The Court in *McMillan* upheld the constitutionality of the mandatory minimum act. It largely deferred to legislatures to define the elements of a crime. Because the Pennsylvania legislature chose not to include visible possession among the defined elements, visible possession was only a sentencing factor. The due process requirements of proof beyond a reasonable doubt traditionally attach only to the elements of a crime, not to sentencing factors....

At the core of *McMillan's* rationale for denying full due process in mandatory minimum sentencing is the Court's view that a conviction authorizes a judge to impose the maximum sentence. The *McMillan* Court affirmed the *Williams* doctrine developed in the context of discretionary sentencing. According to *McMillan*, a defendant convicted under a mandatory minimum statute is not entitled to any more due process at sentencing than a defendant subject to traditional discretionary sentencing. The mandatory nature of the sentence does not change the due process calculus.... So long as the mandatory minimum punishment remains within the maximum the court could impose in its discretion, the defendant suffers no additional harm.

However, *McMillan* explicitly cautioned: "there are constitutional limits to the state's power [to define the elements of a crime]." ... Although the Court declined to delineate all of the circumstances that might trigger Due Process protections for aggravating factors, it did set down certain express boundaries. The Pennsylvania statute, the Court observed, remained within due process boundaries because it did not create any impermissible presumption of guilt or relieve the prosecution of its burden of proving guilt, or change the definition of any existing crime. In addition, as the Court repeatedly noted, a finding of visible possession of a firearm did not subject a defendant to greater punishment than was available for the crime alone. It did not expose a defendant to a higher maximum than he or she might otherwise receive....

Sentencing Guidelines.... Sentencing guideline schemes specify factors which aggravate a crime. With respect to these factors, the guidelines function much like mandatory minimum statutes. A court must impose a sentence in a particular range within the statutory maximum, depending upon the circumstances of the crime and the defendant's criminal history.... Arguably, guidelines create a liberty interest in a sentence below the maximum because a judge is no longer free under the guidelines to impose the statutory maximum by virtue of the conviction alone, as under discretionary sentencing.... The Supreme Court has recognized that due process protects a defendant's interest in fair sentencing, but has emphasized in the same cases that the interest is not defined as a liberty interest in a sentence below the statutory maximum.

Maximum-Enhancing Statutes. One genre of statutes differs markedly from mandatory minimum statutes and sentencing guideline schemes. Maximum-enhancing statutes ... are statutes which permit or require a sentencing court to impose a sentence greater than that available, were the judge to consider only the elements of the crime. For example, assume a kidnapping statute defines the offense as restraining or taking another by force or the threat of force. It allows imprisonment for no more than twenty years if the defendant is convicted of the crime. However, it permits, or requires, a sentence of thirty years if the sentencing judge finds the defendant used a weapon in committing the kidnapping....

Maximum-enhancing statutes create a sentencing structure very different from discretionary sentencing or sentencing under mandatory minimum schemes or guidelines. Under a discretionary sentencing structure, a kidnapping defendant may lose twenty years of liberty, whether or not he or she used a weapon. Under a mandatory minimum scheme, a defendant will forfeit at least five years of liberty if the judge finds the defendant used a weapon. A guideline may require a convicted kidnapper to be sentenced more harshly within the maximum allowed for kidnapping, if the defendant used a weapon. In these instances, in the prevailing view of the circuit courts, all the safeguards of a criminal trial precede any loss of liberty the defendant will suffer by virtue of conviction. The statute set out the maximum term for the crime and the sentence did not exceed the maximum.

Can the same hold true for maximum-enhancing statutes? Under a common-sense view of the matter, the judge adds an extra term to what the crime alone permits. The judge thereby deprives the defendant of more liberty than a bare conviction would entail. What was twenty years for kidnapping becomes thirty years for kidnapping with a gun. Of course, the motive for imposing the "enhanced" sentence is apparent. Such a defendant is worse than one who commits the kidnapping without the aggravating factor. But, however sound the reason for imprisonment, the Due Process Clause guarantees that the state may not imprison a person for a crime without first according the defendant all the protections of a criminal trial. How can a defendant constitutionally suffer the additional loss of liberty without the due process protections of a criminal trial?

Does the *Williams/McMillan* approach to sentencing justify the denial of full due process protections for maximum enhancing statutes? *McMillan* recognized that a statutory scheme different from discretionary sentencing or mandatory minimum sentencing might cross the constitutional line and trigger the safeguards of a criminal trial. Unlike the Pennsylvania statute before the Court in *McMillan*, maximum enhancing statutes expose a defendant to greater punishment than the range "already available to [a court] without the special finding of [an aggravating circumstance]." Indeed, the Court had already held one such statutory scheme violated Due Process. The Court in *McMillan* distinguished *Specht's* maximum-enhancing scheme from the mandatory minimum statute before it. It did not overrule or limit *Specht*. It left *Specht's* reasoning entirely intact. In upholding the constitutionality of the Pennsylvania sentencing structure, the *McMillan* Court relied on the fact that the sentencing factor in *McMillan* did not increase the maximum punishment. Given this reasoning and *McMillan's* continuing adherence to *Specht*, is there any justification for providing anything less than full criminal due process for sentencing findings under maximum-enhancement statutes? ...

Reduced Due Process By Characterization. Legislatures have the power to specify certain conduct as an element of a crime. But not everything a legislature includes in a criminal statute is an element of the defined crime. Statutes contain penalty provisions that are distinct from the elements. The penalty provisions bear on the amount of punishment meted out for the crime. A legislature may exclude specified conduct from the definition of the crime, making it part of the statute's penalty clause. When a penalty clause describes aggravating conduct, courts will refer to the conduct as a sentencing factor or an enhancement, not an element of the crime.

A maximum-enhancing statute singles out particular conduct which serves to increase a defendant's punishment over what it could be without consideration of that conduct. Defendants sentenced under an enhancement statute may receive a greater penalty than they otherwise could. But for the aggravating conduct, the sentence would be less. Understandably, some defendants have argued they were denied due process safeguards when they were subjected to an increased sentence based on conduct described in the criminal statute's penalty provision without the usual due process safeguards associated with the state's right to deprive a defendant of liberty.

In responding to this challenge, some courts have asked whether a legislature intended to make conduct an element of a crime or part of the penalty clause. Conduct determined to be "merely" a sentencing factor automatically justifies reduced due process. They reason that [law only] requires full trial due process only for elements. A sentencing factor is not an element. Therefore, full due process does not attach to such conduct even though it increases the defendant's sentence. Characterizing the conduct as a "sentencing factor" establishes the convicted defendant's rights or, rather, lack thereof.

This reasoning is flawed. *McMillan* expressly noted that facts not formally identified as elements of the offense charged may trigger due process in some circumstances. The Pennsylvania statute did not fall among those circumstances because it did not authorize a sentence in excess of that otherwise allowed for the offenses of conviction. Labeling enhancement conduct as a "sentencing factor" begs the real question: does the factor trigger criminal due process protection?

The judicial treatment of 21 U.S.C. §844(a) of the Drug Abuse Prevention and Control Act demonstrates the labeling approach fails to answer this question. In pertinent part, the Act authorizes a penalty of not more than one-year in prison if a defendant knowingly and intentionally possessed a controlled substance. But the Act authorizes imprisonment for not less than five nor more than twenty years if a defendant possessed more than five grams of cocaine base (crack). Do the criminal due process safeguards of a criminal trial precede a finding that the defendant possessed over five grams of cocaine base? To answer this question, the circuit courts have tried to discern what the legislature intended. Did Congress want quantity to be an element of the crime or a sentencing factor? A defendant's rights hinge on the proper characterization.

With so much in the balance, courts examining §844(a) have expended a great deal of effort to determine whether Congress intended quantity to be an element or a sentencing factor. They have parsed the express wording and structure of the statute, its use of titles and paragraph headings, and the placement of semi-colons. They have reviewed its legislative history. They have teased out the defined elements of the crime from the statute's penalty provisions. Motivating these efforts is the premise that legislative intention determines whether or not a defendant will receive the due process protections of a criminal trial....

Make the Enhancement Disappear. By labeling particular conduct as a sentencing factor, a court is implicitly holding that a statute has not created a separate crime. A court may accurately interpret legislative intent when it finds a legislature intended conduct as a sentencing factor and not a separate crime. It may also be that a "sentencing factor" should wear that label if that is what the legislature intended. But, whatever its label, a maximum sentence enhancer appears to punish the conduct that caused the enhancement. *McMillan* does not offer any justification for reduced due process in such a case. On the contrary, *McMillan* upheld Pennsylvania's minimum sentence increase because it did not "alter[] the maximum for the crime." If the legislative label of "sentencing factor" does not justify elimination of due process safeguards for maximum sentence enhancers, is there anything else that does?

[In] *United States v. Rivera-Gomez*, the First Circuit Court did not merely label the conduct as a sentencing factor. It made the enhanced portion of the defendant's sentence disappear. [A] trial court sentenced the defendant to life in prison for a car jacking in which death occurred. 18 U.S.C. §2119 provided in relevant part [that whoever is convicted of carjacking shall be fined a certain amount or imprisoned a certain length of time "and, if death results," be fined or imprisoned to further extents].

A jury convicted Rivera-Gomez of carjacking. At sentencing, the judge found that death had resulted in the course of the carjacking. The defendant attacked the constitutionality of his sentence. He conceded that "death results" is not an element of carjacking. He claimed that the life sentence punished him for conduct for which he was not charged.

The First Circuit examined the wording and structure of the carjacking statute. In its view, the first section defines the base offense and the following two sections "clear the way for enhanced sentences if either serious bodily injury or death results from the commission of the carjacking offense." According to the First Circuit, Congress did not intend the "death results" provision of the act to be an element of the offense, nor did it intend to create a new species of carjacking offense (carjacking when death results). It intended "simply to augment the sentences for certain aggravated carjackings...."

The court analogized an enhancement sentence to a guidelines sentence. Guidelines sentences, the court reasoned, increase punishment on the basis of aggravating factors. A finding of aggravating circumstances under the guidelines does not require the full safeguards of criminal due process. Therefore, the court concluded, the safeguards are not required under the carjacking act either, when it increases punishment on the basis of aggravating circumstances.

This analogy is flawed. Yes, fact-finding under the guidelines does not require full criminal due process. But that is because any increase the guidelines permit must remain within the statutory maximum. The guideline sentence is valid, as long as the statutory maximum is valid. But it does not follow that the statutory maximum is valid because the guideline is valid.

For example, suppose a statute subjects kidnapping to a penalty of twenty years. A guideline then requires a sentence of at least ten years if the defendant used a weapon to accomplish the kidnapping. Under *McMillan*, the guideline sentence of ten years is valid without full due process safeguards for the weapon finding because the ten years for the weapon remains within the twenty-year statutory maximum for the kidnapping. If, however, the statute called for twenty years for kidnapping, but thirty years for kidnapping accomplished with a weapon, a guideline range up to thirty years would be valid only if the increased statutory maximum itself was valid. The enhanced penalty upheld in Rivera-Gomez was not within the maximum guideline range for simple carjacking. The guideline range does not validate the extra ten years.

Rivera-Gomez's analogy does not explain why the statutory increase, of ten years in this case, over the sentence available for the elements can be imposed without full due process safeguards.... How can the court attribute this sentence to the elements alone when the elements do not permit more than a fifteen-year term? Life in jail is more than fifteen years in jail. Ask any defendant. A life sentence for "death results" alters the maximum penalty for the elements of carjacking.

On the basis of *McMillan*, *Rivera-Gomez* admits "in all probability, there are constitutional limits on the way sentencing factors can be deployed in the punishment of a substantive offense." But faced with one of those limits, an increase in the maximum, the *Rivera-Gomez* court blinked it away. It denied that the sentencing factor altered the statutory maximum. Apparently, the factor did not increase the maximum, but established a new maximum, still based on the same elements. If this view is correct, no sentence alters the maximum available for the elements alone. This approach formalistically respects McMillan's logic but simultaneously guts it of all possible force.

The "Subset" Theory of Enhancements. It is possible to effect the same disappearance using different language. Some courts speak of the enhancers as delimiting a "subset" or "portion" of defendants whose aggravating conduct has made them eligible for an "increased" sentence. This "increase," however, is not considered an increase over the base offense for the elements. Rather, it expands the base. The "increase," therefore, is for the elements alone. This difference in base is justified on the ground that one defendant may commit the elements of a crime in a more aggravating fashion, or with a worse character, than another. The "subset" approach, like that in *Rivera-Gomez*, acknowledges that an enhanced sentence is greater than a lesser term (*e.g.*, life is greater than fifteen years). But both assume the harsher sentence represents punishment for the elements only....

[T]he theory is alluring. Under the subset theory, the penalty clause of an enhancement statute divides the set of all those convicted of the crime into groups deserving differing punishments. The legislature has not created one maximum sentence and then particular appropriate sentences along this range. Rather, the legislature has created different maximum sentences depending on aggravating factors. Assume, for example, a legislature imposes a maximum of twenty years for kidnapping accomplished without a gun and a maximum of thirty years if the kidnapping is accomplished with a gun. Under the "subset" theory, the legislature has not increased the penalty for kidnapping when it is accomplished with a gun. It has simply declared that kidnapping is punishable by thirty years for the subset of persons who accomplish it by use of a gun.

This legislative sentencing structure, it may be argued, is analogous to discretionary sentencing. Traditionally, judges made similar divisions based on their discretion. They divided defendants into those more and less worthy of punishment, depending on the defendant's character and the way in which the offense was committed. Full due process was not required for traditional sentencing procedures. The conviction alone substantially diminished the defendant's liberty interest (or due process rights) to the extent of the maximum period of confinement. Why invoke full due process merely because a statute now guides the dividing process that previously lay within the judge's discretion? Indeed, reply the subset theorists, full due process is not triggered.

This approach leaves something in the shade. Under traditional sentencing, a defendant lost his due process right to liberty to the extent of the maximum sentence under the statute. Thus, a defendant convicted of an offense carrying a maximum of twenty years lost his due process right to twenty years of liberty. The source of that loss included any considerations the judge might entertain about the defendant's character or method of committing the crime. The entire twenty years was initially protected by due process but forfeited upon conviction after a criminal trial. The defendant's liberty beyond the statutory maximum was not threatened. His due process right to that liberty was not lost.

An Objection to Due Process Protections for Maximum Enhanced Sentencing. If courts were to acknowledge that criminal trial safeguards must precede maximum-enhanced sentencing, it may be objected that a legislature might try to circumvent the demands of due process by a simple expedient. A legislature could abandon maximum-enhancing statutes and revert to traditional discretionary sentencing. It could expand the maximum penalties available for the elements alone. For example, instead of penalizing kidnapping by twenty years imprisonment and kidnapping with a weapon by thirty years, a legislature could punish kidnapping itself by thirty years. In such case, under the *Williams* rationale applied to discretionary sentencing, due process protections would not attach to the sentencing finding. The defendant could lose thirty years of liberty on the basis of the conviction alone, whether or not he used a weapon. If a legislature can escape due process safeguards by artfully drafting its statutes, why put the legislature to the trouble in the first place?

In fact, a legislature is unlikely to abandon maximum enhancing statutes in an attempt to avoid due process protections. The graded structure of maximum-enhancing statutes serves a desirable purpose. It protects less culpable defendants from excessive punishment when they commit only the un-aggravated crime. Maximum-enhancing statutes reserve harsher punishment for the worse criminal. If a legislature expanded the penalties available for the simple elements of a crime, it would create greater penalties than it deems appropriate for the simple elements merely to avoid complying with the mandates of the Due Process Clause. Would legislators expose themselves, or their families, or members of their own electorate, to life imprisonment for possessing any amount of cocaine, just to deny the safeguards of criminal trial to those who possess great amounts? [Echoing Justices Marshall and Stevens, dissenting in *McMillan*,] "continued functioning of the democratic process" provides some assurance that legislatures will not increase penalties in order to make an end-run around due process guarantees. A legislature can harshly penalize serious criminals without placing less culpable citizens at risk of draconian punishment. It can maintain the graded structure of maximum-enhancing statutes. But when it does so, the protections of a criminal trial should attach to the enhancing conduct.

Conclusion. Appellate courts have failed to justify the denial of criminal due process protections at sentencing for maximum-enhancing conduct. Judicial efforts to analogize maximum-enhanced sentences to punishment under discretionary statutes fail. An increased maximum sentence cannot be attributed solely to the elements. Perhaps in the rush to "lock up criminals," courts have forgotten that thirty is more than twenty and always will be. The elements alone do not permit the longer sentence. The increased portion is punishment for the aggravated conduct that causes the increase. Characterizing the aggravating conduct as a "sentencing factor" does not change the reality of what the punishment is for. A defendant sentenced to thirty years for kidnapping with a weapon, who could only be sentenced to twenty years for kidnapping without a weapon, is punished with ten years for using the weapon. Call the weapon use an "element;" call it a "sentencing factor." Unless the due process protections of a criminal trial have preceded the finding that caused ten additional years of punishment, the finding deprives a defendant of liberty for criminal conduct without the safeguards of a criminal trial. Granted, a defendant may belong to a "subset" of convicts who deserve additional punishment. Worse criminals deserve heavier penalties. But criminal trial protections should attach in determining whether an accused is a worse criminal deserving a greater penalty than the crime otherwise permits.

Judicial formalism attributes all punishment to the elements of a crime. Consequently, legislatures can create two crimes but call them one. The first is composed of the simple elements the legislature defines. Full due process protections apply to finding those elements. But when a defendant receives a maximum-enhanced sentence, the court imposes punishment for a second, greater crime. Formalism denies the existence of the second crime. It perceives "a mere sentencing factor." Defendants have better eyes. They see they are punished for aggravating conduct that a court found without the due process of law.

Selected References

Susan N. Herman, The Tail That Wagged the Dog: Bifurcated Fact-finding Under the Federal Sentencing Guidelines and the Limits of Due Process, 66 USC Law Review 289 (1992).

David Yellin, Illusion Illogic, and Injustice: Real Offense Sentencing and the Federal Sentencing Guidelines, 78 Minnesota Law Review 403 (1993).

Deborah Young, Fact-finding at Federal Sentencing: Why the Guidelines Should Meet the Rules, 79 Cornell Law Review 299 (1994).

Cases

McMillan v. Pennsylvania, 477 U.S. 79 (1986).

Specht v. Patterson, 386 U.S. 605 (1967).

United States v. Haggerty, 85 F.3d 403 (8th Cir. 1996).

United States v. Rush, 840 F.2d 574 (8th Cir. 1988) (en banc).

United States v. Ryan, 9 F.3d 660 (8th Cir. 1993), *cert. denied*, 514 U.S. 1082 (1995).

United States v. West, 826 F.2d 909 (9th Cir. 1987).

Williams v. New York, 337 U.S. 241 (1949).

Examples of Federal Maximum-Enhancing Statutes

18 U.S.C. §2113(d) (1997) (dangerous weapon in bank robbery).

18 U.S.C. §924(c) (1976) (firearm in a felony).

18 U.S.C. §2119 (1996) (car jacking if death resulted).

Examples of State Maximum-Enhancing Statutes

Mont. Code Ann. §46-18-221(1) (1978) (weapon in a felony).

Cal. Penal Code §12022(a)(1) (West 1990) (same).

Minn. Stat. §609.1352(1)(1) (1989) (offense motivated by sexual impulse and predatory behavior).

Further Reading
(selected work by Frank R. Herrmann, S.J.)

Facing the Accuser: Ancient and Medieval Precursors of the Confrontation Clause, 34 Virginia Journal of International Law 481 (1994) (with Brownlow M. Speer).

Chapter Forty-Two

Catholic Judges in Capital Cases*

Here is an interesting cultural collision. The death penalty is back in fashion in our legal system. Congress has created more than sixty new capital crimes. The Attorney General has used the new laws to prosecute Timothy McVeigh and Theodore Kaczynski. The federal courts have lost some of their authority to review state executions. The Catholic Church, with no sense of timing (or a fine sense of urgency), has picked this moment to launch a campaign against capital punishment. This puts Catholic judges in a bind. They are obliged by oath, professional commitment, and the demands of citizenship to enforce the death penalty. They are also obliged to adhere to their church's teaching on moral matters.

The legal system has a solution for this dilemma—it allows (indeed it requires) the recusal of judges whose convictions keep them from doing their job. This is a good solution. But it is harder than you think to determine when a judge must recuse himself and when he may stay on the job. Catholic judges will not want to shirk their judicial obligations. They will want to sit whenever they can without acting immorally. So they need to know what the church teaches, and its effect on them. On the other hand litigants and the general public are entitled to impartial justice, and that may be something that a judge who is heedful of ecclesiastical pronouncements cannot dispense. We need to know whether judges are sometimes legally disqualified from hearing cases that their consciences would let them decide.

We talk specifically about Catholic judges, but they are not alone in facing this difficulty. Quakers have opposed capital punishment in this country since its founding. The Church of the Brethren has long espoused the same pacifist ideal. The Union of American Hebrew Congregations, in common with a

---

* **John H. Garvey**, *Catholic Judges in Capital Cases*, 81 Marquette Law Review 303 (1998) (co-authored with Amy V. Coney), http://papers.ssrn.com/abstract_id=781344.

large number of liberal Protestant groups, has spoken out against the death penalty during much of this century. Unitarians and Universalists did so both before and after their merger in 1961.... To simplify our exposition we also focus on federal judges.... [in part because] the "drug kingpin" law contains a recent, detailed set of procedures for death cases that will help us explain the various roles judges may play.... Our conclusions would not be different if we were to focus on state judges—indeed, we hope to have most influence on that level. We have chosen to state our case in federal terms in order to make it as accessible as possible.

To anticipate our conclusions just briefly, we believe that Catholic judges (if they are faithful to the teaching of their church) are morally precluded from enforcing the death penalty. This means that they can neither themselves sentence criminals to death nor enforce jury recommendations of death. Whether they may affirm lower court orders of either kind is a question we have the most difficulty in resolving. There are parts of capital cases in which we think orthodox Catholic judges may participate—these include trial on the issue of guilt and collateral review of capital convictions. The moral impossibility of enforcing capital punishment in the first two or three cases (sentencing, enforcing jury recommendations, affirming) is a sufficient reason for recusal under federal law....

Catholic teaching about capital punishment is fairly complicated. Furthermore, it is not possible to say, as some might suppose, that members of the Catholic Church are simply bound by their faith to follow the Church's teaching on this issue. And even if they were, the prohibition against capital punishment has different implications for people acting in different roles. Though one might say that it was simply and unqualifiedly wrong to flip the switch or pull the trigger that kills a human being, this is not what judges do. Judges cooperate in many ways more or less direct with that evil act, and their participation in some of these ways is permissible, even commendable....

[N]ot everyone who plays a role in the system of capital punishment bears the same degree of guilt. Some do not act wrongly at all. In the old Code of Canon Law there was a rule that a person who had served as a public executioner could not be ordained as a priest. His immediate assistants were also disqualified, but only if they had actually taken part in an execution. The judge who imposed the death sentence was also disqualified, but jurors who only made a decision about guilt or innocence were not. Nor were lawyers, witnesses, or even those who built scaffolds. These distinctions might seem too refined, but they are not out of line with our own intuitions. The most adamant opponent of capital punishment today would probably impute no blame to the manufacturer whose needles are used for a lethal injection; nor to the bus driver who brings the executioner to work.

If we are going to make these kinds of distinctions, we will also (though for rather different reasons) have a difficult time with judges, who play a wide variety of roles. At one extreme is the sentencing judge who imposes a sentence of death. This is still a step removed from the actual execution, which the judge will not even see, but it is a role where the judge bears a primary responsibility for what happens to the criminal. At the other end is the Supreme Court justice who votes to deny certiorari to a state prisoner, condemned to death, whose last hope is to convince someone that the trial court improperly denied his suppression motion. Our instinct is to say that the Church's teaching on capital punishment has little bearing on this last case. But how exactly is it different?

In Catholic moral theology, there is an extensive literature on this subject, usually collected under the heading of cooperation with evil. Stated abstractly, these are cases where one person ("the cooperator") gives physical or moral assistance to another person ("the wrongdoer") who is doing some immoral action. In judging the morality of the cooperator's action, the most important distinction the Church draws is between what it calls formal and material cooperation. Here is a simile to help lawyers think about the distinction. In first amendment law there are two "tracks" for judging government actions that sin against the freedom of speech. Track one is for cases where the government acts with a bad intention—where it restricts speech because it does not like what is being said. (Imagine a law forbidding people to make jokes about the Vice President.) This kind of action is almost always unconstitutional. Track two is for cases where the government restricts speech unintentionally, in the course of doing something else. (Imagine a law against littering applied to a politician distributing handbills.) This kind of action is sometimes unconstitutional and sometimes not. The courts will balance the law's good effects against its impact on speech.

Formal and material cooperation are a little like tracks one and two. A person formally cooperates with another person's immoral act when he shares in the immoral intention of the other. Imagine a tenant who, coveting the apartment of his Jewish neighbor, gives his name to the Nazis. Formal cooperation is always immoral. Material cooperation involves an act that has the effect of helping a wrongdoer, where the cooperator does not share in the wrongdoer's immoral intention. Imagine a grocer who sells food to a glutton, or a letter carrier who delivers an extortionate threat. Material cooperation is only sometimes immoral. We judge this by a kind of moral balancing test—weighing the importance of doing the act against the gravity of the evil, its proximity, the certainty that one's act will contribute to it, and the danger of scandal to others.

Rather than say much more about these rules in the abstract, let us see how they might apply to judges. We will examine a few of the roles a federal judge can be asked to play in a capital case arising under the Anti-Drug Abuse Act of 1988 (the "drug kingpin" statute).

This Act authorizes capital punishment where a defendant engaged in a "continuing criminal enterprise" intentionally kills someone or causes such a killing. The United States Attorney must serve notice of the government's intention to seek the death penalty early on, but the sentencing hearing is held after trial on the issue of guilt, generally before the judge and jury who handled the trial. At the hearing the government must prove that there are certain factors present that make the crime an aggravated case, deserving of death. The defendant tries to prove factors that might mitigate against death—his youth, record, state of mind, and so on. The jury can recommend death if it finds the requisite aggravating factors and concludes that they outweigh any mitigating factors. But no matter what its findings, it is not required to impose death. Neither is the judge who sits without a jury. When the hearing is held before a jury and the jury recommends the death penalty, however, the Act provides that "the court shall sentence the defendant to death."

1. *Sentencing With a Jury.* Let us begin by considering the action of the judge who sentences a defendant to death upon the jury's recommendation. Here is an example of such a sentence imposed in *United States v. Chandler*:

> *Sentence*: Based upon the Special Findings and Recommendations of the jury on April 3, 1991, under Count 3, the court hereby imposes upon the defendant a sentence of death. The defendant will be remanded to the custody of the Bureau of Prisons with directions to cause such death sentence to be implemented.

This is a straightforward case of formal cooperation, one in which the judge sets the wheels of injustice in motion. Once the judge enters the order, the government is authorized—indeed unless there is a pardon, bound—to put the defendant to death. And the judge intends that this should happen. That the judge may feel reluctance or regret does not change his intent. One who pulls a trigger reluctantly still intends to fire a gun. One who gives an order cannot protest that he did not intend it to be carried out.

There are two points that might cause some hesitation. Perhaps the judge's act, though it is followed by momentous consequences, is really just a formality, and should not entail the burden of guilt we impute to it. Consider the docket clerk who enters the order. It would be a bit much to accuse the clerk of formal cooperation in the execution. Both acts seem to be routine, ministerial—the cranking of tiny wheels in a machine that runs by itself. Section 848(l) tells the judge that, "Upon the [jury's] recommendation that the sentence of death be imposed, the court shall sentence the defendant to death."

But the judge's and the clerk's acts are not the same. The content of the order does not matter to the clerk. He files death sentences and discovery orders indifferently, as the post office franks love letters, pornography, blackmail, and letter bombs without a thought to their contents. Content matters to the judge, who composes the order. More importantly, he commands that the execution take place. This is an exercise of authority that in our system of government only a judge can have. It is true that the statute obliges him to give the order, but the reason it obliges him (rather than the docket clerk or the court reporter) is that we want the approval of a responsible figure who has seen the proceedings and polled the jurors, and who can assure us that there is no legal reason against the sentence being imposed.

The other point that might cause hesitation concerns the judge's intent. Consider this case. In *Zobrest v. Catalina Foothills School District*, the Supreme Court approved public payment of a sign-language interpreter for a parochial school student. Strict separationists complained that the interpreter would accompany the student even to mass, and that having a state employee deliver religious messages would violate the establishment clause. The Court replied that there was a difference between a teacher and an interpreter: The interpreter is obliged to "transmit everything that is said in exactly the same way it was intended." In passing it on he does not signify his own (or his employer's) approval. Might we say that the judge stands like an interpreter between the jury and the Bureau of Prisons? If the judge hands the message on without endorsing it, might he lack the intent required for formal cooperation?

This comparison leaves out an essential component of what the judge does. He does not merely repeat what the jury has said; he orders it to be done. Under the statute the jury only makes a "recommendation"; the judge "imposes" the sentence. The judge's order says, "the court hereby imposes upon the defendant a sentence of death." It is a performative utterance.

2. *Sentencing By the Judge.* Under the drug kingpin law a defendant can opt, with the government's agreement, to dispense with a jury and have his sentence determined by the judge alone. A judge who imposes the death penalty in such a case is plainly engaged in formal cooperation. Here there can be no suggestion that the judge is acting like a docket clerk or an interpreter. He bears responsibility for the entire decision, and could make it either way. Section 848(k) states that "the court, regardless of its findings with respect to aggravating and mitigating factors, is never required to impose a death sentence."

But suppose that the judge in the end decides not to order death. The judge might in fact make up his mind at the beginning of the hearing that, no matter what the evidence showed, he would not (because he morally could not) impose the death penalty.... [I]f the judge entertained this resolve he would be obliged to recuse himself. But the judge might go through the sentencing hearing with an open mind, and only after all the evidence was in decide on life rather than death. If that is what happens can we say, at the end of the day, that he has done nothing wrong? In order to actually conduct the hearing with an open mind, the judge who accepts that capital punishment is wrong must suspend his moral judgment during deliberation. It is the willingness to do this that we want to focus on.

Conscience is not a uniquely Christian idea—many people subscribe to the notion of an interior faculty that guides our moral judgments. Christians generally maintain, however, that judgments of conscience are more than natural insights. They are judgments illumined by faith (or darkened by error and vice). The Catholic Church teaches its members that they are bound to obey the certain judgment of their consciences. A judge who suspends his moral judgment during sentencing sets his conscience aside. The effect of the decision, though internal, is real—the judge rejects his obligation to obey conscience and consents, at least provisionally, to act contrary to right judgment. He cuts himself loose from his moral moorings.

Because the act lacks any observable effect (the defendant gets life in the end) it is easy to overlook this point. But the Catholic Church, unlike the criminal law, maintains that we can sin in thought as well as action. This is not a moral stance peculiar to Catholics. You may recall the attention Jimmy Carter received when he told an interviewer from *Playboy* magazine that he had sinned by lusting in his heart. He was referring to the injunction in Matthew's gospel: "What I say to you is: anyone who looks lustfully at a woman has already committed adultery with her in his thoughts." The moral problem with suspending judgment in a capital sentencing hearing is like this. It would be wrong for a judge to place himself at the service of evil by getting in a position to go where events may take him.

3. *The Guilt Phase.* Suppose the district judge knows in advance of trial that the United States Attorney will seek the death penalty, and resolves to take no part in sentencing. May the judge nevertheless handle the case up until that point? May he sit in the trial on the issue of guilt or innocence and then withdraw? The statute might allow this. We will explore in Part II whether this solution is legally proper. Let us assume for the moment that it is, and ask whether there might be a moral problem with making such a contribution. The judge who guides the jury to a guilty verdict lays the groundwork for the defendant's execution. Is it wrong for one opposed to the death penalty to do this?

There are several important differences between this case and the first two. There is nothing intrinsically wrong with trying the defendant. Indeed it is a good thing to try and convict criminals who murder innocent people. It is doing justice. This is not like sentencing the defendant to death—a punishment that is wrong despite the defendant's guilt. Moreover, the judge who conducts the trial need not intend to bring about the defendant's death. Think of *Washington v. Davis*. The government gave a verbal ability test to candidates for the police force. There is nothing intrinsically wrong with this. It is a good idea to have cops who can communicate. The test also disqualified more black than white candidates. But the government did not intend this effect; indeed it regretted it. So too here. The judge's unintended contribution to capital punishment is an example of material cooperation.

Unlike formal cooperation, material cooperation is not always immoral. But neither is there a very neat rule for deciding when it is. The rules are, as we suggested earlier, like the balancing test we use on track two in speech cases or like the tort rules of proximate cause, which define an actor's responsibility for far-reaching effects. In judging the propriety of material cooperation an actor must weigh his reasons for participating against such things as the gravity of the evil, the proximity of his cooperation, the certainty that his work will be misused, the probability that his refusal to cooperate would prevent the evil, and the danger of scandal to others.

Consider what this might mean for a Catholic judge sitting at trial on the issue of guilt. The judge has a strong reason to participate in that phase: society needs judges to enforce the criminal law. Those who do so help maintain a peaceful and just society. It is this social good that we must weigh against the harm of material cooperation. The evil of capital punishment is certainly grave—the taking of human life. But the judge does not actually participate in the sentencing. Indeed he does not know for certain whether he is contributing to a death sentence because he does not know what sentence will be imposed at the later hearing. Recusing himself would not prevent the evil, because another judge would replace him at trial. For these reasons we think that the district judge's material cooperation in capital punishment can be morally justified.

4. *Appeal.* The appellate judge, like the district judge, plays a variety of roles, and some of them present more difficult moral questions than others. If the defendant is convicted and sentenced to death under the drug kingpin law, he may appeal both the conviction and the sentence. The judge's role in reviewing a conviction is not very different from his role in conducting a trial on the issue of guilt. Consider some of the claims in *United States v. Chandler*. Chandler was convicted of murder in furtherance of a continuing criminal enterprise in violation of 21 U.S.C. 848(e). He argued on appeal that the indictment failed to allege and the jury instructions failed to require a connec-

tion between the murder and the enterprise. The Eleventh Circuit concluded that the language of both was sufficiently clear on the point. Chandler also charged that the government had called a witness (a police officer who identified a piece of paper seized in Chandler's home) who was not on the witness list that the law requires the government to supply. The court agreed that this was an error, but it did not require reversal because Chandler had made no contemporaneous objection, and it had no effect on the outcome of the trial.

Affirming Chandler's conviction has the effect of sending him to death. And the appellate judge knows this, because he does his job after sentencing (not before, like the trial judge). But his cooperation is also material rather than formal. In reviewing the sufficiency of the indictment, the jury instructions, and the trial procedure he takes no position on the issue of capital punishment. He would reach the same conclusion if the defendant were sentenced to life in prison. Apart from its unintended consequences, his act (reviewing the fairness of the trial) is a good and just thing to do. If he did not sit on the case someone else would, with the same result. On balance, this seems like the kind of material cooperation that is morally acceptable.

The appellate court's review of Chandler's sentence is a closer question. This seems to complete the district court's order, as the district court completes the jury's recommendation. Is there any real difference between the two cases? The statute provides … :

> the court shall affirm the sentence if it determines that
> (A) the sentence of death was not imposed under the influence of passion, prejudice, or any other arbitrary factor; and
> (B) the information supports the special finding of the existence of every aggravating factor upon which the sentence was based, together with, or the failure to find, any mitigating factors …
> In all other cases the court shall remand the case for reconsideration under this section.

In one way this assignment seems to make the appellate judge more culpable than the trial judge. If the jury recommends death, the trial judge has no choice about imposing that sentence. He might therefore say that his action is just a formality, like the docket clerk's entry of the judgment. We found that this excuse does not work, given the nature of the judge's order. But the excuse is not even available to the appellate judge. The statute directs him to review the evidence and the behavior of the judge and jury, and gives him two options: affirm or remand. He (more accurately, the panel) thus has some room to affect the defendant's fate.

Strictly speaking, though, the panel neither condemns nor saves the defendant. The sentencing judge's order in *Chandler* said, "the court hereby imposes upon the defendant a sentence of death." The Eleventh Circuit's order said:

> Upon Consideration Whereof, it is now hereby ordered and adjudged by this Court that the Judgment ... of the said District Court in this cause be and the same is hereby Vacated in Part and Affirmed in Part.

To affirm the sentence is not to approve it, but to say that the trial court did its job. What the court of appeals really decides is that the responsibility for life and death lies somewhere else. When the court of appeals finds an error it does not sentence the defendant itself. It "remands the case for reconsideration."

The appellate judge can thus say, we think rightly, that he does not intentionally direct or promote the defendant's execution. Consider a slightly easier case of the same sort. The defendant, convicted in Alabama state court, seeks direct review in the United States Supreme Court. He claims that the death penalty violates the Eighth Amendment. The Supreme Court would probably reject this claim. It might point out that the text of the Fifth Amendment contemplates executions. But affirming the sentence is not the same thing as authorizing capital punishment. It only means that in our federal system, the federal courts are not empowered to hold up executions if Alabama chooses to carry them out. The responsibility for doing that lies with the voters, legislators, and judges of Alabama. An affirmance under the drug kingpin law makes a more modest, but comparable, point: that the statute entrusts the decision to the trial judge and jury.

Appellate review of a death sentence is not, then, a case of formal cooperation. This does not mean that it is all right. Whatever might be the legal significance of an affirmance, it probably looks to most people like an endorsement of the sentence. This can cause scandal, leading others into sin ... Considerations like this make it exceedingly difficult to pass moral judgment on the appellate review of sentencing. The morality of the acts which fall under that description will, it seems to us, vary from one set of circumstances to another.

5. *Habeas Corpus.* This is a bit of a misnomer if we confine our attention to federal convictions. Section 2255 of the federal code, though it gives federal prisoners relief commensurate with what state prisoners get in habeas corpus proceedings, is a slightly different procedure. A 2255 motion is a further step in the criminal case, not a separate civil action. This means that it is filed with the judge who tried the case and handled the sentence (or if they are different, with the judge who supervised the proceeding being attacked). And that in turn means that orthodox Catholic judges who recuse themselves from capital sentencing proceedings will not ordinarily be assigned 2255 motions attacking the sentence itself. It may nevertheless occasionally happen when the

appropriate judge is unavailable to consider the motion. And of course judges who preside over the guilt phase will be assigned motions attacking that proceeding. Is there a moral objection to deciding either of these questions?

Let us first consider an attack on the underlying conviction. Suppose the prisoner claims that he had ineffective assistance of counsel, or that the court violated the confrontation clause by letting the prosecution use a videotaped deposition of its key witness. We have already explained why we think it would be permissible for a pro-life judge to sit in the guilt phase of a capital trial, where questions like these might arise in the first instance. We see even less reason to worry about deciding them on collateral review. When the movant invokes the right to counsel or the confrontation clause, the judge's job is to interpret the Sixth Amendment. We need judges to do this to maintain the balance between individual rights and government authority. Though the judge must know that the movant's life is at stake, he can act without intending to cause the movant's death. This is a case of material, not formal, cooperation. And as material cooperation goes, one can make a pretty good case for it. It would be unwise from the point of view of death row inmates to leave the interpretation of the constitution to death-qualified judges.

An attack on the sentence itself is a harder question, just as it is on appeal. Suppose the movant charges that the aggravating circumstances relied on by the prosecution are expressed in the statute in unconstitutionally vague terms, or were not proven beyond a reasonable doubt. Would it be wrong for a judge who conscientiously opposes the death penalty to decide claims like these where the movant's life is at stake?

The problem seems rather like the one we identified in appellate review. The movant who makes a vagueness claim asks the judge to invalidate a capital sentencing scheme created by Congress because it does not narrow the sentencer's discretion enough. But a judge cannot just casually strike down laws enacted by democratically elected officials. The power of judicial review created in *Marbury v. Madison* lets the judge intervene only when a law is inconsistent with the constitution. Saying that the Eighth Amendment does not authorize intervention is not equivalent to enforcing or approving what Congress has done. Here is what the court says:

> It is Ordered, Adjudged, and Decreed that all ... claims asserted in Chandler's ... motion to vacate and for a new trial ... are Denied, and a final judgment in favor of the United States is hereby Entered with respect to Chandler's motion to vacate and for a new trial.

In essence the judge declines to get involved. Of course we all know that judicial review is not a mechanical process, that there is a lot of room to maneuver, and that a determined judge can get involved, often without running a serious risk of reversal. But the conscientious judge is not under a moral obligation to save all the prisoners he can. The real responsibility for Chandler's death sentence lies with the Congress that wrote the law, the President who signed it, the prosecutor who invoked it, and the judge and jury who imposed the sentence. The 2255 judge who declines to undo their work has a good reason for standing by if he is respecting a lawful and otherwise useful and morally acceptable division of authority....

Conclusion. Catholic judges must answer some complex moral and legal questions in deciding whether to sit in death penalty cases. Sometimes (as with direct appeals of death sentences) the right answers are not obvious. But in a system that effectively leaves the decision up to the judge, these are questions that responsible Catholics must consider seriously. Judges cannot—nor should they try to—align our legal system with the Church's moral teaching whenever the two diverge. They should, however, conform their own behavior to the Church's standard. Perhaps their good example will have some effect.

Selected References

Thomas Aquinas, 3 The Summa Theologiae IIaIIae, Q. 64, a.7 (Fathers of the English Dominican Province trans., 1981).

Joseph Bernadin, Cardinal Bernadin's Call for a Consistent Ethic on Life (1983), reprinted in 13 Origins 491 (1983).

Catechism of the Catholic Church (1994).

M.B. Crowe, I Theology and Capital Punishment (1964).

Charles Kenneth Eldred, Note, The New Federal Death Penalties, 22 American Journal of Criminal Law 293 (1994).

John Finnis, Natural Law and Natural Rights (1980).

Kent Greenawalt, Religious Convictions and Lawmaking, 84 Michigan Law Review 352 (1985).

Germain G. Grisez, 2 The Way of the Lord Jesus: Living a Christian Life 891 (1993).

Germain G. Grisez, Toward a Consistent Natural-law Ethics of Killing, 15 American Journal of Jurisprudence 64 (1970).

George Kannar, Federalizing Death, 44 Buffalo Law Review 325 (1996).

J. Gordon Melton, ed., The Churches Speak On: Capital Punishment (1989).

John Paul II, Evangelium Vitae (1995).

U.S. Catholic Conference, U.S. Bishops' Statement on Capital Punishment (Nov. 1980).

Cases and Other Materials

Marbury v. Madison, 5 U.S. (1 Cranch) 137 (1803).

United States v. Chandler, 996 F.2d 1073 (11th Cir. 1993).

Washington v. Davis, 426 U.S. 229 (1976).

Zobrest v. Catalina Foothills School District, 509 U.S. 1 (1993).

Anti-Drug Abuse Act of 1988, 21 U.S.C. 848 (1997).

28 U.S.C. 2255

Rules Governing Section 2255 Proceedings, Rule 4(a).

Violent Crime Control and Law Enforcement Act, Pub. L. No. 103-322, 108 Stat. 1796 (1994).

The Antiterrorism and Effective Death Penalty Act of 1986, Pub. L. No. 104-132, 110 Stat. 1214 (1996).

Further Reading (selected work by John H. Garvey)

Religion and the Constitution (Aspen 2nd ed. 2006) (with Michael W. McConnell & Thomas C. Berg).

Modern Constitutional Theory: A Reader (West 5th ed. 2004) (with T. Alexander Aleinikoff & Daniel A. Farber).

The First Amendment: A Reader (West 2nd ed. 1996) (with Frederick Schauer).

What are Freedoms For? (Harvard 1996).

CHAPTER FORTY-THREE

BEHAVIORAL SCIENCE
EVIDENCE[*]

From its earliest use in American courts, when one Dr. Brown offered his "scientific" opinion in a Salem witch trial, expert testimony has posed fundamental issues for our system of adjudication. At its most basic the quandary is: How can we utilize specialists to educate a lay jury about matters beyond their ken without at the same time intruding upon the jurors' central role as ultimate fact finder?

In recent years courts and commentators have focused considerable attention on one dimension of this problem assuring some degree of "reliability" regarding the principles and methodologies underlying the expert's testimony before it is heard by the jury. For much of the twentieth century courts followed the *Frye* decision, which delegated this assessment to the practitioners in the particular field under a "general acceptance" standard. *Daubert v. Merrell Dow Pharmaceuticals, Inc.* and its progeny as well as revised Federal Rule of Evidence (FRE) 702 now assign the trial judge the enhanced role of "gatekeeper," screening expert testimony based on certain reliability criteria. Evidence routinely admitted under the pre-*Daubert* regime from forensic to epidemiological to economic is now subject to close scrutiny and exclusion even before a jury is impaneled. In the age-old contest between judge and jury, the balance has shifted dramatically toward the former.

Daubert's measure of reliability clearly reflects a traditional conception of science, envisioning a model driven by experimentation, replication, and validation. In the context of the "hard" sciences concerning physical phenomena, scientific facts (like the force of gravity) can be validated in these ways. But applying this model to ... the social or "soft" sciences, is far more problematic.

---

[*] **Mark S. Brodin**, *Behavioral Science Evidence in the Age of Daubert: Reflections of a Skeptic*, 73 CINCINNATI LAW REVIEW 867 (2005), http://papers.ssrn.com/abstract_id= 613564.

The social sciences most often find their way into the courtroom as a tool to account for or predict human behavior. The evidence usually consists of general assertions about classes of persons.... Expert testimony concerning child sexual abuse accommodation syndrome (CSAAS), battered woman syndrome, learned helplessness, and rape trauma syndrome is offered by prosecutors to explain conduct of the alleged victim that might appear inconsistent with abuse. For example, an expert may testify to the reasons behind a victim's delay in reporting the events, recantation, or remaining in a relationship with the abuser. Battered woman syndrome evidence may also be offered by the defense for the purpose of establishing that the defendant believed she was in imminent danger, even though the objective circumstances posed no apparent immediate threat justifying self-defense (as where the abuser is killed in his sleep). "Future dangerousness" testimony is offered during the penalty phase of capital cases and in proceedings to commit sexual aggressors.

Derived not from experimentation but observation, there is serious question as to whether much of this behavioral evidence can meet the *Daubert* definition of reliable science. Nonetheless, this evidence continues to be admitted routinely at trial, often with little critical analysis by the court and sometimes even after the evidence has been discredited in its own field. Indeed, researchers tracking *Daubert* have concluded that it has not resulted in significant changes in the admissibility of behavioral and social science evidence. [But] the recent focus on reliability has distracted us from far more basic evidentiary problems with the admission of behavioral science, particularly of the syndrome variety....

Daubert ... provided the vehicle by which the United States Supreme Court reworked the doctrinal structure for weighing admissibility of scientific proof. The decision was written against the backdrop of dissatisfaction with the ubiquitous *Frye* standard, which pinned admissibility on whether the methodology was "generally accepted" as reliable in the particular scientific community. *Frye* produced results that were both overinclusive, admitting dubious evidence merely because practitioners in the field rallied to its support, and underinclusive, excluding reliable evidence merely because a consensus had not yet emerged accepting its validity. *Daubert* was portrayed in the popular media as the "junk science" case after the phrase from Peter Huber's 1991 book *Galileo's Revenge*....

[In *Daubert*, the Court] rejected *Frye's* outward-looking and singular focus on "general acceptance" and concluded that FRE 702 imposed upon trial judges themselves the task of independently assessing the reliability of scientific proof. "[I]n order to qualify as 'scientific knowledge' [within the meaning of FRE 702], an inference or assertion must be derived by the scientific method. Proposed testimony must be supported by appropriate validation *i.e.,* 'good grounds,' based on what is known." General acceptance within the scientific community becomes only one of several factors for the judge to consider under *Daubert*....

Other factors to weigh include whether the testimony grows naturally and directly out of research conducted independent of the litigation, or was prepared expressly for purposes of testifying; whether the expert has unjustifiably extrapolated from an accepted premise to an unfounded conclusion; whether the expert has adequately accounted for alternative explanations; whether the expert is being as careful in court as he or she would be in his or her regular professional work; and whether the field of expertise claimed by the expert is known to reach reliable results....

Social Science in the Courtroom: The Beginnings. It is instructive to consider the most famous example of social science evidence Dr. Kenneth Clark's doll studies in *Brown v. Board of Education,* documenting the injurious effect of segregated schools on the self-esteem of black children. The eminent sociologist testified that he had presented black and white dolls to 16 black children attending a segregated elementary school and inquired which doll they liked the best which was the "nice" doll, which looks "bad," and which "looks like you." Ten children preferred the white doll and eleven identified the black doll as "bad." Dr. Clark testified that these were consistent with previous results he obtained involving hundreds of black school children that revealed negative stereotypes held by them as well as lasting psychological injuries.

The Court's landmark decision relied on Kenneth Clark's work to conclude that *Plessy v. Ferguson* was flat wrong in its assertion that "enforced separation of the two races [did not] stamp the colored race with a badge of inferiority:"

> Segregation of white and colored children in public schools has a detrimental effect upon the colored children. The impact is greater when it has the sanction of the law; for the policy of separating the races is usually interpreted as denoting the inferiority of the Negro group. A sense of inferiority affects the motivation of a child to learn. Segregation with the sanction of law, therefore, has a tendency to [retard] the educational and mental development of Negro children and to deprive them of some of the benefits they would receive in a racial[ly] integrated school system.

Whatever may have been the extent of psychological knowledge at the time of *Plessy v. Ferguson,* this finding is amply supported by modern authority. Any language in *Plessy v. Ferguson* contrary to this finding is rejected.

Dr. Clark asserted that his doll tests were "generally accepted as indications of the child's sensitivity to race as a problem," and neither his methodology nor conclusions were seriously challenged by defense counsel at trial. Yet several attorneys for the plaintiffs (including William Coleman, former clerk to Justice Felix Frankfurter) reportedly had considerable doubt about the tests' validity. Moreover, the results of the doll tests in northern schools also indicated a marked preference for the white dolls, seemingly undercutting any causal connection to a formally segregated environment.

The scientific validity of Dr. Clark's methodology was subsequently subjected to scathing criticism. Doubters questioned the adequacy of the sample tested and whether the group was a representative cross-section, and noted the absence of both control tests on white children and precise standards for interpretation of responses. Dr. Clark himself later conceded that his studies could not isolate the effects of segregated schools and thus did not provide evidentiary proof that school segregation alone damaged the personalities of black children. In short, it is highly unlikely that the legendary doll studies would meet the standards set by *Daubert*. Having said this, the Court's long overdue abandonment of *Plessy v. Ferguson* stands firmly on it's own constitutional footing even if Dr. Clark's evidence (which was, from a doctrinal point of view, arguably irrelevant) is discounted.

Syndrome Evidence. The legal philosopher Edmond Cahn perceptively predicted that *Brown* would invite social scientists into court as expert witnesses with increasing frequency.... Syndrome evidence continues to be widely admitted, yet it does not come close to satisfying [requisite] standards. The concept of psychological syndromes was originally developed by practitioners for therapeutic and not truth-detection, purposes. Mental health professionals are trained to assist patients, not judge their credibility.... It is far from self-evident that methodologies useful in choosing a course of psychotherapy are reliable enough "to provide a sound basis for investigative conclusions and confident legal decision-making." Indeed the American Psychiatric Association's own Diagnostic and Statistical Manual of Mental Disorders (DSM) warns against using these categories for forensic purposes....

Although sometimes confused with one another, syndromes must be distinguished from Post-Traumatic Stress Disorder (PTSD), a generally recognized anxiety disorder (with more precise contours) that has been listed in the DSM since 1980. Syndromes are not recognized in the DSM. [T]here has been substantial criticism of the endeavor to compile a checklist that could serve as an accurate indicator of whether abuse occurred.... When the checklist includes behavioral reactions that may be caused by traumatic events unrelated to sexual abuse, it is not a reliable diagnostic tool. Indeed, testimony from syndrome "experts" often identifies such commonplace symptoms as poor self-esteem, family problems, association with an older peer group, depression, withdrawal, leaving home without permission, and problems with school behavior and performance.

In order to establish the clinical reliability of a syndrome identification, it would have to be shown first that its particular symptoms are distinguishable from those associated with other syndromes or disorders, and second, that different clinicians would agree on a diagnosis for the same patient. Social scientists have demonstrated neither....

Although the literature is somewhat more persuasive in identifying common characteristics among victims of rape and battering than of child sexual abuse, serious questions of evidentiary reliability persist. As Professor Jane Moriarty has put it, syndrome evidence essentially "requires a belief in the meaningful relationship between the criminal activity (the cause) and the observable behaviors or symptoms in the victims (the effect)." But the "empirical pillars" of that belief rest ..."on less than sound foundations." To the extent that the conclusions are based on anecdotal evidence, the reliability problems are self-evident such broad generalizations about social phenomena, without empirical confirmation, have been rejected when asserted by social scientists in court in other contexts....

In pondering the admissibility of syndrome testimony it is instructive to look at another form of behavioral "science" that, although of even more dubious reliability, is regularly admitted in the trial of capital cases. Texas executed Thomas Barefoot for the murder of a police officer after two psychiatrists told the jury that he would commit further acts of violence and represented a continuing threat to society. One psychiatrist testified that there was a "one hundred percent and absolute" chance that Barefoot would commit future acts of criminal violence. Neither witness had examined (or requested to examine) Barefoot; each merely responded to hypothetical questions about the defendant posed by the prosecutor.

In its amicus brief in *Barefoot v. Estelle*, the American Psychiatric Association roundly debunked the accuracy of such predictions, asserting that "[t]he unreliability of psychiatric predictions of long-term future dangerousness is by now an established fact within the profession." Studies acknowledged by the Court indicated that these predictions were wrong two out of three times. The best that Justice White could come up with to support the holding that admission of the evidence did not violate Barefoot's constitutional rights was that "[n]either petitioner nor the Association suggests that psychiatrists are always wrong with respect to future dangerousness, only most of the time;" and thus the Court was "not persuaded that such testimony is almost entirely unreliable" Justice Blackmun derided this "remarkable observation."

Even after *Daubert*, "future dangerousness" evidence continues to be admitted in capital cases, civil commitments, and proceedings to commit "sexually dangerous persons." Psychiatrists routinely testify in Texas courts without even the benefit of an examination of the defendant or his psychological records that in their unequivocal "expert opinion," the convicted murderer poses a future danger. Yet nothing in the years since *Barefoot v. Estelle* has even remotely established the reliability of this evidence, which "virtually compel[s]" juries to choose the death penalty.

Ironically, the form of social science evidence which is most solidly based in "hard" empirical science has met with the most resistance in the courts. Expert testimony concerning the limitations and weaknesses of eyewitness identification is firmly rooted in experimental foundation, derived from decades of psychological research on human perception and memory as well as an impressive peer review literature. Like syndrome evidence, this testimony purports to educate the fact finder about reasons a witness at trial should be believed or disbelieved. The expert is prepared to testify about the factors that adversely affect accuracy (for example, stress, "weapon focus," and confusion of post-event information) and to contradict assumptions likely to be shared by jurors, such as the equation of the witness's level of certainty with the accuracy of the identification.

Despite its clearly "scientific" (in the *Daubert* sense) foundations, expert testimony on eyewitness identification is very often excluded at trial. Courts rejecting it typically conclude it is unnecessary because an unassisted jury is perfectly capable of weighing the weaknesses of eyewitness testimony after cross-examination by defense counsel, a conclusion belied by the empirical data, or that it invades the exclusive province of the jury to assess the credibility of witnesses.

In any event, the frequent exclusion of expert testimony on eyewitness identification despite its scientific reliability, contrasting sharply with the widespread admission of evidence of such dubious reliability as "future dangerousness" and the various syndromes discussed above, strongly suggests that factors other than reliability are playing the determinative role....

Judicial Rationales for Admission of Behavioral Science Evidence. Despite heightened reliability standards, courts persist in admitting behavioral science evidence. In explaining this paradox, it has been suggested that media attention and public sentiment surrounding certain kinds of cases, particularly those involving abuse of children and women, have influenced courts in this regard. Researchers in the fields may have failed to critically test their hypotheses for fear of being labeled politically incorrect. Also playing a part is the reluctance or inability of trial judges to conduct the critical analysis envisioned in *Daubert* ... And in cases like *Barefoot v. Estelle*, the courts seem willing to skirt the reliability question in order to permit statutory schemes like Texas's death penalty, premised on future dangerousness, to operate....

Several other judicial rationales have been invoked to avoid meaningful reliability testing of social science evidence. Some states continue to follow *Frye* and admit such evidence under the more lenient "general acceptance" standard. Others have concluded that expert testimony concerning syndromes is not novel science and thus need not be specially scrutinized. Still other decisions except from screening expert testimony that is based on observation and experience. [Also,] some courts have held that where the social science evidence is not offered as direct proof of what happened, but only as an explanation of a victim's behavior, a reliability showing is not necessary....

Threshold Foundational Issues Regarding Behavioral Science Evidence. As a witness permitted to expound opinions in court, the expert holds great potential sway over fact finder. The trial judge has always served as a gatekeeper to assure that the expert is "qualified" by virtue of "knowledge, skill, experience, training, or education"; that the subject matter to be addressed concerns "scientific, technical, or other specialized knowledge"; and that the testimony will "will "assist the trier of fact to understand the evidence or to determine a fact in issue." It is also of course the judge's responsibility to determine that the expert's evidence is relevant and that its probative value is not substantially outweighed "by the danger of unfair prejudice, confusion of the issues, or misleading the jury, or by considerations of undue delay, waste of time, or needless presentation of cumulative evidence."

A survey of federal district judges recently conducted by the Federal Judicial Center determined that the reasons most often cited for exclusion of expert testimony have to do with these basic foundational requirements for admission, and not concerns about reliability. The most frequent ground for exclusion was that the evidence is not relevant (47%), followed closely by the conclusion that the proffered testimony would not assist the trier of fact (40%). Twenty-one percent of the exclusions were based on FRE 403 concerns that the prejudicial nature of the testimony outweighed its probative value. Reliability concerns accounted for approximately 20 percent of the exclusions.... [B]ehavioral science evidence does not fare well measured against these threshold requirements for admission.

"Helpfulness" and "Fit." A prime consideration with regard to the admissibility of expert testimony is, as Wigmore put it, whether "[o]n This subject can a jury receive from This person appreciable help?" While the traditional formulation required the subject matter to be beyond the ken of average juror, the federal standard of "helpfulness" is more lenient. Although the matter is

one not wholly outside the jury's knowledge, an expert may still be permitted to testify if it will "assist" in resolving the disputed issues. Moreover, as one court explained in a case involving testimony regarding a defendant's susceptibility to making a false confession, "[e]ven though the jury may have had beliefs about the subject, the question is whether those beliefs were correct. Properly conducted social science research often shows that commonly held beliefs are in error."

On the other hand, if the jury is in as good a position to resolve the disputed issues as the expert, the testimony should not be admitted. When the lay juror would be able to make a common sense determination of the issue without the aid of an expert, the testimony is superfluous. Indeed, too pessimistic a view of the jury's capabilities leads to substitution of professional "expertise" for community wisdom.

Courts have allowed expert testimony concerning the "typical" conduct of abuse victims on the assumption that jurors need assistance in understanding why a battered woman does not leave the abusive relationship, or a rape victim fails to report the crime, or a child represses the memory of the traumatic sexual encounter....

Most jurisdictions allow testimony based on child abuse accommodation syndrome to explain the child's apparently self-impeaching conduct, such as delayed reporting or recantation. Testimony concerning both battered woman and rape trauma syndrome is admitted on the same rationale to "dispel common myths and misunderstandings about domestic violence that may interfere with the fact finders' ability to consider issues in the case."

But how valid is this nearly universal, but untested, assumption that the jurors need assistance because they are not sophisticated enough to recognize that victims sometimes recant, give conflicting versions of the event, fail to report promptly, or forget details? Serious questions must be raised about the willingness of courts to take for granted that jurors, left unaided, will misinterpret such behavior. Should we not take into account the increasing sophistication of lay people regarding abuse and its victims due to constant news accounts, movies, TV shows, and other information sources? Is there any real doubt that the general public is more knowledgeable today about sexual harassment than they were when Anita Hill's credibility was challenged during the widely-publicized 1991 Senate confirmation hearing of now-Justice Clarence Thomas because she did not report her allegations and continued to work for him? ...

What little empirical data has been developed presents at best a mixed picture of jury knowledge versus ignorance on these matters. Even some enthusiasts for syndrome evidence concede there is serious question as to whether such testimony tells the jurors anything they do not already know, or, as some courts have put it, "explodes common myths" held by jurors. Yet courts rarely recognize that these may be matters of common knowledge.

Jurors in a bank robbery case do not need a criminologist to inform them that persons like the defendant, who are in substantial debt to bookmakers or loan sharks, may commit robbery to pay their debts this is clearly in the realm of "common knowledge." Nor does a jury need an expert to tell them that crime victims sometimes recant their testimony or feign forgetfulness on the witness stand. We leave it to them to "sort out the truth" after direct and cross-examination. The jury determines whether the witnesses changed their testimony out of fear or an honest reappraisal of the facts. The rules of evidence are designed to facilitate this decision by permitting counsel to make jurors aware of the witness's prior statement, confront the witness with the inconsistencies, and explore the discrepancies on cross-examination. And, jurors certainly need no expert to educate them that people sometimes lie to protect family or friends....

A second equally dubious assumption underlies the admission of behavioral science evidence, namely that the fact finders can receive meaningful assistance from it. In order to be helpful to a jury deliberating whether this complaining witness was in fact abused by this defendant, an expert would have to bring to bear knowledge sufficiently definitive to be readily applicable to the particular case....

Daubert ... emphasizes, as did Wigmore long ago, the need to assure that the testimony "is sufficiently tied to the facts of the case that it will aid the jury in resolving a factual dispute," what the Court refers to as "fit." [But syndrome] theory lacks the precision necessary to truly assist the trier-of-fact in determining what happened on the occasion in question....

.... Dr. Lenore Walker, who in 1979 originated the theory of battered woman syndrome (BWS), concluded that only about half the victims studied actually exhibited BWS. In her later writings she conceded that not all relationships follow the pattern and that inconsistencies and variations can be found. In fact, victim conduct defies characterization as common or typical, and the considerable research that has been conducted in the past decades has failed to provide support "for a single profile that captures the impact of abuse on a woman." ... The originator of child sexual abuse accommodation syndrome has criticized its use by prosecutors in a similar vein ...

Expert testimony must achieve a requisite level of certainty in order to provide assistance to the fact finder. In the medical context this means the physician must testify "to a reasonable degree of medical certainty." Courts have similarly required scientific experts to be able to testify "to a reasonable degree of scientific certainty." Syndrome theory, however, defies such exactitude both because it operates at a level of meaningless generality and makes contradictory claims. By way of example, indicia of abuse include such commonplace behavior as biting lips, clenching fists, tapping fingers, biting nails, stomachaches and nightmares, and "fatigue, poor sleep and headaches, emotional changes including anxiety, irritability, depression and hopelessness, and behavioral manifestations including aggression, cynicism, and substance abuse, leading to poor job performance, [and] deterioration in interpersonal relationships."

If a child is calm during a genital examination, that may be taken as evidence that she is used to being handled in that way; but a child who resists during the exam may also be viewed as having experienced sexual trauma. A victim's relating of conflicting versions of the events is considered a sign of abuse, but so is the consistency of the victim's story over time. Even courts that admit rape trauma syndrome concede that "the behavior exhibited by a rape victim after the attack can vary. While some women will express their fear, anger and anxiety openly, an equal number of women will appear controlled, calm, and subdued." Behavioral response checklists include such opposites as increased or decreased eating or smoking, and preoccupation with or aversion to sex.

This contradictory nature of syndrome evidence distinguishes it from well-recognized medical diagnostic techniques such as that used to determine whether a child's physical injuries are inconsistent with a claim of accidental harm. Instead syndromes look more like drug courier profiles, which have a "chameleon-like way of adapting to any particular set of observations."

Even assuming that behavioral evidence may sometimes aid the jury in understanding conduct that may appear inconsistent with abuse, especially where the defense has pressed the late reporting or retraction to undermine the witness's credibility, such testimony remains problematic. First, expert opinions that "merely tell the jury what result to reach" (like that abuse occurred) are, for obvious reasons, neither "helpful" nor appropriate. Second, where the expert's opinion is based largely or solely on the alleged victim's statements and the testimony therefore translates into a reassertion of the victim's story, the testimony should not be admitted. Third, syndrome evidence may simply and, ironically, substitute one set of stereotypes (*e.g.*, abused women are all passive and helpless) for another (*e.g.*, abused women do not stay with their abusers)....

Vouching for Credibility and Invading the Province of the Jury. It is axiomatic that assessing the credibility of witnesses is the sole prerogative of the jury. Indeed, it has been said that the genius of the jury trial system is to have twelve laypersons perform this task, each bringing his or her common sense and experience to the table, rather than relying on a single judge.

It is thus nearly universally recognized that expert testimony directly vouching for or attacking the credibility of another witness at trial is inappropriate. Courts vigilantly guard against invading the province of the jury on matters they are capable of resolving without the benefit of expert opinion, and the credibility of witnesses is such a matter. An expert, for example, generally may not testify to the damaging effects on perception and memory caused by prolonged use of drugs when offered to impeach the credibility of a witness. Experts have been precluded from testifying that children rarely lie about sexual abuse, or that women rarely lie about rape. An eminently qualified expert conversant with the extensive literature was not permitted to render an opinion that a child witness is likely to falsely accuse a parent of sexual assault when the child is the subject of a stressful custody dispute. And virtually all jurisdictions prohibit behavioral experts from testifying to the ultimate issue that a rape or assault occurred, whether based on consistency with a syndrome or interviews with the alleged victim....

Nonetheless, ... syndrome evidence is widely admitted. Some jurisdictions accept it with the explicit purpose of influencing the credibility judgment, especially where the complaining witness has recanted her testimony.... Nearly all courts permit expert testimony about the common patterns of victim behavior to serve a rehabilitative purpose when defendant seeks to impeach the complaining witness by showing delay in reporting, recantation, and the like. Some allow testimony on the characteristics of "typical" abusive relationships, including the statistical national average for the number of times a woman goes back and forth before ultimately leaving. But not all jurisdictions limit admissibility to situations where the defendant opens the door by way of attempted impeachment, or to use for rehabilitative purposes only. Some will admit it as substantive evidence during the prosecution's case-in-chief, if the trial judge determines the victim's conduct may be misinterpreted, notwithstanding the defendant's strategy....

Syndrome and other behavioral science evidence clearly presents a quandary. The more general the expert's testimony the less intrusive into jury's traditional role, but also the less helpful in resolving disputed facts. Conversely, the more specific the testimony the more helpful, but the greater the risk the jury will defer to the expert's judgment.... Various devices have been proposed over the years to determine the truthfulness of a subject's account, ranging from "truth serum" to polygraphs that measure blood pressure and pulse to counting the rate of eye blinks. But even if we were satisfied with the scientific reliability of a particular method, it is inconceivable that we would permit its use at trial to test the truthfulness of a witness' testimony....

Probative Value and Prejudicial Harm. [T]he probative value of behavioral science evidence, especially syndrome testimony, is often questionable, and a few courts have even excluded it on grounds of relevancy "for failure to make the existence of any fact of consequence more probable or less probable than it would have been without the evidence." If the symptoms associated with a particular syndrome also appear with frequency in the population generally, the testimony adds little to the resolution of the dispute. Moreover, since the diagnosis of post traumatic stress disorder, battered woman syndrome, and child sexual abuse accommodation syndrome is based in part on the victim's version of events, there is a troubling circularity to the logic of this evidence. It sometimes sounds like: The witness recanted, therefore she must have been abused....

On the other side of the ... balance, the risk of jury overvaluation (which the common law handled clumsily by operation of the now discredited "ultimate issue" rule) pervades the evidentiary rules controlling opinion testimony. The concern is particularly acute for testimony carrying a scientific aura, but has been identified as well in the case of non-scientific clinically-based testimony. Moreover the very terminologies used by the witness such as rape trauma syndrome or battered woman syndrome may itself unfairly prejudice the defendant's case....

It has been argued that the risk of overestimation of psychological testimony has been exaggerated, particularly since human behavior (unlike the opaque box of DNA science) is not a subject foreign to jurors. And certainly some of the risk can be addressed in obvious ways, as for example by not referring to witness as an "expert" in front of the jury. Nonetheless, as Justice Blackmun noted in his dissent in *Barefoot v. Estelle*, there is considerable evidence that suggests that juries "are not effective at assessing the validity of scientific evidence." Boilerplate instructions to the jury regarding the assessment of expert testimony could very well exacerbate the problem.

Moreover, the adversary system cannot be counted on to reveal the defects in behavioral testimony because it rests on "psychiatric categories and intuitive clinical judgments not susceptible to cross-examination and rebuttal." Even skilled opposing counsel may have difficulty exposing the flaws....

In certain trials expert testimony is obviously essential in order for the fact finder to reach a rational decision on the issues in dispute. Neither a lay jury nor judge untrained in medicine could determine whether a highly sophisticated surgical procedure had been performed competently or negligently, or whether a nurse had killed her patients deliberately by injections that sent their hearts into "accelerated ideo-ventricular rhythm." But in many trials in which social science evidence is offered it serves a collateral role, such as explaining the behavior of a witness, who (it is feared) may otherwise be misinterpreted by the jury. Given this more tangential function there is serious question about whether its probative value outweighs the downside risks, including distraction from the actual issues in dispute to a focus on the expert's pedigree, poise, and presentation....

Since abuse cases often come down to a credibility contest between the accused and the alleged victim, it is acknowledged that expert behavioral testimony presented by the prosecution may very well be determinative, and its impact has been empirically documented as producing significantly more guilty verdicts, particularly where the testimony refers specifically to the victim in the case, and where no opposing defense expert is presented. But admitting social science evidence of dubious reliability on the untested assumption that it is necessary to counteract jurors' false beliefs about victims may, ultimately, result in the substitution of another set of false beliefs, this time coming from the "expert." ...

Costs and Benefits of Admitting Behavioral Science Evidence. One might ask: Even if there are troubling issues regarding the use of social science in the courtroom, what is the harm in admitting it for whatever value it has to the fact finder? In this regard, it is instructive to note that the Federal Judicial Center survey of judges and attorneys found that the problem most frequently cited by both groups regarding expert testimony was that "experts abandon objectivity and become advocates for the side that hired them," followed closely by the "excessive expense" of expert witnesses. Other recurrent observations were that the conflict among the experts at trial often "defies reasoned assessment," and that there is a "disparity in level of competence of opposing experts." All of these concerns should inform our assessment of social science evidence in the courtroom....

For years it was gospel among most liberals and progressives that an activist Supreme Court was a good thing. But as the Warren Court gave way to the Burger Court and then the Rehnquist Court, views changed dramatically. The weapon of the social science expert could be, and has now certainly been, turned against civil rights plaintiffs. "Hired guns" can be pointed in any direction.

The fair and proper use of social science evidence would require that both litigants have relatively equal access to such experts, to related resources, and to skilled counsel. This is not always, or even often, the case. Particularly in criminal cases, and certainly where defendant is indigent, it is not likely the defense will be able to retain either a testifying expert or one who may be consulted for purposes of challenging the testimony of the government's expert.

Not surprisingly, the most dramatic increase in guilty verdicts has been documented where the prosecution expert is not countered by a defense expert....

Selected References

Lisa R. Askowitz & Michael H. Graham, The Reliability of Expert Psychological Testimony in Child Sexual Abuse Prosecutions, 15 Cardozo Law Review 2027 (1994).

Edmond Cahn, Jurisprudence, 30 N.Y.U. Law Review 150 (1955).

Kenneth B. Clark, The Desegregation Cases: Criticism of the Social Scientist's Role, 5 Villanova Law Review 224 (1959).

David Crump, The Trouble with *Daubert-Kumho*: Reconsidering the Supreme Court's Philosophy of Science, 68 Missouri Law Review 1 (2003).

David L. Faigman *et al.*, Science in the Law: Social Behavioral Science Issues (2002).

David L. Faigman, The Law's Scientific Revolution: Reflections and Ruminations of the Law's Use of Experts in Year Seven of the Revolution, 57 Washington & Lee Law Review 661 (2000).

Henry F. Fradella *et al.*, The Impact of *Daubert* on Forensic Science, 31 Pepperdine Law Review 323 (2004).

Paul C. Giannelli & Edward J. Imwinkelried, Scientific Evidence (3d ed. 1999).

Paul C. Giannelli, The Admissibility of Novel Scientific Evidence: *Frye v. United States*, A Half-Century Later, 80 Columbia Law Review 1197 (1980).

D.H. Kaye, Choice and Boundary Problems in *Logerquist*, *Hummert*, and *Kumho Tire*, 33 Arizona Sate Law Journal 41 (2001).

David McCord, The Admissibility of Expert Testimony Regarding Rape Trauma Syndrome in Rape Prosecutions, 26 Boston College Law Review 1143 (1985).

Andre A. Moenssens *et al.*, Scientific Evidence in Civil and Criminal Cases (1995).

Jane Campbell Moriarty, Wonders of the Invisible World: Prosecutorial Syndrome and Profile Evidence in the Salem Witchcraft Trials, 26 Vermont Law Review 43 (2001).

Robert P. Mosteller, Legal Doctrines Governing the Admissibility of Expert Testimony Concerning Social Framework Evidence, 52 Law & Contemporary Problems (1989).

D. Michael Risinger, Defining the "Task at Hand": Non-Science Forensic Science After *Kumho Tire Co. v. Carmichael*, 57 Washington & Lee Law Review 767 (2000).

Michael J. Saks, The Aftermath of *Daubert*: An Evolving Jurisprudence of Expert Evidence, 40 Jurimetrics 229 (2000).

Symposium: Syndromes, Frameworks, and Expert Testimony: What Jurists Need to Know, 24 Pace Law Review 187 (2003).

Missy Thornton, *State v. Chauvin*: Determining the Admissibility of Post-Traumatic Stress Syndrome Diagnosis as Substantive Evidence of Sexual Abuse, 78 Tulane Law Review 1743 (2004).

Neil J. Vidmar & Regina A. Schuller, Juries and Expert Evidence: Social Framework Testimony, 52 Law & Contemporary Problems 133 (1989).

Laurens Walker & John Monahan, Social Frameworks: A New Use of Social Science in Law, 73 Virginia Law Review 559 (1987).

John Henry Wigmore, Evidence (1940).

Selected Cases

Barefoot v. Estelle, 463 U.S. 880 (1982).
Brown v. Bd. of Educ., 347 U.S. 483 (1954).
Commonwealth v. Francis, 453 N.E.2d 1204 (Mass. 1983).
Daubert v. Merrell Dow Pharm. Co., 509 U.S. 579 (1993).
Frye v. United States, 293 F. 1013 (1923).
Kumho Tire Co., Ltd. v. Carmichael, 526 U.S. 137 (1999).
Logerquist v. McVey, 1 P.3d 113 (Ariz. 2000).
People v. Peterson, 537 N.W.2d 857 (Mich. 1995).
Plessy v. Ferguson, 163 U.S. 537 (1896).
United States v. Hall, 165 F.3d 1095 (7th Cir. 1999).

Further Reading (selected work by Mark S. Brodin)

Criminal Procedure: Examples and Explanations (Aspen 4th ed. 2004) (with Robert M. Bloom).
Civil Procedure: Doctrine, Practice & Context (Aspen 2nd ed. 2004) (with Stephen N. Subrin, Martha L. Minow & Thomas O. Main).
Accuracy, Efficiency, and Accountability in the Litigation Process—The Case for the Fact Verdict, 59 Cincinnati Law Review 15 (1990).
The Standard of Causation in the Mixed-Motive Title VII Action—A Social Policy Perspective, 82 Columbia Law Review 292 (1982).

C. CIRCUMVENTION

Chapter Forty-Four

Doctrine in Dispute Resolution[*]

Mediation—the process through which a neutral third party assists parties in reaching their own agreement—has achieved a prominence in our legal system that belies its youth…. [M]ediation today is touted for disputes of all sizes and in all areas of the law…. Despite such broad encouragement, its success varies widely in different fields of law. While in some areas of law it has achieved dominance, in others its development has been far slower. Two areas where this disparity is particularly puzzling are divorce and will contests….

Mediation has become a widely used method for settling divorce disputes, and based on this success, there has been great interest in encouraging the use of mediation to resolve will disputes. Academics and practitioners alike have written about its value in resolving these disputes, and some courts have established programs specifically geared towards encouraging mediation of probate matters. Yet, despite these efforts, the use of mediation to resolve will disputes has lagged far behind its use in divorce. Judges and lawyers seem reluctant to use mediation to resolve will disputes, and many jurisdictions with well-developed mediation programs recognize that mediation is not commonly used to resolve will disputes. Even professional mediators have noted that will disputes are some of the most difficult disputes to resolve through mediation.

What accounts for this difference? One conventional explanation is that judges and lawyers involved with will disputes lack familiarity with mediation. This suggests that it is only a matter of time and education before mediation is used as commonly in will disputes as it is in divorce. The difficulty with this explanation is that it is counterfactual. In many cases the familiarity with mediation already exists. Family and probate law matters are commonly handled

---

* **Ray D. Madoff**, *Lurking in the Shadow: The Unseen Hand of Doctrine in Dispute Resolution*, 76 USC Law Review 161 (2002), http://papers.ssrn.com/abstract_id=309749.

in the same courthouses by the same judges; lawyers handling significant will disputes often also have significant divorce litigation practices; and mediation programs run by many courts are, at least theoretically, as much geared towards the probate docket as towards the family law docket....

An alternative explanation ... is that parties to will disputes often have such deep-seated feelings of anger against one another that it is almost impossible to get them to sit in a room together—let alone get them to reach an agreement. Yet this explanation is also ultimately unsatisfactory. While it is true that will disputes are often highly charged, many divorces ultimately resolved through mediation also involve similar levels of rancor. Thus, while the level of emotion may play some role in the limited adoption of mediation in resolving will disputes, it cannot provide a complete explanation for the disparity in comparison to the use of mediation in divorce.

Theoreticians in the growing field of dispute resolution might add another dimension to this inquiry. Drawing on insights from psychology and economics, they address the question as to why settlement attempts fail. Since there is some evidence that will disputes are more likely to go to trial than other disputes, this literature may be particularly relevant. Under classic economic theory, parties should reach a settlement when there are settlement options that will leave both parties better off then they would be if they went to trial. Yet, there are many cases where the parties fail to settle even when it is clearly in their economic interest to do so. A variety of factors have been found to contribute to this phenomenon. For example, sometimes there are problems of strategic bargaining, when the parties agree that there is a joint surplus but cannot decide how to divide it. There are also psychological impediments: some evidence suggests that people are reluctant to settle if they believe that they are not being treated equitably. Despite the breadth and rigor of this scholarship, it does not explain the discrepancy between the use of mediation in divorce and will disputes since all of the identified impediments appear to apply (or not) with equal force to both types of disputes.

One factor that has not been accounted for is the role of legal doctrine in shaping how people involved in the dispute conceive of the dispute and its appropriate mode of resolution. In this Article, I argue that legal doctrine—the statutes and case law governing a dispute—plays an important role in encouraging parties and lawyers to engage in mediation or other forms of private negotiation. This builds on the seminal work *Bargaining in the Shadow of the Law*, by Robert Mnookin and Lewis Kornhauser, which examined divorce law through the lens of its impact on the negotiation process. However, rather than looking at the impact of law on the negotiation process, this Article examines how substantive doctrinal law can affect whether parties resolve their dispute through judicial resolution or private negotiation, with or without a mediator.

[T]here is a connection between substantive doctrinal law and the acceptance of alternative dispute resolution. [W]idespread adoption of mediation in divorce disputes would not have been possible without the changes in the substantive legal rules governing divorce brought about by the no-fault revolution. This transformation effectively changed the core story about divorce from one about guilt and innocence to one that minimized the importance of fault and instead created a complex forward-looking inquiry. This new regime effectively discouraged parties from seeking judicial resolution of their disputes and encouraged them to resolve their disputes through negotiation or mediation. The rules governing divorce stand in sharp contrast to the rules governing will contests. Largely unchanged in the United States over the last 200 years, wills law involves a backward-looking inquiry that focuses on testator intent and provides moral condemnation under a winner-take-all system, effectively encouraging parties to seek judicial resolution of their disputes.

The Many Roles of Legal Doctrine.... Legal rules affect dispute resolution in a number of significant ways. First, they establish the difference between a grudge and a claim. People may be angry or upset about any number of things, but only grievances that rise to the level of a legal claim can be aired before a judge. People have much greater leverage over this latter class of grievances because grievances that do not constitute legal claims can only be resolved through negotiation or mediation, whereas grievances that are also legal claims can be resolved through the courts, as well as through negotiation or mediation.

In addition, the legal rules of standing establish which parties have a role in the dispute and therefore whose views need to be considered in structuring a resolution. As a result, standing plays an important role in dispute resolution. The number of recognized parties in a dispute establishes the number of people who have to agree to a settlement. The more players there are, the more difficult it is to reach a privately negotiated settlement. One of the reasons that divorces are relatively easy to resolve through mediation, for example, is that only two people need to agree on a resolution. If our legal system required approval from other parties (such as in-laws and friends) on whether a divorce should be allowed and on what terms, the disputes would be more difficult to resolve in a private negotiation. In will disputes, expansive standing provisions make negotiated settlements more difficult to achieve. The relevant parties to a will contest include all of the people named in the will being submitted for probate, the people who would inherit the estate if the testator had died without a will, and in some situations, all of the people named under a prior will. Conversations with mediators suggest that even coordinating a time in which all of the parties can meet can often take several months.

Legal rules can also affect the negotiation process itself. [L]egal rules indicate an allocation that the court will impose if the parties fail to reach an agreement. These rules create bargaining chips that the parties use in the negotiation process.... [Legal doctrines] frame a core story as to why the state is involved. This story reflects larger cultural values in that a legal claim recognizes that there has been a deviance from desired norms. The remedy reflects a view as to how to correct this deviance. The story of any given claim is outlined in the rules governing liability, but is often most salient in the applicable remedies. Law is a powerful tool for shaping how people think about their dispute.... [Legal rules also] play an important role in how the players in a dispute (including judges, lawyers and the parties) understand the dispute. This understanding, in turn, affects the players' ability and desire to negotiate a settlement outside the courtroom....

Divorce Law Prior to Modern Reforms. Prior to modern reform, the stories of marriage and divorce embodied in the legal doctrines governing divorce were drastically different from the stories provided by the law today. Since marriage was construed as a life long arrangement generally terminated only by death, courts granted divorce only on the basis of serious misbehavior by either the husband or the wife. Divorce was premised on the assumption that one spouse was guilty and the other spouse was innocent. The importance of this predicate finding was so great that if both spouses were found guilty, the divorce would not be granted.

The determination of guilt also significantly affected post-divorce property settlements. If the husband was found guilty, his obligation to support his wife continued after the divorce in the form of alimony. If the alimony payments were insufficient, then a portion of his property could be awarded to the wife to assist in her support. In community property states—in which the wife owned half of the husband's earnings acquired during the marriage—the innocent spouse was eligible for more than half of the community property. If the wife was found guilty, she was not entitled to alimony and could not claim any of her husband's property. This imposed significant hardship in a world in which women largely worked at home without compensation.

The determination of guilt could also affect child custody.... Although custody was most often granted to the mother, she could lose custody if she was not the innocent spouse. The pre-reform standards for divorce imposed a strong bias in favor of preserving the marriage. Individuals could not unilaterally file for divorce unless they could prove that their spouse was guilty of one of the enumerated grounds. However, the effect of these rules was more far-reaching in that even if both members of the couple wanted to divorce, they could do so only by resorting to fiction and fraud.

This system presented a story about marriage and divorce in our society that underscored the state's interest in keeping marriages together. Because marriages were to continue until the death of one of the spouses, the state essentially enforced the marriage contract even if the marriage broke up.... Because the state had an interest in preserving the marriage, the story presented another central theme: the party responsible for its break up deserved punishment and the innocent party was entitled to a form of damages for her suffering....

This paradigm encouraged lawyers and parties to seek judicial resolution of the issues surrounding divorce. The traditional function of courts after all, is to determine what happened in the past and to apply legal standards to those determined facts. In doing so, courts also play a societal role of establishing a winner and a loser, often translated into popular consciousness as a tale of a victim and a wrongdoer. When the legal rules surrounding divorce required the establishment of a guilty and innocent party, and rigidly imposed results based on that determination, judicial resolution was the obvious, if not the only, way to resolve such disputes.

The No-Fault Revolution. Beginning in the mid-1960s, divorce law in the United States underwent a revolution. Fault—which had been the determining factor for the existence and effect of the divorce—was rendered largely irrelevant through the enactment of no-fault divorce provisions. These provisions (which often existed alongside traditional fault-based provisions) generally declare that a divorce will be granted if the marriage has suffered an irretrievable breakdown. They were originally enacted to allow couples who wanted divorce to do so without resorting to fraud. However, the effects of these changes were more far-reaching in that they allowed either spouse unilaterally to end the marriage. In less than thirty years, the changes largely eliminated fault as a relevant factor.

The no-fault revolution also effected changes in the rules governing property distributions and child custody determinations. Property distributions and alimony are no longer based on the notion of preserving the obligations of marriage and of punishing the guilty while rewarding the innocent spouse. Instead, property distribution issues are resolved through equitable distribution statutes, in which each spouse is entitled to a share based on his or her financial and non-financial contributions to the marriage—similar to the unwinding of a partnership in business. Alimony has been transformed as well from a permanent obligation to support the innocent ex-wife (until another man accepted that responsibility), to a temporary transitional payment intended to carry the former spouse (either husband or wife) until he or she becomes self-sufficient. In many states, fault has been completely eliminated as a relevant factor in property division. Even in those states retaining fault as a relevant factor, it is only one of many to be considered.

The rules governing child custody also changed dramatically. Whereas the law prior to modern reforms often provided that child custody was to be awarded to the innocent wife, in the post no-fault world, child custody is awarded "in the best interests of the child." This generally requires courts to consider a variety of factors including the wishes of the child and the parents, the child's adjustment to his home, school and community as well as the mental and physical health of all individuals involved. The pattern has also shifted from awarding custody to a single spouse to a bias in favor of promoting the relationship of the child with both parents.

These changes tell quite a different story about marriage and divorce. In this new story, the state no longer has a basic interest in preserving marriage and divorce is not perceived as an evil caused by a wrongdoer. The new story is that marriage is a private affair and that society is essentially indifferent as to whether any particular couple remains married. The rules governing divorce are based on the assumption that couples break up for a number of reasons. The state is no longer interested in monitoring the validity of these reasons through an inquiry into what happened in the past. Instead, divorce is understood simply as an event with consequences that need to be managed. Therefore, rather than focusing on designating the wrongdoer, societal concern has shifted to the issues of whether the division of marital assets and arrangements for child custody are equitable, practical plans acceptable to all parties.

This new story fits neatly with a mediation model for resolving disputes since mediation is a forward-looking inquiry designed not to evaluate fault and mete out justice, but instead to work on the issues underlying the dispute to achieve a satisfactory resolution for all parties. There are three core features of modern divorce law that encourages the use of mediation: (1) the issues in divorce law are governed by vague standards in which there is broad judicial discretion; (2) the inquiry is primarily forward-looking in nature; and (3) the opportunity for moral vindication has been largely eliminated.

Divorce law is noted for its vague standards and the broad discretion given to judges to resolve disputes.... This imprecision in the law combined with the broad discretion granted judges makes "the law"—and thus the role of the lawyer—less central to the resolution of the dispute....

Wills Law and Dispute Resolution. [W]ill disputes are more likely to be resolved by a judicial decision (made by a judge or jury) than by private negotiation.... What accounts for this likelihood of cases being resolved through court rather than through private negotiation? There are three features of will contests that make these disputes less likely to settle: (1) the role of testator intent; (2) the opportunity for moral condemnation or vindication; and (3) the all-or-nothing nature of the remedy.

The Role of Testator Intent. The touchstone for American wills law is freedom of testation. This is the notion that people are (and should be) able to dispose of their property at death however they choose. The idea is of mythic stature in wills law. It is central to the popular understanding of wills, and it permeates all aspects of the legal doctrine governing wills. When wills are interpreted, the interpretation takes place in the context of testator intent. Even the rejection of a will is often premised on the notion of fulfilling the testator's intent. For example, undue influence, one of the most common grounds for rejection, is described as an influence impeding a testator's true intent.

This dominance of testator intent in wills law acts as a significant impediment to nonjudicial resolutions because not all views can be present at the negotiating table. The person whose "will" is in dispute is dead. In addition, to the extent that people feel they are representing the decedent's views, they are often particularly unwilling to yield their positions.

For a mediation or negotiation to be successful, people must be willing to change their original positions. The theory of mediation is that by creating an opportunity for parties to communicate with each other, they gain a greater understanding of each other's views, thus becoming more willing to change their positions. The emphasis in wills law on the testator's intent is particularly problematic in this context because the person whose views are most relevant to the legal dispute—the decedent—cannot participate....

The focus on testator intent creates another significant impediment. To the extent that parties feel that they are standing up for what the testator wanted, they often assume a strongly positional approach to the dispute, making them less likely to consider settlement.... The centrality of testator intent in will disputes thus seriously impedes private resolution of the dispute....

The Opportunity for Moral Condemnation or Vindication. One of the fundamental factors that motivates people to seek legal solutions to their problems is the opportunity for moral vindication. As those experienced with the legal system acknowledge, this is rarely granted in real life disputes. However, a will contest is one area in which such vindication is possible. The reason for this is that moral judgments are central to will disputes. Disputes that on one level are about money are quickly converted to claims of moral worth. Positions become polarized and this works powerfully against private settlement of disputes.

Consider our typical fact pattern and the will dispute it could generate: A widowed mother has two children. One lives at or near home and takes care of the widowed mother toward the end of her life; the other lives across the country. Mother changes her will toward the end of her life to give everything to the local child who took care of her, disinheriting the child who lives out of town. The out of town child feels that it is unfair that she gets nothing from her mother's will so she goes to a lawyer who tells her that she may have a claim that the care taking child exerted "undue influence" over her mother.

The mediation literature suggests that there are many reasons why this type of dispute ought to be well served by mediation. Litigation is likely to be extremely expensive and highly destructive to the relationship between the siblings. Additionally, it does not provide an opportunity for the siblings to work out any of the additional non-legal issues between them. For example, the at-home sibling may want the other sibling to recognize the sacrifices that he endured in taking care of their mother. The sibling who lives far away may want to be assured that the will does not reflect that their mother loved her less. Although these issues are not central to the legal claim, they may be vital to resolve in order for the siblings to have a good relationship in the future.

The allegation of undue influence is basically a claim that the at-home child exerted so much control, that the mother wrote a will in his favor that she otherwise would not have written. Undue influence, in conjunction with lack of mental capacity, is the most common ground for overturning wills. The desire to share a portion of their mother's estate has now been changed—courtesy of the legal rules—into a different story. Now it is a story that the mother probably wanted her property to go to both children equally, but that the at-home child did something wrong and overcame her mother's wishes, causing her to write a will that she otherwise would not have written.

This conversion to a legal claim has the effect of inflaming the dispute and polarizing the siblings. The at-home child (previously "the good one" for taking care of mother) is now demonized for overcoming the will of the mother. The away child (possibly feeling guilty for not living closer to her mother) can claim victim status. This creates substantial difficulties in resolving this dispute because the claim has been transformed from a claim about money, to a claim about gut-level principles. Note how different this is from divorce today, in which a party may go to a lawyer asserting claims of moral worth (I was good, my spouse was a bad person), and yet the lawyer in effect explains that this dispute is not about right and wrong, but only about how to practically and equitably dissolve the relationship.

Centrality of the Rule of Law—All-or-Nothing Nature of Will Disputes. Will disputes are distinctly legal in nature. Judicial resolution of these disputes involves a backward-looking inquiry in which judges are thought to apply clearly established rules to a set of facts. If the judge misapplies these rules, the lawyer can appeal to a higher court. This is similar to many other areas of the law, but is unlike divorce law which is generally perceived by lawyers to be a system in which judges apply standards, but not rules, to reach results which try to be fair, but are not necessarily right. This difference is conceived of by some lawyers involved in both divorce and will disputes not just as a qualitative difference in law, but as a distinction between legal and non-legal disputes....

The all-or-nothing nature of will disputes may also play a role in encouraging lawyers and parties to seek judicial resolution of their disputes. Under current law, probate judges have limited authority in fashioning remedies to will contests. They can either uphold the will or reject it and have the property pass under the rules of intestacy—or by the terms of a prior valid will, if one exists. The dispute resolution literature suggests that this all-or-nothing nature of the remedy in will disputes should encourage resolution of disputes because it would cause risk averse parties to be more willing to settle. However, it is also possible that an all-or-nothing remedy encourages lawyers and parties to seek judicial resolution by removing one aspect of uncertainty that normally exists under judicial resolution, thereby highlighting the legal nature of the dispute.

Judicial resolution of most legal disputes involves two components: (1) establishing a winner and (2) fashioning a remedy. In most cases, an evaluation of the risks of litigation—and the relative attraction of a negotiated settlement—involves assessing both (1) the likelihood of winning, and (2) the likelihood of receiving a remedy significantly better than that which might be achieved through a negotiated settlement. Litigation of will contests is unusual, perhaps even unique, since the rules provide no discretion to the probate judge to fashion a remedy. Thus the probate judge can either uphold the will (in which case the property passes to the beneficiaries named in the will) or reject the will (in which case the property passes to the legal heirs of the decedent). The court cannot create a remedy that deviates from one of these two polar choices.

One effect of this all-or-nothing system is that it highlights the legal nature of the dispute. Lawyers and parties easily understand they have only limited power to control judicial discretion. If a judge's discretion in fashioning a remedy is limited, however, the lawyers and parties may place greater emphasis on their own understanding of the case. Therefore, they may feel that they have greater control over the outcome. This theory is supported by psychological research suggesting that people are likely to overestimate their abilities as well as their degree of control over a situation. Thus, the all-or-nothing nature of the remedy in wills law could further act to encourage parties to seek judicial resolution of their disputes instead of a negotiated settlement because they feel they have more direct control in the ultimate outcome.

Towards a Less Contentious Wills Law. Is it possible to make our wills law more conducive to private resolution of disputes, and if so, what would the effects be of making such a change? Changing the substantive rules governing wills law to avoid the impediments to private resolution discussed above would be an important step in decreasing contentious litigation and increasing private resolution of will disputes. This could be accomplished by changing the rules governing will disputes to: (1) diminish the role of testator intent; (2) reduce the moral tone of the inquiry; and (3) reduce the role of law by adopting vague standards and giving probate judges broad discretion to resolve disputes.

What would such a wills law actually look like? One interesting example worthy of consideration is the discretionary regime in English wills law known as the Family Maintenance Statute. English wills law is the original source of wills law in the United States and the two systems remain remarkably similar in many respects. Both have a stated ideal of freedom of testation, and both generally share the same formal requirements for executing or revoking a valid will. Yet English law differs from wills law in the United States in one key respect. While both systems provide for freedom of testation, for decades now, English law has provided a limited exception to this right through its family maintenance statute. This statute allows certain people to make claims against a decedent's estate for their support.

The right to make such a claim is open to a fairly broad class of individuals including the decedent's spouse, former spouse, child, current or former-step child, and any other person maintained wholly or partly by the decedent at the time of the decedent's death. The amounts paid under these provisions are somewhat limited since the purpose of these distributions is to provide for reasonable maintenance. In making a family maintenance determination, an English court is directed to consider numerous factors, including: the financial resources and needs that the applicant currently has and is likely to have in the foreseeable future; the size and nature of the decedent's estate; any physical or mental disabilities of the applicant; and any other matter, including the conduct of the applicant or any other person, the court may consider relevant.

The family maintenance regime is similar to the regime now governing divorce law in the United States. It includes, for example, a forward-looking inquiry, vague standards, broad judicial discretion and a reduction in the role of fault. One can easily imagine that parties operating within the family maintenance regime would be more likely to fashion their own settlement because a judicial determination would not implicate hot-button issues such as testator intent. Judicial resolution would not provide moral vindication because the role of fault is so minimized. Also, due to the vague standards and broad judicial discretion, the parties could have only limited confidence in their ability to get a better result through a judicial determination.

To what extent would a system such as the English family maintenance statute change substantive doctrinal wills law? To be sure, enacting a family maintenance statute would somewhat limit the degree of control that people have over the disposition of their property at death. It would grant judges the authority to make dispositions from the decedent's estate to support individuals who may not have been provided for in the will. However, seen in the context of the limitations on freedom of testation that already exist in the United States, the effect of this change would be one of degree, rather than kind.

Existing wills law in the United States already limits freedom of testation, explicitly and implicitly, in a number of significant ways.... Limitations on freedom of testation are imposed on married individuals directly through marital property laws and more subtly through federal tax statutes.... A person does not need to be married in order to be subject to limitations on freedom of testation. Wills law itself provides even more significant, albeit indirect, limitations on freedom of testation. Although wills law explicitly refers to the value of freedom of testation, an individual can only be certain of being able to exercise this freedom to the extent that she provides for her family or otherwise writes a will that conforms to societal norms.

Extensive literature describes the ways in which the doctrines of undue influence and lack of mental capacity have been imposed when the testator has disposed of her property in a way that fails to conform to societal norms. In *The Myth of Testamentary Freedom*, Melanie Leslie shows how courts are even willing to apply the formal requirements of wills (for signature and two witnesses) in such a way as to reject wills that fail to meet a testator's familial duty. Application of these doctrines in this way substantially limits freedom of testation. The effect of the application of these doctrines is to reject the will in its entirety and, instead, to transfer the property to the decedent's spouse and blood relatives through intestacy statutes. In contrast, the limitations on freedom of testation that would be imposed by a family maintenance statute are in many ways less significant than those already in place since family maintenance statutes only apply to the extent that the relevant person needs money for support. Indeed, enacting family maintenance statutes may increase freedom of testation by reducing judicial use of other doctrines (such as undue influence and lack of mental capacity) to address wills that courts believe to be unfair.

Regardless of the minimal impact of English family maintenance statutes on actual freedom of testation, it is unlikely that states will adopt such provisions in the near future. While the adoption of a system such as the family maintenance statute would cause only an incremental change on existing freedom of testation, its effect on the core story of wills law would be far greater. At its heart, wills law tells a story about individual rights which essentially says that (1) people have the ability to control their property at death, and thus the ability to exert their power after death, and (2) people bear no obligation to others (with the exception of their spouses).

Statutes such as the English Family Maintenance Statute directly contradict these tenets. These statutes explicitly send the message that an individual's property is not entirely her own to do with as she pleases. Rather, her family and other dependents have some claim to the property. As such, adoption of this type of provision would change the central wills narrative, and transform it from an individualistic to a communal account.

Conclusion. Mediation—with its promise of less contentious, less expensive resolution of disputes—has been widely recommended for disputes in all areas of the law. Yet, its successes have not been as uniform. While it has flourished in some areas (most notably in divorce and child custody disputes) it has met with much greater resistance in others. This is particularly puzzling for areas of the law, like will disputes, where mediation would seem to provide so many benefits. This Article has sought to explain this conundrum by showing the ways in which legal doctrine—the statutes and case law applicable to a particular dispute—plays an important role in lawyers' and parties' willingness to accept the mediation model.

The [foregoing] analysis ... is not limited to will disputes and divorces. I have also identified features of law that encourage parties to resolve their own disputes. These features include: a forward-looking inquiry, a reduction in the role of fault, adoption of vague standards, and broad judicial discretion. To the extent that there is a desire to encourage negotiation and mediation of disputes, legislatures should consider systems with these features. To be sure, there will be costs associated with such changes. These provisions encourage settlement, but simultaneously send another message as well—that is, that getting along is more important than right or wrong.

Selected References

Kenneth J. Arrow, et al., eds., Barriers to Conflict Resolution (1995).
Linda Babcock & George Loewenstein, Explaining Bargaining Impasse: The Role of Self-Serving Biases, 11 Journal of Economic Perspectives 109 (1997).

Connie J.A. Beck & Bruce D. Sales, Family Mediation: Facts, Myths, and Future Prospects (2001).

Ronald Chester, Less Law, But More Justice?: Jury Trials and Mediation as Means of Resolving Will Contests, 37 Duquesne Law Review 173 (1999).

Robert Cooter, Stephen Marks & Robert Mnookin, Bargaining in the Shadow of the Law: A Testable Model of Strategic Behavior, 11 Journal of Legal Studies 225 (1982).

Russell Korobkin & Chris Guthrie, Psychological Barriers to Litigation Settlement: An Experimental Approach, 93 Michigan Law Review 107 (1994).

Kimberlee K. Kovach, Mediation Principles and Practice (1994).

Melanie B. Leslie, The Myth of Testamentary Freedom, 38 Arizona Law Review 235 (1996).

Lela Porter Love, Mediation of Probate Matters: Leaving A Valuable Legacy, 1 Pepperdine Dispute Resolution Law Journal 255 (2001)

Robert H. Mnookin & Lewis Kornhauser, Bargaining in the Shadow of the Law: The Case of Divorce, 88 Yale Law Journal 950 (1979).

Richard A. Posner, An Economic Approach to Legal Procedure and Judicial Administration, 2 Journal of Legal Studies 399 (1973).

George L. Priest & Benjamin Klein, The Selection of Disputes for Litigation, 13 Journal of Legal Studies 1 (1984).

Austin Sarat & William L. F. Felstiner, Divorce Lawyers and Their Clients: Power and Meaning in the Legal Process (1995).

Jana B. Singer, The Privatization of Family Law, 1992 Wisconsin Law Review 1443.

Aviam Soifer, Law and the Company We Keep (1995).

Further Reading (selected work by Ray D. Madoff)

Practical Guide to Estate Planning (Aspen 2001 & CCH 2005) (with Cornelia R. Tenney & Martin A. Hall).

Mediating Probate Disputes: A Study of Court Sponsored Programs, 38 Real Property, Probate and Trust Journal 697 (2004).

Taxing Personhood: Estate Taxes and the Compelled Commodification of Identity, 17 Virginia Tax Review 759 (1998).

Unmasking Undue Influence, 81 Minnesota Law Review 571 (1997).

CHAPTER FORTY-FIVE

ADVANCE PRICING AGREEMENTS[*]

... In the field of international tax, there has developed a national, and even international consensus that traditional mechanisms for administering the law and resolving disputes have virtually collapsed in the area of transfer pricing (which plays an important role in allocating a taxpayer's income among taxing jurisdictions).... [T]ransfer pricing essentially refers to the prices related parties charge each other in transactions. If the parties agree to an artificially high or low price for the goods, services, intangibles or borrowing, they can strategically place their total profits in the "best" (*i.e.* lowest tax) country. Such off-market pricing is possible because the parties' common control or ownership means they share a common economic interest....

In a bold move in the early 1990s, the United States led its trading partners toward a new model of advance dispute resolution for transfer pricing, the [Advance Pricing Agreement (APA)] program, which relies on a backbone of familiar mechanisms complimented by certain novel features. The APA process is an alternative to the standard taxpayer path of doing the transactions, filing a return, facing audit (some level of audit is more likely with larger taxpayers), and, finally, possible appeal with settlement or litigation. The taxpayer initiates the APA process by approaching the [Internal Revenue] Service (and typically the corresponding tax authorities in the other relevant jurisdictions) before engaging in the related party transactions potentially at issue. At this point the taxpayer voluntarily provides detailed information to the governments regarding its business activities, plans, competitors, market conditions, and prior tax circumstances. The critical piece of this presentation is the taxpayer's explanation of its planned pricing method. Following discussion and negotiation, the parties hopefully reach agreement on how the tax-

---

[*] **Diane M. Ring**, *Advance Pricing Agreements and the Struggle to Allocate Income for Cross Border Taxation*, 21 MICHIGAN JOURNAL OF INTERNATIONAL LAW 143 (2000), http://papers.ssrn.com/abstract_id=772104.

payer should handle the pricing of these anticipated related party transactions. This understanding is embodied in the APA agreement which typically runs for three years.

In order to appreciate the potential issues raised by this innovative procedure it is necessary to outline briefly the features of the process from the perspective of the various parties. First, why would taxpayers participate to the extent it requires disclosure to the government of significant information, some of which might otherwise be withheld? Ideally participating taxpayers obtain tax certainty before actually engaging in their transactions. In addition they obtain a tax treatment that is uniformly accepted by all of the taxing authorities, thereby eliminating conflict. There is also an expectation that this alternative mechanism for dispute resolution might reduce overall costs of addressing transfer pricing problems.

Second, why should governments be willing to engage in this one-on-one process with taxpayers? Governments may hope to gain information about pricing practices and transaction specific issues, to utilize a different forum, and to interact with other countries in a setting conducive to more comprehensive resolutions of transfer pricing "problems." Additionally, governments, have historically borne a significant burden for transfer pricing, both in terms of time and money. They now look to the APA program to provide less costly dispute resolution and to enhance their information base for future improvements to the taxation of related party transactions....

The creation of the APA program illuminates the difficult procedural choices made in a particular administrative regime in response to concrete substantive and procedural problems and goals. But of course, the tax system is not entirely unique. Numerous other administrative agencies confront comparable issues including complex rules, detailed facts, and international players. Thinking about such questions from a more universal administrative law theory perspective allows us to see the connections across a range of administrative regimes and to develop a better understanding of the risks and opportunities in reform....

Overview.... What marks APAs as an unusual procedural device in the tax system is the fact that they permit the taxpayer and the government to discuss and resolve substantive tax issues voluntarily, prior to the transactions occurring, and to reach agreement on their tax treatment. At first blush this may not seem unusual; a student of the tax system could identify other existing mechanisms that allow this kind of interaction. The APA differs because of the precise nature and context of the interaction. Unlike an audit or settlement agreement, the primary function of the APA is to cover future transactions. Although advance tax rulings exist in the United States (for example letter rulings), APAs are different for several reasons: the agreements involve foreign countries; the issues are intensely factual (and the facts very complex) and require significant negotiation between the government and taxpayer; the agreements can cover a number of years; and the terms of the agreements are confidential with no redacted versions released to the public. These APA characteristics stand in contrast to the operation of the most common advance ruling, the letter ruling. Such rulings, which are primarily legal determinations applied to relatively generic facts, involve only the Service and are published in redacted form....

Forum for Testing Administrative Law Theories. The first step in using the APA program as a testing ground for administrative law is to outline the current picture of the theories in question. Obviously such a description is a shorthand and not inclusive of the numerous variations of the different models. Moreover, the goal is not to demonstrate the complete relevance or irrelevance of a given theory, but rather to use a case study to advance understanding in at least two ways: (1) by revealing the complexity of administrative law analysis within a single example; and (2) by indicating directions for the expansion and development of the theories. Three general theories of regulation and the administrative state can be identified: (1) public choice, (2) neopluralist, and (3) public interest. These theories share a common foundation in their view of the function and significance of interest group behavior.

The first theory, public choice, begins with the understanding that administrative law and regulation are justified in part on the ground that such efforts respond to the "market failure" in providing necessary rules or outcomes in the absence of the administrative state. The theory then concludes that the administrative state generally is unsuccessful at repairing this market failure and instead is providing regulatory benefits to well-organized political interest groups which benefit at the expense of the general public. The second theory, the neopluralist, is similar to public choice in that it also places organized interest groups at the center of the regulatory process. Neopluralism notes the dominant role that interest groups play in setting regulatory standards but concludes that their competition produces results very roughly reflecting the general public interest as a whole. This competition oriented picture takes the process and the results to be less imbalanced than the public choice theory and thus is less critical of the regulatory system.

The third theory, public interest, is also more open to a potentially positive regulatory role and process. However, this theory adopts public choice's critical view of interest groups, and holds that only full disclosure of the administrative process to general public scrutiny and monitoring saves an administrative regime from capture by such groups. Where particular processes afford the public this critical scrutiny of regulatory decision making, the theory contends that results tend to reflect the general public interest. In contrast, where the process fails to provide such scrutiny and the decision makers operate without public oversight, results tend to benefit well-organized interest groups at the expense of the public.

Each of these theories contains both positive and normative elements, and it is not completely clear to what degree the theories are contradictory, compatible, or complementary. One of the claims of recent scholarship is that the administrative law debate can be advanced by grounding these theories in the details of specific administrative processes. It is in this capacity that the analysis of the APA program and its operation may be valuable.

One caveat, however, must be noted. Although all regulation moves through administrative regimes and thus theoretical discussions have wide application, important distinctions exist. Social regulation in areas such as environment, food safety, and occupational safety differ from regulation in taxation and social security. The former represent acts of government intervention into conduct otherwise undertaken by the market. The government justifies its intervention on the grounds of market failure. In contrast, redistributive regimes such as taxation and social security, do not redress market failure but instead serve a function entirely separate from the market. Thus, to the extent theoretical discussions focus on normative justifications for the creation of particular administrative regimes, universal answers do not exist. Social regulation and redistributive regimes rely on different foundations. However, to the extent the administrative theories seek to probe what happens in a regulatory regime, both redistributive and social regulation regimes share some common analyses. Understanding the various ways in which power, structure and process interact in a regulatory setting has universal salience....

In considering whether the APA program in particular can provide any support for one of these theories, it is important to consider all three facets of the APA: namely its creation, its modification, and its operation. The creation of the APA program provides little direct support for any of the three theories. The program was initiated at the prompting of the Service itself in response to what it, and many taxpayers, perceived to be serious problems with the operation of the transfer pricing tax rules. However, even more significant than the fact that the Service initiated the program is the fact that the general response of the intended audience—multinational corporations with significant cross border related party transactions—was not warm. It seems unlikely, therefore, that the program was the result of pressure from a narrow interest group of taxpayers as would be predicted by the public choice theory or from a competition among well-organized interest groups as predicted by the neo-pluralist theory. Certainly, of course, a few taxpayers were interested in APAs. Shortly after the program was formally introduced the Service announced the first completed APAs, which obviously had been underway prior to the formal announcement. Nonetheless, the overall factual picture of the development of the program does not really support a strong claim that one or more narrow interest groups were the primary actors behind the program. Nor is it clear that its creation reflects the triumph of narrow interests over the general public interest. To the extent that a significant motivation for and potential outcome of the program is the alleviation of administrative burden and the improvement of transfer pricing regulations, the benefit is both a specific one for taxpayers facing transfer pricing issues, and a general one for the public in terms of improved tax administration. Of course the degree of disclosure poses some difficult questions that are considered below in evaluating the APA program's operation.

The creation of the program also fails to provide much evidence that the public interest theory was at work here. The APA program was presented in 1991 as a complete, new program. The general public, even through their congressional representatives, had little oversight of the creation process. Despite the fact that the creation of the APA program lends little direct support to any particular administrative theory, the subsequent modifications present a slightly different picture.

Two notable changes to the program, the restructuring of the role of foreign governments and the introduction of a special APA route for small businesses, were both responses to concerns raised by particular "interest groups." In the case of foreign countries' place in the APA process, the Service found that under the 1991 structure, other nations considered their role in the development of the taxpayer's transfer pricing treatment inadequate. Given the critical position of foreign nations in preventing the double taxation that the APA was designed in part to eliminate, they served as a significant "interest group" whose needs had to be accommodated. Thus, it is not surprising that the Service reevaluated the foreign countries' role and ultimately revised the program—to the initial dissatisfaction of at least some taxpayers.

On one level this modification seems to support an administrative theory along the lines of public choice, with the foreign countries emerging as the successful interest group. This picture, however, is complicated by the fact that this "interest group" is another foreign government acting in essentially the same regulatory capacity as the Service. Considered in that light, a characterization of the foreign government as an "interest group" may be misleading. Although there is no one valid interpretation of public choice theory and its view of interest group competition, the simple case presumably envisions a single government/regulatory body responding to various interest groups formed from the general public, all portions of which are bound by the final decisions stemming from the regulatory process.

A foreign government with an equal claim to the same regulatory authority does not operate as a traditional interest group in that context. It does not even have the same relationship as a state level agency in a federal system, or even as another federal agency with an interest in the topic. The tax bodies of other countries are in precisely the same position vis-a-vis transfer pricing as the Service without any ultimate supranational authority. Moreover, transfer pricing decisions of one country directly impact those of another. The result is the intersection of two independent, although connected, regimes. This relationship cannot be examined exclusively within the context of traditional administrative law concepts. Thus, it may make sense to seriously explore the applicability of international relations theory in evaluating that dynamic. What this example does clarify is that administrative law theories, as difficult as they may be to work with in the domestic context, become more complicated with the inclusion of other governments and their parallel regulatory bodies.

Regarding the other significant modification of the APA program, the creation of a small business track, more than one administrative theory seems relevant although none exclusively so. Viewed as a response to demands from smaller international businesses that the APA program be more accessible to smaller taxpayers, the modification may seem an example of public choice theory (or perhaps neopluralist theory). However, it may not be accurate to consider the creation of the smaller business track to be a concession counter to the general public's interest, nor a change taking place outside the public's attention. Thinking in terms of the public interest theory, it is relevant to note that the Service continually publicized its desire and intent to provide an APA format more suitable for smaller businesses. The prospect of this particular modification seemed to raise no general or interest group specific complaint. Rather, it aligned with a fundamental view that if the APA program exists it should be accessible to the full range of relevant taxpayers.

... [T]he implementation of the program [provides] fuller clues ... regarding the aptness of various administrative theories in this context. The individualized nature of the APA process and the refusal to consider disclosure until the Service's short-lived announcement suggest that "good" would fail to result from the clash of interest groups because each party who wants to "play" (*i.e.*, negotiate transfer pricing individually with the Service) could engage the government in relative privacy. The APA regime makes it difficult, if not impossible, for competing groups or the public to monitor or challenge the resulting tax treatments and policies. Thus, if one takes the baseline behavior shared by the neopluralist and public choice views, one might see the handiwork of public choice and its dismal portent, as the eventual prospect of the APA program.

Certain additional observations about the program, however, might nullify this prediction. The degree of resistance to the APA program exhibited by taxpayers suggests that the corporations did not see themselves as predominantly in a position vis-a-vis the Service to compete or pressure for desired tax treatment. Rather, the paramount taxpayer concerns regarding the provision of detailed information to the Service suggest they saw a different relationship. Of course, some taxpayers did go forward with the process, but those decisions seem sufficiently explained by their particular risks of possible bad audits, current bad audits, or high transaction costs. Even assuming this description of taxpayers' understanding of their relationship with the government prior to starting the APA process is accurate, it still remains plausible that once engaged in the process, the factors of individualization and nondisclosure (until now) enabled participants to pursue their agendas in a public choice-like arena. However, the more unique aspect of the APA regulatory environment as compared to typical "domestic" settings may impede a participating taxpayer's ability to fully achieve a public choice type result. The fact that most APAs are bilateral or multilateral (and the fact that there is some element of zero-sum to the amount of tax collected by all countries regarding a cross border related party transaction) suggests that the taxpayer cannot easily pursue an aggressively self-interested path under the public choice theory because fiscal "sacrifices" by the Service could be eagerly scooped up by the other country or countries. This is not to suggest that some version of public choice behavior cannot occur, just that the taxpayer's maneuvering is more complicated in this multi-jurisdictional administrative setting.

Moreover, even if a public choice type result might be foreseeable under the program as it has existed thus far, public interest theory may provide a more accurate view of the dynamic under APA processes for the future.... [T]he public interest view refines the other two theories by asserting the ameliorative effect of public monitoring. The theory anticipates that despite the activity of interest groups, when the public can monitor behavior it ensures that general good and not simply individual good is achieved. To the extent this monitoring mitigates the harsh view of the administrative process, its unavailability at all in the APA context until now, has meant that the level of public information on outcomes was limited (even if "public" here is taken to be the larger class of active multinational corporations, policy makers, academics, and tax media) and may have provided opportunity for taxpayers to at least vie for a public choice result behind closed doors. However, ... recent legislation barring disclosure but requiring annual reporting means there will be more information available than there has been, but perhaps less than it could be.

... [T]he real operational impact of the new reporting requirement turns on what is revealed. A very generalized report will leave nonparticipants still unclear on precisely what rules are being applied. Conversely, a rich report increases the awareness in the tax community of the standards to which transactions will be held but also risks the publication of information that might be identifiable by country or industry. This direction could push the APA process towards neopluralist or public interest models as parties other than the relevant taxpayer become part of the process. Although the "public's" interest in APA results may never be high, if the broader tax community including nonparticipating multinationals, other taxpayers, tax media, policy makers, and academics are able to examine the direction of the APA program, they may effectively monitor APA treatments, thus achieving some of the goals of the public interest model.

The first cut observations here support the idea that the particularized administrative setting plays a significant role in what theoretical view is most descriptive. Agencies and administrative processes are not monolithic; moreover the typical interactions among an agency, interest groups, and the public may vary—even within a given agency and process. It is possible that different issues and facets operate more or less under different theories. Perhaps the most interesting observation from the APA program case study is that the move from a domestic administrative and regulatory setting to an international one involving multiple jurisdictions complicates the interpretation of the various parties' actions in very specific ways. The position of the foreign governments in the APA process makes it difficult to classify behavior and determine who is an interest group and who is the bureaucracy for purposes of administrative theories.

Functional Aspect of APA Program Design Choices. While it is possible to sift through the genesis and results of the APA process for evidence of one or another underlying causal theory governing administrative interactions, an alternative approach in administrative law eschews the search for an overarching principle and would instead examine the APA experience for more practical information on administrative design. Instead of accepting the premises of private party-government interactions and the dominant role of interest group behavior and working from there, this alternative operates under the view that new frameworks and formats of administrative and regulatory action can produce different interactions. Thus, a substantial emphasis is placed on what might be done differently if agencies have an opportunity to consider creative, context-specific approaches. The starting point for this functional view is the possible relationship that an administrative regime may construct between and among the government, interest groups, and public. Change in this multifaceted relationship is sought through revised regulatory processes that encourage participation, problem solving, and agency flexibility in ways that permit agencies to establish systems best suited to the regulatory problem at hand.

One version of this approach is "collaborative governance." This basic model has generated a variety of regulatory devices such as negotiated rulemaking and special EPA permitting practices. Very briefly summarized, the suggestion is that more joint, collaborative rulemaking processes may be advantageous because they (1) may produce novel and better solutions if the less adversarial atmosphere allows more information to be generated and debated, and (2) the mutual participation in a consensus building format may improve relations which in and of itself is valuable but also feeds back into other stages and aspects of the administrative process.

Another version is civic republicanism. Positing that regulatory decisions reflect broad judgments about how competing regulatory values should be balanced, the civic republican theory argues that the process of regulation serves as the occasion for collective discussion and deliberation about both the means and ends of the regulation at issue. Such deliberation, properly structured, provides a further forum for refining the requirements of the general public's interest. Reliance on deliberation by expert administrators replaces interest group competition as the key to legitimate rulemaking. Still other paradigms for rethinking administrative law have emerged ... including "reflexive regulation," "cooperative implementation," and "interactive compliance." Regardless of their precise scope or formulation, these theories share a common focus on the value of cooperation in the regulatory process and the flexibility necessary to achieve it.

To ... facilitate successful collaborative governance of some type, an administrative system requires a certain flexibility and discretion to consider new structures and options and retain the possibility of rejecting plans that fail. The government agency functions as an active administrative player in terms of exploring, testing, and developing administrative options. The agency draws parties in by identifying how the process can benefit them, through "cost savings, reduced litigation, or improved relationships."

This ground level approach to administrative and regulatory theory, with its rousing call for creative administrative processes still recognizes the core concerns of accountability and measurement of success. A collaborative approach does not eschew mechanisms for accountability. Instead, it folds that necessary feature into the heart of the theory. Accountability becomes one of the administrative features for which creativity is possible and a range of options and structures must be investigated....

... The connection between the APA program and a more collaborative regulatory model is strong. The goals thought to be achieved by changing the system and presumably the parties' relationships are very much the ones underlying the APA program.... [T]he transfer pricing system appeared in crisis because among other things, it was adversarial, was unsuited to the highly factual content, elicited limited information, and failed to include all of the critical parties in the initial steps. The Service designed the APA program with the expectation that it could provide an improved forum for examining transfer pricing problems, designing appropriate tax treatments, and resolving disagreements. The inclusion of the foreign governments in the process was a novel but ultimately crucial choice in creating a process with a plausible chance for success. Accountability has proven the most contentious issue but is itself in the process of being modified, though the sufficiency of the solution awaits judgment.

The specific criticisms targeted at the APA program reveal the direct tension between a "collaborative" model and the traditional rulemaking/adjudication framework.... [T]he tension [is] captured in the description of the APA program as a hybrid by virtue of its departure from a clear division between rulemaking and adjudication. The same clash exists at the theory level because the division of tasks and functions into the two categories conflicts with a call for flexibility and creativity that could muddle such delineated roles. However, the blurring of roles need not subvert an administrative process. For example, inclusion of a range of personnel at the one and only stage of the APA program does not inappropriately mix administrative roles. Instead, it encourages broader participation and creates an atmosphere of joint responsibility for solving problems. A collaborative approach may, through its departure from traditional patterns of interaction, solve problems without seriously undermining the integrity of the administrative process.

The real value of some version of collaborative administrative theory is that it not only permits agencies the opportunity to design innovative process but in fact it places intelligent creativity at the forefront of regulatory policy. The decision to value the qualities of creativity, flexibility, and innovative structure by supporting a different vision of administrative relations may be most appropriate where certain conditions exist. In particular, the existence of features such as high information costs, fact intensive issues, large stakes, very interdependent decisions, and multiple regulating entities, may outweigh the possible risks. Certainly uncontrolled flexibility and administrative discretion are not a plausible solution to the current ills of the regulatory state. What can be stated with assurance is that refusal to seriously consider reform alternatives and failure to allow some experimentation guarantees little improvement will be made.

Although the APA program cannot unequivocally demonstrate the success and correctness of an approach that emphasizes agency flexibility, creativity and collaboration in rulemaking, it offers a useful example of how such changes can be made to an administrative process. Moreover, even if specific collaborative governance routes prove problematic, and more attention to interest group behavior is needed, some aspects of the program such as creative rulemaking nonetheless remain a valuable alternative for confronting regulatory problems....

Selected References

Gary S. Becker, A Theory of Competition Among Pressure Groups for Political Influence, 98 Quarterly Journal of Economics 371 (1983).

Marshall J. Breger, Regulatory Flexibility and the Administrative State, 32 Tulsa Law Journal 325 (1996).

Steven P. Croley, Theories of Regulation: Incorporating the Administrative Process, 98 Columbia Law Review 1 (1998).

Daniel A. Farber & Philip P. Frickey, The Jurisprudence of Public Choice, 65 Texas Law Review 873 (1987).

Jody Freeman, Collaborative Governance in the Administrative State, 45 UCLA Law Review 1 (1997).

Michael E. Levine & Jennifer L. Forrence, Regulatory Capture, Public Interest, and the Public Agenda: Toward a Synthesis, 6 Journal of Law, Economics & Organization 167 (1990).

Sam Peltzman, Toward a More General Theory Regulation, 19 Journal of Law & Economics 211 (1976).

Richard A. Posner, Theories of Economic Regulation, 5 Bell Journal of Economics & Management Science 335 (1974).

Robert B. Reich, Public Administration and Public Deliberation: An Interpretative Essay, 94 Yale Law Journal 1617 (1985).

Richard B. Stewart, The Reformation of American Administrative Law, 88 Harvard Law Review 1669 (1975).

Cass R. Sunstein, Administrative Substance, 1991 Duke Law Journal 607 (1991).

Further Reading (selected work by Diane M. Ring)

Federal Income Taxation of Corporate Enterprise (Foundation Press 2005) (with Bernard Wolfman).

International Tax (Foundation 2005) (with Reuven Avi-Yonah and Yavi Brauner).

Taxation of Financial Instruments (Clark Boardman Callaghan, 1996) (with Reuven Avi-Yonah & David Newman).

Why Happiness? A Commentary on Griffith's Progressive Taxation and Happiness, 45 Boston College Law Review 1413 (2004).

One Nation Among Many: Policy Implications of Cross-Border Tax Arbitrage, 44 Boston College Law Review 79 (2002).

Fixing Realization Accounting: Symmetry, Consistency and Correctness in the Taxation of Financial Instruments, 50 Tax Law Review 797 (1995).

INDEX OF CONTRIBUTIONS

Alexis Anderson (with Arlene Kanter & Cindy Slane), *Ethics in Externships: Confidentiality, Conflicts, and Competence Issues in the Field and in the Classroom*, 10 CLINICAL LAW REVIEW 473 (2004) [Chapter 6].

Filippa Marullo Anzalone, *It All Begins With You: Improving Law School Learning Through Professional Self-Awareness and Critical Reflection*, 24 HAMLINE LAW REVIEW 324 (2001) [Chapter 5].

Hugh J. Ault (with Mary Ann Glendon), *The Importance of Comparative Law in Legal Education: United States Goals and Methods of Legal Comparison*, 27 JOURNAL OF LEGAL EDUCATION 599 (1975) [Chapter 4].

Charles H. Baron, *Life and Death Decision Making: Judges v. Legislators as Sources of Law in Bioethics*, 1 JOURNAL OF HEALTH & BIOMEDICAL LAW 107 (2004) [Chapter 14].

Mary Sarah Bilder, *The Origin of the Appeal in America*, 48 HASTINGS LAW JOURNAL 913 (1997) [Chapter 38].

Robert M. Bloom, *Judicial Integrity: A Call for its Re-Emergence in the Adjudication of Criminal Cases*, 84 JOURNAL OF CRIMINAL LAW & CRIMINOLOGY 462 (1993) [Chapter 39].

Mark S. Brodin, *Behavioral Science Evidence in the Age of Daubert: Reflections of a Skeptic*, 73 CINCINNATI LAW REVIEW 867 (2005) [Chapter 43].

George D. Brown, *Carte Blanche: Federal Prosecution of State and Local Officials After Sabri*, 54 CATHOLIC UNIVERSITY LAW REVIEW 403 (2005) [Chapter 15].

R. Michael Cassidy, *Toward a More Independent Grand Jury: Recasting and Enforcing the Prosecutor's Duty to Disclose Exculpatory Evidence*, 13 GEORGETOWN JOURNAL OF LEGAL ETHICS 361 (2000) [Chapter 40].

Mary Ann Chirba-Martin (with Carolyn M. Welshhans), *An Uncertain Risk and an Uncertain Future: Assessing the Legal Implications of Mercury Amalgam Fillings*, 14 HEALTH MATRIX 293 (2004) [Chapter 18].

Daniel R. Coquillette, *Professionalism: The Deep Theory*, 72 NORTH CAROLINA LAW REVIEW 1271 (1994) [Chapter 9].

Lawrence A. Cunningham, *Private Standards in Public Law: Copyright, Law-making and the Case of Accounting*, 104 MICHIGAN LAW REVIEW 291 (2005) [Chapter 17].

Anthony Paul Farley, *The Apogee of the Commodity*, 53 DePAUL LAW REVIEW 1229 (2004) [Chapter 30].

Scott T. FitzGibbon, *Fiduciary Relationships Are Not Contracts*, 82 MARQUETTE LAW REVIEW 303 (1999) [Chapter 31].

Frank J. Garcia, *Trade and Inequality: Economic Justice and the Developing World*, 21 MICHIGAN JOURNAL OF INTERNATIONAL LAW 975 (2000) [Chapter 29].

John H. Garvey (with Amy V. Coney), *Catholic Judges in Capital Cases*, 81 MARQUETTE LAW REVIEW 303 (1998) [Chapter 42].

Jane Kent Gionfriddo, *"The Reasonable Zone of Right Answers:" Analytical Feedback on Student Writing*, 40 GONZAGA LAW REVIEW 427 (2005) [Chapter 7].

Phyllis Goldfarb, *A Theory-Practice Spiral: The Ethics of Feminism and Clinical Education*, 75 MINNESOTA LAW REVIEW 1599 (1991) [Chapter 3].

H. Kent Greenfield, *The Unjustified Absence of Federal Fraud Protection in the Labor Market*, 107 YALE LAW JOURNAL 715 (1997) [Chapter 22].

Dean M. Hashimoto, *The Proposed Patients' Bill of Rights: The Case of the Missing Equal Protection Clause*, 1 YALE JOURNAL OF HEALTH POLICY, LAW & ETHICS 77 (2001) [Chapter 26].

Frank R. Herrmann, S.J., *30=20: "Understanding" Maximum Sentence Enhancements*, 46 BUFFALO LAW REVIEW 175 (1998) [Chapter 41].

Ingrid Michelsen Hillinger, *The Article 2 Merchant Rules: Karl Llewellyn's Attempt to Achieve The Good, The True, The Beautiful in Commercial Law*, 73 GEORGETOWN LAW JOURNAL 1141 (1985) [Chapter 34].

Ruth-Arlene W. Howe, *Redefining the Transracial Adoption Controversy*, 2 DUKE JOURNAL OF GENDER, LAW & POLICY 131 (1995) [Chapter 27].

Reneé M. Jones, *Rethinking Corporate Federalism in the Era of Corporate Reform*, 29 IOWA JOURNAL OF CORPORATION LAW 625 (2004) [Chapter 16].

Gregory A. Kalscheur, S.J., *Law School as a Culture of Conversation: Re-imagining Legal Education as a Process of Conversion to the Demands of Authentic Conversation*, 28 LOYOLA UNIVERSITY OF CHICAGO LAW JOURNAL 333 (1996) [Chapter 1].

Daniel Kanstroom, *Deportation, Social Control, and Punishment: Some Thoughts About Why Hard Laws Make Bad Cases*, 113 HARVARD LAW REVIEW 1890 (2000) [Chapter 24].

Sanford N. Katz, *Marriage as Partnership*, 73 NOTRE DAME LAW REVIEW 1251 (1998) [Chapter 32].

Elisabeth A. Keller, *Consensual Amorous Relationships Between Faculty and Students: The Constitutional Right to Privacy*, 15 JOURNAL OF COLLEGE AND UNIVERSITY LAW 21 (1988) [Chapter 33].

Thomas C. Kohler, *The Overlooked Middle*, 69 CHICAGO-KENT LAW REVIEW 229 (1993) [Chapter 21].

Joseph P. Liu, *Copyright and Time: A Proposal*, 101 MICHIGAN LAW REVIEW 409 (2002) [Chapter 37].

Ray D. Madoff, *Lurking in the Shadows: The Unseen Hand of Doctrine in Dispute Resolution*, 76 USC LAW REVIEW 161 (2002) [Chapter 44].

Judith A. McMorrow, *Civil Disobedience and the Lawyer's Obligation to the Law*, 48 WASHINGTON & LEE LAW REVIEW 139 (1991) [Chapter 10].

Mary-Rose Papandrea, *Under Attack: The Public's Right to Know and the War on Terror*, 25 BOSTON COLLEGE THIRD WORLD LAW JOURNAL 35 (2005) [Chapter 23].

Zygmunt J.B. Plater, *Statutory Violations and Equitable Discretion*, 70 CALIFORNIA LAW REVIEW 524 (1982) [Chapter 13].

James R. Repetti, *Democracy, Taxes and Wealth*, 76 NYU LAW REVIEW 825 (2001) [Chapter 20].

Diane M. Ring, *Advance Pricing Agreements and the Struggle to Allocate Income for Cross Border Taxation*, 21 MICHIGAN JOURNAL OF INTERNATIONAL LAW 143 (2000) [Chapter 45].

James Steven Rogers, *An Essay on Horseless Carriages and Paperless Negotiable Instruments: Some Lessons from the Article 8 Revision*, 31 IDAHO LAW REVIEW 689 (1995) [Chapter 35].

Francine T. Sherman (with Marsha L. Levick), *When Individual Differences Demand Equal Treatment: An Equal Rights Approach to the Special Needs of Girls in the Juvenile Justice System*, 18 WISCONSIN WOMEN'S LAW JOURNAL 9 (2003) [Chapter 25].

Mark Spiegel, *Theory and Practice in Legal Education: An Essay on Clinical Legal Education*, 34 UCLA LAW REVIEW 577 (1987) [Chapter 2].

Judith Tracy, *Teaching Fundamental Structure in Legal Writing through the Use of Samples*, 21 TOURO LAW REVIEW 297 (2005) [Chapter 8].

Paul R. Tremblay, *Rebellious Lawyering, Regnant Lawyering, and Street-Level Bureaucracy*, 43 HASTINGS LAW JOURNAL 947 (1992) [Chapter 11].

Catharine Wells, *Situated Decisionmaking*, 63 USC LAW REVIEW 1727 (1990) [Chapter 28].

Carwina Weng, *Multicultural Lawyering: Teaching Psychology to Develop Cultural Self-Awareness*, 11 CLINICAL LAW REVIEW 369 (2005) [Chapter 12].

David A. Wirth, *Legitimacy, Accountability, and Partnership: A Model for Advocacy on Third World Environmental Issues*, 100 YALE LAW JOURNAL 2645 (1991) [Chapter 19].

Alfred C. Yen, *Copyright Opinions and Aesthetic Theory*, 71 USC LAW REVIEW 247 (1998) [Chapter 36].

Scholarly Expertise of Contributors

Administrative Law	Greenfield, Kanstroom, Wirth
Civil Procedure	Bloom, Brodin, Kalscheur, Papandrea, Spiegel
Clinical Training	Anderson, Goldfarb, Herrmann, Kanstroom, Sherman, Spiegel, Tremblay, Weng
Commercial Law	Hillinger, Rogers
Comparative Law	Ault, Baron, Garcia, Wirth
Constitutional Law	Baron, Farley, Garvey, Greenfield, Kalscheur, Papandrea
Copyright Law	Liu, Yen
Contracts	Cunningham, FitzGibbon, Katz, Hillinger, Rogers
Corporate Law	Cunningham, FitzGibbon, Greenfield, Jones
Criminal Law	Cassidy, Farley, Goldfarb, Herrmann
Criminal Procedure	Bloom, Brodin, Cassidy, Goldfarb, Herrmann
Education Law	Keller
Election Law	Brown
Employment Law	Brodin, Kohler
Environmental Law	Plater, Wirth
Evidence	Brodin, Cassidy, Hashimoto
Family Law	Howe, Katz
Federal Courts	Brown, Spiegel
Federalism	Brown, Jones
Feminism/Gender	Goldfarb, Wells
Health Law	Baron, Chirba-Martin, Hashimoto
Immigration Law	Kanstroom
Intellectual Property	Liu, Yen
International Law	Garcia, Kanstroom, Wirth
Jurisprudence	Bilder, FitzGibbon, Garcia, Wells
Juvenile Law	Sherman
Labor Law	Kohler
Law and Accounting	Cunningham
Law and Medicine	Hashimoto
Law and Religion	Garvey, Kalscheur
Legal History	Bilder, Coquillette, Rogers
Legal Writing	Chirba-Martin, Gionfriddo, Keller, Tracy
Poverty Law	Tremblay
Property	Bilder, Liu, Madoff, Plater
Professional Responsibility	Coquillette, Cunningham, McMorrow, Tremblay
Securities Regulation	Cunningham, FitzGibbon, Jones
Sports Law	Yen
Tax Law	Ault, Repetti, Ring
Torts	Hashimoto, McMorrow, Wells, Yen
Trusts & Estates	Madoff

INDEX

A

abatement, 143

abortion, 307. *See also* right to life movement

  indigent rights, 308

  legal treatment of decisionmaking, 156

  rights and patient rights, similarities, 307–8

accounting industry

  accounting standards and public documents, 190

  generally accepted accounting principles (GAAP), 189

  reformed by Sarbanes-Oxley Act, 183

Adamson v. California, 487, 490

administrative agency law, 135

  Administrative Procedure Act, 215, 269–70

  APA program, regulatory theories, 566–68

  exception, publication requirement, 198

  government delegates standards production, 194

  private standards in public law, 191

  proposed issue management, 199–200

  regulatory takings, 200

  standards as law and copyright, 195–96

  standards-to-law conceptual framework, 194–95, 195 *fig*

adoption

  as statutory process, 322–23

  best interests of the child standard, 324

  biracial children, 321–22

  changing placement arrangements, 320–21

  characteristics of adoptable children, 320

  integrity of Black community and transracial placements, 327

  myth, Black adoptive family shortage, 325–27

  open, 323–24

  professional practice ethics, 324–25

  same sex marriage, 395

  statistics and composition, adoptable children, 319–20

  transracial controversy focus, 318

adult learning, 58–59

Advance Pricing Agreements (APA). *See* APA program

advocacy, public interest

  in the US, 214

  partnership legitimacy, 214–15

  partnership rationales in international finance, 213

AEDPA. *See* Antiterrorism and Effective Death Penalty Act, 1996 (AEDPA)

Aesthetic Definition of Art, An, 434
aesthetics
    in copyright law, 431–33, 439–40
    irrelevant to copyright law, rea-
        sons, 441
    legal interpretation in copyright
        law, 439
agency law, taught in comparative
    law course, 47
Ages of American Law, 408
AIPCA. *See* American Institute of
    Certified Public Accountants
    (AICPA)
air pollution, 142
Alesina, Alberto, 229
*Alfred Bell & Co. v. Catalda Fine Arts,
    Inc.,* 438, 444
alimony, 555
allocative decisionmaking. *See also*
    distributive justice
    of legal and medical resources,
        115–20
American Bar Association (ABA)
    Commission on Women in the
        Professions, 54–55
    Ethics Committee, 93
    Model Code of Professional Re-
        sponsibility, 194
    Task Force on Competency, 20
American Dental Association (ADA)
    Code of Ethics, 204–5
    position on dental mercury amal-
        gam, 203, 204, 208
*American Dental Association v. Khor-
    rami,* 206, 211
American Institute of Certified Public
    Accountants (AICPA), 190
Amsterdam, Anthony, 54
Anarchy, State and Utopia, 354, 383
andragogy, 58
antenuptial agreements, 390–92
Anti-Drug Abuse Act, 1988, 522, 524

848(e), 527–28
848(k), 525
848(l), death penalty as jury rec-
    ommendation, 525–26
Antigone
    clinical perspective of, 29–30
    feminist perspective of, 28–29
    legal perspective of, 28
Antiterrorism and Effective Death
    Penalty Act, 1996 (AEDPA),
    283
APA (Advance Pricing Agreement)
    program. *See* APA program
APA program. *See also* Internal Rev-
    enue Service (IRS); taxes
    administrative options, 573–74
    creation, modification, operation
        of, 568–69
    criticisms and value of, 574–75
    functional versions, 572–73
    new reporting requirement, 572
    regulatory theories, 567–68
    relationship with Internal Revenue
        Service, 565–66
    role of corporations, 571–72
    roles of foreign governments and
        small businesses, 569–71
    taxpayer/government cooperation,
        566
    voluntary resolution of interna-
        tional tax issues, 566–67
appeal
    appellate process, medieval Eng-
        land, 473
    as cultural script, 466
    as equitable theory of justice, 471
    as franchise, 473–74
    culture of redress, 467–68
    delegation of power, 474–75
    ecclesiastical history of, 469–71
    equity and justice in early Eng-
        land, 472–73

in literature, 475–76
role of appellate judge and moral
    questions, 527–29
*Appello Caesarem: A Just Appeale from
    two Unjust Informers,* 475
Aquinas, Thomas, 386, 471
Archeion, 473, 475
Arendt, Hannah, 23
Argyris, Chris, 55
Aristotle, 90, 240, 471
    practical reasoning process, 33
art
    definition, fine art, 437
    definition, formalist, 433–34
    definitions, institutionalism and
        intentionalist, 434–35
    formalist theory of interpretation,
        435–36
    intentionalist theory of interpreta-
        tion, 436
*Art and the Aesthetic: An Institutional
    Analysis,* 434
autism, mercury amalgam contro-
    versy, 206

B

Bachman, Steve, 113
Baker, J.H., 469–70
Ballard v. United States, 484, 485,
    490, 505
Bank of Nova Scotia v. United States,
    484, 490, 505
Banks v. Manchester, 191, 201
Barefoot v. Estelle, 537–38, 544, 547
Barefoot, Thomas, 537–38
Bargaining in the Shadow of the Law,
    552
battered women syndrome, 534, 541
BCRA. *See* Bipartisan Campaign Re-
    form Act, 2002 (BCRA)
Beardsley, Monroe C., 434
Bebchuk, Lucian A., 177, 181

behavior science evidence. *See* evi-
    dence
Bell, Clive, 433
Bellow, Gary, 20, 71, 113
Bentham, Jeremy, 227, 268, 343, 352
Berger v. United States, 503, 505
Bernheim, B. Douglas, 233–34
Bernstein, Richard, 23
Bill of Rights, 307, 487, 498
Binder, David A., 123
bioethics. *See also* medicine
    Conroy, In re, 157
    health care proxy law, 158
    informed consent, dental mercury
        amalgam controversy, 203
    McConnell v. Beverly Enterprises,
        159
    Peter, In re, 157–58
    randomized clinical trial (RCT),
        117–18
    right to die, 149–50
    right to refuse treatment, 155, 158
    *Saikewicz v. Superintendent of
        Belchertown State Hospital,*
        156–57
Bipartisan Campaign Reform Act,
    2002 (BCRA), 171
Black Panther Party, 366, 368, 369
Black, Hugo L., 487
Black/White paradigm, 361–63,
    365–67
Blackstone, William, 227, 268
*Bleistein v. Donaldson Lithographing
    Co.,* 437–38, 444
*Bluebook: A Uniform System of Cita-
    tion,* 197
Board of Dental Examiners v. Hufford,
    205, 211
Bok, Derek, 3
Bolling v. Sharpe, 313, 314
Booker, United States v., 509
Boyd v. United States, 289, 290, 295

Brandeis, Louis D., 479–80
Bratton, William W., 181
breach of duty, 65–68
Breiner v. State Dental Commission,
    205, 211
Breyer, Stephen G., 209
bribery, 165, 170, 172
    18 U.S.C. §666, 164, 167–68,
        173
Brilmayer, Lea, 348
Brophy v. New England Sinai Hospital,
    160
Brown v. Board of Education, 313,
    314, 535, 547
Buckley v. Valeo, 171, 174
Burger, Warren E., 20
Burke, Edmund, 239
Burrow-Giles Lithographic Company v.
    Saroy, 437–38, 444

C

Cahn, Edmond, 536
Calandra, United States v., 481, 491,
    498–99, 505
Campaign Finance Reform, 165
Cannon v. University of Chicago, 303,
    304
canon law. *See* ecclesiastical law
capital punishment. *See* death penalty
Cardozo, Benjamin N., 376
carjacking, 516, 520
Carnegie Foundation, 17
Carter v. Carter Coal co., 201
Cary, William, 177, 180
case method/study, 10–11, 53–54
    as theory with criticism of, 17–18
    dialectic process, 9–10
    feminist jurisprudence perspective,
        35–36
    in law school, 12
    justified as teaching analysis,
        16–17

perspectives, clinician and femi-
    nist jurisprudence, 35–36
theory and practice, 15
Castelli, Jim, 243
Catholic theology
    Catholic judges and the death
        penalty, 522
    conscience and moral judgment,
        526
    cooperation with evil, 523–27
    death penalty, 521
    ecclesiastical history of appeal,
        469–71
    ecclesiastical system and appeal
        process, 464
    Jesuit legal education and,
        11–12
    moral consideration of appellate
        review process, 527–29
    moral consideration of trial guilt
        phase, 526–27
    sanctioned and encouraged
        unions, 244–45
    vision in legal education, 11
Center for National Securities Studies
    v. US Department of Justice, 278
certiorari, writ of, 496
Chandler, United States v., 524,
    527–28, 531
Chase, Anthony, 18
Chesterton, G.K., 239
child sexual abuse accommodation
    syndrome (CSAAS), 534, 540,
    541
Childress, James, 116
Church of the Brethren, 521
Cicero, 386
City of Cleburne v. Cleburne Living
    Ctr., 300, 304
civil disobedience, 97, 102–105
civil law, 466
Clark, Kenneth, 535

CLEPR. *See* Council on Legal Education for Professional Responsibility (CLEPR)
client confidentiality
    breaches of duty, 68–69
    in externships, 64–68
    protocols to protect, in externships, 69–71
client empowerment. *See* rebellious lawyering
clinical education. *See also* externships
    and legal ethics, 34
    as apprenticeship system, 20
    as methodology, 20–21
    authoritarianism in, 32, 36
    contextual reasoning and critical inquiry in, 33–34
    Council on Legal Education for Professional Responsibility (CLEPR), 20–21
    ethical inquiry, 37–38
    interdisciplinarian collaboration, 32–33
    interpersonal dynamics in, 31–32
    pedagogical identity of, 30–31
    roles of experiences and affect in learning, 31, 33–34
    study of decisionmaking, 24
    teaching of professional responsibility, 21
    theory and practice, 15
cocaine, 515
Code of Canon Law *See* ecclesiastical law
cohabitation, 392–95
Coke, Edward, 467, 468, 470
Coleman, Jules L., 382
Coleman, William, 536
Colkley, United States v., 501–2, 505
Columbia Law School. *See* Keener, William A.
commercial law. *See* UCC Article 2

Commissioner of Correction v. Myers, 169
Committee of Dental Amalgam Manufacturers and Distributors v. Straton, 209, 211
common law
    appeal, historic origin of, 464–65
    Code of Canon Law, 522
    culture of redress, appeal, 467–69
    equities of court, 152–53
    equity in, 14–15, 135, 142–43
    history of, 149
    lawmaking by, 151–54
    parens patriae, 324
    right to die, development of principles, 154–56
    right to refuse treatment in, 158
Commonwealth v. Francis, 547
community organizing, 109
    mobilization, 113–14
comparative law
    as perspective course, 42–44
    different from traditional basic course, 44
    French, American, German doctrines of apparent authority, 47
    methods of analysis taught in, 43
Comparative Legal Analysis course in Boston College Law School, 43–44
comprehensive law movement, 125–26
conflict resolution. *See* dispute resolution
Conroy, In re, 157, 160
conscience, 471
    and legal decisionmaking, 521
    and moral judgment, 526
Constitution of the US
    commerce clause and corruption, 167

Constitution of the US, *continued*
  due process clause, 150, 292, 307,
    324, 486
  Eighth Amendment, 299
  ex post facto laws, 150
  First Amendment, 163, 268, 457
  Fourteenth Amendment, 150, 156,
    299, 313, 324, 480–83
  Fourth Amendment, 479–83, 502
  freedom of association, 400
  interference in state governments,
    166–67
  no right to adopt, 324
  Sixth Amendment, 290, 294, 487,
    509
constitutional law
  doctrine of deportation, 286, 288
  double jeopardy, 290–91
  due process clause, 150, 292, 307,
    324
  long-term civil commitment, 291
  no right to adopt in Constitution,
    324
Constitutions of Clarendon, 470
Consumer Product Safety Commission (CPSC), 199
contract. *See also* marriage
  as taught in comparative law
    course, 46
  between merchants, signed writ-
    ing, 409–10
  incomplete contracts, judicial ap-
    proaches to, 379–80
  irrevocable offer, 410
contract cohabitation
  economic restrictions, 395
  partnership laws, 396
  recovery in termination, 394
conversion, 9–10
Cooper v. Telfair, 295
cooperation with evil
  formal, 523–25, 529

  material, 527
copyright, 189
  as applied to accounting stan-
    dards, 190
  judicial reference standards exam-
    ples, 197–98
  regulatory takings, 200
Copyright Act, 1790, 445
Copyright Act, 1976, 48, 191–92, 196
  rights ownership over time, 453
  Section 107, 458
copyright law. *See also* art; copyright
  term extension
  aesthetic and legal reasoning, dis-
    tinction, 432–33
  aesthetics, reasons irrelevant, 441
  author reward, justification,
    454–56
  classification scheme by which
    standards become law, 193
  constraints on government strat-
    egy, 196–97
  Copyright Act, 1790, 445
  copyright protection, 450–53
  derivative works, 198
  doctrinal arguments, time and
    scope of protection, 457–58
  fair use defense, 449–50
  form of the work, 440
  government strategy to optimize
    resources using standards,
    195–96
  judicial opinions not protected by
    copyright, 191
  opinions and aesthetic theory, 436
  originality cases, 436–40
  plagiarism, 438
  private sector-generated public
    documents, 192
  private standards in public law,
    proposed issue management,
    191

proposal, political economy argu-
    ments for, 456–57
prospect justification, 453–54
scope of protection, 445–47
time as factor in fair use analysis,
    445
copyright term (time), 445
    constitutional challenges to,
        448–49
    effect on copyright markets,
        447–48
    incentives, 451
    Sonny Bono Copyright Term Ex-
        tension Act, 1998, 447, 448
Coquillette, Daniel R., 471
Corbin, Arthur, 408, 411
corporate constituency, in compara-
    tive law course, 48–49
corporate law
    corporate federalists favor deregu-
        latory bias, 177
    Delaware and Sarbanes-Oxley Act,
        176
    horizontal competition, 178–79
    regulatory competition among
        states for corporate charters,
        175–76
    regulatory regimes compared,
        182–83
    vertical competition, 179–81
corruption, 173
    definition, 165
    federal anti-corruption statutes,
        167
    in union management, 242–43
    local and state, 163
Costello v. United States, 494–95,
    497–98, 505
Council for Institutional Investors, 181
Council on Legal Education for Pro-
    fessional Responsibility
    (CLEPR), 20–21

counseling, ethnocentric model, 124
Court of Delegates, 471
Cowell, John, 467, 469
CPSC. See Consumer Product Safety
    Commission (CPSC)
crack, 515
Creppy Directive, 271–73
Creppy, Michael, 271
critical legal theory, 4, 91
critical pedagogy, 57–58. See also
    legal pedagogy
critical reflection, 57–59
Cromwell, Thomas, 470
Cruzan v. Director Missouri Depart-
    ment of Public Health, 160
CSAAS. See child sexual abuse ac-
    commodation syndrome
    (CSAAS)
Current Dental Terminology, 197–98
Cynics, School of, 91

D

Dante, Alighieri, 386
Danto, Arthur, 435
Danzig, Richard, 414
Daubert v. Merrell Dow Pharmaceuti-
    cals, Inc., 207, 211, 533, 541,
    547
death penalty
    admissibility of syndrome testi-
        mony, 537
    Anti-Drug Abuse Act, 1988, 524
    Catholic Church, 521
decisionmaking. See also clinical edu-
    cation; situated decisionmaking
    contextual decisionmaking,
        336–37
    factual and normative judgments,
        342–44
    Frye, "general acceptance," 533
    interdependence of structured and
        contextual analysis, 340–42

decisionmaking, *continued*
  judicial authority and, 151–52
  justification, 338–39
  legal, 339
  normative models, 335, 339
  rule-centered and case-specific, 340
  situated character and perspective, 333
  structured, 335–36
  structured and normative, compared, 339–40
Delaware
  effect of Sarbanes-Oxley on state, 181–82
  favors mergers, 177
  federal government, main competitor in corporate law, 179–80
  monopoly in chartering public traded corporations, 178
  response to Sarbanes-Oxley Act, 184–85
dental mercury amalgam, 203–08
deportation
  as crime control strategy and retribution, 284
  civil or criminal, 285
  civil/criminal and regulation/punishment distinctions, 288–91
  due process in juvenile justice case comparison, 294
  legal permanent residents, 286
  loss of US. citizenship, 289–90
  models of, 286–88
  policy justifications, 283–85
  substantive due process argument, 291–92
Detroit Free Press v. Ashcroft, 278
Dewey, John, 59
Diagnostic & Statistical Manual of Mental Disorders (DSM), 198, 536

Dickie, George, 434–35
Difficult and Obscure Words and Terms of the Law of this Realm, 467
discrimination
  Brown v. Board of Education, 313
  gender, in the jury pool, 484
  in health care treatments, 308, 311–12
  in mental health, 124–25
  schemas, 129–30
  Title IX of the Educational Amendment, 1972, 303
  VA hospital study, racial differences in health care treatment, 312
dispute resolution. *See also* mediation
  legal rules, effect of, 553–54
  standing, role of, 553
  strategic bargaining, 552
distributive justice, 354
  entitlement theory opposite of, 355
  international relations and libertarianism, 356
diversity, 54
divorce
  alimony, 555–56
  asset distribution, 396–97
  no-fault revolution, 553
  property settlement and child custody, before/after reform, 554–56
  variables in asset distribution, 397
doctrine
  common law wrongful termination, 247–48
  deportation, constitutional law theory of, 286, 288
  informed consent, 203
  internal affairs, 177
  lack of mental capacity, in wills, 558, 561

of consideration, 410
plenary power, immigration and "alienage jurisprudence," 291
silver platter, 480
undue influence, in wills, 558, 561
Williams, 512
wrongful termination, 247–48
domestic partnership. *See* contract cohabitation
Drug Abuse Prevention and Control Act, 515
drug kingpin statute. *See* Anti-Drug Abuse Act, 1988
DSM. See Diagnostic & Statistical Manual of Mental Disorders (DSM)
Ducktown Sulphur, Copper & Iron Co., Madison v., 147
    abatement question and decision, 143–44
due process, 486 *See also* Fifth Amendment
    juvenile justice and deportation, 294
    mandatory minimum sentencing, 511–12
    maximum-enhancing statutes and reduced, 514–17
    objections, maximum enhanced sentencing, 518–19
    restrictions, judicial integrity, 486–88
    substantive argument, deportation, 291–92
    total incorporation, 487
due process clause, 150, 292, 324
    protection choices, 307
    right to privacy, 156
    sentencing scheme violates, 510
Duncan, G.I.O., 472
Dvorkin, Elizabeth, 4, 5
Dworkin, Ronald, 92, 340, 348, 489

E
Easterbrook, Frank H., 264, 375, 376, 380
ecclesiastical law
    Code of Canon Law and death penalty, 522
    conscience and judgments, 472
    ecclesiastical history of appeal, 469–71
Economic Analysis of Law, 380, 382–83
economics. *See also* wealth concentration
    commodity, 378
    commodity, slave as, 359–60
    comparative advantage theory, 353
    dynastic wealth in US, 232–33
    philosophical views of wealth transfers, 227–28
    time value of money in copyrights, 451–52
    utilitarian economic theory, 353
Edgeworth, F.Y., 383
education, and wealth concentration, 230
EFL. *See* Environmental Foundation, Ltd. (EFL)
egalitarianism
    Nozick's objection to egalitarian redistribution, 356
    Rawls' theory of justice, 348–51
Eighth Amendment, 299
elderly
    health care delivery disparities, 308
    study results of care in HMOs, 309–10
Elements of Political Economy, 378–79
Elkins v. United States, 480, 490
Employee Retirement Income Security Act (ERISA), 1974, 254
employment law, 240–41

employment law, *continued*
  collective bargaining, 242
English legal system
  appellate process in medieval England, 473
  appellate system, 465
  chancery courts, 472–73, 475
  culture of appeal, 466–67
  culture of redress, 467–68
  equity and chancellors appealing to tribunal, 139
  franchises, 474
  grand jury, 493, 497
  Inns of Court, 92–93
  substituting king for pope in appellate process, 470
  writ of error, 468–69
Environmental Foundation, Ltd. (EFL), 214, 215
environmental law
  Ducktown Copper case, 141
  forest preservation in Sri Lanka, 214–15
  greenhouse effect, 218
Equal Protection clause, 297
equal rights
  analysis, compared to girls in juvenile justice system, 297–98
  and law, 364
  mask of oppression, 367
  strategy in juvenile justice system, 299
Equal Rights Amendment (ERA), 297
equitable jurisprudence, 136
  abatement and injunction remedy, 141–44
  Aristotle's concept of equity, 139
  categories of refused injunctions in statutory violations, 137–38
  discretionary balancing components, 140–45

discretionary equitable concepts, 140
  equitable discretion, 136–37
  principles and historic concepts, 139–40
equity
  and Puritans, 475
  Aristotle's concept of, 139
  balancing components, 136
  definition, 471
  Ducktown Copper case, 141
  grounding in common law, 135
  in nuisance law, 142
  justice and economic law, 471–72
ERISA. *See* Employee Retirement Income Security Act (ERISA), 1974
estate taxes. *See also* Internal Revenue Service (IRS); taxes
  philosophy of, 228–29
  results in revenue loss, 233–34
  wealth transfer, 235
ethics. *See also* clinical education
  American Dental Association's ethical rules and mercury removal, 204
  ethical inquiry, 36–38
  ethical relativist, 34
  role-defined, 90
  teaching of, 21
Ethics and Economics, 377, 383
Eusden, John Dykstra, 475
euthanasia. *See* bioethics
evidence. *See also* expert testimony
  affirmative defenses, before grand jury, 504
  before grand jury, 495–96
  behavioral science, 538–39, 545
  close scrutiny and exclusion, 533
  evidentiary rules and opinion testimony, 544
  exculpatory, 495–97, 500–504

Federal Rules of Evidence (FRE) 702, 533
Frye, "general acceptance," 533
general assertions about classes, 534
illegal evidence cases, 480–83
intentional omission, *Franks* test, 501
syndrome, 542
testimony as "common knowledge," 541
exclusionary rule, 480–83
exculpatory evidence. *See* evidence
expert testimony. *See also* evidence
  "future dangerousness" as commitment tool, 534
  "helpfulness" and "fit," 539–40
  "reasonable degree of medical certainty," 541–42
  admissibility of scientific proof, 534
  behavioral science evidence, credibility of, 544
  eyewitness identification, 538
  grounds for exclusion, 539
  judicial survey summary, 545
  syndrome evidence, 536–37
  victim abuse symptoms, 542–43
  witness credibility, 543
externships, 55, 64–71

F

family law. *See* adoption; marriage; transracial adoption
Family Maintenance Statute. *See* divorce; wills law
Farrell, In re, 158, 160
FASB. *See* Financial Accounting Standards Board (FASB)
Faucher, Leon, 228
Federal Energy Regulatory Commission, 194

Federal Judicial Center, 545
Federal Register, 191
Federal Rules of Evidence
  Rule 403, 207, 439
  Rule 702, scientific knowledge, 534–35
federalism, 163
  anti-bribery statute, 164
  arguments against incorporation scheme, 182
  basis for challenge to *Sabri v. United States,* 172
  corporate federal law vision, 179
  corruption at state and local level, 168–69
  enumerated powers support anti-corruption law, 167–68
  goal of intervention, 171
  horizontal competition, 178–79
  in corporate law, 177
  preemption, 209–10
  recipient integrity, 173
  regulation of economic conduct, 170–71
  restricted authority over state governments, 166–67
  Sarbanes-Oxley Act as preemptive threat, 184–85
Feller, David, 241
feminist jurisprudence, 27
  and legal ethics, 34
  authoritarianism, 32, 36
  contextual reasoning and critical inquiry in, 33–34
  ethical inquiry, 37–38
  interdisciplinarian collaboration, 32–33
  interpersonal dynamics in, 31–32
  pedagogical identity, 30–31
  roles of experience and affect in learning, 31
Fichte, J.G., 366

fiduciary law
    contractual relationships, 375
    fiduciarius, 381
    fiduciary relationships and utility
        contract, 385–86
    fiduciary relationships as social in-
        stitutions, 381–82
    fiduciary role and responsibilities,
        376
    guardian, fiduciary duties, 385
    prescriptive contractualism,
        382–83
    utilitarianism, 377–78
    utility contracts, elements of, 379
Fifth Amendment
    due process, 150, 290, 313, 487
    due process before grand jury,
        496, 497–98
Financial Accounting Standards
        Board (FASB), 190
First Amendment, 163, 268, 457. *See
        also* right to know
    basis for challenge to *McConnell v.
        FEC,* 172
    challenges to Creppy Directive,
        271–73
    freedom of association, relation-
        ships in educational settings,
        400
    right of access, 269–71
Fischel, Daniel R., 262, 264, 375,
        376, 380
Fischer v. United States, 168, 174
Fisher, Irving, 228
FOIA. *See* Freedom of Information
        Act (FOIA)
Fong Yue Ting v. United States, 286, 295
formalism, 19
Formulation of Rational Choice, The,
        377, 383
foster care, and Black children, 320,
        325

Foucha v. Louisiana, 292, 295
Fourteenth Amendment, 324
    due process, 150
    equal protection, 299, 313
    restrictions on state powers, 487
    right to privacy, 156
Fourth Amendment, 479
    exclusionary rule, cases, 480–83
    valid search, *Franks* test, 502
Frank, Jerome, 18
Frankfurter, Felix, 487, 536
Franks v. Delaware, 500, 505
fraud, 183
    bank, 495–96
    costs, leaving capital and labor
        markets, 262–63
    damages, labor and capital mar-
        kets fraud, 263–64
    employer, 254
    fraudulent information in the
        labor market, 257–59
    in capital market, 253
    in divorce, 555
    justification for antifraud rules,
        265
    labor market and capital market
        compared, 260–62
    mail fraud statute, 167
    market correction, 264
    protection through diversification,
        263
Freedom of Information Act (FOIA),
        198, 269–70. *See also* Privacy
        Act of 1974; right to know
    exemptions, 270
    request for detainee information,
        273–74
Freire, Paolo, 58
French legal system, 45
Fried, Charles, 117
Fukuyama, Francis, 382

G

Gallup, George, 243
Garrison, Charles, 230
Gas Industry Standards Board, 194
Gault, In re, 293, 295, 298, 305
Gee, E. Gordon, 17
Geiger, Jack, 308
gender. *See* feminist jurisprudence
generally accepted accounting princi-
    ples (GAAP), 189
generally accepted auditing standards
    (GAAS), 189
Georgia, United States v., 505
German legal system, 45
Gierzynski, Anthony, 231
Gilchrist, John, 469
Gilmore, Grant, 408, 415
Gilson, Etienne, 249
Glendon, Mary Ann, 390, 394
    rights talk, 312–13
Goebel, Julius, 464
Gornick, Marian, 311
government
    capitalism, slave as capital, 359
    democracy, three models of, 231
    leveraging regulatory function,
        189–200
    loss of citizenship cases, 289–90
    Rawls and Nozick theories of state,
        355
grand jury
    evidence affirmative defenses, 504
    evidence before grand jury, 498
    historic screening function, 497
    integrity and function of, 499
    legal proceedings and inquisitorial
        function, 494
    omission of materially exculpatory
        evidence, 501
    prosecutor, role and responsibili-
        ties, 493–95
    prosecutorial misconduct, 485–86

Gray's Anatomy, 193
Gray, Charles M., 472
Green, Ronald, 116
greenhouse effect, 218
Gregory VII, Pope, 469
Griswold v. Connecticut, 401, 404
Grossberg, Michael, 389
Guy, J.A., 471–72

H

habeas corpus, 488, 489, 530
Hagerty, United States v., 520
Hall, David, 465–66
Hall, United States v., 547
Halper, United States v., 289, 290, 295
Hamdani, Assaf, 177, 181
happiness, 352
Harlan, John M., 292
Harris v. McRae, 308, 314
Harrison, Linda, 368
Harsanyi, John, 377
Harvard Educational Review, 403
Harvard Law School. *See* Langdell,
    Christopher Columbus
Harvard Medical School, 310
Health Care Financing Administra-
    tion (HCEA), 311
health care reform
    abortion rights and patient rights
        compared, 307–8
    health care delivery disparities,
        308
    HMO and fee-for-service, patient
        care disparity, 310–11
    patients' bill of rights, 307
    physician/patient relationship, 311
    proxy law, 158
    rationing medical care to reduce
        medical costs, 309
Helmholz, R.H., 470
Henry VIII, King of England, 470
Herrera v. Collins, 488, 490

Heschel, Abraham, 37
Hewitt v. Hewitt, 392, 398
Hicks v. Friock, 286, 295
Hill, Anita, 540
Hobbs Act, 167
Hoffman, Frances, 403
Holland, Paul, 298
Holmes Devise History of the Supreme Court, 464
horizon, 9–10
Houchins v. KQED, Inc., 268, 278
House of Lords
    appellate process, medieval England, 473
Hughes, Hughes, 160
Hurst, Willard, 465

I

Ibis ad Caesarem, 475
Ignatius, 12
Illegal Immigration Reform and Immigrant Responsibility Act, 1996 (IIRIRA), 283
ILO. *See* International Labor Organization (ILO)
Immigration and Nationality Act, 1952, 290
immigration law. *See also* deportation
    border control, 286–87
    counterterrorism directive, 271
    deportation of legal permanent residents, 291
    federal immigration statutes, 283
    Fong Yue Ting v. United States, 286
    national security access to detainees, 273–75
    Reno v. American-Arab Anti-Discrimination Committee, 285
    social control, 287
    special interest immigration hearings, 271–73
    Wong Wing v. United States, 286

Yamataya v. Fisher, 285, 286
impact litigation. *See* rebellious lawyering
In re [party name]. See[party name], In re
Inns of Court, 92–93
Inoue, Tatsuo, 250
Internal Revenue Service (IRS), 484. *See also* taxes
    relationship with APA program, 565–66
International Labor Organization (ILO), 221
international tax
    transfer pricing, model of ADR, 565
    voluntary resolution of issues using APA program, 566–67
internships, 55
Interpreter, The, 467
IRAC formula, 84
IRS. *See* Internal Revenue Service (IRS)

J

Jackson, Donald W., 17
Jacobs, Michelle, 124, 127
James, C.I.R., 369
Janis, United States v., 481, 491
Jefferson, Thomas, 228
Jesuit law school. *See also* law school
    pedagogy based on Spiritual Exercises, 11–12
    vision in legal education, 11
Jha, Ashish K., 312
Johnson, Samuel, 197
Jordan v. Duff & Phelps, Inc., 376, 388
judicial activism, 489. *See also* judicial authority; judicial integrity
    grand jury selection, 499
judicial authority. *See also* judicial discretion; judicial integrity

appeal, definition, 463

binding precedent in copyright opinions, 441–42

deference to Executive expertise, 273

discretion in equity limited by statute, 138, 140

equity defined by, 145

intervention in review process, 530

judge as gatekeeper, 533

judicial lawmaking, 150–54

judicial opinion rationales, 191–92

recusal, 334, 521–22

reluctance to enforce "right to know," 269–70, 275–76

standards, law by reference, 193

subjectivity, 442–43

supervisory powers, 483

judicial detachment, 333

judicial discretion. *See also* sentencing

balancing of the equities, 136–37

behavioral science evidence, rationales for admission, 538–39

by trial judges, 487

conduct as sentencing factor, 515–17, 519

due process and maximum enhanced sentencing, objections, 518–19

in mandatory minimum sentencing schemes, 511–12

in penalty phase of sentencing, 509–10

in wills dispute, 559

maximum-enhancing statutes and reduced due process, 513–17

sentencing guidelines, 512–13

subset theory of sentencing enhancement, 517–18

judicial formalism, 519–20. *See also* formalism

judicial integrity

Catholic judges and the death penalty, 522

due process restrictions, 486–88

ensuring court procedure, 483–86

exclusionary rule, cases, 480–83

grand jury, 499

leading by example, 479

jury. *See also* expert testimony

assessing reliability of testimony, 542–43

behavior and syndrome evidence, 542

discrimination in the selection, 484

knowledge of syndrome evidence, 540–41

justice

allocations, required and forbidden, 384

appeal as equitable theory of, 471

appeal as equity in early England, 472–73

as equality, 348

as fairness in international trade, 356–57

as viewed by feminist and clinical movements, 36

distributive, 114–16

distributive, international, 353

egalitarian liberalism, 348–51

equity and ecclesiastical law, 471–72

impartial, and recusal, 521

implicit in canons of decency and fairness, 487

in situated decisionmaking, 324

inequalities in distribution of primary goods, 349–50

libertarianism, 354–56

justice, *continued*
  principles of, 92
  Rawls' theory, 116, 351
  social, 110
juvenile justice
  characteristics of girls involved in, 297–98
  due process in delinquency proceedings, 293–94
  gender-based claims, 299–301
  gender-based discrimination, 303
  gender-based state ERA claims, 301–3
  medical model of treatment, 298
  right to treatment, 299
  school and Title IX, 304
  Title IX of the Educational Amendment, 1972, 302–03

K

Kaczynski, Timothy, 522
Kahan, Marcel, 177
Kamar, Ehud, 177
Kant, 343, 348
Karst, Kenneth L., 401
Katherine of Aragon, 470
Katz, Jay, 311
Keener, William A., 16, 17–18
Kefauver, Estes, 323
Kennedy v. Mendoza-Martinez, 289, 295
Klein, Susan, 288
Klinger v. Department of Corrections, 305
Knowles, Malcolm, 58
Kornhauser, Lewis, 552
Krieger, Stefan, 127, 128
Kumho Tire Co, Ltd. v. Carmichael, 547
Kuznets, Simon, 229
Kymlicka, Will, 348

L

labor law, 240–41
  common law wrongful termination doctrines, 247–48
  federal protection in the workplace, 254
  job security analogy, capital markets to securities risk, 255–58
  justification for lack of federal fraud protection, 255
  labor fraud, effect on local area, 261
  participative management theory and self-transcendence, 249–50
  reform, 240–41
  wages, job security and information accuracy, 257–60
  Wagner Act, 242
  work force statistics, 241–42
Labor Management Relations Act (LMRA)
  Section 301, 254
labor union. *See* union
Lambarde, William, 470
Lane v. Candura, 160
Langdell, Christopher Columbus
  developed case method, 4
  Harvard method/model, 16, 17
  judge as spectator and agent, 334
  law as science, 16
  Socratic dialogue in law school, 53
  theory over practice, 17–18
Lattin, Norman D., 408
law
  as ambiguity, 366
  positive, 98, 99–100
  rebellious and regnant lawyering, 110–12
  rule of, definition and as ideal, 99–100

law professor, 42. *See also* legal peda-
    gogy
    improving teaching through self-
        reflection, 56–57
    legal scholarship, 19–20
    role for, 59–60
    role in legal education, 9
law school. *See also* case
        method/study; legal education
    changes in curriculum, 41–42, 54
    clinical and feminist methods in,
        34–35
    comparative law as perspective
        course, 42–44
    culture of argument, 12
    faculty and students, amorous re-
        lationship, 399–404
    legal research, reasoning and writ-
        ing (LRR&W), 81
    legal writing class, writing process
        in, 73–79
    LRR&W curriculum, 82–86
    primary focus, 4
    recommendation of ABA to teach
        clinical skills, 20
    role of Jesuit, 10–11
    social science theory in, 18
    Socratic dialogue in, 53
    teaching methods in, 55
    White's conception of, 9–10
law student, 18–19. *See also* law
        school; legal education
Law's Empire, 489
lawyers
    adherence to rule of law, 100–101
    and civil disobedience, 101–2
    engaging in public protest, 103–4
    held to special standard, 98–99
    Langdell's conception of the iden-
        tity of, 4
    obligation to pursue legitimate
        change, 102–3

    progressive, duties of, 109
    rule of law, definition, 99
    self-regulation, 106
lawyering. *See also* multicultural
        lawyering; practice; rebellious
        lawyering
    Binder-Price model, 123
    client-centered models, 123,
        125–26
Lawyering Process, The, 71
learned helplessness, 534
Lee, Feng-Yao, 230
legal analysis. *See also* case
        method/study
    in comparative law course, 44,
        46–49
    in legal writing class, 73–74
legal doctrine
    as taught in Comparative Legal
        Analysis course, 43–44
    discrepancies in divorce and will
        disputes, 552
legal education. *See also* case
        method/study; law school; legal
        pedagogy
    academic support programs in, 55
    changes in, 41–42
    clinical education, 20–22
    crisis of meaning and value in,
        3–5
    ethics as taught with clinical and
        feminist methods, 36–37
    goal instrumentalism, 93
    goal-based deep theory, 91
    intellectual bias in, 7–8
    law professors' roles in, 9
    legal realism, 18–20
    legal research, analysis and writing
        in law school, 81
    practical side of, 18–19
    practice, 23–24
    process of, 4–5

legal education, *continued*
  reform proposals, 23–24
  studies of, 17–18
  theory, 22–23
  traditions, 15
  use of interdisciplinary tools in,
    35–36
  views of clinical education,
    24–25
  vision of, 10–11
legal ethics, 34
  Canons of Professional Ethics,
    1908, 105
  in externships, 64–65, 69–71
  Model Code of Professional Re-
    sponsibility, 1969, 105
  representational, 99
  utilitarianism, 352–54
legal fetishism, 361, 363–64
  rule fetishism, 367
legal history, 42, 43
  appeal, in common law, 463–66
legal movements. *See* clinical educa-
    tion; feminist jurisprudence
legal pedagogy. *See also* legal writing
    class
  and legal theory, 53
  applied learning theory, 56–57
  changes in, 41–42
  classroom methodology linking
    theory and practice, 36
  critical pedagogy, 57–58
  critical reflection, 55–56
  feminist and clinicians' perspec-
    tives, 36
  legal problem-solving simulation,
    82–83
  reflective practice, 55, 58
  teaching doctrine, 35
legal philosophy, 42, 43. *See also*
    Rawls, John
  conscience and judgments, 472

equity and conscience, definitions,
    471
  freedom, 386
  goal-based, 92
  happiness, welfare and utility, 352
  Llewellyn's theory of, 19
  social scientists as expert wit-
    nesses, 536
  views of wealth transfers, 227–28
legal policy, in Comparative Legal
    Analysis course, 43, 45–46
legal realism, 4, 15, 91
legal science, 19
legal services for the poor. *See*
    poverty law
legal studies
  social sciences and, 18–19
legal theory. *See also* theory
  as "constitutive rhetoric," 5
  factual and normative judgments,
    342–44
  law and bias in intellectual devel-
    opment, 7–8
  law as rules, 4, 8
  law, definition of, 6
  pragmatism, 334–35
  Rawls' theory of justice, 351
  science as, 4
  situated character and perspective,
    333
  study of law as theoretical, 16
  White's theory of law, 5–6
  White's view of law as culture of
    argument, 8–9
legislative lawmaking
  advance directives for health care,
    158
  advantages of, 157–58
  compared to judicial lawmaking,
    151–54
  standard becomes law through
    adoption, 194

Leon, United States v., 482, 491
Leslie, Melanie, 561
Levinson, Harold, 104
liberalism, 348–49
 commitment to equality, 348
libertarianism, 348
 objections to, 355–56
 primacy of individual rights,
  354–56
Libset, Seymour Martin, 243
Linkletter v. Walker, 481, 491
living will, 157–58
Llewellyn, Karl, 18–19
 defense of unconscionability provision, 416
 design behind Article 2, 414–16
 drafted Article 2 merchant rules,
  407–9
 theory of jurisprudence, 19
 vision for merchant rules, 413
LMRA. *See* Labor Management Relations Act (LMRA)
Local 174, Teamsters v. Lucas Flour Co,
  261
Locke, John, 227, 455
Logerquist v. McVey, 547
Lonergan, Bernard, 5
 authentic conversation, definition,
  10
 concept of legal education, 12
 cosmopolis, 8–9
 horizon and conversion, definitions, 9–10
 law as practical common sense, 6–7
 question-distorting biases, 7
Lopez, Gerald, 112
Lopez, United States v., 167, 169, 170,
  174
Luban, David, 116

M
MacIntyre, Alasdair, 380

*Madison v. Ducktown Sulphur, Copper
 & Iron Co.,* 147
Madison, James, 249, 268
Mahoney, Paul, 262
managed care systems, 307
Mapp v. Ohio, 480, 491
Marbury v. Madison, 530, 531
Markets, Morals and the Law, 382
marriage. *See also* dispute resolution;
  divorce
 antenuptial agreements, 390–92
 as a contract, 389–90
 biracial marriage statistics, 321
 concepts, 390
 contract cohabitation, 392–95
 definition, 396
 divorce, 395–97
 interracial marriage, 326
 same sex and adoption, 395
 Uniform Marriage and Divorce
  Act, 397
Martineau, Robert J., 469
Marvin v. Marvin, 392, 398
Mathews v. Eldridge, 295, 324, 329
matrimonial property, in comparative law course, 48
Matthews, Connie, 368
maximum sentence enhancements.
  See sentencing
May v. Anderson, 324, 329
Maynard v. Hill, 389, 398
McCahery, Joseph A., 179, 181
McConnell v. Beverly Enterprises, 159,
  160
McConnell v. FEC, 173, 174
 Campaign Finance Reform deci-
  sion, 163–64
 compared to *Sabri v. United States,*
  171–72
McFarland, Douglas, 59–60
McKeiver v. Pennsylvania, 298, 305
McMillan v. Pennsylvania, 511, 520

McNabb v. United States, 483, 491
McNabb, United States v., 484
McVeigh, Timothy, 521
mediation
    analysis, in will disputes and di-
        vorces, 562
    in wills and divorce, 551–52
    model of divorce, 556
Medicaid managed care, 310
    coverage for indigent patients,
        308–9
    indigent rights to abortion and
        health care, 308
    preventive care for children, 313
    size of, 309
Medical Device Amendments (MDA),
    209
Medicare program, §666(b) benefits,
    168–69
medicine. *See also* bioethics; expert
    testimony; health care reform
    allocation of resources debate,
        115–17
    Conroy, In re, 157
    freedom from regulation, 155–56
    Gray's Anatomy and copyright, 193
    macroallocation in Oregon, 119
    McConnell v. Beverly Enterprises, 159
    rescue, or crisis, 115–16
    right to die, 149–50
    *Saikewicz v. Superintendent of
        Belchertown State Hospital,*
        156–57
    testimony, "reasonable degree of
        medical certainty," 541–42
Medtronic, Inc. v. Lohr, 209–11
Meiklejohn, Alexander, 268
Meinhard v. Salmon, 376, 388
Menkel-Meadow, Carrie, 5
merchant rules
    application of 2-205 to non-mer-
        chants, 417–18
    commercial rules in noncommer-
        cial context, 417
    Llewellyn's vision for merchant
        rules, 413
    merchant, definition, 407
mercury amalgam. *See* dental mer-
    cury amalgam
Meyer v. Nebraska, 324, 329
Mezirow, Jack, 59
Mickey Mouse, 453–54
Middletown, 231
Middletown In Transition, 231
Mill, John Stuart, 227, 343, 348, 352,
    377–78
Miranda, 307
Mlyniec, Wallace J., 298
Mnookin, Robert, 552
mobilization. *See* community organ-
    izing
Model Code of Professional Respon-
    sibility, ABA, 194
    lawyer's relationship to the law,
        104
Model Rules of Professional Conduct
    (ABA), 105
    lawyer's relationship to the law,
        104
    test case technique, 103–4
Model Rules of Professional Respon-
    sibility, 68
Montague, Richard, 475
Montesquieu, 240
moral relativism, 91
morality, 522, 526–29
    moral relativism, 91
Moran v. Burbine, 487, 491
Moriarty, Jane, 537
Morone v. Morone, 393, 398
Morrison, United States v., 170, 174
Moulton, Bea, 71
multicultural lawyering, 126–29

N

Nash v. Lathrop, 201
National Center for Health Statistics (NCHS), 321
National Conference of Commissioners on Uniform State Laws (NCCUSL), 323
National Council for Adoption (NCFA), 320
National Institute of Standards and Technology, 196
National Institute of Trial Advocacy, 20
National Labor Relations Act, 254
national security, 271–74
National Technical Information Service, 199
National Technology and Transfer Act, 198
Nationality Act, 1949, 290
Natural Resources Defense Council (NRDC), 214, 215
NCCUSL. *See* National Conference of Commissioners on Uniform State Laws (NCCUSL)
NCFA. *See* National Council for Adoption (NCFA)
NCHS. *See* National Center for Health Statistics (NCHS)
nepotism, 171
Neumann, Richard, 127, 128
New Federalism, 165–66, 173. *See also* federalism
spending power statutes, 163
New Jersey Media Group, Inc. v. Ashcroft, 278
New York Stock Exchange, 422
Nixon v. Shrink Missouri Government PAC, 171, 174
Nixon v. Warner Communications, Inc., 278
Nozick, Robert, 348, 354, 383, 385
entitlement theory, 355
objection to egalitarian redistribution, 356
NRDC. *See* Natural Resources Defense Council (NRDC)

O

O'Connor, Sandra Day, 209, 210
O'Lone v. Estate of Shabazz, 300–302, 305
Olmstead v. United States, 400–401, 404, 479, 491
opinion
aesthetics in, 431
binding precedent in copyright, 441–42
judicial aesthetic preference in copyright law, 440–41
judicial law making, 151
not copyrightable, 191
organizational theory
group conscience management, 250
participative management theory and self-transcendence, 249–50
principle of subsidiarity, 246
risk and security theory, 256–57

P

Page, United States v., 496, 505
palimony, 394
Pargo v. Elliot, 305
patents, prospect theory of, 453
patients' bill of rights, gag clauses, 311
Payner, United States v., 484, 491
PCAOB, 197
pedagogy. *See* legal pedagogy
pedagogy, critical. *See* critical pedagogy
Pegram v. Herdrich, 309, 314

Pell v. Procunier, 278

Pellegrino, Edmund, 116

People v. Peterson, 547

Perotti, Roberto, 230

persistent vegetative state (PVS),
    149–50, 153, 156

Peter, In re, 157–58, 160

plagiarism, 438

Plessy v. Ferguson, 535, 547

Poe v. Ullman, 292, 295

police
    acting in good faith case, 482
    execution of officer-murderer, 537
    misconduct during interrogation,
        487–88
    omissions, search/arrest warrant
        applications, 500–501
    unlawful action cases, 480–81, 483

pollution, greenhouse effect, 218

Ponder v. Graham, 389, 398

Posner v. Posner, 391, 398

Posner, Richard A., 379, 380, 382–84

Post-Traumatic Stress Disorder
    (PTSD), 536–37

Poterba, James, 234

Pound, Roscoe, 464

poverty law, 109–10

practice
    definition, 15
    scientific view of, 22
    theoretics of, 125

preventive medicine. *See* medicine

Price, Susan C., 123

priest, historic disqualifications for
    ordination, 522

Privacy Act of 1974, 215

professionalism, deep theory, 90–93

progressive lawyer, 109. *See also* re-
    bellious lawyering

prosecutor
    alibi evidence before grand jury,
        504
    duty to disclose exculpatory evi-
        dence, 500–504
    prosecutorial misconduct, 485–86
    responsibilities and role, grand
        jury, 493–95

prostitution. *See* juvenile justice

PTSD. *See* Post-Traumatic Stress Dis-
    order

Public Company Accounting Over-
    sight Board (PCAOB), 190

public law, 190

Puritans, 475

Q

Quakers, 521

Quinlan, In re, 160
    decision, 154–55

R

race theory, critical. *See also*
    Black/White paradigm; slave
    as social construct, 361–69
    health care delivery disparities,
        308
    pleasure of hierarchy, 362–63
    poverty and property, 366
    rights as loss of power, 365–70
    white-over-black, 361–68

race-to-the-bottom, 177

race-to-the-top, 177, 180

randomized clinical trial (RCT),
    117–18

Rankets Case, 147

rape trauma syndrome, 534

Rastell, John, 467

Rawls, John, 92, 343
    civil disobedience, 102
    just rules, 150–51
    justification of international trade
        law, 357
    objections to libertarianism,
        355–56

social contract theory of justice, 116

taxes for wealth distribution, 227

theory of egalitarian liberalism, 348–51

theory of justice, 351

RCT. *See* randomized clinical trial (RCT)

rebellious lawyering, 125
  client voice, 112, 114, 120
  collectivist argument theme, 113–14
  defects of, 111–12
  deferral thesis, 112–14
  definition and elements of, 111
  distributive justice, 114–16
  resource allocation, 117–18

Redlich, Josef, 16–17

Reed, A.Z., 17

regnant lawyering, 110, 112

relational positivism, 386

Reno v. American-Arab Anti-Discrimination Committee, 285, 287, 295

reparations, 360, 364, 367

resource allocation. *See* distributive justice

Ricardo, David, 228

Richmond Newspapers, Inc. v Virginia, 268–69, 272, 279
  history-and-logic test, 271

Ridley, Thomas, 471

right of access, after September 11, 2001, 270–71

right to know
  disparaged by courts, 277–78
  Freedom of Information Act (FOIA), 267
  history of, 267–68
  threat to, 276–77

right to life movement, 152. *See also* abortion

development of principles, 154–56

right to privacy
  limits, 402–4
  relationships in educational settings, 400–402

Rivera-Gomez, United States v., 515

Robinson, Ian, 118

Rochin v. California, 487, 491

Rodrik, Dani, 229

Roe v. Wade, 152, 160, 307, 314, 402, 404
  right to privacy, 156

Roe, Mark, 179

Roman law. *See* economics

Rosenstein, Elizer, 249

Rush, United States v., 520

Ryan, United States v., 520

S

Sabri v. United States, 167, 169, 173, 174
  bribery, 164
  compared to *McConnell v. Beverly Enterprises*, 171–72
  recipient integrity rationale, 170

Saikewicz v. Superintendent of Belchertown State Hospital, 156–57, 160

Salinas v. United States, 168, 174

same-sex cohabitation. *See* marriage

Sandel, Michael, 348

Sarbanes-Oxley Act, 176, 182–85

Saxbe v. Washington Post Co., 279

Schlegel, Henry, 19

scholar. *See* law professor

Schuck, Peter, 284

securities
  certificate-based system, 422–23
  indirect holding system, 425–26
  interests, possession, 427–28
  intermediary transaction, 427
  investment, negotiability rules, 426–27

securities, *continued*
    pricing and fraud, 253
    Securities and Exchange Commission (SEC), 189
    transfer property interests, 424–25
segregation, 313
    effects on Black school children, 535
Sen, Amartya, 377, 378, 383
sentencing
    Anti-Drug Abuse Act and death penalty, 525
    conduct as factor, 515–17
    enhancement to guidelines analogy, 516
    judicial discretion in penalty phase, 509–10
    judicial discretion, mandatory minimum sentencing schemes, 511
    maximum-enhancing statutes, 513–14
    objections, due process protection for maximum enhanced, 518–19
    rights at, 509
    subset theory of enhancement, 517–18
sexual harassment
    Anita Hill, 540
    faculty and students, amorous relationship, 399–404
sexual offender, 510–11
    civil commitment, 291
    future dangerousness, 534, 537–38
    Sexual Offender Act, Colorado, 510–11
Shakespeare, William, 475
Shakur, Afeni, 366, 369
Shalleck, Anne, 124
Shaw, Lemuel, 149
Shulman, Harry, 247

Sierra Club Legal Defense Fund, 218
Silent World of Doctor and Patient, 311
situated decisionmaking
    agent-centered theories, 323–24
    just decisionmaking, 335
Sixth Amendment, 290, 294, 487, 509
slave
    as commodity, 359–60
    as mark, 360
    as property, 361, 362, 366
    conditioned training, 362
    reparations, 360, 364, 367
Smith, Adam, 228, 249, 383
Smith, Thomas, 467
social science
    Brown v Board of Education, 535
    evidence, 539
    syndrome evidence, 536–37
    syndrome in courtroom, 534
society
    based on participation and training, 363
    correlation of decline in unions and religious organizations, 243–44
    interdependence of social structures, 239–40
    social fragmentation and unions, 248
Sonny Bono Copyright Term Extension Act, 1998, 447, 448
Sophist School, 91
Souter, David H., 292, 293
South Dakota v. Dole, 174
Specht v. Patterson, 510, 520
Spring, In re, 160
St. German, Christopher, 471
Stanley v. Illinois, 324, 329
stereotyping, 128
    schemas, 129–30

Stigler, George, 377
Stone v. Powell, 482, 491
Stratton, 210
Strauss, George, 249
Sue, David, 124
Sue, Derald, 124
syndrome. *See* expert testimony

T

taxes. *See also* estate taxes; Internal
 Revenue Service (IRS)
 effects on savings, 235–36
 marriage to preserve estate plan,
  390–91
 to prevent wealth concentration,
  233
 wealth distribution, 227–28
testimony, expert. *See* expert testimony
theory
 definition, 15
 scientific view of, 22–23
Theory of Justice, 349–50
theory-practice relationship. *See* clinical education
Third World. *See also* World Bank
 American advocates and World
  Bank, partner benefits,
  217–18
 American partnership purposes,
  219
 American partnership responsibilities, 218
 partnership limitations, 220
Tiebout, Charles, 179
Title IX of the Edcucation Amendments, 1972, 297
Tocqueville, Alexis de, 228, 239–40,
 244, 248
Tolhurst, William, 436
tort law
 doctrines and equity, 144–45

equitable standards in, 142–43
injunction, 145
proximate cause, 527
Ranketts Case, 142
trade law, international.
 distributive justice, 353
 justice as fairness, 356–57
 Rawlsian justification of, 357
 securities trades, transfer concept,
  424–25
 trade and inequality, 347–48
 wealth and, 347
Transformation of Family Law, The,
 394, 395
transracial adoption
 evaluating perspective parents, 317
 foster care system, 326
 same-race placement preferences,
  318
Treatise on Commerce, 474
Trembley, Paul, 127, 128
trial advocacy, 20
trial, rights at, 509
Trop v. Dulles, 289, 295
trust, taught in comparative law
 course, 47
*Trust: The Social Virtues and the Cre-
 ation of Prosperity,* 382
Tuebner, Gunther, 246
Turner v. Safleyn, 300–302, 305
Twining, William, 18

U

UCC Article 2. *See also* merchant
 rules
 1-102(3), 417–18
 2-201(1), 411
 2-201(2), 412, 413
 2-205, 409, 417
 2-302, 416
 2-509(2), 407
 2-601, 412

UCC Article 2, *continued*
  2-603 Comment 1, 413–14
  merchant firm offer rule, 410
  merchant, definition, 407
  statute of frauds, 411
UCC Article 8
  8-102(a)(17), 423–24
  8-106, 428
  8-313, 425
  8-501(b), 425–26
  8-502, 427
  concept of control, 428
  direct and indirect holding, distinction between, 423
  history of revisions, 421–22
  security entitlement, definition, 423–24
  three revisions, 421–22
UN Commission on Human Rights, 221
UN Human Rights Committee, 221
Uniform Marriage and Divorce Act, 397
union, 239
  alternatives to, 245–46
  collective bargaining agreements, 254
  decline in membership, 242–43
  Local 174, Teamsters v. Lucas Flour Co., 261
  monitor management fraud in labor markets, 264
  sanctioned and encouraged by Catholic Church, 244–45
  trade, Poland and international right to organize, 221
Union of American Hebrew Congregations, 521–22
United States v. [party name]. See [party name], United States v.
US Sentencing Guidelines, 509
utilitarianism, 348, 377–78

ethical theory of liberalism, 352–54
fiduciary relationships and utility contract, 385–86
freedom, 386
preference, 377, 384
relative to economy, 385
utility enhanced by unjust project, 384

V

Veeck v. Southern Building Code Congress International, Inc., 192, 201
View of Civil and Ecclesiastical Law, 471
vocation, 89

W

Wagner Act, 242, 245–47
Waldron, Jeremy, 348
Walker, Lenore, 541
Ward, United States v., 290, 295
Ware, John, 309
WARN Act. *See* Worker Adjustment and Retraining Notification (WARN) Act
Washington v. Davis, 532
Washington v. Glucksberg, 292, 295
wealth concentration
  economic growth, studies of, 229–30
  effects, 228–29
  effects on local politics, 231–32
  investment in education, 230
  redistribution, 354
  sociopolitical instability, 230–31
  taxation effect, 234–35
  taxes to prevent, 233
Weber, Max, 116, 247
Weeks v. United States, 491
welfare, 322, 352

West, United States v., 520
Weyrauch, Walter O., 391
Wheaton v. Peters, 191, 201
Wheeler, John, 474
White, James Boyd, 5
    conception of law school, 9–10,
        12
    view of law, 8–9
Wigmore, John Henry, 539, 541
will, living, 157–58 *See also* bioethics
Williams v. New York, 520
Williams, John, 284
Williams, United States v., 484, 491,
    494, 495, 497–98, 505
wills law. *See also* dispute resolution
    common grounds for overturning,
        558
    disputes, 551
    English system, Family Mainte-
        nance Statute, 560–62
    imposition of doctrines to over-
        turn wills, 561–62
    judicial resolution more likely,
        556–57
    less contentious option, 560
    nature of wills dispute, 559
    testator intent, 553, 557
Winter, Ralph, 177, 180
wiretap, 479

*Women Prisoners of the D.C. Depart-
    ment of Corrections v. District of
    Columbia,* 305
Wong Wing v. United States, 286, 288,
    295
Wood v. Georgia, 499
Woodward, Calvin, 19
Worker Adjustment and Retraining
    Notification (WARN) Act, 254
World Bank
    adjudicatory mechanisms, 220–22
    partnership model of advocacy,
        216–17
    primary mandates and institu-
        tional accountability,
        215–16
    structure dilutes influence, 216
    US influence on, 215
writ of certiorari, 463, 496
writ of error, 463, 464, 467–68

Y
Yamataya v. Fisher, 285, 286, 295
Yates, John, 475

Z
*Zobrest v. Catalina Foothills School
    District,* 525, 532